Cambridge Companions to Culture

The Cambridge Companion to Modern German Culture
Edited by EVA KOLINSKY *and* WILFRIED VAN DER WILL

The Cambridge Companion to Modern Russian Culture
Edited by NICHOLAS RZHEVSKY

The Cambridge Companion to Modern Spanish Culture
Edited by DAVID T. GIES

wrote the English-language version of *Crime and Punishment* recently directed by Yury Liubimov at London's Lyric Theatre, Hammersmith.

The Cambridge Companion to
Modern Russian Culture

edited by
NICHOLAS RZHEVSKY

CAMBRIDGE
UNIVERSITY PRESS

PUBLISHED BY THE PRESS SYNDICATE OF THE UNIVERSITY OF CAMBRIDGE
The Pitt Building, Trumpington Street, Cambridge, United Kingdom

CAMBRIDGE UNIVERSITY PRESS
The Edinburgh Building, Cambridge CB2 2RU, UK   http://www.cup.cam.ac.uk
40 West 20th Street, New York, NY 10011–4211, USA   http://www.cup.org
10 Stamford Road, Oakleigh, Melbourne 3166, Australia

First published 1998

Printed in the United Kingdom by Biddles Limited, Guildford and King's Lynn

Typeset in 9/13 pt Lexicon (*The Enschedé Font Foundry*), in QuarkXPress®   [SE]

A catalogue record for this book is available from the British Library

Library of Congress Cataloguing in Publication data
The Cambridge Companion to modern Russian culture / edited by Nicholas
Rzhevsky.
       p.   cm. – (Cambridge companions to culture)
Includes bibliographical references and index.
ISBN 0 521 47218 0 (hardback)
ISBN 0 521 47799 9 (paperback)
1. Russian – Civilization.
2. Russia (Federation) – Civilization.
3. Arts, Modern – Russia.
4. Arts, Modern – Russia (Federation)
I. Rzhevsky, Nicholas, 1943–.
II. Series.
DK32.C33   1998   947.08 – dc21   98-3850 CIP

ISBN 0 521 47218 0   hardback
ISBN 0 521 47799 9   paperback

Contents

List of illustrations ix
List of contributors xi
Chronology xiv
Note on names and transliteration xxviii

1 Russian cultural history: introduction *1*
NICHOLAS RZHEVSKY

Part I Cultural identity

Origins

2 Language *19*
DEAN S. WORTH

3 Religion: Russian Orthodoxy *38*
DMITRY S. LIKHACHEV

Boundaries

4 Asia *57*
MARK BASSIN

5 The West *85*
PIERRE R. HART

6 Ideological structures *103*
ABBOTT GLEASON

7 Popular culture *125*
CATRIONA KELLY

Part II **Literature and the arts**

8 Literature *161*
DAVID M. BETHEA

9 Art *205*
JOHN E. BOWLT

10 Music *236*
HARLOW ROBINSON

11 Theatre *264*
LAURENCE SENELICK

12 Film *299*
NIKITA LARY

Suggested reading 330
A select filmography 347
Index 355

Illustrations

4.1 Vasily Ivanovich Surikov, "Yermak's conquest of Siberia in 1582" (1985). Oil on canvas. By permission of the State Russian Museum, St. Petersburg. 63

7.1 Zemstvo statisticians in a Russian village. From Harold Williams, *Russia of the Russians* (London, 1914). Taylor Institution, Oxford. 130

7.2 Pilgrims at a Russian monastery. From Rothay Reynolds, *My Russian Year* (London, *c.* 1912). Taylor Institution, Oxford. 132

7.3 "The four loving hearts who spend their time in gaming and amusements." Late eighteenth-century woodcut. From Iu. Ovsiannikov, *The Lubok* (Moscow, 1968). Taylor Institution, Oxford. 139

7.4 "The sirin-bird." Old Believer watercolor in the style of an engraved *lubok*. Probably early nineteenth century. From Iu. Ovsiannikov, *The Lubok* (Moscow, 1968). Taylor Institution, Oxford. 140

7.5 Girls using *kacheli*, a Russian swing, and a seesaw, both popular amusements since medieval times. Russian lithograph, *c.* 1850, author's own collection. 150

7.6 "Tsar Saltan's feast": illustration by Ivan Bilibin to Pushkin's verse folk-tale stylization *Skazka o tsare Saltane*, Moscow 1905. Author's own collection. 154

11.1 Griboedov's "Woe from Wit" at the Moscow Maly Theatre in the 1850s: L. V. Samarin as Chatsky, Mikhail Shchepkin as Famusov, and G. S. Olgin as Skalozub. Phototype by Panov. Laurence Senelick collection. 268

11.2 Korsh's Theatre, Moscow, designed by the architect M. N. Chicagov. Laurence Senelick collection. 270

11.3 The last act of Chekhov's *The Three Sisters* at the Moscow Art Theatre, directed by Stanislavsky in the setting by Viktor Simov (1903). Laurence Senelick collection. 271

11.4 Michael Chekhov as Hamlet. Laurence Senelick collection. 279

11.5   A Blue Blouse troupe demonstrating "Fordism in the factory."
       Laurence Senelick collection.   283
11.6   Act II of *Armored Train 14–69* at the Moscow Art Theatre (1927).
       Laurence Senelick collection.   286

Contributors

MARK BASSIN: Lecturer, University College London. Author of *Geographical Imaginations and Imperial Power: The Russian Annexation of the Amur River 1840–1865*, essays and articles on Russian perceptions of the East, the history of geopolitics, and the history of environmentalism in the *Slavic Review, American Historical Review, Journal of Modern History*, and *Transactions of the Institute of British Geographers*. Former fellow in the Institute for European History, Kennan Institute, and the Remarque Institute.

DAVID M. BETHEA: Vilas Professor of Slavic Languages, University of Wisconsin–Madison, Senior Associate Member, Russian Centre, St. Anthony's, Oxford (1994–95), former Director, Middlebury College Russian School. Author of *Khodasevich: His Life and Art, The Shape of Apocalypse in Modern Russian Fiction, Joseph Brodsky and the Creation of Exile*, articles and essays in *Slavic Review, PMLA, Slavic and East European Journal, Russian Review, California Slavic Studies*, and the *NY Times Book Review*. Editor of *Pushkin Today* and *Pis'ma V. Khodasevicha k N. Berberovoi*.

JOHN E. BOWLT: Professor, University of Southern California. Director, Institute of Modern Russian Culture at Blue Lagoon, Author of *The Russian Avant-Garde: Theory and Criticism 1902–34, Russian Art 1875–1975, The Silver Age: Russian Art of the Early Twentieth Century*, articles and essays in *Form, Art Journal, Soviet Studies, Slavonic and East European Review, Apollo, Art News, Russkaya mysl, Russian Review, Journal of Russian Studies, Metropolitan Museum Journal, Performing Arts Journal, Twentieth Century Studies, Cornell Review, Times Literary Supplement*, and *New York Review of Books*. Editor of works in Russian art studies and co-editor of *Russian Formalism* and *Kazimir Malevich*. Curator and consultant for numerous exhibitions of Russian art, stage, and costume design.

ABBOTT GLEASON: Professor, Brown University. President, American Association for the Advancement of Slavic Studies. Author of

*Totalitarianism: the Inner History of the Cold War, Bolshevik Culture:
Experiment and Order in the Russian Revolution, Young Russia: the Genesis of
Russian Radicalism in the 1860s, European and Muscovite: Ivan Kireevsky and
the Origins of Slavophilism*, essays, articles, and reviews in *Journal of
Interdisciplinary History, Contemporary European History, Russian Review,
Slavic Review, American Quarterly*, and *The Journal of Modern History*.

PIERRE R. HART: Professor and Chair, Louisiana State University. Author
of *G. R. Derzhavin: A Poet's Progress*, articles, essays, and reviews in *Slavic
and East European Journal, Canadian–American Slavic Studies, Slavic Review,
Russian Language Journal, Modern Fiction Studies, Modern Language Journal,
The Modern Encyclopedia of Russian and Soviet Literature*, and the *Handbook
of Russian Literature*.

CATRIONA KELLY: Reader in Russian and Tutorial Fellow of New College,
University of Oxford. Author of *Petrushka, the Russian Carnival Puppet
Theatre, A History of Russian Women's Writing, 1820–1992*, articles in
numerous collections of essays and professional journals. Editor of *An
Anthology of Russian Women's Writing, 1777–1992*, and co-editor of
*Discontinuous Discourses in Modern Russian Literature, An Introduction to
Russian Culture Studies*, and *Constructing Russian Culture in the Age of
Revolution*.

NIKITA LARY: Professor, York University, Toronto. Author of *Dostoevsky
and Soviet Film: Visions of Demonic Realism, Dostoevsky and Dickens*, essays,
articles, and reviews in *Slavic and East European Journal, Sight and Sound,
Slavic Review, Slavic and East European Arts, Kinovedcheskie zapiski,
Eisenstein Rediscovered, Echoes of Glasnost' in Soviet Ukraine, Eisenstein No. 2,
Chas-Pik, Rossiia, Epicene, The Penguin Companion to Literature: Britain and
Commonwealth, Historical Journal of Film, Radio and Television, Victorian
Studies, Dostoevsky Studies, Globe*, and *Mail*.

DMITRY S. LIKHACHEV: Academician, Institute of World Literature,
Russian Academy of Sciences, St. Petersburg. Former head Soviet
Culture Foundation and Deputy, Congress of Russian Deputies.
Author and editor of numerous works on Russian literature and
language. Widely regarded as the primary modern authority and
conscience of Russian culture. Advisor on cultural matters to the
Soviet and Russian Federation governments.

HARLOW ROBINSON: Professor and Chair, Northeastern University.
Author of *The Last Impresario: the Life, Times, and Legacy of Sol Hurok, Sergei
Prokofiev: a Biography*, articles, essays, and reviews in *Musical Quarterly,
Opera News, Opera Quarterly, Dance Quarterly, Dance Magazine, Russian
Review, Slavic Review, Slavic and East European Journal*, and the *New York
Times Book Review*. Radio and television commentator on Russian
music and culture. Editor of *The Operas of Sergei Prokofiev and their*

Russian Literary Sources, musical compositions, and *Selected Letters of Sergei Prokofiev.*

NICHOLAS RZHEVSKY: State University of New York, Stony Brook. Author of *Russian Literature and Ideology*, articles and essays in *Encounter, Nation, Modern Drama, Russian Review, Slavic Review, New Literary History,* and (with Yury Liubimov) an English-language adaptation of *Crime and Punishment.* Editor of *An Anthology of Russian Literature. Introduction to a Culture*, and co-editor of *Media><Media, Dramaturgs and Dramaturgy*, and *Slavic and East European Arts.*

LAURENCE SENELICK: Fletcher Professor of Drama and Oratory at Tufts University, Honorary Curator of Russian Drama and Theatre at the Harvard Theatre Collection. Recipient of the St. George medal of the Ministry of Culture of the Russian Federation. His many books include *The Chekhov Theatre: A Century of His Plays in Performance, Serf Theatre: The Life and Art of Mikhail Shchepkin, Anton Chekhov, National Theatre in Northern and Eastern Europe, 1749–1900: A Documentary History,* and *Gordon Craig's Moscow Hamlet.* He has edited and translated *Russian Dramatic Theory from Pushkin to the Symbolists, Cabaret Performance: Europe 1890–1940, Russian Satiric Comedy, Russian Comedy of the Nikolaian Era.* His dramatic adaptation of *Dead Souls* was staged in Boston.

DEAN S. WORTH: Professor, University of California, Los Angeles. Past Chair, American Committee of Slavists, member Academic Council of the Kennan Institute for Advanced Russian Studies. President, Western Slavic Association and Vice President, International Committee of Slavists. Author of fifty-plus publications on Russian culture and approximately 160 on linguistics, Paleosiberian languages, and Russian folk poetics.

Chronology

History	Literature	Performing Arts, Art, Architecture
Third to eighth centuries Tribal migrations		
Ninth century c. 750–800 Vikings reach central Volga c. 862–879 Slavs invite Riurik, Sineus, Truvor Beg. reign Kiev Great Princes 882 Oleg unites Kiev, Novgorod	***Ninth century*** c. 863 Saints Cyril, Methodius, Glagolitic alphabet 2nd half ninth century Greek *Teacher's Gospel* Late ninth century first trans. Bible	
Tenth century 907 Oleg attacks Constantinople c. 955 Olga baptized Christian faith c. 962 beg. reign Sviatoslav c. 968 Sviatoslav defeats Bulgarians 969 Kiev besieged by Pechenegs 978 Beg. reign Vladimir 988 Vladimir accepts Byzantine Christianity	***Tenth century*** 988 trans. Bible, liturgical texts, saints' lives	***Tenth century*** c. tenth century Church of Ilia, Kiev 991–96 Assumption Church (Tithe); Kiev
Eleventh century 1016 Saints Boris and Gleb d. 1019–54 Reign Yaroslav ("the Wise") 1037 Victory over Pechenegs 1051 Hilarion, first Metropolitan Russian origin	***Eleventh century*** c. 1017 beg. *Novgorod First Chronicle* 1036 *Sermon of Luka Zhidyata* c. 1040 first chronicles Kievan Rus' c. 1050 Hilarion's *Sermon on Law and Grace*	***Eleventh century*** 1036 Transfiguration Cathedral, Chernigov 1036–41 St. Sophia, Kiev 1045–50 St. Sophia, Novgorod 1046–67 St. Sophia Russo-Byzantine mosaics

1070–88 Archangel Michael Cathedral, Vydubetsky Monastery, Kiev
1073–78 Monastery of Caves Russo-Byzantine mosaics
1089–90 Church St. Michael, Pereyaslavl
c. eleventh century *znamenny raspev* (choral singing)
c. eleventh to twelfth centuries *kriukovye noty* (musical notation)

Twelfth century
c. first half twelfth century Vladimir Mother of God icon
1103 Annunciation Church, Novgorod
1114 Monk Alipy d.
1115–23 Cathedral Saints Boris and Gleb, Chernigov
1117–19 Cathedral Nativity of Virgin, Antoniev Monastery
1119–20 Cathedral St. George, Yuriev Monastery
1128 Spassky Monastery, Polotsk
1135–44 Church Dormition, Kanevo
1140 Kirillovsky Monastery beg. near Kiev
1145 Church Boris and Gleb, Smolensk
c. 1150 Church Boris and Gleb, Kideksh
1152 Church of Savior, Pereiaslavl-Zalessk
c. 1152 St. Olaf's Church, Novgorod
c. 1158 Uspensky Cathedral, Vladimir
1165 Church Intercession of Virgin on Nerli
1179 Church Annunciation, Miachino
1185–92 Church Saints Peter and Paul, Sinichia Hill
1190–92 Church St. Basil, Ovruch
1194–97 Cathedral St. Dmitry, Vladimir
1198 Church of Savior, Novgorod

1051–54 *Russian Pravda*
1056–57 *Gospel of Ostromir*
1079–85 *Boris and Gleb*
c. 1088 Nestor's *Life of Theodosius*
1089 Ioann's *Church Regulation*
c. 1093–95 Primary Compilation, *Primary Chronicle*
1095 *Novgorod Monthly Readings*

Twelfth century
1096–1117 *Instructions of Vladimir Monomakh*
c. 1110–13 Nestor's *Primary Chronicle* (*Tale of Bygone Years*)
c. 1117 Silvester's second redaction *Primary Chronicle*
1128–57 Synodal copy *Novgorod First Chronicle*
c. 1187 *Tale of Igor's Campaign*

1061 Kiev troops defeat Polovtsy (Kumans)
1074 St. Theodosius d. (founder Kiev-Pechersky Monastery)
1078–93 Reign Vsevolod
1093–1113 Reign Sviatopolk, Iziaslav's son
1096 Polovtsy occupy Kiev

Twelfth century
1113–25 Reign Vladimir Monomakh
1136 Novgorod breaks away from Kiev
1154–57 Kiev reign Yury Dolgoruky, founder Moscow
1169 Andrei Bogoliubsky, Prince of Vladimir, sacks Kiev
1170 Novgorod forces defeat Suzdal
1174–1212 Vsevolod ("Big Nest") Great Prince of Vladimir
1185 Igor's unsuccessful campaign against Polovtsy

History

Thirteenth century

1223 Mongols victory, Kalka River
1237–40 Mongol invasion. Cities devastated
1240 Kiev taken; beg. Mongol "Yoke"
Aleksandr Nevsky defeats Swedes, Neva River
1242 Aleksandr Nevsky's "Battle on the Ice"
1252–63 Reign Aleksandr Nevsky
1263–72 Yaroslav reign in Vladimir
1270 Novgorod treaty Hanseatic League

Fourteenth century

1317–22 Reign Yury of Moscow
1326 Metropolitan Peter moves see to Moscow
1328–40 Ivan I ("Kalita")
1359–89 Reign Moscow Prince Dmitry ("of the Don")
1380 Dmitry defeats Mongols, Kulikovo Field
1389–1425 Vasily I reign Moscow
1389–95 Tamerlane attacks Golden Horde

Fifteenth century

1425–62 Vasily II ("The Dark")

Literature

Thirteenth century

c. late twelfth–early thirteenth century *Supplication of Daniil the Exile*
c. 1223–before 1246 *Tale of Ruin Russian Land*
1237–40 *Tale of Battle on River Kalka*
c. 1239 *Tale of Batu's invasion*
mid. thirteenth century trans. Greek *Aleksandriia*
1263 *Life of Aleksandr Nevsky*

Fourteenth century

1340s *Tale of Battle Novgorod with Suzdal*
1377 *Laurentian Chronicle*
c. 1393 *Zadonshchina (Beyond the Don)*
1396 d. Stefan of Perm

Fifteenth century

c. 1400 *Tale of Battle with Mamai*

Performing Arts, Art, Architecture

Thirteenth century

1202–06 Birth of Mother of God Monastery, Vladimir
1216–24 Cathedral Transfiguration of Savior, Yaroslavl
1222–25 Cathedrals Nativity of Virgin, St. George, Vladimir-Suzdal
1292 Church St. Nicholas on Lipna, Novgorod

Fourteenth century

1326 Uspensky Cathedral, Moscow Kremlin
1330 Church Savior in Forest, Moscow Kremlin
1333 Archangel Cathedral, Moscow Kremlin
c. 1335 Sergius of Radonezh's Trinity-Sergius Monastery
c. 1350 Icon Savior of Fiery Eye; Assumption Cathedral, Moscow
1361 Church St. Theodore Stratilates, Novgorod
1367 Kremlin stone walls, Moscow
1370–80 Assumption Church, Volotovo Field, Novgorod
1374 Church Savior on Elijah Street, Novgorod
1378 Theophanes' icons and frescoes, Church Transfiguration, Novgorod
1379 Church Nativity of Virgin, Mikhailitsa
1383–84 Church St. John the Divine, Radokovitsi, Vitka river

Fifteenth century

c. 1400 Uspensky Cathedral, Zvenigorod

1439 Council of Florence
1448 Russian Church autocephalous
1453 Fall of Constantinople
1462–05 Ivan III ("the Great")
1470 "Judaizers" heresy, Novgorod
1472 Ivan m. Sophia Paleologue
1472–85 Moscow rules Perm, Rostov, Novgorod, Tver
1497 Code of Ivan III (*Sudebnik*)

Sixteenth century
1503 Church council; "Possessors" – "Non-Possessors" debate
1505–33 Reign Vasily III
1533–38 regency Elena Glinskaya
1533–84 Reign Ivan IV ("the Terrible")
1550–51 Hundred Chapters Council (Stoglav)
1552 Kazan taken
1555 English Moscow Trade Company
1558–83 Livonian War
1565 Ivan introduces *Oprichnina*
1569 Metropolitan Philip strangled
1571 Crimean Tartars raid Moscow

1406 *Arsenian Edition* saints' lives
c. 1420 *Hypatian Chronicle*; Epiphanius the Wise d.
1433 b. Nil Sorsky
1442 Pachomius Logothetes' *Russian Chronograph*
c. 1474 d. Afanasy Nikitin author, *Journey beyond Three Seas*
c. 1475–1556 Maksim Grek

Sixteenth century
c. 1540s Macarius' *Chet'i Minei*
1547 Sylvestr's *Domostroy*
1550 Peresvetov's *Tale of Sultan Mahmed*
1551 *Stoglav*
1560–63 Athanasius' *Book of Generations*
1564 Fedorov, Mstislavets' *Apostol* printed
1568 *Psalter* printed
1560s–70s *Correspondence* Ivan IV and Kurbsky
1581 *Ostrog Bible*

1405 Rublev, Theophanes, Prokhor icons *Nativity, Baptism, Transfiguration*
1406 Church Saints Peter and Paul Kozhevniki, Novgorod
c. 1408 Rublev and Daniel the Black's *Christ in Majesty*
c. 1410–22 Rublev's *Old Testament Trinity*
1443 Church St. Basil on Hillock, Pskov
1420 Rublev interior Cathedral, Trinity-Sergius Monastery
1421–22 Church St. John the Compassionate, Lake Miachino
c. 1430 Rublev, d.
1441 first mention *demestvennyi* form singing
1450 Icon "*Battle Suzdal and Novgorod*"
1479 Fioravanti's Assumption Cathedral, Moscow Kremlin
1484–89 Annunciation Church rebuilt, Moscow Kremlin
1484–90 Ivan III's Novgorod citadel
1485–1516 Moscow Kremlin reconstruction
1487–91 Armoury Chambers, Moscow Kremlin

Sixteenth century
1500–02 Dionisius and sons' frescoes, Ferapont Monastery
1505 Novy's Archangel Michael Cathedral
1510–14 Cathedral Intercession Mother of God, Suzdal
1515 Transfiguration Cathedral, Khutyn Monastery
1524–25 Cathedral Smolensk Mother of God; Novodevichy Convent
1529 Church St. Prokopy
1530–32 Vasily III's Trinity Cathedral, Trinity-Danilov Monastery
1532 Ascension Church, Kolomenskoe

History

1582 Yermak conquers Khanate Siberia
1584–98 Reign Fedor I, Boris Gudunov regent
1589 First Patriarch Iov
1591 Ivan's son Dmitry d. Uglich
1592–97 Restrictions on peasant mobility
1598 Fedor d.; end House of Riurik
1598–1605 Reign Boris Gudunov

Seventeenth century
1601–03 Drought, famine, plague
1604 First False Dmitry invades Russia
1605 Boris Gudunov d.; beg. "Time of Trouble"
1605 Reign Fedor Gudunov; killed same year
1605–06 Reign False Dmitry
1606–10 Reign Vasily Shuisky
1607–10 False Dmitry II
1610 Polish forces occupy Moscow
1610–13 Vladislav of Poland, tsar elect
1611 Swedes occupy Novgorod
1611–12 Armed resistance, Minin and Pozharsky
1613 Beg. Romanov Dynasty, Landed Assembly chooses Mikhail
1613–45 Reign Mikhail
1619–33 Filaret (Mikhail's father) Patriarch
1632 Kiev Academy

Literature

Seventeenth century
1600 Chudovsky *Chet'i Minei*
1614 Moscow Printing House founded
1653 Nikon reforms, *Nomokanon*
1669–76 Avvakum's *Life*
1677–78 Polotsky's *Many-Flowered Garden*
1680 Polotsky's *Rhymed Psalter, Rifmologion*
late seventeenth century *Misery-Luckless-Plight; Shemyaka's Judgement, Frol Skobeev, Savva Grudtsyn*

Performing Arts, Art, Architecture

1535–37 Church St. Nicholas rebuilt, Pskov
1536 Church Saints Boris and Gleb, Plotniki
1547 Church Decapitation John the Baptist, Moscow
c. 1548 Morality plays, Novgorod
c. 1553–1600 Cathedral Virgin of Intercession on Moat (St. Basil's the Blessed), Red Square, Moscow
1557 Trinity Church, Holy Ghost Monastery, Novgorod
1559–85 Dormition Cathedral, Trinity-Sergius Monastery
1571 *Skomorokhi* mentioned *Novgorod Chronicles*
1589 *Code Tsar Fedor Ivanovich*, regulation *skomorokhi*
c. 1598 Trinity Church, Moscow

Seventeenth century
1613 Performance chambers, Moscow court
1615 Kiev religious puppet shows
1628 Dormition Church, Uglich
1634–35 Intercession Church, Moscow
1635–36 Kremlin "terem" palace
1635–37 Church Saints Zosima and Savvatii, Zagorsk
1643 Holy Trinity Church, Nikitinki, Moscow
1647–50 Church Prophet Elijah, Yaroslavl
1648 Tsar Aleksei forbids *skomorokhi*
1649–52 Church Nativity of Virgin, Putinki, Moscow
1649–54 Church Ioan Zlatoust, Korovniki, Yaroslavl
1658 Vasily Likhachev on Italian theatre
1672 Pastor Gregory stages adaptation *Book of Esther*
1673 Ballet *Orpheus and Eurydice*; Tsar Aleksei funds theatre

1632–34 War with Poland
1637 Don Cossacks seize Azov
1645–76 Reign Aleksei
1647 Russian-Polish alliance against Turks
1648 Ukrainian liberation war, Boghdan Khmelnitsky
1649 *Ulozhenie*, code of laws
1652 Nikon Patriarch
1654 Beg. Schism (*Raskol*); Old Believers
1654 Ukrainian Rada allegiance to Russian tsar
1654–57 Russo–Polish War
1659 Pan-Slavist Yury Krizhanich in Moscow
1661–72 First Russian expeditions Kamchatka
1664 S. Polotsky's Latin school (Moscow)
1665 Mail service established
1666–67 Church council deposes Nikon
1669–71 Stenka Razin rebellion
1676–82 Reign Fedor III, regent Prince Vasily Golitsin
1682–1725 Reign Peter I "the Great" (initially with brother Ivan)
1687 Greek-Latin-Slavonic Academy (Moscow)
1695 War with Turkey/Crimean Tartars
1696 Naval fleet; Turks surrender Azov
1697–98 Peter travels West
1698 *Streltsy* revolt
1699 Trading companies formed; Julian calendar

Eighteenth century
1700 Beg. Northern War with Sweden
1701–03 Foundation St. Petersburg
1705 Military draft instituted
1708 Administrative reforms; provinces created
1709 Battle of Poltava
1710 War with Turkey

Eighteenth century
1703 first Russian newspaper *Vedomosti* (News)
1710 new "civil" alphabet
1711–27 five printing presses open St. Petersburg
1735 Trediakovsky's *New and Brief Method for Composing Russian Verses*
1743 Lomonosov's *Ode on Conquest of Khotina*

1676 Tsar Fedor evicts theatre from court
1678 Ushakov's *Saviour Not Done by Hands*
1678–83 Potekhin's Trinity Church, Ostankino, Moscow
1679–82 Church St. Nicholas, Kamovniki, Moscow
1684–93 Epiphany Church, Yaroslavl
1687–95 Church Resurrection in Kadashi, Moscow
1690–1704 Church Icon of Sign at Petrovo, Moscow
1695 Church of Ascension, Suzdal
1697–1703 Nativity Church, Bell Tower, Nizhny-Novgorod
1698–1704 Church St. Anne, Uzkoe, Moscow

Eighteenth century
1701–7 Church Archangel Gabriel (Menshikov Tower)
1702 Kunst's theatre troupe arrives
1703 Peter and Paul Fortress
1705 Peter I decree on comedies; Prokopovich's *Vladimir*

History

1711 Senate replaces boyar duma
1712 St. Petersburg new capital
1713 Conquest Finland
1718 Poll tax; judicial reform
1721 Treaty Nystad. Peter Emperor. Patriarchate abolished
1722 War with Persia; Table of Ranks instituted
1723 Treaty gives Russia Caspian Sea's southern shores
1725 Academy of Sciences opens; First Kamchatka expedition
1725–27 Reign Catherine I
1727 Treaty with China; Bering discovers strait
1727–30 Reign Peter II
1730–40 Reign Anna I
1735–40 War with Turkey
1739 Tatishchev proposes Urals Europe–Asia divide
1740–41 Reign Ivan VI
1741–61 Reign Elizabeth I
1744 Russia joins Warsaw pact
1755 Moscow University founded
1757 Treaty with France, Austria; Russia invades Prussia
1759 Russian forces occupy Berlin
1761–62 Reign Peter III
1762–96 Reign Catherine II ("the Great")
1764 Government takes church lands and peasants; women's education Smolny Convent
1767 Catherine's Legislative Commission
1768–74 War with Turkey
1772 First partition Poland

Literature

1747 Sumarkov's *Khorev*
1748 Lomonosov's *Short Guide to Rhetoric*
1757 Lomonosov's *Russian Grammar*
1763 Voltaire–Catherine II correspondence
1766 Trediakovsky's *Tilemakhida*
1769–70 Novikov's *Truten*
c. 1770 *Brigadier*
1779–89 *Moscow News*
1782 *The Minor*; "Felitsa"
1786 Catherine II's plays
1790 Radishchev's *Journey from St. Petersburg to Moscow*
1791 *Moscow Journal*
1792 "Poor Liza"
1797 Karamzin beg. *Letters of Russian Traveler*
1799 Pushkin b.

Performing Arts, Art, Architecture

1711–14 Summer Palace
1712 Imperial court moves to St. Petersburg
1712–33 Trezzini's Saints Peter and Paul Cathedral, St. Petersburg
1714 Kunstkammer; Church Transfiguration, Kizhi
1714–52 LeBlond, Braunstein, Michetti, Rastrelli's Peterhof
1715 Aleksandr Nevsky Monastery, St. Petersburg
1716 Princess Natalie stages plays
1716–24 Second Winter Palace
1720 Peter I hires Prague actors
1722–26 Saints Peter and Paul Cathedral, Kazan
1722–41 Twelve Colleges, Vasilevsky Island, St. Petersburg
1724 Bidlow play, Moscow
c. 1727 Leshchinsky theatre, Siberia
1729 Volkov, actor, b.
1731–34 Church Saints Simeon and Anna
1733 Dmitrevsky. b.
1734 Winter Palace Theatre, St. Petersburg
1732–38 Admiralty, St. Petersburg
1735–39 Korobov's Church, St. Panteleimon
1738 Dance school, St. Petersburg
1741–43 Rastrelli's Summer Palace
1741–50 Rastrelli, Zemtsov's Anichkov Palace
1743 *Musical Rose without Thorns*, St. Petersburg court
1748–64 Resurrection Cathedral, Rastrelli's Smolny Convent
1749 Nobleman's Corps' production *Khorev*
1750 Elizabeth encourages Russian actors; Yaroslav troupe's *About Penance of Sinful Man*

1752 Volkov's Yaroslav performances; formal actors' training
1754–62 Rastrelli's Winter Palace
1756 Opera *Taniusha*
1757 Academy of Arts, St. Petersburg
1762 Actors given noble rank
1763 Volkov d.
1768–82 Falconet's *Bronze Horseman*
1768–85 Rinaldi's Marble Palace, St. Petersburg
1772 M. Popov's *Anyuta*; Synodal Typography prints *znamennyi* chants
1773 D. Levitsky's women's portraits
1774 Journal *Musical Entertainments*
1776 Bolshoi Theatre of Opera and Ballet; Trutovsky's collection folk songs
1779 D. Bortniansky, Dir. Imperial Chapel Choir; Dmitrevsky head dramatic school
1780–1801 Cameron's architectural ensemble, Pavlovsk
1782–86 Cameron's Temple of Friendship, Pavlovsk
1783 Bolshoi Kamennyi Theatre
1784–86 Bazhenov's Pashkov House, Moscow
1788 Shchepkin b.
1797 V. L. Borovikovsky's *Portrait of M. I Lopukhina*
1799 Kozlovsky's Statue Suvorov, Field of Mars

Nineteenth century
1800 Mochalov b.
1802 Karatygin b.
1804 Glinka b.
1804–18 Martos' sculpture Minin & Pozharsky, Red Square
1805 decree instituting Imperial Theatres
1806–23 Zacharov's Admiralty, St. Petersburg
1808 Smolny Institute; Didelot's *Zephyr and Flora*; *Drama News*

Nineteenth century
1802–03 *Herald of Europe*; A. N. Radishchev's suicide
1803 Karamzin's *Marfa Posadnitsa*; *Discourse on Old and New Style in Russian Language*
1808 Zhukovsky's *Lyudmila*
1809 Krylov's *Fables*
1811–16 Collegium of Amateurs of Russian Word
1815 "Arzamas" literary circle
1816 Karamzin's *History of Russian State* (completed 1829)

1773 Diderot visits Russia
1773–75 Pugachev rebellion
1783 Crimea annexed. Dashkova heads Academy
1784 Alaska settled
1785 Charter of Nobility
1787 War with Ottoman Empire
1788 Sweden declares war
1794 Kosciusko rebellion
1796–1801 Reign Paul I
1796 Prussian military reforms

Nineteenth century
1801–25 Reign Alexander I
1802 Creation government ministries
1804–06 Expansion Caucasus
1805–06 V. Kruzenshtern's expedition
1806–12 War with Turkey
1807 Battle Friedland; Treaty Tilsit
1808 A. Arakcheev Defense Minister
1808–09 War with Sweden, annexation Finland
1810 Lyceum Tsarskoe Selo, founded

History

1812 Invasion of Napoleon; Battles Borodino, Smolensk
1812 Fort Ross, California, founded
1813 Battle Leipzig
1814 Russian forces in Paris
1814–15 Vienna Congress
1815 Holy Alliance signed
1819 St. Petersburg University founded
1819–21 Exploration Antarctica
1825 Decembrist revolt
1825–55 Reign Nicholas I
1826–28 Russian-Persian War
1830–32 M. Speransky Russian Code of Laws
1833 S. Uvarov Minister Public Education
1834 Herzen-Ogarev circle arrested; Kiev University founded
1834–59 Shamil' rebellion Caucasus
1842–51 Railroad track St. Petersburg–Moscow
1849 Petrashevsky circle arrested
1854–56 Crimean War
1855–81 Reign Alexander II ("the Tsar Liberator")
1856 N. Lobachevsky d.
1857 Herzen's and Ogarev's *Kolokol* journal begun, London
1858 Treaty with China; Amur region acquired
1859 Conquest Caucasus
1860–73 Expansion railways
1861 Emancipation peasants
1864 Local government (*Zemstvos*); education, judicial reforms
1867 Russian trans. Marx's "Das Kapital"; Alaska sold

Literature

1817 Batyushkov's *Dying Tasso*
1818 *Fatherland Annals*
1819 Society of Lovers of Russian Letters
1820 *Ruslan and Liudmila*
1821 Pushkin's *Prisoner of Caucasus*; Dostoevsky b.
1823 Society of Wisdom; *Polar Star*
1824 *Mnemozyne*; *Woe from Wit*
1825 *Moscow Telegraph*; *Boris Godunov*
1827 *Moscow Herald*
1828 Tolstoy b.
1829 Yury Miloslavsky or *Russians in 1812*
1830 *Belkin Tales, Little Tragedies*
1831 *Evenings on Farm near Dikanka, Telescope*
1833 *Eugene Onegin, Bronze Horseman*, "Queen of Spades"
1834 Belinsky's *Literary Reveries*
1835 *Arabesques, Mirgorod; Masquerade*
1836 *Captain's Daughter, Contemporary; Inspector General*, "Nose"
1837 Pushkin d.; Lermontov's "Death of Poet"; Chaadaev's *Apology of Madman*
1839 *Fatherland Notes*
1840 *Hero of Our Time, Mtsyri; Aksakov's Family Chronicle*
1841 Lermontov d.
1842 *Dead Souls*, "Overcoat," *Marriage,*
1846 *Russian Nights*
1846 *Poor Folk, Double*; Herzen's *Who is to Blame?*
1847 Gogol's *Selected Passages*; Goncharov's *Common Story*
1850 *Diary of Superfluous Man, Month in the Country; From the Other Shore*

Performing Arts, Art, Architecture

1810 Stock Exchange Building, St. Petersburg
1811 Voronikhin completes Kazan Cathedral
1812 First Russian vaudeville Shakhovskoy's *Cossack Poet*
1818 Sadovsky, b.
1818–58 Montferrand's St. Isaac's Cathedral
1819–29 Rossi's General Staff Building
1823 V.A. Tropinin's *Lace-Maker*
1824 Maly Theatre, Moscow becomes state theatre
1827 Kiprensky's *Portrait of A.S. Pushkin*
1828–32 Rossi's Alexandrinsky Theatre
1829–37 Orlovsky's sculpture Kutuzov and Barclay de Tolly, St. Petersburg
1830–33 Briullov's *Last Day of Pompei*
1832 Briullov's *Horsewoman*
1833 Borodin b.
1836 *Life for the Czar; Inspector General*
1839 Mussorgsky b.
1839–49 Ton's Bolshoi Kremlin Palace
1840 Tchaikovsky b.
1842 Glinka's *Ruslan and Liudmila*
1844 Rimsky-Korsakov b.; Repin b.
1848 Glinka's *Kamarinskaia*
1856 Vrubel b.
1857 Ivanov's *Christ's Appearance to the People*
1858 I. Molchanov's folk chorus
1860 Levitan b.
1862 St. Petersburg Conservatory; Mighty Group (*kuchka*); Mikeshin's sculpture *Millennium of Russia*, Novgorod; Balakirev, Lomakin's music school
1863 Stanislavsky b.

1868 Russians occupy Samarkand
1869 Dmitry Mendeleev periodic law of elements
1870–77 N. N. Miklukho-Maklai expeditions Malaysia
1870–85 N. M. Przhevalsky expeditions Central Asia
1871–72 Conservative education reforms
1874 Populist movement "going to the people"
1875 Treaty with Japan; Russia acquires Sakhalin
1876 Revolutionary group Land and Liberty
1877–78 Russo–Turkish War; Treaty San Stefano; Berlin Congress
1880 K. N. Pobedonostsev head Holy Synod
1881 Alexander II assassinated
1881–94 Reign Alexander III
1882 Artistic-Manufacturing Exposition, Moscow
1885 Anglo-Russian conflict Afghanistan
1889 S. Kovalevskaya first woman member Academy of Sciences
1891 Trans–Siberian railroad begun
1891–93 Famines
1892–1903 Witte reforms
1894–1917 Reign Nicholas II
1895 Lenin, Social Democrats arrested; textile workers' strikes
1896 Treaty with China
1897 Socialist Revolutionary Party founded
1898 Social Democratic Party founded

1852 *Notes of Hunter*; Tolstoy's *Childhood*
1854 Tiutchev's *Verses*; Ostrovsky's *Poverty's No Vice*; Tolstoy's *Boyhood*
1855 *Sevastopol's Stories*; Afanasiev's *Russian Folk Tales*
1856 *Rudin*; Saltykov-Schedrin's *Provincial Sketches*
1857 Tolstoy's *Youth*
1858 *A Thousand Souls*
1859 *Oblomov*; *Nest of the Gentry*; *Storm*; Dobroliubov's "What is Oblomovism?"
1860 *On the Eve*
1860–62 *House of the Dead*; Chekhov b.
1862 *Fathers and Children*
1863 *What is to Be Done?* Nekrasov's *Who is Happy in Russia?*
1864 *Notes from Underground*
1865–69 *War and Peace*
1866 *Crime and Punishment*
1868 *Idiot*; *Fatherland Notes*.
1869 Goncharov's *Precipice*
1871 *The Devils*; Ostrovsky's *Forest*
1872 Leskov's *Cathedral Folk*
1873 *Anna Karenina*
1876 Dostoevsky's *Meek Woman*
1877 Turgenev's *Virgin Soil*
1878–80 Soloviev's *White Lily*
1880 *The Golovlyovs*; *Brothers Karamazov*
1881 Dostoevsky d.
1882 Tolstoy's *Confession*
1883 Fet's *Evening Fires*
1887 *The Power of Darkness*
1888 Chekhov's "Steppe"
1889 *Kreutzer Sonata*
1892 Chekhov's "Ward No.6"; Merezhkovsky's *Symbols*
1893 Chekhov's *Sakhalin Island*
1894 *Russian Symbolists*
1895 *Russian Word*

1866 Tchaikovsky's *Symphony No: :*; Kandinsky b.; Moscow Conservatory
1869 Mussorgsky's *Boris Godunov*
1872 Diaghilev b.; Scriabin b.; Kramskoy's *Christ in Desert*
1873 S.V. Rachmaninov b.; Repin's *Volga Barge-Haulers*; Chaliapin b.
1874 Mussorgsky's *Paintings from an Exhibition*; Roerich b.
1876 *Swan Lake*
1878 Tchaikovsky's *Eugene Onegin*
1880 Opekushin's Pushkin's statue, Moscow; *Khovanshchina*
1881 Mussorgsky d.
1882 Rimsky-Korsakov's *Snow Maiden*; Stravinsky b.
1883 Cathedral Christ the Savior, Moscow
1884–87 Surikov's *Boyarina Morozova*
1888 *Scheherazade*; Stanislavsky's Society of Art and Literature
1890 Tchaikovsky's *Queen of Spades, Sleeping Beauty*, ch. M.I. Petipa; Vrubel's *Demon*; *Prince Igor*
1891 Rachmaninov's 1st Piano Concerto
1892 *Nutcracker*; Tretiakov donates art collection, Moscow
1893 Tchaikovsky's *Symphony No: 6*; Tchaikovsky d.
1894 Levitan's *Above Eternal Peace*; Rachmaninov's *Aleko*; A. Bakhrushin museum
1895 *Swan Lake*, chs. M. Petipa, L. Ivanov
1896 First film showing, St. Petersburg
1897 *Raymonda*; Borodin d.; Moscow Art Theatre
1898 *World of Art*; Vasnetsov's *Bogatyrs*; Eisenstein b.; MAT's *Tsar Fedor Ivanovich, Sea Gull*
1899 First World of Art Exhibition; MAT's *Uncle Vanya*

History

Twentieth century

1900 Boxer Rebellion; Russian occupation
Manchuria

1902 Lenin's *What Is to Be Done?*; strikes, unrest
villages

1903 Split SR Party, Bolsheviks and Mensheviks;
Kishinev pogroms

1904 V. Phleve assassinated; I. Pavlov Nobel Prize

1904–05 Russo–Japanese War

1905 "Bloody Sunday"; Tsushima, Cadet Party;
Lenin returns Russia

1906 First Duma; Petr Stolypin Prime Minister;
agrarian reforms

1907 Second Duma (dismissed); Third Duma

1910 First Russian automobiles and airplanes

1911 Stolypin assassinated. *Pravda* first number

1913 Three Hundredth Anniversary House of
Romanovs

1914 Beg. WWI; St. Petersburg renamed Petrograd;
Battle Tannenberg

1916 Rasputin murdered; numerous strikes

1917 February (March) revolution; Tsar Nicholas
abdicates; Provisional Government; Council
Russian Orthodox Church; October (Nov.)
Revolution

1918 Constitutional Assembly disbanded; Treaty
Brest–Litovsk; Tsar, family murdered; "Red
Terror"

Literature

1896 *Sea Gull*

1897 *Uncle Vanya*

1898 *Father Sergius*

1899 Foma Gordeev; *Resurrection*

Twentieth century

1901 *Three Sisters*

1902 Bely's *Symphonies*; *Lower Depths*

1904 *Cherry Orchard*; *Verses of a Beautiful Lady*; *Hadji-
Murat*; *Scales*

1905 Kuprin's *Duel*

1906 Briusov's *Wreath*

1907 *Mother*

1908 Second vol. Blok's verses;

1909 *Vekhi* (Landmarks)

1910 Tolstoy d.; *Apollon*

1911 Guild of Poets

1912 *A Slap in the Face of Public Taste*

1913 St. Petersburg; Mandelstam's *Stone*; Rozanov's
Fallen Leaves (1913–15); *Rose and Cross*

1914 Akhmatova's *Rosary*

1915 *Cloud in Pants*; *Backbone Flute*; Kuprin's *The Pit*

1916 Gorky's *In the World*; Esenin's *Radunitsa*; *St.
Petersburg* (revised 1921)

1917 Proletkult

1918 *The Twelve*, *Scythians*; Bely's *Christ is Risen*;

1919 GOSIZDAT. Nabokov's family emigrates

1920 VAPP; "The Smithy"

1921 *Naked Year*; Serapion Brothers; *Red Virgin Soil*;
Formalism; *Change of Landmarks*; Blok d.;
Gumilyov executed

1922 Left Front of Art; *Kotik Letaev*; Akhmatova's *Anno
Domini MCMXXI*; Mandelstam's *Tristia*;

Performing Arts, Art, Architecture

Twentieth century

1900 Vrubel's *Swan Princess*; Benois' *Monplaisir,
Petergof*

1901 MAT's *Three Sisters*; Somov's *In Park of Versailles*

1901–03 Repin's *Meeting of State Council*

1901–07 Nesterov's *Holy Rus'*

1901–09 Rachmaninov's concertos

1902 Vrubel's *Demon Downcast*

1904 MAT's *Cherry Orchard*

1905–07 Scriabin's *Poem of Ecstasy*

1906 Glazunov's *8th Symphony*; Shostakovich b.;
Blok's, Meyerhold's *Puppet Show*

1907 Parland's Church of Resurrection, Savior on
Blood; Blue Rose Society; Rachmaninov's *2nd
Symphony*

1908 Rimsky-Korsakov d.; *Chopeniana*, ch. Fokine;
Stravinsky's *Nightingale*; Drankov's first feature
film, *Stenka Razin and Princess*

1909 Trubetskoi's sculpture Alexander III, St.
Petersburg; Somov's *Young Lady Asleep*; Grabar's
art history

1910 Vrubel d.; Scriabin's *Prometheus*; "Jack of
Diamonds"; Stravinsky, Fokine's *Firebird*; MAT's
Brothers Karamazov; Piatnitsky Folk Chorus

1911 Stravinsky, Fokine's *Petrushka*, Ballets Russes;
Larionov's *Relaxing Soldier*

1911–14 Kandinsky's "Blue Horseman" group; *On
Spiritual in Art*

1918–21 Civil War
1919 Decree state ownership land
1920 Soviet-Polish War; nationalization small businesses
1921 Kronstadt Rebellion; NEP; 10th Party Congress; Gosplan
1922 Stalin General Secretary; expulsion intellectuals
1923 USSR constitution
1924 d. Lenin; Petrograd named Leningrad; Atheist League
1925 14th Congress; TASS
1927 Trotsky, Zinoviev expelled from Party; 15th Congress
1928 First Five Year Plan; beg. collectivization; 6th Komintern Congress
1929 Trotsky deported; policy "kulak liquidation"
1930 Gulag started; 16th Congress
1931 "Work days" on collective farms; White Sea Canal
1932 Internal passport system; famine (esp. Ukraine)
1933 Diplomatic relations with USA
1934 Kirov murdered; 17th Congress; USSR in League of Nations
1935 New Soviet constitution; Moscow metro; Stakhanov movement
1935–38 Purges, political trials
1936 Soviet aid anti-Franco forces
1938 Beria replaces Ezhov head NKVD; third Five Year Plan
1939 Beg. WWII; Molotov–Ribbentrop pact; 18th Congress; invasion Finland
1940 Trotsky assassinated; creation Baltic republics
1941 Germany invades; army approaches Moscow
1941–44 Siege Leningrad
1942 National mobilization; Battle Stalingrad;

Khodasevich's *A Heavy Lyre*
1923 *On Guard*; *Pereval*; Mandelstam's *Noise of Time*; Tsvetaeva's *Craft*; Babel's *Odessa Tales*
1924 Leonov's *Badgers*; Esenin's *Moscow of the Taverns*; *Iron Flood*
1925 *White Guard*; *Cement*; Esenin suicide
1926 *Red Cavalry*
1927 *Envy*; *The Rout*; *Tale of Unextinguished Moon*; *We*
1928 *Quiet Don*; *Twelve Chairs*; *Bedbug*; Tsvetaeva's *After Russia*; Gorky returns; RAPP
1929 A. N. Tolstoy's *Peter the First*
late 1920s Platonov's *Chevengur*
1930 Shklovsky renounces "formalism"; Mayakovsky suicide
c. 1930 Platonov's *Foundation Pit*
1931 *Golden Calf*; Pasternak's *Safe Conduct*; G. Ivanov's *Roses*
1932 *Time Forward!*, *Virgin Soil Upturned* (1932–60); *How Steel Was Tempered*; Union of Soviet Writers
1933 Bunin Nobel Prize;
1934 Mandelstam arrested
1935 Akhmatova's *Requiem* (1935–40)
1936 Gorky d.
1937 B. Pilnyak arrested; Nabokov's *Gift*
1938 Mandelstam arrested, d.; Nabokov's *Invitation to a Beheading*
1939 I. Babel arrested
1940 *Master and Margarita* (1928–1940)
1941 Tsvetaeva suicide; *Vasily Tyorkin*
1942 *Russian People*
1943 *Days and Nights*; *Before Sunrise*
1945 *Young Guard*
1946 Fedin's *Early Joys*; Nekrasov's *In Trenches of Stalingrad*
1948 Fedin's *No Ordinary Summer*
1954 Ehrenburg's *The Thaw*

1912 Petrov-Vodkin's *Bathing of Red Horse*; Malevich's *Taking in Rye*; Donkey Tail Exhibition; Craig, Stanislavsky's *Hamlet*
1913 Rachmaninov's *Bells*; Stravinsky, Nizhinsky's *The Rite of Spring*; Malevich's *Black Square*; *Victory over the Sun*
1915 Scriabin d.; Kustodiev's *Woman Merchant*; Malevich's *Black and Red Squares*
1916 Korovin's *Fish, Wine and Fruits*
1917 Stravinsky's *Soldier's Story*; Meyerhold's *Masquerade*
1918 MAT First Studio; *Mystery Bouffe*; State Film School
1919 Prokofiev's *Love for Three Oranges*; theatres nationalized; Bolshoi Dramatic Theatre
1920 Evreinov's *Taking of Winter Palace*
1922 MAT tour abroad; Popova, Meyerhold's *Magnanimous Cuckold*; AkhRR; Vakhtangov's *Turandot*
1923 Stravinsky, Nizhinsky's *Noces*, Grand Opera
1924 Protazanov's *Aelita*
1925 Vasilenko, Goleizovsky's ballet *Joseph the Splendid*; OST "4 Arts"; Eisenstein's *Strike*, *Potemkin*; TRAM (Theatre of Young Workers)
1926 Maly Theatre's *Liubov Yarovaya*; MAT's *Days of the Turbins*; Meyerhold's *Inspector General*
1927 Stravinsky's *Oedipus Rex*; Grieg's *Ice Maiden*; MAT, Ivanov's *Armored Train 14–69*
1928 Filonov's *Formula of Spring*; Stravinsky's *Apollo Musaget*, Ballets Russes; Eisenstein's *October*
1929 Prokofiev's *Gambler*; Eisenstein's *Old and New*
1930 Shostakovich's *Nose*, *Golden Century*; Dovzhenko's *Earth*
1932 Shostakovich's *Lady Macbeth of Mtsensk District*
1933 Nissky's *On the Track*; Vishnevsky's *Optimistic Tragedy*

History

Accords U.S. and Great Britain
1943 Battles Kursk, Rostov, Kharkov
1943–44 Deportations (Kalmyks, Chechens, Crimean Tatars)
1944 Soviet forces counter-attack; Dumbarton Oaks; Vlasov anti-Soviet army
1945 Soviet forces enter Germany; War Japan; end WWII; UN; Potsdam
1945–48 Communist governments Eastern Europe
1947 USSR rejects Marshall Plan
1948 Berlin blockade
1949 FRG and GDR; NATO; USSR atom bomb
1950 Treaty with China; Korean War
1952–53 Anti-Jewish campaign; 19th Party Congress
1953 d. Stalin; Beria shot; Malenkov, Molotov, Khrushchev gov; USSR nuclear bomb
1954 Crimea made part Ukrainian Republic; first Soviet nuclear plant
1955 Warsaw Pact; Khrushchev's "corn campaign"
1956 20th Party Congress; Khrushchev's "secret speech"; Hungarian revolt
1957 Molotov, Malenkov, Kaganovich expelled Central Committee; Sputnik
1959 Camp David meetings; beg. anti-religious campaign
1960 U2; USSR supports Castro, Lumumbo
1961 Gagarin first manned space flight; 22nd Congress
1962 Cuban missile crisis
1963 USSR, US, Great Britain Nuclear Treaty
1964 Khrushchev resigns; Brezhnev Party Secretary, Kosygin chairman, Council of Ministers

Literature

1955 Doctor Zhivago
1956 Dudintsev's Not by Bread Alone; Fadeev suicide
1958 A. Tvardovsky's New World; Pasternak Nobel Prize
1959 Fedin First Secretary Union of Soviet Writers
1960 Pasternak d.
1961 Nekrasov's Kira Georgievna; Vasily Aksenov's Ticket to Stars; Evtushenko's "Babi Yar"
1962 Bondarev's Silence; One Day in Life of Ivan Denisovich
1963 Tyorkin in Other World; "Matryona's Home"; Paustovsky's Story of a Life
1964 Okudzhava's Merry Drummer
1965 Sholokhov Nobel Prize; Brodsky's Poems and Narrative Verse; Sinyavsky imprisoned
1966 Shalamov's Kolyma Tales, Bulgakov's Master and Margarita pub.
1968 First Circle, Cancer Ward pub.
1970 Erofeev's Moscow-Petushki, Iskander's Goatibex Constellation; Solzhenitsyn Nobel Prize
1971 August 1914
1972 Brodsky emigrates
1973 Arkhipelag Gulag, 3 vols. (1973–75); Iskander's Sandro from Chegem; A. Sinyavsky emigrates
1974 V. Nekrasov, V. Maksimov, A. Galich emigrate
1975 Voinovich's Life and Extraordinary Adventures of Chonkin
1976 Rasputin's Farewell to Matyora; Trifonov's House on Embankment
1977 Brodsky's End of Beautiful Epoch, A Part of Speech
1978 Bitov's Pushkin House
1980 V. Voinovich, V. Aksenov, L. Kopelev exiled

Performing Arts, Art, Architecture

1934 Vasiliev's film Chapayev; Okhlopkov's Iron Flood
1935 Meyerhold's Queen of Spades; Kandinsky's Movement I
1936 Stanislavsky's Actor Prepares; Rachmaninov's Symphony No. 3
1937 Shostakovich's Symphony No. 5; Mukhina's Worker and Kolkhoznitsa; Pimenov's New Moscow
1938 Aleksandr Nevsky; Alexandrov's Volga-Volga
1940 Rachmaninov's Symphonic Dances; Prokofiev, Lavrovsky's Romeo and Juliet
1941 Shostakovich's Leningrad Symphony; Kuleshov's Fundamentals of Film Direction
1941–43 Prokofiev's War and Peace
1942 Plastov's Fascist Flew Past
1943 Rachmaninov d.; Kandinsky's Around the Line
1944 Kandinsky d.; Ivan the Terrible Part I
1947 Roerich d.
1948 Eisenstein d.
1951 Stravinsky's Rake's Progress; Plastov's Tractor Driver's Supper
1954 Shostakovich's Preludes & Fugue for Piano
1955 Prokofiev's Fire Angel
1956 Jakobson, Khachaturian's Spartacus
1957 Grigorovich's Stone Flower; Neizvestnyi's Atomic Explosion; Tovstonogov's Idiot; Kalatozov's Cranes Are Flying
1958 Ivan the Terrible Part II; Contemporary Theatre (Moscow)
1959 Chukhrai's Ballad of a Soldier
1961 Kremlin Palace of Congresses
1962 Shostakovich's Symphony No. 13; Tovstonogov's Woe from Wit; Manège Exhibition; Tarkovsky's

Ivan's Childhood

1965 Paradzhanov's Shadows of Forgotten Ancestors
1967 Television tower Ostankino
1968 Grigorovich's Spartacus, Bolshoi Theatre
1969 Shostakovich's Symphony No. 14; Rabin's Violin at Cemetery
1970–72 Popkov's Father's Overcoat
1971 Bulatov's Horizon; Shostakovich's Symphony No. 15; Stravinsky d.; Liubimov, Vysotsky's Hamlet; Tarkovsky's Andrei Rublev; Kozintsev's King Lear
1972 Popkov's After Work; Tarkovsky's Solaris
1973 Efros' Don Juan; Contemporary's Ascent of Mt. Fuji
1974 Bulldozer Exhibition, Moscow; Shukshin's Red Snowball Tree; Liubimov, Abramov's Wooden Horses
1974–75 Schnittke's Requiem
1975 Shostakovich d.; Tovstonogov's Story of a Horse; Riazanov's Irony of Fate
1977 Shchedrin's Dead Souls; Schnittke's Concerto grosso; Liubimov's Master and Margarita
1977–80 Neizvestnyi's Scream
1978 Liubimov's Crime and Punishment
1980 Denisov's Requiem; Kabakov's On Gray and White Paper
1982–86 Shemyakin's Carnivals of St. Petersburg
1985 Dodin, Abramov's Brothers and Sisters
1986 5th Congress Filmmakers' Union
1987 Shchedrin's Millennium of Christianization
1990s new const. Cathedral Christ the Savior, Moscow

1981 Aksenov's Island Crimea; Aitmatov's Day is Longer Than a Century
1987 A. Rybakov's Children of Arbat; Brodsky Nobel Prize

1967 Yury Andropov heads KGB; treaty on cosmos
1968 "Prague Spring"; Brezhnev Doctrine
1969 Helsinki meetings US and USSR
1972 USSR–Iraq pact; Nixon visits Moscow
1974 Expulsion A. Solzhenitsyn; Nuclear Arms accords
1975 BAM construction
1976 25th Congress; Nuclear Arms accords; 10th Five Year Plan
1977 New USSR constitution
1979 Invasion Afghanistan; Strategic Arms Treaty
1980 Boycotted Moscow Olympics; Sakharov exiled Gorky
1981 26th Party Congress; Geneva talks
1982 Suslov d.; Brezhnev d.; Yury Andropov General Secretary
1984 Konstantin Chernenko General Secretary; Stockholm talks;
1985 Mikhail Gorbachev General Secretary; Reagan–Gorbachev Summit
1985–87 Boris Yeltsin, Mayor of Moscow
1986 27th Congress; perestroika; Chernobyl
1987 Strategic Arms Treaty
1988 19th All-Union Party Congress; party reforms; Millennium Russian Orthodoxy
1989 First Congress People's Deputies; Second Congress; Bush–Gorbachev summit
1990 Gorbachev President USSR; 28th Party Congress; Yeltsin head Russian Republic
1991 Warsaw Pact dissolved; attempted putsch; USSR dissolved; Gorbachev resigns; Commonwealth of Independent States
1992 Russian Republics pact
1993 Yeltsin dissolves Parliament; new parliamentary elections

Note on names and transliteration

Names are transliterated from their Russian forms with the exception of familiar examples (Leo Tolstoy, Alexandre Benois). The Library of Congress transliteration system predominates although contributors were allowed some leeway, in part to adjust to their sense of common usage.

1

Russian cultural history: introduction

What are the lessons of Russian culture, what does it have to offer 1
us and our time? Fortunately, Russian cultural studies have a rich history
– including the works of Nikolai Berdiaev, Pavel Miliukov, George
Vernadsky, Nicholas Riasanovsky, Wladimir Weidle, Georges Florovsky,
Dmitry Chizhevsky, James Billington, Mikhail Bakhtin, and Dmitry
Likhachev (who is a contributor to this volume and a link to the earlier
tradition), and more recently Alain Besançon, Yury Lotman, Caryl
Emerson, Katerina Clark, Boris Groys, Mikhail Epstein, Irina Paperno,
Boris Uspensky and Geoffrey Hosking among others – that offers orientation and points of engagement in answering such questions. In spite of a
rich diversity of approaches that have changed over time and in reaction
to historical and social context, these and other cultural analysts most
often depend on certain basic vantage points they assume in common,
whether in part or in whole. They are: the language origins of a culture,
its geographic location, its religious and ideological attachments, and its
broadly based folk ethos. Yet other points of view exist in aesthetic texts
that are equally open to history and later uses by cultural observers but
that have some material permanence in their media of transmission.

Such is the basis of the present book's structure. It is divided into two
parts: the first combining approaches to culture which frequently influence both observers and participants; the second, offering brief histories
of Russian contributions to the arts and emphasizing the modern period
from 1860 on. The intersections of these analytical and creative concerns
as well as the intersections within them of different personalities, events,
and artifacts provide a comprehensive overview, although considerations of space and general readership have limited the contributors to
introductions of many of the complex and varied parts of the Russian

cultural experience. Guidelines for further study and interpretation are provided in the suggested reading sections that accompany each chapter and in a chronological chart of major historical and cultural events.

Surprisingly, and notwithstanding a marked tendency among observers to see centrifugal and authoritarian tendencies as dominants, Russian cultural history suggests an openness to others, passionate but rapidly changing commitments, and a precarious existence for authorities. Geography – and particularly the open steppe noted by Mark Bassin – is a site and metaphor of this free-flowing cultural space. Russian boundaries can be seen to be constantly transgressed, most often by the Russians' own initiatives, beginning with the invitation noted in the *Primary Chronicle* issued to the Vikings to assume political leadership, continuing with Peter the Great's modernization project, and including the new Westernization of Boris Yeltsin. At other times transgressions occurred thanks to unwelcome intrusions: of the Mongols, the Poles, the French forces under Napoleon, and the German armies of Hitler. As a result both of such violent and more peaceful forms of intercourse with North and South, East and West, the Russians came to share the significant movements of the civilizations around them.

Major agents of cultural and historical development described in the following chapters included first the Scandinavians, who arrived in the eighth century to help organize tribes into the typical fiefdoms of the medieval world and to shape an economic trade route by water from the North Sea to the Black Sea. From the ninth century on, the Greeks, via Byzantium, provided the common religious and philosophical heritage that the Russians shared with the West. From the twelfth to the fourteenth century – subsequently defined as the "Tatar Yoke" by the Russians themselves – the Mongols stimulated political structures such as that for the central gathering of taxes, and helped create a strong distrust of politics on the part of the Russian people. The East also provided Russia's broadest frontier – the conditions F. J. Turner's *The Frontier in American History* defined as contributing to American national identity and comparable to what the Russians think of as the Siberian element in their character. The Western turn from the sixteenth century on enabled the Russians to share, with various degrees of enthusiasm, the cultural inclinations commonly noted as the Renaissance and the Enlightenment, the nineteenth-century ideological syndromes Abbott Gleason outlines culminating with Marxism, and the rival economic and political processes of the end of the twentieth.

On the whole, there are unlikely to be surprises when emphasis is placed on such cross-cultural conditions. There are, however, elements of history that carry unusual weight in this particular culture and that give it specific directions. The Mongol invasion was not merely a fleeting moment, as say the German presence in Paris in the Second World War, but lasted for over 250 years; the Renaissance occurred late in Russia and at a considerable distance from its original cultural energy in the West; the economic and political programs of Peter the Great and Stalin were brutal and extreme by any world standards. Other frequently noted geopolitical, economic, or social circumstances are: the lack of fresh water ports, the presence of numerous rivers for commerce, the drive to expansion encouraged by the fur trade, an insecure middle class, late industrialization and modernization, and the instabilities of an unusually large empire – by the modern era Russia included many different ethnic groups and religions and their proximity and intersections served both for mutual cultural enrichment, and the familiar social tensions and dilemmas of cultural diversity. If these conditions are not taken to be exclusionary or too important, thus reducing and simplifying what is richer and more complex than all of them put together, they can be seen to provide the economic and social superstructures on which the Russians built their cultural history.

Much of what Russian cultural identity is all about is suggested by the ways in which the Russians themselves reacted to such particularities of their geographic space and contacts throughout history. What were the basic directions and emphases of their response? The introductions to literature, art, music, theatre, and film included in this book are especially helpful in answering questions of this sort. The histories of aesthetic media indicate not only cultural processes, but cultural products transmitted through history and forming its strongest links. Books, paintings, opera scores, records of stage performances, and cinema recordings, are lasting, material evidence of explorations in a civilization's consciousness; they open cultural history to the creative engagements that show a society's highest aspirations, achievements, and doubts. They are both different from the hard evidence of social or economic acts, and often the most telling record of them. A strong indication of cultural directions – and a measure of validity for their interpretation – is the central and recurring responses of this creative record and the evidence it brings to the fundamental viewpoints of historical process.

The introductions to language and religion written by Dean Worth and Dmitry Likhachev – which assume divergent perspectives but arrive at the same decisive events – give us one starting point of definition. The investigation of cultural origins, Homi Bhabha and others have pointed out, is a risky business, subject both to the absurdity of continual regress in a search for first causes and continual reappraisals according to the predilections of observers arriving later in history. Most of what we know about early Russian culture comes down to us through the chronicles, those first expressions of both self-definition and literacy created by monks that begin with the intent of clarifying "the origins of the land of Rus'." As Dmitry Obolensky noted in an earlier Cambridge Companion (Robert Auty and Dmitry Obolensky, eds., *An Introduction to Russian Language and Literature*, 1977), the chronicles not only provided a universal framework within which the Russians could orient themselves, but were incomplete and thus ever open to future interpretations of the meaning and directions of the originary condition. Nevertheless, the chronicles make clear that literacy and religion were vital to the beginnings of cultural consciousness, and that their bonded early histories, thanks to the work of missionary representatives of Greek civilization, were of fundamental importance for later cultural development.

The Byzantine legacy – particularly in the aesthetic inclinations noted by Professor Likhachev – became a critical element of Russian Orthodoxy and Russian self-definition, although it is equally clear that Russian Orthodoxy itself did not become a fixed and unchanging doctrine based solely on Greek tradition but continued to evolve through a cross-cultural and open-ended process. Over time such interreligious transmutations included not only the Hesychast influence transmitted by the Greeks and striking in similarity to Sufi Moslem mysticism, but Ivan IV's extremist interpretations of the Judaic tradition and the Old Testament, the strong influence of Catholics such as Yury Krizhanich in the seventeenth century and Joseph de Maistre in the nineteenth, the Protestant inclinations shown in Peter the Great's time by Feofan Prokopovich, and various other fecund contacts.

The history of the Russian language charted by Dean Worth was part of this free-flowing and cross-cultural process. By Peter the Great's epoch – the time when Professor Worth ends his observations – modern Russian was essentially in place, although still evolving through interaction with other languages, particularly French, German, and later English. The continual flux of language and its natural propensity to undermine stable meanings was reflected in specific Russian instabilities. During the early nineteenth century French, not Russian, was the language of choice of the aristocracy and it is not surprising, therefore, that Petr Chaadaev, a young man who had a prolonged stay in Paris along with the Russian army that had defeated Napoleon, was sufficiently impressed by such contacts with other cultures to suggest that Russia had too little of its own and to argue that Catholicism best served humanity's universal obligations.

Chaadaev's often-cited example of cultural self-consciousness and insecurity is symptomatic of larger contrary patterns of stability and instabilities. On the one hand, the impermanence and flux of language did not stop the Russians from using their own language to grapple with the same religious concerns throughout their history, or to formulate beliefs in a transcendent realm of God's "truth of truths." Words of this sort create the ethical codes and borders that organize civilization, and the issues of aesthetic–ethical conjunctions, of love and its expression in universal engagement, of humility, and the self's obligations funda-mental to Russian Orthodoxy, were explored by language masters of the stature of Aleksandr Pushkin, Fedor Dostoevsky, Vladimir Soloviev, and Mikhail Bakhtin. On the other hand, the very nature of language's inevitable diffusions and a basic volatility at the religious core made such concepts problematic. The play of language and the attraction of sym-bolic formations over material ones, in combination with intransigence before earthly imperfections and the yearning for beauty and the absolute, if pushed far enough, can lead to a condition of perpetual dis-satisfaction, abstraction, and withdrawal from society, all manifested in Chaadaev's later life.

Withdrawal – to the desert, the monastery, the wanderer's roads, the philosopher's or theatre director's quiet rooms – was, in fact, one typical Russian cultural gesture. The urge or necessity to leave society, however, often stimulated by political considerations as during the Mongol era of St. Sergius of Radonezh or Constantine Stanislavsky's and Sergei Eisenstein's times of Stalinist terror, was frequently followed by subver-sion of the separate place by a sense of obligation. St. Sergius, thus, went on to build the monastery of Trinity-Sergius in Zagorsk that became an emblem of moral–social commitment and Russian cultural identity, and Stanislavsky and Eisenstein devoted the last part of their lives to students who continued the strong traditions of Russian theatre and film. The gesture of withdrawal was part of a larger cultural pattern for the Russians that combined intransigence, initial separation to better one's self, and optimism that such betterment could be put to good uses in the world at large.

Nevertheless, the optimistic reach for transcendent truths through self-betterment and the self-placement in a universal context that began with the chronicles contributed to excessive abstractions and neglect of the practical local realities – material things to satisfy human needs and political and legal structures to regulate them. That is not to say the Russians did not develop strong legal and political systems – the law codes of the early *Russkaia Pravda* (Russian Truth) or those implemented after the reforms of 1862 and 1912 were progressive for their day – but that their functions in society were always subverted by a larger yearning for the transcendent. A state of grace, the Russians held in their heart of hearts, could not be determined by the inevitable corruptions and hypocrisies of earthly laws and earthly politicians. The religious imperative of Russian culture, in André Malraux's words about Byzantine art, was "the charm of the absolute"; it resulted both in an inability to lower its sights, and the inevitable shocks of the real to the ideal that followed.

Communism, of course, was one such major shock. The Russians led the way in bringing Marx's upside-down religious principles to ideological and social-political realization and in discovering the consequences of pushing such ideologies too far. The prophecies of the Slavophiles, Soloviev, and Fedor Dostoevsky that Russia had a unique universal mission to contribute to humanity turned out to be true in the twentieth century, except the contributions they imagined were replaced by a cautionary tale of the central principles played out in historical communism – the diminution of human beings to social and economic categories implemented by force – and by the tragic earthly resolution of the perennial hopes of complete freedom, complete human mastery of the world, complete equality and moral being. This course of Marxism was the result of cultural predilections we have already noted: an eager welcome and use of ideas from the outside were only possible for an open culture; the radical intelligentsia's maximalism encouraged by its origins in the clerical class made political gradualism and concern for legal niceties unlikely; the notion that earthly means were secondary to ultimate ends sanctioned the expediencies of Soviet terror in serving the communist future; the moral obligations of sacrifice, humility, and disrespect for material things supported the party's programs and allowed its failures in servicing the everyday needs of USSR citizens.

An obvious lesson of Soviet cultural history, then, lies in the dangers of forcing utopias upon reality – or at least in excessively trusting those who advocate them – but to confine ourselves to such pessimistic modalities of the Russian cultural experience would be to underestimate it. For Aleksandr Herzen, Soloviev, Dostoevsky, and a host of other Russians who envisioned cultural utopias were fully aware of the quandaries and unrealities of their hopes, and the interesting cultural fact is that they did not stop hoping. They arrived at visionary realizations of ambitions shared by most civilized peoples, and they themselves, seeking the ideal, continued to question their discoveries in the most unrelenting ways. The larger lesson they provide – forgotten during communism – was not that one should stop hoping but that one should not stop questioning by accepting ideological reductions; the Soviet period of Russian culture was a moment when cultural questioning stopped and a mindless faith, encouraging Soviet citizens to live myopically and hypocritically, pre-dominated.

A central tenet of this faith was the notion of the *narod*, the people. As pointed out in Catriona Kelly's overview of popular culture the concept has been much abused, in the Russian instance, across the ideological spectrum. Social conditions – the sheer number of peasants who made up 80 to 85 percent of the Russian population at the end of the nineteenth century – provided the foundation for a vast and complex popular culture and combined with a moral sore point – serfdom – to make the peasants and their mores a central issue for upper-class culture as well. Both those who wanted to find native strengths in Russian history – the historian Mikhail Pogodin, the Slavophiles, Dostoevsky, Tolstoy – and those who looked to paradigms of progress from the outside – the Westernizers and the various socialists – imagined the peasant world to be a peculiar Russian advantage. The historical realities of poverty and servitude stimulated rather than undermined this vision, and serfdom, which ended in 1861 one year before Lincoln's proclamation freeing Afro-Americans, was as long-lasting in cultural repercussions and social retributions as American slavery. A crucial factor, reminiscent of American liberal angst in the 1960s, was the upper classes' feeling of guilt. It impelled the 1870s "going to the people," a specific historical event, but also a description of fundamental directions in Russian social and political agendas in the modern period.

And again, a maximalist insistence on this agenda of "the people" guided Russian cultural history on its problematic course in the modern era. Popular culture in the Soviet period became an object of ideological insistence, a central principle – *narodnost'* – of socialist realism and its mandate to develop easily understandable forms of communication to propagandize and impose the government's wishes. The beneficial effects of political concern for mass culture included the huge financial outlay the state injected into amateur organizations – theatres, dance troupes, choruses – that came to form part of the ubiquitous Palaces of Culture and that encouraged the ordinary citizen's participation in the arts. The negative effects of an imposed *narodnost'* was that it had neither the subversive benefits of free folk laughter and questioning of authorities Mikhail Bakhtin defined in a true people's culture, nor the opportunity for its participants to rise above the mediocre intellectual and creative standards encouraged by the government. As the Italian Marxist Antonio Gramsci once noted, all human beings, whatever their class origins, are potential intellectuals, but not all perform the social function of intellectuals. Soviet culture was predicated on the principle of totally controlling or eliminating this social role.

A historical event organized by the young Bolshevik government in 1922 serves as an emblematic moment of Russian culture's deintellectualization. Ostensibly motivated by moral disapprobation of the hostile upper classes, but in reality wary of ideological competition, Lenin's government put over 160 men and women of letters on a train and forcibly expatriated them to the West. This one-way journey was not the only instance, of course, and the trains continued to transport Russia's best minds and talents not only to the West but also east – to prison camps – well into the time when trains were replaced by airplanes carrying Aleksandr Solzhenitsyn and Joseph Brodsky. One result of the Russian emigration was very noticeable repercussions in cultures beyond the former Russian borders; the introductions to literature, art, music, theatre, and film offered in this book remind us how hard it would be to imagine the modern Western course of the arts without Sergei Rachmaninov, Vasily Kandinsky, George Balanchine, Vladimir Nabokov, or Igor Stravinsky. The other result was a vastly impoverished culture at home, marked by the banality, obtuseness, and prejudices of a people's state deprived of many of its best people.

The Soviet period, however, also included a counterculture of men and women like Boris Pasternak, Anna Akhmatova, Vsevolod Meyerhold, Stanislavsky, Eisenstein, Mikhail Bulgakov, Dmitry Shostakovich, and Mikhail Bakhtin. They and many others continued the struggle to maintain high standards and to push the arts forward even in the face of the most brutal repressions of Russian history in the modern era. Compromises were unavoidable, social-political forces vitally damaged their works and their lives, but one can hardly deny their achievements. The cultural roots of these men and women, as well as those who emigrated, sank deep into the past and were nurtured in a specific historical period of unusual brilliance and creative vitality: the end of the nineteenth century and the early decades of the twentieth. This was the central moment of modern Russian culture, its historical crux, and, as Abbott Gleason notes, a primary point of orientation and hope after the collapse of the Soviet Union.

What cultural processes gave this period – sometimes undervalued with the label of the Silver Age – its staying power and its influence? One such cultural imperative underlying many of the aesthetic and intellectual achievements noted in the following chapters, was that the end of the nineteenth century and the beginning of the twentieth saw Russia produce a body of theoretical works on philosophy and the arts unprecedented in its history. The singular analytical spirit derived considerable energy from an impulse to take stock of past accomplishment in the light of the new century's possibilities. A propensity to retrospection and assessment before the uncertain course of the future was given voice by Sergei Diaghilev in a much discussed speech delivered in 1905. The occasion was a banquet given to commemorate Diaghilev's influential retrospective exhibition of portraits and the closing of the journal *World of Art*. It was "the hour of summations," Diaghilev noted, a "grandiose historical moment of summations and endings in the name of a new unknown culture."

The second keynote speaker, Valery Briusov, together with other participants of that dinner such as the merchant-patron Savva Mamontov and the painters Valentin Serov and Konstantin Yuon, had already felt strong impulses of appraisal and change. Two men, Nietzsche and Vladimir Soloviev – a philosopher we have already noted – provided particular directions for the cultural milieu in which they worked. Soloviev was as, if not more, important to the Russians as Nietzsche; he died in 1900 but left for his followers – considerable both in number and influence – a philosophical system comparable in scope and the creative energy it stimulated (if not in ultimate achievement) to Hegel's work. A host of original, at times brilliant, thinkers followed Soloviev, including the Trubetskoy brothers Sergei and Eugene, Dmitry Merezhkovsky,

Sergei Bulgakov, Semen Frank, Nikolai Berdiaev, Lev Shestov, Pavel Florensky, and others such as Mikhail Bakhtin.

The respect and attention accorded ideas were not only philosophically driven, however, but were sustained at their core by religious tradition and its intellectual revival. The end of the nineteenth and beginning of the twentieth century was a period of new accomplishment in Russian theology. The exploration of religious issues, with Soloviev again at the center of influence, responded to deep-rooted values and cultural attachments and inspired all other forms of cultural activity, whether historical, philosophical, or aesthetic.

By the beginning of the twentieth century religion had taken on firm ideological functions. Transcendent notions of self and the world continued to motivate basic intellectual and ethical commitments in Russia but without the faith of the past and in conditions of secularization. Dostoevsky's defense of Christian verities even in the face of atheism's strong arguments, Tolstoy's demystification of the Gospels, and Soloviev's insistence on theocracy and faith before his own strong sense of irony, were all symptomatic of this ideological condition and contributed equally to the complexity of intellectual discourse and to its intensity. Added cultural impetus was provided by a revival of mysticism and interest in life beyond death, ranging from Nikolai Fedorov's resurrection project to P. D. Uspensky's *Fourth Dimension* published in 1909, and an epidemic of séances reminiscent of the occult vogue in the reign of Alexander I.

This religious sensibility, combining skepticism with passion, was at least consistent in the old Russian intransigence before life's realities. It continued to measure the nature of things and to invariably find them lacking. The turn to history was partially the result of such dissatisfaction with the present and with prophetic warnings of the "Age of the Lout" as Merezhkovsky called it. Attacks on louts in their middle-class prototypes (made vivid through a biblical connotation of the Russian word for lout, *ham*, also given as a name to Noah's son) were already familiar to Russian intellectual history in the works of Herzen, Dostoevsky, and Konstantin Leontiev, while Nietzsche's dissatisfaction with the bourgeois type Leontiev called "the average man, average European" added a new stimulus. In theatre, of course, Alexander Ostrovsky had created an immense body of dramatic texts evoking the "kingdom of darkness" and the grotesque mediocrity of the developing middle class. At the beginning of the century, the sense of evil attached to the average was so strong that

Satan became banal in one of the more popular novels of the time, Fedor Sologub's *Petty Demon*.

As pointed out by Professor Likhachev, one of the most interesting social phenomena in this period – another example of religious forces transformed into new secular structures – was the role played by patrons of the arts from Old Believer families. Much of the avant-garde cultural activity outlined in this book was the result of an exemplary model of capitalist intervention and support on the part of such sponsors as Savva and Ivan Morozov, Pavel Tretiakov, and Sergei Shchukin. Among the interesting questions of modern Russian culture are: what attracted these powerful merchants and industrialists to the arts and what gave them the insight to recognize the significance of the young and yet unknown Stanislavskys, Picassos, Gorkys, and Matisses? One likely explanation is that familiarity with the non-representational elements of old Russian icons supported a capacity to recognize the value and directions of modern art and to encourage its reach for truths beyond realism. In such instances as Stanislavsky's, in which traditional representational forms were favored, the impulse to develop realism to extremes of perfection found equal inspiration in religious sensibilities (Stanislavsky, it will be remembered, hoped to turn the theatre into a temple). In any case, the activity of these Russian patron-merchants provides strong historical evidence arguing against the pessimistic appraisal of late capitalism's role in culture. Their commitment to the arts suggests that the determining factor is often not the ostensibly harsh laws of capitalism itself but who the capitalists happen to be in their moral and intellectual makeup.

In a related potential lesson for the late twentieth century, Marxists turned idealists expressed a religious-based dissatisfaction, given a sharp edge by their insiders' knowledge, with social–political categories. Their cultural presence was strongly felt in the Ivanov and Merezhkovsky–Gippius gatherings – social occasions for intellectuals and artists to engage in passionate debate – and in essay collections such as *Problems of Idealism* (1902), *From Marxism to Idealism* (1903), *Landmarks* (1909), and *From the Depths* (1918). *Landmarks* brought together Nikolai Berdiaev, Michael Gerzhenzon, Sergei Bulgakov, Semen Frank, and Peter Struve, rapidly went through five editions, and was the most notorious. Cultural scandal was inevitable; despite the political temper of the times and the obvious need for government reform after the Russo-Japanese War and the 1905 uprising, the contributors offered devastating (and still provocative) attacks on the Russian intelligentsia's social–political approach to human nature and destiny.

Discontent with hackneyed perceptions of the social-political sort obtained intellectual energy from a dissatisfaction with traditional modes of perception themselves. The attempt to arrive at a greater complexity of definitions of what personality and existence are all about accompanied a new concern for how one arrives at knowledge of such things. To paraphrase a familiar generalization, the battles of German idealism fought on the fields of epistemology by generals Schelling and Kant were, in this regard, as important for modern Russian culture as the social disruptions caused by the Russo-Japanese War.

In considering the nature of consciousness and knowledge the Russians shared the general discontent of Western modernism with the cruder strategies of empirics and positivists in philosophy and the sciences, and with naturalists and fetishists of realism in the arts. The Russians, like their Western counterparts, viewed the general tendency to reductive epistemological assumptions in the humanities and sciences as fostering a particular neglect of the complex roles of the self in consciousness. Western modernism, in Berlin, Paris, and Vienna, reacted by placing new emphasis on psychology, individual perception and creativity, and, in the process, rediscovered philosophers of the ego such as Max Stirner. For the Russians, such accentuations of the self were old hat, as old as the 1840s and the Russian translation of Ludwig Feuerbach's *Essence of Christianity* at the time the young Dostoevsky was beginning his literary career. In the early years of the twentieth century the texts of Viacheslav Ivanov, Eugene Trubetskoy, and Vasily Kandinsky, among many other works prompted by religious sensibility, continued explorations of the self in terms of its epistemological functions, moral and psychological complexities, interaction with social context, or aesthetic fulfillments.

In their epistemological explorations the Russians also arrived at the underlying concept of language relativity shared by Ferdinand de Saussure and Stéphane Mallarmé, and separated sign from signified in the notion of *uslovnost'* or conditionality. The meaning of language, Valery Briusov pointed out as early as 1902, was relative to its context and uses and not firmly attached to some unchanging material referent. One did not, for instance, have to drag actual or even cardboard trees into a dramatic performance to convey the setting; one could, instead, remember the Elizabethans and create an efficient act of aesthetic communication by writing the word "Forest" on a stage column. Among other cultural possibilities, that insight opened the performing arts to Meyerhold's nonrealistic theatre, but, as the century progressed, it also served manipulations of language for purposes of social-political control. One did not have to worry quite as much about providing actual food for a starving citizenry when images of collective farm bounty were available in socialist realist art to distract the yearning for real eggs and wheat.

Before the Russian men and women of the arts lost their independence to such political manipulations they at times abetted, the first three decades of the twentieth century saw them attain the highest professional standards and technical mastery of modern culture. The following pages are rich in instances of creative achievement and innovation on the part of a generation of men and women of unprecedented talent: in poetry – the symbolists, followed by the acmeists Nikolai Gumilyov, Anna Akhmatova, and Osip Mandelstam, the daring futurists Vladimir Mayakovsky, Velemir Khlebnikov, and the young Boris Pasternak, the imagist and "peasant poet" Sergei Esenin, and leading examples of a new role for women in the arts, Marina Tsvetaeva and Zinaida Hippius; in prose – Fedor Sologub, Maksim Gorky, Andrei Bely, Alexei Remizov, Mikhail Bulgakov, Mikhail Zamyatin, and Yury Olesha; in drama and the performing arts – Anton Chekhov, Konstantin Stanislavsky, Vladimir Nemirovich-Danchenko, Aleksandr Blok, Vsevolod Meyerhold, Nikolai Evreinov, Aleksandr Tairov, Evgeny Vakhtangov, Anna Pavlova, and Fedor Chaliapin; in art – Vasily Kandinsky, Kazimir Malevich, Natalia Goncharova, Mikhail Larionov, Vladimir Tatlin, Marc Chagall, Aleksandra Exter, Aleksandr Rodchenko, and Kuzma Petrov-Vodkin; in music – Igor Stravinsky, Sergei Prokofiev, Aleksandr Scriabin, Sergei Rachmaninov, and Aleksandr Glazunov; and in film – Vsevolod Pudovkin and Sergei Eisenstein.

This period of high cultural achievement was followed by a profound plunge into cultural devastation lasting from the late 1920s to the dissolution of the Soviet Union in 1991. Government manipulations of moral codes of sacrifice and humility for purposes of social-political control were combined with a high dependence on past traditions and continued technical mastery – if not innovation – in the arts. Eventually, with the collapse of the Soviet Union and its underlying ideological supports, the Russians arrived at the shared cultural processes of the late twentieth century in which, as noted by Jürgen Habermas, Frederic Jameson, and many others, much of the aesthetic world responded to the demands of commodity production. The political domination of the arts in Stalin's time gave way to their economic manipulation as entertainment and to media uses by politicians – at times former professional performers and writers – in the interests of gaining power in democratic societies.

After the fall of communism the openness of Russian space and the numerous ethnic and religious groups within it brought attention, once again, to Asia and the West as ways of delineating national identity. The war with Chechen separatists, the exclusionary arguments of Ukrainian nationalists who would expel all Russians from the cradle of their civilization, and the continued presence of a huge Chinese population in Siberia coupled the issue of identity with political and economic forces – not unlike the issues behind illegal immigration in the United States or behind immigration itself in France and Germany. Through the media and its crossovers with the formal arts the Russians demonstrated with gusto – as both Abbott Gleason and Catriona Kelly point out – elements of late twentieth century culture: an erosion of standards and of notions of taste or technical excellence, a rapid succession of images and sensations providing the quick fix of postmodern entertainments, and the narrow concern for an immediate local effect rather than some larger, unifying sense of things. With growing access to computers, the Russians joined in the Internet's unprecedented communication possibilities, as well as its anonymity, irresponsibility, and the free pirating of software. Moscow and Petersburg, along with New York, London, and Zagreb, thus, experienced the same strange combinations of globalization and ethnic aggrandizement, ethical instability and ethical longing felt throughout the world.

The depth and intensity of the culture explored in this book give it some opportunity for dealing with such dilemmas. The Russian tradition of using aesthetic languages – despite their fictional status and relativity – as serious and sustained ways of grappling with social reality offers constructive possibilities in a period when shallow entertainment and a mindless flow of images are cultural norms. The emphasis Russian culture places on values of humility and universal responsibility, a reflective self-placement in history, intransigence before the imperfections of life, and even the sometimes naive persistence in the face of disquieting odds, suggest ways of transcending skepticism and cultural diminutions. Russian culture is fundamentally helpful in dealing with those numerous cultural selves – heirs of the great ideological ploymasters of the past – who smuggle in their own agendas by making all other selves yet another logocentric fallacy. The Russian experience includes a master narrative – and not only a narrative but real women, men, and actions – defining the idea of self in its fulfillment with others, emphasizing the inescapable presence and responsibilities of the self, and challenging those modern definitions and systems in which the full human individual is reduced to economic status, race, gender, or body parts.

The complex lessons of humility and sacrifice that Russian culture found in searching for transcendent and social truths are equally to the point in the modern era. It is telling that the true heroes of Russian history and the arts are not the political leaders and the power they represent: Ivan the Terrible, Peter the Great, Catherine II, or Stalin. They are, rather, the victims of political necessity and moral compromise: Saints Boris and Gleb, Dmitry, the son of Ivan whose murder was unjustly attributed to Boris Godunov, and more recently the children of Nicholas II and Alexandra. Or to put it another way, the major political figures who wield authority and power in Russian history are always accompanied by moral representations of sacrifice and humility in Russian culture or themselves act as such cultural emblems.

At the time of this book Russia has felt the full force of yet another culural challenge operating across national boundaries. This challenge to cultures is not in the familiar relativism and aggrandizements of twentieth century sensibilities but in a loss of memory, a subversion of civilization's achievements through forgetfulness rather than mere disillusionment or analytical quandaries. Pride of race and cultural ethos turning into racism and tribal insularity, the breakdown of morality expressed in rampant crime, the sense that the vulgar and physical – the material girls and boys of popular culture – are all we really are, the brutal manipulations of economic systems which repudiate the infirm and elderly are all part of this cultural amnesia encouraged by the transience and simplifications of late twentieth-century media forms and marked by neglect of the complex lessons of written narratives from the past.

It is useful in the attempt of recovery from such reductions of civilization to remember the rich diversity within Russian cultural origins, the borders that provided Russian cultural identity and order and the crossings that enriched them, the fruitful conjunctions of Russian popular and high culture, and the complex ideological struggle for values and ideas to live by in a secular age. Late twentieth-century cultural debate also suggests lessons to be gained from remembering that Tolstoy tried not to limit his creative vision to social class or economic power and imagined all women and men engaging universal moral codes, or the consequences of their neglect; that Dostoevsky managed to integrate female–male differences into his harsh insights of shared human personality without exclusionary gender reductions; that Aleksandr Borodin was profoundly involved in a variant of Orientalism but as a vehicle for enriching Russian music and not for hostility to other ethnic groups or racial aggrandizement; that Stanislavsky – son of an industrialist – fully appreciated the financial necessities of theatre, but never reduced performance to commodity values; that Eisenstein was well aware of the importance of ideology for film, but did not confine his creative vision to its Stalinist demands. This cultural history has its failures and impracticalities, but given such men and women it also has lessons and hope – those indispensable elements of any healthy culture – to offer. The preservation and reintroduction of these complex insights and lessons is this book's way of reaffirming modern Russian culture's necessary hopes.

I
_____

Cultural identity

DEAN S. WORTH

2

Language

Background material

Introduction

Among the Slavs, as among many other peoples, cultural identity tends to be defined by language: in a way that would be difficult for a Québequois, a Mexican, or an American to understand, to be Russian is primarily to have Russian as one's mother tongue. This is especially true in a preliterate society with its limited comprehension of time and space, but remains substantially accurate as a society develops into a modern nation. Historical and geographical awareness, the ability to respond to psychological and aesthetic dimensions of literature, the challenge and pleasure of intellectual interchange, even the possibility of truly understanding non-verbal experience like music and art – all are mediated by language. Some, perhaps exaggerating, have averred that the form of our language determines the form of our thought, while others, more convincingly, maintain that language is the primary modeling system through which we view all our surroundings and through which all other systems must be filtered. At the very least, it is obvious that language plays an essential role in culture, and in defining culture. This is especially true of Russian cultural history.

947
.08

Russian and Slavic

Russian, like Belorussian and Ukrainian, is an East Slavic language,[1] distinct from West and South Slavic. West Slavic includes Polish, Czech and Slovak, Sorbian, and a few minor or extinct languages, while South Slavic includes Slovene, Serbian and Croatian, Bulgarian, and (since 1945) Macedonian. At the end of the first millennium AD, the three territorial groups were already distinct from each other, but had not yet separated into the individual languages we know today. At this time, for example, there was no separate Russian, Ukrainian, or Belorussian language, but a linguistically more or less homogenous East Slavic language, spoken with only minor dialectal differences from the Novgorod-Pskov area in the North to Kiev in the South. This territory is known as Kievan Rus' (with the word Rus' referring originally to the Scandinavians who had colonized the area in the ninth century and only later to its Slavic inhabitants), and the language spoken there is referred to as Rusian (from Rus'), to distinguish it from Russian, the language of the nascent Muscovite empire of the fourteenth and subsequent centuries.[2]

The three branches of Slavic had themselves developed out of a single linguistic entity known as Common Slavic, located north of the Carpathian mountains around the present Polish-Belorussian border, and spoken in various stages of development as long ago as 1500 BC, by which time the Slavic language family had become differentiated from such other families as the Germanic, Romance, Celtic, Armenian, and Indo-Iranian, several of which later split into more local groups, the Romance family, for example, separating into French, Italian, Spanish, Portuguese, Romanian, etc. All of these families (Slavic, Germanic et al.) had themselves developed out of a common ancestor language known as Indo-European, originally spoken (according to one hypothesis) somewhere north of the Caucasus, but later, as its daughter languages developed and spread out, stretching from the Indian subcontinent in the East to Ireland in the West.

The Germanic group eventually gave rise to English (along with German, Dutch, and the Scandinavian languages), so that our own speech is genetically related to that of the Russians. The correspondences between the two languages are sometimes clear (English *three* = Russian *tri*, English *mother* = Russian gen.sing. *materi*, English *cat* = Russian *kot*), sometimes less so (English *wagon* = Russian *voz*, English *two* = Russian *dva*), and at other times completely obscure (English *in* = Russian *v* "in," English *comb* = Russian *zub* "tooth," English *hundred* = Russian *sto*).

Overview of Russian cultural history

Premodern Russian culture, from its Rusian origins to the late seventeenth century, has consisted of three major components, one inherited and two acquired. The inherited component is the pre-Christian and pre-literate culture of the Rusians, due partly to their Common Slavic and even Indo-European heritage, partly to developments specific to East Slavic itself. The acquired components result from two powerful waves of foreign influence, which, each in its own way, totally transformed the local Rusian and then Russian societies. These waves of foreign influence, which have been referred to as the two great "macroevents" of Russian cultural history, are the Christianization and Byzantinization of Rusian culture from the ninth to the fifteenth centuries and the secularization and Westernization of Russian culture from the sixteenth century to the present. Needless to say, both of these macroevents were complex processes replete with internal contradictions and counter-currents, nor do they fit smoothly into the suggested temporal limits. Taken together, however, they do suggest that throughout the pre-national period, that is, roughly until the ascension of Peter the Great to the Romanov throne in the late seventeenth century, Russian culture developed primarily by response to and partial adaptation of foreign models, rather than by internally motivated evolution, such as one sees, for example, in the Italian Renaissance. In other words, the history of Russian culture is to a substantial extent derivative. To say this is not to denigrate Russian cultural accomplishments, which are entirely obvious in, say, the churches of Novgorod and Suzdal' or the icons of Andrei Rublev, any more than it would denigrate Roman culture to point out that it copied Greek statuary.

The Rusian heritage

Introduction

With the exception of some interesting but unreliable material from the Gothic chronicler Jordan in the sixth century and accounts from Arabic travelers in the eighth, East Slavic recorded history begins towards the end of the first millennium AD, at which time we find ten or so East Slavic tribes scattered across Kievan Rus', i.e. primarily the territory drained by the Dnepr and its tributaries and by the Dvina in the north. The surrounding territories were occupied by a succession of nomadic warrior tribes to the southeast, by largely Finnic tribes to the east and north, Baltic tribes to the northwest, Poles to the west, Hungarians to the southwest, and the Byzantine Empire to the south.

The Scandinavian conquest

When the expansion of the Arab world cut off the Mediterranean trade routes from Western Europe to the Near and Middle East in the late eighth century, this trade was diverted northward, through the Baltic Sea and up the northwestward-flowing rivers of North Russia and thence down the Dnepr to the Black Sea. By the latter part of the ninth century, roving clans of Scandinavian warrior-traders (Normans or "Varingians," Russian *varjagi*) had subjugated the Slavic population along the major waterways and established trading connections with the Byzantine Empire across the Black Sea, the famous "route from the Varingians to the Greeks."[3] The major Scandinavian centers were Novgorod on Lake Ilmen in the north and Kiev on the middle Dnepr in the south, whence the Norman invaders could lead their Slavic troops to Constantinople for fighting or trading. Great as the political and economic impact of the Scandinavians was, their cultural impact was insignificant, a sign, perhaps, that they brought little of cultural interest with them. Linguistically, they were soon absorbed into the indigenous Slavic population: with the exception of the phrase "bloody and blue" (< Old Norse *blar et blopuger*) in the Rusian legal code (*Rusьskaja Pravьda*),[4] a few dozen loanwords preserved in modern Russian (Old Norse *askr* "box" > Russian *jaščik*),[5] there is hardly a trace of Old Norse in the preserved Rusian documents. Aside from language, the only indication that the governing Scandinavians considered themselves different from the Slavs is found in a few *Primary Chronicle* episodes indicating that in the mid tenth century the Scandinavians still considered the Slavs their cultural inferiors.

Of the native culture the Scandinavians encountered, very little is known, and only a bit more can be conjectured. What has been recovered of material culture (weapons, beads, etc.) seems irrelevant to the changes to come. Early chronicle texts refer to wooden architecture, for example the princely "palace" (*terem*), but there is no reason to equate such structures with the splendidly elaborate wooden architecture of northern Russia of a much later period.

Of spiritual culture, we know that there was a pagan religion, but we know next to nothing about its beliefs or practices other than that they practiced human sacrifice. It is true that in 980, only eight years before he introduced Christianity as the official state religion in Rus', Vladimir I erected large statues of a pagan pantheon on a hill behind his palace in Kiev, "a wooden Perun [thunder god] with a silver head and a golden mustache" and several associate deities, Xorš and Dažbog the sun gods, Stribog the wind god, Simargl and Mokoš, whose functions remain unclear.[6] How many of these deities had actually been worshiped in Rus', and for how long, is uncertain. Perun was also known to Procopius in the sixth century as an East Slavic deity and can be assumed to be of Indo-European origin (cf. Old Norse Thor), Xorš and Simargl appear to be Iranian borrowings, as is the word for "god" itself (cf. Avestan baγa "lord"), and Mokoš may have been a local East Slavic tribal deity. In spite of the paucity of knowledge about specific gods and their functions, it is certain that, at the least, quasi-religious superstitions played an important role in pre-Christian Rus'; otherwise, there would be no explanation for the fact that these beliefs remained powerful psychological forces, as manifested in the so-called "dual-faith" (*dvoeverie*) that plagued the official church for centuries after Christianization.

Language and its uses

By the tenth century, the language of the Eastern Slavs had developed a number of characteristics that distinguished Rusian speech from that of the other Slavic areas, but most of them are of interest primarily to comparativists and do not significantly affect verbal culture; those that do will be examined in the following section below. What we know of Rusian verbal culture is largely inferential. We can infer, for example, that there was a religious cult language, and typology would suggest that it differed from everyday speech and was accessible only to the local priests (shamans?). The legal code, as pointed out above, had been handed down orally, probably from the Common Slavic period. Contrary to widespread assertions, there is no reason to equate this legal language with the tenth-century spoken Rusian of the time, since typology again suggests that the "keepers of the code" would maintain their privileged status by using language that was not easily accessible to the profane. On the other hand, the fact that the code was transmitted orally forced it into the form of short and easily memorized "if . . . then" sentences like "if one man kills another, then a brother shall revenge his brother." Some genres of folk literature, such as folk tales and proverbs, may well have existed but are not attested even indirectly, while others, such as the epic (*bylina,* or more authentically *stárina*), have been shown to be descended from the Common Slavic period (this is true specifically for the ten-syllable poetic line), although actual texts are available only from the seventeenth century and only from the north, notwithstanding the fact that their scenery and motifs clearly originated in the south. About folk songs, including laments, we can infer less, although some of their phraseology is so common across time and space (again, in the north) that it cannot be of recent origin.[7] It has been suggested that fixed military expressions (e.g. exhortations to proceed into battle) be treated as literary forms, but even if one concedes this dubious proposal, they must be attributed to the Scandinavian warriors and not to the East Slavs.

All in all, the little we know about Rusian culture suggests that it was not highly developed, particularly when compared to the vigor and success of Rusian military and economic activity or to the rich and flourishing Byzantine culture to the south. It was not surprising, then, that this Byzantine culture soon flowed north.

Christianization

Background

In the year 988, the *Primary Chronicle* tells us, Prince Vladimir I of Kiev declared Christianity the official state religion of Rus'. Two contradictory motivations for Vladimir's decision are adduced in the *Chronicle*. According to the one, he promised to be baptized if he won at Chersonese; the other, more elaborate, has him sending envoys to investigate several faiths and settling on the Greek Orthodox because of the beauty of the Byzantine church service. Whatever his motivation – and one suspects that politics and diplomacy played more of a role than a beautiful church – Vladimir dragged the statue of Perun down to the Dnepr and sent it floating seaward, and had the remaining wooden deities chopped up or burned. Inhabitants of all ranks were commanded to participate in a mass baptism in the waters of the Dnepr. Vladimir then had churches built and priests appointed "in all cities and towns," collected children from the upper classes of the Kievan population and set them to learning to read. Thus was Rus' launched in a direction which would determine its cultural development for the next six hundred years, and to an extent even to our own days.

In reality things were more complex. Photius tells us that there had been Greek Orthodox missionaries in Kievan Rus' as early as the mid ninth century, i.e. about the same time as the original Christian mission to the Slavs in Greater Moravia in 862. In 912 the Emperor Leon showed Rusian envoys the beauty and the wealth of the Byzantine rite, "teaching them his faith and demonstrating the true faith to them." Of the Rusian warriors at this time (still Scandinavians) who swore an oath to support the 945 treaty with Byzantium, the Christians took their oath in a church, the pagans theirs over their arms. More importantly, in 955 Olga, the widow of Igor I, was converted to Christianity in Byzantium. Her son

Svjatoslav refused to join the church, saying that his retinue would mock him if he did so, which left Olga's grandson Vladimir to complete the task in 988,[8] the date which serves as a peg on which to hang this century of preceding events.

Byzantinization

The advent of official Christianity opened Kievan Rus' to a powerful stream of Byzantine influence, both directly from Constantinople and indirectly via Christian Bulgaria, where Byzantine influence was strong and where the disciples of Cyril and Method had been welcomed after being driven out of Greater Moravia in the late ninth century. The Byzantine culture transplanted to Rus' was above all the culture of the Orthodox Church: architecture, frescoes and icons, music, and literature (on which below). Some of the finest results of this influence are still visible today, for example the cathedral of St. Sophia in Kiev with its tenth century frescoes of the princely family, or the stately churches of Chernigov to the east. Compared to the splendors of Byzantium itself, the Rusian reflex was of course pale and provincial, but it nonetheless represented a total change in the cultural life of the Rusians, whose consciousness would for centuries be filtered through that of the church. We should not forget, of course, that what we know of the Rusian response to this new culture was recorded precisely by churchmen, who had a vested interest in the new state of affairs: when we read in the *Chronicle* of 988, "Blessed is the Lord Jesus Christ, who came to love new people, the Rusian land, and enlightened it with holy baptism," this is not the voice of a hunter or an oarsman, but that of a monk.[9]

Literacy

The widespread use of writing, and verbal culture in general, also came from Byzantium. Writing was not unknown in pre-Christian Rus', but its use was very restricted. We have a puzzling but obviously Cyrillic inscription on a ninth century pot from Gnezdovo, and the treaty of 912 between Rus' and Byzantium is recorded only in the much later *Chronicle*, but was surely concluded in 912 and kept in the princely archives, as, one assumes, were other important documents. The missionary efforts which had been underway since the mid ninth century must have made use of the Bible and liturgical works. On the other hand, the ninth century *Life of St. Cyril*, preserved only in much later copies, refers to the gospel and a psalter "written in Russian" (*rusьskymi pismeny pisano*), but the *rusьskymi* is now generally taken to be a scribal error for the *surьskymi* "Syriac" (that is, the Aramaic language).

Literacy in the period following Christianization was largely passive, since what was needed to spread the new faith was priests who could read the liturgical works used in celebrating the mass. People learned to write by copying syllabaries: "a – b – v – g – d . . ." then "ba – va – ga – da . . ." then "be – ve – ge – de . . ." eventually proceeding to reading from the Psalms. One infers that active command of the written language was restricted to a small number of monks and members of the power elite, but we have no direct evidence of this. Prince Yaroslav established a scriptorium in 1037 which was active in copying religious works and in translating from Greek, and such copying and translation served as a link between passive and active knowledge of the written language. In Novgorod far to the north, writing began to be used at about the same time, but for entirely different purposes: the oldest of a remarkable set of birchbark letters, dealing primarily with petty domestic affairs and written nearly entirely in the vernacular, can be dated to roughly 1025–75.

As was the case with material culture, the written culture brought from Constantinople to Kiev was oriented almost exclusively toward the church. What existed in Kiev had, almost without exception, been translated from the Greek, sometimes well but often enough awkwardly, in ninth-century Greater Moravia, tenth-century Bulgaria, or in Kiev itself. Rusians with training and inclination had access to the Bible (the entire New Testament, some books of the Old, and some apocrypha, at that time not clearly distinguished from approved versions), a variety of liturgical texts, homilies (e.g. from John Chrysostomos), hagiography, a few exegetical works, usually in excerpts, monastic statutes (especially the Studite statute, translated in the latter part of the eleventh century at the behest of Feodosy, abbot of the Kiev Monastery of the Caves), and canon law. Only a very restricted choice of secular literature was available: the Hamartolos and Synkel Chronicles, Flavius' *Jewish Wars*, Xoiroboskos' treatise on tropes (incomprehensible in translation), an imaginative but uninformative *Journey to India*, and a few tales of Middle Eastern or Indian origin. There is no Homer, no Plato, no Aristotle, and even the religious literature was more oriented toward establishing proper monastic habits than toward serious systematic theology or philosophical inquiry. In effect, what happened to Kievan Rus' was not Byzantinization but semi-Byzantinization, and as far as verbal culture is concerned, it was not the finest part of Byzantium that came north to Kiev. With time, of course, the Rusians developed their own writers, and there is no shortage of talented storytelling in the *Chronicle* (e.g. the four revenges of Olga after the Derevljane had killed her husband Igor, or the tale of the blinding of Vasily of Terebovl with its thoroughly modern use of narrative retardation), not to mention the sharply etched vignettes of monastic life (including a vivid if unsuccessful seduction scene) in the *Kievan Caves Patericon*, or the moving lyric of the *Tale of the Loss of the Russian Land* at the beginning of the *Life* of Prince Aleksandr Nevsky of Novgorod. Overall, however, there can be little doubt that the dogmatically narrow framework served to retard rather than encourage the development of verbal culture.

The problem of "Slavonicisms"

Saints Cyril and Method, the originators of Slavic writing, came from Thessaloniki in northeastern Greece, where urban speech was Greek but a South Slavic dialect was still spoken in the countryside.[10] The bilingual brothers were ideal translators, and their translations naturally showed South Slavic features. After the Moravian mission had been forced to move south to Bulgaria in the late ninth century, the South Slavic foundations of Old Church Slavonic underwent a century of further strengthening in Prešov and Ohrid, whence a number of important texts came to Rus', for example the miscellany known as the *Izbornik of 1073*. The language of texts from the Greater Moravian and Bulgarian period, called Old Church Slavonic (OCS), differed in a number of obvious ways from the East Slavic Rusian of the time.

One language or two? Diglossia

Differences between the written language of Cyril and Method and the spoken tongue of Rusian scribes meant that Slavonic texts (those of OCS, including Bulgarian provenance)[11] were immediately identifiable as such. Furthermore, since the overwhelming majority of texts brought to Kiev in the oldest period (or copied there) dealt specifically with religious matters, the Slavonic language elements were associated specifically with religion, and more generally with solemn subject matter and high style, while the Rusian, by default, were associated with the quotidian details of secular life.[12] Rusian Slavonic developed its own norms, derived from but not always identical to OCS. The bulk of written Rusian, especially in the first century or so after the advent of literacy, was in a language that consistently differed, in some obvious ways, from the spoken language of those who were reading and writing it. This fact has been taken by some to mean that Slavonic and spoken Rusian were two different languages, albeit closely related, and to suggest that the relation between them was one of diglossia, in which the two languages are used in complementary distribution, the high language (Slavonic) for spiritual or otherwise exalted matters and the vernacular for everyday affairs. In this view, diglossia defines verbal culture until the seventeenth century, when the lengthy period of mixing of Slavonic and vernacular elements results in a breakdown of the hitherto rigid functional distinction between them, and Russia enters a period not of diglossia but of bilingualism (*dvujazyčie*) in which both types of language can be used for one and the same purpose.

However, there is good reason to doubt that educated Rusians had any reason to look on Slavonic as a foreign language. There are three reasons for this view. First, the obvious differences between East and South Slavic are precisely obvious, that is, they lie on the very surface of language and could easily and nearly automatically be substituted by their vernacular counterparts. A Rusian would have no more trouble converting Slavonic *vremja* and *grad* to Rusian *veremja* and *gorod* than the British and American speakers of English have in writing *colour* or *color*, pronouncing *laboratory* with stress on the *o* or the *a*, or remembering that they can ride up to their offices in either a *lift* or an *elevator*. Differences like these are as insignificant as they are obvious (for genuinely significant differences, see below). The second reason why these surface differences could not create any important structural distinction between Slavonic and Rusian is that the Rusians in their writing were, almost from the very beginning, mixing South and East Slavic elements in single texts. In some cases, the motivation was merely to keep the right margins straight and not to waste precious parchment. Finally, the third reason why the choice of Slavonic forms in such contrasting pairs had no major effect on the Rusian perception that they were nonetheless dealing not with a foreign but with their own language is that the South Slavic–East Slavic contrasts themselves were a relative rarity in the great mass of forms which were neither specifically Southern nor specifically Eastern but both (or neither). For example a ten-page sample of the *Life of Feodosy* has 267 identifiable South Slavic forms (13.7 percent of the total), 114 identifiable East Slavic forms (5.9 percent), and 1,562 forms which are not geographically localizable (80.4 percent), not counting prepositions and monosyllabic conjunctions.

"Slavonic" = "difficult"

The conclusions noted above are valid for relatively simple narrative texts such as the Gospel stories and the bulk of the material in saints' lives. Such texts usually show an iconic correspondence between the order of narrated events and the order in which these events actually took place, so that the text consists of a series of brief phrases, none at all complex, coming in a simple 1 – 2 – 3 order, e.g. "At that time John was standing and [= 'with'] two of his disciples, and he saw Jesus going and he said, this is the lamb of God." Their vocabulary is simple and largely Common Slavic in origin, so that little of it would be difficult for a native Rusian to understand. Finally, such texts show a minimum of anaphora (repetition of lexical referents or clauses), each segment being sufficient unto itself, with little or no reference to preceding or following segments, and equally little embedding (inclusion of a subordinated predication into a principal predication, usually by means of participles). However, in addition to such simple narrative texts, there existed other and far more complex forms of Rusian Slavonic. These were exegetic or meditative texts expressing complex ideas with highly metaphoric imagery. Such texts cannot be broken down into a series of simple fragments. Their syntactic complexity is often compounded by a vocabulary which consisted not of easily recognizable Slavic words or obvious borrowings, but of calques on Greek models, i.e. of morpheme by morpheme translations of Greek words. The resulting vocabulary was superficially Slavic, but the meanings of such calques would have been obscure to those – and they were many – who did not know the original Greek. The combination of entangled syntax and vague vocabulary resulted in texts that must have been as hard to understand in the twelfth century as they are now.

The role of original literature and mixed genres

As time passed, an increasing amount of literary activity was devoted to original writing rather than to copying imported works. If Rus' was full of translated lives of Near and Middle Eastern saints, it also had the *Life of Feodosy* and three different versions of the martyrdom of Saints Boris and Gleb. The translation of Flavius' *Jewish Wars* finds an echo in the *Tale of the Destruction of Rjazan'* in 1237 and a series of other and later military tales, not to mention the *Hypatian Chronicle* account of the 1185 battle on the river Kajala and its lyric transformation in the *Igor Tale*. Original literature is at its most impressive in the Rusian chronicles: the *Laurentian* of 1377, the above mentioned *Hypatian* of c. 1425, both containing the *Primary*

Chronicle as the first part, and a series of Novgorod Chronicles in the north. The chronicles represent an important step in the development of verbal culture, not least because they range across a variety of subject matter and styles.

As original literature grew more frequent, its authors had at their disposal a range of choices on different linguistic levels, choices that could be exploited for stylistic reasons. When Prince Mstislav Vladimirovič recorded his gifts of lands to the St. George Monastery near Novgorod in 1131, the document begins, "*+ Se az M'stislav Volodimir' s[y]n*" (This is I, Mstislav son of Volodimir) with the solemnity of the occasion marked by the initial cross and by the Slavonic pronoun *az*, while the patronymic "son of Volodimir," being the fixed name of the individual permitted no such choice.[13] Later, in the less solemn part of the document, Mstislav refers to himself as *jaz* while Mstislav's son Vladimir uses the yet more vernacular *ja*. Even the Novgorod birchbark letters, stylistically unadorned as they are, make use in the older period (to *c.* 1250) of stylistic devices to solemnize their beginnings: they too prefix a cross to their texts and use a Slavonic salutation. This is but one of the many ways in which originally geographical distinctions (*grad-gorod* [city], etc.) developed into stylistic markers of the higher versus lower styles. This process would continue until the present, with former South versus East differences additionally exploited as lexical distinctions (*glava* "chapter" – *golova* "head"), derivational devices (*vorota* "goal [in soccer]" – *vratar'* "goalkeeper"), et al.

Neoslavonisms

In the period from the eleventh to the fourteenth centuries the Rusian language underwent several far-reaching structural changes. The so-called jer shift, in which "weak" jers were dropped and "strong " jers vocalized to /o/ or /e/, nearly stood the phonological system on its head: where eleventh century Rusian distinguished many words from each other by back versus front vowels, by the fourteenth century the distinction was carried by plain versus palatalized consonants, thus nearly doubling the number of consonantal phonemes and halving the vowels. More importantly, entire grammatical categories were eliminated: the vocative "case," the dual number, the aorist, the imperfect, perfect, and pluperfect tenses, declined short adjectives, the "dative absolute." Eliminated too were a number of morphophonemic alternations that had once helped to distinguish certain case forms from others. As a result of these and similarly radical changes, entire classes of forms which had been perfectly natural in spoken Rusian three centuries earlier were now perceived as artificial, bookish, that is, as "Slavonic." The large numbers of neoslavonisms made Rusian writing increasingly inaccessible to even literate Russians.

The archaistic movement

The widening gap between spoken and written language was made wider yet by a church-driven archaizing movement in the fifteenth to seventeenth centuries. Often wrongly attributed to the influence of South Slavic intellectual refugees from the Turkish conquest of the Balkans, the misnamed "Second South Slavic Influence" was in fact the result of the growing hegemony of Moscow among the East Slavic territories.[14] As Muscovy swallowed up one East Slavic territory after another, the increasingly powerful princes of Moscow, and the church which supported them, sought historical legitimacy not only by falsifying genealogy but also by editing scripture and other serious writing to what they (usually wrongly) took to be the correct Rusian norms, reintroducing imperfects and aorists (and often confusing them in the process) and several dozen other archaisms and pseudo-archaisms. The same period was one of rhetorical effusion, often patterned on devices used in Kievan Rus', e.g. by Metropolitan Hilarion in his eleventh-century *Sermon on Law and Grace*, but grotesquely exaggerated, as in Epifany Premudryj's *Life of Stephen of Perm*. Such a text, while rhetorically "exuberant," as one investigator put it, poses no particular linguistic difficulty and passages of it can be approximated to a murkily overwritten piece of modern Russian. Overall, however, the combination of the rapid evolution of spoken Russian and the deliberate archaization of the written language rendered the latter increasingly incomprehensible; one educated cleric even complained that liturgical texts were unreadable.

The chancery language

The only significant exception to the growing gap between written and spoken Russian was the language of civil administration or chancery language. Administrative texts (treaties, records of charitable donations, legal disputes, land surveys, etc.) had existed since early Kievan times (birchbark letters, many of which record business transactions, go back to the eleventh century, and the oldest preserved charitable donation dates to *c.* 1131). The growing hegemony of Moscow in the latter part of the fifteenth and early sixteenth centuries concentrated official record-keeping in the Muscovite chanceries and imposed a quasi-unified administrative language upon the scribes who labored there. Dialectisms were eliminated (e.g. the various forms of the first person plural present of "to be"). And, in spite of the adoption of a limited number of originally Slavonic terms and phrases, a new form of written Russian evolved that was readily accessible to literate speakers of the fifteenth and sixteenth centuries. The fact that this occurred in Moscow, which lies in a narrow transitional dialect belt between the greater masses of North and South Russian dialects, would later be important for the developing standard language, since speakers of this dialect use a mixture of North and South Russian forms, taking for example their consonantal system largely from the North, but their vocalic system largely from the South. The new chancery language itself became fixed, even rigid, in its bureaucratic formulas, and by the late sixteenth century there were two established forms of written Russian, vying not only with the still-evolving vernacular but also with each other.

New genres

A number of new secular genres of written Russian arose in the sixteenth century. Disputes about the proper relation of church to state and whether or not the church should own land and exploit peasants took the form of extended disputations between Joseph Volocky and his followers, who backed a worldly church with financial power and a close relation with the tsar, and the so-called Trans-Volga Elders led by Nil Sorsky, who, influenced by the mystical notions of South Slavic Hesychasm, preached an impecunious and meditative monasticism far from the sources of civil power. This polemical pseudo-correspondence appears to have been intended more for the public than for private consumption, as was that between Ivan IV and the renegade Prince Kurbsky. The sixteenth century also saw the rise of diplomatic reports as a new written genre, and of tales, both native and imported. Such new genres, unhampered by traditional constraints of the Slavonic versus Russian type, were free to draw from whatever models they chose, and this freedom is reflected in a wide range of stylistic variation within genres, one diplomat reporting in a more Slavonic and another in a more vernacular or chancery tone. The interpenetration of Slavonic and vernacular idioms, which had been growing since Kievan times, led to a state of stylistic confusion that would ultimately be resolved only in the eighteenth century. In the meantime, however, as the growth of secular genres weakened the older connection between Slavonic and solemnity, a new and powerful cultural force was approaching, this time not from the South but from the West.

Westernization

Historical background

As the Muscovite state consolidated its hold on other East Slavic fiefdoms, the southwestern territories of Kievan Rus' (roughly = Ukraine and Belarus) were drawn into the political orbit of Poland. As early as the fourteenth century the Grand Duchy of Lithuania had taken control of the territories of Kiev and Smolensk. After the marriage of Jagello of Lithuania to Jadwiga of Poland in 1386 Lithuania was Christianized as a Catholic state and attempted to impose this faith on the Orthodox East Slavic population it controlled. This attempt intensified in the sixteenth century, especially after the official Polish-Lithuanian union in 1569, which brought large East Slavic territories under Polish control. Latin as the language of proselytization was also learned by the latter's Orthodox opponents, and it was not long before Polish political and cultural influence permeated the southwestern territories, resulting in a new legal codex, known as *Litovsky Statut*, which was introduced in the late sixteenth century but preserved some elements of the older *Russkaja Pravda*. The Polish language exerted considerable influence on Russian, often via the Ukrainian intermediary. This influence is visible on such different levels as word formation, syntax (introduction of the predicate instrumental) and, above all, vocabulary. Many Polish words became permanent members of the Russian lexicon, while a probably greater number was used briefly and soon disappeared. Latin vocabulary, sometimes in Polish guise, poured from Poland into such cultural centers as Kiev, Vilnius, Lvov, and Ostrog, both as direct loans and as calques. Older Hellenisms were replaced by Latinate forms.

Southwestern Rus', with its contacts with the centers of learning not only in the Polish-Lithuanian state but also in Germany, Italy, and the scholarly monasteries of Mt. Athos in northeastern Greece, was culturally far more advanced than the economically flourishing but intellectually impoverished Muscovite state.[15] The educator and religious activist Melety Smotritsky, for example, was educated by Jesuits in Vilno and attended lectures at Leipzig and Wittenberg, while Archbishop Iosif of

Suzdal' had been educated at Padua and spent some years as a monk on Mt. Athos before coming to Moscow in 1625.[16]

Education and literature

Formal education, too, came first to Southwestern Rus'. Some schools had existed there since the late sixteenth century, but higher education really began with the founding of the so-called Brethren school in 1615 and a school in the famous Kiev Monastery of the Caves in 1631; in 1632 these two institutions were combined to create the Kiev-Mogila Academy, the first institution of higher learning in East Slavic territory. It was from the Southwest that educators left for Moscow to found the first schools there, Simeon Polotsky a Latin school in 1664 and the Greek Lixudi brothers the Greek-Latin-Slavonic Academy in 1687.

In addition to education, Muscovite musical and literary culture was also greatly enriched under Southwestern influence. Ukrainian choral groups had come to Moscow in 1652, and soon there were at least four such groups performing. Drama in Moscow began in the 1670s, one of the principal playwrights being Simeon Polotsky, whose very name shows his non-Muscovite origin.[17] At the same time, and partly thanks to the same author, Polish-style syllabic verse was introduced to Russia's capital, where it would remain the only accepted form of serious verse until the reforms of Vasily Trediakovsky three generations later. Overall, it would be hard to exaggerate the Southwestern contribution to Russian cultural development in this period. This is not to say that literary culture itself was invariably on the level, say, of Polotsky's coeval Molière (1622–73); indeed, it at times barely skirted the risible, as in the love scene between Holophernes and Judith, from the play *Comedy from the Book of Judith* of 1673. One may smile at the awkwardness of such efforts, but one must also wonder at the linguistic and cultural development that gave us, a bare 160 years later, Pushkin's exquisite "I loved you . . ." This was, after all, only the beginning.

Normalization of Slavonic

Grammatical treatises in manuscript, translated from or based on Greek models and in most cases originating in Bulgarian and Serbian scriptoria (with the exception of the Donatus *Ars Minor*, translated from Latin in Russia itself) were extant in Russia from the fifteenth century, but it was with the advent of printing, which reached East Slavic lands only in the latter sixteenth century, that language standardization began. What was standardized was of course the high Slavonic variant of written Russian, and where standardization began was in the Southwestern territories that had long been subject to Polish (and, via Polish, generally Western) culture, but which were completely reunited with Moscovite Russia in the seventeenth century.

The first printed grammars of Slavonic appear at the very end of the sixteenth and in the early seventeenth century: Lavrenty Zizany's *Grammatika slovenska* (1596); Melety Smotritsky's *Grammatiki slavenskija pravilnoe sintagma* (1619), which was later reedited in 1648 in Moscow and again there by Feofan Prokopovič in 1721 and was *the* grammar for educated Russians until the appearance of Mikhail Lomonosov's work later in that century. The first dictionaries appeared at the same time, e.g. Zizany's Slavonic-Russian *Leksis . . .* of 1596, in which over a thousand Slavonisms were defined in the vernacular, providing some doubtless welcome guidance for those who wished to write in Slavonic and, incidentally, proving that for many users Slavonic was becoming difficult to distinguish from the vernacular. The grammars and dictionaries of this period are the first attempts to normalize Slavonic, although the normalization usually took the form of trying to force Slavonic into a Greek or Latin mold, for example with only four cases for nouns but as many as six genders. The artificiality of these early attempts at standardization rendered them impractical as a guide to even the loftiest intended style, especially since actual writing practice had long since departed from the rigorous separation of vernacular from Slavonic elements, although solemn and/or religious passages tended to use more of the latter.[18]

Summary

As we have seen, by the late seventeenth century the situation of written Russian was close to chaotic, a term that is usually reserved for the innovations of the reign of Peter the Great (b. 1672 – d. 1725). Formal grammars of Slavonic decreed the use of forms which had disappeared from the spoken language centuries earlier, and the idea of describing systematically the spoken language simply never occurred to anyone in Russia.[19] In the vocabulary, Polonisms, Latinisms, Polonized Latinisms, Slavonisms, Slavonic calques from the Greek, and Polish, Ukrainian, or Russian calques from Latin all competed for the attention of those hardy enough to try to formulate a message with some consistency and clarity. Poetry was written in a syllabic verse scheme foreign to Russian folk verse (the poetic reforms of Trediakovsky were still decades away), dialog in the theatre was in a sort of tardy Slavonic that, while comprehensible, was totally incompatible with the panoply of human emotions that the theatre must convey. In effect, the verbal culture of late seventeenth century Russia had not yet freed itself of the stultifying norms of an out-lived and unassimilated Slavonic, nor had it yet found a newer and more natural norm in the chancery language or in the vernacular, or in any combination of these two elements with Slavonic and Western European. One might say that Russians of that time had more linguistic material than they could cope with, and no sense of how this material might be blended and systematized. Such systematization would only come in the next century with Trediakovsky and especially Lomonosov. Before such systematization could begin, however, Russian verbal culture would undergo its greatest trauma, as Peter the Great dragged his unwilling country, and its language, definitively into the Western world.

NOTES

1. Unless otherwise noted, "Russian" and other labels will be used as cover terms for the given language, the people speaking this language, and the culture of this people.

2. Where ambiguity is unlikely, the term "Russian" will be used to refer to both Rusian and Russian *sensu strictu* developments; thus, "Russian cultural history" includes the Rusian period.

3. The Russian *Primary Chronicle* (Povest' vremmenykh let), the oldest part of which was composed *c.* 1030, but which is preserved in a copy only from 1377, claims that Slavs had invited the Scandinavians (Rus') to come and rule them, "for there is no order among us," but this invitation has all the credibility of that tendered to the Russians by the Czechs in 1968.

4. This legal code, probably inherited orally from the late Common Slavic period some centuries before, was first set down in writing in the 1030s under Jaroslav the Wise, and is preserved in a Novgorod manuscript of 1282.

5. There are perhaps an additional hundred in Russian dialects.

6. Equally unclear is why the otherwise well-known cattle god Volos/Veles was omitted from this *Chronicle* list.

7. A very lament-like passage known as Jaroslavna's Lament (*Plač Jaroslavny*) occurs in the *Igor Tale* of 1187 (if, of course, the *Tale* is authentic).

8. This transgenerational Christianization repeats, and perhaps not by chance, the story of Ludmila and Václav in Bohemia.

9. Although dated 988, this passage was probably not set down until some fifty years later, when the earliest version of the *Chronicle* is assumed to have been written.

10. Slavic tribes had occupied nearly all of Greece in the seventh century, but the Slavic waves receded in the eighth and the ninth.

11. The term "Slavonic" is short for "Russian (or Rusian) Church Slavonic" and refers to Rusian texts, translated or original, which show a preponderance of linguistic features that go back, directly or indirectly, to South Slavic.

12. In discussing Slavonic–Rusian contrasts, it should not be forgotten that South and East Slavic were after all closely related dialects and that the great bulk of their phonology, morphology, and lexicon was identical.

13. Use of the Slavonic *Vladimir* as a princely appellation and eventually as an everyday first name was a later development; note that even today the affectionate hypocoristic of *Vladimir* is *Volodja*.

14. The economic and military power of such older centers as Kiev and Novgorod, located along the "road from the Varingians to the Greeks," had long since been declining, partly because the Crusades had reopened the more convenient Mediterranean trade routes, partly because of the devastating Tatar conquests of the early thirteenth century (Kiev fell to the Tatars in 1240, and they would not be decisively defeated until 1480).

15. An adequate measure of the cultural distance between the two areas might be the fact that in the mid seventeenth century there were nineteen printing shops operating in the Southwest and but a single one in Muscovy.

16. This experience seems not to have been exploited for the common good, as Iosif had no record as either scholar or theologian; furthermore, one of his contemporaries complained that he "sinned in secret and ate meat with a sinful woman."

17. "Polotsky" is a sobriquet conferred on Simeon by his Moscow associates; he was born Samuil Gavrilovič Petrovsky-Sitnianovič (b. 1625 in Polock, d.1680 in Moscow).

18. In Russian legal language, Slavonisms had been gradually increasing over the period from the *Russkaja Pravda* of 1287 to the *Sobornoe Uloženie* of Tsar Aleksei Mixailovič in 1649, but the *Uloženie* uses more Slavonic forms in the sections dealing with the Church than elsewhere. Similarly Grigory Kotošixin's *O Rosii v carstvovanie Alekseja Mixailoviča* uses more Slavonic in the first chapter, devoted to the royal family, than in the rest of the work.

19. The first published grammar of vernacular Russian was authored by the Oxford Professor Heinrich Wilhelm Ludolf in 1696.

3

Religion: Russian Orthodoxy

In Rus' the official conversion from paganism to Christianity took place in the tenth century. Paganism, thriving in the vast East European territory inhabited by different Slavic, Finno-Ugric, Lithuanian, and Turkic tribes was not an "organized" religion, which could be viewed as some kind of unified whole with common gods for all tribes or with a common level of world understanding. There were, instead, higher deities unifying the tribe or several tribes, and there were local deities, of particular settlements, and even of homes (for example, the house spirits or *domovye*).

With the adoption of Christianity in the population centers, only the higher deities, such as Perun (in Finno-Ugric Perkun, god of thunder and war), Veles (god of household animals and trade), and Dažbog (god of the harvest), were deposed. The "lesser" deities, the house gods, those imagined by the people to inhabit swamps, forests, rivers, and outbuildings, continued to be objects of worship – or, more exactly, superstition – into the twentieth century. Faith in them coexisted with belief in Christianity, just as superstitions continue to exist to the present day in different varieties of omens, fortune-telling, and so on.

Such cultural conditions among the lower classes – including the pre-existing beliefs regarding the land and nature that supported the ethics of common agricultural labor – made the transition from paganism to Christianity in the official sphere fairly rapid and painless. The need for a single religion to bring together the Russian tribes was fully recognized by Vladimir at the end of the tenth century. In 980, when he, the Prince of Kiev who already had done much in the way of Russian unification, gathered and placed the idols of all the major tribal gods on the highest ground of the city no great new unity between the tribes resulted.

Paganism was unsuitable for centralization and Vladimir chose another more fortuitous path to his goal: the official recognition of a single state religion from the ones available.

Christianity was adopted from Byzantium in 988–89 to serve this function. Vladimir's task was prepared by other historical conditions: Eastern Christianity previously had spread in a spontaneous fashion along the Black Sea shore, and had taken root in the great Slavic centers of Tmutarakan (at present Taman) and Korsun (now Khersones in the Sevastopol region). Vladimir brought into widespread social and political practice many of the values of Christian culture already introduced in these areas: they included charity and education (the "study of books") both noted in the *Primary Chronicle*, democratic ideals, and the virtues of an austere way of life.

Certain differences between Eastern (Byzantine) and Western (Roman) Christianity, important for the future course of Russian history, were already determined in the tenth century. A general disposition of Byzantine religiosity that differed from Western tendencies was more significant than the commonly noted local divergences – perceptions of the Holy Spirit's origin, the ways in which the Eucharist sacrament was celebrated, or other ritual practices. In the words of the great Russian philosopher Vladimir Soloviev, this crucial feature of Byzantine Orthodoxy was – and continued to be into the modern era – its firm and stubborn commitment to the traditions of the past. Christianity for the Orthodox was: "something consummated and complete, God's truth of truths; it figured only as a ready-made object for mystical contemplation, pious worship, and dialectical interpretation."[1]

Soloviev, in the main, saw this religious preoccupation to be a negative phenomenon. It was, however, precisely the vigorous adherence of Eastern Christianity to church traditions that helped it to survive the Ottoman Turks' occupation of the Byzantine Empire, Bulgaria, and Serbia, and in Russia to withstand the reign of Peter I, and to live through seventy years of the Soviet government's unrelenting atheism in the twentieth century. Consciously or unconsciously the same sense of tradition led Orthodox believers to hold on to values from the past partly de-emphasized by Christians of other denominations.

In any case, Prince Vladimir was very conscious and deliberate in selecting the Eastern Christian creed with its strong external and ritual practices. When Vladimir began choosing a faith in 986 he received representatives from Islam, Judaism, and Rome; he heard them out but responded immediately to his own ambassadors, who had returned from Constantinople after attending a service in St. Sophia and who recounted their amazement at the grandeur of the church and the beauty of the service. Vladimir made his choice on the basis of their testimony, and that act shaped a cultural leitmotif – the idea that the Russian religion was determined by aesthetic qualities (of Byzantine ritual and St. Sophia itself). Beauty determined the nature of Orthodoxy in Russia.

Vladimir's decision was not his personal whim. The chronicles of the eleventh and twelfth centuries typically note the construction of new churches, and, if they are beautiful, describe their external facade along with their internal design and the splendor of the service. That is precisely why the concepts of the church as a building and the church as a congregation of believers often converge and blur in ancient Russian religious practice.[2] Beauty beyond intellectual justifications allowed the content of church doctrine and its sanctity to be preserved. The often-quoted words of Fedor Dostoevsky "Beauty will save the world," are evidently to be interpreted in this light: beauty will not allow faith to collapse or disappear. As Soloviev points out: "In the East, the Church was understood and defended mainly as a sanctuary, steeped in tradition – in its immobile [static] elements. This [tendency to preserve tradition] corresponded to the general spiritual disposition of the East."[3]

Churches constructed in keeping with this aesthetic sense of religious tradition mark the subsequent history of Russian architecture. After the building of St. Sophia in Kiev (1037–41) and St. Sophia in Novgorod (begun 1045), with their overt references to Byzantium, a very abbreviated list of notable examples includes: the Uspensky (Assumption) Cathedral built in Vladimir (1158–60) for which Andrei Rublev and Daniel the Black painted icons in 1408, the Church of the Virgin of the Intercession on the Nerl, Bogoliubovo (1165), the Church of the Assumption on Volotovo Field near Novgorod (1370–80), the Moscow Kremlin Church of the Annunciation with an iconostasis (the partition of icons separating altar from worshipers) decorated by Theophanes the Greek and Andrei Rublev in 1405 and rebuilt by native Pskov architects in 1484–89, the Kremlin Cathedral of the Assumption informed by the Renaissance vision of Aristotle Fioravanti (1479), the Church of the Ascension in Kolomenskoe near Moscow (1532), the Cathedral of the Virgin of the Intercession (known as St. Basil's the Blessed) on Moscow's Red Square (completed 1560), the Church of the Holy Trinity in Nikitinki, Moscow (1643), the Church of Ilia the Prophet in Yaroslavl'

(1647–50), and a series of architectural projects combining Western and native Russian elements such as Domenico Trezzini's Saints Peter and Paul Cathedral (1712–33), Francesco Bartolomeo Rastrelli's Smolny Cathedral (1748–64), the Kazan Cathedral (1811), and St. Isaac's Cathedral (1818–58) all in St. Petersburg. One should also note the intricate wood construction of the Church of the Transfiguration of the Savior on the Island of Kizhi (1714), the imitation of Moscow's St. Basil's in Petersburg's Church of the Resurrection (built after Alexander II's death in 1882 on the place where he was assassinated and known as "Savior on the Blood"), and the monumental Cathedral of Christ the Savior opened in 1883, blown up by the Soviet government in 1930, and totally rebuilt in the 1990s.

The attention that the Russian ambassadors paid to external beauty in choosing a faith, thus, left its mark on the entire subsequent course of Russian culture. Within church history, it is most evident in the Eastern Orthodox – especially Russian Orthodox – emphasis on ceremony, church singing, and the pleasing architectural forms we have noted, and church ornament and decoration. In the society at large the religious beginnings influenced a long history of profound and tangible interactions between the search for knowledge and theology, and the artistic forms of culture. Theology in Russia expressed itself through the painting of icons, through architecture, prose, and, especially, through poetry. This essential cultural characteristic was evident both in the nineteenth and the twentieth centuries. For the most part, Russian theologians were – poets; poets such as Gavrila Derzhavin (particularly the ode "God"), Aleksandr Pushkin toward the later part of his life, Mikhail Lermontov, Fedor Tiutchev, and Vladimir Soloviev. A poetic sensibility inspires the religious works of the greatest Russian theologian of the twentieth century, Pavel Florensky, and it lives on in the reflections of the philosopher Nikolai Berdiaev.

In all probability this preference for beauty influenced the composition of Russian hagiography; the saints' lives do not so much communicate the facts of their existence as they use ceremonial aesthetic forms to embellish the few facts that are known. The ritual format conveying the beautiful is linked firmly with another characteristic element of the saints' lives which gives the concept of beauty ethical and social dimensions: the saints, in the main, lead lives full of labor and creation – they originate monasteries and build churches. Work, for them, often replaces physical asceticism.

Labor is one of the basic elements of saintliness in the cases of Theodosius of the Caves, ascetic leader of the Kiev Monastery of the Caves founded in the eleventh century, Sergius of Radonezh, founder of the Holy Trinity Monastery northeast of Moscow in 1337, Metropolitan Filipp, Ivan the Terrible's moral antagonist in the sixteenth century, Pafnuty Borovsky (d. 1477) descendant of Tatars and founder of the monastery which bears his name, Yulianiia Lazarevskaia, the matron-saint (d. 1604), Ksenia of Petersburg (*Ksenia Piterskaia*), the female holy fool of the eighteenth century who dressed in men's clothing and was widely respected for her untiring work, and others. And the most holy feat of labor was considered to be the copying of books. From the eleventh century on this form of promulgating literacy and church doctrine becomes a central occupation of monks and entire monasteries. Monasteries were established a certain distance away from the towns, and from the time of the Mongol-Tatar conquest monastic life "departs" to the forests and to the north. Even in the wilderness, however, the monasteries continued to maintain contacts between themselves and to exchange manuscripts for copying. It was at this time of the Tatar invasion that the church center of Russia shifted away from Kiev. In 1300, the Kiev based Metropolitan of All Russia, Maksim, moved to Vladimir, and then to Moscow, retaining the title of "Metropolitan of Kiev and Vladimir."

In the middle of the thirteenth century – during the period of their Russian conquests – the Tatars were pagan and they were extremely cruel to the local inhabitants. It is known from the chronicles that if the people of a town or village opposed them in any way, the entire population was destroyed. Nevertheless, the Tatars were tolerant to the church and even granted it certain favors. The reason for this attitude is probably that as believers in "multi-gods" the Tatars were ready to recognize even Christian saints "just in case." Their superstitions, however, were not consistent in consequences, particularly after they began to convert to Islam following the conquest of Russia.

One more historical factor complicated the external situation of the Russian church. Metropolitan Isidor, representing the Russians at the Council of Florence, accepted unification with the Catholic church and announced the decision in Moscow in 1441. The union was rejected (Isidor was imprisoned), and the Russian church was confined to its national boundaries, which, in turn, led to reinforcement of its state and political attributes: subjugation to the Moscow princes on one hand, and submission to Tatar power on the other. Moreover, at the outset, the Tatars themselves were interested in reinforcing the influence of the Moscow princes on the church since the princes tended to be obedient executors of the Khans' will. Thus, the tradition of church obedience to the state – although violated from time to time in short bursts of protest – was established as early as the fourteenth century. And in consequence, by the eighteenth and nineteenth centuries, the church's submission to the state was complete, which led to the creation of sharply critical attitudes toward the church and toward religion as a whole. Eventually, this negative perception of the church predominated in the intelligentsia and took an especially virulent form among the revolutionary semi-intelligentsia.

On this historical background the fourteenth century saw religious life flourish in particular forms connected with the development of hermit monasticism in the Byzantine Empire and the Balkans, with seclusion, and with the search for profound prayer. In the fourteenth and fifteenth centuries, a large number of monasteries were founded in forest tracts and on lake and sea islands (Lake Seliger, Ladoga, Siver, the White Sea). During this period importation of South Slavic and Greek manuscripts intensified. Particularly noticeable among them was ascetic literature, such as the works of Isaac the Syrian, Maksim the Confessor, Simeon the New Theologian, Vasily the Great, and Gregory Palamas.

Of the newly built monasteries, the Troitsky cloister, later named the Trinity-Sergius Monastery, founded by one of the most revered Russian saints, Sergei Radonezhsky (the name comes from the small town of Radonezh where he was born), assumed particular importance. Former monks of Trinity-Sergius created an entire network of monasteries. Among the major and most attractive of them are: the Kirillo-Belozersky Monastery, the Ferapont Monastery, where the famed frescoes of Dionysius are still preserved, the Spaso-Kamennyi Monastery on Kubenskoe Lake, the Valaam Monastery on Lake Ladoga, the Solovetsky Monastery on the White Sea, and the Spaso-Prilutsky Monastery close to the Vologda region. The monasteries not only spread spiritual enlightenment, but were large agricultural and craft organizations as well.

If the culture of Western Europe predominantly was a university culture – with all the specific features of university tolerance of other cultures past and present, Russian culture, from the fourteenth century and up to the beginning of the eighteenth, was one of monastic literacy and a monastic type of economic structure.

The flourishing of monastery culture was supported not only by an abundance of holy places, but by the large number of saintly ascetics living in the monasteries. Thanks to them basic Russian ideals of moral conduct were created during this time. This ideal moral structure was most fully embodied in the *Izmaragd* which received widespread distribution. In the sixteenth century, a collection of texts dealing with practical advice on household and everyday matters and titled *Domostroi* was compiled out of excerpts from *Izmaragd*. Although *Domostroi* was not at all as influential as *Izmaragd*, thanks to a lack of discernment on the part of many in the nineteenth century, it became a source for false evidence regarding the backwardness of Russian mores. To the present day, it should be noted, *Izmaragd* has not been made available in a scholarly edition and, for all practical purposes, is unknown even among educated readers.

The non-possessors movement, led by monks who maintained that poverty in the monastery was a condition for profound spiritual life, marked Russian church history in the period toward the end of the fifteenth and the beginning of the sixteenth centuries. Chief among the non-possessors was Nil Sorsky, who advocated the abolition of monastery rights to land during a church council held in 1503. In addition to Nil Sorsky, other intellectuals among the clergy such as Vassian Kosoi, Artemy Troitsky, and Maksim Grek (well known due to his past life in Italy as a supporter of Savonarola), argued that spiritual fulfillment was unattainable except in conditions of personal poverty. Nil Sorsky and the other non-possessors also supported evangelical tolerance of other points of view, and wrote on the problems of spiritual self-realization, the dependence of spiritual life upon external stimuli, and the corporeal nature of man.

The non-possessor movement of Sorsky and his followers, to a considerable extent, continued to inform the most important and morally cultivated tendencies in the further history of Russian Orthodoxy.

At the same time, one cannot overlook the culturally vital and multifarious offshoots of the official church among the Russian people.

The Old Believer movement, in particular, not only exemplified but also developed many characteristic features of Russian religiosity. The Old Believers demanded that nothing be altered in the Russian service, texts, or rituals. The Russian church had always followed this principle earlier, attempting to fix "distorted" texts and to deal with mistakes in

Russian orthography that were the result of countless copying. So, for example, the orthographic reforms undertaken by the Bulgarian patriarch Evfimy in the fourteenth century were adopted in Russia because they were considered to be an attempt to return to the past and to traditional ways. The same goal of reviving past tradition led to an invitation to the learned monk Maksim Grek (a member of Aldo Manuci's circle of Italian humanists under his secular name Mikhail Trivolis) to come from Mt. Athos to Russia at the end of the fifteenth century.

In 1550, at the Stoglav Council of leading religious figures which took place during the reign of Ivan the Terrible, attention once again concentrated on the revision of theological books (the minutes taken at this council were written in a hundred chapters and that is why their compilation and the conference itself took on the name "Stoglav" or "Hundred chapters"). In his keynote address to the council, Tsar Ivan observed: "the scribes copy books from inaccurate translations, and having copied, do not correct them." It should be noted, once again, that this tendency toward tradition in the external forms of belief was typical of Orthodoxy throughout the length of its history.

The issue of divergence among the Russian, Greek, and Ukrainian ceremonial practices and the texts of church books became especially acute after the so-called Time of Troubles – the period of anarchy and Polish invasion at the beginning of the seventeenth century. After the restoration of the Printing House (the main Moscow printing facility) which had been destroyed during the unrest, it became not only a center for printing books but also a type of learning establishment, where the editing of theological editions to be published was undertaken. This work began in 1616 and was initially considered to be a "local" task, concerning only the Russian church and predominantly carried on by Russians editing Russian texts. Subsequently, members of the Printing House began working with Greek books, since they considered the Greek texts to be older than the available Russian ones. One of the most important stages in the verification of Russian books was two trips of a Russian scholar named Arseny Sukhanov to the East, from where he brought back approximately 500 Greek manuscripts. His detailed research in the material he gathered allowed Sukhanov to compile a detailed account – named by him *Proskinitarii* – regarding the differences between Russian and Greek rituals.

The establishment of contacts with Kiev scholars complicated the task of correcting texts and rituals, since the Ukrainian scholars' studies were, as a rule, in Latin. As a result, many of the corrections made in the texts were considered to be heretical, which included many of the differences in ritual practices existing then between Kievan and Russian services. Adherents of the old rituals held the following major points to be deviations from Orthodoxy: in the eighth part of the Creed the word "truthful" was omitted from the line "and in the Holy Spirit, God truthful and life-giving," the form of address to God in the Lord's prayer was changed, and the spelling of Jesus' name was slightly altered. In ritual changes five prosphoras (pieces of communion bread) were used instead of seven, the "hallelujah" was sung three times instead of two, and it was suggested that priests walk around the altar to face the sun's movement (instead of moving with it). The most important change for all worshipers was the manner in which fingers were to be held in crossing oneself. The established practice in Russia since days of old had been to cross oneself using two fingers, while in the East the custom (indeed of newer origin) dictated making the cross with three fingers. At present Old Believers are still identified in Russia by the act of crossing themselves with two fingers.

In the middle of the seventeenth century, Patriarch Nikon, the head of the church, began to impose these changes in a stubborn and cruel fashion, creating conditions that eventually led to the *Raskol* (Schism). The churchgoers unhappy with his reforms complained to the Tsar Aleksei Mikhailovich, and accused Nikon of heresy. Nevertheless, Nikon and the tsar gathered a council in 1654, that agreed on the necessity of correcting the church books. The "corrected" books began to be printed; however, more than a quarter of the population from various social groups (boyars, noblemen, merchants, craftsmen, and peasants) refused to accept these innovations.

The struggle of the Old Believers on behalf of the earlier customs and rituals gradually took an extremely violent course, especially from the time when Avvakum – "the intransigent archpriest" – became the head of their movement. Archpriest Avvakum (1620–82) stands out among the leading supporters of the Old Belief thanks to his enormous gifts as a preacher and a writer, and the unyielding defense of his convictions. His works provide exceptional examples of authorial passion, spontaneity, originality of language and thought. He defended the Old Belief, above all, as one sanctioned by tradition – as the faith of the Russian forefathers. After a series of unsuccessful attempts to subjugate him to state-approved doctrine (including monastery imprisonment and exile to Siberia)

Avvakum was defrocked and sent to Pustozersk in the Far North, where he was held for fifteen years confined to a damp hut dug into the earth. It was here that his main works were written – including interpretations of Holy Writ, epistles, and his famous autobiographical *Life*, now considered to be among the outstanding works of Russian literature of the seventeenth century. It was in Pustozersk, as well, that Avvakum was burned at the stake along with three of the supporters exiled with him.

The Old Belief spread throughout the entire North, the Urals, and to Siberia, where it is held even today. In order not to acquiesce to the church innovations after the Schism the people resorted to mass self-immolations, that often included hundreds of believers. The largest *"gar'"* (burning) took place in 1687 when around two thousand people and children voluntarily immolated themselves. An armed resistance of monks from the Solovetsky Monastery on the White Sea continued from 1667 to 1676 (the tsar's troops were able to seize the monastery only because of the treachery of one of the monks, who showed them a secret passage). Although they strongly resisted attempts to crush their movement with military force, the Old Believers never themselves attacked the authorities. Defending their convictions and the right to live according to them, they left for the North – to the shores of the White Sea, the Urals, and to Siberia.

Fairly early in its history the Old Belief branched out into various sects. After the last Old Believer bishop, Pavel Kolomensky, was burnt at the stake, there was no one left to ordain priests. It became impossible to perform a number of rituals in accordance with the church canon. As a result, there appeared a sect named *bespopovtsy* or "The Priestless," among whom many of the clerical functions were taken up by laymen – i.e. the most respected and educated members of the church community. Eventually, another branch of the Old Believers was able to have their priests ordained by the Bosnian bishop Amvrosy, who accepted their faith in 1841. In this way, the priesthood was restored to this particular group, subsequently named the *popovtsy* or "The Priestly."

The Old Believers maintained values characteristic of Orthodox monasticism such as attention to industriousness, cleanliness, precise workmanship, honesty, and a high level of general education which later helped them to assume leading roles in Russian industry. From the eighteenth century on the Old Believers were prominent in the metallurgical industry, silver and gold mining, and in commerce. They came to be known for their practical acumen, reliability, love of work, and high ethical standards that did not permit fraud and subterfuge in commercial activities. It may very well be that all these qualities were developed in them precisely because of their adherence to the strict fulfillment of rituals, the view of all actions as a holy task or as a religious feat. As we have already noted, physical labor and the arduous work of copying manuscripts were considered to be holy acts in old Russia. In any case, due to hard work the Old Believers, together with monasteries engaged in the Russian economy, prospered.

During the eighteenth century Old Believers built their own cultural center in the wilderness of Karelia, on the banks of the stormy and deep river Vyg. This most famous of all Old Believer settlements continued to maintain the legacy of ancient Russian culture even in the epoch when Peter I attempted to break with established traditions. With all his Westernization, in fact, Peter the Great eased the persecution of the Old Believers, and did not move against the Vygovky settlement. He understood its value for the industrial and cultural development of Russia's North, a process that had in turn moderated the excesses of the Old Belief faith. In the second half of his reign, however, Peter began to deal with the Old Believers in a much harsher fashion, seeing in them a political threat to the state.

By the end of the nineteenth and the beginning of the twentieth century the Old Believer milieu had produced a number of enlightened patrons of the arts and charities, creators of innovative industrial technology, and collectors. Thanks to their knowledge of ancient Russian art, the most prominent of the last group were able to take a leading role in the European art world in gauging the merits of impressionist and post-impressionist works, and in putting together the outstanding collections which now grace Russian museums. They also played a considerable role in the development of the performing arts by supporting theatres and creating "private operas." And they acted as patrons of scholarly research. In these activities the contributions to world culture of people such as Pavel Tretiakov (after whom the gallery in Moscow is named), Savva Morozov (without whose patronage the Moscow Art Theatre could not have survived) and his numerous relatives, the Mamentovs, the banker and publisher of *The Golden Fleece* Nikolai Riabushinsky and his family, the six Shchukin brothers (particularly the great art collector Sergei), I. Ostroukhov, and others, were substantial by any measure.

Despite all the persecution that the Old Belief experienced at the hands of the Russian state, it managed to preserve its cultural and moral potential into the twentieth century. The disparities between this productive cultural presence and the religious notions supported by the government are of some importance for an understanding of Russian culture. A core difference between the official church and the Old Believers was the official church's vision of itself as a universal institution – a church for all nations. The Old Believers also took every opportunity to emphasize the universality of their church but they saw it, in the first instance, as a Russian institution, and as such based in Russian customs and rituals. The Old Belief, to some extent, intensified the dominant elements of Orthodoxy, formed in the earliest period of its existence. Nevertheless, the Old Believers were not characterized by nationalism; they easily managed to coexist with all the different nationalities and races next to whom they lived in the course of saving themselves from persecution. In many ways, their religious vision expressed an underlying idea of Russian culture, that the relationship between church and state in its ideal condition should be a "symphony" – a complete, harmonious agreement. On Palm Sunday this vision was annually represented to the people in a procession through Red Square, in which the Orthodox patriarch rode on a horse led by the tsar himself, on foot.

The persistence of the Old Believer movement finally brought the state to strive toward total subjugation of all religious institutions. During Peter's reign, for more than twenty years after the death of Patriarch Adrian in 1700, no new patriarch was selected to head the reigning "Nikonian" church (that is, that part of it that followed the reforms of Patriarch Nikon). As a result, worshipers became accustomed to the absence of a patriarch and comparatively easily agreed to substitute a composite governing body – what became the Synod – for a single church leader. For Peter this was an advantageous state of affairs, since it is always more difficult to subjugate a separate person than a collective body.

It is said that during one of the Synod meetings, while discussing the necessity of electing a patriarch, Peter replied in gestures – with one hand he unsheathed his dagger and with the other he struck his chest, saying, "Here's your patriarch!" That is, Peter made it clear that he himself assumed the functions of the patriarch and that he would rule by force. It was Peter the Great who introduced absolutism to Russia; earlier autocracy was limited by councils and an assembly of boyars, the duma, which at times did not submit to the monarch. Strange as it may seem, true despotism came to Russia along with Westernization and Peter was the medium for both one and the other.

In order to help him completely subjugate the church Peter devised a clever ploy – he appointed a Ukrainian, Stephan Yavorsky, and not a Russian, to manage all its affairs. Yavorsky was a loyal and totally obedient follower of Peter's, and the tsar could rest assured that he would never side with the Old Believers. Among the other supporters of Peter's church politics, another outstanding personality was Feofan Prokopovich (also a Ukrainian), who drafted the *Spiritual Order* that provided the official rationalization for collective administration of the church. In this way, the Holy Synod was created. At its head was a government appointee who acted as a liaison with the monarch and represented him or her at meetings. Gradually, this government official assumed responsibility for all church matters and took on the role of its leader.

Let us note that the dependence of the church on the state was not a novelty for church life; in the past, the Byzantine emperor was considered to be the protector of all the Orthodox churches. After the conquest of Constantinople by the Turks, this view contributed to the gradual formation of the concept of merger between church and state – in Rome. In Russia, this concept received its own continuation in the theory of "Moscow, the Third Rome."

The widespread notion that Peter "turned" Russia onto the European path of development is very inaccurate. The European character of Russia was formed out of its conversion to Christianity (which was much more important for culture) and not out of Peter's reforms. Russia's ties with Europe were never completely severed, although they grew weak from the thirteenth to the fifteenth centuries, when Russia was under the power of the Golden Horde. The ties were maintained through the northern ports of Novgorod and Narva (where the majority of residents were and still are Russian). In turn, large numbers of foreigners lived in Moscow, and the Germans formed an entire settlement. Peter, thus, did not establish but continued ties with Europe, which had been already strengthened by his father Tsar Aleksei Mikhailovich. Peter only gave the existing cultural conjunctions an externally visible presence, by attempting to change dress codes, the design of Russian towns, and the mores of the Russian citizens.

As we have already noted, a principal difference between European and Russian culture was that European culture was based in universities while the cultural centers for Russians were monasteries. The importance of religious institutions for Russian history explains why a crucial part of Peter's attempt to establish political absolutism included limiting monastery resources,[4] abolishing the patriarchate, and generally subjugating religion to political concerns to the extent of restoring the Byzantine system of church–state relations. Peter, in fact, brought back the emperors' power into Russia, and he stopped convening the institutions of a democratic nature – assemblies (both of the church and of the citizenry in general). Having fashioned the state on Byzantine lines, Peter tried to give Russia the appearances of a European power, taking his model not from south or central Europe but from the northern Baltic region.

For Russia such an aggressive attitude toward the church and church spirituality was extremely risky in essence, since secular government and bureaucratic administration damaged central achievements of the religious tradition based on non-possessor values and the striving for pure spirituality.

As signaled by the positions of power achieved by Feofan Prokopovich and Yavorsky, the end of the seventeenth century through the entire eighteenth century saw Ukrainian prelates assume dominant roles in the Russian Orthodox hierarchy. The close attention paid to rituals and to all the external aspects of religious practice, which earlier had helped to preserve church tradition, now turned against it. The musical element of the rituals, the language and pronunciation of the services, were all strongly Ukrainianized, becoming in their turn traditional and binding. Among the positive effects, however, the strong musical talents of Ukrainian singers who were enlisted into the Imperial Chapel Choir and composers such as Dmitry Bortniansky enriched the divine service (without entirely replacing older traditions – especially in the provinces). The art of oratorical prose was also developed, and sermons composed by Dmitry Rostovsky exemplified a new type of scholarly asceticism.

The evolution of scholarship among ascetic hermits was particularly noticeable in the eighteenth century in the activities of Tikhon Zadonsky (1724–82). Tikhon studied at Latin schools both in Tver and Novgorod and he enjoyed reading Western mystics such as Johann Arndt (whose works were translated by Simeon Todorsky, the Ukrainian son of a converted Jew, and an outstanding Orthodox theologian). Tikhon named his own main work in imitation of Arndt, giving it the title of *About True Christianity*. Tikhon's language is colored by Latinisms but is smooth and readable. The principles of Tikhon's asceticism support his high moral standing among the Russians together with his diverse examples of prayer, pastoral duty, teaching, and compassionate advice. Many of his characteristics, along with those of Father Ambrose, the elder often visited by Fedor Dostoevsky, found their way into the depiction of Father Zosima in *The Brothers Karamazov*.

Another outstanding prelate was the founder of the famous Optyna Pustyn (Wilderness of Optyna) monastic community near the town of Kaluga, Paissius Velichkovsky (1722–94), the son of a Ukrainian priest and a converted Jewish woman. He studied at the Kievan Theological Academy, but left it early to travel, to visit Mt. Athos, and to live in Moldavian cloisters. His readings consisted mainly of the Church Fathers but he preferred Greek to Latin writings, following the precepts of Nil Sorsky. He actively translated Greek ascetic essays in a Moldavian monastery, organized a school of translation there, and published a collection of translated texts which is famous even today as the multi-volume *Dobrotoliubie* (Love of the Good).

The end of the eighteenth and the beginning of the nineteenth century was marked by a religious revival – that sometimes took secular forms such as Masonry or Alexander I's notion of a Holy Alliance – and by new Russian interactions with Catholics and Protestants. Particularly important was the influence of Joseph De Maistre and the Jesuits, who established a new branch of their order in St. Petersburg and who were allowed to open a seminary in Polotsk. Protestant Pietism and the mystical writings of Heinrich Jung-Stilling and Karl Eckartshausen provided strong competition for Catholicism. Much of the appeal of Pietism was, once again, the vision of a universal church, a new union of Christians that would transcend all religious differences and creeds.

Closer to home, and partially under the influence of Paissius Velichkovsky and Tikhon Zadonsky, intellectual asceticism was renewed in Russia in the nineteenth century. In Optyna Pustyn the work of monastery elders once again flourished in the form of the so-called "wise activity" typical of Mt. Athos. The monastery obtained a widespread resonance in Russian society thanks to the regular visits of Russian authors like Nikolai Gogol, Konstantin Leontiev, Dostoevsky, and Soloviev. In the 1840s, the Optyna elder Makary (1788–1860) and the well-known Slavophile philosopher I. V. Kireevsky began printing literature, which exerted a strong influence throughout Russian culture. In 1910, it was to

Optyna that Leo Tolstoy intended to go after leaving home before his death. Here also many Russian intellectuals found consolation in dialog with the elders during the earlier years of Soviet power, when the church was subverted by the destructive "movement for church renewal," promulgated skillfully by an atheist state. This leading role for maintaining religious life was continued by the monastery after the death of Patriarch Tikhon and up to its closure in the 1920s. In the last decades of the twentieth century the monastery once again experienced a revival of intellectual and cultural activity.

The great saint of the Russian Orthodox Church in the nineteenth century was Seraphim Sarovsky (1759–1833), whose personality and indubitable oratorical gifts influenced many men and women of the Russian intelligentsia to turn to the church. Seraphim founded his Sarovsky Monastery and a convent for women, the Diveevsky Pustyn, close to the town of Arzamas; they became favored places for pilgrimages.

The separation of the clergy into an isolated social class during the eighteenth and nineteenth centuries seemed to alienate it from the Russian intelligentsia. Nevertheless, the church remained an important and familiar cultural presence for poets and artists. Aleksandr Pushkin, Mikhail Lermontov, Nikolai Gogol, Fedor Tiutchev, Sergei Aksakov, Nikolai Leskov, Konstantin Leontiev, Vladimir Soloviev, and many writers and philosophers of the "Silver Age" of Russian culture dating from approximately 1900 to 1928, all arrived at religious issues by complex and diverse ways.

The religious engagements of the Russian intelligentsia are most typical in the life of the great Russian poet Alexander Pushkin, who later became a Russian national symbol. Despite his premature death (he only lived for thirty-seven years), Pushkin was able to pass through an entire lifetime of spiritual change. At the beginning of his creative path lay atheism, exemplified in his works by the anti-church poem "Gavriiliada." At the end of his life, in his last year, he created a poetic version of one of the favorite prayers of the Russian people – the supplication of Ephraim the Syrian – which is repeated many times throughout Lent. The text delineates the sins and virtues of man's destiny, which most fascinated Russians and especially Pushkin himself.

The prayer begins with repentance. The penitent asks to be delivered first from four minor, very ordinary sins: such as feelings of indolence (laziness), despondency, love of rule (i.e. the striving for power), and idle talk. He then prays for four virtues: integrity (chastity), humility, patience, and love. At the end, of particular importance is a request for the ability to perceive one's own sins and to not condemn one's brother. In totality all these virtues were the characteristic features of Russian saints; they are, in fact, the moral qualities of the Optyna elders and Seraphim Sarovsky reproduced by Dostoevsky in the elder Zosima.

Pushkin's journey from non-belief to belief was repeated by most of the major Russian philosophers of the first half of the twentieth century, including Nikolai Berdiaev, Sergei Bulgakov, Semen Frank, and many others. The key figures of the spiritual renaissance, which was inter-linked with the Silver Age of the first quarter of the twentieth century, were not only poets, prose writers, and philosophers but also intellectu-als from the clergy itself. The clergy and the intelligentsia began a vibrant dialog in religious-philosophical meetings, the first of which was held at the end of 1901, and which were eventually banned by the head of the Holy Synod, K.Pobedonostsev, in 1903. The debates, however, continued in print in the collection *Vekhi* (Landmarks, 1909) and the journal *Novyi put'* (The New Way). One of the eminent theo-logians of this time was the priest Pavel Florensky (1882–1939), who, in the short life allotted to him before he was shot, managed to do out-standing work not only in philosophy and theology but in the sciences and humanities as a mathematician, philologist, technical engineer, museum scholar, and art historian.

One should also note publishing firms such as *Put'* which flourished and printed an extensive series of books under the rubrics of "Logos," "Musaget," and "Orpheus." Various gatherings of intellectuals who dis-cussed religious topics flourished as well, including the circle organized by M.A. Novoselov (among the most democratically inclined) and that of A. Meier, which was the most free-thinking and well-attended.

Atheism continued to be typical of the revolutionary and, I would say, terrorist-inclined semi-intelligentsia. A form of radical atheism was widespread among the newly enlarged class of service workers (postal and railroad workers, accountants, technicians, petty merchants) who often had not received a higher education and, at times, not even a sec-ondary education. The church's subservient position in the monarchial state played a significant role in generating this attitude toward religion. For growing numbers of the semi-intelligentsia the church was the per-sonification of reactionary ideology. Typically, having inaccurately taken Rasputin to be a church dignitary, the semi-intelligentsia ascribed all his vices to the church. Thanks to these widespread attitudes, when the Revolution succeeded in overthrowing the existing order in 1917 and the semi-intelligentsia came to power, the church, as well as the real intelligentsia, underwent a form of persecution seldom seen in the histories of either Christianity or world culture. The negative attitude of the semi-educated classes of society toward theology and higher culture was further reinforced by a general suspicion of everything which was in one way or the other incomprehensible to them, or which testified to the cultural inadequacies of the governing semi-intelligentsia.

The church attempted to respond quickly to the social upheaval, and in August 1917 convened the first church council since the times of Peter I. Finally acting independently of the state the council elected a patriarch, the former head of the Russian Orthodox Church in North America, Tikhon. The new patriarch demonstrated qualities of modesty, kindness, firmness, and broad-mindedness, typical of the best representatives of Russian religious practice: Theodosius of the Caves in the eleventh century, Metropolitan Filipp Kolychev during the reign of Ivan the Terrible in the sixteenth, and Seraphim Sarovsky in the nineteenth. As a result, Tikhon was widely respected and attempts by the political authorities to discredit him failed. Until his death in 1925 he continued an intelligent and courageous defense of the interests of the church. The "progressive" movement of the so-called Renovationists supported by government organs in opposition to Tikhon's administration ultimately faltered because the people refused to believe in their innovations and preferred traditional church practices. The true representatives of the religious element in culture, the thinking intelligentsia, were sentenced to annihilation in jails, concentration camps, and in mass executions.

It is typical of this persecution, concentrating on the intellectual opposition to Soviet ideology in the 1920s–1940s, that the church suffered the same fate as the Academy of Sciences, various universities, and eventually entire cultural movements. They were labeled as "anti-Marxist" and "anti-scientific" and were eliminated by force and terror. Such was the fate of the Indo-European theory in linguistics, of its direct opposite "Marrism," of genetics, of cybernetics, of the formalist method in literature and the humanities, and so on.

Nevertheless, the majority of the people, brought up for centuries to respect tradition, the external form of church services, and the performance of church rituals, preserved its faith in Orthodoxy. No small role in maintaining the cultural vitality of religion was played by Russian

Orthodox theologians who continued the productive conjunction of the church and the intelligentsia in emigration. The beginnings of a new renaissance of Russian Orthodoxy could be seen at work in both the broad base of worshipers and in the intellectual sphere after the 1988 celebration of the millennium since Russia accepted Christianity.

NOTES

Translated and adapted by Nicholas Rzhevsky with the help of Rama Sohonee.

1. Vladimir Solov'ev, "Velikii spor i khristianskaia politika," *Sobranie sochinenii,* vol. IV (St. Petersburg, 1911–14), p. 64.

2. Platon Sokolov, *Russki arkhierei iz Vizantii* (Kiev, 1913), p. 550.

3. Solov'ev, "Velikii spor i khristianskaia politika." IV, p. 55.

4. In 1701 Peter created a new monastery administration to which he turned over control of the extensive land holdings of the clergy.

4

Asia

Grattez le russe et vous trouverez le tartare!
(Scratch a Russian, find a Tatar!)

57

NAPOLEON BONAPARTE (attr.)

Let it be clearly understood that the Russian is a delightful person till he tucks in his shirt. As an Oriental he is charming. It is only when he insists upon being treated as the most easterly of western peoples instead of the most westerly of easterns that he becomes a racial anomaly extremely difficult to handle.

RUDYARD KIPLING, *The Man who Was*[1]

No less than other peoples, Russians have traditionally been open to the proposition that there is a logical meaning and significance to be read into their geographical position in the world. And because they are further inclined to believe that this significance of location has direct implications for the most basic questions about their national identity and destiny, it has commonly been the object of rather intense preoccupation. In the case of Russia, "location" is to be understood first and foremost in terms of a gradient running east and west, that is to say from the Orient to the Occident. The country, it is well appreciated, had the peculiar historical-geographical fate to emerge and develop in a vast intermediary space between highly differentiated zones of global civilization, and the ensuing sense of occupying some sort of critical middle ground has been pervasive, throughout modern Russian history at least. To be sure, Russia is not the only society to see a significance in its intermediate position (one thinks immediately of Germany, or indeed Turkey) but it is fair to say that in no other country has this awareness worked to provoke such an enduring and profoundly disquieting ambivalence in the national psychology. In Russia, this ambivalence assumes the form of a sort of existential indeterminacy between East and West, a veritable geo-schizophrenia which for nearly three centuries has penetrated irresistibly and tormentingly to the very core of the society's self-consciousness. The specific question of Russia's relationship to Asia forms a component element of this dilemma, and thus can only be understood within the context of the larger juxtaposition. The foundations of this relationship rest upon a tangible historical legacy of social interaction, conquest and defeat, and state building, the main contours of which we will examine in the early sections of this chapter. At the same time, however, the perceived *meaning* of these contacts – and more broadly of Russia's location between East and West – is of critical importance for Russian culture, and will consequently represent our principal focus. We will see that the Russian vision of Asia and of Russians' relationship to it – whether as victims, civilizers, or fellow members – was in the final analysis a profoundly ideological one, and one which could be manipulated to suit the broader exigencies of Russia's national sentiments.

Earliest contacts

The concept "Asia" acquired its full meaning for the Russians only in the early eighteenth century, that is to say at a very late date. By virtue of this circumstance, it is something of an anachronism to draw a distinction at all between Russia and Asia in regard to interactions and perceptions in the period which preceded Peter the Great. This is not to say that pre-Petrine Russian society did not clearly differentiate between itself and the peoples of the East, for it most certainly did, but rather that the contrast was conceived in somewhat different terms. Indeed, such distinctions were being drawn already in the very earliest period of Russian civilization, that is to say in Kievan Rus'. On its eastern and southeastern fringes, Kievan Rus' came into protracted contact with a number of distinct societies which a much later period was to recognize as Asiatic. Concentrated for the most part on the prairie grasslands of the west Eurasian steppe, these groups had migrated west over the centuries in successive waves from the continental depths of inner Asia. As historians since the eighteenth century have been at pains to emphasize, the ancient Russians were fundamentally set apart from these groups by a variety of aspects of their social and economic life. These would include their "Western" political institutions of monarchy and aristocracy, the economic foundations of

Kievan Rus' in the commerce and agriculture of the Dnepr valley, and of course (from the second half of the tenth century) their Christianity. The material existence of Russia's neighbors to the east, by contrast, was founded almost entirely on nomadic animal husbandry, and in marked contrast to the Christian Slavs, these pastoralists practiced a variety of shamanistic-pagan religions, and in later centuries Islam or (in one case) even Judaism.

From its earliest origins, Kievan Rus' was confronted with a succession of these nomadic groups. The Khazars, whose state had taken shape by the mid-seventh century, were eventually replaced by the Pechenegs, who were in their turn displaced by the Polovtsy or Cumans. There was an appreciable degree of social contact and economic intercourse between the Russians and the nomads, but relations were frequently hostile as well. In the course of these conflicts, the Russians were able to score some impressive victories against their neighbors, such as Sviatoslav's eastern campaign against the Khazars in the 960s or Yaroslav the Wise's spectacular victory against the Polovtsy in 1037. By virtue of the devastating effectiveness of the mounted warfare waged by the nomadic cavalries across the open grasslands, however, the clashes between the two groups became increasingly costly for Kievan Rus'.

In the early decades of the thirteenth century, the Mongolian prince Ghengis Khan was directing his armies from the steppes of inner Asia in a series of spectacular conquests, the grand result of which was the creation of one of the largest and mightiest land empires that world history has known. At the height of its glory, the Mongol empire extended from China to Persia, Turkestan to the Euphrates and the Mediterranean, and the Korean peninsula to eastern Europe. The first notice of the Mongols' advances to the west reached the Russians in the early 1220s, but the energies of the Mongolian armies were absorbed for over a decade by the struggle against the intervening nomadic groups, and it was only in 1237 that they finally launched a concentrated campaign against Kievan Rus' itself. The ensuing onslaught was devastating, for the Russian princes, having been caught disunited and militarily unprepared, were unable to offer significant resistance, and the Mongol victory was rapid and very nearly absolute. By 1241, when the capital city itself fell, all of Kievan Rus' had been invaded and conquered; as Nicholas Riasanovsky notes, it was the only instance of total subjugation to a foreign invader throughout Russia's long history.[2] The single region to escape conquest was the "republic" of Novgorod, which enjoyed the natural protection of its remote northwestern isolation in a zone of dense forests and marshes. The ruthlessness with which the Mongols pursued their conquest, and the absolute depredation which ensued from it, have been accorded legendary dimensions in the Russian chronicles of the period, and indeed the ravaging and wholesale destruction of towns and agricultural regions, with the accompanying slaughter and enslavement of entire populations, all represented a national holocaust quite without precedent.

The city of Sarai on the lower Volga served as the capital of what became known as the "Golden Horde," or that part of the Mongol state located on the conquered Russian domains west of the Urals. From here, the Mongols maintained effective control over the battered remnants of Kievan Rus' for about a century and a half. They exercised their authority not through direct physical occupation, but rather by proxy through the agency of Russian princes, whom they appointed and supported on the condition that they acknowledge Mongol authority, most importantly through regular payments of tribute. From this standpoint, the influence of the Mongols on Russia was geographically remote and, in a real sense, mediated. As time wore on the subject Russians became ever more obstreperous, at first limiting or neglecting their tribute obligations, and eventually attempting to resist Mongol domination altogether. In 1380, one of the most celebrated battles in Russian military history was fought at the fields of Kulikovo south of Moscow, where the Muscovite prince Dmitry engaged and defeated the opposing Mongol armies. Although the latter were subsequently able to make a comeback of sorts, their authority had been fundamentally undermined, and it continued to erode over the following century. Russian allegiance to the Mongols was formally renounced by Ivan III in 1480.

The terrified souls of Kievan Rus', so the chronicles tell us, were inclined to perceive their unsparing predators in eschatological terms as a ghastly heathen scourge deliberately set upon them by God Himself in retribution for their worldly transgressions. The "Tale of the Destruction of Riazan'," for example, includes the following grim account of the taking of that city in 1237.

> And in the city they hacked men, women, and children to pieces with their swords. And others were drowned in the river. The priests were all hacked, to the last man, and the whole city was set afire. And all of the riches of Riazan' . . . were taken. The churches of God were plundered and much blood was spilled in the holy altars. And in the

whole city not a single person was left alive. All perished, all drank from the same cup of death. Not a single person was left to groan or cry, not fathers or mothers with their children, nor brothers, nor relatives, for all were lying dead. And all this happened to us for our sins.[3]

Traumatic as these experiences undoubtedly were, it should be noted that the Russians did not have any specific notion of their predators as *aziaty* or Asian in the sense that the designation came to be understood in more recent centuries. Regardless of this fact, however, the entire legacy of encounters with the steppe nomads, and most importantly its fateful culmination in the Mongol conquest, has in modern times been imbued with a profound significance as the opening chapter in an unfolding pattern of interaction between Russia and Asia.

The precise meaning of these early events continues to be the subject of vigorous debate, and an assortment of more or less distinct positions has been articulated. One popular position has been to downplay or even deny any enduring significance to the experience of nomadic "Asiatic" domination. Kievan Rus' had been developing as a proto-European society, and when Russia emerged from under the sway of the Mongols it simply took up where it had been interrupted. Two other interpretations, by contrast, underscore the critical significance of the Mongol period as a major caesura in Russian history. Both concur that the political, social, and cultural structures of Kievan Rus' were smashed in the course of the nomadic invasions, and that the society which emerged out of its rubble – now centered in the entirely new geographical hearth of the Moscow-Oka region, far to the northeast of the Dnepr valley – differed fundamentally from its predecessor. Rather than continuing the legacy of Kiev, the nascent Muscovite state was very much a new beginning for the Russian nation, one which was oriented to the east rather than to the west and whose political and social institutions betrayed the strong and unmistakable influence of its steppe rulers. The divergence in the two interpretations arises precisely in regard to how they qualify or assign a value to this influence. One perspective, also quite popular, judges it entirely negatively, seeing Mongol domination as the source of Russia's peculiar political culture of autocracy or the unlimited and unchallengeable authority of a single individual. The great nineteenth-century historian Vasily Kliuchevsky among others gave expression to this view, identifying in Russian society and the state "common characteristics of states of an Oriental Asiatic structure, even if decorated by a European facade."[4] Tsarist despotism, it is argued, was nothing more than a Russian variant of what Karl Wittfogel has so famously identified as "Oriental Despotism," and had no real precedent in Kievan Rus'.[5] In later periods, the institution of Russian autocracy served to differentiate Muscovite and imperial Russian society quite fundamentally from the more politically plural countries of Europe, and proponents of this view identified the communist Soviet Union as the modern expression of Russia's now genetic nature as an Oriental Despotism.

The alternative interpretation, finally, while accepting Russia's basic differentiation from Europe that was the result of the Mongol experience, nonetheless pronounces a positive evaluation of the influence of the nomads. The Mongols had in fact played a creative role as the very first to recognize the imperative to political unity which was the true "geopolitical destiny" of the vast territorial expanses of the East European plain and Northern Asia. When Muscovy finally emerged triumphant, it was to take over this project and indeed carry it on to completion. The civilization that grew organically and naturally out of this process was a complex blend of Slavic, Mongol, Turkic, and other indigenous elements, all of which served to give it a unique "Eurasian" identity, quite apart from the Occident and Orient alike. As we will see, this latter perspective was to be advanced with particular vigor in the early decades of the twentieth century, and indeed is being reasserted in our own day.

Expansion and state-building in the east

Whatever may or may not be said retrospectively about the character of ancient Russia as a proto-European or alternatively Oriental society, there is no disputing the fact that the massive empire which took shape in the centuries after Russia freed itself from the Mongol yoke was located overwhelmingly in geographical realms commonly identified as part of Asia. The reasons for this preponderance are not to be sought so much in some vague eastern bias embedded deep within Russia's imperial inclinations as in the simple circumstance that the Russians found easier and more practical opportunities for convenient expansion in these directions. Indeed, the various factors which impelled Russia to expand into Asia – the need for natural resources or agricultural land, commercial imperatives, considerations of security and defense, or the simple drive for imperial aggrandizement – did not as a whole differ substantively from those operating on the western frontier. The first moves toward

4.1 Vasily Ivanovich Surikov, "Yermak's conquest of Siberia in 1582" (1895).

assembling this agglomeration were made in the mid-sixteenth century by Tsar Ivan IV, more popularly known as Ivan the Terrible. At this time, the principality of Muscovy succeeded in definitively establishing its pre-eminence and control over the other Russian principalities, and became thereby the geographical heart of an essentially new political entity, to which it lent its name. When this process came to an end some three-and-a-half centuries later, Russia's imperial boundaries in the east would be pushed far out to the islands of Alaska, the Manchurian frontier, Korea, Mongolia, Persia, and Turkey. Russia's Asian empire was the product of a highly complex process of formation, which for the purposes of a summary overview may be best visualized and examined in terms of the three specific directions which the expansion followed, that is to say to the east, the south, and the southeast.

The push due east opened the first and, in terms of the raw quantities of territory involved, by far the most dramatic arena for Russian expansion and assimilation. Fixing his sights on the remnant domains of the Golden Horde, Ivan undertook a campaign in the 1550s against the Khanates of Kazan, Astrakhan, and Crimea. With the success of the first two endeavors by the end of the decade, the entirety of the Volga basin was securely in Russian hands. These advances were then considerably augmented in the early 1580s, when the Cossack Yermak – the "Russian Cortez," as nationalist-minded historians of the nineteenth century celebrated him – led a ragged band across the Ural mountains in an attack on the capital of the Siberian Khanate at Tiumen'. The Cossacks obtained their victory with surprising ease (although it cost the unfortunate Yermak his life), and after this resistance had been overcome the road to the east across the frigid *terra incognita* of Siberia lay open and essentially unobstructed. Despite Siberia's forbidding natural regime, this road proved to be appealing for the Russians, so much so indeed that the vast region was traversed and occupied in a remarkably short period of time. By 1639, the Russians had already emerged onto the shores of the Pacific, which is to say that in the space of a little over half a century a decidedly meager assortment of Cossacks, moving by foot and in primitive log boats, had crossed several thousand miles of some of the most rugged and difficult terrain on the face of the globe.

What drew these Russians so quickly and resolutely across the north Asian continent was the fabulous wealth of sable, ermine, mink, and fox pelts available in the coniferous forests of Siberia. The great profits that these furs could fetch west of the Urals, both on domestic Russian as well as foreign markets, dictated that they would be hunted intensively, and thus the rapidity of Siberia's occupation was proportionally matched by the depletion of the fur-bearing population. Indeed, the latter was exhausted to a significant extent already by the end of the seventeenth century. After this time, attention shifted to the sea-otter pelts harvested in the waters of the North Pacific, and the main center of the Russian fur trade migrated yet further to the east, off of the Siberian mainland onto Kamchatka (briefly), across the Aleutian islands, and finally beyond Asia altogether, settling on the North American continent. The Russian occupation of Alaska began in the 1780s, and lasted until its sale to the United States in 1867. At the southeastern terminus of Russian expansion across Siberia, the Amur river valley on the Pacific-Manchurian frontier was briefly occupied in the seventeenth century, but the determined resistance of the Chinese forced the Russians to abandon the region. Russian claims were successfully reasserted in the 1850s, after the encroachment of Britain and other European powers had weakened the Middle Kingdom to the point where it could no longer resist the demands of its northern neighbor. Russia annexed the Amur and Ussuri valleys in 1860, thus establishing its current border with China in the Far East.

The Russian drive to the south focused first upon the northern and northeastern littoral of the Black Sea, with its prize jewel of the Crimean peninsula. As we have noted, Ivan the Terrible's campaign against the Crimean Khanate in the 1550s was unsuccessful, as were all further attempts to conquer and incorporate these remaining territories of the Golden Horde over the following two centuries. The endeavor was frustrated by the fact that the Crimean Tatars enjoyed the protection of the

Turkish sultan, and success on this front eluded the Russians until the late eighteenth century, when Catherine II was finally able to defeat the Turks and secure Russia's annexation of the entire northern extent of the Black Sea coast. The definitive pacification of these territories made it finally possible for the Russians to open up the steppe grasslands, so long the exclusive domain of nomadic groups more or less hostile to the Russian state, to large-scale agricultural colonization by Russian and Ukrainian peasants. After this point, Russian expansion continued to penetrate south, across the Caucasus mountains on the broad isthmus between the Black and Caspian seas. The ancient kingdom of Georgia in the North Caucasus, whose conversion to Christianity predated that of the Russians themselves, accepted the authority of the Russian tsar in 1801, and Armenia further to the south in 1827. Other regions of the Caucasus succumbed far less readily, however, and it was to cost the Russians decades of bitter internecine warfare with a variety of small but tenacious mountain peoples before the region as a whole could be completely pacified and absorbed into the empire. When this had been accomplished, by about 1860, the Russian Empire incorporated the entire western coast of the Caspian Sea, and its borders extended clear across the Caucasus to abut the Ottoman Empire and Persia.

The final line of expansion took the Russians to the southeast, across the semi-arid steppe regions beyond the lower Volga, through the broad gate between the Caspian and the southern terminus of the Ural mountains, and further into the deserts and oases of Turkestan. A major bastion was constructed in the 1730s at Orenburg, on the Ural river, and by mid-century the Russians had extended their line of fortifications across southern Siberia to the headwaters of the Irtysh rivers. Further advances against the fragmented states of Central Asia were undertaken only well into the nineteenth century, however, and the first major foray – General Perovsky's 1839 expedition against the Khanate of Khiva – was an unmitigated disaster for the Russians. Subsequent movement proceeded at a more moderate and deliberate pace, and throughout the 1840s and 1850s the line of Russian fortresses was gradually extended south to the Aral Sea, the Syr Darya, and Lake Balkhash. It was only in the heady aftermath of Russia's territorial acquisitions in the Amur valley, however, that the final advance began in the mid-1860s. The cities of Tashkent and Samarkand were occupied quickly, and by the end of the 1880s virtually all of what was to be called Russian Turkestan had become a colonial province of the empire. Across the southern frontier of the region, the

Russian advance was halted by the mountains of the Kopet Dag, the Hindu Kush, the Pamirs, Tian-Shan, and Altai, which together provided apparently secure natural boundaries as well as an impermeable partition between Russian and British zones of colonial influence in the center of the Asian continent.

Thus as a geopolitical entity the Russian empire was fully formed by the end of the nineteenth century, and the fact that such a preponderant portion of it was located in the Asian realm insured that Russia's imperial identity would be deeply imbued with an awareness of its position in the East. In this, it should be noted, Russia was not really different from any of the other European empires of the time, for they were all highly differentiated global conglomerates of metropolitan and colonial domains. From this standpoint, Russia's close intimacy with Asia seemed entirely natural, and it caused no more confusion for its self-image as an European empire than the incorporation of India did for the British – which is to say absolutely none at all. The situation was very different, however, in regard to Russia's sense of itself not as an empire but rather as a nation, at which point the comparison with Britain, or indeed any of the European empires, faltered. For while it was perfectly apparent to anyone just how England as the European national core of the British empire could be fundamentally distinguished from the latter's colonial dominions – geographically, ethnographically, culturally, and in a myriad of other respects – the parallel distinction between the national core of the Russian empire on the one hand and its imperial domains in Asia on the other was by no means so clear or straightforward. Quite to the contrary, the distinction was a profoundly obscure one, no less for the Russians than for the rest of the world, and this obscurity insured that as the Russians began to be concerned with defining themselves as a national entity, they would consistently return to and attempt to resolve what had now become the "problem" of their position in and relationship to Asia. It is to this fundamental process – the problem of Asia in the Russian imagination – that we shall now turn.

Russia versus Asia: the geography of national identity

Despite the rich legacy of early contacts and protracted involvement, it was only in the early eighteenth century that the relationship between Russia and Asia was suddenly recognized as a conundrum in need of explanation and solution. This is not to say that medieval Russians were unaware of the geographical distinction between the continents of Europe and Asia that Western scholarship had been emphasizing for centuries, but simply that, by all indications, this distinction was not one that carried a great deal of meaning for them. In its perceptions of foreigners, isolated and xenophobic Muscovy showed some inclination to equate Europeans with Tatars or Turks – all of whom were negatively marked by their failure to acknowledge the one true faith of Orthodoxy – at the same time that it drew distinctions between them. There is little evidence that the Russians of the sixteenth or seventeenth centuries endorsed or were even particularly cognizant of the conceit brewing among the Europeans that the quality of their civilization was "the best of the world," as Samuel Purchas put it with admirable immodesty,[6] and almost none of any subjective Russian desire that they should be counted as a part of this civilization.

These attitudes were to change dramatically as a result of the revolution in Russian society initiated by Peter the Great during his long and turbulent reign (1682–1725). Most fundamentally, the Petrine upheaval was driven by the novel conviction that Russia was, or at least ought to become, a European country. In his relentless pursuit of this objective, Peter initiated a far-reaching program of economic, political, and cultural reform, all of which was directed in one way or another toward what – for want of a better term – has come to be called the "Europeanization" of Russian society. The success of the Petrine project, however, was frustrated by a number of factors. Among the most tenacious of these was the reluctance of Europe itself to affirm conclusively the validity of the new dogma regarding Russia's identity. To be sure, there was an encouraging amount of positive response from the West, at least in the eighteenth century, when some of the most illustrious representatives of European letters and culture traveled to Russia's new European capital on the estuary of the Neva river to sing paeans of praise to Russia's "enlightened" autocrats. Underlying this apparent openness, however, remained a persistent residual of doubt, a skepticism about whether the vast, little-known, and – for many, at least – apparently still semi-wild society on the remote eastern fringe where Europe passed into Asia had really come so suddenly to possess those attributes necessary to gain it admission into the most advanced and exalted realm of civilization. These reservations emanating from the West, in turn, had the ineluctable effect of undermining the strength of the Russians' own convictions about their Westernizing endeavor. How legitimate, after all, could their claims that they were an intrinsic part of Europe be in the absence of unconditional confirmation from Europe itself? It was squarely in the context of Russia's highly charged anxieties and frank insecurities about its new European identity that the juxtaposition between itself and the East began to attract special attention, for it was recognized that Russia's connection to Asia might be of considerable use for the purposes of enhancing its new, Western-oriented ideology. Put most simply, if it were possible to distinguish Asia fundamentally from Russia, and perhaps even to oppose the two as counter-categories or anti-types, then this differentiation could cast Russia in a new light and assist significantly in confirming its own asserted identity as a European society.

This process of differentiation could obviously proceed only on the basis of clear and unambiguous geographical boundaries, for which reason the very first order of the day was to establish the definitive line of continental demarcation between Russia *qua* Europe and Asia. Owing to a heritage of rather profound historical-geographical confusion, this task was considerably easier said than done. The Greek cosmographers who first distinguished Europe from Asia had been under the very mistaken impression that the two were completely separated by an aquatic boundary – specifically, the river Tanais (present-day Don) – which they believed to originate in the Arctic and flow south across the entire landmass to empty into the Sea of Azov and the Black Sea. In fact, however, the river flows over only a small portion of this territory, and thus for the most part Europe and Asia adjoin over an unbroken stretch of dry land, with no obvious physiographical demarcations whatsoever to mark their separation. As Western geographers began to become uneasily aware of this situation in the fifteenth to sixteenth centuries, they quickly proposed an assortment of topographical landmarks, which could replace the Tanais in representing the continental divide. The fact that down to the eighteenth century, the Russians showed virtually no interest in or even understanding of this academic problem may be taken as a clear indication of just how little the whole problem of Europe and Asia actually meant to them. In the wake of the Petrine reforms, however, this indifference evaporated literally overnight, and the question of locating the appropriate boundary between Orient and Occident acquired a national-political significance of the first magnitude.

The problem was resolved already in the decade after Peter's death by the geographer and historian Vasily N. Tatishchev, one of the most committed partisans of the tsar's reforms. In the 1730s, Tatishchev proposed that it was not a river at all but rather the Ural mountain range, running from the Arctic coast due south, which should be seen as the physical-geographical representation of the continental division between Europe and Asia. With this boundary, Russia's old fur colony of Siberia was transformed in a stroke into an Asiatic and thus quintessentially foreign region, clearly and cleanly set off from a metropolis west of the Urals which could now be portrayed indisputably, indeed objectively, as a part of Europe. The geopolitical dichotomization of the Russian realm produced by this continental bifurcation along the Urals was formalized in the notions of "European" and "Asiatic" Russia, which came into currency precisely at this time and have endured ever since. The southernmost extent of the boundary, moreover, continued below the Urals such that the Caucasus mountain region – despite its relatively westward location – was nonetheless relegated to Asia, and thus after its incorporation by Russia a century later could serve to embellish this particular imperial model yet further. In this manner, the deliberate "Europeanization" of Russia's own image set in motion by the Petrine reforms not only engendered but to a significant extent actually depended upon an inverse and no less deliberate "Asianizing" of its vast colonial domains in the east. These domains which comprised Asiatic Russia were seen as being joined with Russia proper only in a political sense, by virtue of their common inclusion in an imperial state. In terms of their natural environment, culture, and ethnography their affinities were now held to be with an entirely different world.

Exploiting to the full this basic geographical differentiation, Russia's nascent self-image as a European country was further embellished through the articulation of an imperial mentality which resembled that of the Western empires in all important details. The Russians actively fostered the belief in their own inherent cultural superiority over the collective nations of the East, both their own colonial realm as well as the rest of Asia, and adduced this quality as yet further evidence of an essential commonality with the other advanced European powers. The ubiquitous feature by which Asian society as a whole was increasingly characterized – its *nepodvizhnost'* or stagnation – appeared to offer a suitably backward contrast to the creative and progressive dynamism of the West, a dynamism which Russia as well now claimed as its own. The absolute contempt which this stagnation could excite was well expressed in Petr Chaadaev's summary conclusion from the 1820s that the Orient represented "only some dust left for us to look at," preserved as if intentionally by Providence itself as a grim lesson of the depths to which humanity was capable of sinking.[7] It was not, however, in such deprecatory terms that this sentiment found its most common and effective expression, but rather in the firm conviction that Russia, along with the other leading representatives of European-Christian civilization, had been providentially charged with the mission of bringing enlightenment and civilization to these ossified societies of the East. As the Orientalist Vasily Grigoriev wrote in 1840, "I do not know if there can be on earth a higher, more noble calling for a people and a state than the calling of Russia in regard to the tribes of Asia: to preserve them, set their lives in order, and enlighten them."[8]

It is significant to note that Grigoriev was speaking here about Asia in its most expansive and all-inclusive form, and the "noble calling" which he described was accordingly valid in Asiatic Russia as well as all other Eastern societies. What this meant, quite practically, was that Russia's mission of civilization and spiritual salvation was to be realized not only through a program of enlightened internal imperial administration, in Siberia and other benighted zones of the empire, but through one of active political expansion as well. Indeed, the conflation of these two rather different projects seemed to be entirely natural. The result was that Russia's eighteenth- and nineteenth-century territorial acquisitions in the Far East, Central Asia, and the Caucasus were assimilated into the popular consciousness not only, and perhaps not even primarily, as simple and self-serving territorial aggrandizement and empire-building, but rather as an ultimately self-sacrificing positioning which would allow Russia to proceed expeditiously in rendering those onerous obligations to the heathen realm with which it had been providentially charged. The essential similarity of this attitude to that of the other European powers toward their own imperialist ventures hardly need be pointed out, and it was one which the Russians themselves were at pains to emphasize. "We will say it with the words of the Western powers," observed a steamship captain participating in the occupation of the Amur valley in the 1860s, "WE ARE SPREADING CHRISTIANITY AND CIVILIZATION AMONG WILD TRIBES AND PEOPLES."[9]

Thus it was that the new and considerable importance the Russians were investing in their relationship with Asia derived to a significant extent from the exigencies of their highly problematic relationship to Europe. And far from operating at some obscure subliminal level of the national psychology, this peculiar correlation and synergism between

East and West was both widely appreciated and warmly endorsed, for it was seen by many in Russia as providing the country a valuable opportunity to prove that it indeed possessed those "credentials," as they expressed it, by means of which their homeland could conclusively establish its European identity. "If in Europe we Russians are the younger brothers in a moral sense," wrote Mikhail Petrashevsky, an early opponent of tsarist autocracy, from his Asiatic-Siberian exile in the late 1850s, "then in the circle of Asian peoples we are justified in claiming seniority." For this reason, it was only in Asia – either within Russia's imperial realm or outside of it – where "the moral and industrial strengths of Russia can manifest themselves freely and independently, with the least constraint." In Asia, the Russians would have their chance. By exploiting this opportunity to its fullest, he concluded, that is to say by being diligent and credible civilizers of a stagnant and backward Orient, Russia "was destined . . . to achieve a diploma with the title of a truly European people!"[10]

Asia as Russia's alternative to Europe

We have remarked upon the absence of definitive Western endorsement for Russia's European identity as a complicating factor for the success of the new dogma. In the course of the nineteenth century, a yet more problematic source of resistance to the Petrine project took shape among the Russians themselves, in the wake of the emergence of a vigorous nationalist movement. Russian nationalism – of which the Slavophiles represented only one important expression – was inspired by a heterogeneous and not always consistent assortment of beliefs and ideals. A common point of agreement for many adherents, however, was the emphatic rejection of the notion that Russia's destiny lay in its ability to "Europeanize." Quite to the contrary, many nationalists argued, Russia already possessed an entirely worthy national identity of its own, one which was well nurtured by Russia's very special historical and cultural heritage and thus stood in no need of infusions from without. The quest to become a part of Europe was pronounced not only to be misguided but actually malicious, for the nationalists were convinced that in its heart of hearts Europe remained coldly antipathetic to Russia, with no sincere inclinations to extend it any support or good will. For the future, they concluded, Russia would have no choice but to define its national concerns and interests independently of and in clear opposition to those of the West.

The nationalists by no means discarded the vision of a God-given imperial mission to the East – indeed, for them it took on an enhanced significance – but they understood it in rather different terms. To begin with, it was a mission which by all historical and geographical rights belonged to Russia more legitimately than to anyone else. "The East belongs to us unalterably, naturally, historically, voluntarily," exclaimed Aleksandr Balasoglo, a radical-nationalist *protégé* of Petrashevsky in the early 1840s. "It was bought with the blood of Russia already in the pre-historic struggles of the Slavs with the Finnish and Turkish tribes, it was suffered for at the hand of Asia in the form of the Mongol yoke, it has been welded to Russia by her cossacks, and it has been earned from Europe by [Russian] resistance to the Turks."[11] Beyond these simple historical-pro-prietary rights, Russia's prerogatives in Asia came from the fact that the Russians were in fact far better civilizers and enlighteners than the other Europeans. "The Russians do not annihilate – either directly, like the Spanish at the time of the discovery of America, or indirectly, like the British in North America and Australia – the half-wild tribes of . . . Asia," wrote the geographer Petr Semenov, they rather "gradually assimilate them into their [own] civilization, their social life, and their national-ity."[12] Russia's natural preeminence in Asia was felt to be guaranteed by the factor of territorial contiguity as well, which it possessed alone of all the European colonizers. In consideration of this latter circumstance, even the Western-oriented Petrashevsky was moved to point out that the Russians were not "strangers from across the ocean who, sticking to the coast like polyps, can be thrown back into the sea at the first movement of discontent among the native peoples. For the peoples of Asia, the Russians . . . are like old neighbors." The coastal "polyps" Petrashevsky had most immediately in mind were obviously the British in China, but his point was valid for all Westerners who, like them, were oceanic strangers from an entirely different part of the planet. This "simple territorial fact," he concluded with emphasis, "has great political significance."[13]

Under the influence of this nationalist perspective, the significance of Asia for Russia's own sense of self-identity began to be subtly trans-formed. Instead of serving as a means to help elucidate Russia's commonality and shared universal destiny with Europe, it was increas-ingly viewed as an arena which offered Russia the opportunity to demon-strate effectively the opposite, namely its elemental difference from and superiority to the West. Indeed, it was not at all uncommon for nationalists to envision their homeland's destiny in terms of the basic geographical choice with which they believed their juxtaposition between East and West confronted them. In an apparently categorical rejection of Peter's "turn to the West," voices were now raised demanding that Russia turn its attention and energies *away* from an unwelcoming and ungrateful Europe, and direct them instead toward the beckoning realm of Asia, where Russia's genuine and enduring interests were to be pursued. Such sentiments found expression for the first time during the Crimean War of the 1850s, which was seen universally in Russia as a demonstration of the natural belligerence toward Russia harbored by the Western powers. It was a tragic shame, declared the aging Slavophile Aleksei Khomiakov in the early days of the war, that Russia's insane preoccupation with Europe had led the country to ignore for so long its "natural instincts" and "true advantages," all of which rightfully "summoned the country [instead] to intensified activities in the East, which could have become ours very easily."[14] The nationalist historian Mikhail Pogodin, to whom Khomiakov addressed these thoughts, commented upon the same point even more explicitly, and the breathless exuberance with which he laid out his vision of Russia's impending destiny in the East was surely fired by desperation at the stunning military defeats on the Black Sea, which Russia was enduring at that very moment. "Leaving Europe in peace and in the expectation of better circumstances, we should turn all of our attention to Asia . . . Half of Asia – China, Japan, Tibet, Bukhara, Khiva, Persia – belongs to us if we want . . . Asia, Europe, influence on the entire world. What a magnanimous future for Russia!"[15] The image of Asia as an alternative to Europe for Russian national self-assertion and even salvation was to become firmly rooted in the Russian imagination, and it continued to affect attitudes into the present century.

As this vision was subsequently articulated, however, it became clear that it was fraught with ideological intricacies which made it far more complex than suggested by the apparently straightforward geographical choice upon which it was premised, that is the choice between East or West. For the fact was that despite the conviction and even truculence of its anti-Western tone, Russian nationalism proved in the final analysis to be incapable of purging itself entirely of those impulses and attitudes that had stimulated the original turn to Europe in the eighteenth century. At a deep psychological level, that is to say, even the most uncompromising nationalists continued to carry at least two rather substantial pieces of baggage of the Petrine legacy: the nagging belief, on the one hand, that Western civilization indeed represented the desirable standard for themselves and the rest of the world, and the distress on the other at the thought that their native Russia somehow fell short of it. The persistence of this legacy, in turn, meant that the intimate correlation and synergism between Asia and Europe in the Russian mind that it had spawned, a correlation Pogodin sought to neutralize and sunder, was sustained as well. The ultimate result of this situation was that defiant calls such as his for an absolute turn away from the West and a redirection of all activity and attention to the East were in fact nothing of the kind. Regardless of all rhetoric to the contrary, at the most fundamental level Asia continued to represent not an autonomous field of activity in its own right, but rather an arena upon which the much more essential engagement with Europe could be pursued. The irresistible appeal of such an arena for the Russians, moreover, continued to come from the fact that in Asia they believed they had a unique opportunity to manipulate this engagement in their own favor.

The full scope of these ambivalences came to light in an essay by Fedor Dostoevsky, composed on the occasion of the fall of the Turkmen fortress at Geok-Tepe to Russian troops in 1881, an important milestone in Russia's advance across Central Asia. Repeating the theme which we have described of the pointlessness of further activity in Europe, Dostoevsky depicted Asia as an alluring and untapped field on which Russia could work out its destiny, and he urged his readers to direct their attention to it. "Don't you see," he demanded of them, "that with a new turn to Asia, with a new view of it, something like what happened with Europe at the discovery of America can happen with us? . . . The mission, our civilizing mission in Asia will give us spirit . . . if only we would get on with it!" Here then was a restatement of Pogodin's vision of Asia as Russia's promising alternative to Europe, and a future source of national rejuvenation.

Yet at the bottom of it all, even such a strident nationalist as Dostoevsky could understand Russia's need for this special rejuvenation only in terms of its deficiencies as measured against a Western standard, deficiencies which insured, as he bitterly put it in his essay, that in Europe the Russians could never hope to be accepted as anything more than "unschooled smatterers and dilettantes." In Asia, however, Russia would have the opportunity not merely to rearrange this image, but indeed to transform itself wholesale. "We will become serious" in the East, he asserted, "we will become masters, instead of toadies, which is all that we are presently." Ultimately, Dostoevsky was to return to Petrashevsky's point that it was precisely in Asia – and *only* in Asia – that Russia would be able to find its "Europeanness," and he asserted the idea with the blunt eloquence that was a mark of his expressive genius. "In Europe we are hangers-on and slaves, but in Asia we are masters. In Europe we are Tatars, *but in Asia we too are Europeans.*" And it was, of course, not at all for the sake of the hapless indigenous populations of the East that this final point would need to be demonstrated – in the final analysis, they were quite irrelevant to the entire calculation – but rather for the Europeans themselves, as it was only through their acquiescence that Russia could possibly feel secure in its own Western identity. Through the medium of Asia this acquiescence would finally be forthcoming. "Europe is sly and intelligent," he reassured his readers, "it is guessing what is going on, and believe me, will begin to respect us immediately."[16] As ever, the real salvation awaiting Russia on its road to the East lay in the fact that it would lead the country finally and definitively to the West.

Scythianism and the vision of Eurasia

The deep-running tensions and ambivalences which permeated all of these attempts to valorize Russia's relationship with Asia and thereby to articulate more clearly its own national identity achieved a creative apotheosis of sorts during Russia's *fin-de-siècle*, in the form of a cultural movement called Scythianism. Playing upon the image of an obscure but exotic tribe of nomadic Eastern warriors who had roamed the southern steppes and the Black Sea coasts in pre-Slavic times, a collection of leading writers and poets at the turn of the century began to refer to themselves and to Russians in general demonstratively as "Scythians." With this unprecedented preparedness to avow an Asian identity, it seemed that these Russians were at long last conceding that they actually were the very "Tatars" who, so Dostoevsky insisted, Europe had always believed them to be. The critical difference was that this identity was now cast in a positive rather than a negative light. The Scythians were committed nationalists, and the point of the image was to deepen and lend more substance to the distinction they were anxious to draw between their native Russia on the one hand and a philistine and all-too-civilized West on the other. Russia's new Scythian personality, accordingly, was asserted with a vigor tinged by an unmistakable element of hostility. During a sojourn in Paris in the early years of the century, for example, the symbolist poet Viacheslav Ivanov used precisely this image to evoke the sense of unbridgeable foreignness and alienation he felt in the West. In a poem entitled *A Scythian Dances*, he wrote

> The wild Scythians do not feel at home
> Within the walls of liberty and rights.
>
> . . .
>
> We, formless ones, need our willful freedom.
> We need our nomadic life! We need our open spaces!
> We need our boundlessness! We need our expanses!
> Borders are for you to bicker about.[17]

Yet even such defiant assertions of Russia's nomadic-Oriental affinities, and the ensuing antinomies with the civilization of the West, were not entirely what they seemed to be. For the *fin-de-siècle* image of Russia *qua* Scythia was not so much a new vision of Russia as a part of Asia, as it was a newer version of the old notion of Russia as the mediator of the juxtaposition between Europe and Asia. In the final analysis Russia's new casting as Scythia relinquished neither the abiding desire to be accepted into the Western fraternity, nor the associated conviction in the legitimacy of these pretensions. All of these points were set forth with a singularly powerful eloquence in what is unquestionably the best known and most celebrated of the Scythian proclamations, namely the remarkable poem *Skify* (The Scythians) by Aleksandr Blok. Composed in the early weeks of 1918, *Skify* was addressed to the Western belligerents in the First World War, in particular Germany, with whom the Soviet government was negotiating at that moment for a separate peace. Blok began with a defiant assertion of Russia's Scythian-Asian identity that was even more emphatically anti-European than Ivanov's:

> Of you, there are millions. We – are numberless,
>   numberless, numberless.
> Just try to fight with us!
> Yes, we are Scythians! Yes, we are Asiatics!
> With slanting and greedy eyes!

Despite the raw belligerence of this assertion, however, Blok maintained a careful distinction in his poem between his Scythia and the rest of Asia proper. Russia's intermediacy between East and West, rather than its full identification with the former, was apparent in his point that its historical mission had been to "hold the shield between two warring races: the Mongols and Europe," as well as his warning that, in the future, Russia had the option of withholding this protection, in which case it would observe from afar the ravaging of Europe as the latter is overrun by "wild Mongolian hordes." That these rapacious multitudes would be not Scythian but rather genuinely Asiatic, he left very little doubt.

Thus Blok's Russia–Scythia was not fully Asian, but rather lay somewhere between Asia and Europe. Still, it was not even equidistant from the two, for it was the relationship with the latter which ultimately was the most important. Although the poet gave full voice to the painful ambivalence with which Russia's relationship to the West was fraught, his poem nonetheless made clear the desire that his homeland should now at long last be accepted and welcomed by the rest of Europe.

> Russia is a sphinx. Exulting and grieving,
> And bathed in black blood,
> She looks, looks, looks at you,
> With hatred and with love.
>
> ...
>
> Come then to us! From the terrors of war,
> Come receive our peaceful embraces.
> While there is still time – we can still sheathe our swords
> Comrades! We shall become – brothers![18]

The notion that Russia's Scythian rudiments logically provided the basis for a parallel or even alternative *rapprochement* with the East clearly did not occur to Blok, and he most certainly would have found the suggestion blasphemous.

Thus the Scythians were among the first to intimate that the sources of Russia's differentiation from Europe lay in a putative Asiatic bias in its national ethos. As Blok's masterpiece illustrates, however, they were not prepared to press this insight very far, and ultimately were unable to resist the pervasive Eurocentric influences of the Petrine legacy, although they submitted to them only partially and in their own rather charismatic manner. It therefore remained for others to draw out some of the deeper implications of Scythianism and mount a genuine, full-scale challenge to this legacy. Such a challenge took shape in the chaotic aftermath of World War I and the Russian Revolution. Beginning around 1920, a group of Russian intellectuals already forced into European emigration boldly set forth a new perspective on Russia's relationship to the Europe–Asia juxtaposition, and with it proclaimed the inception of a new movement, *Evraziistvo* or Eurasianism. Emphatically repudiating

Tatishchev's proposition of the 1730s that the "natural" boundary of the Ural mountains split the Russian state into separate European and Asiatic entities, the Eurasians argued instead that the entire landmass from the Baltic to the Pacific had to be seen, despite its immensity, as a single, tightly cohesive territorial entity. Indeed, this entity constituted an actual continent unto itself, roughly equivalent to the territory of the Russian empire or the USSR, which was set off geographically from the adjacent continents by the unique arrangement of its four ecological zones: tundra, taiga, steppe, and desert. It was in effect a third and middle world between East and West, an entirely distinctive geographical space which they christened Eurasia. Although the name suggested that the region absorbed both Asian and European influences, these were nonetheless understood to have combined in such a manner as to create a civilization which stood quite apart from the other two.

From the standpoint of the Eurasians, Russia was part of an autonomous cultural-ethnographic complex, which had developed out of a protracted period of intermingling with the Finno-Ugric, Tatar-Turkic, and Mongolian peoples who cohabited the vast expanses of the Eurasian "melting pot." The defining moment in the formation of this complex was the conquest of ancient Russia by the steppe nomads that had so fatefully ruptured the country's early evolution, and the Eurasians focused upon the protracted experience of Mongol domination as the essential crucible in the history of the Russian people and the Russian state. Needless to say, they did not repeat the disparaging characterization of this period, typical of Russian historiography, as one of national calamity at the hands of Oriental barbarians, but celebrated it instead as a sort of creative national catharsis. The Russia which finally emerged out of it was neither European nor even Slavic, but rather an integral part of the complex amalgam that was Eurasian civilization. The Eurasians spent much of their energy identifying the spectrum of those affinities which demonstrated the blending of the region's diverse elements into a single anthropological entity, including a common historical heritage, shared patterns in their respective folk cultures, extensive linguistic ties, and even racial similarities. More than anything else, however, Russia was a part of Eurasia by virtue of its political-geographical destiny, for the vast territorial expanses of the region had been destined from the very beginning for consolidation into a single political entity. It was the creative contribution of the Mongols to have been the first to recognize this imperative, and the Muscovite state, emerging from under Mongol control, took over and actually consummated the project in the form of its extended empire. The Eurasians stressed this continuity in no uncertain terms. The "historical mission of Russia," observed one of their early leaders, was to be the "political unifier of Eurasia and the heir and descendant of Ghengis Khan."[19]

With the Eurasians, the discourse about Russia and Asia was moved to an entirely new level. For the first time, a picture had been crafted of a Russia which, by virtue of its geographical, political, and cultural genesis, was irrevocably disengaged from the West and firmly fixed instead in a kind of synthesis with the East. Within the framework of their elaborate and impressive scholarly hypotheses, the question about Russia's relationship to Europe ceased to be subject to the ambivalence and moody irresolution we have repeatedly observed in this chapter, for the separation of the two became absolutely incontrovertible. With their vision of the self-contained middle world of Eurasia, therefore, the Eurasians may be credited with having finally cut the Gordian knot of the "problem" of Russia's schizophrenic position between Europe and Asia, a knot that had been tied some two centuries earlier. In order to accomplish this, however, they were constrained to develop a vision of Russia that was radically beyond what even the most vociferous nationalist sentiment could support, for the fact we have stressed throughout still remained the case, namely that Russian public opinion had not by and large divested itself of the Petrine legacy. When the Eurasians set forth their extreme identification of Russia with the Asian civilization immediately adjacent to it, therefore, they were attempting to neutralize and render obsolete a Eurocentric perspective which – however distressing and painful it may have been – practically no one aside from themselves truly wanted to get rid of. This circumstance insured, paradoxically, that whatever success they could claim in their endeavor to eliminate the ambiguities which debilitated and compromised Russia's identity as a self-standing entity would only work to undermine their ultimate appeal. Despite the committed support it attracted during the interwar period from some of the Russian *intelligentsiia*'s most illustrious representatives, Eurasianism failed to receive broad endorsement, either in the international *émigré* community or indeed within the Soviet Union itself. In its original form, the movement did not survive the Second World War.

The USSR and beyond

With the entrenchment of a uniform communist ideology in the Soviet Union by the late 1920s, the issue of Russia and Asia that had so pre-occupied the immediate post-revolutionary period ceased to be a central concern. Within the strictures of the new orthodoxy, the traditional debate about Russia's national identity that had served as the incubus for this issue had no real place. Moreover, while the question of the country's relationship to the West did not lose its former significance, it was now conceived in the non-geographical Marxist categories of a progressive workers' state pitted against a reactionary capitalist world. The homogenization and ever closer political and economic integration of the regions of the former empire undertaken by the new regime were superficially resonant enough with *émigré* Eurasianism to win some political support from the latter in the 1930s, but the Soviets, for their part, unceremoniously denounced the movement as bourgeois nationalism (and summarily executed those adherents unwise enough to return from their European exile). Instead, they emphatically endorsed the old notion that the USSR was divided naturally-geographically into European and Asiatic sections by the Ural mountains, and they actually codified this division by incorporating it into their internal system of territorial administration.

On the highest official levels, the only ideological significance that the country's physical-geographical identity as a part of the Asian continent retained was strictly for the purposes of political propaganda. This was apparent, for example, in Lenin's argument from the 1920s that the position of the USSR in Asia gave it a natural leadership role in the colonial revolutions that were taking shape there, or, rather more trivially, in the toast raised by the Georgian Stalin to the visiting Japanese foreign minister in 1941: "You are an Asiatic, so am I."[20] With an eye toward securing a position for the USSR in Pacific affairs, Mikhail Gorbachev found it expedient to reaffirm, and quite loudly, the Asian identity of the Soviet Union in a famous speech delivered in Vladivostok in 1986. By the same token, however, the Communist Party's last general secretary made even more concerted endeavors in the opposite direction, namely his attempt to confirm the necessity of accepting the Soviet Union into a "common European home" by resuscitating Charles de Gaulle's faded geographical vision from the 1950s of a Europe "from the Atlantic to the Urals."[21] On non-official levels, the celebrations in the early 1980s of the 600–year anniversary of the Russian victory at Kulikovo stimulated some crypto-Eurasian efforts to demonstrate the positive significance of the Mongol-Russian legacy for the Soviet present, but these scattered pronouncements remained very much at the ideological fringes.[22]

Developments in post-communist Russia, however, have demonstrated quite clearly that the silence of the Soviet period on the deeper historical, cultural, and political significances of Russia's relationship to the East was only a moratorium. In the aftermath of the collapse of the USSR, the ever thorny problems of Russia's national identity and destiny reemerged with undiminished vigor, and as before these problems were connected with a debate over the meaning of Russia's geographical position in the world. Indeed, to a significant extent the conflicting political tendencies in Russia of the 1990s characterized themselves precisely in terms of their geographical orientations, and elements of the perspectives which we have examined throughout this chapter were once again clearly manifested in their various positions. As was the case in the past, a strongly articulated (although by no means preponderant) orientation – dubbed "Atlanticism" – was to the West. Its goal was the fullest possible integration of Russia into the ranks of the developed industrial (or post-industrial) Western world, which in the language of the 1990s can be expressed concisely as becoming an eighth member of the "group of Seven" leading nations. This goal was to be achieved, among other things, through the rapid assimilation of parliamentary democracy and free-market capitalism.

In emphatic opposition to Atlanticism, however, an outspoken current of opinion took shape which emphasized the enduring importance of Russia's connections to the East and its legacy in Asia, imperial as well as Soviet. Russia's path to the future, it asserted, could only be constructed on the basis of these connections and on their absolute prioritization above relations with the European and trans-Atlantic West. In order to bolster this position ideologically, the doctrines of the original Eurasians were resurrected and freshly embraced, and the term *Evraziistvo* – whatever the relation to the *émigré* movement of the 1920s – became one of the most important political keywords of the day. Indeed, despite the wide array of obvious dissimilarities, there are a number of palpable affinities which serve meaningfully to link the two movements and periods. The most important of these is the character of Eurasianism – then and now – as a reaction against the political fragmentation and dissolution of Russia as an imperial entity. Eurasianism's insistence on Russia's deep-running kinship with the adjacent Asian world has always pointed in the first instance to the absolute imperative for maintaining the lost or threatened geopolitical cohesiveness and unity of the greater region, be it in the form of the old Russian empire, the Soviet Union, the "Commonwealth of Independent States," or something else. As Aleksandr Prokhanov, one of the main ideologues of this movement, wrote in the ultra-nationalist newspaper *Den'* (now renamed *Zavtra*) in 1992:

> Eurasia is a magnetic field, a plasma, a primal bouillon, out of which the continental landmass of a great state is recreated time and again with new contours.... Eurasian unity [*obshchnost'*] – this is a geopolitical necessity, an immutable fusion of all those plains and mountains, military frontiers and battlefields. The unrelenting pressure from the west, east, and south has pressed these peoples into a single defensive entity, an entity which counters this pressure with a thrust of its own and gathers together the resources of the land and nature.[23]

Prokhanov's mysticism has a distinctly contemporary ring, but fundamental echoes of the 1920s resonate nonetheless in his vision of Eurasia as a transcendental "geopolitical necessity" for all time. Along with this, moreover, Eurasianism in the 1990s was characterized by an anti-Westernism that is implacably hostile. "A new empire of the Chingizids is Eurasia's possible answer to the restructuring of Russia according to the plans of the West," defiantly proclaimed another article in *Den'*, which took as its title the same epigraph used by Aleksandr Blok for his poem *Skify* ("Panmongolizm! Khot' imia diko,/No mne laskaet slukh ono").[24] In a tone yet more intensely bellicose, the journalist Aleksandr Dugin wrote with grotesque bravura about the conflagration to come between Russia and the West: "The *Endkampf*, the final struggle will burst upon us very soon... The decisive hour is already at hand, the hour of Eurasia. The GREAT WAR OF THE CONTINENTS is approaching."[25] To be sure, Dugin's vision of impending Armageddon between East and West, which incidentally is laced with far more crank mysticism than that of Prokhanov, has quite as much to do with the unresolved legacy of superpower hostilities of the Cold War as with that of Eurasianism. The fact is, however, that he found it meaningful and appropriate to express these sentiments using the terminology of the latter. The contemporary revival of Eurasianism is an unmistakable indication of the persistence and enduring vitality in today's Russia of that ideological process which we have attempted to trace in this chapter, namely the attempt to articulate a vision of Russia's own character and national destiny in terms of its juxtaposition and relationship to Asia.

NOTES

1. "The Man Who Was," in *A Choice of Kipling's Prose*, ed. W. Somerset Maugham (London: Macmillan, 1952), p. 28.

2. Nicholas V. Riasanovsky, "Asia through Russian Eyes," in Wayne S. Vucinich, ed., *Russia and Asia: Essays on the Influence of Russia on the Asian Peoples*, (Stanford, CA: Hoover Institution Press, 1972), pp. 3–29, here p. 5.

3. "Povest' o razorenii Riazani Batyem," V. P. Adrianova-Peretts, ed., *Voinskie povesti drevnei Rusi* (Moscow-Leningrad: AN SSSR, 1949), pp. 12–13. All translations in this chapter are by Mark Bassin.

4. V. O. Kliuchevskii, *Kurs Russkoi istorii*, 5 vols. (Moscow: Gos. Sots.-Ekon. Iz-vo, 1937), vol. IV, p. 352.

5. Karl Wittfogel, *Oriental Despotism. A Comparative Study of Total Power* (New York: Vintage, 1981). Wittfogel's was only the most well-known of the characterizations of Russia as an Oriental Despotism; it was hardly the first. See Joseph Schiebel, "Aziatchina: The Controversy concerning the Nature of Russian Society and the Organization of the Bolshevik Party," Ph. D. thesis, University of Washington (1972).

6. *Purchas his Pilgrimes*, Haklyut Society, Extra Series, 20 vols. (Glasgow: James MacLehose, 1905), vol. I, p. 248.

7. Raymond T. McNally, *The Major Works of Peter Chaadaev. A Translation and Commentary* (Notre Dame, IN: University of Notre Dame Press, 1969), pp. 144, 151.

8. V. V. Grigoriev, *Ob otnoshenii Rossii k Vostoku* (Odessa: n.p. 1840), pp. 4, 7–9.

9. "O parakhodstve na Amure," *Irkutskie Gubernskie Vedomosti* no. 14 (15 August 1857), section II, pp. 2–4, here p. 2; emphasis in original.

10. Quoted in Mark Bassin, "A Russian Mississippi? A Political-Geographical Inquiry into the Vision of Russia on the Pacific, 1840–1865," Ph. D. thesis, University of California, Berkeley (1983), pp. 221–24.

11. V. A. Desnitskii, ed, *Delo Petrashevtsev*, 3 vols. (Moscow: AN SSSR, 1937–51), vol. II, p. 44.

12. P. P. Semenov, "Obozrenie Amura v fiziko-geograficheskom otnoshenii," *Vestnik Imperatorskogo Russkogo Geograficheskogo Obshchestva* 15:6 (1855), pp. 227–54, here p. 254.

13. Quoted in Bassin, "A Russian Mississippi?" p. 223.

14. N. P. Barsukov, ed, *Zhizn' i trudy M. N. Pogodina*, 22 vols. (St. Petersburg: Tip. M. M. Stasiulevicha, 1888–1906), vol. XIII, p. 16.

15. M. P. Pogodin, "O russkoi politike na budushchee vremia" [1854], *Istoriko-politicheskie pis'ma i zapiski v prodolzhenii Krymskoi voiny 1853–1856. Sochineniia M. P. Pogodina*, vol. IV. (Moscow: V. M. Frish, 1874), pp. 231–44, here pp. 242–44.

16. F. M. Dostoevskii, *Dnevnik pisatelia*, 3 vols. (Paris: YMCA Press, n.d.), vol. III, pp. 609–12; emphasis added. An English translation of *Diary of a Writer* is available (trans. Boris Brasol, 2 vols. [New York: C. Scribner's Sons, 1949]).

17. Viacheslav Ivanov, "Skif pliashet," *Stikhotvoreniia i poemy* (Leningrad: Sovetskii pisatel', 1978), pp. 75–76.

18. Aleksandr Blok, "Skify," *Stikhotvoreniia, poemy, teatr*, 2 vols. (Leningrad: Khudozhestvennaia literatura, 1972), vol. II, pp. 196–98.

19. Nikolai S. Trubetzkoy (*sic*), "The Legacy of Ghengis Khan: A Perspective on Russian History not from the West but from the East" (1925), in *The Legacy of Ghengis Khan and other Essays on Russia's Identity*, trans. Anatoly Liberman (Ann Arbor: Michigan Slavic Publications, 1991), pp. 161–232, here p. 226.

20. Quoted in John J. Stephan, "Asia in the Soviet Conception," in Donald S. Zagoria, ed., *Soviet Policy in East Asia* (New Haven: Yale University Press, 1982), pp. 29–56, here p. 36.

21. Mikhail Gorbachev, *Perestroika* (New York: Harper and Row, 1987), pp. 180, 191, 194–95, 197–98; Gorbachev, *Toward A Better World* (London: Hutchison, 1987), pp. 344, 348.

22. See Fedor Nesterov, *Sviaz' vremen. Opyt istoricheskoi publitsistiki* (Moscow: Molodaia Gvardiia, 1980); Lev N. Gumilev, "Epokha Kulikovskoi bitvy," *Ogenek* 36 (September 1980), pp. 16–17; Vasilii Lebedev, "Iskuplenie," *Molodaia Gvardiia* 8 (August 1980), pp. 47–156, and 9 (September 1980), pp. 62–155.

23. Untitled essay, *Den'* 7 (87) (21–27 February 1993), p. 3.

24. Aleksandr Anisimov, "'Khot' imia diko . . .': Novaia imperiia chingizidov – vozmozhnyi otvet Evrazii na perestroiku Rossii po planam zapada," *Den'* 31 (59) (2–8 August 1992), p. 4. Blok's epigraph was taken from the poem "Panmongolizm" (1899) by Vladimir Soloviev.

25. Aleksandr Dugin, "Velikaia voina kontinentov," *Den'* 15 (93) (12–18 April 1992), p. 2; emphasis in original.

5

The West

Throughout her history, Russia has assumed an ambivalent attitude toward the West, an attitude conditioned by the diverse sources of
initial contact. The influence of Byzantium, realized through Russia's
conversion to Christianity toward the end of the tenth century, was of
signal importance. By devising an alphabet for the spoken language, her
missionaries gave the Kievan state access to an established literature and
facilitated the further development of an indigenous culture based upon
the tenets of Orthodoxy. Yet the Greek heritage common to the cultures
of Europe assumed particular forms of expression in Russia.

Many of the documents which were available in translation contributed to a conservative definition of the relations between church and
state and of the ruler's rights and duties. Together with Christian doctrine, they were "incorporated into the political structure of the state of
Kiev . . . [and] became a basis for Russia's further evolution."[1] With the
decline of more democratic traditions during the ensuing period of
Mongol conquest, this autocratic inheritance from Byzantium gained
the ascendancy, putting its stamp upon the emerging state of Muscovy.

The fragmentation of Kievan Rus' altered the primary means of
communication with the West, Novgorod assuming central importance
by virtue of its location on the trade routes linking Northern Europe with
the Middle East. A high rate of literacy among its landowning classes and
the assembly of free citizens in the *veche* or town council contributed to
the success of a republican form of government quite unlike Moscow's.
Its function as one of medieval Europe's most important manufacturing
towns and its close commercial ties to the Hanseatic League further
strengthened its identity with the West. As early as the twelfth century,
a foreign quarter populated by Germans and Scandinavians lent a

cosmopolitan quality to the city. The Sigtuna Doors of Novgorod's Cathedral of St. Sophia might be considered representative of the manner in which Europe and Byzantium joined in shaping that society. Inspired by the Kievan cathedral which, in turn, drew its inspiration from Constantinople's Hagia Sophia, the church served as a political and religious center. Its doors, cast in bronze at a foundry in Magdeburg, Germany in 1050, had originally graced a Varangian fortress from which they were stolen and relocated to Novgorod in 1117. Richly detailed with biblical scenes, they provide a significant addition to the building's Byzantine design.

Although but vaguely realized, Novgorod's Western impulses were sufficient to arouse the suspicions of Muscovy, their culturally influenced antagonism prefiguring the opposition between St. Petersburg and Moscow that would follow Peter the Great's decision to construct a new capital on the European model. Moscow's conquest of Novgorod in the late fifteenth century, an important milestone in the unification of East Russia, signaled a retreat from Europe at the height of the Renaissance. Even though little of European culture's revitalization found direct expression among the Eastern Slavs, the rupture was never complete. Italy served as a sporadic source for both humanistic ideas and new forms of artistic expression. Architects and craftsmen from Florence and Venice were brought to Moscow in the late fifteenth century to assist in the reconstruction of the Kremlin, leaving their imprint on several of its important buildings. Unlike the example of the Sigtuna Doors, the Western involvement was now immediate, even though resolution of the differences between native and borrowed elements would require several centuries more.

As Muscovy grew in prowess, it recognized the necessity of employing Western technology for its own political purposes. Under Ivan IV (1533–84) contacts with the West expanded considerably, his appeal to England, Denmark, and Germany for commercial and military expertise anticipating Peter the Great's strategy by more than a century. Yet the xenophobic tsar's motivation had to be quite different; while realizing the practical advantages to be gained from such assistance, he did nothing to encourage cultural *rapprochement*.

The first of the Romanovs continued a cautious cultivation of European sources. Foreign residents in Moscow occupied a separate quarter, the German *sloboda*, which attracted the interest of certain members of Russia's upper class. Especially after the middle of the seven-

teenth century, with the accession of Tsar Aleksei, emulation of the foreigners' life style could be detected among the Muscovites. Tsar Aleksei
established Moscow's first school for ballet and drama in 1673 as the result
of his personal interest in those art forms. His suburban estate at
Izmailovo featured massive gardens designed in accordance with
Western models. One of his closest counselors, Artemon Matveev, hosted
numerous foreign residents in his home, which was appointed in a
manner reflecting European tastes. The personal portraits on his walls
attested to an interest in secular art that was condemned by the Orthodox
church. Moreover, their particular subject matter reflects what has been
described as the century's most distinctive feature: "The aggrandizement
of the role of personality as against the medieval subordination of the
personal to the collective element."[2]

An early indicator of the humanistic impulse, this newfound awareness of the individual traced to its European origins through intermediate sources, most notably Kiev. That city's academy, founded under
Catholic Poland's rule, was modeled after Jesuit centers of learning.
Kievan monks were invited to Moscow to found similar institutions, in
1682 opening one for instruction in the liberal arts. The official language
of instruction, reflecting a persisting distrust of the Catholic West, was
Greek. Latin was briefly taught in the early 1690s before being removed
from the curriculum, along with philosophy and theology, for the
remainder of the decade. Its subsequent reinstatement and recognition
as the language of scholarship is consistent with the pro-European bias
introduced with the reforms of Peter the Great.

Russia's growing sense of national identity presented its eighteenth
century men of letters with the same issue that had engaged other
European writers and thinkers since the Renaissance: the relative weight
to be assigned to the combined legacy of Greece and Rome as opposed to
the distinctive contributions of indigenous sources. "The Quarrel
between the Ancients and the Moderns," as it had been known in France,
centered about the issue of an absolute standard of cultural achievement,
inherited from antiquity, which could be approximated but never surpassed.

The Russians' debate was further complicated by its belated initiation; even as they discussed the application of classical aesthetic standards to their own works, Western Europe was moving quickly toward a
resolution that favored modern national norms. What had evolved over
the course of several centuries elsewhere was compressed into a period of

about fifty years in Russia. During that time, the neoclassical canon, as it had been elaborated in Europe, was tested against the Russians' increasing sense of cultural distinction. Although elements of the neoclassical impulse would persist well into the nineteenth century, other ideas struck more responsive chords among Russian thinkers at century's end, resulting in a stronger expression of nationhood.

The application and adaptation of European standards found their most tangible expression with Peter the Great's decision to construct a new capital at the beginning of the century. Created by imperial decree from the swamps bordering the Baltic, St. Petersburg did not have to accommodate established urban patterns, as did Moscow or the cities of Western Europe. Rather, it could unambiguously express the prevailing concepts of urban design. Its first planners were largely French and Italian but as the century progressed, Russians assumed increasing responsibility for the city's shape. Although particular details might impart a national flavor, the predominant impression remained cosmopolitan European.

Louis Mumford's concept of the baroque city is reflected in the several plans commissioned during the eighteenth century for the development of the new capital: "[its] abstract mathematical and methodical side, expressed to perfection in its rigorous street plans, its formal city layouts, and ... its geometrically ordered gardens and landscape designs."[3] In the particular case of St. Petersburg, its planners declared that "no effort should be spared to make the city ... beautiful and ... magnificent." To achieve this effect "all the buildings of the ensemble would follow one overall general line with all the building facades arranged in such a way as to form a continuous front, without projecting porticoes, and of equal height."[4] The central city was defined by the three-pronged effect of its broad central prospects, all of which converged upon the Admiralty building located on the Neva River. From any vantage point along these streets, one's gaze was directed toward the golden spire of the Admiralty, a symbol of the new secular state's prowess. Similarly, the view of the central city from the river was profoundly affected by the combination of the massive granite embankments and the assemblage of architecturally unified buildings facing the water. The cumulative effect of this consciously orchestrated array of structures was to evoke a powerful emotional response from those who experienced it. Such disparate countries as Russia and the United States confirmed, in their construction of new capitals during the eighteenth century, the Age of Reason's calculated promotion of nationalism through architecture.

What has been termed the "facade planning" of St. Petersburg would become a central element of tsarist urbanism, to be employed throughout the empire: "Whether on the borders or in the hinterland, these cities were the frontier posts of autocratic power and European civilization."[5] Yet in no other instance was the baroque design so fully realized, and to generations of Russians, the capital city would visually affirm the nation's indebtedness to Western concepts. (Although Moscow would experience neoclassical architectural amendment, particularly after the fire of 1812, its fundamental character remained Slavic.) The vocabulary for its expression, inherited from antiquity, was regarded as having universal validity, but in the case of St. Petersburg, the architectural text would be read in strikingly different fashion by successive generations. The eighteenth century panegyrists considered it further evidence of Peter's successful reforms, both the tone and substance of their praise continuing to echo in Aleksandr Pushkin's famous poem, "The Bronze Horseman." His celebration of the city's "stern, graceful appearance" derives from the basic features of its neoclassical design. Detractors, including Fedor Dostoevsky, would seize upon those same traits as proof of its impersonal, alien essence.

If the capital in its entirety can be considered an example of cultural borrowing for the promotion of national consciousness, Etienne-Maurice Falconet's equestrian statue of Peter the Great, the symbolic subject of Pushkin's poem, offers a more explicit demonstration of the adaptive process. Commissioned by Catherine the Great and erected in 1782 to commemorate both the enlightened rules of her predecessor and herself, the work challenged certain received aesthetic attitudes. Although its creator was a French national, the monarch chose him for his progressive views, having rejected an earlier casting designed by the architect Rastrelli for Empress Elizabeth. It was Falconet's qualified attitude toward the sculpture of antiquity which placed him among the "modern" proponents of particular national cultures.

The source of inspiration for many eighteenth-century equestrian statues was that of Marcus Aurelius, a Roman work of the second century AD. As was commonly the case, Europe regarded it as a perfect realization of its subject and the later sculptor could not do better than to attempt an approximation of its absolute perfection. Had Falconet chosen to use it as his model, it might have conformed perfectly to the design principles informing the capital as a whole. But Falconet objected to servile imitation of the ancients, based upon uncritical judgments rather than judicious appraisal of the particular work. It is clear that he did not consider the static image of the Roman emperor a felicitous example of classical sculpture and he was particularly critical of the unrealistic rendering of the horse. He was encouraged in his position by Catherine, who advised him to disregard the statue and to pursue his own ideas. Falconet's own comments reflect a desire to create a specific tribute to his subject, rather than a generalized association with the person or concept of the Roman ruler: "I have tried during my work on the model of the statue of Peter I to capture as faithfully as possible the true character of the Russian Emperor . . ."[6] Even his choice of an enormous unhewn piece of native granite as the base, rather than a more regular and polished pedestal, conveys his interest in the particular image of the Russian ruler. Moreover, the very placement of the statue, relative to immediately adjacent structures, might be construed as affirmation of a rather different aesthetic standard: "The unique and inimitable charm of Falconet's siting is based precisely on the noncompliance to the strict axiality of all the other elements within the space of the central squares . . ."[7]

The attempt to impose rational order from without was not limited to the spheres of literature and urban planning. Catherine the Great's enthusiasm for the French Enlightenment, evidenced by her personal correspondence with the *philosophes*, motivated her ambitious proposal to reform the existing legal codes in accordance with the rule of reason and natural law. The *Instruction,* which she issued to the Legislative Commission convened to draft the revisions, proceeded from the assumption that Russia was a European state, amenable to a comparable system of justice. Careful examination of her proposals has revealed, however, that she had thoroughly perverted the spirit of her French source. And, despite lengthy deliberations, the Commission failed to enact any reforms.

In the realm of literature, Catherine proved equally equivocal; her earlier promotion of satire as a means of moral improvement quickly faded as she became the target of those writers' barbs. For the most part, however, French neoclassicism provided the foundations for the development of a secular literature during the first half of the century. Because of the small number of Russians conversant with aesthetic issues, and the disparate European sources for their views, it is impossible to speak of an artistic consensus. Thus, Mikhail Lomonosov, the nation's most distinguished scientist, brought to his literary judgments the increasingly outmoded notions of the German baroque as the result of his studies in that nation. His contemporary and intellectual rival,

Aleksandr Sumarokov, while endorsing the current tenets of French neo-classicism, was amenable to the recognition of minor genres, including those of distinctively Slavic provenance, such as the folk tale and song.

Despite differences in matters of style and genre hierarchy, these writers shared an interest in russified content. Whether composing panegyrics or satires, Russia's eighteenth-century authors sought to convey a sense of the national experience through their art, rather than restricting it to classical thematics. In the case of the panegyric, the celebration of coronations and military victories prevailed, while the satirists sought to improve the moral character of their readers, castigating the servile imitation of foreign dress and manners. Yet their message was necessarily ambiguous; while critical of the excesses in European influences, they could not speak with confidence of superior domestic traditions. Nikolai Novikov, a writer who would assume a leading position among the Freemasons (see below), typifies the Russians' attitude toward Europe: "He realized that Russia was not a world sufficient unto herself and that she could not yet live exclusively by her own cultural and intellectual heritage. This made his resistance to uncritical borrowing a call for self-awareness, a call for a more discriminating reception of the West, not its rejection."[8]

As this suggests, much of the reaction to Europe was based upon observations of Russian practices rather than immediate experience of Western culture. With increased opportunities for travel, however, there were explicit comparisons which did not necessarily reflect favorably upon Europe. Novikov's contemporary, the playwright Denis Fonvizin, made several trips to France and Germany, during which he recorded his impressions. In describing the city of Paris, he drew the distinction between form and substance that he would apply to the whole of French culture; by contrast to its surface grandeur, there lay hidden a squalor which Russia would do well to avoid. Despite their own shortcomings, he continued, his compatriots had no reason to feel inferior and, in matters of heart and feeling, they were superior to their neighbors.

Fonvizin's repudiation of the West as intrinsically flawed, whatever its superficial attractions, reflects the *ressentiment* that came to characterize much of the Russian nobility toward the end of the eighteenth century. It was impossible for them to deny Europe's importance to the very sense of nationhood yet Russia's obvious cultural inferiority made the realization of equality a seemingly hopeless proposition: "Unable to tear themselves away from the West, to eradicate, to efface its image from their consciousness, and having nothing to oppose to it, they defined it as the anti-model and built an ideal image of Russia in direct opposition to it."[9] Fonvizin's affirmation of his compatriots' superiority in matters of heart and feeling is one expression of this attitude. The cult of reason, so closely identified with the Age of Enlightenment, pales in comparison with such qualities. Even the stock character who champions reason in Fonvizin's celebrated play, *The Minor*, emphasizes its insufficiency in the absence of a soul.

The search for alternative bases that might define a separate, presumably superior, national character led the nobility not to indigenous sources but to other, countervailing currents of English and German thought. Chief among these was Freemasonry, which gained considerable popularity among the aristocracy in the mid eighteenth century, reflecting a reaction to the culture of reason. Introduced from England, its original purposes were broadly commercial and social, but members such as Novikov were not satisfied with what they regarded as the superficial conviviality of the English club. Rather, they were attracted to the order's mystical rites, to its promise of moral perfection through self-knowledge, and to its philanthropic ideals which satisfied a growing sense of civic concern. In the later portion of the century, those Russian masons gravitated toward the more esoteric Rosicrucian Order, centered in Moscow. The internal distancing from its original English source and its increased emphasis upon both mystical and civic elements have led some critics to regard the Moscow permutation as a first indication of the Slavophile response to the Westernizers which would be fully articulated in the following century. Interestingly, the ultimate source for the Moscow reaction was also Western, Rosicrucianism being of German and Swedish origins.

Closely associated with the quasi-religious appeal of Masonry was the "philosophy of feeling" that increasingly attracted Russia's writers. English Sentimentalism, filtered through French and German translations, enjoyed a considerable vogue and the emphasis which writers such as Edward Young and Laurence Sterne placed upon the central role of genius was quickly endorsed by the Russians, who felt that "the rule and line of neo-classicism must be abandoned and free genius must return to healthy nature, to feeling, and to the idealization of one's native land."[10] Affirmation of the individual's experience, as contrasted with the universalizing tendencies of the neoclassical writer, marks the 1780s and 1790s as a turning point in Russian letters; from that point forward, the artist as an engaged social commentator will be a fixture on the cultural scene. One of the first of these, Aleksandr Radishchev, would take his inspiration from Sterne's *A Sentimental Journey*. Rather than introspective reflection upon his own self, however, Radishchev employs pathos for purposes of political and social criticism, indicating the adaptive pattern frequent among Russian borrowers.

A combination of political, social, and cultural developments at the beginning of the nineteenth century heightened the national consciousness and altered Russia's appraisal of her indebtedness to the West. The search for indigenous roots of a distinctive folk culture, which would legitimize a sense of nationhood, engaged her just as it did Europe. Historical fiction, popularized by Sir Walter Scott, seized the popular imagination with its idealization of the nation's past. Napoleon's defeat confirmed Russia's prowess and her claim to equal regard among the community of nations. A generation educated in the European manner, weighing these developments, was divided on the question of its country's historical mission and destiny.

Nikolai Karamzin's increasingly reduced estimate of Russia's indebtedness to Europe serves as one measure of this changing perception. Inspired by Freemasonry and Sentimentalism, he began his career in sympathy with the era's liberals. Although he quickly lost his initial enthusiasm for the French Revolution, it was only when he turned to the task of writing a comprehensive history of the nation that his skepticism about the impact of Westernization became clear. In his *Memoir on Ancient and Modern Russia*, he criticized Peter's excessive zeal for European customs, which had resulted in the sacrifice of ancient Russian practices. St. Petersburg itself was a tangible example of the tsar's mistakes, although Karamzin did not take issue with its embodiment of foreign notions about urban planning and architecture. Rather, he faulted Peter for situating the new capital in a desolate, inhospitable location on the Baltic rather than amidst the natural beauty of Russia's interior. (Although he did not mention Moscow explicitly, his comments might be taken as an early expression of the juxtaposition of Moscow and St. Petersburg, symbolizing the Slavophile–Westernizer controversy.) Despite the negative consequences of Europeanization, however, Karamzin acknowledged the irrevocable nature of the new institutions established by Peter and Catherine. He would argue for autocracy as the only means of maintaining order in a society so profoundly altered by reforms.

Other members of the aristocracy, while equally persuaded of their nation's own accomplishments, continued to regard Europe as a source of inspiration, particularly in the realm of political theory and practice. By virtue of their experiences in the West as military officers after Napoleon's defeat, they became convinced of the advantages of a relatively open society. Confronted with the reality of an increasingly repressive government at home, they banded together with the intention of working within the confines of existing society to achieve liberalization of the autocracy. Russia's Decembrists, the group of officers who attempted to preempt Nicholas I's ascension to the throne with calls for a constitution, were not successful in achieving their objectives; their attempted revolt, staged on St. Petersburg's Senate Square, in the city that ostensibly represented the nation's receptivity to Western ideas, resulted in death and exile for those advocates of reform. Despite its failure, the movement marks a transition from aristocratic reformism to an active revolutionary spirit equally fueled by Western ideology.

Among those subscribing to the Decembrists' position was Petr Chaadaev, a young aristocrat whose prolonged residence abroad resulted in his absence from the scene of the revolt. Although he was arrested and briefly detained upon his return to Russia in 1826, his importance stemmed from the *Philosophical Letters* which he subsequently wrote. Their effect was to crystallize the issues of central concern to the budding intelligentsia and to initiate the decades-long debate between Westernizers and Slavophiles about Russia's future path. The tone of his critique was set by its dateline, Necropolis. To so designate the actual place of composition, Moscow, was to effectively discredit its claim to being "the third Rome" and thus the true center of Christian civilization. Rather, Chaadaev saw his country as existing in a spatial and temporal limbo, between East and West, without a sense of past or future. The decisive moment had occurred when, "driven by a baneful fate, we turned to Byzantium . . . for a moral code that was to become the basis for our education." Although he does not further elaborate on that code, it is evident from his description of the history of Christian Europe that Moscow's moribundity derives from its Byzantine legacy. The salutary union of secular and religious impulses at the time of the Renaissance stimulated Europe while Russia "hibernated." The latter's effort to compensate by borrowing had proved insufficient because of a lack of "that long succession of events and ideas that caused the present state of society."

Chaadaev's pessimistic analysis of Russia's position led him to the conclusion that, while she did not seem to "make up an integral part of the human race," her destiny was "to teach the world some great lesson."[11] In his subsequent writings, he would modulate his criticism of his own culture and emphasize Russia's potential for assuming a positive role of leadership *vis-à-vis* the West.

During the decade (1838–48) which followed, members of the intelligentsia explored various French and German philosophies in their efforts to further define Russia's place in history. The German philosopher, Georg Hegel, held a particular attraction for them, his concept of historical progression through the synthesis of opposing forces being applied to the political and social arenas. Increasingly, the Russian Hegelians became convinced that revolution was an inevitable element in this process, that the state would be destroyed rather than elevated. Mikhail Bakunin, whose early interest in Hegel was philosophical rather than political, departed for Berlin in 1840 where he rapidly and completely converted to the cause of revolution.

His essay, *Reaction in Germany*, with its apocalyptic vision of annihilation as a necessary precursor of individual freedom, had application to his native land where, he asserted, "the dark storm clouds were gathering." Particularly after the 1848 revolutions throughout Europe, he saw Russia as the nation which would lead by example. Bakunin's response to events of that year anticipate some of the articles of revolutionary faith that would sustain Russian radicalism during the latter half of the century. Europe's bourgeoisie had proved itself counter-revolutionary, the prospects for future action resting with the proletariat. In the absence of the latter group as a force for positive change in Russia, he and others invoked the peasantry as the necessary instrument for the destruction of the established order. Bakunin would become known as one of the fathers of anarchism, in part because of his confidence in the unorganized power of the mob.

Other students of Hegel extended his ideas to contemporary Russian culture. Vissarion Belinsky, the most important of the nation's literary critics, elaborated an aesthetics which was strongly influenced by the German philosopher, as well as by various French utopian socialists. Of particular importance to Belinsky were the Hegelian emphases on realistic and objective art, its social universality and national specificity.[12] Individual authors and their works were to be judged relative to the era's realization of the national spirit and certain genres were deemed appropriate to particular stages of that realization. Thus, Belinsky argued that the epic, being expressive of a positive national ideal, could not be successfully produced in the negative conditions of Russia; the novel was a more suitable vehicle for depicting modern society.

During the latter portion of his brief career, Belinsky was to focus less upon abstract rational principles and more upon their application to the circumstances of contemporary society. His conception of literature as the means of creating a strong social consciousness was one inspired by the French. He wrote approvingly of those socially engaged authors, such as Eugène Sue, whose purpose was to expose the inequities of society. But, although he endorsed tendentious literature, he reiterated the utopian socialists' view that the writer should be concerned with the aesthetic qualities of his work and not allow himself to become a pamphleteer.

The next several decades would see the finest examples of the Russian realistic novel as Russian writers, inspired by Belinsky's ideas in concert with those of his European sources, assumed a leading role in fiction. Fedor Dostoevsky's rise to prominence was especially noteworthy, involving as it did his repudiation of an early enthusiasm for Western socialism and an affirmation of the Slavophile position in his mature works. It is impossible to define a point at which his conversion occurred; doubtlessly, the transformation was gradual during the period of exile that followed his arrest for political activities in the 1840s. Of particular interest, however, are his observations published as *Winter Notes on Summer Impressions*, following his trip to Western Europe in 1862. As had Fonvizin almost a century earlier, he reacted negatively to the moral complacency and hypocrisy that he observed. He reserved some of his most damning criticism for the West's equation of progress with material wealth, as evidenced by London's Crystal Palace. Both as a structure and a symbol of the International Exhibition of 1851, that building epitomized the secular course of European civilization. Visitors to the enormous glass enclosure spoke of it with the same reverence as earlier generations might have reserved for cathedrals. It housed all of those manufactured products which attested to the triumph of technology and rational organization. Yet Dostoevsky, upon viewing the exhibits and building could only express apprehension at all that the Crystal Palace represented: "Yes, the Exhibition is astonishing. You feel the terrible force which has united these countless numbers of people from all over the world into a single herd, you become aware of a colossal idea, you sense

that something has been attained here, that here there is victory, triumph
... You sense that much spiritual resistance and denial would be needed
eternally so as not to submit, not to surrender to the impression, not to
bow to fact and not to deify Baal ..."[13]

The example of the Exhibition did not elicit a uniformly negative
response among Dostoevsky's compatriots. Indeed, the Russians staged a
series of less ambitious industrial fairs during the nineteenth century,
culminating in the All Russian Artistic-Manufacturing Exhibition of
1882 in Moscow. The architectural design of its main structure was
inspired by the Crystal Palace and the whole exhibition's purpose was to
assert Russia's equality with the West, as its organizers emphasized: "The
outstanding order reigning at the exhibition makes Russia appear to be a
fully European country, enlightened and well-ordered."[14]

Coming after Dostoevsky's death, the Moscow Exhibition could not
have been remarked upon in his writings, but Western notions of
material progress had already been challenged in his fiction. His novel
Crime and Punishment, set almost entirely within the confines of St.
Petersburg, elaborates his views about Europe's impact upon Russia. The
squalid, cheerless urban landscape through which the hero of that novel,
Raskolnikov, moves is reminiscent of the London street scenes described
in *Winter Notes on Summer Impressions*. There is an enormous disparity
between the magnificent neoclassical facade and the reality of the back
streets. Napoleon III's ambitious reshaping of mid-century Paris is
echoed in Raskolnikov's thoughts about restoring the Russian capital to
its original orderly design. The latter's notions complement his theoretical justification for crime, being "based on the assumption that a rational superman can control and change his environment."[15] Dostoevsky's
repudiation of pernicious Western influences is confirmed by the novel's
conclusion; his hero will only experience spiritual rebirth once he is
removed from the stifling confines of St. Petersburg and exiled to Siberia.

The literary centerpiece in the debate between Slavophiles and
Westernizers was Ivan Turgenev's *Fathers and Children*. Although far
removed from the capital in its setting on the estates of several members
of the gentry, its action is informed by the Western ideas emanating from
that source. Members of the younger generation, the "men of the
sixties," profess increasingly radical social views. "Nihilism," a term
earlier used to denote materialism as opposed to idealism, now serves to
justify the condemnation and destruction of all institutions and practices lacking in objective, scientific validation. Thus, its hero Bazarov's

categorical rejection of the village commune and the peasant family, staples of the Slavophiles' system of beliefs.

Although Bazarov will die without implementing any of his radical notions, the readers' response to the novel indicated the complexities of the underlying controversy. The majority of the activist Westernizers regarded him as a parody but at least one of their leading members, Dmitry Pisarev, found much to commend in his character. By the same token, the opponents of Westernization were divided in their assessment of the novel's representation of the generation of the fathers. Both groups agreed, however, on the significance of the literary work as a shaping influence upon society.

As the century advanced, failure to effect fundamental changes either through acts of revolutionary terrorism or artistic example produced an atmosphere of pessimism. Although many Russian intellectuals shared with their European contemporaries an enthusiasm for Western economic determinism, others distanced themselves from social and political analyses. Mystical idealism, elaborated by Vladimir Soloviev over the last quarter of the century, contended for the nation's attention as a philosophic alternative to that offered by the Marxists.

The central thrust of Soloviev's work, after an initial period of interest in theosophy, was the reunion of the Eastern and Western churches. He thus attempted to close, at least on the religious plane, the gap between Westernizers and Slavophiles, retaining the latter's confidence in the spirituality of the Russian people while disputing their criticism of the Western church and culture. The universal church envisioned by him would transcend national identities and restore theocracy as the supreme authority in Christian nations. In the final decade of his life, however, Soloviev identified an alien force emanating from the East and threatening the realization of the new church. Russia's historic memory of Mongol conquest was revived in his poem "Pan Mongolism" (1894). Its prophecy of destruction anticipated the outcome of the Russo-Japanese War of 1904–05 in which Russia suffered a heavy defeat.

Soloviev's mystical religious ideas and apocalyptic vision found a sympathetic audience among Russia's symbolists, whose members were initially influenced by the aesthetic principles of the French symbolist movement. The latter's emphasis on art for art's sake, so contrary to the socially engaged stance of nineteenth-century realists, found graphic expression in *The World of Art*, a sumptuously published periodical of cosmopolitan cast, which included both Russian and European contributors to its issues. During its brief existence (1898–1904) it provided a forum for discussing contemporary movements, particularly in the visual arts, and it sponsored exhibitions of paintings and art objects from various countries. Short-lived though it was, *The World of Art* stimulated the Russian intellectual community, reaffirming its ties to that of Western Europe.

To those associated with the *World of Art*, the city of St. Petersburg, in its original baroque conception, was a source of aesthetic satisfaction. Haphazard development over the previous century had obscured its visual integrity and a number of artists and architects, led by Alexandre and Leonty Benois, set about reviving a sense of the historical city and ensuring that its architectural heritage be preserved. An attempt was even made, in the final decade of tsarist Russia's existence, to plan urban expansion in the spirit of the eighteenth century, the proposed New Petersburg embodying that same combination of the monumental and the functional which had distinguished the original conception.

Renewed appreciation for the capital as a physical testament to Russia's successful adaptation of Western values coincided with the culminating literary treatment of the Petersburg theme. The symbolist poet and novelist, Andrei Bely, published *Petersburg*, as the second installment of an intended trilogy entitled "East or West" in 1916. The first volume had described an ex-urbanite's tragic involvement with a mystical religious sect in the Russian countryside and the subsequent novel may well have been intended as the secular Western antithesis. Yet the synthesizing final volume was never written and, within *Petersburg*, there is continuing evidence of the East–West opposition. In one of its central scenes, the vexing question "Whither Russia?", inspired by the rearing Bronze Horseman, is addressed in a narrative digression: "Once it has soared up on its hind legs, measuring the air with its eyes, the bronze steed will not set down its hooves. There will be a leap across history. Great shall be the turmoil. The earth shall be cleft . . . As for Petersburg, it will sink."[16] Even though the novel deflects this apocalyptic expectation, the sense of an end to the Western chapter of Russian civilization permeates this and other works written during the period of war and political revolution.

Shortly after the Bolsheviks seized power, the nation's capital was moved to Moscow and, in 1924, the former St. Petersburg was further divested of its symbolic ties to Europe when it was renamed Leningrad in honor of the Revolution's leader. It would remain under that name until the final collapse of communism, when its original designation was restored. The cyclical renaming process mirrors the society's retreat into Great Russian nationalism and a xenophobic attitude toward the West which would gain in intensity under Stalin before finally relaxing in the last decades of this century.

In the years preceding the Revolution of 1917, the intelligentsia had been fully involved in modern high culture and, as such, its members were part of an international community which tended toward apolitical inquiry. Yet it was also true in Russia, as it has subsequently proved to be in other less developed nations, that the intelligentsia continued to be drawn by its faith in modern culture "in a practical direction toward engagement in such mundane or even sordid affairs as politics."[17] Increasingly, the Bolsheviks identified "bourgeois" high culture with the capitalist West and, while tolerating the presence of well-trained specialists as essential to the establishment of a new order, ultimately sought its suppression. The intelligentsia's responses to the changing environment varied; those who opted to pursue purely apolitical objectives often chose to emigrate to the more receptive environments of Europe and the United States; others believed that they could maintain the integrity of their inquiry while serving the new society. Many of the latter sustained their enthusiasm for the Revolution through the 1920s, but the eclecticism of that decade yielded to an ideological uniformity, imposed from above, that tended to be anti-Western in its nature.

Professionals in a wide range of disciplines confronted the problem of reconciling the basic tenets of their practice with those of Marxist-Leninism. Artists and writers experienced particular pressure to reflect the new political realities but scientists were also subjected to condemnation and persecution for engaging in "bourgeois, pseudoscientific" activities. Of particular note was the repudiation of Western principles of genetics. Russia's need to improve crop production in the 1920s led to a plant-breeding program which accepted the classical notion of the gene as the determinant of inherited traits. Its foremost member, Nikolai Vavilov, was President of the Lenin All-Union Academy of Agricultural Sciences, a position which did not spare him from attack by those who, citing Engels as their authority, insisted upon the inheritance of acquired characteristics. At issue was the possibility of altering the genetic nature of a species, in this instance wheat, by subjecting it to cold treatment. Proof of the latter possibility would discredit genetic theory as elaborated in the West and prove the superiority of Soviet science. An obscure agronomist, T. D. Lysenko, persuaded Stalin of his success in wheat genetics, for the next three decades precluding any research like that being conducted in the West. That their position was based upon national political considerations rather than experimental data is evidenced by the remarks delivered at the infamous Academy of Agricultural Sciences session in August 1948: "We will not debate with Morganists [those subscribing to classical genetics principles] but continue to unmask them as representatives of a detrimental and ideologically foreign and essentially pseudoscientific trend imported from abroad."[18]

Subsequent to Stalin's death, the most virulent political attacks against Western thought diminished but Aleksandr Solzhenitsyn's Harvard commencement address of 1975 served to remind the world of a persisting, deeply-rooted suspicion that transcends the particulars of the Russian political system. Although the critical tone of his analysis of Western culture left many in his audience nonplused, it was consistent with the Slavophile tradition. The "soulless and smooth plane of legalism" that he saw as the defining element of the West's self-indulgent materialism offered little for his compatriots to emulate: "Through deep suffering, people in our country have now achieved a spiritual development of such intensity that the Western system, in its present state of spiritual exhaustion, does not look attractive."[19]

With the precipitous disintegration both of political and economic structures, the sense of crisis in Russia became ever more acute. Her pride of place among nations diminished, her citizens divided sharply about the means of restoration. The risks and uncertainties of a market economy, compounded by the contention inherent in pluralistic systems of democratic government, provoked strong reaction in many quarters. If communism has been disavowed, authoritarian rule has not been. Solzhenitsyn's vision of a theocratic state, morally distanced from the West, is but one of the proposed solutions to the nation's dilemma. "Whither Russia?" in relation to the West remains as pressing a question as at any point in her history.

NOTES

1. Francis Dvornik, *The Slavs in European History and Civilization* (New Brunswick: Rutgers University Press, 1962), p. 76.
2. William Brown, *A History of Seventeenth-Century Russian Literature* (Ann Arbor, MI: Ardis, 1980), p. 8.
3. Lewis Mumford, *The City in History. Its Origins, Its Transformations, and Its Prospects* (New York: Harcourt, Brace, & World, Inc., 1961), p. 351.

4. Quoted in I. A. Egorov, *The Architectural Planning of St. Petersburg*, trans. Eric Dluhosch (Athens: Ohio University Press, 1969), p. 86.

5. Daniel R. Brower, *The Russian City between Tradition and Modernity, 1850–1900* (Berkeley: University of California Press, 1990), p. 11.

6. Egorov, *The Architectural Planning*, p. 222.

7. *Ibid.*, p. 178.

8. Hans Rogger, *National Consciousness in Eighteenth-Century Russia* (Cambridge, MA: Harvard University Press, 1960), p. 75.

9. Leah Greenfeld, *Nationalism: Five Roads to Modernity* (Cambridge, MA: Harvard University Press, 1992), p. 255.

10. Ernest J. Simmons, *English Literature and Culture in Russia, 1553–1849*, Harvard Studies in Comparative Literature, 12 (Cambridge, MA: Harvard University Press, 1935), p. 165.

11. Petr la. Chaadaev, *Philosophical Letters and Apology of a Madman*, trans. with an introduction by Mary-Barbara Zeldin (Knoxville: University of Tennessee Press, 1969), pp. 42, 47, 38.

12. For a thorough discussion of Belinsky's indebtedness to these European sources, see Victor Terras, *Belinskij and Russian Literary Criticism* (Madison: University of Wisconsin Press, 1974), pp. 59–76.

13. Fedor M. Dostoevsky, *Polnoe sobranie sochinenii v 30-ti tomakh*, vol. v (Leningrad: Nauka, 1973), p. 70.

14. Quoted in Brower, *The Russian City* , p. 73.

15. Adele Lindenmeyr, "Raskolnikov's City and the Napoleonic Plan," *Slavic Review*, vol. 35, no. 1 (March 1976), p. 43.

16. Andrei Bely, *Petersburg*, trans. Robert A. Maguire and John Malmstad (Bloomington: Indiana University Press, 1978), p. 65.

17. David Joravsky, "Cultural Revolution and the Fortress Mentality," in Abbott Gleason, Peter Kenez and Richard Stites, eds., *Bolshevik Culture* (Bloomington: Indiana University Press, 1985), p. 97.

18. Unattributed quotation in Zhores A. Medvedev, *The Rise and Fall of T. D. Lysenko*, trans. I. Michael Lerner (New York: Columbia University Press, 1969), p. 117.

19. Aleksandr Solzhenitsyn, "A World Split Apart," in Ronald Berman, ed., *Solzhenitsyn at Harvard* (Washington: Ethics and Public Policy Center, 1980), p. 12.

6

Ideological structures

It is a special Russian irony that the eighteenth century – during
which explicitly religious values lost a great deal of their position and
power within Russian culture – should have seen an influential if subtle
reaffirmation of religious attitudes, however disguised, towards its end.
Much, though not all, of this reaffirmation was connected to the development of Russian Freemasonry. The attitudes, activity, and organization
of Russian masons played a vital role in the very early stages of the creation of a "civil society" in Russia, a frequently arrested process not complete to this day. At the same time, however, the culture of the educated
elite – particularly that portion of it eventually to be called the intelligentsia – took on many attitudes significantly colored by religious values
and aspirations which have never disappeared from the culture. The
Russian church, however, failed to recover the grip it lost on Russian
society during and after the reign of Peter the Great.

When Peter told the Russians that he wanted them to become
"European," he basically meant that he wanted to endow them with
European energy and dynamism. He wanted to wake them from what he
understood to be a sleep of lethargy and barbarism, to make entrepreneurs of the traditionalist merchantry, to make statesmen, administrators,
generals, admirals, and scientists of the gentry. (The peasants had to
undergird and support this "Westernization" with their meager
resources, since there was nobody else to do so.)

When Catherine the Great came to the throne in 1762, she could regard
a good deal of Peter's program as realized, or at least launched. In her
vision of Russian progress, the stress could thus fall on achieving full
Russian participation in the high, French-international court culture of
the eighteenth century, with its powerful component of political radical-

ism. She never abandoned, of course, the orientation to material power which lay at the base of Peter's Westernization efforts.

So the St. Petersburg court continued to be the center from which Western influence radiated in Russia. The creation of Western-style plays, poetry, art, and architecture, the definition of Western-oriented fashions, the creation of a *beau monde*, "society," with its language (French) – all this and much more was fundamentally the work of the court and the empress. Even the politically subversive ideas of the Enlightenment and the means for diffusing them in society – journals – were at first stimulated by Catherine's desire to produce Russian versions of the famous English journals *Spectator* and *Tatler*. Once begun, of course, the discussion of serious issues – corruption, obscurantism, even the abuse of peasant serfs – in periodicals could not be contained and ultimately played a central role in the development of oppositional political cultures over the following century and a half.

Until something like the last quarter of the eighteenth century, Russian aristocratic society thus struggled – with greater or lesser expenditure of effort – to be Westernized. There were a few voices of opposition, like the aristocratic Mikhail Shcherbatov, but their points of view were diverse, uncoordinated, and – like his subsequently famous *On the Corruption of Morals in Russia* – seldom heard in public.

Beginning in the 1770s, Russia's cultural apprenticeship to Western models began to grow more complex. To steal a phrase from historians of England, Russia's court society began to be faced with a "country" opposition. This happened in various ways. The lengthy and arduous effort to organize and educate the Russian gentry and harness it firmly to the national enterprise had already begun to create a nostalgia for rural life, a kind of elegiac feeling about lost simplicity that one finds elsewhere in Europe among aristocracies dominated by court and state power.[1] Further, young gentry publicists and educators like Nikolai Novikov began to feel that court society (and the European model that lay behind it) was alien to and in important ways opposed to something particularly Russian, to Russian ways, to the traditions of "our fathers"; yet they were by no means ready to repudiate Peter the Great's Westernization root and branch.

These issues were easier to feel than to formulate. There was as yet no generally agreed picture of what traditional Russian ways actually were or what their meaning was, and no coherent new view of what Peter's reforms had meant. Novikov simply sensed that the old Russian ways were valuable because they were ancestral, "ours."

The dominant classicism that marked court-sponsored literary culture contained within itself the desire to formulate and live by a universal ethical ideal, but the search for that ideal gradually became more agonizing, more implicitly religious, and related to some powerful but indefinite idea of the national past. A growing number of educated Russians began to feel themselves alienated from the world of court and career, to the point of experiencing confusion, longing, and occasionally deep estrangement.[2]

None of this was uniquely Russian. Many of these impulses could be found elsewhere in Europe. But in Russia their importance was particularly great because issues of national and cultural identity were so acute. This was the beginning of the first effort by educated Russians to decide who they were and what they believed, independent of the Petrine reforms and the court-sponsored Westernization which had increasingly dominated Russian life since the end of the seventeenth century.

Compared to most of the nations of Western Europe, however, educated Russians in the last third of the eighteenth century were a small and isolated group, powerfully dependent on their lifeline to court. Yet they did what many other Europeans were doing in the eighteenth century: they created clubs and other forms of "voluntary organizations."

But Russian society, unlike most of the nations of Western Europe, lacked guild or confraternal traditions, and only a small and highly Westernized segment of the Russian gentry was prepared for the work of self-organization. As a result, the new impulse to create a social life independent of the court was at first concentrated almost entirely in the lodges of Russian Freemasonry. And it was in those same lodges where the initial efforts to define a new world view and a more "Russian" individual were concentrated.

The first Masonic lodge in Russia of which we can be certain dates from 1731.[3] For the next thirty years or so the number of lodges in Russia remained uncertain, but they played no significant role in Russian culture and their membership seems to have been heavily foreign. But in the late 1760s and 1770s, Freemasonry increased its influence in the culture of the Westernized Russian elite.

At the same time, the general character of Russian Freemasonry changed. Older "English" masonry, with its three degrees (apprentice, craftsman, master) and even Scottish masonry, which added two more, gave way to a variety of mystical and occult masonries from the Continent with many "higher degrees" and links to secret organizations and coteries. Whether the mythologies and organizational forms of these newer lodges were of the Swedish system, of the "chivalric" type (purporting to be a continuation of the medieval crusading Knights Templar), or of the mystical and alchemical Rosicrucians, all claimed to make available some form of "ancient wisdom," which was represented to the Masonic seekers as the cure for their spiritual malaise. A fundamentally theosophical idea of ancient wisdom, derived from Renaissance Neoplatonism, Western mysticism, and piety was transmitted to Russians via masonry and became the intellectual staple of these seekers, who reacted against the fashionable Voltairean skepticism of the court "as if it were an illness."[4]

Historians have certainly not uncovered the entire network of Russian lodges, but in a pioneering study, George Vernadsky estimated that around 1780 there were considerably more than two thousand masons in at least several score lodges (perhaps as many as a hundred), the bulk of them in Moscow and St. Petersburg.[5] The names of the more prominent mystical masons read like a muster roll of Russia's great families: Kurakin, Chaadaev, Trubetskoy, Turgenev, Lopukhin, Volkonsky, Vorontsov. There were many masons with less well-known names, to be sure, and many foreigners, but very few Russians from merchant or other non-noble backgrounds. Because of the segregation of Russian society, Russian masonry was more purely aristocratic than most Western masonries.

The literature introduced into general circulation by the publishers of higher order masonry was of several kinds; in its overall impact it had a profound effect on the education of cultivated Russians for several generations (and hence far into the modern period). A great deal of it could be called "pietistic," both in a broad sense that would suggest older classics of Western piety like Thomas à Kempis' *Imitation of Christ*, and in the narrower sense of putting into Russian circulation a number of the classics of the German Pietist movement, such as Johann Arndt's *On True Christianity*.

All over Europe Pietism was seized upon by those reacting against the skepticism of the Enlightenment, but nowhere was its impact more powerful than among Russian intellectuals between the 1780s and around 1820. "The heart of pietism," Gordon Craig wrote

> was the moral reformation of the individual, achieved by passing through the anguish of contrition into the overwhelming realization of the assurance of God's grace. This experience was the result of introspection and prayer and was completely personal and unique to the believer. He had no need of theologians to point the way for him,

nor could he derive any benefit from religious hierarchies dominated by the [state]. Help could be provided only by searchers for grace like himself, and the true Christian life could be lived only in small communities of awakened Christians.[6]

Philanthropic activities, so notable in the Masonic program, were also undertaken by organized Pietism in Germany and elsewhere. Schools for poor children and publishing houses for religious literature were established, as were libraries and, when necessary, organized famine relief.

The second new category of literature introduced into Russian culture by higher-order masonry was Western mystical occultism. Not only did the recognized mystical classics – works of Meister Eckhart, for example – appear in Russian translation, but also those of the esoteric traditions of Renaissance Neoplatonism and alchemy: Hermes Trismegistus and Paracelsus, as well as unclassifiable theosophists like Jacob Boehme.[7]

For two generations, many of the most intelligent, broadly educated Russians sought the meaning of their lives in these sacred and secret books, which were in vogue elsewhere in Europe and played an important part in the rise of a conservative opposition to the Enlightenment. "The newborn Russian intelligentsia," wrote Georges Florovsky, "all at once acquired a complete system of mystical enthusiasms and embraced the western utopian tradition and the rhythm of post-Reformation mysticism. The intelligentsia studied and grew accustomed to quietist mystics, pietists and (to some extent) the Church fathers."[8]

Whether or not one can yet speak of the birth of the Russian intelligentsia, one can at least discern the emergence of a distinctly new kind of Russian person. This figure, exclusively male at first, was preoccupied, at times morbidly, with his spiritual health, determined to forge an integrated moral personality, but prone to distraction and revery, to abrupt and extreme swings in mood from wild optimism to deep discouragement. This Masonic type was given to searching for the meaning of life in an endless series of books from abroad. The patient himself gradually became aware that there was something particularly "Russian" about his struggle.[9]

A spiritual seeker like Novikov's friend Ivan Lopukhin, for example, who died in 1816, read the literature of Pietism, Neoplatonic treatises, and mystical literature going back to the Middle Ages. Nearly all of it was in some sense "Western." But he and many of his contemporaries cherished the idea that the Byzantine and Orthodox tradition was particularly nourishing to their piety, although they were not yet able to say how or why this was so. But out of their sense of old Russia's religious past, they began to develop the much more modern idea that Russians as a people were distinguished by a particular religiosity or a particular spiritual vocation.

Ultimately, Freemasonry was important in Russian culture partly because it provided a way for Russians to discover the Orthodox church as a vital part of their sense of themselves as a nation. But the way was long and winding. Georges Florovsky stressed that the religiosity characteristic of Freemasonry was ultimately Western, corresponding in a way to the institutional and theological Protestantization of Orthodoxy by the reforms of Peter the Great and what followed. Masonry, he wrote, rather disapprovingly, was characterized by "dreaminess and imagination." The soul of these semi-Protestant seekers, he thought, "developed an unhealthy inquisitiveness and mystical curiosity."[10] This "dreaminess" is surely connected to the abstractness and visionary impracticality of the Russian intelligentsia's subsequent commitment to the creation of a new world for Russia.

Not all Russian freemasons, however, became such explicitly religious seekers as Novikov and Lopukhin. Nor were all of them so preoccupied with reexamining their attitude toward what was "ours" and "not ours," indigenous and foreign. Aleksandr Radishchev was a mason for a time, but his famous critique of Catherine's regime was built upon his absorption of the ideas of the radical Enlightenment.[11] He is properly described as the first Russian *philosophe*, and his education to European Enlightenment culture helped him transmute the Petrine ideal of service to the state into a new ideal of service to the people. But despite the obvious influence of Enlightenment radicals like Helvétius and Holbach on his views, despite his exposure to social contract thinking, Radishchev never really abandoned the moralistic German natural law point of view that he encountered during his university years at Leipzig. And the German natural law tradition was also deeply connected to pietist ideals of duty and service.

It is customary to regard Novikov and Radishchev as forefathers and to contrast them: Novikov as a crucial harbinger of the Slavophiles and Radishchev as the first radical Westernizer. But especially in these notions of duty and service to the collectivity, the two are not so far apart; both are errant sons of Peter the Great; both were arrested and exiled by Catherine.

The Alexandrine period in Russian culture saw the inchoate blend of

Enlightenment mysticism and rationalism grow ever more bizarre and exotic. Freemasonry and Pietism were revived and non-Orthodox religious cults, sponsored by non-Russian individuals and organizations, flourished until the Orthodox authorities persuaded the increasingly conservative Alexander I to clamp down in the 1820s. Perhaps even more significant, the development of literary societies, social clubs, and finally political discussion groups (along varyingly Masonic lines) continued to provide Russia with the embryo of a civil society. The Decembrist Revolt of 1825, however, which demarcated the reign of Alexander I from that of his younger brother Nicholas, seemed to suggest that the traditions of Novikov had been superseded, or at least overwhelmed, by the more explicitly radical ones of Radishchev.

But this impression is illusory. The decades of the 1820s and 1830s saw the creation of the first ideological structure in Russia that made a serious and successful attempt to describe pre-Petrine Russia's unique qualities and what the reforms of Peter, therefore, had cost. Drawing on German romantic and counter-revolutionary thought, the first generation of Slavophiles – Ivan Kireevsky, Aleksei Khomiakov, Konstantin and Ivan Aksakov in particular – created what their leading student of recent years has called a "conservative utopia."[12] It was conservative, in that it exalted tradition and the past, but it was utopian, in that it projected an ideal Russia, distinct from and superior to "the West," that would influence all future generations of Russians, down to the present time. As Iu. M. Lotman and B. A. Uspensky have reminded us, Russian culture always appealed to "the old ways" when it was making its most radical and definitive breaks with the preceding period.[13]

The ideological structure of Slavophilism applied to European history the well-established Christian view that, against all appearances, the day was coming when the last should be first. The individualism, secularism, and rationalism of Europe – the aggregate mythologies of Faust and Prometheus – were leading the European world in the direction of an Armageddon of national and class conflict, fueled by a rapacious industrialization. Beneath the overweening and prideful facade of secular European culture were blight and decay, already far advanced.

To this attack on European civilization, the Slavophiles added an apotheosis of Russia's past, centering on new and startling hypotheses about the role played in that past by the autocracy and the church. The pre-Petrine monarchy, the Slavophiles claimed, had not played the role of autocratic state-builder as claimed by the rival Westernizers; even the claim to have "gathered the Russian lands" was soft-pedaled. The monarchy's historical role was startlingly limited to that of judge, protector of the church, and guardian of sacred tradition. To use terminology later stressed by Max Weber, the tsar was both reduced and idealized into a traditional "patrimonial monarch."

The political passivity of the Russian church in modern times was glorified, rather than being subject to criticism. The church was understood to have permeated Russian society (often referred to as "the land," as opposed to "the state") with a kind of benevolent, mild, communal spirit, equally apparent in the communality of church organization and practice and in the social communalism of the Russian village and its governing structure. The communalism (or "conciliarism," as the Russian term [*sobornost'*] has sometimes been translated) of the Orthodox Church differed from the religious autocracy of papal government, on the one hand, and from the anarchic and subjective individualism of the Protestant response on the other.

To many contemporaries and to future critics the Slavophile idyll of pre-Petrine Russia seemed startlingly at variance with the facts and also, to progressives, a scandalous and reactionary glorification of Russia's dreadful past of barbarism and stagnation. The weakest aspect of it, in fact, was its vulnerability to better founded historical views. But it was more than just a reactionary figleaf. Even perspicacious Westernizer critics noticed that there was something critical about the Slavophile ideologues, that they were not right-thinking celebrants of the government and dynasty, like their friends and contemporaries, the so-called "official nationalists."[14]

In fact, the Slavophile view that the proper balance in the Russian political and social system had been terribly damaged by Peter the Great contained a barely concealed subtext, critical of the autocracy of Nicholas I. It suggested that the dynasty's frequently coercive sponsorship of Westernization had been a mistake and an affront to Russia's past; despite the regime's ostensible glorification of Orthodoxy, it had humiliated and damaged the church. Perhaps worst of all, it indicated that the true values of Russia were communal, embodied in the peasant masses of Russia and their way of life in the village – not at all in the European-derived culture of the court or the upper class. The Slavophile discovery of the people (*narod*) did not amount to socialism, not even democracy, but it could seem at times to be either or both. In any case it did not have much in common with the sterile and reactive dynastic nationalism that the court was sponsoring.

Aleksandr Herzen and other Westernizers, who continued to speak of Peter the Great with respect, recognized the difference between the Slavophiles and their sometime official nationalist allies. Herzen referred to the Slavophiles and the Westernizers as a single "Janus-faced" individual, looking creatively forward and backward at the same time. The gaze of the official nationalists, by contrast, was focused almost entirely on the achievements of the Romanov dynasty.

Nevertheless, the differences between the Slavophiles and the Westernizers in the 1840s were profound. Herzen, Vissarion Belinsky, and other of the Westernizers continued to disbelieve in the Slavophile romance with Russia's past. To them, Russia's hope lay in becoming part of a progressive Europe, developing the liberal or socialist inheritance of the French Enlightenment. Their commitment to a Russian version of the utopian socialism of Western Europe was developed during the latter 1840s by younger and more plebeian circles of Westernizers, the most important grouping of which was the so-called "Petrashevsky Circle." Among its members were two whose mature views were to be very different from their youthful fling with Charles Fourier, the guru of the circle: the novelist Fedor Dostoevsky and the Panslav theoretician Nikolai Danilevsky.

The question of Russia's national identity (usually then referred to as its "nationality" [narodnost']), how the country should develop, and what its relationship with Europe should be continued to bedevil Russian intellectuals, even as new movements and social points of view developed. The extraordinary longevity and power of this cluster of problems – not exhausted to this day, most observers would say – suggest some of the anomalies of Russian culture, in which old problems seem to reappear, badly disguised in new costumes, generation after generation. It is the view of some scholars that the powerful anti-Westernism of these ideal images of Russia has played an important role in the failure of "modern" and democratic ideas to take root in Russian soil.[15]

The more open political and ideological debates of the 1850s and 1860s tended to diminish the utopianism exhibited by the first generation Slavophiles. Their stress on the religious essence of the Russian people and their hostility to "abstract reason" were taken over by – among others – the novelist Fedor Dostoevsky and the so-called "people of the soil" (*pochvenniki*), who revealed the potential messianism within Slavophilism and developed it. The Russian people, Dostoevsky came to think, were a "God bearing people," a more explicit reworking of the Slavophile point of view, which widened and dramatized the contrast between Russian religiosity and the desiccated secularism of the West.

Among the Panslavs, on the other hand, we see the anti-dynastic, anti-modernist "utopia" of the Slavophiles evolving into a more ordinary nationalism; the messianic potential of Slavophilism here developed into something parallel to other "pan" movements of European history, suggesting geopolitical conflict between the Slavic sphere, inevitably dominated by Russia, and the British Empire or the even more threatening political world of the Germans. In Nikolai Danilevsky's *Russia and Europe*, the Slavophile notion of the decay of European civilization and the redemptive rise of Russia was incorporated into a worldwide "system" of the growth, maturation, and decay of civilizations, which anticipated the more celebrated theories of Oswald Spengler and Arnold Toynbee.

The preservation of the idea that Russian civilization had a special destiny or "separate path" was perhaps most strikingly preserved in the new radicalism that developed during the 1860s and 1870s, broadly known as populism. The populists (*narodniki*) inherited from the radical Westernizers of a slightly earlier period the commitment to an egalitarian and socialist future, which necessitated major social-political change, if not revolution.

Nikolai Chernyshevsky, despite his interest in the Russian village, was profoundly Western in orientation. He espoused a set of radical Enlightenment views, including a strong commitment to feminism, which he embodied in his remarkable novel, *What Is to Be Done?*, which may have had a greater impact on the evolving Russian Revolution than any other book. Subtitled "Tales about New People," the novel sketched out a political program for the young leftists of the 1860s – the creation of artels and other kinds of socialist communes. Even more valuable to the radicals of the day were the characters – providing what today would be called role models for the movement. These were not abstract formulas, but pictures of how people should live and what they should do, including the first sketches of new, much more egalitarian relations between the sexes. Lenin, who took the title for his most famous pamphlet, was only the most famous of the scores of leftists who delighted to confess the profound impact on them of *What Is to Be Done?* The radical critic, Nikolai

Dobroliubov, was even more militant in his rationalism, atheism, and hatred of "old Russia" than his friend and mentor Chernyshevsky.

But many features of this fascinating "Russian socialism" derived from Slavophile points of view: the idea that Russia's socialism would be an evolution of the communal institutions of the peasantry, especially the village communal structure of governance; and the conviction that this particular evolution would be unlike (and superior to) anything found in Western Europe. Furthermore, after this "Russian socialism" had been accomplished, it was believed, it could be adapted by Western Europe and would ultimately constitute its salvation. This self-serving socialist messianism aroused the particular ire of Karl Marx.

Just as the Slavophile utopia soft-pedaled the role of aristocratic intellectuals who would nevertheless have to take the lead in its realization, mainstream populist culture minimized the role of radical and revolutionary youth in bringing self-consciousness to the peasant village. At the same time, however, young people, the majority from the newly exciting world of Russian universities, began to make their pilgrimages to peasant Russia, to learn from the people and to teach them at the same time. These touching projects came to be individually and collectively known as "going to the people."

But on the fringes of this apparently ultra-democratic movement (and sometimes mingling with it) were rather different points of view, destined for a long career in Russian culture. Russia's Westernization always suggested a set of elitist possibilities or even necessities, revolutionary Westernization in particular. Western culture had to be imported into Russia and disseminated. This enterprise would have to be the work of individuals or groups. At first, of course, the Romanov dynasty itself had been the sponsor, but it ceased to pursue Westernization seriously (that is, progressively) after 1825, when it became clear that many "Western values" – greater liberty and equality, individualism – were antithetical to the social and political goals of the Russian monarchy. The "Westernizer" intellectuals of the 1840s, who opposed the Slavophiles, saw people like themselves performing this heroic task, often in a quasi-Hegelian framework of dialectical progress.

The so-called "nihilists," a rather distinct fragment of the 1860s radical spectrum, represented a particular, rather narrow, evolution of radical Westernism. Young literati, like the famous critic Dmitry Pisarev, refused to bow down before the creativity of the people, as did their

Populist colleagues. They insisted instead that the spread of science, scientism, and radical individualism was what Russia needed. This project presupposed a cadre of educated, Westernized intellectuals who knew that Russia needed these things and was committed to bringing them, come what might. This point of view was immortalized by the novelist Ivan Turgenev in his most famous work, *Fathers and Children*.

As the populists, at this time largely groups of radical students, pressed their agitation against the government and tried to bring their message to the Russian village, their inexperience and guilelessness often made them easy prey for the police and other government agents. Alongside populist openness therefore, there gradually developed a more ruthless politics, which gained increasing influence among the radical youth.

Radicals who came to be known as "Russian Jacobins," for instance, took the view that the role of radical intellectuals would have to be much greater in making the revolution and creating the new society than mainstream populists supposed. These men and women (who were not part of a single organized group with a single set of beliefs) came to support not only an enhanced role for non-peasant intellectual ideologues, but also for secrecy, careful and tight organization, and for a series of tough ethical positions which might be called revolutionary machiavellianism – the proposition that the revolution is so difficult in a closed society and yet so vital that no means should be ruled out, including systematic lying, deception, and the sacrifice of one's own colleagues if necessary – what Albert Camus later called "violence done to comrades." The classic manifestation of such attitudes is revealed in the life of Sergei Nechaev, whose remarkable career provided the basis for Dostoevsky's novel, *The Devils*.

These political attitudes must be understood in light of the regime's refusal of even minimal political liberty to its subjects and its commitment to the maintenance of the most conservative and oppressive old regime in Europe right into the twentieth century. Such attitudes were also an important legacy that pre-Marxist radicalism left to Russian Social Democracy, especially to the faction that became known in 1903 as the Bolsheviks, led by Vladimir Il'ich Lenin.[16]

Broadly speaking, the ideological conflicts in Russian culture at the turn of the century were paradoxical. In the forty years or so since the end of the Crimean War, Russia's political leadership had reluctantly and unevenly embraced an economic project that later scholars would call "modernization." But economic modernization does not take place in a void. The economic policies of late tsarism recall those of Peter the Great earlier (and to some degree of Stalin later): force industrialization from above, but make as few concessions to "liberal" points of view as possible, socially or politically.

This policy turned out to be a catastrophe. The drive for industrialization, often globally characterized as the "Witte system," after tsarism's most effective and committed industrializer, brought real, but limited economic successes. At the same time, however, both the right and left extremes flourished, each in their own way characterized by agrarian and politically nostalgic and romantic points of view. Not even the modernizing right-center of the political spectrum was really committed to opening up the political system and to accepting greater pluralism or diversity of values.

In the last quarter century of the monarchy's existence, Russian literary and political culture developed a rich bouquet of nostalgic romanticisms, which mixed oddly with the continuing effort to industrialize, on the one hand, and with the first wave of literary modernism on the other. In some ways, Russian high culture began to look more like certain European cultures: Ireland, or even France. Literary movements like symbolism flourished. Russia also participated in the neo-Kantian revival that was centered in Germany; and Slavophilism was finally accepted by the conservative leaders of the Orthodox church, giving rise to an important religious revival, of great interest to Russian thinkers of the post-Soviet period.[17]

Meanwhile, as industrialization continued to be pushed by the finance ministry, the monarchy itself implicitly repudiated what remained of its Petrine commitment to modernize Russia and substituted for it a post-Slavophile myth of "Holy Russia," which drew on medieval sources.[18] On the political right, monarchist politics and cultural chauvinism flourished. During and after the 1905 Revolution, a fringe of right-wing populist leaders and groups developed, anti-Semitic and violence-prone; under different circumstances these "Black Hundreds" might have evolved into an explicit Russian Fascism.

On the left, the revolutionary machiavellianism that had increasingly characterized the late phases of populism became an important aspect of Russian Social Democracy, especially of Bolshevism. The relatively open and "European" Marxism of Georgy Plekhanov, which gave serious (if reluctant) support to bourgeois development as a prerequisite for socialism, was unable to stand against the profound revolutionary elitism of Lenin.

Thus the political extremes of Russia's political culture were more polarized than those of any other major European power, but both were violently hostile to "bourgeois" liberalism and political compromise. Both acted out of what tended to be closed intellectual systems in which compromise was understood as betrayal. If, as two important students of Russian culture have recently suggested, "negotiation," "compromise," and "contracts" were unusually slow to gain acceptance in Russian culture, the process of Russian industrialization during the last years of the monarchy did surprisingly little to accelerate their development. Principle, not process, was central to the declared values of educated Russians, and Russians were polarized and fragmented in their commitment to principles.[19] In 1909, a group of intellectuals attacked the intransigent politicization of Russian intellectuals – the well-known symposium called *Landmarks* – but liberals and Marxists alike maintained their positions and even went on the offensive against their critics.[20]

This cultural arena created extraordinary obstacles to the industrial process which continued to unfold in Russia. Politics on all sides were more "principled" than elsewhere in Europe; extremists were more powerful and there was little room for compromise that could be regarded as honorable. The monarchy vacillated in a schizoid way between an uneasy promotion of industrial culture and open detestation of it.

"Practical" statesmen like Sergei Witte at the finance ministry and Petr Stolypin, who strove to bring order back to Russia after the Revolution of 1905, thus had an extraordinarily constricted arena in which to work. They wanted the tsar and court to sponsor a conservative, controlled (but economically vital) capitalist development that would provide a middle-class underpinning for the monarchy. Not only did the Russian left regard them as the deadliest of enemies, but neither Witte nor Stolypin gained the trust and support of Nicholas II, engaged in his closed, family-centered *folie* of neo-medieval mysticism and magical remedies for Russia's ills. Nor was there enough reliable support elsewhere among Russia's agrarian conservatives.

The war and the Revolution of 1917 appeared to change Russia's cultural landscape entirely. The possessing classes were largely swept away or submerged in the enormous mass of workers and especially peasants. This left two very different powers facing each other uneasily: the old village culture of the Russian peasantry and its peasant-worker offshoot on the one hand, and the Bolshevik variant of radical intelligentsia culture on the other. (The apparently powerful non-Bolshevik cultural left – socialist, modernist, and feminist in inspiration – turned out to have little support among either the Bolsheviks or the masses.)

It has seemed to many students of the subject that Russian peasant culture was remarkably self-contained, socially undifferentiated, and tenacious in its ability to resist challenges from outside, but the rigid separation of urban and rural, upper and lower, indigenous and foreign was breaking down by the first decade of the twentieth century.[21] The catastrophe of the war, however, disrupted this process, and so did the period of the Revolution and Civil War. One result of these terrible years was that by the mid-twenties the working class had grown smaller and some of Russia's urbanized population had returned, for at least a portion of the year, to the village. The old peasant commune had been partially reconstituted and the Stolypin reforms, which had aimed at creating an independent, middle-class stable peasantry, had suffered a defeat. The village society which confronted the victorious Bolsheviks in the 1920s appeared to be in key ways more archaic than it had been on the eve of the war.

As earlier noted, the Bolshevik viewpoint was in many ways an extreme variant of the old Westernizer ethos. Lenin, Maksim Gorky, and others regarded the patriarchal Russian village with loathing, and fear as well; in gloomy moments they regarded themselves as a pocket or an island of civilization and progress in a sea of "darkness" and counter-revolution. Their feeling of being beleaguered increased as the proletariat shrank in size during the early 1920s, decimated by the Civil War, in many cases driven back to the village, its most promising elements absorbed into the Communist Party and its growing *apparat*. The Bolsheviks' determination to modernize this brutal, backward, and benighted peasant society increased, however, and they were the more prepared to use force, as they considered rural Russia a powerful and ultimately deadly enemy. As Marxists, they thought political power to be ultimately dependent on economic power, as embodied in social classes.

Thus a traditionally minded, isolated, suspicious, closed, rural society faced an ideologically inspired enemy, with a utopian commitment to a vast industrial transformation and a determination to stop at nothing to achieve it. The Bolsheviks saw the capitalist world outside *and* the vast majority of their own citizens as enemies – different kinds of enemies, to be sure, but enemies in a peculiar alliance against Bolshevik progress. There was almost no place in this confrontational situation for liberal viewpoints, for the development of pluralism or a commitment to compromise. And the industrialization that ensued was desperate (as well as on occasion triumphalist), focused, utopian, and highly coercive. It helped focus the attention of Stalin and the leadership to an extraordinary degree both on unrealizable goals and on enemies, with unspeakably dreadful results.

The Soviet variant of Russian culture evolved in strange and unexpected ways over the course of its existence. Official Soviet cultural norms, derived from the peculiar Soviet brand of Marxism that I have described, inevitably evolved in the direction of something much more conservative. In order to facilitate the massive and coercive upheaval entailed by his industrial policies, Stalin abandoned almost all that remained of the cultural avant-garde and social utopianism that had flowered across the revolutionary divide from late tsarism. The generous and liberationist aspirations of feminism and socialism were replaced by iron industrial discipline, hierarchy, and command.[22] All academic disciplines were brought under much tighter state control and cultural freedoms almost totally curtailed. Art, literature, and even music were supposed to conform to a standard officially known as "socialist realism." This doctrine demanded a "realism" that could speak to ordinary people, but also a politically correct depiction of the inevitable march, under socialism and communism, toward a brighter future. The difference between such ideas and the old "critical realism" of the nineteenth century – almost invariably directed against the dominant powers – must be clear.

The era of the Five Year Plans brought an enormous increase in the urban and factory population, but at the same time it resulted in a kind of peasantization of the new working class, blending with the desired proletarianization of the peasantry. In conjunction with the purges of the late 1930s, Stalinist terror reached its apogee.

There were a few carrots for the upwardly mobile, along with many sticks. Bourgeois and Victorian styles in the arts and design were sponsored, and the upwardly mobile workers and peasants of the late 1930s and 1940s were permitted a kind of semi-middle-class life style in return for political acquiescence.[23] The upper echelons of the Stalinist elite did better still.[24] The puritanism of Soviet culture, along with its Victorianism, gave the visitor an eerie sense of nineteenth-century European provincial life in a society often described as "totalitarian."[25]

Official Soviet ideology was, in some ways, the twentieth-century equivalent of the dynastic nationalism of the age of Nicholas I. It profoundly affected the already idiosyncratic Soviet Marxism, drenching it in Russian nationalism, beginning in the late 1930s and coming to the first of several climaxes in the years after the Second World War. "We will never rouse the people to war with Marxism–Leninism alone," Stalin is supposed to have told one of the few surviving Old Bolsheviks, and his wartime speeches celebrated the victories of Dmitry Donskoy over the Mongols and those of the tsarist generals Kutuzov and Suvorov in the eighteenth and nineteenth centuries.

After the Second World War was over, it gradually became the subject of a remarkable state-sponsored cult, organized by the leadership but fueled by the patriotism of ordinary people and by their terrible losses. By the 1980s, the mythic celebration of the "Great Patriotic War" (as it was known in the Soviet Union) had come almost to replace the cult of Lenin and the October Revolution as the founding myth of the Soviet state.[26] Ultimately the Great Patriotic War also lost much of its power for younger people, but the themes of military might, physical courage, love of the motherland, loss and suffering were for many years highly resonant for almost all Soviet Russians. There was much pride in the Soviet Union's rise to superpower status; and the traditional Russian tendency to divide the world rather sharply into "ours" and "not ours," "we" and "they," helped fuel the cult as well.

Thus Soviet culture at a quasi-official level could be seen as largely the triumph of a Soviet version of the nineteenth-century Westernizer point of view, if in a distorted and maximally illiberal form. (Stalin, however, should surely also be regarded as a twentieth-century version of "Little Father Tsar," mysterious, exalted, all-powerful.) But such industrial-urban cultural dominance in a country where the rural had played such a powerful cultural role was virtually impossible over the long run; already in the 1950s a reaction was gathering. Despite the highly regulated quality of Russian cultural life, a powerful anti-urban point of view, often simply described as "village prose," developed and even flourished in Russia for thirty years or so.[27] As the Soviet Union came to an end, the mark left by the village writers on the Russian cultural scene was profound, although the dislocation and chaos of the first few post-Soviet years have in different ways weakened all traditional cultural points of view.

Lying at the base of the village prose movement was a reaction in favor of sincerity and truthfulness in creative writing and against the tired, stereotypical, and implausible depictions of the countryside in the so-called "collective farm literature" – and also, as time passed, against consumerism, in both its Western and Soviet forms. The imposed "progressive" point of view of official culture was not only false to the realities of rural life, as these writers understood them, but also to the writers' understanding of creative authenticity. They, like the more official writers, were interested in history, but in a totally opposite way. In the Soviet Union, their work suggested, "big history" was false. Truth is small and private, something discovered in walks along country roads, in a handful of pebbles, or an old story. No more direct challenge to the official point of view of early Soviet culture can be imagined. And although it is not possible to speak authoritatively about the audience of the village prose writers, they certainly expressed values that could be found in more diffuse form elsewhere in the culture.

The themes that dominate village prose hearken back to pre-revolutionary, even nineteenth-century, culture. Village prose sounded notes common to certain Westernizers, like Ivan Turgenev, in his *Sketches from a Hunter's Album*, who tried to see the peasant world faithfully, accurately, and distinctly. By and large, however, their work extended the Slavophile tradition. Village prose displayed a profound sympathy for the past, and especially for the rural past. Village writers sympathized with the old – places, people, words, points of view – and the young, those who had not yet entered into the disconcerting history of their time, and the specific. "Each village," wrote Kathleen Parthé, "is [for them] a separate *rodina* (motherland)" (*Russian Village Prose*, p. 6).

Just as the Slavophiles had defended Russia's despised past against outsiders who scorned it and insiders who had betrayed it, the village writers gave their hearts to the premodern, the out-of-the-way, the particular – the little rutted path "alongside the railroad tracks," not the new highway, certainly not to the railroad tracks themselves.[28] In the nineteenth century, both Slavophilism and especially Populism had strongly influenced ethnography, and so it was again with village writers. The boundary between folklore and fiction was porous in their work.

Insofar as Russia's Soviet experience was seen to have ruined the village, the thrust of the village writers was anti-Soviet, for all the obliqueness of the way they expressed themselves. Their work was pessimistic, saturated in a sense of loss, of the intolerably high costs of Soviet modernity (perhaps by implication of all modernity). The passing of childhood is the ultimate tale of loss, and the return of the writer to the highly specific place of his origins and his inability to recover it is one of the master narratives of these writers. It is entirely opposed to Maksim Gorky's famous memoirs, archetypically Bolshevik in their hostility to the countryside and their orientation to the future.

The bridge between this literary movement (and there were visual artists who expressed similar attitudes) and the political establishment was nationalism. Despite its anti-Soviet essence, village prose had its sympathizers and private defenders within the government. This is apparently why, in spite of numerous conflicts with the authorities, village prose more or less ran its generational course, producing, in the process, much of the best literary work to appear in Russia since before the First World War.

There were, in the nineteenth century, significant connections between the thematics of Slavophilism and the development from it of Russian nationalism, Panslavism, and related movements. Many of these movements (with the honorable exception of the first generation of the Slavophiles) were explicitly chauvinistic in their outlook. Dostoevsky's hostility to Poles, Jews, and Americans was extreme. The Panslavs saw the German world as blocking the epochal future of the Slavs. And interlaced with the conservative and nostalgic themes of village prose was a general chauvinism, which focused explicitly – again – on Jews, but also on those "others" who had led Russian innocence astray with their international-ism, secularism, hostility to tradition, devotion to technology, orienta-tion to material power, etc.

With the passing of the Soviet phase of Russian history, we can discern a cultural crisis in Russia perhaps as severe as the economic and political crises and of course related to them. Formally speaking, Russia's political orientation under Boris Yeltsin would seem to represent a moderate Westernizer point of view. But Russian political culture is powerfully marked by its violent and contradictory past. Despite very substantial gains in education, and the creation of a peculiar form of smokestack industrial culture, in terms of values it is clear that Russia has changed less in the last century than we had come to believe, as we watched what we regarded as the enormous changes in the culture, broadly speaking, of the Soviet Union. This is true both among ordinary working people and the intelligentsia.

Soviet political culture was, at its demise, a very peculiar amalgam. Its deepest stratum was a peculiar derivative of the autocratic and peasant past – but overlaid with seventy-five years of communism. It fostered very conservative, negatively egalitarian, and risk-averse attitudes (especially among rural dwellers) and its legacy to the post-Soviet era was great. There was clearly a continuing tendency among Russians to believe strongly in "leveling down" and to believe that in their world it is impossible to "level up." As people saw their neighbors doing well or getting something new, there was increasing resentment and demands that they be cut down to size. This is, according to the sociologist Igor Kon, "the dictatorship of envy disguised as social justice."[29] Such attitudes, originating in Russia's ancient peasant culture, were hardly conducive to the growth of capitalism or market relations. (Fortunately they were somewhat less marked among young people and urban dwellers.)

The situation was made much worse by the fact that capitalism in Russia *was* more marked by banditry, bribery, intimidation, and fraud than Western capitalism, at least in much more than a century. In the world of early post-Soviet capitalism, it was difficult for ordinary Russians to believe that success in the new world is a matter of industry, thrift, skill, or cleverness (long stigmatized in Russian culture as "guile"). Many Russians believed and acted as if the pie could not get larger (so one could only get ahead at someone else's expense) – well, the pie, in fact, *shrunk!* At least, under communism, there was a minimal "social contract," which in return for political acquiescence, guaranteed a minimal safety net. Now much of the *nomenklatura* became capitalist. In the eyes of many ordinary people, the same elite continued to run things, for its own benefit, but it abandoned the "social contract."

Intellectuals and those who created culture in the post-Soviet world were in a state of crisis. They experienced greater freedom but cultural conviction, where it existed, was often forced and desperate. Resources fell largely into the hands of people with little interest in the arts, so that publications, performances, exhibitions became harder to create, and forms of nostalgia for the communist past grew. The values of unfettered capitalism continued to be anathema to both educated Russians of the intelligentsia, broadly defined, and to the working classes, if in somewhat different ways. The audience for traditional Russian high culture, or some contemporary development of it, shrunk.

Many intellectuals and creative people aspired to return to the cultural world as it existed prior to 1917, but it was difficult to reestablish connections in any practical way. Intellectuals displayed considerable interest in the culture of the "Silver Age" – its religiously tinged philosophy, its pioneering forms of literary modernism, its bohemian aristocratism. But it is not at all clear that the philosopher and cultural historian Nikolai Berdiaev – however acute his understanding of the "Russian idea" or the "origins of Russian communism" – could provide a living link between Russia's pre-revolutionary past and its chaotic present. Both foreigners and Russians showed marked interest in the remarkable critic Mikhail Bakhtin, but foreigners saw him as connected to Marxism; Russians stressed his hatred of "dialectics" and totalizing systems.

Russia's Soviet isolation broke down; Western high culture became increasingly available in Russia, but in no very coherent way. Alongside the influx of Western literature and the episodic and struggling revival of early twentieth-century Russian culture came far less helpful phenomena. Post-Soviet Russia learned to deal with (occasionally in creative ways) a new commercial literature characterized by the worst elements of Western culture – trivial, pornographic, violent – rather than its best. The recurrent struggles between what appears to be native and what appears to be foreign entered a new, disorienting, and potentially dangerous phase. In the second half of the 1990s, everyone had a different idea of who is to blame but no one had a plausible idea of what to do.

NOTES

Some of the research which undergirds the early section of this essay was done at the Russian Research Center of Harvard University. Thanks to two generations of directors, Adam Ulam and Timothy Colton. Thanks also to Sarah Gleason, Lisa Meloy, and David Gehrenbeck for helpful criticism.

1. See the very suggestive chapter, "The Sociogenesis of Aristocratic Romanticism," in Norbert Elias, *Court Society* (New York, 1983), pp. 214–67.
2. The best general account of these developments in English remains Hans Rogger, *National Consciousness in Eighteenth-Century Russia* (Cambridge, MA, 1960). On the ethical ideal of Russian classicism, see Ilya Serman, *Russkii klassitsizm* (Leningrad, 1973).
3. There is a large literature on Russian Freemasonry, but much of it is more than a half century old. For orientation, see Stephen Lessing Baehr, *The Paradise Myth in Eighteenth-Century Russia* (Stanford, CA, 1991) and the bibliography therein. See also W. Gareth Jones, *Nikolay Novikov, Enlightener of Russia* (Cambridge, 1984), esp. pp. 127–48 and the notes.
4. Georges Florovsky, *Ways of Russian Theology*, Part I (Belmont, MA, 1979), p. 148.
5. George Vernadsky, *Russkoe Masonstvo v tsarstvovanie Ekateriny II* (Petrograd, 1917), pp. 84–85.
6. Gordon Craig, *The Germans* (New York, 1982), p. 87.
7. Vernadsky, *Russkoe Masonstvo*, pp. 126–27.

8. Florovsky, *Ways*, p. 152.

9. The experience of A. M. Kutuzov is instructive. See Iu. Lotman, "'Sochuvstvennik' A. N. Radishcheva A. M. Kutuzov i ego pis'ma k I. P. Turgenevu," *Uchenye zapiski Tartuskogo universiteta*, no. 139 (1963), esp. pp. 298–301.

10. Florovsky, *Ways*, p. 155.

11. Aleksandr Nikolaevich Radishchev, *A Journey from St. Petersburg to Moscow* (Cambridge, MA, 1958). The Russian original was published in 1790.

12. Andrzej Walicki, *The Slavophile Controversy* (Oxford, 1975).

13. Iu. M. Lotman and B. A. Uspensky, "The Role of Dual Models in the Dynamics of Russian Culture (Up to the End of the Eighteenth Century)," *The Semiotics of Russian Culture* (Ann Arbor, MI, 1984), pp. 3–35.

14. Nicholas V. Riasanovsky, *Nicholas I and Official Nationality in Russia, 1825–1855* (Berkeley and Los Angeles, 1961).

15. This is an essential point of Tim McDaniel, *The Agony of the Russian Idea* (Princeton, NJ, 1996).

16. The essential book on Russian Populism is still Franco Venturi, *Roots of Revolution* (New York, 1960). On Populism's debt to Slavophilism, see Abbott Gleason, *Young Russia* (New York, 1980).

17. Nicolas Zernov, *The Russian Religious Renaissance of the Twentieth Century* (New York, 1963).

18. Richard Wortman, "The Dethroning of Peter the Great," Seminar, Kennan Institute, 27 April 1982.

19. Lotman and Uspensky, "'Agreement' and 'Self-giving' as Archetypal Models of Culture," *Semiotics of Russian Culture*, pp. 125–40, esp. p. 130.

20. Boris Shragin and Albert Todd, eds., *Landmarks* (New York, Karz Howard, 1977).

21. Jeffrey Brooks, *When Russia Learned to Read* (Princeton, NJ, 1985); Stephen P. Frank and Mark Steinberg, *Lower-Class Values, Practices and Resistance in Late Imperial Russia* (Princeton, NJ, 1994).

22. Richard Stites, *Revolutionary Dreams: Utopian Vision and Experimental Life in the Russian Revolution* (New York, Oxford, 1989).

23. Vera S. Dunham, *In Stalin's Time: Middleclass Values in Soviet Fiction* (Cambridge, 1976).

24. Many of these cultural changes were summed up as "becoming cultured (*kulturnyi*)." As Svetlana Boym has written, becoming cultured in this specific Russian-Soviet sense "offered a way of legitimating the formerly despised bourgeois concerns about status and possession; it both justified and disguised the new social hierarchies and privilege of the Stalinist elite." (*Common Places: Mythologies of Everyday Life in Russia* [Cambridge, MA, 1994], p. 105). See also Dunham and Sheila Fitzpatrick, *The Cultural Front: Power and Culture in Revolutionary Russia* (Ithaca, NY, 1992), pp. 247–48.

25. Abbott Gleason, *Totalitarianism: The Inner History of the Cold War* (New York, Oxford, 1995).

26. Nina Tumarkin, *The Living and the Dead: The Rise and Fall of the Cult of World War II in Russia* (New York, 1994).

27. Kathleen Parthé, *Russian Village Prose: The Radiant Past* (Princeton, 1992).

28. The phrase is taken from Aleksandr Solzhenitsyn in his *Letter to the Soviet Leaders* (New York, 1974), p. 20. Solzhenitsyn began as a village writer. Valentin Rasputin (*Farewell to Matyora*) and Vladimir Soloukhin (*A Time to Gather Stones*) are two others whose work is available in English.

29. Quoted in Boym, *Common Places*, p. 149.

7

Popular culture

Introduction: problems of terminology

Russian peasants, factory workers, artisans, and small traders have by tradition lived in a world made colorful by endless shades of difference, one not easily demarcated under the typical definitions and categories of popular culture. Their first loyalties have been to kinship groups, to work collectives, to the villages or districts where they lived, rather than to their own class or social group in a broad sense. For those traditional villagers who lived all their lives close to home, the opposition *svoi/chuzhoi* ("our own/strange," but close to the English polarization "us and them") was fundamental to organizing life. *Nenash* ("Not-ours") was one of the many dialect terms for the Devil, and considerable hardship awaited the *nevesta* (bride, but literally "unknown woman"), displaced by patrilocal tradition to her husband's parents' family, and treated there as a stranger, though she might herself come from a village only a few miles away, or even from a household in the same village.

The industrialization of Russia, which led to a massive population movement from villages into cities, did much to soften conservatism, but did not erode it entirely; nor did peasants who went to the cities necessarily change attitudes overnight. Loyalty to a particular village was replaced by the wider, but still extremely concrete, affiliations of *krai* and *rodina* (birthplace). Like Irish contractors in London who only employ brickies and plasterers from their own county of origin, and who rely on a network of local contacts to recruit them, the Russian peasants who settled in St. Petersburg or Moscow during the nineteenth and early twentieth centuries attached great importance to the ties of *zemliachestvo* ("land where you were born"), which meant in the first place their *guberniia*, later *oblast'* (an administrative region roughly equivalent to a county). *Zemliaki* ("fellow-countrymen"), identifiable by dress, custom, and especially by dialect, as well as by name, helped incomers find their feet, as well as work and accommodation. Particular occupations were under the domination of peasant incomers from particular places. And the same solidarity ties aided Russian peasants torn from their roots by another violent upheaval afflicting the lower classes, conscription into military service.

If living in cities tended to make the region one came from as important as the village, it could also make Russians sharply aware of themselves as Russians – probably for the first time unless they came from an ethnically mixed area such as the west or southeastern fringes of European Russia. Particularly in St. Petersburg, with its communities of Tatars, Finns, Germans, Jews, French, British, Italians, and Swedes, its Western Christian churches, synagogues, and by the early twentieth century, mosque and Buddhist temple, Russian peasants found themselves in a fundamentally different atmosphere from the village community with its single Orthodox church. Their commercial transactions (buying food, clothes, and goods, or borrowing money) were likely to alert them to the presence of foreigners, many of whom worked as small traders; so, too, were their experiences at work, since many factory-owners and some foremen were of foreign origin. (In the Soviet and early post-Soviet period, trading at street markets was dominated by non-Russians, in this case Azerbaijanis, Uzbeks, Chechens, and other migrants from Central Asia and the Caucasus.) The result was that chauvinism was and is a far from an unknown phenomenon in Russian cities, flaring alarmingly at times of social unrest.

Yet for all the prevalence of chauvinist feeling, chauvinist activism generally remained small-scale. It has been estimated that the early twentieth-century groups of reactionaries known as the "Black Hundreds" had the support of no more than 20,000 (out of a total population of 150 million) at their peak, and a similar estimate could perhaps be ventured for the proportion of active neo-fascists in Russia after communism. Nationalism in a negative sense (that is, suspicion of outsiders) has not necessarily, or even generally, cohered into positive nationalism. There is little evidence that Russians from outside the educated classes generally had or have a very strong sense of ethnic identity, other than a vague sense of pride in "our" achievements (from the Orthodox church to space travel).[1]

Another typical form of abstraction, "class identity," has played an equally ambiguous role in popular history. Pre-revolutionary peasants and workers knew that a *muzhik* and *baba* (peasant or working man and woman) were not at all the same thing as a *barin* or *barynia* (gentleman or lady, though "toff" or "nob" would be closer to the coloration of the Russian nouns), and spoke of such people in the polite third person plural ("His Excellency have already arrived"). They were also sensitive, particularly if they worked as servants or had relatives who did, to the vast divide between those who had money and those who did not. Occasionally, resentment fed violence. The brutality of peasant rebels was renowned. And many lower-class Russians used the opportunities afforded by the Revolution and the Civil War in order to exact personal revenge on those they considered to be their oppressors. The campaigns for dekulakization organized when Russian villages were collectivized in the 1930s, while directed from above, were also able to draw on the resentment toward the better-off that was felt by some Russian peasants themselves. Once violent social conflict was over, the studied rudeness of Russians working in the service industries, and carrying out official duties (depicted most effectively in the tragicomic stories of Mikhail Zoshchenko), provided low-level evidence that worker resentment continued. And since 1988, as post-Soviet Russian society stratified, resentment again began to boil; violent crime moved in from outlying districts to the centres of cities, with the expensive Western cars and clothes considered *de rigueur* among the Russian new rich becoming targets of robbery and vandalism.

Even here, though, appreciations of identity in a negative sense ("we're not rich") have by no means always transmuted into positive perceptions of identity. Deprivation has been a fluid and undependable motivating force, because the stigma of poverty has discouraged identification (as in other European countries, the "respectable working class" has been reluctant to demonstrate solidarity with lawbreakers, beggars, and other marginal figures, while peasant communities have traditionally shown a very nice sense of status, in which property ownership, occupation, and family honor all play a part). Accordingly, the most successful populist groups have been those, such as the Socialist Revolutionaries, Father Gapon's Association of St. Petersburg Workers, and the Tolstoy movement, which have advanced rather broadly based programs of social justice linked with utopian visions of communality.[2]

In any case, much of lower-class Russians' propensity for violence has always been directed against each other. *Kulachnye boi,* mass bouts of ritualized fist-fighting, were a regular holiday occupation from medieval times. The infamous custom of *dedovshchina* (domination through bully-ing) was and is widespread. Apprentices at factories and workshops, mil-itary conscripts, newcomers to prisons, all had to endure violence and abuse before being accepted by "senior" comrades (*dedy,* literally "grand-fathers"). Street (or tavern) brawls of less carefully organized kinds, not to speak of domestic violence, were also rife. Such conflicts have persisted into more recent times; if *kulachnye boi* have long been a thing of the past, fighting between members of rival gangs has been a fact of life at every stage of Russian history at which police control has slackened; today, membership of peer-group gangs plays almost as large a role in the youth culture of urban districts in Russia as it does in American cities. And the relationships between different subcultural groups (punks, hippies, football, horseracing or ice-hockey fans, heavy metal enthusiasts, or break-dancers) remain at best distant; overt antagonism is common, sup-ported by private forms of slang (*zhargon*). *Dedovshchina* lives on, especially in the army. Among "outsiders," only animals have suffered as much from casual acts of cruelty: among Moscow workers in the 1900s, a favorite custom was to inundate a rat with paraffin, set it alight, and watch the creature gyrate to its death.[3]

All in all, then, solidarity amongst the lower classes, the key bearers of popular culture, is of a rather nebulous kind, based on negative ideas (we are not foreigners, we are not rich) rather than positive ideas, and under-cut by numerous subjectively significant distinctions, with age playing as great a part as regional origin. The working-class Russian's path from cradle to grave was and is marked out by "rites of passage," celebrations initiating and sustaining transitions to different phases of life. The early and late stages of childhood, apprenticeships at work, courting and mar-riage, childbearing, funerals, all had and have their own particular texts, costumes, gestures, and actions, their proper performance ensured by "tradition," which is to say the patterns laid down by consciously guided imitation, or simply by osmosis. Gender difference has also been enor-mously important, determining occupations, status, family role, cloth-ing, and even leisure preferences.

Such demarcations have not been entirely inflexible. The age hierar-chy has weakened considerably over the last century, and so to some extent has the gender hierarchy, as women took up supposedly male occupations at times when male labor was short (notably, during the

Second World War). Likewise, in the field of popular entertainments, it is possible to trace shifting roles. In Russian villages, women were especially associated with certain rites and genres (fertility rituals, laments for the dead, lullabies, and certain types of folk tale – the animal tales traditionally told to children, and tales of women's rivalry and resourcefulness, such as *Kosoruchka* [Lophand], the story of a sister mutilated by her brother as a result of his wicked wife's calumny, who contrives to bear three heroic sons and vindicate herself). In the early genres of urbanized popular culture, such as street puppet shows and dancing songs, women played a lesser role as disseminators of folklore; they were ordinarily invoked and represented as the objects of male lust, and ritually insulted. In new genres from a still later period, such as film melodrama, one can see the tastes of women viewers themselves accommodated by the assignation of much larger roles to women characters, and by the emergence of female stars (such as, in the 1910s, the "gypsy singer" Vera Panina and the film actress Vera Kholodnaia). But in all these overlapping phases of the history of popular culture, the belief that differences between men and women were vital and insuperable has shown a stubborn persistence, surviving even the concerted campaign of gender egalitarianism carried out during the first decade of the Soviet regime. Part of this is no doubt connected with the still heavily ritualized character of Russian popular life, in which, though many rites have atrophied or been pared down almost to vanishing point, others, such as drinking and eating ceremonies, or customs such as laying out the dead, yet lead a vigorous existence, albeit in diminished form.[4]

"Popular culture," then, is to some extent a meaningless term if one is speaking from the perspective of workers and peasants. Yet the fact remains that, whether peasants and workers have comprehended it or not, their culture has been affected in fundamental ways by the manner in which it is perceived by observers. The very regions according to which Russian peasants identified themselves, once in cities, were, like their equivalents in Western Europe or America, the inventions of centralizing administrators, not of the local population (with the exception of the few places with old civic traditions, such as Novgorod or Pskov). In other ways, too, Russian villagers and factory workers necessarily came into more or less direct contact with outsiders' conscious efforts to transcribe and analyse their lives. Villagers upon whose villages had descended folklorists wishing to record "old" legends, tales, or songs, or to learn the local words for ploughshare, bucket, pump, basket, thistle, blackbird,

7.1 Zemstvo statisticians in a Russian village. From Harold Williams, *Russia of the Russians* (London, 1914).

and so on, or health workers persuading groups of women that the use of dirty rags as infant pacifiers might be directly connected with the high rates of infant mortality, necessarily themselves developed a more self-conscious attitude to the values and meanings of material that they formerly took for granted. The same was true of factory workers whose homes and customs became the subject for the equally intense scrutiny of ethnographers and of philanthropists. Traditional hostility to outsiders could be overcome when those outsiders' efforts led to genuine improvements in villagers' or workers' lives; xenophobia vied with the drive to self-betterment. The Soviet notion of *kul'turnost'* (cultivation, the art of being a refined and cultured person, involving everything from reading the right books to using a flush lavatory and taking off your coat in restaurants), was not simply impressed on an inert mass from outside, but reflected very real desires, amongst working-class people themselves, to acquire an education and lead a "decent" life, escaping the squalor of the past, and built on a legacy of populist educational programs developed in Russia since the 1860s.[5]

Equally important has been the influence of other forms of populism, as political leaders attempted to manipulate aspects of what they perceived as lower-class mentality in return for political legitimation. An especially striking illustration of such assimilation was Stalinist nationalism's governing symbol of *Rodina-mat'* (Mother Russia). This term drew most effectively on popular feeling for the "home patch" (*"rodina"* having the original sense of "birthplace," or "native village"; the tsarist term for Russia, *otechestvo*, had no such popular resonance). At the same time, the synthesis *Rodina-mat'* evoked the time-honored patriotic sense that Russia was a nation under the particular protection of the Mother of God, exemplified, for example, in the *Kazanskaia Bogomater'*, an icon of the Virgin which, legend had it, was miraculously discovered after the Russian conquest of Kazan'. It also resonated with the still older respect for *Mat' syra zemlia* (Mother Damp Earth), that is, for the land as giver of life. Furthermore, to an intensely patriarchal culture, the symbol of "nation as mother" urgently suggested the need for a controlling "father" of the nation, the "strong leader" around whom monarchist feelings in the lower classes had traditionally crystallized. Not merely passively recording lower-class mentality, the idea of *Rodina-mat'* also altered the character of that mentality by becoming, for millions of people, a nationalist symbol that could stand alongside affiliation to *zemlia* and work-group. Yet the exploitation of a form of nationalism with strongly peasant overtones also had its effects on the modernization desired by the Soviet state; it was certainly one factor in the survival of traditional time-budgeting and client–patron relations in Soviet agri-culture and industry into the late twentieth century.[6]

The evolution of popular culture as concept and reality

It is evident, then, that lower-class culture can itself be directly depen-dent upon outsiders' perceptions of "the lower class." One could even go further, and say that "popular culture" cannot exist independently of such perceptions. With no governing concept of "the people," medieval Russia also lacked not only the concept, but also the reality, of a "popular culture." Though there was a clear and important distinction between ecclesiastical and secular culture, this was not necessarily associable with any distinction between "elite" and "popular" as such. According to the simplistic historiography of the Soviet period, "the people" were dis-tinguished from "the elite" by their *dvoeverie* ("double-faith," the reten-tion of pagan beliefs alongside, or indeed more prominently than, their commitment to Christian belief). The Russian scholar T. A. Bernshtam, however, has cogently argued that the term *dvoeverie* should be replaced by *mnogoverie*, or "multifaith," a term which certainly does better justice

7.2 Pilgrims at a Russian monastery, c. 1912.

to the proliferation and fragmentation of religious practice in Christianized Russia than a simple dichotomy allows. For example, the *Trebnik*, or collection of "occasional offices," includes prayers used for the dedication of new houses and wells, and the casting-out of demons, and even the stern *Domostroi*, the famous sixteenth-century manual of house management, accepts without question such non-Christian wedding rites as the breaking of pottery.

Religion underpinned no easy division between "elite" and "masses"; the same was true of many other areas of culture. Entertainments and leisure activities were shared by all levels of society. The *skomorokhi* (fools) performed the same coarse jesting shows at palaces and in villages; the toboggan slides, see-saws, and swings which delighted Russians of low birth were enjoyed by upper-class Russians, although more discreetly. Social privilege was so deeply enshrined in the legislation and customs of feudalism – its minute orderings of precedence by occupation and status – and in material culture (architecture, furnishings, costume, means of transport) that those of noble birth had no need to emphasize, in their customs and beliefs, the separation of their lives from those of their underlings, whether *meshchane* (burgers), or *kholop'ia* and *smerdi* (slaves and peasants).

In the mid-seventeenth century, the stability of social relations began to be unsettled, with lasting effects on the evolution of popular culture.

There was an increasing emphasis on appropriate behavior, beginning, under Peter the Great, with the introduction of European dress and of guides to etiquette translated from French and German. As etiquette books were translated, so appeared versions of foreign status terms such as *siiatel'stvo* (from "Durchlaucht," "highness") *vysokoblagorodnyi* ("hochwohlgeboren," "high-born"), and *prostoliudina* (from "das gemeine Volk," "the common people"). By the time of the publication of the first standard dictionary of the Russian language, published by the Russian Academy in 1796, indigenous entertainments such as swings or ice-hills had begun to be described as "for the common people," a phrasing that was without doubt intended to work incentively as well as descriptively, communicating to a wide readership of nobles the ideology of separate social spheres for different classes that had been set down in clear terms by Catherine II's project for a Russian legal codex (*Nakaz*, 1767–68). The nobility itself had reason to accept the significance of the idea that cultivation was the fundament of social distinction, given that its legal constitution as a class was ill defined, and its access to political authority limited.[7]

But, as social stratification was fostered in ideology and education (the early *gimnazii*, grammar schools, having separate programs for those of noble birth and those not of noble birth, with a greater emphasis on intellectual matters in the former), there also came the first hints of a growing interest in, and condescension toward, the culture of those outside the nobility. The earliest such hint was that orally transmitted texts began to be collected and published. The writer Mikhail Chulkov (himself chameleonized to gentility from humbler origins) published in 1770 a collection of songs that included, besides stanzaic romances for performance in salons to musical accompaniment, some transcriptions of unrhymed ballads and plaints ("historical songs" and "lyrical songs") with sources in oral tradition. Chulkov was also the author of an alphabetical commonplace book of superstitious beliefs, the *Alphabet of Russian Superstitions*, published in 1784, an intriguing compilation of unlikely anecdotes and fanciful "little-known facts" of the kind then fashionable in the West too, but also including some convincing close observations of Russian peasant custom and ritual. The *Writing Manual* (*Pis'movnik*) of Nikolai Kurganov, first published in 1769, included a selection of authentic Russian proverbs as well as stories translated from Italian, French and German. In 1804, these were followed by the publication of *The Oldest Russian Poems, collected by Kirsha Danilov*, selections from an anthology of oral epic set down in manuscript at some period in the early eighteenth century. The collection, which appeared in an enlarged second edition in 1818, was one of the most influential early nineteenth-century sources for conceptualizations of what was later to be described as *fol'klor*.

Like Grimm, Percy, Scott, and other early publishers of folklore in the West, the Russian pioneers of folklore publication often "improved" their material, smoothing out dialect irregularities, eliding obscenities, and correcting incoherences or what they saw as needless repetitions. Still further "improvements" were carried out by the imitators of folklore, whose productions, with rare exceptions (such as Aleksandr Pushkin's *Tale of the Priest and his Servant Balda,* a piece not intended for publication), resembled their originals about as closely as Scott's poems, or Wordsworth and Coleridge's *Lyrical Ballads,* resembled actual ballads of the Scottish borders. For Pushkin himself, though, as for Wordsworth, the attraction of folkloric material was to a large extent as a source of what Wordsworth, in his *Preface to the Lyrical Ballads*, had called "the language of men," the non-standard conversational locutions preserved even by the "improved" versions of ballad, story, and epic. In his representation of his own biography, Pushkin's strategies bore strong relation to those of the *Modernes* in late seventeenth- and early eighteenth-century France; his depiction of his nurse as informant on folklore, often naively cited as a statement of plain fact, was a literary *topos* going back at least to the works of Jeanne-Marie Lhériter (1644–1734), salon authoress of folk-tale adaptations.[8]

By the early nineteenth century, however, there was far more at stake than a purely aesthetic squabble between salon lions about the appropriate language for lyric verse. The interest in folklore, which had also been voiced in some pioneering magazine articles published in the first decades of the nineteenth century, was part of an explosive political debate whose origins lay in fear of the French Revolution's "mob rule." Even for the covert opponents of autocracy, the French Revolution appeared as an awful warning of how legitimate authority, and in particular the "rule of law," might be overturned. This consideration (added to the self-interest felt by a group of potential rebels who themselves depended on serf income) led the Decembrist theorists on the one hand to make rather equivocal statements about the abolition of serfdom (freedom for all Russian men was seen as an ideal achievable in the long, rather than the short, term), and on the other to emphasize the virtues of the Russian people as legitimation for their own authority. For its part, the tsarist autocracy, especially during the reign of Nicholas I, made constant references to the harmonious existence of the lower orders in the course of propagandizing the official policy of *narodnost'* (national populism).[9]

The first manifestation of populism as political ideology in Russia consisted, then, of appeals to a vague and abstract notion of "the people," who were apostrophized rather like the quaintly dressed chorus in some early nineteenth-century opera or ballet. In the first half of the nineteenth century, there were no Russian ideologists who resembled, say, William Cobbett, a British radical who had gained his knowledge of "the people" by birth, and by day to day contact with grassroots politics. Nor could there have been, given that Russia still had no representative elected assembly, thus precluding discussion of the key issue in British populism, extension of the suffrage; given also that the persistence of serfdom made the gulf between commentators and *narod* nothing less than enormous. It was not until the 1840s, therefore, that the first systematic recording of popular texts began, with P. V. Kireevsky, N. N. Iazykov, and the writer (later lexicographer) Vladimir Dahl the most important early collectors. Also working at this period, though a compiler rather than a collector, was A. N. Afanas'ev, whose eight-volume *Russian Folk Tales* (*Narodnye russkie skazki*, 1855–64) contained more than 600 texts from all over Russia.

But it was not until the 1870s that genuine populist activism, in the form of the movement known as *khozhdenie v narod* ("going among the people"), became established in Russia. The movement, whose main rationale was the establishment of broadly based political activities among the lower classes, had important spin-offs not only in the area of philanthropy (the founding of democratic cooperatives, schools, and medical facilities for peasants and workers in Russian villages), but also in the domain of academic ethnography (the collection of material relating to every aspect of village life, from material culture to agricultural practices, from seasonal rituals to musical and verbal texts). Between 1860 and 1917, collection of folkloric material was more wide-ranging, more energetic and enthusiastic than it had ever been before. These years also saw the publication of several superb collections of Russian folklore, notably of folk song, ritual, and epic.[10]

The populists' agenda was significantly larger than that of their romantic Slavophile predecessors, such as Kireevsky, who were attracted on the one hand by the picturesque quaintness of folk diction, and on the other by the hope of finding material that would demonstrate a Russian "literary" tradition (of an Ossianic kind) preceding Westernization. But this is not to say that they were free from bias. Like their predecessors in Russia and Western Europe, they had a marked preference in favor of "folklore" in the most conventional sense: material circulating in small rural communities which appeared to reflect the stability, over long periods of time, of peasant customs and practices, and which was elevated and rarefied in tone. Epics of the distant past were collected and analyzed more assiduously than topical ballads of the present day; "magic tales," stories of questing princes and princesses, appealed more than "everyday tales," comic narratives of resourceful peasants; vulgar jokes and proverbs exercised a lesser fascination than laments or incantations. In other words, there was an emphasis on genres that were the province of "professional" culture-bearers and remote from the ordinary life of the peasantry, rather than on those which were actually most familiar and widespread in villages and cities at the time. Additionally, the secular preferences of Russian ethnographers made them, like their counterparts in Britain or Ireland, especially assiduous in seeking out beliefs and customs which could be held to derive from those held by "common Slavonic" tribes in the pre-Christian era. Besides operating positive discrimination in favor of high-flown and "pagan" material, the populists also discriminated in a negative sense. They disparaged and dismissed material which they did not see as "proper" folklore: which was of recent date, or "contaminated" by modern interpolations, and especially by interpolations which had leaked into the oral milieu from printed literature.[11]

Such prejudices persisted in Russian culture during the twentieth century too. Though the modernist movement in Russia, with its strongly pro-urban bias, led to there being something of a preference for "modern" genres of popular culture between 1910 and the late 1920s, the decades of Stalin's domination saw a reversal to conservative forms of populism, with folklore occupying something approximating to the place that it had in official culture during the reign of Nicholas I. In the 1920s, the key genre for agitprop purposes had been the irreverent, limerick-like *chastushka*; in the 1930s, folk poets (the most famous of whom was the Onega peasant woman Marfa Kriukova) were kept busy in the more decorous genre of *bylina* (folk epic), celebrating the virtues of Stalin and Lenin as *bogatyri* (traditional folklore heroes). In Kriukova's *The Tale of Lenin*, the meeting of Lenin and his wife Nadezhda Krupskaia is a touching (if also unintentionally humorous) marriage of the stereotypes of political hagiography (Lenin's tireless work at his desk) with deeds of magical derring-do and romance, and of folk literature formulae such as "magic ring," "silver moon," and "oaken door," with naive references to Bolshevik ideology.[12]

If such texts hymned the myths of Soviet history, enamel boxes painted with fairy-tale scenes, or recordings of trained choirs in neatly ironed embroidered blouses singing melodious adaptations of folk melodies, formed an idealized, pastoral drop-curtain to veil the famine and repression that overwhelmed actual Russian villages. Even after 1953, when more disinterested treatments of village culture again became possible, publications of, and studies dealing with, "vulgar" urban genres were few. Though interest in urban culture has intensified since the late 1970s, amongst Western scholars as well as Russians, the amount of secondary material dedicated to it still remains insignificant by comparison with the many volumes dedicated to village *fol'klor.*

Yet, like certain other "top-down" attitudes, the prejudice against "vulgar" popular culture has also had its effect in the social strata where "popular" texts are themselves most at home. In the late nineteenth century, visitors to Russian fairgrounds were delighted by the idea that the spectacles they were watching were old, though in fact most of them had been established in Russia for only a hundred years. Dolls dressed as medieval jester versions of the puppet theatre hero Petrushka (in fact a variant of the Italian Pulcinella) were eagerly purchased; popular magazines, such as *Niva* (The Meadow) and *Vsemirnaia illiustratsiia* (Universal Illustration) carried pictures of "traditional" customs as practiced by well-fed peasants in improbably lush, prosperous Russian villages. At the same time, the readiness to dignify the past led peasants and workers themselves increasingly to save indecorous songs for private occasions, such as wedding receptions, to abandon, or even destroy, old houses and craft objects, and to adopt the standards and values of elite art and culture, or those of what some ethnographers call "fakelore," in place of, or alongside, the standards and values of folk custom.

As will already be obvious, the "folklore/fakelore" dichotomy is in any case problematic. Even by the early nineteenth century, Russian redactions of medieval Western romances, such as *Bova Korolevich, Eruslan Lazarevich,* and *Frantsyl' Ventsian,* already enjoyed a wide readership; they were to remain amongst the favorite reading of peasant households until after the Bolshevik Revolution. Printed song-books, another genre of

popular literature that reached Russia in the eighteenth century, made
such an impression that collections of rural folk songs made in the late
nineteenth century invariably include songs whose composition betrays
their literary origins (they are set down in rhymed quatrains rather than
in the unrhymed running lines of authentic Russian folk song). The
popular ballad *Van'ka the Steward* was adapted as a poem by the writer V. V.
Krestovsky in 1860; from here it moved back into popular tradition, the
new stanzaic version replacing the old unrhymed one. Another type of
printed material, the *lubok* or popular print, in general circulation from
about 1700, was ubiquitous, from the early nineteenth century, in lower-
class settings: taverns, *izbas* (peasant homes), the lids of the trunks in
which workers and servants kept their belongings in cities. What were
popularly called *kartinki* ("little pictures"), were originally borrowed
from Germany (some early plates preserve traces of erased German
script), but made such an impact on popular consciousness that even the
most conservative lower-class group, the Old Believers, began, during
the early nineteenth century, to imitate their techniques in manuscript
paintings.[13]

In the twentieth century, new forms of dissemination – gramophone
records, films, picture postcards, newspapers, radio, domestic tape-
recorders, and television – have in their turn contributed to the irre-
versible transformation of Russian popular culture, including the
culture of villages. As in many cultures where the spoken word has traditionally had a central role, television has had a particularly powerful
impact, not only effacing older methods of entertainment, such as tale-
telling sessions, but also giving rural youth a sense of the easier and more
prosperous life that could be theirs if they migrate to cities. And so
bizarre combinations of material were and are common. Popular
printmakers of the nineteenth century shamelessly plagiarized motifs
from engravers, etchers, or lithographers working for a monied public,
placing them alongside motifs of their own composition; in the twentieth century, the formulaic love token of the past, the "gold ring," has been
replaced in folk songs by a "snapshot."[14]

No wonder, then, that most Russian observers who are not specialists
cannot distinguish "genuine" *fol'klor* (in their terms) from the reimag-
ined *narodnaia kul'tura* ("people's culture") represented by restaurants
called *The Chamber* or *The Izba*, by professional choruses singing "*Kalinka*"
and "*Katiusha* " (popular Second World War songs in a folksy "romance"
idiom), and by political reactionaries' idyllic visions of Russian peasant

ЧЕТЫРЕ ЛЮБАЧИ СЕРДЕЧЪ, ВЫГРАХЪ IBЗАБАВЛАХЪ ВРЕМА ПРОВОДАЮ
IЗДРАВIE ЛЮБЕЗНЫХЪ, IIОПОЛНОИ IСПОЧТЕНИЕМЪ ВЫПИВАЮТЪ,
ХОТА БЫЛИ РДЗГОВОРЫ, НЕНАВИРША ХЪ А ЛЮБЕЗНЫ IПЛЕННЫ:
IOTВЗГЛАДОВЪ АРУГЪ КОДРУГУ, ВЛЮБОВНОИ СТРАСТI РАСПДЛЕННЫ
ЗГОВОРIВШIСД. БУДЕТЪ КОЗЫРЬ, ТОМУ ВССЛЮБЕЗНО ПОПОЦАЛУЮ А ДТЬ
IСТАЛI ТАКЪ МОЛЧДIВО, ЧТО КОМПАНИА СКУЧНА БУДЕМЪ ЛУТЧЕ ВРД
ОДIНЪ ОТВЕРНУЛСА, ЗДРУГОИ УЛЫБНУЛСА, АРУГОИ ДДЕТЪ ЗНАКЪ
КДКУЮ КАРТУ ДДТЬ.   ВЕНЕРД ОТБАХУСД ПРИСЛАНА УГОФДЕТЪ
СКОРО ИХЪ ИГРУ АРУГОИ ИГРОИ ОКОНЧДЕТЪ,

7.3 "The four loving hearts who spend their time in gaming and
amusements." Late eighteenth-century woodcut. Printed from an imported
block: the original German text has been effaced and an ill-spelt Russian text
making use of some Roman letters inserted.

families not as extended collectives tied together by often bitter economic necessity, but as happy nuclear families joyfully enacting conventional bourgeois gender roles. No wonder that the *matreshka*, "Russian
doll," invented by the Art and Craft movement in the late nineteenth
century, became so "traditional" that it eventually was parodied for the
purposes of political satire (an immense Gorbachev, or later Yeltsin, gives
birth to a smaller Brezhnev or Gorbachev, and so on down to a tiny, shape-
less, fetus-like Lenin). No wonder that, during the last century, rural
culture has come to resemble an alternative form of urbanized mass
culture, whose idiosyncratic qualities become more and more hard to
identify. Because of this, and because any overall survey of "popular
culture" in the broadest sense – all the genres of text, classes of ritual, and

7.4. "The sirin-bird." Old Believer watercolor in the style of an engraved *lubok*. Probably early nineteenth century. An originally secular motif (Sirin is a corruption of the Greek "Siren") adapted to religious purposes as the "Bird of Paradise", a bird-woman messenger from Heaven.

types of object that were not explicitly produced for an upper- or upper-middle-class audience – would turn into an interminable and dizzying enumeration, I shall concentrate below on material of urban origin, most of it originating from the period after 1900. The traditional "folklore" of Russian villages – the ritual and fixed-form genres that did not get imported to Russian cities – will be dealt with only fleetingly, and generally from a comparative perspective.

Popular culture: general characteristics and genres

One significant dynamic in the development of popular culture during the nineteenth and twentieth centuries has been the evolution of a rigid binary opposition between "work" (activities practiced for professional gain) and "entertainment" (passive consumption of material produced by other professionals). In villages, much folklore had been intimately related to work practices: seasonal festivals such as the bonfire-lighting and dancing organized for Ivan Kupala (the popular celebration of St. John's Night, coinciding with the summer solstice) commemorated the important dates of the agricultural calendar (here, the height of the hay-making and harvesting season). Both festivals of this kind, and the traditional work-songs that had accompanied work in the fields, such as scything, digging, or water-hauling, were irrelevant to life in cities; what is more, they were not replaced, in the twentieth century at any rate, by work-songs specific to the new environment.

Less quickly eroded were other types of functional or utilitarian text, such as spells, incantations, and divinatory texts. True, beliefs in other-worldly forces as such, for example *domovye* (house spirits) or *leshie* (wood demons), seem to have been subdued, if not forced out, by urban life, as noted in a sketch by the writer Valery Briusov, an acute observer of popular beliefs.[15]

Not all non-scientific or commonsense beliefs vanished easily, of course. Urban Russians continued to believe in signs and portents (for example, that sparrows take dust baths before rain, or that it is unpropitious if a black cat crosses your path). They continued to treat ailments with herbal remedies (honey, for example, being recommended for everything from sore throats to dry skin). Not only alternative medicine, but also many other alternative belief systems, from yoga to the symbolism of dreams, from divination by coffee-grounds to numerology, from hypnotism to astrology, all had and have their adherents. The rationalistic Soviet disapproval of "primitive" and "perverted" "survivals of the past" meant that such practices could not be openly discussed, and led a clandestine existence, but political liberalization after 1986 provoked an explosion of overt interest, which nearly a decade later showed no signs of abating. Whilst admiration for *ekstrasensy* (mesmerists and mediums) was by no means universal, it became widespread, even among some doctors, scientists, and other members of the intelligentsia.

Here though, as with religion in a narrower sense, we have an area where the term "popular culture" itself gets called into question, one where anti-rationalism flourishes regardless of education and class. The central area, therefore, where the term "popular culture" still carries weight, is that of leisure activities. In a certain sense, the years since 1930, or even since 1890, have seen a reversal of the situation that obtained in medieval times – as clothing, architecture, manners, and diet become increasingly standardized, it is taste in entertainments that has acted as the litmus test of class.[16]

Admittedly, the divide between "popular" and "elite" preferences is not unbridgeable. The decline of seasonal festivals (Christmas, Shrovetide, Easter), accelerated, after 1917, by an aggressive official policy of secularization, and the reduction of workloads, has made leisure, potentially at least, part of the everyday timetable for workers and peasants, not just a feature of a few important holidays or occasional Sundays. Universal elementary education, and the emphasis placed by successive Soviet administrations on the fact that elite art forms (opera, theatre, music, and literature) should be generally accessible, irrespective of occupation, have eroded the division between leisure for the intelligentsia and leisure for the lower classes. So, too, have the development and propagandization of "democratic" art forms (the cinema, popular music, television). Visiting the cinema, listening to the songs sung by Vera Panina, Aleksandr Vertinsky (cabaret singers of the 1910s and 1920s), or Vladimir Vysotsky (an actor and "guitar poet" of the 1960s and 1970s), or watching football or ice-hockey matches, were, and to a lesser extent still are, activities enjoyed amongst Russians more or less irrespective of class.

To some degree, then, the Soviet regime genuinely did realize the vision set down by its laureate, Demian Bedny, in his 1930s poem "Worker Leisure Then and Now": "Now workers' leisure is *kul'turnyi* [cultured] / And clean and wholesome through and through."[17] But for all these brave words, working-class Russians remained, not only in the 1930s, but also in the 1960s and indeed the 1990s, a good deal more likely to visit the beer-bar than the ballet, or the stadium than the concert hall. Their tastes in music, art, and literature, whilst marked to some extent by schoolroom exposure to the Russian classics, still remained fundamentally different from those of the metropolitan intelligentsia (if not always from those of, say, the provincial middle classes, such as schoolteachers, doctors, or minor party officials). In many other ways, too, their manner of spending their leisure has changed surprisingly little. Films, records, and mass media have altered the manner of transmitting popular materials, and presentation of performances is usually smoother and more sophisticated, but in terms of content many performances, when closely scrutinized, still resemble their counterparts a century ago. Conversely, members of the intelligentsia, whilst they do appreciate and disseminate some "popular" genres, above all songs and jokes, do so in a conscious spirit of self-irony, or at the very least regard such pleasures as only part of what constitutes acceptable leisure activity.

This situation partly derives from the ephemeral nature of much popular culture, in particular orally transmitted material. Well before the Revolution, solemn, celebratory genres of rural folklore, such as the *bylina*, the *istoricheskie*, and *dukhovnye pesni* (historical and devotional songs), and the *protiazhnaia pesn'* (sad, long-drawn-out melody of woe) had more or less disappeared. These genres, as well as "lyric songs," wedding songs, and laments, still survive in some areas, but according to fieldwork statistics published in the journal *Russian Folklore (Russkii fol'klor)* in 1972, 1976, and 1977, recordings of them are now at most in dozens, while thousands of recordings are made of different satirical genres. Since the late nineteenth century, aphoristic, comical phrasing has been valued more highly in oral tradition than folk poetic motifs, such as "white swan" or "grey dove," and topical material has been more popular than tales of the heroic past.

All these elements are abundantly present in what has, during the twentieth century, been the most productive genre of orally transmitted song, the *chastushka*, a four-line ditty whose themes sometimes include love and friendship, but which is more often of humorous or indeed scabrous content. *Chastushki* express an age-old humor of bodily functions that was accommodated just as readily in the songs and dances of the *skomorokhi*, the anecdotes of Russian villages, and the raree shows, popular street comedies, and cheap prints of Russian cities during the eighteenth and nineteenth centuries. Very often, though, the *chastushka* is the vehicle of a much more aggressive topicality than was found in these genres, even in the most news-aware of them, the raree show (*raek*) in which perspective prints, or later, pictures from magazines, were accompanied by doggerel texts on satirical topics. Before the Russian Revolution, the "topicality" of the *chastushka* tended to mean its suitability for jesting insults. Although this use of the *chastushka* did not disappear entirely with the Revolution, it was to become more noticeable, and notorious, as a vehicle for popular discontent that could not otherwise be expressed. The following example, recorded in about 1920, satirizes the domestic privations characterizing the years of war communism:

> We Moscow folk, we live damn well,
> Snug as corpses, don't you think?
> Me and the wife sleep in a drawer,
> Her mother's tucked up in the sink.

The topicality of the *chastushka* was well appreciated by the Soviet authorities themselves; especially in the 1920s, it was a genre particularly widely used for propaganda purposes. Like most appropriations of subversive genres in order to put across worthy messages, the effort was doomed to failure. Propaganda *chastushki* lacked the obscene wit, the pithiness, and often even the accentual meter, of their models, and are not part of the popular repertoire that can still be heard at weddings in Russian cities and villages today.[18]

Apart from the *chastushka*, the other most viable orally transmitted genre is probably the narrative joke *(anekdot)*. Again, the flowering of this as a topical genre appears to be post-revolutionary.[19] Some of the most popular *anekdoty* turned out to be serial in nature, such as the immensely productive Radio Erevan series, which draws on the age-old folklore tradition of the "wise fool" (represented in village culture by the well-loved figure of "Ivan the Fool," and in nineteenth-century cities by the puppet hero Petrushka). The question-and-answer format allows for witty one-liners, as well as reviving the defunct genre of the riddle.[20] In other serial anecdotes, further "wise fool" figures such as the brave Red Army commander Chapayev, hippies, Cheburashka (a sort of large-eared bear featured on Russian children's programs), and Cornet Rzhevsky have replaced Ivan the Fool. The last character (travestied from the hero of a 1940 play by Fedor Gladkov, and of a 1962 film, *The Hussar's Ballad*, directed by E. Riazanov) is an exceptionally boorish officer of the 1812 campaign, whose activities fly in the face of the official and intelligentsia myth that the early nineteenth century epitomized refinement. Cornet Rzhevsky, like Cheburashka and Chapayev, is especially popular with schoolchildren, no doubt as a reaction to indoctrination in proper behavior.[21]

A third enduring, if less productive, genre of orally transmitted popular culture is the proverb or saying, frequently used by populist politicians to give a folksy flavor to their speeches ("when you live with the wolves you must howl with the wolves" – Lenin), but also spontaneously employed in colloquial speech for the purposes of emphasis. Here, too, humor (of a scatological or sexual kind, in the right contexts – the resources of Russian swearing are notoriously rich) is usually the primary requirement.

Besides making and narrating jokes, lower-class Russians (indeed, all Russians in moments of relaxation) have always been avid spectators of comedies, from the street theatre shows of pre-revolutionary Russia to the satirical "clownades" of the Soviet circus and television, to television shows featuring comedians such as Arkady Raikin. This is not to say that seriousness has altogether disappeared from popular culture during the last two centuries; the point is that orally transmitted material is no longer looked to for solemnity or edification. (One possible exception to this generalization is the urban myth, which purports to communicate suppressed facts, and is meant to be shocking, but not implausible. An example with much currency in Leningrad during 1980 was a story that the party leader, Romanov, had commandeered the Aurora, flagship of the Revolution, in order to stage a wedding reception for his daughter, at which a dinner service of Catherine II's was smashed to pieces "for luck" by drunken guests. In the 1990s similar stories were told about the millionaire mafiosi of St. Petersburg and Moscow.) The deficiency of the oral tradition was made up by books, films, television, and newspapers, and though Soviet newspapers generally aimed to cut across class barriers, in the 1990s some newspapers, such as *Moskovsky komsomolets*, began self-consciously aiming at a lower-class audience in the manner of Western tabloids, or of such pre-revolutionary "boulevard newspapers" as *Peterburgskii listok* and *Gazeta-kopeika*.

Even before the Revolution, many mass-print-run volumes had begun to cater for readers' need to feel that they were being uplifted and educated as well as entertained. Anastasiia Verbitskaia's bestseller *The Keys of Happiness* (1908–13), for example, interwove conversations about fashionable ideas with scenes of passion. An equally notorious novel by a male contemporary of Verbitskaia's, Mikhail Artsybashev's *Sanin* (1907), switches from scenes depicting the heroine's thigh-trembling desire for a cynical, "rough trade" officer to portrayals of the tormented situation of her male contemporaries, "superfluous" in the wake of the 1905 Revolution – all, that is, but for the Nietzschean superman of the title, Sanin himself. In more recent years, the genres of science fiction and historical novel have both catered to readers wanting information-heavy narrative. *Riches*, a 1978 novel by one of the most popular writers of recent years, Valentin Pikul, even has footnotes filling in historical background. Like many other works by Pikul, this piece of "faction" introduces historical figures under real or altered names, alongside wholly invented characters, in the manner made canonical by Tolstoy's *War and Peace*.[22]

The fact remains, though, that most consumers of popular culture do not look upon the books, films and music that they like as substitute encyclopedias. They expect, in the first instance, to be entertained – to read, see, or hear material that is interesting or involving. This has been regularly indicated by audience surveys over the years, from a questionnaire given to spectators at worker theatres in St. Petersburg at the turn of the century, to investigations of cinema audiences in the 1920s, to canvassing of fiction audiences in the 1970s.[23] The artifacts that make up popular culture also themselves suggest that many consumers of it would agree with Tolstoy, who argued in *What Is Art?*, chapter v, that emotional truth, rather than factual truth or aesthetic pleasure, was the primary requirement of works of art: "The effect of art is based on one man's perceiving, visually or aurally, the expression of another man's feeling, and being able himself to feel that very same feeling." Emotion – preferably extreme emotion – is a key desideratum in the popular arts. The need for feeling is satisfied by direct, human-centered, narrative-heavy modes of creation: whether in song, film, or literature, character is the key. The absorption into popular culture of types from literature, the prevalence of star cults (from Vera Kholodnaia, through the "Soviet Garbo," Liubov Orlova, to the actor and bard Vladimir Vysotsky, whose funeral was attended by thousands, and such luminaries as the singers Alla Pugacheva and Boris Grebenshchikov, or the actress Natalia Negoda, star of *Little Vera*), and the popularity of figurative art, especially portraits, all suggest how important is the concentration on remarkable individuals.

That is not to say that irony is unknown in popular genres. Parody, "alienation effects" such as the play-within-a-play or film-within-a-film, or nudging addresses to the reader or viewer reminding him or her that he or she is consuming a play, a novel, or a song, are all reasonably prevalent (occurring, for example, in turn-of-the-century "cruel romances," street plays, and in the novels of Pikul, whose eighteenth-century romance *The Favorite* [1984] begins with a fairly lengthy disquisition on the traditions of historical fiction). But these devices are seldom used in order to play down emotional effects – the pattern is closer to the double-think implied in the term "romantic irony" than to the rational detachment required by, say, Brechtian alienation, or for that matter Renaissance tragedy. The point is to arouse readers' or spectators' identification with the characters. Narrative perspective matters little – complex techniques such as stream-of-consciousness are not favored, but first-person discourse, as used in song or popular poetry, seems to be considered neither more nor less effective than narrative in the third person. Because subtle delineations of psychology are not what is required, the voice "speaking from within" is accorded no extra authority. The point is to present readers or viewers with a schema, an archetype, over which they can float their own complex and ambivalent perceptions of the world. Hence, as is routinely pointed out in studies of popular culture, descriptions of people's appearances and feelings are formulaic. Women are pale, sensitive, and interesting, or buxom, seductive *femmes fatales*; men are strong and handsome (often too handsome if they are villainous). Hearts swell, bound and leap, stomachs churn, eyes flash, roll, or narrow to slits, teeth are gnashed. Love is always uncontrollable, overwhelming, and accompanied by shaking limbs, shining eyes, and other involuntary physical gestures. Any surprise effects, therefore, result from accumulation rather than the nature of any specific part of the description.[24]

The stars of Russian theatre and screen, like those in other countries, have played up to this simplification of human existence by making their performances depend on a few easily recognizable mannerisms. Particular characters – the passionate artiste, the tyrannical tycoon, the exotic and usually also devious foreigner – surface in generation after generation of popular texts. Schematism of characterization, and of character contrast, is, however, offset by extremity of situation. No disaster is too bizarre, no death too horrendous, no illness too languishing. Murder, revenant spirits, monstrosities, and especially forbidden love, are the essential constituents of popular melodramas (in the broadest sense) of all generations, from the translated romances of the late seventeenth century, such as *Bova the King's Son*, to the popular novels and films of the 1990s. In ballads, the most "modern" genre of Russian villages, not only murder but adultery and even incest were preferred topics. Later texts have contrived ever more ingenious catastrophes.

In cases where lurid disasters are averted, the theme of sudden reversals of fortune is frequently used in order to heighten sensation. Two genres very popular in today's Russia, the soap opera and the game show, both depend on knife-edge *peripeteiai* (in the former case emotional as well as financial). These genres continue preoccupations that were evident in texts written before the Revolution too, recounting, for example, the woeful adventures of a country boy (or occasionally girl) in the big city, a subject treated also in the puppet text *Petrushka* and the popular novel *Bandit Churkin*.[25]

The adventure narrative also manifests another persistent feature of popular tradition: its preference for sinners over saints, for flaws over perfection. Many of the most popular Russian stars (amongst the men, at least) have been vulnerable neurotics with a propensity for a drop too many (Vysotsky is the classic example of the late Soviet period). It is scarcely surprising that the myth of art produced in suffering should suit an audience that has to work extremely hard for its living, that wants to see performers such as Vysotsky, Piaf, and Garland, perform their hearts out on the edge of collapse. But the attitude to actors and singers perpetuates an aesthetic applied to ambivalent fictional characters too. In recent years, the huge success of Iulian Semenov's Stirlitz novels, especially *Seventeen Moments of Spring* (1968: filmed for television in 1973) is partly attributable to the ambiguity of the hero's status (he is a double agent successfully chameleonized to life in decadent fascist Germany).[26] No wonder that, like Chapayev, Stirlitz has become the hero of countless anecdotes.

Such stereotypes have been played on (one could say cashed in on) by the autobiographical statements of Boris Yeltsin and of the right-wing politician Vladimir Zhirinovsky, both of whom spin the "I'm a hard man, but I had a hard childhood" line for all it is worth. In Zhirinovsky's *The Last Thrust to the South* (1993), the harrowing portrait of a loveless childhood (no birthday presents, perpetually hungry, cooped up in a bookless communal flat stinking of cheap Prima cigarettes and an over-used lavatory) is skilfully juxtaposed to the confessions of the adult extremist politician whose experience has hardened him and made him a true populist, but also rendered him incapable of finding "that one woman to love that I so need."

Perhaps the most popular type of ambiguous or flawed hero or heroine is the sexual sinner: the virtuous woman who, like Madame de Tourvel in Laclos' notorious eighteenth-century novel *Les liaisons dangereuses*, sacrifices her chastity to the wrong man, or the rake who, like Valmont, enforces the sacrifice in the first place. Mikhail Kalatozov's film

The Cranes are Flying (1957) offers classic examples of such a heroine and hero: so, too, does Evgeny Bauer's 1916 melodrama *A Life for a Life,* in which the beautiful daughter and stepdaughter of a woman magnate both languish for a handsome young aristocrat (played by the matinee idol Vitold Polonsky).

Forgiveness toward the errant has also led to a high degree of tolerance (despite Russian society's long tradition of public puritanism) toward the representation of "deviant" behavior. Even the most prudish works produced for mass circulation, for example socialist realist novels and paintings, occasionally allowed whispers of eroticism to be heard (for example, the denigratory, but still enticing, portraits of self-serving, flirtatious young women in the novels of Anna Karavaeva or Vera Panova, or the lip-smacking paintings of nubile, bosomy young women produced by official Soviet artists during the 1940s).[27]

The demand for sensation, even titillation, at all costs means that Russian popular culture is fluid in its attitude to genre convention. Techniques are mixed – musicals have spectacular lighting effects, whilst atmospheric music is essential in films; theatrical shows are mounted on ice (so mixing narrative and sport), popular songs are quoted in novels, plays are based on popular songs, novels adapted for television or the big screen.[28] Whilst all this is familiar enough in the West as well, one major difference in the manner of conveying sensation is suggested by the fact that Russian popular genres display a much smaller emphasis on structure, on tight plotting, than their Western counterparts. Blockbusters (whether books or films) often seem, by Western standards, over-extended and flaccidly paced.

In a similar manner, popular prints and paintings (from shop signs to film posters), are often, by the standards of Western post-Renaissance elite art, chaotically organized, but also extraordinarily vivid and energetic. They ignore the demands of conventional geometric perspective in favor of semantic perspective (in which objects are represented according to their narrative importance), or simply suspend motifs randomly in a flat field, relying on brilliant color to hold the eye. This, it has to be said, succeeds better in the overtly non-naturalistic style of, say, *lubok* prints, pre-revolutionary shop signs, and wooden utensils than it does in the work of some recent populist painters such as Ilia Glazunov.[29]

Apart from the emphasis on motif rather than structure (perhaps an indication of some residual influence from folkloric tradition, though in fact random *bricolage* was not always characteristic there; in so-called

7.5 Girls using *kacheli*, a Russian swing, and a seesaw, both popular amusements since medieval times. Russian lithograph, *c*. 1850. "P. A.", the creator of this low-quality work, which was almost certainly intended for mass consumption, has plagiarized the right half from a series of fine English engravings on Russian subjects published in the 1820s. The left half is his own, hence the peculiarities in perspective.

"fixed-form" genres, such as the folk tale, shaping devices as strict triple repetition and the use of opening and closing formulae were considered requisite), popular culture's concentration on sensation is also evident in its hospitable attitude toward novelties of all kinds. From the early nineteenth century, song-books, divination manuals, tales, and other volumes aimed at a lower-class market were regularly marketed with the enticing term "new" or "newest" in their titles (*A New and Complete Song-Book* [*Novyi polnyi pesennik*, 1869], or *A Brand-New Letter-Writer* [*Noveishii pis'-movnik*, 1883], for example). Though enthusiasm for novelty has not generally been articulated with quite such naive directness in the twentieth century, its effects have persisted – dampened, but never extinguished, by the artificial closing of borders to Western influence between the late 1930s and the mid-1950s. Under the regimes of Khrushchev and Brezhnev, Soviet popular culture became more and more receptive to external influences. By 1980, Western groups such as the Beatles or the Rolling Stones, and mass-market Indian films, were just as much part of Russian popular culture as the songs of Alla Pugacheva, and a great deal more so than officially sponsored folk-music ensembles – these, whatever their appeal for tourists, were regarded with indifference by most Russians of the younger generation, at any rate. And, in the late 1980s, Russian popular culture began to be saturated with Western texts and artifacts, from hamburgers and t-shirts to magazines and videos. In fact, not since the late eighteenth century had Russia experienced such an intensive period of Westernization, and such an enthusiasm for all things foreign; almost all native products were despised in favor of imports.

Yet comparison with the late eighteenth century also suggests that the arguments advanced by nationalists, according to whom Russian popular culture has entered a period of terminal decline, may be exaggerated, indeed alarmist. Foreign visitors to Russia around 1800 frequently commented on the preference of Russians, working-class as well as aristocratic, for foreign goods, customs, and entertainments. During this period such novelties as glove-puppet shows, circuses, peep shows, panoramas, clown shows, and pantomimes performed by foreigners were ubiquitous. Yet by 1830 at the latest, things had settled down once more, and these entertainments had begun being absorbed into Russian tradition. In the same way, the rage for popular Western fiction, such as Agatha Christie, the *Angélique* novels, Mexican or Spanish television soap operas, is likely to be replaced by some new fusions of Western and native traditions – a domestically made soap, perhaps, or a new and less moralistic tradition of detective-story writing, in which the security services do not always have the last word. In the second half of 1994, Russian television advertisements – which in the early 1990s consisted of a single shot of some product, usually Western, or sales outlet, with voice-over – had already begun to show a much higher level of sophistication and sensitivity to indigenous preferences (they now include narrative scenes obviously set in Moscow, and in-joke references to television series, while the hero of the MMM Savings Bank advertisements, Lenia Golubkov, became a Chapayev-like folk hero in 1993–94).

That said, the adaptability and flexibility of urban popular culture should not be exaggerated (as we have seen, successful formulae display a remarkable longevity); nor should its benevolence. In the late 1980s and early 1990s, some of the most popular events in Moscow included topless beauty contests, pornographic video showings, and live revues with nude dancing of a stunning crudity. Though this was the first time in Russian history when such material had been on general view (a fact that goes some way toward explaining its popularity), and although working-class people are not its only or main consumers, the preference for material that is offensive and anarchic is deep-rooted in popular culture. Though, as argued earlier, it is doubtful whether the random, everyday (*bytovoi*) chauvinism often present in popular entertainment and popular life can in its own right be the basis of a coherent and effective nationalist ideology, it can at the very least cause a great deal of distress to individual "outsiders," whether they be people's neighbors, workmates, fellow townsdwellers, or even spouses or partners, who are made the target of hostile jokes and nicknames such as *zhidovskaia morda* ("yid face"), *khokhol* ("dirty Ukrainian"), *chernomazyi* ("black mug," also used for those from the Caucasus and Central Asia), or for that matter *sterva* ("bitch") or *bliad'* ("whore"). Further, some forms of popular culture have proved excellent vehicles for propagandizing repellent political ideologies. The "class hatred" dogma of the early Soviet period was easily grafted onto the traditional structure of Russian fairground farces, in which a streetwise clown figure pitted himself against grotesquely caricatured outsiders (officials, foreigners, or women). Traditional detective-story and thriller plots proved all too congenial to the xenophobic cold-war fictions about power-crazy Americans engaged in germ warfare that were demanded by the Soviet regime in the late 1940s; later, they became the vehicle for a different kind of chauvinistic horror film, tales of encroachment on heroic border-guards and fishermen by cold-eyed Chinese invaders. A worrying development was the increasingly effective manipulation by nationalist right-wingers of certain sectors of popular culture – a fact that suggests, at the very least, these groups' ability to exploit the vacuum left by the disappearance of Soviet nationalist agitprop. At the aborted Moscow mayorial elections in January 1992, "Pauk" (Wolfspider), the lead singer of the heavy metal group "Corroded Metals," was intending to stand as a candidate for the chauvinist National Radical Party. The group's songs included a number dedicated to the opponents of "Zionists and *natsmeny*" (a derogatory term for non-Russian racial minorities), with a chorus (sung – with an irony of which the performers were apparently unconscious – in English), running "Kill, kill, kill, kill the bloody foreigners." And there is no doubt that Zhirinovsky's description of Caucasian and Central Asian migrants as "fly agaric toadstools [*sic*] and cockroaches crawling over the Urals" was well in tune with popular xenophobia.[30]

It is not, then, just the prejudices of educated Russians that have made them suspicious of urban popular culture; these suspicions have on occasion been all too well justified by the popular culture itself. For those, too, who (unlike Tolstoy) value art above all as a source of beauty, the noble themes and articulation of "folklore" in a selective sense – traditional Russian magic tales, epics, laments, "lyric songs," spells, and seasonal rituals – is far more attractive than the low farce, strained emotionalism, and general garishness often evident in modern forms of popular culture. Firebirds, bright-feathered falcons, snow maidens, men with moons on their foreheads and stars on their temples, have an immediate and obvious appeal to post-romantic art (which has for the most part ignored more disturbing motifs such as *Svinoi chekhol*, "Pigjacket," the Russian version of "Donkeyskin," in which a princess disguises herself in a skinned pig to avoid incest with her father). Few writers in the nineteenth century would have thought of turning street theatre or tavern songs into art, but rural folklore inspired (in however distant a sense) figures as diverse as Aleksandr Pushkin, Aleksandr Ostrovsky, Petr Tchaikovsky, Igor Borodin, Modest Mussorgsky, Viktor Vasnetsov, Mikhail Nesterov. The early twentieth century witnessed a "golden age" of folklore imitations: Igor Stravinsky's *Firebird*, Marina Tsvetaeva's *Tsar' Maiden*, the poems of Aleksandr Blok and Anna Akhmatova, the paintings of Ivan Bilibin and Nikolai Rerikh, the paintings and sculptures of Mikhail Vrubel, are only some of the most significant works derived from folklore sources. Even in the anti-rural 1920s and 1930s, folk tradition sustained the anti-Soviet lyric of one of the greatest twentieth-century Russian poets, Nikolai Kliuev, himself from a peasant background, as well as the remarkable imagery of *Happiness*, the collectivization myth of film-maker Aleksandr Medvedkin (who was also of peasant descent). Besides such direct adaptations, folklore, and especially folk tales, have left surprising and quixotic traces in some of the classics of Russian realism: in Ivan Goncharov's *Oblomov*, where the hero's memories of his birthplace are colored by folkloric fantasies of plenty and happiness; in Anton Chekhov's *Three Sisters*, where the character of Natasha, the spiteful daughter-in-law, bears a strong relation to the evil women of folk tale; most surprisingly perhaps in *War and Peace*, in which another Natasha is a "princess" competed for by three suitors (Andrei, Anatole, and Pierre), and won, as in the tales of "Ivan the Fool," by the least promising of them, the ugly innocent who travels by the slowest road.[31]

Both the intrinsic beauty of the solemn genres of rural folklore, and the enigmatic mystery that derives from their remote origins (the traditional peasant mentality being at least as strange to moderns as the pagan

7.6 "Tsar Saltan's feast": illustration by Ivan Bilibin to Pushkin's verse folk-tale stylization *Skazka o tsare Saltane*, Moscow 1905.

beliefs of pre-Christian Russia), make it unsurprising that appropriations should proliferate. Yet popular art, precisely because of its rough-hewn, ironical, even ugly self-presentation, has been of value to those of different sensibilities in their desire to avoid the wistful and the elegiac. The announcement by the "Eccentrics" of Soviet cinema in their manifesto of 1922 that "a Pinkerton [detective novel] cover is worth more than a painting by Picasso" was silly and callow, but the aesthetic that it expressed prompted such magnificent achievements as the "lumpenproletarian" scenes of Sergei Eisenstein's *Strike*, with their abundant references to the trick-photography of popular cinema, and to the "attractions" of circus and music-hall. The absurdist stories of Daniil Kharms, dating from a generation later, are closely related to popular jokes and urban myths, as is the later work in the same vein of Nina Sadur; similar material inspired Nikolai Gogol's superb stories "The Nose" and "Diary of a Madman"; even earlier, in the eighteenth century, generally something of a desert for interesting prose, the populist narratives of Mikhail Chulkov (*The Mocker* and *The Comely Cook*) have a vitality that is absent from the more polished fictions of Nikolai Karamzin. If the traditions of folklore proper inspired Chekhov in some works, his remarkable long story *In the Ravine* draws on Westernized romance tradition: with her lashless eyes, penchant for green, and sibilant name, the villainess Aksinia is a bizarre recreation of snake-women such as Melusina. Among the many excellent twentieth-century Russian painters who have appropriated the popular arts of Russian cities are Natalia Goncharova, Igor Larionov, Alexandre Benois, Marc Chagall, Boris Kustodiev, Mstislav Dobuzhinsky, and Aleksandr Tyshler, whilst Stravinsky and Dmitry Shostakovich were both drawn to the "trash music" of urban areas.

And so, while arguing that all art must be based on popular themes or texts in order to be successful would be as absurd as positing that all art must appeal to a mass audience if it is to be worthwhile, it is evident that there is, for all that, something in the hypothesis, voiced most eloquently by Mikhail Bakhtin in his study of Rabelais, that the cultural energy essential to the production of significant works of art is likely also to be expressed in a strong and lively popular culture, which will in its turn provide a positive source of inspiration for many artists, whether or not they themselves work with a mass audience in mind.

NOTES

1. On *zemliachestvo*, the effects of emigration, and worker culture generally see particularly Victoria Bonnell, *Roots of Rebellion: Workers' Politics and Organizations in St. Petersburg and Moscow, 1900–1914* (Berkeley, CA, 1983); Victoria Bonnell, ed., *The Russian Worker: Life and Labour under the Tsarist Regime* (Berkeley, CA, 1983); Diane Koenker, *Moscow Workers in the 1917 Revolution* (Princeton, NJ, 1981); S. A. Smith, *Red Petrograd: Revolution in the Factories 1917–1918* (Cambridge, 1985); Jeffrey Baxter, *Muzhik and Muscovite: Urbanization in Late Imperial Russia* (Berkeley, CA, 1985); Daniel Brower, *The Russian City between Tradition and Modernity 1850–1900* (Berkeley, CA, 1990); Robert B. McKean, *St. Petersburg between the Revolutions: Workers and Revolutionaries, June 1907–February 1917* (New Haven, CT, 1990); on village culture Ben Eklof and Stephen P. Frank, eds., *The World of the Russian Peasant: Post-Emancipation Culture and Society* (Boston, 1990); Esther Kingston-Mann and Timothy Mixter, eds., *Peasant Economy, Culture and Politics of European Russia 1800–1921* (Princeton, NJ, 1991); Marjorie Mandelstam Balzer, ed., *Russian Traditional Culture: Religion, Gender, and Customary Law* (Armonk, NY, 1992); Stephen P. Frank and Mark D. Steinberg, eds., *Cultures in Flux: Lower-Class Values, Practices, and Resistance in Late Imperial Russia* (Princeton, NJ, 1994). On popular chauvinism, A. Avakumovic "The Black Hundreds," in *The Modern Encyclopedia of Russian and Soviet History*, ed., J. L. Wieczynski, 50 vols. (Gulf Breeze, FL, 1976–93), vol. IV, pp. 197–200; Hubertus F. Jahn, "For Tsar and Fatherland? Russian Popular Culture and the First World War," in Frank and Steinberg, *Cultures in Flux*: pp. 131–46.
2. On Russian utopianism generally see Richard Stites, *Revolutionary Dreams: Utopian Vision and Experimental Life in the Russian Revolution* (Oxford, 1989). On the Socialist

Revolutionaries, Maureen Perrie, *The Agrarian Policy of the Russian Socialist-Revolutionary Party, from its Origins through the Revolution of 1905–7* (Cambridge, 1976).

3. On pre-revolutionary public violence see Joan Neuberger, *Hooliganism: Crime, Culture and Power in St. Petersburg, 1900–1914* (Berkeley, CA, 1993); recent academic studies include Beatrice Farnsworth and Lynne Viola, *Russian Peasant Women* (New York, 1992); Christine D. Worobec, *Peasant Russia: Family and Community in the Post-Emancipation Period* (Princeton, NJ, 1991); on post-revolutionary gang culture, Alan M. Ball, *And Now My Soul is Hardened: Abandoned Children in Soviet Russia, 1918–1930* (Berkeley, CA, 1994); John Bushnell, *Moscow Graffiti: Language and Subculture* (Boston, 1990); Il'ia Erenburg, *Liudi, gody, zhizn'*, vol. I (Moscow, 1990), p. 58.

4. The topic of gender and popular culture, formerly neglected, is now widely explored, e.g. Barbara Engel, *Between the Fields and the City: Women, Work, and Family in Russia, 1861–1914* (Cambridge, 1994); Rose Glickman, *Russian Factory Women: Workplace and Society, 1880–1914* (Berkeley, CA, 1984); Catriona Kelly, "'Better Halves'? Women and Russian Urban Popular Entertainments, 1890–1910," in Linda Edmondson, ed., *Women and Society in Russia* (Cambridge, 1992), pp. 5–31; Hilary Pilkington, "'Good Girls in Trousers': Codes of Masculinity and Femininity in Moscow Youth Culture," in Marianne Liljestrom, Eila Mantysaari, and Arja Rosenholm, eds., *Gender Restructuring in Russian Studies: Slavica Tamperensia* 2 (1993), pp. 175–91.

5. On the transformation of popular mentality through official ideology, see especially Abbott Gleason, Peter Kenez, and Richard Stites, eds., *Bol'shevik Culture* (Bloomington, IN, 1985); Peter Kenez, *The Birth of the Propaganda State* (Cambridge, 1985); Sheila Fitzpatrick, *The Cultural Front: Power and Culture in Revolutionary Russia* (Ithaca and London, 1992); Vera Dunham, *In Stalin's Time: Middle-Class Values in Soviet Fiction* (Cambridge, 1976).

6. On *Rodina-mat'* see Mary Buckley, *Women and Ideology in the Soviet Union* (London, 1989); on the mother cult before 1917, Adele M. Barker, *The Mother Syndrome in the Russian Folk Imagination* (Columbus, OH, 1986); Joanna Hubbs, *Mother Russia: the Feminine Myth in Russian Culture* (Bloomington, IN, 1988). On the "strong ruler" cult, see Maureen Perrie, *The Image of Ivan the Terrible in Russian Folklore* (Cambridge, 1987). On the persistence of peasant values in the Stalin period, see Donald Filtzer, *Soviet Workers and Stalinist Industrialization: the Formation of Modern Soviet Production Relations* (London, 1986); Sheila Fitzpatrick, *Stalin's Peasants: Resistance and Survival in the Russian Village after Collectivization* (Oxford, 1994).

7. On medieval religious tradition, see James Billington, *The Icon and the Axe: an Interpretive History of Russian Culture* (London, 1966); Eve Levin, *Sex and Society in the World of the Orthodox Slavs, 900–1700* (Ithaca, NY, 1989); *The Domostroi: Rules for Russian Households in the Time of Ivan the Terrible*, trans. and ed. Christine Johnston Pouncy (Ithaca, NY, 1994); on popular entertainments: Russell Zguta, *Russian Minstrels: A History of the Skomorokhi* (Oxford, 1978); Catriona Kelly, "The Origins of the Russian Popular Theatre," in V. Borovsky and R. Leach, eds., *The Cambridge Companion to the Russian Theatre* (Cambridge, 1998). On class attitudes before 1700, Richard Hellie, *Slavery in Russia 1450–1725* (Chicago, 1982); in the eighteenth century, Marc Raeff, *The Origins of the Russian Intelligentsia: The Eighteenth-Century Russian Nobility* (New York, 1966).

8. The Introduction to Felix J. Oinas and Stephen Soudakoff, eds., *The Study of Russian Folklore* (The Hague, 1975), is an excellent short survey.

9. A useful English-language anthology of Russian nineteenth-century sources on

nationalism and political ideology is D. Offord and W. Leatherbarrow, *A Documentary History of Russian Thought, from the Enlightenment to Marxism* (Ann Arbor, MI, 1987).

10. On Russian populism, see Franco Venturi, *Roots of Revolution: A History of the Populist and Socialist Movements in Nineteenth-Century Russia*, trans. F. Haskell (London, 1960); Richard Wortman, *The Crisis of Russian Populism* (Cambridge, 1967); Derek Offord, *The Russian Revolutionary Movement in the 1880s* (Cambridge, 1986); Barbara Engel, *Mothers and Daughters: Women of the Intelligentsia in Nineteenth-Century Russia* (Cambridge, 1983). On populism's links with folklore, see the brief observations in Catriona Kelly: "Life at the Margins: Women, Culture and Narodnost' 1880–1920," in Liljestrom, Mantysaari, and Rosenholm, *Gender Restructuring*, pp. 139–53.

11. See Julia Vytkovskaya, "Russian Mythology" in Carolyne Larrington, ed., *The Feminist Companion to Mythology* (London, 1992). A Western source with similar attitudes is Hubbs, *Mother Russia*.

12. On adaptation of folklore during Stalin period, see Felix J. Oinas, *Essays in Russian Folklore and Mythology* (Columbus, OH, 1985), pp. 77–95; Frank J. Miller, *Folklore for Stalin: Russian Folklore and Pseudofolklore of the Stalin Era* (Armonk, NY, 1991).

13. On the sources and dissemination of early Russian popular fiction, see D. L. L. Howells, "The Origins of Frantsel' Ventsian and Parizh i Vena," *Oxford Slavonic Papers* vol. 19 (1986), pp. 29–45; on popular prints, Alla Sytova, ed., *The Lubok* (Leningrad, 1984). On turn-of-the-century culture, Richard Stites, *Russian Popular Culture: Entertainment and Society since 1900* (Cambridge, 1992); Jeffrey Brooks, *When Russia Learned to Read: Literacy and Popular Literature, 1861–1917* (Princeton, NJ, 1985).

14. Elizabeth Warner and Evgenii Kustovskii, *Russian Traditional Folksong* (Hull, 1990), contains examples of "photograph" for "gold ring" substitutions.

15. V. Ia. Briusov, "Rasskazy Mashi, s reki Mologi, pod gorodom Ustiuzhna" (1905), *Literaturnoe nasledstvo* vol. 85 (1976), p. 88.

16. On popular medical beliefs, see e.g. Rose Glickman, "The Peasant Woman as Healer," in B. E. Clements, B. A. Engel, and C. D. Worobec, eds., *Russia's Women: Accommodation, Resistance, Transformation* (Berkeley, CA, 1991), pp. 148–62. On the history of leisure activities, see Stites, *Russian Popular Culture;* James Riordan, *Sport in Soviet Society: The Development of Sport and Physical Education in Russia and the USSR* (Cambridge, 1977).

17. Dem'ian Bednyi, *Stikhotvoreniia i poemy* (Moscow and Leningrad, 1965), pp. 258–9.

18. Irina Odoevtseva, *Na beregakh Nevy* (Washington, 1967), p. 381. On performance of the *chastushka*, see Eduard Dune, *Notes of a Red Guard,* trans. and ed. Diane P. Koenker and S. A. Smith (Urbana and Chicago, 1993), p. 8.

19. See A. Shepievker, ed., *Smekh – vopreki vsemu: sto russkikh anekdotov* (n.p., 1982); L. Shturman and S. Tiktin, eds., *Sovetskii soiuz v zerkale politicheskogo iumora* (London, 1985); Iurii Borev, ed., *Fariseia: poslestalinskaia epokha v predaniiakh i anekdotakh* (Moscow 1992) (also includes urban myths).

20. See *Govorit Radio Erevan: izbrannye voprosy i otvety*, N. Olin, comp., 3rd edn (Munich, 1970).

21. For Chapayev anecdotes see Nicholas Rzhevsky, ed., *An Anthology of Russian Literature. Introduction to a Culture* (Armonk, NY, 1996), pp.509–10.

22. For other examples of "faction" by Pikul, see e.g. his novel about the court of Catherine II, *Favorit*, 2 vols. (Leningrad, 1984).

23. Reception sociology is a much under-studied area of popular culture. For brief

remarks on the preferences of turn-of-the-century theatre audiences, see Catriona Kelly, "Urban Popular Theatre and Entertainments, 1821–1917," in Borovsky and Leach, eds., *The Cambridge Companion to the Russian Theatre;* on cinema audiences, see Denise Youngblood, *Movies for the Masses: Soviet Popular Cinema in the Twenties* (Cambridge, 1993); on fiction audiences in the 1970s, see Klaus Mehnert, *The Russians and their Favorite Books* (Stanford, CA, 1983).

24. For examples: Anastasiia Verbitskaia, *Kliuchi schast'ia*, 2 vols. (St. Petersburg, 1993), vol. I; Valentin Pikul', *Favorit*, vol. I.

25. On Petrushka see Catriona Kelly, *Petrushka, The Russian Carnival Puppet Theatre* (Cambridge, 1990); on Bandit Churkin, Brooks, *When Russia Learned to Read.*

26. Iulian Semenov, *Semnadtsat' mgnovenii vesny* (Minsk, 1984).

27. See e.g. Vera Panova, *Sputniki* (Moscow, 1947); for sentimental 1940s girlie paintings, Matthew Cullerne Bown, ed., *Soviet Socialist Realist Painting 1930–1960s* (Oxford, 1992).

28. On one such work, *Intergirl*, see Anna Lawton, *Kinoglasnost': Soviet Cinema in Our Time* (Cambridge, 1992), pp. 211–13; Lynne Attwood, ed., *Red Women and the Silver Screen: Soviet Women and Cinema from the Beginning to the End of the Communist Era* (London, 1993), p. 118, pp. 200–01.

29. See Alan Bird, *A History of Russian Painting,* Oxford 1987, plate 16; Aleksandr Sidorov, "Il'ia Glazunov: a Career in Art," in Matthew Cullerne Bown and Brandon Taylor, eds., *Art of the Soviets: Painting, Sculpture and Architecture in a One-Party State, 1917–1992* (Manchester, 1993), pp. 188–95.

30. My information on Corroded Metals is from the documentary *Stars, Tsars, Swastikas,* shown on British television (Channel 4) on 21 April 1994. Vladimir Zhirinovskii, *Poslednii brosok na Iug* (Moscow, 1993), p. 117.

31. On Goncharov, see Faith Wigzell, "Dream and Fantasy in Goncharov's *Oblomov*," in Arnold McMillin, ed., *From Pushkin to Palisandria: Essays on the Russian Novel in Honour of Richard Freeborn* (Basingstoke, 1990), pp. 96–111; on Chekhov, Marina Warner, *From the Beast to the Blonde: On Fairy Tales and their Tellers* (London, 1995), p. 230.

II

Literature and the arts

8

Literature

Any national literature is to some significant extent a mirror held up to its people's collective countenance: its myths, aspirations, national triumphs and traumas, current ideologies, historical understanding, linguistic traditions. But it is also more than that – more than a reflection in the glass of what has come before and what is now, even as one glances into it, passing from view. It is, in a real sense, generative of new meaning, and thus capable of shaping that countenance in the future. For the society that takes its literary products seriously, the text of a novel or poem can be a kind of genetic code for predicting, not concrete outcomes or actual progeny, but something no less pregnant with future action: the forms of a culture's historical imagination. The variations seem limitless, and yet how is it we are able to determine any given work of literature is clearly identifiable as Russian? Why could Flaubert's Emma Bovary in some sense not be imagined by the great realist who created Anna Karenina? How is Dostoevsky's Marmeladov both alike, but more importantly, unlike Dickens's Micawber? What, in short, can be shown in a mirror that *speaks back*?

Few societies have been more dependent on their literature for overall meaning (social, psychological, political, historical, religious, erotic) than the Russia of the modern period (1800 to the present). For a variety of reasons we will touch upon in the pages to follow, Russians have turned repeatedly to their literature as the principal source of their national identity and cultural mythology. But this relationship to the written word is a two-edged sword. It gives Russian literature both a high seriousness that can be genuinely inspiring and at times an intrusive didacticism that can be annoying to a more pluralistic (or "secular") Western audience. Regardless of one's orientation as reader, however, Russian culture is unthinkable without this literature – and not only the great novels of Tolstoy and Dostoevsky out of which Westerners have for decades constructed their own versions of "Russianness." The purpose of the present chapter is to acquaint the non-specialist reader with the basic cultural contours necessary to read and understand this literature. In the first part, I will outline some of the formative influences and salient themes of modern Russian literature; in the second, I will provide a skeletal framework in terms of periods, genres, and major literary figures. Along the way, and where appropriate, I will also discuss how certain important Russian writers and cultural figures creatively engage aspects of contemporary Western thought. The goal here cannot be historical thoroughness or authoritative canon-formation, but rather a reasonably accurate readerly orientation – that is, an attitude toward the subject that takes its cultural values seriously and tries to understand its various verbal traces in their proper context.

Formative influences, salient themes

In recent times, culture has been compared to a kind of "supraconsciousness" hovering over the physical globe in a circumambient cloud. It manipulates on a massive scale the same communicative codes that every human being operates in his/her individual world. Building on discoveries in cell biology, organic chemistry, and brain science, the Russian theorist and literary scholar Yury Lotman has devised the term "semiosphere" to capture this notion of human communication writ large as cultural ecosystem: the place where intracranial brain function (i.e. the relationship between right and left hemispheres), meaning production, and the shapes and symbols we project onto (or extract from) the external world coalesce into our collective organism's psychic drive for growth and discovery. That this site is a metaphor, a product of language and therefore invisible like the atmosphere over the earth, does not make it any less "real" to those constructing meaning out of their interactions with others. In this regard, literature has traditionally been seen as a rich source of communication (i.e. new information) because, potentially, many different codes and "languages" (in the sense of stylistic registers, dialects, idiosyncratic speech patterns, etc.) can coexist and be artfully juxtaposed within its boundaries.

Modern Russian literature, as I have already intimated, has played a dynamic, even crucial role in the larger "ecosystem" of Russian culture.

To appreciate this role, let us propose another metaphor – an interior photograph, or what neurosurgeons call a CAT scan, of the Russian literary "brain." This figure of speech is, of course, inexact, in that it registers likeness more than difference (as all metaphors do); and it cannot do justice to subtle changes over time or to the historical specificity of certain phenomena. Still, as a means of isolating global psychic tendencies that become, as it were, imprinted on the larger social organism's memory, it is not without heuristic value. Exceptions to these tendencies exist, to be sure, some of them very significant, but the fact that these exceptions take the tendencies into account (i.e. they thwart them or undermine them but they do not *ignore* them) means that this psychic mapping is not invisible. Why these tendencies and not others have become salient in the Russian context is buried deep in the past, and is as much a question of cultural mythology (Russians' sacred legends about themselves and about their destiny as a people) as of history *per se*. The list could of course be expanded, but the following seem a good place to start:

(1) Religious sensibility (*dukhovnost'*)
(2) Maximalism
(3) Writer as secular saint
(4) Heterodox literary forms
(5) Belatedness
(6) Literature as social conscience
(7) Problem of personality (*lichnost'*)
(8) Space–time oppositions (East/West, old/new)
(9) Eros-cum-national myth

(1) *Religious sensibility*. Perhaps the first and arguably the most important formative influence/psychological trait to come to mind is Russian culture's pervasive spirituality (*dukhovnost'*) and, correlatively, the written word's traditionally sacred status. Russia (Kievan Rus') was Christianized under Prince Vladimir in the year 988, and from roughly that point until well into the seventeenth and eighteenth centuries, the entire notion of literature as a secular form of pleasure or edification was largely moot. There were saints' lives (*vitae*), sermons, chronicles, and even epics (e.g. *The Igor Tale*), but what is interesting from a modern vantage is that the category of "fiction" (i.e. a self-contained world wholly created through words that is understood by its reader to be artificial, hence "untrue") came late to Russian literature. Indeed, it can be argued that much of the attraction of the great works of Russian literature is due to this tendency of reader reception/perception: Russian "fictions" about

the world are more "real" than the real-life context into which they are read and absorbed. Russian writers have long operated under the conviction that they are writing, not one more book, but versions, each in its way sacred, of The Book (Bible). Thus, when some modern Russian writers have taken a militantly materialist, anti-spiritualist approach to reality, the fervidness and single-mindedness of their commitment to new belief systems often suggest a replay of various medieval models of behavior, replete with the latter's thematics of conversion. Likewise, Leo Tolstoy's anti-clericalism and his sharp criticism of Orthodox dogma and ritual are, significantly, not in the name of Voltairean enlightenment and urbane secularism but in that of a *new* religion, which came to be known as "Tolstoyanism."

One of the attributes of this religious sensibility that continues in the shadow life of some of the most influential Russian poems, novels, and dramas is the transposing of medieval forms of sacred writing (especially hagiography) to later secular works. Examples include Ivan Turgenev's "Living Relics," Nikolai Chernyshevsky's *What Is to Be Done?*, Fedor Dostoevsky's *Idiot* and *The Brothers Karamazov*, Sergei Stepnyak-Kravchinsky's *Andrei Kozhukhov*, Maksim Gorky's *Mother*. What the *vita* requires is that the personal become sanctified, monumentalized, subsumed within the impersonality of holiness, which means – if one considers how much the modern novel in the European and Anglo-American "bourgeois" traditions depends on individual, concrete examples of an open, *developing* biography and history (e.g. the *Bildungsroman*) – that in many instances the Russian novel will be acting against prevailing trends in Western practice. Saintly behavior can be actively submissive (the "meek" model of the martyred brothers Boris and Gleb) or defiantly subversive (the "holy warrior" model of Aleksandr Nevsky), but what it cannot be is consciously concerned with its own needs as a separate ego with a merely personal mission.

Another important attribute of the literary expression of Russian spirituality is the latter's emphasis on what might be termed, after the pioneering work of the mathematician-priest Pavel Florensky, liminality or "iconic space." The icon, with its physical materials (painting on wood), its other-worldly, two-dimensional figures, and its notion of divine authorship (the icon painter is merely the instrument of the higher power), is not perceived by the viewer as a representation of holiness, but as holiness itself: when the penitent individual kisses the icon, he or she as it were steps *through* its frame from the realm of the profane to the realm of the holy. There is no middle ground or expandable space *en route* to this miraculous transformation, just as the icon itself cannot be understood in Western terms of mediation (i.e. the three-dimensional figures that, increasingly, as a result of the Renaissance, stood in for humanity in representational paintings). One could argue that when a writer such as Dostoevsky describes heroes and situations – Myshkin before the portrait of Nastasya Filippovna and the Holbein painting of Christ; Alyosha Karamazov recalling his half-crazed mother in the context of an icon of the Virgin – that are constructed around the psychological dynamics of liminality, we are in the presence of this same iconic space: the space of religious conversion (or, in its demonic opposite, the space wherein all faith is lost).

Likewise, the reason the *iurodivyi* (holy fool, fool-in-Christ) is such a potent figure in Russian literature, from Aleksandr Pushkin's character who says to the tsar what no one else dares (*Boris Godunov*) to Yury Olesha's Ivan Babichev who tells campy versions of Gospel parables to the drunks and outcasts of Soviet society (*Envy*), is because he captures in one person, with great economy and expressive force, this principle of iconic liminality. He voluntarily humiliates himself, thus re-traversing Christ's path, in order to, as it were, rub society's nose in its own pride and exclusionary logic (ostracizing the "pure" from the "impure"). By plunging into the midst of "polite society" naked or with the carcass of a dog strapped to one's waist, the *iurodivyi* forces the issue of his own degradation and marginalization.[1] And the reader must make a choice: is this simply a fool or a fool whose antics reveal the workings of divine wisdom? Do I judge and join the ranks of the modern Pharisees or do I imitate Christ and celebrate the carnival logic of role-reversal, laughter, and folly?

(2) *Maximalism*. Russian spirituality has a powerful maximalist streak, a fact which should not seem surprising in light of the tragic character of Russian history. "There are," as the philosopher Nikolai Berdiaev once wrote in *The Russian Idea*, "two dominant myths which can become dynamic in the life of a people – the myth about origins and the myth about the end. For Russians it has been the second myth, the eschatological one, that has dominated."[2] Likewise, some of the best known works in modern Russian literature (Pushkin's *Bronze Horseman*, Nikolai Gogol's *Dead Souls*, Dostoevsky's *The Devils*, Gorky's *Mother*, Andrei Bely's *Petersburg*, Aleksandr Blok's *The Twelve*, Evgeny Zamyatin's *We*, Andrei Platonov's *Chevengur*, Mikhail Bulgakov's *The Master and Margarita*, Boris Pasternak's *Doctor Zhivago*, etc.) have possessed a "deep structure" of bib-

lical/apocalyptic or utopian myth. Meaning is sought in a dramatic, usually violent, "right-angled" resolution: either God the Author, standing outside/beyond, decides to put a flaming end (*ekpyrosis*) to his story (human history), or else mankind, realizing that it is the sole author (God is dead) and that perfectibility on earth is possible, devises its own ideal polis (a secular City of God) as a conclusion to history's plot.[3] In either case, whether meaning comes from without or from within, an equals sign is placed between "revelation" (the final truth) and "revolution" (violent social/political upheaval). Indeed, not only charismatic popular leaders (Stenka Razin, Emelyan Pugachev), whose rebellions were inevitably portrayed as apocalyptic scourges striking at the godless state with its "new" religion, but Peter the Great himself, perhaps the most famous of all tsars, was viewed among some segments of the populace (e.g. the Old Believers) as the Antichrist and among others (e.g. Pushkin) as an arch-revolutionary.

But it is not only historical conditions that have forced on Russians this maximalist mentality. One can argue that the very structure of their religious imagination has in a way guaranteed certain outcomes. For example, Russian holy men and religious thinkers have traditionally shown great impatience with any axiologically neutral or "middle ground" – from the Purgatory of the Catholic Church, where one can gradually (cf. the notion of "progress") atone for one's sins *en route* to Paradise, to the notion of "middle class values," where one can see to one's individual well-being even as those less fortunate are excluded or allowed to become invisible. Likewise, it has been traditional for Russians to evince a profound skepticism for the rhythms of everyday life (*byt*): it seems this quotidian space/time can only, with great difficulty, "mean." Furthermore, as Lotman and others have shown, Russians, and perhaps (Eastern?) Slavs in general, have felt that such compromising notions as "negotiation" and "agreement" (*dogovor*) are the province of the devil, whereas in the Western tradition of Roman law and the Catholic church such concepts were more or less unmarked: i.e. one could "arrange" one's position (or one's loved ones) in the other world by doing good deeds, making donations, etc. in this one. But as in Florensky's iconic space, where any believer can instantaneously step through the frame from the profane to the holy, this concept of agreement, or "giving with strings attached," has often proved anathema to the "all or nothing" Russian religious mind. It is by no means strange in this context, therefore, that Russian culture has produced a number of modern thinkers, most notably Vladimir Soloviev and Nikolai Fedorov, whose ambitious visions for the realized transfiguration of humanity are virtually unimaginable in the West. Soloviev, for instance, made the case for a theocratic marriage of Western and Eastern Christian churches, while Fedorov assayed nothing less than the actual biological (as in molecule by molecule!) resurrection of our ancestors. Moreover, these and other philosophers (including the already mentioned Florensky) exerted considerable influence on modern writers: their ideas surface in modified form in the works of Gorky, Fedor Sologub, Blok, Bely, Vladimir Mayakovsky, Bulgakov, Platonov, Nikolai Ognyov, Nikolai Zabolotsky, Pasternak, etc.[4]

(3) *Writer as secular saint.* Because Russian society was slow to adopt the worldly ways of the West and because the written word was carefully scrutinized and censored by church and state (its "sacred" status thereby implicitly recognized and controlled), the writer in general and the poet in particular became a secular saint and, very often, a martyr (or suffering "holy fool").[5] The Ur-text in this regard was Pushkin's 1826 poem "The Prophet" (*Prorok*), whose speaker has his formerly sinful tongue ripped out by a six-winged Seraphim (the source is Isaiah) and whose words are henceforth meant to "burn the hearts of people" with their message. The list of "martyred" writers is very long and the role of "suffering for the faith" must be acknowledged as one of the truly defining traits of the Russian literary imagination: Vasily Trediakovsky, Aleksandr Radishchev, Pushkin, Mikhail Lermontov, Gogol, Chernyshevsky, Dostoevsky, Blok, Velimir Khlebnikov, Nikolai Kliuev, Evgeny Zamyatin, Isaak Babel, Osip Mandelstam, Anna Akhmatova, Marina Tsvetaeva, Bulgakov, Pasternak, Aleksandr Solzhenitsyn, Varlam Shalamov, Andrei Sinyavsky, Joseph Brodsky. Even famous suicides – Aleksandr Radishchev, Sergei Esenin, Mayakovsky, Tsvetaeva – did not "simply" kill themselves but were written into this larger martyrology (i.e. they were "killed" by society/the state). The Russian writer became a lightning rod (or scourge) in a society that was anything but "civil" and in a faceless, sprawling bureaucratic state (tsarist, then Soviet) that had little respect for individual rights and the rule of law.

How did this martyrology work, what were its psychic mechanisms? In the poet Vladislav Khodasevich's phrase (borrowed again from Pushkin), Russian society and its writers entered into a kind of fatal contract, or "bloody repast" (*krovavaia pishcha*). It was a contract with little of the spirit of compromise about it. The poet/martyr was persecuted and eventually killed (like Christ) because of his service to a higher ideal (Russian culture, the Russian poetic word), while society played the role of Pontius Pilate or the Roman soldiers at the foot of the cross. The persecutors could not, according to this logic, act otherwise. By bringing the sainted figure to his death they were fulfilling a larger dispensation: giving the Christ-figure the chance *to redeem them* through his sacrifice. Even those who survived persecution (Akhmatova, Pasternak) or those who emerged alive from the hell of the camps (Solzhenitsyn, Shalamov) did so with the martyr's aureole intact and the myth of their semi-religious witness confirmed. Hence one of the more fascinating questions of Russian literary studies is how poets have seemed to fashion their own "fated" ends (Pushkin's is again the archetypal example) out of this contract with their wayward, needful flock. Rather than meekly accepting God's will, as in the famous *vita* of the murdered brothers (and first "passion sufferers") Boris and Gleb, the Russian poet has tended to model his life on that of the indomitable and "plain-speaking" Archpriest Avvakum, who was burned alive with his sectarian followers in 1682 for not accepting the official faith of the church and state.

(4) *Heterodox literary forms*. Russian writers have developed a reputation in the West for their eccentric understanding of literary form. Henry James, for example, in a famous phrase that captured well his and other contemporaries' puzzlement at the extravagant shape of Russian novels, called the latter (he was discussing Tolstoy's *War and Peace*), "loose baggy monsters." However, the issue goes deeper than James and his tradition could have imagined. From at least the time of Gavrila Derzhavin, Nikolai Karamzin, and Pushkin (late eighteenth, early nineteenth centuries) right up until the recent work of Solzhenitsyn and Sinyavsky, Russian literature has produced major exemplars that both take into account Western genre systems *and* boldly use those same systems against themselves in order to create something distinctly Russian. Here we must keep in mind two factors: (a) the Russians' need not merely to copy/imitate Western forms but to make something their own, and (b) the fact that Western trends (schools of thought, current "-isms," etc.) were not, beginning with the modern period, imported and assimilated in strict chronological sequence, but often mixed together in a heady, asynchronous brew (see no. 5 below).

Thus, Russian writers were intensely aware of the fact of their belatedness and of their need to outstrip (or remake in their own image) existing models in order to arrive as equals at the "feast" of European culture. In most cases their frustration of genre expectations could not be called naive. The list of great works of Russian literature that are also generic "misfits" is astonishing, in some sense a logical extension of that same maximalism ("doing the impossible" and "undoing the expected") observable in the national identity, with its spiritual strivings: Derzhavin's jocular odes ("Felitsa"), Karamzin's belletristically shaped history (*History of the Russian State*), Pushkin's novel-in-verse (*Eugene Onegin*), Gogol's novel-*poema* (epic poem) (*Dead Souls*), Chernyshevky's anti-novelistic novel (*What Is to Be Done?*), Dostoevsky's novel-memoir (*Notes from the Dead House*), Tolstoy's monstrous historical novel (*War and Peace*), Pasternak's novel-plus-poetic-cycle (*Doctor Zhivago*), Solzhenitsyn's "experiment in literary investigation" (*The Gulag Archipelago*). Also adding to this hybridization is the fact that several of Russia's most celebrated creative writers have either tried their hands at professional historiography (Karamzin, Pushkin) or openly competed with academic historians in their attempts (neither wholly fictional nor non-fictional) to reconstruct the past (Tolstoy).

(5) *Belatedness*. Russian writers, thinkers, and cultural figures have long grappled with their country's belated status *vis-à-vis* the West. Due to a variety of factors, no doubt the most important being the Mongol invasion and occupation of the Russian lands from the thirteenth through the fifteenth centuries, Russia did not benefit directly from the two most seminal movements of modern humanistic thought: the Renaissance and the Reformation. Over and over again in later centuries Russians were faced with the dilemma of how to "catch up" with Europe. Some saw Russia as hopelessly backward and doomed to outsidership (Petr Chaadaev), others saw their country's anomalous position as an opportunity to avoid Europe's mistakes (Aleksandr Herzen), and still others turned this very lack into nothing less than a salvational mission, a scenario in which Russia "saved" Europe from barbarism in order that Europe could now learn from this supreme gesture of Christian love and sacrifice (Dostoevsky). Whatever the case, it is clear that Russian writers could not ignore this time-lag: it had to be dealt with and in some way "overcome." Virtually all the major movements in Russian thought and culture of the nineteenth century, beginning with the debates between the Slavophiles and Westernizers (late 1830s–1840s), addressed this problem of belatedness, placing either a plus or a minus sign over the "other" values and institutions that had been forcibly foregone or those that were "ours" and indisputably native. When Western movements,

such as classicism, romanticism, realism, symbolism, did come to Russia, it was often with the sense that there was something profoundly artificial about their application to the Russian context (an autocratic/ bureaucratic state with a tiny oppositional intelligentsia surrounded by a huge and illiterate peasant mass). One of the problems of belatedness was that Russians often felt they were "playing" at being Westerners and that this was sinful: e.g., the boyars whom Peter tried to force to wear Western dress thwarted the emperor by wearing hair-shirts underneath the new fashions.

(6) *Literature as social conscience*. As Nadezhda Mandelstam once wrote about the role of poetry in Russian culture, "People can be killed for poetry here [in Russia] – a sign of unparalleled respect – because they are still capable of living by it."[6] She was of course speaking not only about poetry (and literature) in general, but also about the work of her husband, Osip Mandelstam, one of the great poets of the twentieth century, who died in a Stalinist labor camp because his writing was judged to be a crime against the state (and more crucially an affront to its leader). The point is that, ironically, the state has shown – until very recently – "unparalleled respect" through its relentless persecutions of its writers because its attempts to silence them has only further emphasized the roar of independent protest in their written words. And because the state has not only not protected the individual, but made a mockery of any notion of basic human rights, it has traditionally been literature's job to serve as social conscience: advocate for the downtrodden (peasant, "little man" *chinovnik*/bureaucrat, factory worker, women and children) and critic of the despotic tsarist regime, with its instruments of power (censorship, secret police, court system, labor camps). It is this tendency to give voice to concerns, however partially muffled by censorship and "Aesopian" encodings and circumlocutions, that were incapable of being uttered through other social institutions that has given Russian literature its strong didacticism and sense of moral rectitude. It is arguable that this same urge to use "literature" (broadly defined) in the service of social change has always been present in Russian culture, but its rise in modern times is usually associated with the name of the great *raznochinets* critic Vissarion Belinsky and his literary journalism of the 1830s and 1840s. The questioning titles of works by various leading practitioners of the "Belinskian line" speak forcefully of this notion of literature as conscientious opposition to the *status quo*: Aleksandr Herzen's novel *Who Is to Blame?* (1847), Nikolai Dobroliubov's essays

"What Is Oblomovism?" (1859) and "When Will the Real Day Come?" (1860), Nikolai Chernyshevky's novel *What Is to Be Done?* (1863).

(7) *Problem of personality (lichnost')*. Closely related to Russian literature's function as social conscience (no. 6) is the problem of *lichnost'* (personality, personhood). If the tradition of Belinsky and the civic critics relentlessly exposed the negative sides of Russian existence (what the state had denied its citizens in terms of basic dignity and self-respect), then the concern on the part of many other writers was to find a *positive content* – expressed in the search for a "positive hero" (*polozhitel'nyi geroi*) – for *lichnost'*.7 Russian literature of the nineteenth and twentieth centuries is heavily populated by personality "types": the "superfluous man" (*lishnii chelovek*) who is gifted and often "noble" (in both senses) but has no historically viable arena for action and thus repeatedly suffers a loss of will (Aleksandr Griboedov's Chatsky, Turgenev's Rudin, Ivan Goncharov's Oblomov); the "new man" of the 1860s (and then of the Soviet period), who is precise, unsentimental, scientific, materialist, but who inevitably must wait for society to "catch up" to him (Turgenev's Bazarov, Chernyshevsky's Rakhmetov, Gorky's Pavel Vlasov); and the "strong woman" who is often made to represent Russia's hidden potential and who possesses the courage and resolute idealism that the weaker male characters lack (Pushkin's Tatiana Larina, Goncharov's Olga Ilyinskaya, Fedor Gladkov's Dasha Chumalova, Bulgakov's Margarita). Again, in a way that suggests a religious/"maximalist" as opposed to secular/"skeptical" approach to the written word, the Russian reading public has often made a direct, prescriptive link between the portrayal of charismatic activity in fiction and the rules for behavior in phenomenal reality outside the text. As is the case with Florensky's iconic space, the word does not stand in, metaphorically, for the person, but *is* the person, his most real, sacred trace.

(8) *Space–time oppositions (East/West, old/new)*. From the time of its earliest formation Russia has faced the problem of how to view itself in the "history of nations" (e.g. which version of Christianity, Eastern or Western, should it choose for itself?). Many of the turning points in its history and many (if not most) of its cultural monuments have centered on the issue of whether this increasingly vast and diverse country and its people are "Western," "Eastern," or some significant, new combination of the two. But what has not been, until recently, sufficiently commented upon is how another opposition, the temporal old/new, is simultaneously embedded in the spatial East/West. In other words,

these oppositions, which are necessary for constructing meaning, can in certain highly charged situations be viewed as extensions of each other. Their respective values (plus/minus, good/bad, we/they) can change depending on the circumstances, but that they are implicated in each other in the Russian historical imagination seems by now beyond doubt.

To mention a few prominent examples: Hilarion, in his early "Sermon on Law and Grace" (c. 1037–50), likens the "new" faith of the Russians to the enfranchised bride Sarah (hence to New Testament grace) but the "old" faith of Byzantium to the handmaiden Hagar (hence to Old Testament law). Several centuries later, the Archpriest Avvakum would reverse these values during the Great Schism (raskol) of the 1660s – i.e., the "new" Nikonian reforms imposed by the church/state were now perceived as the province of the Antichrist and a betrayal of the Old Belief. Likewise, Moscow's role as Third (and last) Rome, with its tsar as basileus (the emperor who was simultaneously spiritual and secular leader of the Christian realm), became clear when Constantinople (the "Second Rome") fell to the Ottoman Turks in 1453. And Peter the Great's reforms, including his spelling with a foreign alphabet, his passion for Western architecture, and his new calendar, galvanized the Old Believer sectarians precisely because these innovations conflated and made interchangeable the unholy categories of new/Western: they demonstrated that this tsar could not be the true basileus and so had to be an impostor, which is to say, the Antichrist. In recent centuries these binaries have become especially marked in Russia's myth-saturated geography: the "old," more native city of Moscow versus the "new," more Western city of St. Petersburg. Generally speaking, Russian cultural and political figures, and writers a fortiori, tended to face the problematic present by either looking to a positive future ideal (a modern urban or technological utopia emerging out of new/Western ideas) or to a positive past ideal (an archaic village utopia – the peasant mir/obshchina – emerging out of old/native ideas).

(9) Eros-cum-national myth. The pagan roots of Russian/Slavic culture were not forgotten with the coming of Christianity. Indeed, as the scholar Boris Uspensky has indicated, those roots were often "remembered" through inversion in the forms of the adopting mythology: the pre-Christian gods became the devils of the Russian Christian world (e.g. Volos/Veles → volosatik or "wood goblin"). In this respect, one of the inevitable developments in the mythologization of Russian time and space by its writers and thinkers is that the pagan concept of "Mother Earth" (mat' syra zemlia) and the Christian concept of "Holy Russia"

(*Sviataia Rus'* – the term was first used in the sixteenth century by Prince Andrei Kurbsky in his correspondence with Ivan IV) were telescoped – again, made extensions of each other. As a result, perhaps the greatest of all modern Russian literary plots, expressed in a stunning variety of works over the past two centuries, involves the rescuing/redeeming of a heroine, who represents the country's vast potential, by a Christ-like paladin. The logic of the fairy tale and the logic of the Christian hierogamy (the marriage of the Lamb and the Bride in Revelation) join hands.

This indicates that the national Russian myth has, at its core, become profoundly eroticized and at the same time strangely sublimated/ abstracted: personal love cannot have meaning outside this higher calling. Pushkin's Tatiana, Dostoevsky's Nastasya Filippovna, Tolstoy's Anna Karenina, Soloviev's Sophia, Blok's Beautiful Lady/Stranger, Bulgakov's Margarita, Pasternak's Lara – all these heroines, and more, have their fates linked with Russian history (broadly speaking), primarily in its tragic incarnation. Many of them die for their love. In a sense their lives and loves cannot have a happy ending until the right "Prince Charming" appears in a historical context that is ready for him – and this, given the belatedness of Russian culture, is almost never. Even the great women poets, Tsvetaeva and Akhmatova, participate as suffering wives, mothers, and lovers in the tragedy that is Russian historical time: Tsvetaeva's roles as Amazonian freedom fighter (it is *she* who must rescue the swain) and as archetypal heroine trapped in male role-playing (Ophelia, Gertrude, Phaedra); Akhmatova's realized metaphor of Suffering Mother in *Requiem* (her first husband the poet Nikolai Gumilev executed by firing squad, her close friend Mandelstam dead in a Stalinist camp, her own son Lev also serving time in prison). In sum, the erotic theme in Russian literature has traditionally been played for infinitely more than the stakes of bourgeois love and family happiness. If the heroine is portrayed as some combination of heavenly mother and earth-bound demiurge – e.g. the Stranger is both streetwalker and other-worldly enchantress, Margarita is both the spirit of hope/forgiveness and a witch who flies naked, Lara is both a Mary Magdalene figure and an image of Russia waiting to be reborn – then the hero is also just as likely to appear as Christ-like paradox: the leader of marauding Red Guard disciples as androgynous apparition (*The Twelve*), the poet-doctor Zhivago as weak-willed Red Cross Knight, the Master as great artist who is also hopelessly paranoid and on the verge of insanity.

With some notable exceptions (e.g. Pushkin), therefore, Russian literature of the modern period is plagued with its own special brand of cultivated repression or "Victorianism." Sex for its own sake, as a source of bodily pleasure, or sex merely for the sake of procreation, to produce children, can be equally "insulting" to the quixotic Russian truth-seeker. By the same token, the number of influential writers and thinkers (Soloviev, Fedorov, Blok, Bely, Mayakovsky, etc.) who felt the act of copulation to be essentially humiliating and/or the prospect of biological children frightening is striking. The rare exception of someone such as the philosopher Vasily Rozanov, whose championing of sex and family life in their everyday, non-hieratic guises was scandalous for its time, only proves the general rule. The fear was not so much sin, as in the Catholic and Protestant West, but cosmic indifference, meaninglessness. Perhaps the strongest condemnation of the "demonic" source of erotic pleasure in all Russian literature belongs to Tolstoy in his novella "Kreutzer Sonata," who in typical maximalist fashion would prefer celibacy, and hence the end of the human race itself, to "sex without meaning."

Genres, periods, major figures

For the purposes of this chapter, Russian literature can be broken down into the three standard genre categories, poetry, prose, and drama. Each of these in turn contains numerous formal variations/sub-genres: *poetry* – ode, ballad, elegy, lyric, sonnet, narrative poem (*poema*); *prose* – novel, tale (*povest'*), short story, travel account; *drama* – comedy, tragedy. (In general, little will be said about Russian theatre and drama, which is being covered elsewhere in this volume.) An important detail of Russian literary history not always understood or appreciated in the more prose-oriented West is the role poetry has played in Russia as bellwether genre. In the so-called "Golden" and "Silver Ages" of Russian literature, the first commencing in the early nineteenth century and the second in the early twentieth, it was poetry and poets who led the way. Indeed, in terms of national mythology, Pushkin has been considered the primary source of the culture's "gold reserve" and of its "light" (thus *Golden* Age) ever since Vladimir Odoevsky proclaimed, on the day the poet died as a result of wounds suffered in a duel (29 January 1837), "The sun of our poetry has set." Likewise, the mysterious death in 1921 of the greatest poet of the Silver Age, the symbolist Aleksandr Blok, was perceived by the post-revolutionary reading public on the verge of new Soviet time as the passing of an epoch and a kind of "lunar eclipse."

It is logical that Russian literature has made its way to the West primarily through the most accessible, most translatable genres – the story, the play, but above all the novel. Still, for the Russian literary imagination it is poetry that has been the prime mover; the great novels tended to follow upon the innovations, the doors opened and passed through, of poetry. Many educated Russians would consider their country's supreme writers to be its poets: Pushkin, Evgeny Baratynsky, Lermontov, Fedor Tiutchev, Nikolai Nekrasov, Afanasy Fet in the nineteenth century; Blok, Mayakovsky, Khlebnikov, Pasternak, Akhmatova, Mandelstam, Tsvetaeva, and Brodsky in the twentieth. Both the inherent possibilities in the language (e.g. its inflected endings generate endless rhyming combinations) and the tragic core of the outer historical reality (its belatedness, its failed rebellions, its dreary present, its compulsion to "leap over" the past) conspired to make the Russian poet the master of vertical/metaphorical time, the myth-weaver *par excellence*.

At this point, it may be helpful to see Russian literature in its general periodization, as adapted from a recent history (*Cambridge History of Russian Literature* [2nd edn. 1992]):

(1) Old Russian literature (988–1730)
(2) Neoclassicism/Enlightenment (1730–90)
(3) Sentimentalism/preromanticism (1790–1820)
(4) Romanticism (1820–40)
(5) Naturalism and its aftermath (1840–55)
(6) Age of realism (1855–80)
(7) Transition from realism to modernism (1880–95)
(8) Modernism (1895–1925)
(9) Socialist realism (1925–53)
(10) Twilight of Soviet era (1953–87)
(11) *Glasnost'* and post-*glasnost'* (1987–   )

No schematization can contain every important figure within its temporal boundaries and regnant trends. To cite only two of the more glaring problems, Pushkin falls directly in the period of romanticism, but in many ways is *not* a romantic, just as Gogol is both more and less than the "naturalist" Belinsky hailed him to be. Nevertheless, this schematization is reasonably accurate for the majority of Russian writers, and we will be referring back to it in the discussion to follow.

Old Russian literature is important for modern Russian writers primarily as a spiritual frame of reference and shared heritage. Chronicles, hagiography, translated and original liturgical texts (prayers, hymns, sermons), military tales/epics, travel accounts – all these, to be sure, left an indelible mark on Russian culture. However, the texts of Old Russian literature, inasmuch as the vast majority of them were not considered by their readers as "belletristic" or "fictional," could not provide the actual forms, or genres, for a modern, secular literature. Hence their shadow existence as "deep structures" or "master plots" for their secular counterparts: e.g. the *vita* that can be seen through the novelistic structure of Dostoevsky's *The Brothers Karamazov* or Chernyshevsky's *What Is to Be Done?* Only in the eighteenth century, with the advent of Russian neoclassicism and the importation of Enlightenment values, did the notion of Western genre systems and poetics (e.g. Nicolas Boileau's *L'Art poetique*) become a central concern of educated Russian writers and readers. Vasily Trediakovsky (1703–69) and Aleksandr Sumarokov (1718–77) developed rules for an elaborate system of literary genres, Trediakovsky and Mikhail Lomonosov (1711–65) devised a new system of syllabo-tonic versification, and Lomonosov adapted a variant of the classical system of three styles (high, middle, low) to the Russian literary language.

Two figures stand out as the principal precursors who made possible the phenomenon of Aleksandr Pushkin and the Golden Age of Russian poetry: Gavrila Derzhavin (1743–1816) and Nikolai Karamzin (1776–1826). Derzhavin, the soldier, statesman, and advisor to Catherine, became the greatest poet of his age at a time when the writing of verse was an avocation rather than a profession. He made the neoclassical genres, above all the ode, strangely and charmingly Russian. His mature language was not imitative (the curse of Russian neoclassicism) but was full of colors and sounds, unorthodox diction and mixed "high" and "low" styles (Old Church Slavic archaisms together with striking realistic details), possessed of a kind of shaggy splendor and love of the phenomenal world. In his famous "Felitsa" ode (1782) he found a way of praising Catherine while slyly making fun of her wayward courtiers, and in his last ("Anacreontic") period his verse becomes a brilliant kaleidoscope of tables bursting with food and wine, of charming peasant girls in their native dress, and of the graying, jovial, slightly satyr-like master who knows such moments are few and precious.

Derzhavin's antipode in every way is Karamzin: urbane and stylized, where Derzhavin is blustery and magniloquent; European and especially "Gallic" where Derzhavin is archaic and "Russian"; "sentimental" in the spirit of Sterne and Rousseau where Derzhavin's orientation is primarily neoclassical (with an admixture of "baroque" exuberance). Nevertheless, Karamzin's major works, more particularly *Letters of a Russian Traveler*

(1797, first complete edn. 1801), the cult-status story "Poor Liza" (1792), and above all the monumental *History of the Russian State* (1818–26), succeeded on an unprecedented level in both reforming the literary language and cultivating a new more aware, more cosmopolitan Russian reader (particularly among women). If Derzhavin reminded his readership that no Russian literature worthy of the name could manage without its own archaic, Old Church Slavic roots, then Karamzin reminded his of the opposite: Russians would not be Europeans until they had a historical consciousness of themselves in this larger context. It seems in retrospect appropriate, if not "fated," that Derzhavin and Karamzin represent the *maîtres* of the two language groups – the archaist Colloquy of Lovers of the Russian Word and the Gallorussian Arzamas – out of whose witty polemics the young Pushkin would be born. Likewise it seems fitting that the aging Derzhavin was present at the schoolboy Pushkin's first public reading at Tsarskoe Selo, thereby, in Lotman's phrase, "knighting" him into the ranks of poets, and that in the second half of his career Pushkin would try to duplicate on his own terms, with his investigation into the Pugachev rebellion, Karamzin's "deed of an honorable man" (*podvig chestnogo cheloveka*) – the writing of an independent, factually accurate and impeccably researched history in the shadow of the tsar.

Aleksandr Pushkin (1799–1837) stands at the center of nineteenth- and twentieth-century Russian poetic culture. While his early work resonates with that of the preromantics Vasily Zhukovsky (1783–1852) and Konstantin Batiushkov (1787–1855), especially the latter's Russian adaptation of Anacreontic themes from *The Greek Anthology*, his mature work sets an unparalleled agenda for all Russian writers, and above all poets, coming after. It engages prominent foreign and domestic precursors (Derzhavin, Karamzin, Byron, Shakespeare, Scott) as confident equal, defines issues of history and national destiny (Time of Troubles, legacy of Peter, Pugachev Rebellion) without taking sides, provides a gallery of character types for later writers (the strong woman [Tatiana in *Eugene Onegin*], the "superfluous man" [Onegin], the Byronic anti-hero [Aleko in *The Gypsies*, Sylvio in "The Shot"], the "Napoleonic" striver [Germann in "The Queen of Spades"], the "little man" [Samson Vyrin in "The Stationmaster," Evgeny in *The Bronze Horseman*]), and expands the boundaries of genre (lyric poem/elegy, verse narrative, novel-in-verse, blank verse drama, prose fiction, historiography) in an intoxicating variety that earned him the name "Russian Proteus." No less important,

the event-filled story of Pushkin's life – mythical beginnings as precocious schoolboy, exile because of the "freedom-loving" nature of his
verse, secret affairs of the heart, friendship with Decembrists, troubled
relationship to the tsar Nicholas, fatal duel protecting his wife's honor –
is central to his overall significance because, in Khodasevich's astute
formulation, his was "the first Russian biography in which life is organically and consciously merged with art . . . [Pushkin] was the first to live
his life as a poet, and only as a poet, and *for that reason perished*" (my emphasis).[8] In short, Pushkin's was the quintessential poet's life, a fact which
Lermontov, Blok, Mandelstam, Akhmatova, Tsvetaeva, and Pasternak
knew better than anybody.

Thus Pushkin is the magic fulcrum or, better, mythopoetic "sling-
shot" of the early modern period in Russian literature. By being the
perfect combination of old/new and East/West (eighteenth-century
French Enlightenment values, nineteenth-century romanticism,
Russian historical and folk consciousness, the first glimmerings of
realism), he catapulted those coming after into an intense competition
to, artistically speaking, overtake the West. He made Russian writers
aware that their culture had come of age. Through the "Pushkin Pleiad"
– contemporary poets such as Anton Delvig (1798–1831), Evgeny
Baratynsky (1800–44), and Petr Vyazemsky (1792–1878) who shared his
"aristocratic party" leanings – Pushkin gave nineteenth-century Russian
poetry one of its defining (if not always popular) attributes: a primarily
aesthetic/private/meditative character as opposed to one that was ideological or socially activist. (This has been called the Fet as opposed to
Nekrasov line.) Through his association with Delvig's journal *Northern
Flowers* and through his own journal *The Contemporary*, Pushkin came to
personify the new class of independent professional writers, those who
had to support themselves by their own writing and publishing ventures
without collaborating, as did Pushkin's chief opponent and foil Faddei
Bulgarin, with the state. And finally, through his association with and
support of younger writers and publicists, especially Gogol and Belinsky,
at a time when his own work had fallen off in popularity, Pushkin forged
a living link with the next generation.

Mikhail Lermontov (1814–41), Nikolai Gogol (1809–52), and Vissarion
Belinsky (1811–48) represent three powerful strands in immediate post-
Pushkin literary culture: high romanticism in poetry and prose,
"romantic realism" (Donald Fanger's term in *Dostoevsky and Romantic*

Realism) in prose, and naturalism as critically inspired method or school of writing, respectively. (As an aside, the non-specialist reader should be aware that the great metaphysically inclined romantic poet and Pushkin contemporary Fedor Tiutchev [1803–73] is a rather solitary figure and, at least until his rediscovery by the symbolists in the next century, one of the nineteenth-century tradition's "roads not taken.") In some ways, Lermontov is a natural outgrowth of the Pushkin phenomenon: a career publicly inaugurated by a poem (the 1837 "The Death of A Poet") that excoriated society and the court for Pushkin's demise and that eventuated in the young poet's exile; a precocious, meteoric poetic talent that also gravitated toward prose and dramatic genres; and a "fated" life that projected, with eerie exactitude, its own death in a duel. But here the typological similarities must stop, for at base Lermontov is quite unlike his great predecessor. There is both a youthful seamlessness to Lermontov's romantic donning of masks and a "pure" psychologism that are alien to the more code-conscious "eighteenth century" Pushkin. And while Lermontov is certainly not Byron (cf. the poem "No, I'm not Byron, I'm another"), he represents in rather distilled form what a Russian Byron (i.e. the brooding, tortured, socially cynical, recklessly talented personality) might have been like. With Pushkin one always feels, at least from the 1824 *Gypsies* onward, that the author invokes the Byronic type with the strong whiff of parody and self-deflation. With Lermontov, however, the mask becomes the man, so that the "human" is not allowed to wink mockingly at its role-playing. Even "demonic" sarcasm and social satire are relentlessly "romantic," the reverse side of, and direct reaction to, a former "angelic" faith. In a way, Lermontov seems not to have had the inclination (or the time?) to develop beyond the early "titanic" Byron of, say, *Manfred* to the later, more playful Byron of *Beppo* and *Don Juan*. Nonetheless, he has earned a place of honor on the Russian Parnassus as haunting nature worshiper and landscape painter (he was also an accomplished graphic artist, especially of the Caucasus), eternal youth (his literature's "rebel without a cause" who died at twenty-seven), and lonely, wandering soul (see *The Demon* [1829–39]). Without question his greatest mask is Pechorin in *A Hero of Our Time* (1840), the "fatalist" who is so adept at trapping others in their melodramatic roles because he is more ruthless, more willing to play out the deadly consequences of his society's masquerades, to the bitter end.

Gogol is Russian literature's most enigmatic figure. An utterly brilliant stylist, he used his native ties with Ukrainian folklore and a dark Christianity laced with pagan elements to create a world that was, by turns, comic and haunting. Central to Gogol's "creative path" (*tvorcheskii put'*) was the problematic fact that, boundlessly ambitious, secretive, and peripatetic, he both accepted (with Belinsky's help) Pushkin's mantle as the leader of Russian literature and at the same time became innerly tormented at his own charlatanism (the theme of the impostor) and lack of durable inner substance. Himself a comic actor of genius, Gogol needed only to be given an external situation (he was notorious for having his plots suggested to him by others, beginning with Pushkin) in order to endow it with bizarre, manic life. He has no essence outside his linguistic exuberance, with its madcap mimicking and embellishing (e.g. the endlessly unpacking "Homeric similes" that take on a life of their own). Even in his greatest works, "The Overcoat" (1842), *The Inspector General* (1836), the first part of *Dead Souls* (1842), Gogol's characters have no inner world, but are constructed totally out of external details: the melon rinds that drop on Akaky's hat displaying his obliviousness to his surroundings, the carefully inventoried but utterly arbitrary paper items that mysteriously form the "content" of Chichikov's traveling box. As opposed to the "brightness" of Pushkin's "life of the poet," Gogol's martyrdom involves modern Russian literature's first great wrestling match with the devil: a country that is a shimmering potentiality of space and time without substance (Gogol's famous patches of purple prose, such as Chichikov's troika ride); an "epic novel" (*Dead Souls*) based on Dantesque verticality that can never manage to show its readers the way up and out of Russia's hell; a writer who burns his life's work, drives himself mad with religious mania, and dies in a paroxysm of self-imposed starvation. His last work, *Selected Passages from Correspondence with Friends* (1847), which is probably more famous for Belinsky's response on behalf of an exasperated intelligentsia than for its own reactionary message, shows how sadly banal and predictable is the writer's "substance" once the envelope of his verbal panache is stripped away. Still, Gogol's "ornamental" prose and "laughter through tears" will be crucial for other great nineteenth- and twentieth-century stylists, including Dostoevsky (who is reputed to have said "we all came out of Gogol's overcoat"), Nikolai Leskov, Bely, Bulgakov, and Sinyavsky.

One of the inevitable byproducts of the "Gogol paradox" (linguistic genius searching for ethical substance) is that it could, in powerful hands that did possess their own substance, be made to say different things to different audiences. And Vissarion Belinsky was nothing if not *substantial*, the moral content and conscience of Russian literature – single-handedly responsible not only for discovering some of the greatest nineteenth-century writers but also for explaining to them, both subtly and not so subtly, what their works *should* be saying. Belinsky combined various roles – *intelligent* (a well-educated, politically radical activist), *raznochinets* (of non-noble or non-gentry origin), *zapadnik* (Westernizer) – to become Russia's first professional critic. As Richard Peace explains, "Belinsky was the founder of a canon. He decided what Russian literature *was*, and his instinct for the writers of importance was almost unerring. Pushkin, Gogol, Lermontov, Turgenev, Goncharov, Dostoevsky built the high road of Russian literature, and Belinsky was its 'civic engineer.'"[9] Belinsky's social message, passion for rational system (e.g. his "Hegelian" phases), and martyr's crown (he died young from tuberculosis, having worked himself into the grave) would be picked up by the "men of the 1860s" (the radical critics Chernyshevsky, Dmitry Pisarev, Dobroliubov) and then worked into official dogma by the architects of socialist realism during the Soviet era. But in his lifetime Belinsky's role was, among other things, to tell the Russian audience what Gogol really meant (e.g. the writer is a "realist") as he fixed on the "warts" of Russian life. Belinsky coined the term "Natural School" – an approach that exposed with unvarnished, "naturalistic" details the daily plight of the urban poor – so that Gogol's fiction might be given a name and a method. And, to be sure, writers such as Dmitry Grigorovich (1822–99), Vladimir Dahl (1801–72), and the young Nikolai Nekrasov (1821–78) and young Dostoevsky took Belinsky's lead and expanded substantially the boundaries of acceptable subject matter within this school. They even developed their own sub-genre, the Balzac-inspired "physiological sketch." However, just as the motive force behind Gogol's satiric strafing missions was not (or not only) "realism" (as in exposé, social criticism), so too would it be impossible to contain the pre-exile Dostoevsky of *Poor Folk* (1846) and *The Double* (1846) within Belinsky's "naturalist" agenda. Dostoevsky's polemic with Gogol over the inner psychological dignity of the little man (Akaky Akakievich of "The Overcoat" versus Makar Devushkin of *Poor Folk*) and his investigation of the psychically aberrant as opposed to environmentally determined factors leading to madness (Golyadkin's Hoffmannesque bifurcation in *The Double*) already point to the themes of the mature writer rather than to Belinskian social commentary of the 1840s.

The Age of Realism in Russian literature is associated with the great "fat" novels that appeared, roughly speaking, from 1855, or the end of Nicholas I's reign (ruled 1825–55), until 1880, or Tolstoy's "conversion." (Tolstoy's conversion and rejection of the self that authored *War and Peace* and *Anna Karenina* is usually taken as a convenient *terminus ad quem* because it was also followed quickly by the deaths of Dostoevsky [1881], Aleksei Pisemsky [1881], and Turgenev [1883].) Among the novelists whose most important works appeared during this period are Ivan Goncharov (1812–91), Ivan Turgenev (1818–83), Aleksei Pisemsky (1821–81), Fedor Dostoevsky (1821–81), Mikhail Saltykov-Shchedrin (1826–89), Leo Tolstoy (1828–1910), Nikolai Leskov (1831–95). One might also mention in this regard the prolific playwright of merchant life, Aleksandr Ostrovsky (1823–86), whose early dramas had been linked with the Natural School and Slavophilism but whose most famous (and most romantic) creation, *The Storm* (1859), belongs to this later period. The "fat" (as in filled with many pages and multiple rubrics) journal, in which numerous famous novels were first serialized and various ideological battles fought over their meaning, was a vital element in the literary culture of the epoch (e.g. the radical *Russian Word* [*Russkoe slovo*] and *The Contemporary* [*Sovremennik*]; *Fatherland Notes* [*Otechestvennye zapiski*], where Belinsky was based and which became increasingly populist; the politically conservative *Russian Herald* [*Russkii vestnik*]; and the moderately liberal *Herald of Europe* [*Vestnik Evropy*]).

As Lydia Ginzburg has argued in her book *On Psychological Prose*, a major shift in mental patterns took place in the post-Decembrist generation coming of age in the literary circles of the 1830s and 1840s (Nikolai Stankevich, Mikhail Petrashevsky). This shift, toward greater psychological analysis and self-revelation, was typified by the thought and autobiographical writings of Aleksandr Herzen (1812–70), especially in his *My Past and Thoughts* (written 1852–68). Ginzburg's main point is that, due to the breaking down of poetic conventions that had sealed off (or stylized) the private realm in the age of Pushkin, a crucial watershed was passed and the way made clear to the "prosaic culture" of the realist novel. Whereas Pushkin's generation had revealed its hidden inner life "neither in conversation with one's friends, nor in letters and journals," but only in the "aesthetically transmuted form" of poetry, now that life was rigorously examined in a manner that Tolstoy and Dostoevsky would have understood implicitly.[10] A single standard began to be applied to individual behavior. If previously certain aspects of private space were "invisible" in Russian literature, so that a Decembrist's clothing or food or everyday gestures could be included only if they "signified" (i.e. meant something in terms of the civic myths that organized or "modeled" this generation's behavior), then for this intermediate generation the private/public, poetic/prosaic "fault lines" became more visible, more open to analysis, and more readily transgressed.[11] The result of this shift is that Tolstoy and Dostoevsky could describe, in a manner virtually unthinkable to Pushkin, aspects of their characters' inner and outer worlds, beginning with guilt, shame, and self-analysis. The poetic conventions (what could and could not be said in a lyric, for example) that Pushkin knew were artifice but still took seriously, Tolstoy now subjects to corrosive irony as both artificial and false (see the famous "making strange" scene of Natasha Rostova at the opera in *War and Peace*).

Goncharov and Turgenev are often paired as the "minor key" realists to the great duo of Tolstoy and Dostoevsky. This is certainly unfortunate because their finest creations, including *Oblomov* (1859) and *Fathers and Children* (1862), have come down to today's reader as examples of Russian realist prose at its best. Indeed, the lead characters in these novels – the feckless but lovable Oblomov, who takes many pages simply to get out of bed, and the nihilist Bazarov, who is undone by his own humanity – raged at the center of the epoch's ideological and cultural debates over "types" and were the subjects of essays and reviews by Pisarev, Dobroliubov, and fellow radical critics. Nevertheless, in the mature prose of these writers there was, temperamentally, a "softer," more forgiving irony, a sense of wistful reconciliation with the paradoxes and injustices of the world, that did not go at all with the "maximalisms" of Tolstoy and Dostoevsky. Bazarov dies literally because he exposes himself to a disease – typhus – that his scientific model of the world is dedicated to curing. (The rationalist logic goes that, had he been more circumspect, more "scientific," he might have avoided this needless death.) But Turgenev's irony is subtler than that: consciously or unconsciously, Bazarov "punishes himself" because he has made the ultimate error for one of his type – passionate and full of life, he has fallen in love with the cool, unreciprocating Odintsova. Like his foil the brittle and aristocratic Pavel Kirsanov (one of the "fathers"), Bazarov asks too much of life and consequently is broken by it. Those who survive and bear issue, such as Bazarov's friend Arkady and Odintsova's younger sister Katya, are more in touch with the primordial rhythms of the seasons and family life. It was this sense that Turgenev, who was writing not only for the moment, had seemed to "kill off" Bazarov and to affirm in the end Russia's agrarian roots (i.e. the old order) that infuriated the radicals and caused the disenchanted liberal writer to break with the younger generation and quit Russia.

No writer has been more important to the understanding and/or reception of Russian literature in the West than Fedor Dostoevsky. Many of the cliches about Russian literature (e.g. the "Russian soul") so beloved in the West and many of the characters and situations we have come to associate with the "paradox of Russia" (the Underground Man, Raskolnikov, Sonia Marmeladova, Myshkin, Nastasya Filippovna, Stavrogin, the Grand Inquisitor, the Karamazov brothers) are quintessentially, irreducibly "Dostoevskian." The narrating consciousness that so despises and challenges itself that its language is hopelessly unreliable (*Notes from Underground* [1864]); the brilliant young man who kills another human being in order to find out if he can do it (*Crime and Punishment* [1866]); the prostitute who saves herself and others by religious faith (*Crime and Punishment*); the prelapsarian "positively good man" who drives those around him to frenzy because he denies the existence of their postlapsarian ego needs (*The Idiot* [1868]); the peasant who is prepared to slit his friend's throat for a gold watch and then ask for forgiveness all in the same breath (*The Idiot*); the revolutionary who commits suicide to prove that death does not exist (*The Devils* [1872]); the "infernal woman" who tests and torments those she loves because someone has abused her in the past (*The Idiot, The Brothers Karamazov* [1880]); the intellectually rebellious brother who "returns his ticket" to God's universe because innocent children suffer (*The Brothers Karamazov*) – these are Dostoevskian types, and it would be hard, if not impossible, to imagine the Russian or the Western European literary tradition without them. Dostoevsky is the artist who more than any other provided the melodramatic plots and the "hot" (some would say overheated) verbal consciousness that anticipated and gave necessary narrative form to major trends in twentieth-century thought: Marxism (politics without God), Freudianism/psychoanalysis (psychology without God), Nietzscheanism (philosophy without God), poststructuralism/deconstruction (linguistics without God/Logos).

For earlier Russian generations, Dostoevsky was for the most part read within the politically conservative context ("mature" Slavophilism) out of which he himself wrote. His works were seen as harbingers of the 1905 and 1917 revolutions: accurate barometers of the *ressentiment* of the "men of the 1860s," full of the anxiety that went with the breakdown of polite society and patriarchal forms, the major novels seemed to prophesy the coming of a brazen new leader such as Lenin. However, for more recent generations, especially those influenced by the seminal theories of the philosopher of language Mikhail Bakhtin (1895–1975), Dostoevsky's political conservatism has been played down in the name of his radical refiguring of the "dialogic" word and his pioneering efforts to develop a new form for the novel. As regards Russian literature, Bakhtin's terminology has entered into the critical lexicon mainly in connection with Dostoevsky, whom the philosopher saw as a culminating point in the history of European culture's drive toward "novelization." In his books on Rabelais and Dostoevsky and in his many essays, Bakhtin traced his rather eccentric (implicitly Hegelian) history of this move toward greater communicative openness and, simultaneously, individuation – of verbal forms ("dialogism"), of novelistic structure ("polyphony"), of space–time relations ("chronotope"), of language that revels in stylistic multiplicity and argues with itself ("heteroglossia"), of the "authorizing" process (*chuzhaia rech'*/"another's speech"), of bodies that celebrate role-reversal and their multiple orifices ("carnival"). Dostoevsky was supposedly at the center of this development because his works most fully embody (literally) this formula of liminality + transgression + opening up. Bakhtin's claim that Dostoevsky, despite his own anxieties and political agenda, has created a form (the polyphonic novel) in which each character is a fully alive consciousness who speaks on terms of equality, not only with other characters but with the author himself, is certainly debatable. After all, did the author, knowing that a didactic approach would not succeed, develop a decentered strategy as a Trojan horse to smuggle in his own ideas (as he suggests in his correspondence), or was the political message "declawed" as it made its way into the world of the novel? Still, Bakhtin's ideas have been tremendously influential, both for Dostoevsky studies and literary theory in general, and he has become one of the most powerful voices in Western postmodernist thought as well.

As critics from Dmitry Merezhkovsky to George Steiner have argued, Tolstoy is Dostoevsky's fundamental opposite: visual, painterly (as in three-dimensional, "representational," not "iconic"), metonymic (as in less interested in the "metaphoric" axis of mythical time), patriarchal and aristocratic, analytic and positivist. He is the old order's last and greatest apologist, but as opposed to Turgenev or Goncharov, he will not settle for nostalgia or reconciliation. Like his foil, he is one of the supreme fighters in the tradition. He will not stand still, and it is somehow symbolic that he died *en route*, at a village train station. Some of the most outrageous judgments in the entire tradition belong to Tolstoy's pen: his dislike of Pushkin's lyric poetry, his censure of Shakespeare, his rejection of his own two epoch-making novels as false and wrong-headed. In *War and Peace* (1863–69), Tolstoy created a historical novel that had everything: fictional characters, historical personages, families in everyday time and in time of crisis, a plot (the Napoleonic Wars) that brought these strands together, and pages of analysis explaining how best historical events might be interpreted. By joining fiction writing and historiography within the covers of one book, Tolstoy, in a move quite representative of his age, succeeded in radically transgressing the rules of generic propriety laid down by none other than the tradition's main authority figure, Pushkin, who had written his *History of Pugachev* and *The Captain's Daughter* as two simultaneously composed, but different, self-enclosed works.[12] The honesty, the analytic rigor and fearlessness, of Tolstoyan "fiction" (Pierre on the battlefield of Borodino) could get at a "truth" that the military historians, with their different criteria for accomplishment and honor, could not.

Likewise, in *Anna Karenina* (1873–77), the author could develop a heroine who was so "real," and her living out of the tragedy of contemporary Russian womankind so compelling, that the reader loses sight completely of the novel's artifice and enters into its world as one that is utterly "verisimilar" (the mark of classic Realism). Again, Anna's plight is so meticulously embodied that, as in the case of Dostoevskian polyphony, we can no longer tell whether Tolstoy/God is "punishing" her (the "Vengeance is mine; I will repay" epigraph, with its imputed authorial intention) or whether she, the woman in love who has given up everything and therefore is mortally afraid of falling out of love, is punishing herself. Tolstoy the monologic moralist does pitched battle with Tolstoy the dialogic personalist/artist.[13] "Though feminist opinion may deny Tolstoy's achievement in creating Anna Karenina," writes Richard Freeborn, "natural justice must allow that, for all its faults, the portrait has a vital likeness, an appeal and vulnerability that make Anna's death seem as wanton as any sad suicide at the end of love. Despite himself, Tolstoy breathed life into her, and her death has outlasted his morality."[14] The fact that Tolstoy after 1880 turned his back on these great realist works as mere artifice and moved toward a position where his various roles as social activist, educator, and didactic writer could be united in a seamless countenance of pragmatic Christianity ("Tolstoyanism") only shows how maximalist this part count, part tight-fisted *kulak* was.

Anton Chekhov (1860–1904) is the figure most associated with the "twilight" of Russian literature's Golden Age – its transition to modernism and its preparation for the "hothouse" atmosphere of symbolism/decadence and the pre-revolutionary years. Other writers and thinkers who dominated the last two decades of the century include: the later Tolstoy, the later Leskov, the later Afanasy Fet (1820–92), Vsevolod Garshin (1855–88), Vladimir Korolenko (1853–1921), the poets Semeon Nadson (1862–87) and Konstantin Sluchevsky (1837–1904), and the important philosopher and symbolist "godfather" Vladimir Soloviev (1853–1900). Even so, this period of reaction, gloom, and soul-searching following the assassination of Alexander II (1881) seemed tailor-made to Chekhov's "tubercular muse." A doctor-writer who was also the son of a shopkeeper and the grandson of a former serf, Chekhov had an angle of vision that was equally alien to the apocalypticism of Dostoevsky and to the epic grandeur of Tolstoy. His clinical eye and compassionate questioning irony, his penchant for smaller, "transitional" genre forms (absurdist miniature, travel sketch, longer story, one-act play, etc.), his implicit understanding of life's "gray areas" and lack of resolution both grew out of his epoch and gave form, definition, to it. As the leading Russian Chekhov scholar Aleksandr Chudakov formulates this "peripheral" vision, Chekhov is the poet of the minimalist, "interrupted idea": in his work, "the idea is not dogmatic . . . [nor is it] ever followed to its conclusion; and it is not accompanied by consistent or thorough argumentation . . . A few propositions are uttered, at which point the development of the idea is interrupted by the daily flow of life and sometimes is completely broken off."[15]

It is characteristic, for example, that Chekhov's "Anna"s (the heroines of the stories "Anna on the Neck" and "Lady with a Pet Dog") give us the prosaic version of Anna Karenina – i.e. that version that cannot opt for the suicides of romantic French novels (what Tolstoy's heroine read and compared herself to) but must live on with the reduced expectations, frustrations, and confusions of having a lover and a husband and no clean way out. Chekhov is remarkably free of the didacticism so prevalent in Russian literature before and after him (in this he is akin to Pushkin). His women (and his men) are neither idealized nor demonized. Tolstoy does not "punish" his favorite characters for their bad timing (e.g. Levin still wins Kitty even though she had first fallen in love with Vronsky and all had seemed lost); Chekhov, on the other hand, leaves his characters with the results of their prior "mistimings" – his Anna ends up staying with

"Karenin" and his oversized ears; his Kitty really marries someone like Vronsky, but not necessarily for the right reasons. In Chekhov the prose of life invariably wins out over its grander, more "literary" opposite. Some of Chekhov's stories – "The Steppe" (1888), "The Name-Day Party" (1888), "A Nervous Breakdown" (1889), "Ward No. 6" (1892), the 1898 trilogy of "Man in a Case," "Gooseberries," and "About Love," "The Darling" (1899), "Lady with a Pet Dog" (1899), "In the Ravine" (1900) – are among the undisputed gems of Russian literature; his mature plays – *The Sea Gull* (1896), *Uncle Vanya* (1899), *Three Sisters* (1901), and *The Cherry Orchard* (1903) – are crucial to the canon as well and have in their way been as important in exporting Russian culture to the West, especially Great Britain, as the novels of Tolstoy and Dostoevsky.

Twentieth century Russian literature is tremendously varied and complex. Speaking impressionistically, one might say that while the nineteenth century had several "K-2s" and "Mt. Everests" (the titanic presences of Pushkin, Dostoevsky, Tolstoy), the twentieth century has had a number of entire mountain ranges, dense groups of fantastic (though perhaps slightly lesser known) peaks that are equally awesome in terms of their artistic talent and charismatic personalities. Some of the works of this century – Mandelstam's and Tsvetaeva's poetry, Bulgakov's *The Master and Margarita*, Vladimir Nabokov's *The Gift* – can stand alongside, and by no means in the shadow of, Pushkin's poetry, Dostoevsky's *The Brothers Karamazov*, Tolstoy's *Anna Karenina*. As before, however, the problem of translation is crucial: just as Pushkin, arguably the central figure in the entire tradition, is less appreciated in the West because his poetic genius is difficult, if not impossible, to capture in another language, so too are the legacies of the great modernist (and now post-modernist) poets (Blok, Mayakovsky, Khlebnikov, Akhmatova, Mandelstam, Tsvetaeva, Zabolotsky, Brodsky) exceedingly hard to pass on outside their specific linguistic contexts. Also important to realize in this connection is that the Russian (and more generally "Slavic") literary tradition in this century has grown up in a tight symbiotic embrace with some of the greatest theoretical and philological minds in the history of literary studies: Roman Jakobson and the Russian formalists (Viktor Shklovsky, Boris Eikhenbaum, Boris Tomashevsky, Yury Tynyanov) and Prague School structuralists (Jan Mukařovsky), Bakhtin and his group, Lydia Ginzburg, Yury Lotman and the Moscow-Tartu School of semiotics (Boris Uspensky, Viacheslav Ivanov, Vladimir Toporov). Here one might say, and not entirely polemically, if in previous centuries Russian culture was in a hurry to overtake the West, then in this century the West has been slow in learning what the Russians have already discovered.

As our earlier schematization indicated, twentieth-century Russian literature can be conveniently divided into four periods: modernism (1895–1925), socialist realism (1925–53), the "thaws" and twilight of the Soviet era (1953–87), and the current decade of *glasnost'* and post-*glasnost'* (1987–   ). Given the context, these rubrics have inevitable historical and political connotations. Just as the previous century had various "watershed" dates, including the Decembrist Uprising and ascension to the throne of Nicholas I in 1825, the European revolutions of 1848, the liberation of the serfs in 1861, and the assassination of Alexander II in 1881, that dramatically shifted the sociopolitical *status quo* and its relation to literary production, so too does this century have its epochal turning points: the October Revolution of 1917, the forced expulsion in 1922 of over 160 prominent members of the intelligentsia, the death of Lenin in 1924 and the rise to power of Stalin in 1925–28, the liquidation of separate literary groups and the establishment of socialist realism as official method of Soviet Russian literature (1932–34), the effect of the Second World War (1939–45) on the psychology of the nation, the death of Stalin in 1953, the three "thaws" (1953–54, 1956, 1961–63) and subsequent freezings-up in the literary culture, the establishment of *glasnost'* under Gorbachev in 1987 followed by the astonishing fall of communism in Eastern Europe – and then in Russia itself – within three years.

Running parallel to this chronological frame and to the general history and development of Soviet literature is the shadow life of Russian *émigré* literature. This oppositional phenomenon flowed to the West (and sometimes to the East) in three distinct "waves" and spanned most of the century from the immediate post-revolutionary years right up to the period of *glasnost'*, at which point it lost its primary *raison d'être*. The Western reader needs to bear constantly in mind a fact that otherwise reliable accounts of modern Russian literature have often glossed over or ignored as irrelevant – i.e. the vagaries of geopolitical manipulation: the "Soviet" status, whether of official apologist (i.e. "socialist realist") or of "other-thinking" (*inakomysliashchii*) man of letters merely residing in the Soviet Union, does not fit some of the greatest Russian writers of this century, including the magnificent prose stylist and his country's first Nobel laureate Ivan Bunin (1870–1953), the quixotic teller of stylized folk tales Aleksei Remizov (1877–1957), the post-symbolist poet Vladislav Khodasevich (1886–1939), the *à rebours* romantic poet Marina Tsvetaeva

(1892–1941), the "Russian" Vladimir Nabokov (1899–1977), and the nihilist poet Georgy Ivanov (1894–1958). In recent decades, perhaps the three most important Russian writers writing today have lived in emigration and defined themselves largely (though by no means exclusively) in opposition to Soviet reality: Aleksandr Solzhenitsyn (1918–   ), Joseph Brodsky (1940–96), and Andrei Sinyavsky (1925–97). With Brodsky's recent death, Solzhenitsyn has become Russia's only surviving Nobel laureate for literature.

Russian modernism was dominated by forebodings of the two revolutions (1905, 1917) and of an old world increasingly on the brink of collapse. The positivism and materialism of the previous century, still powerful in the logic of certain movements (Marxism), was thoroughly undermined in the practice of many avant-garde artists (some of them even Marxists, e.g. Maksim Gorky), whose new-found idealism and Nietzschean romanticism burned with a feverish, one might even say "neurasthenic" brightness. Those who spoke most in the spirit of the times felt the force of history, in Blok's evocative phrase the "music of revolution," gathering behind them and searched in these gale winds for what W. B. Yeats, a contemporary and his culture's version of a symbolist, called a "spume that plays upon the ghostly paradigm of things."[16] Poetry was again the dominant genre, and even such a leading exemplar of symbolist prose as Bely's *Petersburg* (not to speak of the same writer's "symphonies") was orchestrated metrically (or as Bely might have blurred these boundaries, "musically") and close to "exploding" (the novel's core metaphor) with various poetic tropes. Above all, writers of this crisis period were consumed by the millenarian impulse to see through pressing political and social realities to a higher reality of apocalyptic *Endzeit* beyond. They read the "text" of the world through the codes of Revelation, the last book of the Bible; in the symbolist poet and theoretician Viacheslav Ivanov's formulation, they tried to see "from the real to the more real" (*a realibus ad realiora*). Perhaps the period's most prominent model and source of "prophetic" intuition was, along with Nietzsche, the philosopher-poet Vladimir Soloviev, who died, significantly, at the turn of the new century, who made apocalyptic predictions in his later works, and whose personal life was dramatically interwoven with the "initiations" of several younger symbolist adepts (i.e. he played the role of John the Precursor to these potential self-anointed Christ figures). His vivid antipode was contemporary Vasily Rozanov (1856–1919), a philosopher of dubious political persuasion and a brilliant aphoristic stylist who adored "Old Testament" family life and incarnated sexuality as much as Soloviev and his heirs loved to transmogrify all that was bodily and three-dimensional into an abstract anagogic system.

The early decades of the century contained numerous movements, but today it is chiefly remembered for three, all fundamentally poetic: symbolism/decadence (early 1890s–1910), which stressed the new aestheticism and the truth of *dvoemirie*, or the mythical correspondences between "this" and the "other" world; futurism (including ego-futurists, mezzanine of poetry, centrifuge, cubo-futurists; 1910–30), which rejected the "effete" idealism and other-worldliness of the symbolists, embracing instead experimental forms, *engagé* politics, social *épatage* (as in consciously cultivated outrageousness), urban technology, "trans-sense" language and "the word as such"; and acmeism (early 1910s–early 1920s), which reacted against both the symbolists (too abstract) and the futurists (too iconoclastic) in favor of human-centered cultural continuity and of poetic language as craft (the metaphor of building, constructing) as opposed to theurgy. These aesthetic positions were contested vigorously in the manifestos of the respective groups. Central figures in the theory and practice of symbolism, futurism, and acmeism include: the "older" symbolists (sometimes termed "decadents") Dmitry Merezhkovsky (1865–1941), Valery Briusov (1873–1924), Konstantin Balmont (1867–1942), Zinaida Gippius (1869–1945), Fedor Sologub (1863–1927); the "younger" Symbolists Aleksandr Blok (1880–1921), Andrei Bely (1880–1934), Viacheslav Ivanov (1866–1949); the futurists Vladimir Mayakovsky (1893–1930), Velimir Khlebnikov (1885–1922), Aleksei Kruchonykh (1886–1969?), Igor Severyanin (1887–1941), and the young Boris Pasternak (1890–1960); the "pre-acmeists" Innokenty Annensky (1856–1909) and Mikhail Kuzmin (1875–1936), and the acmeists Nikolai Gumilev (1886–1921), Anna Akhmatova (1889–1966), Osip Mandelstam (1891–1938). Two talented "peasant poets" also played significant roles in the pre- and post-revolutionary poetic culture: Sergei Esenin (1895–1925), who was associated with the imaginists, and Nikolai Kliuev (1887–1937). Russian prose was still represented by such "neo-realists" of the Znanie (knowledge) group as the immensely influential Maksim Gorky (1868–1936), the early Bunin, Leonid Andreev (1871–1919), and Aleksandr Kuprin (1870–1938).

It is curious that each of these three major movements has spawned a psychology of "pairing" in the modern reader's mind, as though the contrasts-within-sameness of a group's two leading figures define the parameters of poetic possibility in a way no single personality or body of work can. Thus, Blok and Bely are often linked as the "Siamese twins" of symbolism: "the yolk and the white of the one shell,"[17] to invoke Yeats' version of Plato's parable. Blok's verse epic *The Twelve* (1918) and Bely's novel *Petersburg* (in various editions, especially 1916 and 1922) are symbolist culture's two greatest statements about the Revolution: the former shows the movement's leading lyric poet moving as far as he is able in the direction of narrative *mythos*, the other its most powerful abstract thinker and mathematical logician testing the boundaries of poetic prose. As these two friends' voluminous correspondence reveals, they are drawn to that in the other which they lack on their own: in Bely, it is his fixation on Christian Logos (a "male" principle); in Blok it is his overriding concern with the passivity of "fallen" matter and the sensual world (Beautiful Lady-cum-Stranger, or the "feminine" principle). Their lives and their works are in constant, heated dialog (cf., e.g., Blok's *The Twelve* and Bely's *Christ is Risen*); born in the same year and "miraculously" brought together as "brothers," both feel preternaturally close to Soloviev and see Blok's wife Liubov Mendeleeva as the now alluring, now terrifying incarnation of the philosopher's Eternal Feminine.

Likewise, one could say of Mayakovsky and Khlebnikov that they are futurism's tragicomic buffoon and holy fool, respectively. Their best works, including Mayakovsky's two famous pre-revolutionary narrative poems *A Cloud in Trousers* (1915) and *The Backbone Flute* (1915) and Khlebnikov's poem on the Revolution *The Nocturnal Search* (1921), comprised one of essential simultaneous "planes" on the "cubist" face of the avant-garde, and the creative ferment with which these poets and their colleagues worked with leaders in the visual arts (David Burliuk, Kasimir Malevich, Natalia Goncharova, Mikhail Larionov, Vasily Kandinsky, Tatlin), music (Mikhail Matiushin), the theatre (Vsevolod Meyerhold), the new medium of film (Sergei Eisenstein), and literary theorists (the formalists), was genuinely intoxicating. Both remarkable innovators, Mayakovsky and Khlebnikov pushed the possibilities of a revolution in language to its outer limits: Mayakovsky working from the outside or "edge" of the poetic line (his signature being the syntactically or semantically offbeat rhyme and *lesnitsa* – i.e. the strophic design that moved up and down the page like a ladder), Khlebnikov from within (his fanciful etymologies and proto-mythic coinages). In this respect, very "Russian" and "futurist" is the fact that Mayakovsky and Khlebnikov lived out, to the point of suicide and death by willful neglect, their movement's political/aesthetic imperative of "making it new": once that newness and cutting edge were no longer relevant (since revolutions are finite), there was nothing left to do but put a bullet in one's head (Mayakovsky) or lie down to die as a forgotten tramp in a provincial hospital (Khlebnikov). Mayakovsky in particular, as Pasternak realized retrospectively in *Safe Conduct* (1931), was a fatal amalgam of the Revolution's forward momentum; talented organizer, propagandist, and public personality of Whitmanesque sweep, both player and director in his own self-promoting street theatre, scandalous scourge of "bourgeois" values and yet vulnerable lover of unattainable ice-goddesses, he captured the dramatic contradictions of his moment as no one else. He was the Prospero-Caliban creative axis of the avant-garde; Khlebnikov the Prospero-Ariel.

Mandelstam and Akhmatova are the two greatest acmeists and, while their individual reputations certainly outgrew the temporal and narrowly factional confines of the original movement, it is also true that in some sense they remained faithful to the basic tenets of acmeism (enunciated by Mandelstam in his programmatic statements "Morning of Acmeism" [published 1919] and "On the Nature of the Word" [published 1922]) to the end of their days: clarity, precision, restraint. In them was reborn the "St. Petersburg/Pushkinian" ethos in Russian poetry: an emphasis on rising up against the gravity of existence in a tense, joyful equilibrium (see Mandelstam's famous cathedral poem "Notre Dame" [1912]); the poetic word/Logos as something physically palpable, living and breathing, unbidden and miraculous (the darting "swallow-soul"); culture as a fire in the Acropolis that civilized man gathers around for warmth and protection in moments of historic crisis; Christian sacrifice as the basis of the creative act. Mandelstam and Akhmatova are paired through their close friendship, their shared biography of suffering and persecution, their deep culture and love of world literature (especially their 1930s idol and indispensable interlocutor Dante – see, e.g., Mandelstam's "A Conversation About Dante"), their remarkable growth from earlier to later stages of their careers, and their inspiring roles in the poetic mythology of the century (charismatic Son tortured by an arbitrary Father [Stalin], suffering Mother at the foot of the cross). Essential to this pairing is the implicit understanding that Mandelstam, like Gumilev (Akhmatova's first husband), died prematurely as a victim of the Soviet politicization of literature, while Akhmatova lived on to bear tragic witness, particularly in her two late masterpieces, the poetic cycle

Requiem (written 1935–41) and the verse epic *Poem without a Hero* (written 1940–66).

Osip Mandelstam is the most breathtakingly allusive ("intertextual") poet in the history of Russian poetry. An entire school of philological reconstructive ("subtextual") scholarship (Kiril Taranovsky, etc.) has grown up in an effort to identify the many layers of his "reminiscenses" (*reministsentsii*) from other poets and traditions. However, Mandelstam's poetry, its intoxicating cadences, and subtle "deep-breathing exercises" (one of the poet's favorite metaphors is air and the difficulty or ease of breathing), is not, it might be maintained, generated primarily out of an urge to display his culture. The allusions, in his "holy-foolish" way, are more real to the poet than that. Rather, he appropriates culture, or "steals" it like his beloved thief François Villon, in order to prove to himself and his reader how it is still alive ("yesterday has not yet been born"), how it cannot stop moving, how Dante, to cite another example, is not dead but very much audible in the poetic feet and "body language" of the irritable outcast and exile Mandelstam himself. Mandelstam's first books of verse, *Stone* (1913) and *Tristia* (1922), showed their author to be a prodigiously gifted Jewish-Russian outsider who saw his assimilation of Western high culture as the necessary entry pass to the feast of Russian "Christian" culture he associated with the coming new era ("Pushkin and Scriabin"). However, in time these hopes were dashed and the "initiation," already turning dark and bloody in *Tristia*, did not come about. In his later poetry, collected in notebooks and preserved by his wife until they could be published, Mandelstam takes renewed pride in his outcast, Jewish status: he becomes a tragicomic, agile, infinitely inventive Charlie Chaplin – Stalinist Russia's little tramp. These poems, especially the "Voronezh notebooks," written on the eve of the poet's arrest, imprisonment, and ultimately death in the camps, stand comparison with any in the modern tradition.

Of all the modern Russian poets, none has been a richer source of controversy and art-to-life mythologization than Marina Tsvetaeva. Her collections of verse, especially *Craft* (1923) and *After Russia* (1928), and her many long poems, dramas and essays constitute an artistic legacy inexhaustible and exhausting in its energy and variety. Because Tsvetaeva is such a powerful and unique voice in the tradition, the question for recent scholarship has often been: what comes first, her position as a poet or her position as a woman? Does the fact that she is a woman enable her as poet, so that she has produced new forms (the so-called "*écri-*

ture feminine") that only one of her gender could, an essentializing gesture the poet herself would have rejected, or does the fact that she is a female poet make her biography, her own "life of the poet," particularly exemplary even for the tragedy-saturated Russian context (the issue of the female poet and suicide)? How to understand, for example, Tsvetaeva's lesbian tendencies, her insistence on giving voice and agency to the literary heroines fetishized by male myth (Ophelia, Phaedra, Eurydice), her shedding of the domestic semantics of the more "feminine" Akhmatova and her taking of women readers out on to the "high road" of life, her subverting of the traditional suffix in "poetess" and her refusal to become a muse herself, and her embracing of her own male "genius" (masculine in Russian) in *On the Red Steed* and other poems? It is precisely this challenge of *what comes first* that has made Tsvetaeva the object of intense interest for both traditional poetry experts and for the well-known feminists and poststructuralists of the continental (e.g., Julia Kristeva, Hélène Cixous) and the Slavist (e.g., Barbara Heldt, Svetlana Boym) varieties.

Tsvetaeva is also in a class by herself because her biography coincides in fascinating typological (or allegorical) ways with those of other major poets and yet always manages to stay outside, "beyond," and hence to get in a "final word." This stepping beyond occurred with Blok (if he was the epoch's knight searching for the "Beautiful Lady" in his sinful maleness, then she was its "Amazonian" warrior searching for the "male muse" in hers); with Mandelstam (he was the tender swain her forceful presence introduced to Moscow and the latter's myths); with Rilke (his ties with the German language and spirituality were strong magnets in her poetry); with Akhmatova (the female poet as muse versus anti-muse); with Pasternak (he was her closest soulmate and an object of impossible, half-Platonic, half-real desire); and Mayakovsky (his fear of *byt*, hatred of bourgeois values, and his extravagant self-absorption were also hers). But looming over all these parallels was the undeniable fact that Tsvetaeva's fierce loyalty to family (husband and children), on the one hand, and to poetry, on the other, sealed her fatal return to the Soviet Union and suicide by hanging in a way that surpassed even the Russian penchant for this "bloody repast." Whereas the great male poets could take their rightful places in the tradition as tragic Christ figures, and Akhmatova, Tsvetaeva's chief foil (and the sort of woman and poet she could never become), could shift her role from that of alluring temptress or misunderstood wife (early poetry) to that of all-suffering mother (later poetry), Tsvetaeva could not "fit in"; and she managed somehow to take pride in her outlaw status as "tavern queen" and "convict princess." She was always alone, never part of any movements or "isms": the breathtaking acceleration of her enjambments, her bold shifting and mixing of meters and her special signature of the dash (as expansive and aggressive as Emily Dickinson's dash was introverting and self-protecting) all imitate on a stylistic level her urge to "leap into the abyss." Tsvetaeva's "monstrous" problem is that of the powerful signifying woman who cannot enter, except through language, the other; she cannot project a "female" screen (the muse) of supporting roles for herself in the manner of a male poet, nor can she work within the traditional gender roles allocated by her culture in the manner of Akhmatova. She is supremely, tragically solitary. Curiously, this Akhmatova–Tsvetaeva dichotomy is apparently being revisited in contemporary poetry in the work of Olga Sedakova and Elena Shvarts.

Socialist realism became the official method of Soviet literature during the period of "high" Stalinist culture (1932–53). Its definition, as the dissident writer Andrei Sinyavsky has argued in a provocative essay ("On Socialist Realism"), combined elements of "classicism" (the static binary ideal), "romanticism" (what socialism is moving toward, or "should be") and "realism" (socialism's current phase of historical development, or "what is") into an unwieldy modal paradox. The first recorded use of the term was by the president of the Organization Committee of the newly founded Writers' Union (Ivan Gronsky) in May 1932, with the actual definition following two years later: "socialist realism, being the basic method of Soviet literature and literary criticism, demands from the artist the truthful, historically concrete depiction of reality in its revolutionary development. At the same time, truthfulness and historical concreteness of the historical depiction of reality must be combined with the task of ideologically remolding and educating the working people in the spirit of socialism" (*Literaturnaya gazeta*, 3 September 1934). The fact that this method "demanded" that the writer be historically truthful and concrete, i.e. objective, on the one hand, and ideologically right-minded and properly didactic, i.e., prescriptive, on the other, meant that the mold pulled both ways and could be made to say different things in different contexts. What it could not be, however, was openly critical of the Party's official position at any given time.

In her 1981 landmark study *The Soviet Novel: History as Ritual*, Katerina Clark succeeded for the first time in making the often dreary exemplars of the socialist realist novel interesting in their own right as texts of popular culture. She turned the focus away from a set of rules for writing (i.e. a fixed definition passed down by the Party to its writers) toward the concept of an interchangeable "master plot" which replicated, in terms of human biographies the average Soviet reader could understand and identify with, the heroic march of socialism from a mythical past (what the scholar of myth Mircea Eliade would call the "Great Time" of the Revolution) through a problematic present to a mythical future (the attainment of communism). It now became clear that official Soviet fiction had more in common, in Bakhtinian terms, with medieval "epic" time than with modern "novel" time. The master plot, the *topoi* of which might coincide with certain aspects of saints' lives and the goal of which was never "high literature" *per se* (hence much of the criticism of the genre was misplaced) but ritual bonding of the population, was then repeated with small but always context-sensitive variations/reversals in a whole series of "classics." Several of these classics actually predated the adoption of the methodology, which means that this popular expression of a historical consciousness was at work in the culture well before the theorists and literary politicians enshrined it as dogma: Gorky's *Mother* (1906), Dmitry Furmanov's *Chapaev* (1923), Aleksandr Serafimovich's *The Iron Flood* (1924), Fedor Gladkov's *Cement* (1925), Aleksandr Fadeev's *The Rout* (1927), Aleksei Tolstoy's *Road to Calvary* (1921–40), Nikolai Ostrovsky's *How Steel was Tempered* (1932–34), Mikhail Sholokhov's *Quiet Flows the Don* (1928–40), etc. Clark's study has taught many how to read anew these works in the light of Western/Russian critical thought (Bakhtin, Vladimir Propp, Eliade, Victor Turner, Dmitry Likhachev, etc.), and it has been supplemented more recently by the *émigré* intellectual historian Boris Groys's provocative study of the compatible interrelations between totalitarianism and the avant-garde.

It is against this background of socialist realism, either in its pre- or post-"doctrinal" phase, that the major non-official prose works of the Soviet period, including Boris Pilnyak's *The Naked Year* (1921), Zamyatin's *We* (corrupt text 1927, complete text 1952), Isaak Babel's *Red Cavalry* (stories written early 1920s, first published in book form 1926), Olesha's *Envy* (1927), should be situated. However, even among these landmarks of "other-thinking" (e.g. "fellow travelers," "internal" and actual *émigrés*) there are four exceptional novels that define the period (and its *émigré* counterpart) as no others: Platonov's *Chevengur* (written late 1920s, first published in West 1972), Bulgakov's *The Master and Margarita* (written 1928–40, published 1966–67), Nabokov's *The Gift* (1937–38), and

Pasternak's *Doctor Zhivago* (first published in West 1957). One can assume that it is these works that, over time, will come to represent the best in twentieth-century prose in the way that *Fathers and Children*, *Oblomov*, *Anna Karenina*, and *The Brothers Karamazov* have done for the previous century.

It is intriguing that all four of these novels provide parodic anti-versions of the socialist realist master plot, problematizing the narrative structure (the boundaries of author/narrator/character) and the ideological message (the positive hero's collectivist pathos) with an irony totally absent from their official counterparts. Their plots involve both love stories (the familiar theme of eros: Sasha/Sonia and Kopenkin/Rosa, the Master and his Margarita, Fedor and Zina, Yury and Lara) and the encoding of larger "fairy tales" about Russian history (in the apolitical Nabokov, Russian *cultural* history). These novels also differ fundamentally from the official "canon" by intentionally mystifying the issue of authorship and narrative hierarchy: in Platonov, for example, there is no cognitive distance (or privileging) between narrator and character, between intellectual worker "smarty" (*umnik*) and visceral worker "fool" (*durak*); in Bulgakov, the reader can never tell unequivocally whose consciousness is the source of the constantly shifting inner and outer narratives (the Moscow/Yershalaim stories), the Devil's (Woland's) or God's (Yeshua's), although the Faustian epigraph about the Devil being that power that "forever wills evil and forever does good" clarifies the matter somewhat; in Nabokov, the "he" and "I" narrators alternate perspectives in a magical, Escher-like structure of optical illusion that points to the differences between Fedor the character and Fedor the future author; and in Pasternak, the prose narrative about the Revolution provides episodes that are then mythically encoded in the poems of Yury Zhivago that come after and enclose, again in a blend of cyclical, "Christian" rhythms, the prior novelistic text.

Also revealing is the fact that, with the exception of Platonov, who has been called Soviet literature's "metapoet" (Thomas Seifrid), these major novelists incorporate in their masterworks a "magic box" structure that undoes the linear logic of Marxism and dialectical materialism. The Master and Margarita die in the novel, but the story does not end with their deaths; instead, Bulgakov tips the scales of cosmic justice and vouchsafes a view of his autobiographical hero and heroine being rewarded in a special limbo-like afterlife. It is a double ending that, paradoxically, is both "out of this world" and yet continues to speak to this one (the voices and visions of Ivan Homeless). Likewise, the Onegin stanza that is embedded in the final sentences of *The Gift* returns us slyly to the novel's opening, so that Fedor the character becomes Fedor the author, whose first mature work we are now reading. It is only the failed utopian Platonov, rather than the triumphant apocalypticists (Bulgakov, Pasternak) and gnostic (Nabokov), who opts out of Christian culture's magic boxes and Dantesque optical illusions: his hero Sasha Dvanov commits suicide because the spatial and temporal hopes embedded in the new Soviet language (and embodied in the Bolshevik city of the sun, Chevengur) have not been realized – and there is no way out, "high cultural" or otherwise. Hence these novels, in addition to the fact that they are exceedingly rich and multi-voiced fictions appearing at a time when Russian literature was undergoing fierce "monologization," seem to answer a need that has never fully disappeared in the culture: the writer as wandering truth seeker and potential martyr (Platonov, Bulgakov, and Pasternak were all persecuted by the regime, while Nabokov had to make his way in exile). These novelists are all creators of eccentric worlds that subvert the *status quo* and test the boundaries of faith and consciousness.

Post-Stalinist Soviet Russian literature was, until the recent heady days of *glasnost'*, dominated by two phenomena: the three "thaws" that provided brief windows of opportunity to rehabilitate previously repressed writers and to discover young or neglected talent and that are associated with the Khrushchev years (1953–64), and the subsequent period of "stagnation" (*zastoi*) that takes its name from the stifling mediocrity and grey stolidity of the Brezhnev era. There are several *causes célèbres* that punctuate these years, including the famous "Pasternak affair" (1957–58) that came in the wake of the Italian publication of *Doctor Zhivago* and the awarding (*in absentia*) of the Nobel Prize; the arrest and sentencing to hard labor of the young Leningrad poet Joseph Brodsky in 1964 for "social parasitism"; the imprisonment and trial of the dissident writers Yuly Daniel (Nikolai Arzhak) and Andrei Sinyavsky (Abram Terts) in 1965–66; the arrest and expulsion of Aleksandr Solzhenitsyn from the Soviet Union in 1974 following the publication abroad of *The Gulag Archipelago*; and the "*Metropol* affair" of 1979 that grew out of efforts by Vasily Aksyonov and his colleagues to force the state to allow uncensored publication of their unofficial writings. In addition, many prominent writers came of age in these three decades, some as outright dissidents and others as semi-official authors who still published some of their works clandestinely, either through "self-printing" ("*samizdat*") or "printing there/abroad" ("*tamizdat*"). Among the leading literary figures of this post-Stalinist period, a number of whom eventually left (or were expelled from) the Soviet Union under Brezhnev, are: the prose writers Konstantin Paustovsky (1892–1968), Vasily Grossman (1905–64), Varlam Shalamov (1907–82), Viktor Nekrasov (1911–87), Solzhenitsyn (1918–   ), Aleksandr Zinoviev (1922–   ), Sinyavsky-Terts (1925–97), Yury Trifonov (1925–81), Yury Kazakov (1927–83), Chingiz Aitmatov (1928–   ), Fazil Iskander (1929–   ), Yuz Aleshkovsky (1929–   ), Georgy Vladimov (1931–   ), Aksyonov (1932–   ), Vladimir Maksimov (1932–), Vladimir Voynovich (1932–   ), Andrei Bitov (1937–   ), Valentin Rasputin (1937–   ), Venedikt Erofeev (1938–90), Sergei Dovlatov (1941–90), Sasha Sokolov (1943–   ); the poets Arseny Tarkovsky (1907–89), Boris Slutsky (1919–86), Naum Korzhavin (1925–   ), Evgeny Evtushenko (1933–   ), Andrei Voznesensky (1933–   ), Evgeny Reyn (1935–   ), Aleksandr Kushner (1936–   ), Natalia Gorbanevskaia (1936–   ), Bella Akhmadulina (1937–   ), Yunna Morits (1937–   ), Brodsky (1940–96); the "bards" (popular singers/poets) Aleksandr Galich (1918–77), Bulat Okudzhava (1924–97), and Vladimir Vysotsky (1938–80).

During the post-Stalinist period four names stand out for the unique quality of their artistic visions and writing talents: Solzhenitsyn, Brodsky, Aksyonov, and Sinyavsky-Terts. Solzhenitsyn is the tradition's belated inheritor of the "large form" and the moral/prophetic dimension associated with the great high realist novels of Tolstoy and Dostoevsky: a man of daunting earnestness, integrity, and first-hand experience of the camps, in his early novels he also is a remarkable prose stylist whose ingenious play with semantic substrata and narrative tone (from the deadly serious to the savagely sarcastic) give his writing the unmistakable stamp of authenticity. Brodsky was perhaps Russia's last great poet in the "bardic" mode: a uniquely (for Russian poetry) "metaphysical" amalgam of Western and domestic exemplars (John Donne, W. H. Auden, Tsvetaeva, Mandelstam), he deployed a "neo-acmeist" poetic logic and convoluted, highly cerebral syntax in order to make his native tradition aware of what the Soviet years caused it to forget or neglect. From his years as the leader of the "young prose" movement and one of the "men of the sixties" to his recent status as leading *émigré* prose writer in the non-traditional mode, Aksyonov has used language in its subversive guise as popular culture (the importation of "forbidden" Americanisms and spontaneous jazz-like improvisations) to allegorize the fate of late (in both senses) Soviet culture (see *The Island Crimea* [1981]). Sinyavsky has developed two dialogically intertwined personas, the retiring, scholarly "Sinyavsky" and the provocative, "fantastic" Terts, to re-suture his generation's lost limbs to the body of an earlier, more vital tradition (Pushkin, Gogol, Rozanov). Not surprisingly, given the culture's abiding faith (until recently) in the writer's calling and status as secular saint, each of these four writers has been implicated in "political" crimes against the state and, in one form or other, actively persecuted. Moreover, and no less significant, three have been at one time or other imprisoned and internally exiled. And all four have ultimately chosen, or rather been forced to choose (a preferred tactic of the Brezhnev years), life abroad. As of May 1994, the eldest among them, Solzhenitsyn, returned to his homeland; Brodsky and Sinyavsky died abroad in 1996 and 1997 respectively; while Aksyonov, it is assumed, will retain his affiliation as an essentially *émigré* writer. To be sure, with the new permeable borders, this distinction is no longer as fatally ostracizing as it once was.

The case of Solzhenitsyn is perhaps most symbolic of the change in cultural values now confronting Russian literature. Whereas Brodsky, in a manner more successful than any *émigré* writer since Nabokov, made his way as an American man of letters and poet laureate who happened to have been born and raised in the former Soviet Union, Solzhenitsyn, as befitting one of his generation and moral compass, insisted on the primacy of his Russian roots and of his links with the best in pre-revolutionary culture. Much like Tolstoy, who turned his back on his two great novels and devoted himself after 1880 to the even larger task of ethical leader of the Russian (and perhaps not only Russian) world, Solzhenitsyn, in his advancing years, has gone far beyond the remarkable middle-aged author of *One Day in the Life of Ivan Denisovich* (1962) and "Matryona's Homestead" (1963) who was "discovered" by Aleksandr Tvardovsky at *Novy mir* and bizarrely championed by none other than Khrushchev. In a reprise of the Slavophile-Westernizer debate of the previous century, Brodsky tried to raise the consciousness of Russian culture by making it more "cosmopolitan" in such collections as *The End of a Beautiful Epoch* (1977) and *A Part of Speech* (1977), while Solzhenitsyn has seen the path of the West, including its materialism and its lack of moral fiber parading as democratic pluralism and "cost-free" free speech, as false. And just as Dostoevsky saw his mock execution and Siberian exile as redemptive and reinitiating into the Christian faith following the "atheistic" experience of the Petrashevsky Circle, so now does Solzhenitsyn see his experience in the camps and the re-igniting of a

Christian vision ensuing therefrom as the great authenticating turning point in his life and artistic career.

In a way, despite the return of many Russians to the Orthodox faith in recent years, Solzhenitsyn's remains a voice in the wilderness (*glas vopiushchego v pustyne*) raised against the desert winds of increasing secularization, materialism, and the popular youth culture that comes with Western "bourgeois values." From the stunning realism and piercing moral integrity of *One Day*, "Matryona's Homestead," and the fine large novels *First Circle* (first published in the West 1968) and *Cancer Ward* (first published in the West 1968) Solzhenitsyn has now passed on to projects of Tolstoyan magnitude – the reconstruction of suppressed Soviet history (the resurrection of the camps in *Gulag* and now the investigation of the Bolshevik rise to power during the First World War in the novel cycle *The Red Wheel*) and, ultimately, based on this new knowledge, its re-imagining along pre-revolutionary lines. In Solzhenitsyn sits a "maximalist" comparable to "old man" Tolstoy; he would, if he could, turn back the tide of history, stand at its sluices and channel it in a different direction. And his yearning for meaning, while inspirational, needs to be tempered with the knowledge that not all suffering is redemptive and "authenticating": sometimes, as in the *Kolyma Tales* (first published in the West 1978) of Shalamov, who was Solzhenitsyn's chief foil in bearing witness to the atrocities of the Gulag, the reader sees how fragile and easily trampled are the institutions of "civil society" and thus how Russia needs those "middle ground" institutions perhaps as much as, if not more than, the fierce spiritual beauty and maximalist strivings of a Solzhenitsyn or a Tolstoy.

With the coming of the post-*glasnost'* era, the two streams in twentieth-century Russian literature, Soviet and *émigré*, have at last been united. Names that have been important to the three "waves" of *émigré* writing – the prose writer and memoirist Nina Berberova, the bohemian surrealist Boris Poplavsky, the poets Ivan Elagin and Nikolai Morshen – are now being discovered and reclaimed in Russia. This merging of all streams into a powerful, varied current has also crossed gender lines, so that important woman prose writers and playwrights (genres traditionally dominated by men), such as Tatiana Tolstaya and Liudmila Petrushevskaia, as well as poets (Shvarts, Sedakova), are now at the forefront of the literary scene. Equally significant, it looks as though the age of Western skepticism and irony that Russian maximalist spirituality had managed to resist or keep at bay has at last arrived in earnest. The "high" cultural values of Pushkin, Tolstoy, Dostoevsky, Blok, Mandelstam, Bulgakov, and Tsvetaeva – the writer as secular saint, his work as providing a model for life – are being subjected daily to the same rules of the capitalist marketplace that we find in the West. Mandelstam, a difficult poet under any circumstances, must now compete with Agatha Christie and sex manuals on the bookstands in metro stations and on street corners. Contemporary writers who understand (and to some extent probably secretly resent) the fatal allure of the "prophetic" and "bardic" voice, such as the impish pop artist Dmitry Prigov and the intentionally "scandalous" Venedikt Erofeev and Vladimir Sorokin, are at present mounting full scale assaults on all stable cultural values, whether they be socialist realist or messianic/"truth-seeking." They are smashing the cultural icons of the past, and with them traditional reader expectations and notions of "propriety," in order that Russians may at last, to paraphrase the title of a recent essay by Erofeev, taste their version of Baudelairean "flowers of evil" – a self-consciousness no less questioning and no less aware of the "abysses" of meaning than anything in the West. It is, in short, a "deconstruction" more massive and far-reaching than the elitist academic trend in the West. To many of this newest generation of Russian writers the return of Solzhenitsyn is already old news – a mummy ready for a museum exhibit whose writings no longer speak to them. But once again there is a maximalism here, one not unknown to Dostoevsky's Petr Verkhovensky and to the Bakunin who claimed that "the desire for destruction is also a creative desire."[18] What will be left standing when the current iconoclasts have finished their work is a tale for the twenty-first-century.

NOTES

1. Harriet Murav, *Holy Foolishness: Dostoevsky's Novels and the Politics of Cultural Critique* (Stanford, CA, 1992).

2. Nikolai Berdiaev, *Russkaia ideia* (Paris, 1946), p. 35.

3. David Bethea, *The Shape of Apocalypse in Modern Russian Fiction* (Princeton, NJ, 1989).

4. Irene Masing-Delic, *Abolishing Death: A Salvation Myth of Russian Twentieth-Century Literature* (Stanford, CA, 1992).

5. Marcia Morris, *Saints and Revolutionaries: The Ascetic Hero in Russian Literature* (Albany, NY, 1993).

6. Nadezhda Mandelstam, *Hope Abandoned*, trans. Max Hayward (New York, 1974), p. 11.

7. Rufus Matthewson, Jr., *The Positive Hero in Russian Literature* (Stanford, CA, 1975).

8. Vladislav Khodasevich, "Pamiati Gogolia" (To the Memory of Gogol), in N. Berberova, ed., *Literaturnye stat'i i vospominaniia* (New York, 1954), p. 89.

9. Richard Peace, "The Nineteenth Century: the Natural School and its Aftermath,

1840–55," in Charles Moser, ed., *The Cambridge History of Russian Literature*, rev. edn. (Cambridge, 1992), p. 196.

10. Lydia Ginzburg, *On Psychological Prose*, trans. and ed. Judson Rosengrant (Princeton, NJ, 1991), p. 32.

11. Yury M. Lotman, "The Decembrist in Daily Life (Everyday Behavior as a Historical-Psychological Category)," in Alexander D. Nakhimovsky and Alice Stone Nakhimovsky, eds., *The Semiotics of Russian Cultural History* (Ithaca, NY, 1985), pp. 95–149.

12. Andrew Wachtel, *An Obsession with History: Russian Writers Confront the Past* (Stanford, CA, 1994).

13. Gary Saul Morson, *Hidden in Plain View: Narrative and Creative Potential in* War and Peace (Stanford, CA, 1990).

14. Richard Freeborn, "The Nineteenth Century: the Age of Realism, 1855–80," in Moser, ed., *The Cambridge History of Russian Literature*, pp. 321–22.

15. A. P. Chudakov, *Poetika Chekhova* (Moscow, 1971), pp. 246–47.

16. W. B. Yeats, "Among School Children," in *The Collected Poems of W. B. Yeats*, ed., Richard J. Finneran (New York, 1989), p. 217.

17. *Ibid.*, p. 216.

18. Michael Bakunin, "The Reaction in Germany: a Fragment from a Frenchman," in James M. Edie, James P. Scanlan, and Mary-Barbara Zeidin, eds., *Russian Philosophy*, vol. I (Chicago, 1965), p. 406.

9
_____

Art

To assert that a particular historical moment marks the beginning of a particular cultural movement is a hazardous proposition inasmuch as any such moment is only one link in a chain of preceding and subsequent conditions that characterize or define such a movement. However, while precedents to, and consequences of, a "magic moment" (e.g. 1917) can always be found, there is often a constellation of events and circumstances that hastens or emphasizes what may have been a latent action, giving rise to its manifestation as a cultural expression (e.g. constructivism after the October Revolution) and there is at least a conventional wisdom in pursuing this method. The decade of the 1850s is such a moment, for it marked an important juncture in the evolution of Russian culture and gives us a strategic date for establishing a division between what could be called the "classical" and "modern" eras of the Russian visual arts.

From the mid-eighteenth century onwards, the Russian school of painting and sculpture, as opposed to the Moscow and regional schools of icon painting, had been centered in St. Petersburg, where the Imperial Academy of Arts held sway, supporting the neoclassical, idealist canon. Distant from the wellsprings of native culture, the St. Petersburg Academy had elaborated its artistic ideal according to the techniques and aesthetic canons of classical antiquity and cultivated the models set by the Old Masters. But with the passing of Karl Briullov and Aleksandr Ivanov, its greatest sons, in the 1850s, the autocracy of the Academy quickly waned and its official style became increasingly conservative. At the same time, a new generation of Academy students became increasingly aware of the discrepancy between their routine assignments and the sociopolitical issues of contemporary Russia. Undoubtedly, the flowering of the democratic movement led by Nikolai Chernyshevsky contributed directly to the development of this new artistic commitment, and, both then and later, his essay *Esteticheskie otnosheniia iskusstva k deistvitel'nosti* (The aesthetic relations of art to reality) (1855) attracted a number of artistic disciples such as Ivan Kramskoi and Vasily Perov.

Discovering a philosophical justification for their own sentiments in dicta such as "that object is beautiful which displays life in itself or reminds us of life,"[1] the new artists gave increasing thought to the expository and didactic force of art and to how it should respond to the "accursed questions." One effect of Chernyshevsky's tract was the revolt of the fourteen Academy students in 1863, who, led by Kramskoi, rejected the set assignment for the annual Gold Medal competition and resigned *en masse*. Seven years later some of these same students established the Society of Wandering Exhibitions. Supported by the outspoken critic Vladimir Stasov and later sponsored by the collector Pavel Tretiakov (founder of the gallery in Moscow that still bears his name), the wanderers *(peredvizhniki)* formulated a new artistic doctrine that prompted artists to emphasize social and political dimensions rather than mere formal attainments, a stance that coincided with the realist tendency in literature represented by Dostoevsky and Tolstoy. Painters such as Kramskoi, Perov, and Ilia Repin, who were in touch with the progressive writers of their time, sometimes painting their portraits, were primary contributors to the new visual realism of the 1860s–90s. This is clear from their trenchant scenes of the "real" Russia such as Perov's *Easter Procession* (1861, Tretiakov Gallery, hereafter cited as TG) and Repin's *Volga Barge-Haulers* (1870–73, Russian Museum, hereafter cited as RM).

The attitude of the wanderers to Western culture was ambiguous. Certainly, their leaders were conscious of European movements, and parallels can be drawn between, say, Perov and Courbet or Repin and Menzel, but their own agenda was "Russian" rather than "international" and among their constant themes were the Russian peasantry, the Russian landscape, the Russian clergy, etc. Artists such as Repin recognized the innovations of French impressionism, but, in general, they professed a preference for "content" over "form," something that discouraged, rather than encouraged, the flowering of impressionism in Russia, at least until the 1890s. At the same time, the relative introversion of the wanderers and an often desultory technique contributed to their general lack of recognition in the West. Consequently, because of this organic attachment to Russian life, the wanderers must be judged, inevitably, in the context of contemporary social and political reality: "Repin," wrote one critic in 1915, "is unthinkable outside Russia. Accept him or reject him, he is outside personal evaluations, he is from the people and is popular in the real sense of the word."[2] Yet for all their sincerity of purpose and love of the motherland, the artistic ideals of the wanderers soon tarnished as the group was joined by less radical colleagues such as Konstantin Makovsky who, far from exposing the ills of Russian society, lapsed into eclecticism of style and sentimentalism of theme, a decline that affected other areas of the Russian visual arts at that time, including the applied arts and architecture.

The deep changes in Russian culture after 1850 were prompted, or, at least, paralleled by, Russia's rapid industrialization and new social mobility, something felt especially strongly in the countryside, as peasants abandoned their patriarchal way of life for the temptations of the big city. As far as the arts were concerned, an entire diapason of traditional manual methods such as icon-making, wood-carving, and embroidery were suddenly replaced by objects of mechanized, mass production. But conscious that an entire cultural heritage might soon be lost, a few enlightened individuals tried to reverse this pernicious trend by trying to record and save peasant art at its source. Ironically, the operation was orchestrated by those same classes that had weakened this indigenous tradition, i.e. Russia's *nouveaux riches* and members of the industrialist aristocracy such as Savva Mamontov and Princess Mariia Tenisheva, whose commercial interests spurred Russia's new capitalist economy and yet whose aesthetic taste contributed to the cultural renaissance of Russia's Silver Age. Both Mamontov and Tenisheva, for example, were sponsors of Sergei Diaghilev's magazine *Mir iskusstva* (The World of Art) and his exhibitions.

In 1870 Mamontov acquired an estate near Moscow called Abramtsevo. This idyllic hideaway near the Sergiev Posad (Zagorsk) soon became an artists' retreat and a veritable artistic laboratory, where many of Russia's *fin de siècle* painters, actors, and critics resided and researched. An enthusiast of William Morris and much drawn to the traditional arts and crafts, Mamontov and his wife Elizaveta encouraged their artist colleagues such as Konstantin Korovin and Viktor Vasnetsov to reexamine the conventions of old Russian culture and incorporate them into their paintings and their designs for woodwork, ceramics, and the theatre. It was an aspiration that was closely identifiable with the Abramtsevo workshops and Mamontov's own private opera company and that attracted many talented artists, among them, Elena Polenova, Mikhail Vrubel, and even Repin.

Similarly, Princess Tenisheva's estate and retreat, Talashkino, near Smolensk, was an undertaking that shared many of the characteristics of Abramtsevo, although its primary strength lay in the fabric and furniture designs supervised by Sergei Maliutin and then Nikolai Rerikh (Roerich). Talashkino also attracted painters, designers, and musicians (Igor Stravinsky worked on the *Rite of Spring* there), but while its wares were represented in outlets in Moscow, London, and Paris, and were often described in the press, Talashkino was overshadowed by Abramtsevo, in part because of Mamontov's more exuberant and engaging personality, in part because of the Princess's constant emphasis on commercial solvency. Be that as it may, both enterprises marked a closer and more beneficial interaction between traditional Russian art, professional studio painting, and industrial design, a development that attained its climax in the scintillating designs of the Ballets Russes and the utopian projects of post-revolutionary Constructivism. True, the artistic accomplishments of Abramtsevo and Talashkino were by no means pure and simple. Often the artists compounded local motifs and methods or mixed them with the strands and whiplashes of art nouveau and Jugendstil that artists such as Aleksandr Golovin and Vrubel knew well, a tendency that expressed itself clearly in the stage designs for Mamontov's opera company and Tenisheva's private theatre. But the very fact that graduates of the Academy of Arts and the Moscow Institute of Painting, Sculpture, and Architecture, i.e. studio artists, were now working as designers was in itself a radical progression and prepared the way for the more spectacular design achievements of the St. Petersburg World of Art and the Ballets Russes.

The symbolist aesthetic

Despite the restoration of certain traditional art forms at the instigation of Abramtsevo and Talashkino, the position of studio art in the 1880s and 1890s had reached a state of relative decline quickened only by the powerful figures of Isaak Levitan, Repin, and the remarkable Valentin Serov (see his portrait of the dancer Ida Rubinstein of 1910, RM). The exhausted doctrines of both the Academy and the wanderers created an impasse that bore the fruits only of weak technique and repetitive theme. Just as forty years before, Russian art had needed, above all, a thematic and stylistic resuscitation, so now, on the threshold of the twentieth century, Russian art demanded a new discipline, a new school. This was provided by the World of Art group, led by Alexandre Benois and Diaghilev, through its journal, its exhibitions, and its many other artistic and critical accomplishments.

To a considerable extent, the decorative output of the World of Art group derived much strength from the bold stylization and vigorous colors of the Abramtsevo and Talashkino experiments. The fact that the first number of *Mir iskusstva* in November 1898 concentrated on the work of Vasnetsov was symptomatic of this debt, for Golovin, Korovin, Vasnetsov, and Vrubel' were among many artists whose peasant motifs and simplified compositions already carried the "geometrization," stylization, and retrospectivism that figured prominently in the work of the principal World of Art artists such as Lev Bakst, Benois, and Konstantin Somov. Contrary to accepted opinion, however, the World of Art was not an avant-garde group, and despite their dislike of the realists, members such as Benois, Bakst, and Somov were traditionalists at heart, unready to accept the later achievements of the neo-primitivists and cubo-futurists. This is one reason why, from their Parnassian heights, they looked askance at the burgeoning avant-garde in Moscow, accusing its first sponsor, the banker Nikolai Riabushinsky, of rashness and vulgarity, even though his magazine *Zolotoe runo* (Golden Fleece) and exhibitions did much to advance the cause of Russian modernism.

The World of Art is a complex rubric that accommodates a group of artists, writers, musicians, and critics, a journal edited by Benois and Diaghilev, and cycle of exhibitions (1899–1906, 1910–24). Diaghilev, now remembered as the impresario of the Ballets Russes, was the practical inspiration to many of the World of Art undertakings, and it was through his services that his artist-colleagues, including Bakst, Benois, and Roerich, achieved their fame in Europe and America as set and costume designers for the ballet productions. Still, it would be misleading to associate the World of Art too closely with any one individual or aesthetic doctrine, even though it evinced a particular sympathy with the first wave of symbolist writers (Konstantin Balmont, Valery Briusov, Zinaida Gippius, and Dmitry Merezhkovsky). But the multifarious interests of the World of Art stimulated a world view much broader than this and in spite of the group's inclination to interpret art as "craft" rather than as "religion," it also supported the later symbolists such as Andrei Bely, Aleksandr Blok and Viacheslav Ivanov, and promoted the Moscow group of mystical painters, the Blue Rose, inspired by Viktor Borisov-Musatov and led by Pavel Kuznetsov.

However, suffice it to remember the critical and philosophical interests of the Russian symbolist poets, especially Bely and Blok, to appreciate their enthusiasm for the non-literary art forms and their mutual striving to create a *Gesamtkunstwerk* – manifest, for example, in Blok's remarkable essay "Colors and Words" of 1905 and in the general enthusiasm for Richard Wagner. True, the World of Art emphasized the visual and performing arts, but it was in touch with the leading representatives of all the humanistic disciplines and acted as a platform for the cross-fertilization of aesthetic concepts. Consequently, the World of Art accommodated the most varied artistic phenomena – the febrile visions of Vrubel' such as *Demon Downcast* (1902, TG) and the stylized neo-Russian style of Vasnetsov's *Bogatyrs* (1898, TG), the *blanc et noir* of Aubrey Beardsley and the Arts and Crafts designs of Mackintosh, the poetry of Briusov, and the literary commentary of Vasily Rozanov. Such eclecticism was evident at the World of Art exhibitions both at home and abroad – for example, the first, in St. Petersburg, in 1899, contained not only group members, but also Western contemporaries such as Degas, Monet, and Puvis de Chavannes. The most radical exhibition was that of 1906 at which Aleksei von Jawlensky, Kuznetsov, Mikhail Larionov, and other innovators were well represented – as indeed they were in the Russian section organized by Diaghilev at the Paris "Salon d'Automne" in the same year.

It is often forgotten that Vasily Kandinsky was also a member of the World of Art, contributed to the journal, and, in general, sympathized with the general aspirations of the group. Indeed, Kandinsky's move toward abstraction, while prompted by many conditions, owed much to the aesthetic and philosophical culture of the Russian *fin de siècle*. Kandinsky's rejection of materialism in favor of the spiritual constitutes the leitmotif of his *Improvisations* and *Compositions* and also of his many essays, especially *On the Spiritual in Art* (1911). In interpreting art as a vehicle of transcendence and in aspiring from the concrete to the abstract, Kandinsky shared a common desire of the Russian symbolist writers such as Bely, Blok, and Vladimir Soloviev. These and many other Russian poets, artists, and musicians, often associated with the World of Art, were important to Kandinsky then – such as the theosophist composers Foma Gartman and Alexandra Zakharina-Unkovskaia, the painter and physician Nikolai Kul'bin, and the theosophical and then Giurdzhievan philosopher Petr Uspensky, and reference to their activities helps to clarify some of Kandinsky's basic artistic positions. Like Kandinsky, these individuals were convinced that the phenomenal world concealed the "real" world, and that the former, therefore, had little or nothing in common with the spirit.

Most of the World of Art artists, Kandinsky included, distanced themselves from the pressing demands of social and political reality, preferring the order and tranquility of Petergof or Versailles as we sense in Benois' *Monplaisir, Petergof* (1900, TG) and Somov's *In the Park of Versailles* (1901, TG). Consequently, the World of Art painters such as Benois and Somov were foreign to the tendentious statements of the Realists, and their logo, "Art is Free, Life is Paralyzed," embodied their conception of art as an expression of the spirit that transcended the harsh realities of everyday existence. True, a few of the World of Art artists such as Ivan Bilibin and Mstislav Dobuzhinsky confronted the insurgent questions of their society by drawing cartoons and caricatures for satirical reviews during the 1905 revolution, such as *Zhupel* (Bugbear) and *Adskaia pochta* (Hellish Post). But the measure of their ideological commitment was uneven and, ultimately, they preferred the serenity of their retrospective musings even at moments of great social transformation such as the October Revolution and the Civil War.

The comparative disregard of contemporary realia identifiable with much of the artistic and literary output of the World of Art was countered by a strong emphasis on the notion of artifact, something that linked the World of Art with its symbolist predecessors in France and Belgium. Artists such as Bakst, Benois, and Somov stressed the value of technical expertise and of syntagmatic qualities such as line, color, mass, weight, and texture – while often confining a given narrative within a theatrical format, as if the action were on stage. Perhaps this marked attention to formal elements on the part of the World of Art prefigured the peculiar emphasis on geometric configuration that the artists of the Russian avant-garde cultivated in the 1910s and 1920s. After all, Bely endeavored to formulate an exact aesthetics, while Briusov spoke of the need for a "scientific poetry"; and Bely's assertion that "we didn't trouble about form or style, but about inner vision," notwithstanding,[3] his exhortation to renew the stylistic and formal arsenal demonstrated the opposite. Even with a deeply philosophical and introspective poet such as Blok, who also published on the pages of the *Mir iskusstva,* the manifest interest in the poetical fabric parallels the schematic landscapes of Benois and Somov with their central axis and symmetrical planes.

Nevertheless, the emphasis of the World of Art on the autonomy of the artifact does not justify a universal application of the term "art for art's sake." Indeed, while promoting the symbolist pantheon of Ibsen, Nietzsche, Soloviev, and Oscar Wilde, the World of Art also acknowledged the achievements of the realists Repin and Tolstoy as well as the transcendental idealism of Bely and V. Ivanov. In other words, the World of Art served as a cultural intersection, rather than as the advocate of a single idea, for, as one of its members remembered, "it was the cult of dilettantism in the good and true sense of the word."[4]

It was in the graphic and scenic arts that the World of Art artists manifested their technical bravura, where an abundance of detail has to be included within strictly curtailed limits. Perhaps the greatest book illustrator was Somov, whose love of the *commedia dell'arte* inspired his striking cover to the first edition of Blok's dramatic works (1907); in the same year, he executed his equally famous covers for V. Ivanov's *Cor Ardens* and Balmont's *Zhar-ptitsa* (Fire-bird). Mention might be made also of Bilibin's exquisite covers and illustrations for the series of Russian fairy tales published in 1901 onward and the edition of Pushkin's *Queen of Spades* published in 1911 with illustrations by Benois. In broader terms, the graphic expertise encountered in the decorative and ornamental pieces of the World of Art artists might be interpreted as the consequence of their "non-philosophical" world view, because in lacking a concrete ideological reference, their art was left literally to its own devices and to manipulate its own ingredients of line, color, and mass.

Still, the World of Art artists did not ignore philosophical dimensions completely. They shared mutual ground with their writer colleagues in an intense concern with the mythological, the erotic, and the necrological, not only choosing similar subjects, but also codifying them in analogous styles. Symbolist poetry, for example, might convey the sensation of inescapability or tedium by recourse to a circular poetical structure or a choral repetition, while a World of Art painting might capture an *intérieur* replete with objects, but lacking human presence. This conception was shared by Dobuzhinsky, whose incisive graphic scenes of St. Petersburg, Riga, and London seem to illustrate the triumph of mechanical technology over human sensibility. A similar anonymity and crystalline stillness are found in Somov's evocations of the seventeenth and eighteenth centuries, such as Somov's *Young Lady Asleep* (1909, TG). In contrast to Bakst, Benois, or Roerich, who turned to antiquity as the embodiment of moral and social integration, Somov often caricatured and parodied his subjects, using them perhaps as allegories for his own perverse and artificial era or to illustrate his own complex ego. On the other hand, Benois, Diaghilev's mentor and friend within the World of Art, opposed such narcissism, declaring that: "Chaos reigns, something turgid which has scarcely any value and which, strangest of all, has no physiognomy . . . Individualism is heresy mainly because it denies communication."[5] Indeed, Benois' own often humorous and cordial depictions of Versailles seem to elicit some remote, yet beloved childhood.

The World of Art artists looked backward rather than forward, although their "retrospective dreams" were not limited to any one historical epoch. Apart from Egypt, Greece, and Versailles, they also cultivated a deep interest in "primitive" culture as is demonstrated by their promotion of V. Vasnetsov and Vrubel', whose art they regarded as the incarnation of an archaic, barbaric force, a world of ancient myth and elemental unity. Bakst's integration of ethnographical fact and magic fantasy in his interpretations of Hellas (as in his *panneau Terror Antiquus* of 1908 [RM]) crystallized the Symbolists' demand that humankind recapture an earlier and more pristine condition, a concept that Bakst also developed in his important essay of 1909 on "The New Paths of Classicism": "Painting of the future calls for a lapidary style, because the new art cannot endure the refined . . . Painting of the future will crawl down into the depths of coarseness."[6] Bakst was anticipating not only the advent of a fresh and adolescent culture, but also the demise of the World of Art itself, for its fragile, epicurean dreams were no match for the abrasive pressures of the new generation, i.e. the Russian avant-garde.

The avant-garde

The avant-garde was a complex mosaic of many individuals and styles that changed the course of Russian culture in the 1910s and 1920s. Naturally, the Russian avant-garde did not suddenly appear, but, rather, was the creative extension and integration of previous tendencies: the neo-nationalists' attention to folk art at Abramtsevo and Talashkino in the later nineteenth century prefigured the neo-primitivist movement led by Natalia Goncharova and Mikhail Larionov; the symbolists' rejection of the material world gave an immediate impulse toward abstraction; and even the St. Petersburg Academy of Arts, despite its pedantry, supplied deductive analyses in the form of tabulations and physiological schemes that return in the minimal compositions of suprematism and constructivism. After all, it may not be so very far from the nineteenth-century pedagogical textbooks showing how spheres, cubes, and rectangles should be depicted to Kazimir Malevich's suprematism, from anatomical atlases to the expressionist heads of Pavel Filonov, or from conventional perspectival renderings to Liubov Popova's "painterly architectonics".

On 10 December 1910, an exhibition called the "Jack of Diamonds" opened in Moscow, which, when judged from any viewpoint, was certainly unusual. Unaccustomed to such novel titles for art exhibitions, the public assumed that the "Jack of Diamonds" was a gambling-house or a brothel, but in no way an art exhibition. However, the Jack of Diamonds group, its exhibitions, debates, and publications are now acknowledged as being essential to the evolution of the Russian avant-garde. Led by Larionov, the Jack of Diamonds invited immediate associations with the uniforms worn by prisoners, encouraging other outsiders and radicals to slap the face of public taste. The central members of the Jack of Diamonds, i.e. Goncharova, Kandinsky, Larionov, Aristarkh Lentulov, Malevich, and Vladimir Tatlin, upset the conventions of Russian art through their explorations of outlandish artistic systems such as neo-primitivism, cubo-futurism, and rayonism, which paved the way for the veritable explosion of isms in the 1910s and early 1920s, e.g. suprematism, everythingism, nothingism, and constructivism.

Rejecting nineteenth-century reportorial realism and the uneasy visions of symbolism, the new wave of artists contended that Moscow was now the center of contemporary culture and that they were bringing a purity and vitality to the jejune routine of Western culture, although they also acknowledged their debt to the West. Seeking fresh ideas, the Jack of Diamonds artists paid close attention to their indigenous arts and crafts such as the toy, the icon, the *lubok* (a cheap, handcolored print), and urban folklore, transferring methods and motifs to their own pictorial vocabulary – resulting in the formulation of the neo-primitivism aesthetic. Recognition of Russia's patriarchal traditions played a vital part in the evolution of the Russian avant-garde, for, as Aleksandr Shevchenko asserted in his neo-primitivist statement of 1913: "icons, *lubki*, trays, signboards, fabrics of the East, etc. – these are specimens of genuine value and painterly beauty."[7] The Burliuk brothers, David and Vladimir, Marc Chagall, Larionov, and Malevich were excited by the bright colors, rough lines, and rude humor of Russian folk culture, translated this native legacy into their own pictorial language, and even revived it as a sociopolitical weapon in patriotic posters for the First World War. True, the advent of the neo-primitivists was to be expected, because they were students (*c.* 1910) just when the traditional Russian arts and crafts were being rediscovered by scholars, critics, and collectors – as witnessed by the large "Exhibition of Ancient Russian Art" that the Moscow Archaeological Institute organized in 1913.

Like Gauguin in Polynesia, Goncharova, Larionov, Malevich, and their colleagues also "went native" in their search for a more pristine artistic expression, paying particular attention to the life and culture of their indigenous people – the Russian and Ukrainian peasant exemplified by Malevich's *Taking in the Rye* (1912, Stedelijk Museum, Amsterdam). These artists also examined children's drawings, Black African art, and Siberian relics, concluding that these artifacts expressed a higher reality as yet untouched by the artificial values of urban civilization. Surely, Goncharova was heeding this call of the past, when she painted common episodes from rural life (peasants working in the fields, fishing, harvesting, treading wine, round dancing) as in *Fishing* of 1909 (Thyssen-Bornemisza Collection, Madrid), a theme that, in turn, exerted a permanent influence on Malevich. On the other hand, Larionov, Goncharova's companion, was more attracted to the metropolis and the provincial city with the graffiti, store signs, barracks, and taverns that we recognize in paintings such as *Relaxing Soldier* (1911, TG).

Most of the avant-garde artists were Orthodox and the components of the Russian church service such as the icon and the iconostasis left a profound visual effect. Goncharova aspired to revive medieval Russian art within her innovative art, painting scenes from the Bible, and eliciting the dissatisfaction of the Moscow censors. A case in point was her four-part *Evangelists* (1910) that she contributed to the "Donkey's Tail" exhibition in 1912, which was banned by the censor at the instigation of the Holy Synod, because of alleged incompatibility between image and title. Malevich also seems to have remembered his religious upbringing when he placed his most radical painting, the *Black Square*, in the *krasnyi ugol* or "holy corner" at the exhibition "0.10" in Petrograd in 1915–16. Kandinsky's explorations of iconic subjects such as St. George and the Dragon (e.g. 1911, TG) also contributed to the development of his abstract style in *c.* 1912. Still, the Russian avant-gardists tended to consider the icon and the *lubok* as an exercise in formal configurations rather than as a ritualistic accessory, a viewpoint that Larionov supported in arranging his "Exhibition of Icons and *Lubki*" in Moscow in 1913: it was the inverted perspective, anatomical elongations, and bright colors of such artifacts that inspired artists – and not only Russians – to pay particular attention to this cultural legacy. After his visit to Moscow and St. Petersburg in 1911 Henri Matisse even remarked the icons in the Kremlin were "the best thing that Moscow has to offer."[8]

Conversely, the artists of the Jack of Diamonds, and of the three other groups that Larionov established between 1912 and 1914 (the Donkey's Tail, the Target, and No. 4) also responded to French post-impressionism and cubism. Some, such as Chagall, Larionov, and Lentulov, traveled to Paris for longer or shorter periods, others knew Braque, Gauguin, Matisse, and Picasso from the great collections of the Moscow business-men, Ivan Morozov and Sergei Shchukin, still others read the many appreciations and reviews of contemporary French and German art in the Russian press. Larionov's *Gypsy in Tiraspol* (1908, TG), for example, is a clear reminiscence of Gauguin's Polynesian beauties, while Malevich's still lifes and schematic figures of *c.* 1912–13 such as his portrait of Mikhail Matiushin (1913, TG) owe much to Picasso. Still, the Russians used the words cubism – and futurism – as generic terms, even combining them into a single word, cubo-futurism, so as to accommodate all kinds of "new" ideas, including vorticism and the Delaunays' simultanism, which exerted an appreciable influence on the work of Aleksandra Exter, Lentulov, and Georgy Yakulov. In other words, the Russians were well aware of the latest tendencies in Europe, although their own artistic experimentation and patriotic pride supplanted any sense of duty toward cubist Paris, expressionist Munich, or futurist Milan. Indeed, after their initial apprenticeship, Filonov, Goncharova, and Malevich contended in their different ways that Russia was about to experience a cultural Renaissance, and that Velasquez and Raphael were mere "philistines of the spirit" in comparison to the great artists that Russia was about to produce.[9]

Only an extreme self-confidence and a youthful energy could have induced such sentiments, and the Russian avant-gardists seemed to find these same qualities in the everyday life of the street with its flea markets, funfairs, and sports meets, and the rude words, ostentatious clothes, and scandalous gestures of these dissidents echo such sources. David Burliuk, for example, used to wear a top hat, a wooden spoon and a lorgnette, Vasily Kamensky and Vladimir Mayakovsky gaudy vests, while

Goncharova, Larionov, and Ilia Zdanevich painted hieroglyphs on their faces and bodies. Such antics reflected an eager aspiration to reduce "high" art to "low" and raise "low" art to "high". Even Larionov's elegant abstract system called rayonism seems to have been inspired by street-lamps and car headlights rather than by studious investigations into optical refractions (see *Street with Lamps* of 1913, Thyssen-Bornemisza Collection, Madrid).

In the 1910s the avant-garde "shocked the bourgeoisie" not only in boisterous Moscow, but also in demure St. Petersburg. The northern response to the Jack of Diamonds, the Union of Youth, promoted the work of many different artists – from D. Burliuk to Filonov, from Malevich to Olga Rozanova, from Ivan Puni (Jean Pougny) to Tatlin, and it also maintained contact with both Scandinavian and German artists such as the Blaue Reiter group in Munich, including Kandinsky. The Union of Youth sponsored many activities, but perhaps its most tangible contribution to the cause of the avant-garde was its sponsorship of the cubo-futurist opera *Victory over the Sun* in 1913. With discordant music by Mikhail Matiushin, neologistic libretto by Velimir Khlebnikov and Aleksei Kruchonykh, and schematic sets and costumes by Malevich, *Victory over the Sun* explored new aesthetic ideas such as *zaum'* (transrational language), melisma, and geometric reduction – if Malevich's back-drop of black and white triangles for Act 2, Scene 5, can be read as a non-objective composition. True, Malevich came to his abstract system after a fertile investigation into neo-primitivism, but he is now remembered for the suprematist or non-figurative exercises that he displayed for the first time at "0.10" in 1915 alongside other radical paintings by Ivan Kliun, Popova, Rozanova, et al. Among his contributions there were his *Black and Red Squares* (1915, TG and RM), the latter of which, incidentally, was subtitled "Peasant Woman in Two Dimensions."

Malevich never hesitated in his suprematist commitment and he attracted an extensive following. For example, after Malevich ousted Chagall from the directorship of the Vitebsk Practical Art Institute in 1919, he inspired and nurtured an entire generation of new suprematists such as Ilia Chashnik, El Lissitzky, and Nikolai Suetin. Wearing tiny black squares on their clothes, these artists established their own society, i.e. Unovis (Affirmers of the New Art), and until their mentor's departure for Petersburg in 1922, they did much to elaborate the suprematist system. Under the aegis of Malevich, for example, Lissitzky developed his notion of the Proun ("Project for the Affirmation of the New") as an extension of the suprematist doctrine (*Proun 1c* of 1919 in the Thyssen-Bornemisza Collection, Madrid, is an excellent example), and much affected by the cool configurations of suprematism, the Unovis artists soon transferred their lessons to the functional arts – architecture, ceramics, book design, even clothing. Their geometric vocabulary left an indelible imprint on early Soviet design.

At heart, however, Malevich was a painter fascinated with the pictorial plane, a painter who, ultimately, concluded rather than renewed a hallowed artistic tradition. In contrast, Tatlin, who started his career as a sailor before turning to painting, blazed a new trail that led to constructivism. This constructor rejected the idea of transcendental inspiration and the personal genius, arguing for an alliance with engineering, an aspiration symbolized by the models for his Tower or Monument to the III International (1919–20, not built) and his industrial designs for clothing, a stove, furniture, and even an airplane (his so-called Letatlin of *c.* 1930). Tatlin's reliefs of 1914 onward such as *Assemblage of Materials* (1914, TG) were also a gesture to this rationality, attracting a number of other, like-minded artists, especially Popova and Aleksandr Rodchenko, who went on to develop the aesthetic of constructivism. Function as the determinant of form, tactile material, and rational structure became central concepts of the new language, reinforcing a commitment to Tatlin's rather than to Malevich's world view and preparing a new generation for direct involvement in the industrial and democratic demands of the revolutionary ethos.

The October Revolution

The Revolution of October 1917 exerted a formative influence on the development of Russian art, even though the extent of its influence is often misconstrued. Naturally, the Revolution destroyed or damaged many cultural institutions, but, as the real extension of radical politics, it also mandated radical artists such as Malevich, Rodchenko, Tatlin, and even Kandinsky to adopt positions of great ideological and pedagogical power. Their ranks were swelled as *émigré* sons – Chagall, Naum Gabo, and David Shterenberg among them – returned from abroad. Many were welcomed by Anatoly Lunacharsky, head of the People's Commissariat of Enlightenment, who appreciated or at least tolerated the more extreme manifestations of cultural investigation, inviting Rodchenko, Shterenberg, Tatlin and many other leftists to join the Visual Arts Section of his agency. This Section, in turn, did a great deal to propagate the ideas of the avant-garde – by purchasing works for museum collections, by restructuring the old art schools into Svomas (Free Studios), by establishing think tanks such as InKhuk (Institute of Artistic Culture) and RAKhN (Russian Academy of Artistic Sciences), and by orchestrating major enterprises such as Lenin's Plan of Monumental Propaganda (1918 onward) and Tatlin's Monument to the III International. This combination of circumstances enabled many artists to assume influential positions in the new republic, something that led to the short-lived dictatorship of the left, especially in Moscow.

The first question that confronted the artist now was how to define the proletarian style. To many, constructivism, formulated in 1921, seemed to be the clearest expression of the new ideology, because, like communism, it also claimed to be a global and democratic movement inspired by modern technology and the factory. The constructivists also affirmed that the old artistic disciplines such as studio painting and sculpture were moribund and that the new arts of the cinema, photography, commercial advertising, industrial design, and athletics would replace them. Impatient of opposing views, the constructivists voiced their ideas with loud rhetoric, and their extreme intolerance was a curious prelude to the cultural dictatorship of the Stalin epoch – in word, if not in deed. However, the geometric sobriety of constructivism, with its orientation toward industrial design (the printing arts, textiles, and architecture), was a direct response not necessarily to socialist demands, but rather to preceding aesthetic trends and to the significant attainments in applied design by radical artists *before* the Revolution – posters and book designs by Malevich and Tatlin, accessories by Exter and Puni, dresses by Goncharova and Rozanova, etc. In any case, the constructivists did not always practice what they preached (Popova and Rodchenko, for example, continued to paint studio paintings in spite of their avowed commitment to industrial design).

Even so, the constructivist program was much indebted to the ideological pressures of the Revolution, and its leading advocates – Rodchenko, and the critics Aleksei Gan and Nikolai Tarabukin, hastened to prove their political allegiance. In this sense, Rodchenko was the constructivists' constructivist, for as a radical artist he responded immediately to the political, social, and cultural demands, identifying industrial design and photography as the primary media of the new Russia. As early as 1916, Rodchenko contributed six compass-and-ruler drawings to

Tatlin's Moscow exhibition called "The Store," and then went on to produce a series of "minimalist" paintings that depended upon the simple interplay of textures, colors, rhythms, and forms, including a triptych of red, yellow, and blue (Rodchenko family, Moscow), that Rodchenko showed at the "5 x 5 = 25" exhibition in 1921. With this farewell gesture to studio painting, Rodchenko turned his attention to more "relevant" media such as polygraphical design, photography, and stage design. Popova, too, moved from her architectonic paintings of 1917–18 (various collections) to more utilitarian applications, especially in her projects for Vsevolod Meyerhold's theatre and the textile and haberdashery trade. Her constructions for the plays *The Magnanimous Cuckold* (1922) and *Earth on End* (1923) seemed to be walk-through sculptures that were entirely functional and universal in the sense that the actors were invited to use them as props at any time, in any place, and for any performance. Regarding the installation on stage as a scenic relief, Popova also interpreted the human body as a kinetic construction, emphasizing its articulated mobility in her light, efficient, and hygienic dress designs of 1923–24.

Actually, their loud declarations notwithstanding, the constructivists were in the minority, for the more we study the last stages of the avant-garde, the more we are struck by the continued wide diapason of ideas and movements, at least until the total imposition of socialist realism in the early 1930s. Many other artists felt their particular artistic expressions to be revolutionary and engagé, but by no means were they all attracted to constructivism. For example, Filonov and his pupils were always convinced of the potential of studio painting and created some of their most striking pictures in the 1920s, such as *Living Head* (1926, RM). Expressionism and surrealism left a strong imprint on Soviet artists of the mid-1920s, particularly the members of OST (Society of Studio Artists) such as Aleksandr Deineka and Yury Pimenov, whose awareness of the concurrent work of Otto Dix and George Grosz seems clear in paintings such as *Defense of Petrograd* and *Give to Heavy Industry* (both 1927, TG). The OST artists argued that studio painting could, indeed, render the new themes of sports, industry, and aviation in an engaging, if still experimental style. In other words, despite the inexorable move back toward realism in the late 1920s, there was still an artistic plurality, and even as late as 1929, the Tretiakov Gallery in Moscow granted Malevich his first one-man show, just as the Russian Museum in Leningrad was planning one for Filonov, and just as Tatlin was designing his Letatlin.

But by that time Malevich and Tatlin, the owners of the "heavens" and the "earth" of the avant-garde,[10] were middle-aged, and their utopian visions were fast fading in a society caught up with the exigencies of the first Five Year Plan, collectivization, and the glorification of the leader. What was now required was an art form that could be read easily and unambiguously, one that reflected commitment to Stalin's socialist reconstruction, and that could still elicit popular recognition and respect through its emphasis on the classical canon. Advocated in 1934 as the only permissible cultural style for Soviet Russia, socialist realism fulfilled the demands of an ideological and bureaucratic elite, and its basic ideas informed a strict codex that guided Soviet art for the next half-century.

Soviet socialist realism

Socialist realism was not born in a vacuum, but, to a considerable extent, epitomized tendencies that had been manifest all along. Even during the tempest of avant-garde activity immediately after the Revolution, some critics argued that "realism is coming into its own,"[11] a sentiment reinforced by a series of structural and organizational developments throughout the 1920s.

The most far-reaching of these measures was the establishment of AKhRR (Association of Artists of Revolutionary Russia) in Moscow in 1922 – just after the forty-seventh exhibition of the Society of Wandering Exhibitions. The first goal of the *akhrovtsy* was to present revolutionary Russia in an unpretentious and legible manner by emphasizing the common life of the proletariat, the peasantry, the Red Army, etc., a desire that they expressed in their first declaration of 1922: "We will provide a true picture of events and not abstract concoctions discrediting our Revolution in the face of the international proletariat."[12] Cultivating the documentary value of art, AKhRR refurbished the traditions of nineteenth-century realism and was quick to censure those who disagreed. AKhRR attracted many young artists such as Fedor Bogorodsky, Isaak Brodsky, Aleksandr Gerasimov, Evgeny Katsman, and Georgy Riazhsky, who accepted the didactic function of painting and sculpture and who lent their talents to the depiction of the new reality (e.g. Riazhsky's *Woman Delegate*, 1927, TG). Most of the AKhRR members were of proletarian families and their exhibitions such as "Revolution, Life, and Labor" (1924) were extremely popular both with the masses and with the military and political elites – a status that inspired several key commissions such as Brodsky's portrait of Mikhail Frunze in 1929 (Central Museum of the Armed Forces, Moscow).

Eager to transmit the ideological message, the AKhRR artists often neglected technical expertise and their reportorial style was sometimes desultory and even amateur. While taking their cue from the nineteenth-century realist style and giving particular attention to the *tematicheskaia kartina* (the painting with committed subject matter), they were sometimes accused of being photographic and superficial. The Hungarian critic Alfred Kurella, who became an eager advocate of Soviet socialist realism in the 1930s, initiated an ardent polemic in 1928, arguing that AKhRR had not produced a revolutionary style, that even its selection of motifs merely paraphrased traditional ones, and that, if it were not for their external emblems, the AKhRR paintings and sculptures might have been done by the wanderers. The result, he concluded, was a *petit bourgeois* art, a "Pinkerton daubing" that had little to do with revolutionary Russia.[13] Strangely enough, this was the same kind of argument that hostile critics applied to the avant-garde. In the wake of the Revolution, artists such as Lissitzky, Malevich, Rodchenko, and Tatlin affirmed that their revolutionary artistic systems had anticipated the sociopolitical revolution of the Bolsheviks, inferring, for example, that geometric abstraction was close to the technological world of the industrial proletariat and that it could be applied to the world of industrial design, including architecture, posters, furniture, and clothing. A persuasive argument – until it was pointed out that geometric abstraction and the "International Style" were even more fashionable in bourgeois France and capitalist America.

Arguments such as these were part of the intense debate surrounding the Party's status in matters of artistic form and content, the appropriateness of cultural plurality, and, in general, the ramifications of a proletarian or communist style. In order to set up the complex mechanism that would generate a legitimate Soviet style, a more rigorous control of culture had to be established – and, to a considerable extent, this was accomplished through the passing of the Party decree "On the Reconstruction of Literary and Artistic Organizations" in April 1932 and through the proceedings of the First All-Union Congress of Soviet Writers in August 1934.

The direct result of "On the Reconstruction of Literary and Artistic Organizations" was the liquidation of all art and literature factions and the demand that professional art workers join their respective unions;

and although a Union of Soviet Artists was established only in 1960 with the First Congress of Artists of the Russian Federation, a special committee was established to assume responsibility for all art affairs. This drastic reorganization of the Soviet art world prepared the way for the conclusive advocacy of socialist realism two years later at the First All-Union Congress of Soviet Writers in Moscow. Chaired by Maksim Gorky, the Congress played a decisive part in the evolution of Soviet culture not only because it constituted an impressive symbol of solidarity (almost 600 delegates from almost fifty Soviet nationalities were present as well as forty-one guests from abroad), but also because it chose socialist realism as the only artistic medium adequate to the needs of Soviet literature and art. The contributors to the Congress, especially Gorky and Andrei Zhdanov (Secretary of the Communist Party of the Soviet Union), proposed that tenets such as "revolutionary romanticism," "reality in its revolutionary development," "typicality," and "Party spirit" were essential components of the socialist realist formula. Stalin himself was credited with coining the term Socialist Realism, a "definition of genius,"[14] while for the next twenty years critics repeated that "Soviet painting is obliged to the brilliant leadership of Stalin for its development."[15] But the politician's role as art critic and historian was played by other Party leaders, too. Zhdanov, of course, was responsible for some of the most scathing criticisms of modernist art and literature, and even Lavrenty Beria took time out from his duties as head of the secret police to co-organize the "Exhibition of Works by Georgian Artists" in Moscow in 1937.

Delegates to the Congress argued that Gorky's writings, particularly his novel *Mother* (1906), were at the cornerstone of the socialist realist style, since they carried the seeds of its basic principles. But within the context of the visual arts, a precedent of such stature was missing, although the wanderers provided a firm traditional basis, and artists such as Abram Arkhipov and Nikolai Kasatkin, members of the wanderers and then AKhRR, were an important bridge between the critical and socialist realisms. In any case, while the Congress stressed the importance of the written word, its general conclusions were relevant to Soviet culture as a whole, especially to the visual arts, and there could no longer be any doubt that artistic policy in the Soviet Union was now reliant upon "the great and invincible doctrine of Marx-Engels-Lenin-Stalin, a doctrine that has been put into practice by our Party and by our soviets."[16]

In advocating the new realism, the Soviet establishment embarked upon a merciless dismantling of the old avant-garde and the eradication of an entire era of artistic discovery. Since all channels of artistic endeavor – exhibitions, acquisitions, stipends, supplies – were now under Party control, any non-conforming artist was automatically denied exhibition rights and financial support. Even the modernist artists such as Kuzma Petrov-Vodkin who had deviated only slightly from the realist tradition were now reminded of their past sins and deemed alien to the masses. Some courageous individuals continued to experiment: for example, Lissitzky and Rodchenko produced exciting photomontage work for the propaganda magazine *USSR in Construction;* in the early 1940s Rodchenko painted a number of abstract expressionist canvases, curiously reminiscent of Jackson Pollock's; and Filonov continued to follow his expressionist style. But these were exceptions to the rule, and the avant-garde, if it did survive, maintained its momentum only in emigration (Chagall, Gabo, Kandinsky, etc.).

The socialist realist style, as practiced in the 1930s, was meant to be "national in form, socialist in content"[17] and devoid of "class connections." Nevertheless, it still depended upon an internal hierarchy, and if, for example, new media such as film and photography (multiple and "democratic") had been regarded as revolutionary in the 1920s, they now surrendered their primacy to the oil painting in the gilt frame, the monumental sculpture, and the Stalin "wedding-cake" architecture. The theoretical and practical results of socialist realism were propagated through a sophisticated, well-financed structure of exhibitions such as "XX Years of the Red Army and Navy" (Moscow, 1938) and "I. V. Stalin in the Visual Arts" (Moscow, 1949), through didactic monographs by critics such as Rafail Kaufman and Vladimir Kemenov, and through a steady production of masterpieces such as *Higher Ever Higher* (1934, Kiev Museum of Art) by Serafima Riangina. Such measures constituted an efficacious engine that promoted and propagated the principles of socialist realism universally.

Perhaps the most memorable productions of socialist realist art lie in the depictions of industrial and urban complexes, in which the younger generation proved to be especially inventive. Such vivid paintings as *On the Track* (1933, TG) by Georgy Nissky showed an optimistic society at work building a technological future; and the same positive interpretation of socialism was manifest in collective farm scenes by Semeon Chuikov, Sergei Gerasimov, and Arkady Plastov. Still, despite strict control, socialist realism was not impervious to change, and as with any artistic program, its quintessential terms and ideas were open to interpretation. Phrases such as "reality in its revolutionary development"[18] or "working on the image of Stalin is the embodiment of the basic, central theme of socialist realism"[19] are rhetorical approximations, as abstract as words such as "freedom" and "democracy." Consequently, although the subject matter of the Stalin style was predictable, its interpretation was not. Was Stalin to be depicted alone or with a group? Would the political heroes of today continue to be so tomorrow? Such questions fueled the polemical environment of the 1930s–40s, leading to the frequent recantations by writers and artists and to the modification of works of art in accordance with proposals dictated from above. For example, the first title that Aleksandr Gerasimov gave to his *Comrades Stalin and Voroshilov in the Kremlin* (1938, TG) was *Peace Watch*; in 1940 Boris Ioganson painted his *Leaders of October*, but was criticized for underplaying its "psychological aspect," so in 1948 he repainted it, achieving a more adequate "rhythmical construction."[20] After Khrushchev's exposure of the personality cult in 1956, Stalin himself was overpainted and his statues removed from public places, even as socialist realism was still being advocated as the only legitimate cultural canon.

The Second World War engendered a renewed ideological mobilization of Soviet artists. Painters were sent to the front not only to depict actual events, but also to obtain material for large-scale landscapes and portraits, some of which were completed after the war. Infected by the upsurge of patriotism, artists turned to great men and moments of Russia's past, inspiring the triptych, *Aleksandr Nevsky* (TG), by Pavel Korin, for example; and those who had been satisfied with the rendering of innocent landscapes and domestic interiors were now expected to reinforce their paintings with military and nationalistic messages: Plastov, for example, moved from his depictions of rural pleasures to more tendentious pictures such as *A Fascist Flew Past* (1942, TG) and, similarly, Sergei Gerasimov moved from his village celebrations such as *Collective Farm Harvest Festival* to a harsher reality, as in his *Mother of a Partisan* (1943, TG). Of particular interest were the war canvases of Aleksandr Deineka: technically well executed, but not merely photographic, scenes such as *The Defense of Sevastopol* (1942, RM) and *Outskirts of Moscow. November* (1941, TG) supplied an emotional commentary on the horrors of war, while Pimenov and Vladimir Serov tried to document real-life events such as *Meeting on the Neva. Breach of the Blockade* (1943, RM, by Serov and others), a moment that Serov witnessed personally. Apart from their anti-German caricatures and cartoons, for which they are famous, the Kukryniksy trio (the abbreviated names of Mikhail Kupriianov, Porfiry Krylov, and Nikolai Sokolov) also directed their talents into topical studio paintings such as *The Fascists Flee From Novgorod* (1944–46, RM).

Although affected by the strictures of the Zhdanov administration, Soviet art of the post-war period manifested a new element of romanticism, even of nostalgia – apparent in some of the war pictures of the mid-1940s, such as Bogorodsky's *Glory to the Fallen Heroes* (1945, TG). What in the 1930s had often been a powerful and uplifting realism became more reminiscent of salon painting, a sentimental development exemplified by pictures as Plastov's *A Tractor Driver's Supper* (1951, TG).

Developments after Stalin

Obviously, the dictatorship of Stalin did not tolerate open deviation from the established code of socialist realism, but with his passing in 1953, Soviet culture – slowly, but surely – entered a more liberal era. Since its inception after Stalin's death, dissident art in the Soviet Union was constantly associated with the political mechanisms that both nurtured and opposed it and with the various ideological agents that, in their ardent inertia, were slow to accommodate new artistic ideas. For a long time the Ministry of Culture of the USSR, the Union of Artists, and the Academy of Arts were the immediate extensions of the Party machine, and the doctrine that they supported, socialist realism, continued to be reinforced by edict, decree, and statistical analysis in the same way that foreign policy and Five Year Plans were conceived. The process of emancipation followed an uneven, zig-zag path, and the shadows of 1937 returned during the Brezhnev administration, but, even so, the history of modern Soviet art is a history of its inexorable advance from a single canon to a plurality of styles – and, strange to say, from its status as an exclusive and almost sacred expression to that of a profane and marketable commodity.

The external chronology of unofficial art in the Soviet Union has been compiled many times and only the primary facts need be repeated here, i.e. Nikita Khrushchev's reactions to the first dissident showing at the exhibition of "Thirty Years of the Moscow Union of Artists" at the Manège in 1962 (which included works by Eli Beliutin, Ernst Neizvestny, and Vladimir Yankilevsky), the Stevens exhibition in Moscow in July 1970 (which included works by Viacheslav Kalinin, Lev Kropivnitsky, Vladimir Nemukhin, Dmitry Plavinsky, and Evgeny Rukhin), the "First Fall Open Air Show of Paintings" (the "bulldozer exhibition") in Moscow in September 1974, the "Exhibition at the Bee-Keeping Pavilion" at the Exhibition of Economic Achievements, Moscow, in January 1975, and the many provocative exhibitions on Malo-Gruzinskaia and Begovaia Streets in Moscow. The denouement came in the mid-1980s with the accession of Mikhail Gorbachev, the announcement of *glasnost* and *perestroika,* and the Sotheby's auction "Russian Avant-Garde and Soviet Contemporary Art" in Moscow in July 1988, with a record price being paid for one of the *Alefbet* panels by the young Jewish-Russian artist Grigory Bruskin.

Certainly, the way in which the new art deviated from convention was often the result of direct confrontation with clear political symbols – Neizvestny's famous polemic with Khrushchev at the Manège exhibition, the police intervention at the bulldozer exhibition, the KGB interrogations and subsequent imprisonments or expulsions of artists and collectors such as Oskar Rabin, Yakov Vinkovetsky, and Aleksandr Glezer. Such artists and their literary colleagues were labeled as "traitors to the motherland" and "agents of hostile powers"; and their action painting or painted actions were construed as pernicious not only to the aesthetic welfare of Soviet youth, but also to the cause of international socialism: "Thanks to the aesthetics of Marxism and Leninism, these laws have become the foundation of a profound investigation into man and the conditions of his existence. From these laws it follows that everything that is anti-artistic in art becomes automatically anti-humane and anti-human."[21] In Western coverage, these associations led to a plethora of conventional epithets such as "persecuted artists" and "forbidden artists"[22] – which often had little to do with the actual paintings or poems in question. Symptomatic of this tendency to equate the search for artistic freedom with the search for political freedom was the particular attention that the Western press gave to institutional expulsions and enforced exiles. True, expulsion from an art school or science laboratory often anticipated emigration, but in some cases the act was a purely "artistic" one in the sense that when, for example, Oleg Tselkov was expelled from the Academy of Arts in 1955, the accusations were not of anti-government perpetrations, but of "formalism," even though from the viewpoint of the Party, the latter could also constitute an act of treason.

Be that as it may, any analysis of the dissident movement in the Soviet Union must begin with the basic question of iconographic sources: if the artists were nurtured on the principles of socialist realism and were surrounded by the omnipresent mechanism of Party propaganda, how did they learn about "bourgeois formalism" and abstract art? The answers are complex, but at least two main avenues of relevant inquiry can be delineated. One was the slow but sure rediscovery of the avant-garde of the 1910s and 1920s; the other was the sporadic encounter with contemporary Western culture.

As with any artistic or political force, the Soviet nonconformist movement has its pioneers and disciples, luminaries and epigones. Without the initial, iconoclastic statements of Mikhail Kulakov, Neizvestny, Nemukhin, Rabin, Rukhin, Ullo Sooster, and Tselkov in the 1960s and early 1970s the dissident movement would hardly have found the strength to grow further. The abrasive imagery of these artists and their bold polemics with the political *status quo* tested the weaknesses of the Soviet structure, establishing behavioral codes and strategies that helped subsequent generations face the apparatus of the KGB and the threats of imprisonment, hospitalization, and banishment. No doubt, these searing experiences prompted the marked expressionist orientation of that first underground – the brooding urban ugliness of Rabin (e.g., *Jewish Passport,* 1972, private collection), the ruptured objects of Rukhin, and the gestural explosions of Yury Dyshlenko and Vinkovetsky (e.g., his *Major Virginian Series,* 1978, private collection).

In the 1950s, as the first wave of dissident artists and writers emerged, represented by Beliutin, Ilia Glazunov, Neizvestny, Evgeny Evtushenko, and Andrei Voznesensky, some of the old avant-garde artists were still alive – not perhaps the real pioneers such as Filonov and Malevich, but at least artists who could remember and recount: Nikolai Akimov, Robert Falk, Kuznetsov, Vladimir Sterligov, and Aleksandr Tyshler played a major role in bridging the generation gap, and although their own art may not seem especially experimental, they were revered as apologists of artistic freedom and their paintings seen as symbols of aesthetic purity. These survivors also formed a delicate link with the international heritage of post-impressionism and cubism that had long been concealed and maligned. After all, during that epoch of *zapasniki* (storage rooms) and *spetskhrany* (special collections), the average Soviet citizen was denied any possibility of seeing Dali, Kandinsky, or Picasso either at home or abroad or of reading literature that treated of "modern art." That is why the few collectors of the Russian avant-garde such as George Costakis and Yakov Rubinshtein were especially important to the new generation, for their apartments provided artists with a firsthand knowledge of the works of Kandinsky, Malevich, Popova, Rodchenko, etc. Costakis even acquired works by the new avant-garde, e.g. by Dmitry Krasnopevtsev and Plavinsky, although the major dissident collections in the Soviet Union were assembled by other individuals such as Glezer, Tatiana Kolodzei, Georgy Mikhailov, Evgeny Nutovich, and Leonid Talochkin.

A second way in which artists learned about abstract art was through encounters with contemporary Western culture. Nowadays it is hard to imagine the keen appetite for pop art, beatnik poetry, rock and roll, and jazz that young Soviets had in the 1960s and the indignation that these artistic expressions elicited among their elders. It is also difficult to understand the problem of availability – when possession of a Presley record or of a Magritte reproduction could lead to interrogation and hard labor. There were, however, "legal" channels of distribution such as exhibitions of foreign art and official condemnations of abstract art that carried reproductions of the objects of abuse. Of particular importance was the "Exhibition of American Painting and Sculpture" that the Archives of American Art organized in Moscow in 1959, for this was the first public showing in the Soviet Union of works by Jackson Pollock, Willem de Kooning, Georgia O'Keefe, etc. Artists such as Neizvestny and Nemukhin who visited the exhibition tell how it transformed their cultural lives, reinforcing their doubt in the solvency of socialist realism and their endeavor to establish alternative systems.

However complex these conditions, they informed and influenced much of the dissident output. Abstract expressionism (Beliutin and his students), kinetic art (Lev Nusberg and the Movement group), environmental art (Francisco Infante), action painting (Kulakov), geometrism (Mikhail Chernyshev, Mikhail Roginsky, and Eduard Shteinberg), lyrical abstraction (Genri Elinson, Lidiia Masterkova, and Evgeny Mikhnov-Voitenko), and even magic realism (Mikhail Shemiakin [Chemiakin], Vladimir Ovchinnikov, Igor Tiulpanov) were some of the interpretations that prospered in the dissident era. True, leaders of the underground such as Erik Bulatov, Kalinin, and Rabin did interpret Soviet reality in a narrative and often tendentious fashion, questioning and inverting ideological messages that relied heavily on an informed "reader." However, there were many other artists, sometimes less familiar, who rejected this approach, as they endeavored to reconnect with the Russian avant-garde on the one hand and the New York School on the other.

The *émigré* historian Igor Golomshtok has maintained that there are two kinds of artistic innovation – of form and of the spirit.[23] Even though the Western observer may find the Russian insistence on the primacy of the spirit to be overwhelming, the intense aspiration toward the spiritual condition has been a guiding force in twentieth-century Russian culture, from Kandinsky's *On the Spiritual in Art* to Vasily Chekrygin's belief in the resurrection of souls, and although it can be hazardous to connect the "godseekers" of Russia's philosophical renaissance (Nikolai Berdiaev, Sergei Bulgakov, Vladimir Soloviev et al.) with the artistic accomplishments of the avant-garde, there can be no question that, in some contexts, the experimental art of Filonov, Kandinsky, Malevich, and their colleagues owed much of its energy to the theurgical explorations of the Silver Age. In rediscovering this lost heritage, many contemporary artists were also drawn to the spiritual quest of their forefathers and felt an immediate sympathy with Orthodoxy, Theosophy, Judaism, and the Oriental religions. As far as dissident painting is concerned, artists accepted these traditions either as a thematic source, depicting Russian churches, saints, the Purim, etc. or used it in a more private, cryptic, and abstract fashion.

Masterkova, for example, seemed to be following a spiritual path through the mystical cosmos that Malevich created with his suprematist geometries. The apparent equilibrium suggested by her restrained colors and forms and the pregnant silence of her untitled compositions of the early 1970s (as in the Norton Dodge Collection, Zimmerli Art Museum, New Brunswick, New Jersey) generate the same evocatory force as prayers offered to a distant deity, unidentifiable yet omnipresent. Obviously, for Masterkova, as for Kandinsky and Malevich, non-figurative painting, which she began to investigate in the early 1960s, is a vehicle of spiritual engagement with a higher harmony, a painted liturgy that invites the spectator to commune with her art in reverent solitude. Kulakov, on the other hand, broadened the Russian mystical experience to include substantial references to Zen Buddhism, investigating and depicting concepts such as "cosmos" in 1959 and "embryo" in 1962 (artist's collection, Rome). For Kulakov, as for Vinkovetsky, abstract painting held an ecstatic, transcendental power and he used it as an allegory of the ostensible disorder of the universe – controlled, however, by its Creator in the same way that the painted composition is controlled by the artist. To some extent, Lev Kropivnitsky pursued the same avenue of inquiry in his occasional abstractions, visualizing invisible concepts such as "existence," "trajectory," and "fury" as manifestations of the supreme energy of the cosmos. A student of Chinese philosophy, Kropivnitsky retained and expressed a psychological distance and inner peace, establishing a defense system that not even long years of war, imprisonment, and persecution could weaken. Masterkova, Kulakov, Vinkovetsky, and Kropivnitsky teach us that beyond the brutal confrontation of tectonic shifts there exists a grandiose symmetry of silence and that the artist's primary mission, like the priest's, is to trace and transmit this ultimate truth.

In this respect, Nemukhin's constant game of cards has particular significance, for it draws upon the leitmotif of gambling and divination central to Russian culture. Pushkin's *Queen of Spades* and Dostoevsky's *Gamblers* are obvious literary refractions of the theme, but the visual commentary is also manifold, from Aleksei Venetsianov's *Divination by Cards* (1842, Russian Museum, St. Petersburg) to the Ace of Clubs in Malevich's *Aviator* (1914, Russian Museum, St. Petersburg), from Pavel Fedotov's *Gamblers* (1852, State Museum of Russian Art, Kiev) to Olga Rozanova's pictures of playing cards of *c.* 1915. As the nineteenth-century *lubok* called *The Demon of Card Playing* tells us, playing cards is a satanic ploy that undermines social mores and unleashes sinister powers, and in holding up his cards to the Establishment, the sorcerer Nemukhin seemed to be fully aware of these connotations. In other words, what might appear to be an abstract painting, dependent for its effect on a formal counterpoint of textures and rhythms is, in fact, an intricate narrative charged with an ideological message that places it firmly within the Russian esoteric tradition. *Poker on the Beach* of 1974 (Norton Dodge Collection, Zimmerli Art Museum, New Brunswick, New Jersey) is a case in point.

A fervent apologist of abstract or near abstract art during the 1950s–60s was Beliutin, whose tempestuous insurgency and uncompromising behavior led to his expulsion from the Moscow Polygraphical Institute in 1959 and to continued harassment thereafter. Yet in many ways, Beliutin is an organic extension of the very regime that punished him, for he was no less dogmatic in his artistic belief than the socialist realists were in theirs and condemned the cultural establishment for bigotry and corruption in the same way that the Party accused the dissident movement of treachery and treason. Since 1946 he has led a studio of committed students which now, tucked away in the woods of Abramtsevo, leads a dedicated, almost monastic way of life, just as Filonov and his School of Analytical Art did in the 1920s. Beliutin is jealous of his artistic behests, is eager to explain them to the sincere observer, and, paradoxically, also like Filonov, recognizes and ratifies the pedagogical methods of the Academy, even though his artistic practice may seem antipodal. Beliutin's painting demonstrates the sheer force of his artistic talent, unbridled and raw in the same way that Neizvestny's is, although the numerous watercolors on paper are a pale substitute for the enormous fresco that, surely, Beliutin is destined to paint – just as all of Neizvestny's sculptures can be regarded as preparatory studies for his visionary opus, the *Drevo zhizni* (Tree of Life).

In this context, the activities of the Movement group and its subsequent metamorphoses are more contemporary and more international, and both in theory and in practice are among the most exciting manifestations of the abstract tradition in Soviet culture. Founded by the mercurial Nusberg in Moscow in 1962, Movement led a turbulent life checkered with personal antagonisms, jealousies, and internecine warfare. Generally speaking, the primary artistic service rendered by Movement is that it transferred the suprematist and constructivist systems to a more synthetic environment in the form of functional design (e.g. urban designs celebrating the fiftieth anniversary of the October Revolution in 1966) and interior design, and outdoor performance (e.g. the Galaxy Kinetic Complex of 1967). In this way, Movement operated on two social levels – as an "official" design team receiving state commissions and also as a group of "unofficial" artists, provoking public anger for the "frivolity" of their kinetic actions.

By the early 1970s a division of loyalties and personal incompatibilities had undermined the solidity of Movement, and its interests in kinetic art were modified and expanded by members such as Infante and Viacheslav Koleichuk who soon defined new circles of influence. Infante and his group ARGO (Author Working Group) began to give serious attention to the "geometric object introduced into the natural environment."[24] This is not, however, the mechanical and calculated placement of a foreign body in virgin territory, but rather an action based on fortuity and instantaneity – a "discrete displacement," as Infante explains.[25] For example, the artists place mirrors and other reflective surfaces in the natural landscape, using earth, water, snow, foliage as partners in a formal dialog. In their lightness and ephemerality, these constructions evoke the sensation of organic continuity with the landscape, even though the deformed images of their reflections communicate that they are not. Consequently, Infante creates a discourse between the natural landscape, the artist, and the spectator that treats of the entire issue of ambiguity, veracity, and artificiality. He then photographs each scenario, sometimes rearranging the sequence of frames into new series such as the album *Prisutstvie* (Presence). For Infante and his colleagues such as Nonna Goriunova, the artist is a mediator between nature and the artifact, affirming at once that nature has no boundaries and that elemental, artificial forms in metal and plastic can also assume a natural character. This was particularly evident in the snow performances that Infante and Goriunova undertook in the 1970s in which outlandish figures moved across the theatre of the snow or in the addition of silver foil to tree trunks and bushes. The very interplay of these conditions undermines the conventional notions of "symmetry" and "asymmetry," "here" and "there," "start" and "finish."

Thanks to the unrelenting course of protest after Stalin's death, the Russian artists and critics of the 1990s operated in an atmosphere of unprecedented freedom, and the new generation that continued the struggle for self-expression in the Commonwealth of Independent States began to flourish in an ambience vastly different from that of the 1960s–70s. Artists such as Afrika (Sergei Bugaev), Igor Chachkin, Aleksandr Mareev, and Konstantin Zvezdochetov took to emphasizing irony, pollution, and indiscretion as principal themes and to decorating their ailing body politic with gaudy colors, furious beasts, and salacious jokes, as in the latter's series called *Fartville* (various collections). But the mystery is missing, and in their shrill and merciless messages, the artists seemed to create instant puzzles and rebuses as mere surrogates for style and idea. As Vadim Zakharov wrote in 1990: "In the end . . . I would like to hide. Thrust myself in a corner, disappear behind a wall, where I can feel fine and be calm, where I will finally be able to die peacefully, after having misled everybody."[26] Naturally, it is tempting to dwell on the accomplishments of the new wave and to identify them as characteristic of the contemporary art scene in Russia. Indeed, the works of Afrika, Yury Albert, Zvezdochetov, and their colleagues are smart, abrasive, and entirely in keeping with the directions of the international art market of post-modernism. At the same time, we should remember that their actions are some of many and that "realism," for want of a better word, is alive and well and that many Russian artists, young and old, from Vladimir Brainin and Leonid Baranov to Tatiana Nazarenko and Dmitry Zhilinsky, continue to paint or sculpt in ways that often follow the softer styles of the nineteenth century. Even so, unlike their predecessors, all contemporary Russian artists after the demise of the Soviet Union operate in a social vacuum where point and counterpoint, center and opposition merge and where the heated debates on the spiritual in art and the meaning of God are replaced with the rush to capitalize and consume. Some retain a nostalgia for socialist realism, while others serve the dictates of the Western art market, but at least Russian art has become part of the international mainstream and, for better or for worse, has lost its false status as a special, exotic, and alternative commodity.

NOTES

1. Nikolai Chernyshevsky: *Esteticheskie otnosheniia iskusstva k deistvitel'nosti* (Moscow: Gosizdat, 1948), p. 10. (The translations in this chapter are by John Bowlt.)

2. Stepan Yaremich on Repin (1915). Quoted in I Vydrin: "S. Yaremich o Repine-portretiste," in *Iskusstvo* (Moscow, 1969), no. 9, p. 60.

3. Andrei Bely: *Vospominaniia ob Aleksandre Bloke* (Letchworth: Bradda, 1964),p. 31.

4. Dmitry Filosofov. Quoted in A. Grishchenko and N. Lavrsky: *Aleksandr Shevchenko. Poisiki i dostizheniia v oblasti stankovoi zhivopisi* (Moscow: IZO NKP, 1919), p.3, where the original source is not cited.

5. Alexandre Benois: "Khudozhestvennye eresi," in *Zolotoe runo* (Moscow, 1906), no. 2, pp. 80–81.

6. Lev Bakst: "Puti klassitsizma," in *Apollon* (St. Petersburg, 1909–10), no. 3, p. 60.

7. Aleksandr Shevchenko: "Neo-primitivizm," (1913). Translation in J. Bowlt (ed.): *Russian Art of the Avant-Garde* (London: Thames and Hudson, 1988), p. 45.

8. Matisse in interview with the newspaper *Protiv techniia* (1911). Quoted in Yury Rusakov: "Matisse in Russia in the Autumn of 1911," in *The Burlington Magazine* (London May 1975), p. 289.

9. Benedikt Livshits: *Polutoraglazyi strelets* (1933). Translation in John Bowlt: *Benedikt Livshits. The One and a Half-Eyed Archer* (Newtonville: ORP, 1977), p. 81.

10. The critic Nikolai Punin referred to Malevich and Tatlin respectively in these terms. See Evgenii Kovtun: "K. Malevich. Pis'ma k M.V. Matiushinu," in *Ezhegodnik rukopisnogo otdela Pushkinskogo doma na 1974 god* (Leningrad: Nauka, 1976), p. 183.

11. David Aranovich: "Desiat' let iskusstva," in *Krasnaia nov'* (Moscow, 1927), no. 11, p. 219.

12. From "Deklaratsiia Assotsiatsii khudozhnikov revoliutsionnoi Rossii" (1922). Translation in Bowlt, *Russian Art of the Avant-Garde*, pp. 266–67.

13. Alfred Kurella: "Ot 'iskusstva revoliutsionnoi Rossii' k proletarskomu iskusstvu," in *Revoliutsiia i kul'tura* (Moscow, 1928), no. 6, p. 42.

14. German Nedoshivin: "Stalinskii printsip sotsialisticheskogo realizma v razvitii sovetskoi zhivopisi," in *Uchenye zapiski* (Moscow: Akademiia obshchestvennykh nauk, 1951), no. 2, p. 165.

15. Aleksei Fedorov-Davydov: "Obraz I.V. Stalina v sovetskoi zhivopisi i risunke," in *Uchenye zapiski* (Moscow: Akademiia obshchestvennykh nauk, 1951), no. 2, p. 141.

16. From Zhdanov's speech at the First All-Union Congress of Soviet Writers (1934). Translation in Bowlt, *Russian Art of the Avant-Garde*, p. 293.

17. Quoted in Aleksandr Gerasimov: *Za sotsialisticheskii realizm* (Moscow: Akademiia khudozhestv, 1952), p. 80.

18. Zhdanov, speech, in Bowlt, *Russian Art of the Avant-Garde*, p. 293.

19. Fedorov-Davydov, "Obraz I. V. Stalina," p. 128.

20. *Ibid.*, pp. 148–50.

21. Vasily Zvontsov: "Esli tebe khudozhnik imia . . ." in *Leningradskaia pravda* (Leningrad, 16 October 1975), p. 3. The writer was reviewing the "official unofficial" exhibition at the Nevsky District House of Culture, in Leningrad, at which many non-conformist artists were represented.

22. "Persecuted Artists in Moscow," in *Der Spiegel* (Hamburg, November 1974), no. 39; K. Herwig: "Forbidden Artists in the USSR: the Glezer Collection," in *Die Furche* (Vienna, 1 March 1975).

23. As reported by Aleksandr Glezer in *Russkie khudozhniki na Zapade* (Paris: Tret'ia volna, 1986), p. 5.

24. Francisco Infante: "Nature and Art," in *The Structurist* (Saskatoon, 1983–84), no. 23–24, p. 95.

25. Infante: "On My Concept of the Artefact," in *Francisco Infante,* Catalog of exhibition at International Images (Sewickley, 1989), p. 18.

26. Vladim Zakharov: untitled statement in *Contemporary Russian Artists/Artisti Russi Contemporanei.* Catalog of exhibition at the Museo d'Arte Contemporanea (Prato, 1990), p. 65.

10

Music

236   The Russian musical tradition has grown from two basic sources over the last one thousand years: the liturgy of the Russian Orthodox Church and the folk tradition. Running side by side, these two streams have provided a rich flow of melodic and emotional inspiration to many generations of composers, eventually intertwining in the music of nineteenth-century Russian masters such as Mikhail Ivanovich Glinka, Modest Petrovich Mussorgsky, Nikolai Andreevich Rimsky-Korsakov, Aleksandr Porfir'evich Borodin and Petr Ilych Tchaikovsky. In the twentieth century, liturgical and folk sources continued to be essential ingredients of the music of such composers as Sergei Vasil'evich Rachmaninov, Igor Fedorovich Stravinsky, Sergei Sergeevich Prokofiev and Dmitry Dmitrievich Shostakovich.

Particularly in works like Mussorgsky's historical operas *Boris Godunov* and *Khovanshchina*; Rimsky-Korsakov's *The Legend of the Invisible City of Kitezh and the Maiden Fevronia*; and Prokofiev's score to Sergei Eisenstein's film *Ivan the Terrible*, the materials of Russian folk and liturgical music were combined and transformed through the techniques of Western harmony and counterpoint into what has become immediately recognizable as the Russian classical tradition.

But post-1917 Russian music (like all areas of Russian culture) was also profoundly affected by the cultural policies of the Soviet communist regime. Of particular importance for the musical tradition was the official persecution of the Russian Orthodox Church. For Soviet composers, this meant that the use of church music in classical compositions was almost entirely forbidden (with the exception of a brief period of relaxation during World War II). As in other fields of modern Russian culture, the advent of the 1917 Bolshevik Revolution also led to the permanent emigration of numerous prominent composers and musicians to Europe and the United States. This group included Stravinsky, Rachmaninov, and the pianist-composer Nikolai Karlovich Medtner, among many others.

Owing to various geographical, political, and religious factors, music developed very differently in Russia than in Europe. Russian "classical" music came of age only in the mid-nineteenth century, when the first Russian conservatories were founded in the 1860s – centuries after comparable institutions had been established in Europe. The main reason behind this retarded development of European-style classical music was the dominant role of religion in Russian culture until 1700.

The music of Russian Orthodoxy – like Russian Orthodoxy itself – originally came to Russia from Byzantium in the tenth century. After the official adoption of Eastern Orthodoxy as the state religion of Kievan Russia in 988 AD, church personnel from Byzantium were imported to Kiev to instruct in various aspects of religious culture, including the painting of icons and frescoes, and the writing and performance of music. Byzantine Orthodoxy did not allow the use of any instruments during the liturgy, a feature which would have enormous implications for the future development of Russian music. Indeed, the use of instruments was considered a serious sin (and was a punishable crime) until the mid-seventeenth century.

Singing in the Orthodox liturgy was a form of monodic unison chant, entirely vocal, performed *a capella* by male choirs. (Even during the Soviet era, such choirs existed in a few remaining operating monasteries, notably at Zagorsk outside Moscow.) Occasionally, for purposes of dramatic contrast, a drone (singing on one pitch) was added as background, or the choir was divided into two antiphonal groups.

Over time, the chant imported to Russia from Byzantium began to evolve independently – just as the tradition of icon painting increasingly diverged from its Byzantine model. This divergence was facilitated by several external political factors: the conquest of Byzantium by the Ottoman Empire, and the Mongol invasion of Russia. Both of these events served to isolate Russia from the outside world from the early thirteenth century until the seventeenth century. During this period, Russian liturgical music developed its own highly individual character. This phase ended around 1700, when Peter the Great's policies of forced Westernization began to have a profound impact on Russian religious and musical practice.

In the concluding measures of his opera *Khovanshchina* (written

1872–80, left unfinished and later completed by Rimsky-Korsakov), Mussorgsky provides a brilliant illustration of the changes that came to Russian cultural and musical life with Peter I's ascension to the throne. Set in the closing years of the seventeenth century, *Khovanshchina* describes the sharp ideological and cultural conflict that separated the Westernizers (those who wanted Russia to emulate Europe, led by Peter I) and the conservative Orthodox Old Believers, who rejected change as sinful. In the opera's final scene, the Old Believers, intent on holding onto their age-old ways, sing traditional liturgical chants as they set fire to themselves in protest against the government's enforced policies of Westernization. In contrast, we hear the Western-style military band of Peter's victorious army as the curtain falls.

The form of chant which developed in Russia beginning around the twelfth century is called *znamenny raspev* – *znamenny* chant. The word *znamenny* is derived from the Russian word *znamya*, or "sign," referring to the symbols used in notating the chant. The *znamenny* chants were classified into a system of eight "voices" (*glasy*). These corresponded not to different modes (the standard scales used as the basis of the contours of Byzantine and Gregorian chant), but to different melodic patterns. Each "voice" or melodic pattern had many possible variations (as many as ninety), but all the variations possessed a general similarity of sound.

According to musicologist Alfred J. Swan, *znamenny* chant (and the whole tradition of Russian liturgical music) was also deeply influenced over time by Russian folk music.

> To be appreciated, *znamenny* chant as a whole must be singled out as a *corpus melodiarum*, a type of music unlike anything else whether in the Middle Ages or in more modern times, and must be placed side by side with other bodies of music. Then it will gradually become clear that it is akin not so much to Gregorian, Ambrosian, or other liturgical dialects, as to the vast domain of the Russian folk-song. It is its Russian character that is the determining factor, and not its appurtenance to purposes of worship, prayer, and glorification, though the latter in their turn determine its flow and dignity, its elevated, solemn progress.[1]

Also characteristic of *znamenny* chant is its reverence for the text. The purpose of the music is to glorify the word, not to obscure it with excessive harmonic or contrapuntal ornamentation. The language of the Russian Orthodox liturgy was originally Greek, but by the twelfth century was mingling with the Old Church Slavic native to Russia. By the fourteenth century, Greek had disappeared from the liturgy entirely, supplanted by Old Church Slavic. Old Church Slavic is an older version of modern Russian, and has remained the language of the Russian Orthodox liturgy and its music.

Perhaps the most difficult obstacle facing modern scholars and performers of Russian Orthodox liturgical music is the issue of notation. For centuries, *znamenny* chant was written in neume notation, which indicates the contour of the melody but not the exact pitches. It was largely up to the performers to memorize and pass on, through oral tradition, what they were singing. Once the continuity with this tradition was interrupted in the late-seventeenth century, however, it became virtually impossible to decipher the primitive neume notation.

In the eighteenth century, when Western-style musical notation flooded into Russia along with numerous imported Western musicians who served at the Romanov court, some attempts were made to record the ancient *znamenny* chants on staves. The most successful of these occurred in 1772, when the Moscow Synodal Typography printed a collection of various unison chants in the *znamenny* and related styles. This anthology served as the basis for the many Western-style harmonizations of Orthodox music which were created by Russia's newly emerging secular composers.

One of these was Dmitry Bortniansky (1751–1825), often called the "Russian Palestrina," after the Italian master of choral polyphony. Bortniansky's career was also very typical of the first few generations of Russia's post-Petrine composers. A Ukrainian brought to St. Petersburg as a boy to sing in the Imperial Chapel, Bortniansky studied with the Italian composer Baldassare Galuppi, director of the opera company of Catherine the Great. She, of course, was a great admirer of European culture, including its music. Bortniansky went to Italy with Galuppi in 1768, and studied there for eleven years. After returning to Russia in 1779, Bortniansky was appointed director of the choir of the Imperial Chapel, a post he occupied until his death.

Bortniansky's compositions sound more Italian than Russian, and exerted an enormous (and perhaps not entirely healthy) influence on the subsequent Russian liturgical tradition. A good example of the composer's Italianate style is "To Thee, Oh Lord, We Sing Praise" (*"Tebe boga khvalim"*), which belongs to the genre of liturgical concert chorus. Ornately polyphonic, it was intended to be performed before Confession on high holy days, including Easter.

Considerable confusion about the authenticity of existing published versions of Russian liturgical music persisted throughout the nineteenth and twentieth centuries. This is very clear from a letter Tchaikovsky (1840–93) wrote to his brother in 1881, while he was working on a setting of the Orthodox Vesper Service (Op.52). By this time Tchaikovsky had already composed the ballet *Swan Lake*, four of his six symphonies, and many other compositions which were making his reputation as Russia's first internationally recognized "professional" composer.

> Lately my work has consisted in getting acquainted with the "regulations," or laws, of old church music and making choral arrangements of some ancient church melodies; those sung during a Vesper Service. Great chaos reigns over all. Many lovers of the old want to return church music to its original purity and character. I do not know the history and alas! I have come to recognize that this is impossible. In the last century European habits have forced themselves into our church in various vulgar forms as, for example, the dominant seventh chord etc. They have sent down such deep roots, that even in the most remote corners of our land the cantors, after studying in town seminaries, sing something far removed from the original form of the music. This is written down in accordance with old rules, but the singing is much nearer to what is sung in Petersburg, at the Kazan Cathedral. Every cantor knows them and sings the troparion appropriate to the day, the Song to the Mother of God, and the Sedalion to the appropriate "voice." But the most recent methods of singing only faintly remind you of those that are traditional. In respect of harmony, what comes from a choir assembled by chance is nothing more than the most awful and vulgar conglomeration of European commonplaces.[2]

In his own setting of the Vesper Service, Tchaikovsky also deviated significantly from the all-male monodic chant originally imported from Byzantium. The piece is scored for a mixed chorus in a Westernized harmonic and rhythmic style.

Acutely aware of the problems Tchaikovsky describes, certain composers and musicologists began in the final decades of the nineteenth century to make a more scholarly and systematic investigation into the origins of Russian liturgical music. Their efforts clearly corresponded to what Russian artists (particularly the group known as the "wanderers") were doing at the time in painting: rediscovering "the colors, designs and motifs of peasant art and beginning to restore old frescoes and icons."[3] This investigation of authentic Russian folk and liturgical music was also an important part of the aesthetic of the *fin de siècle* impresario Sergei Diaghilev (1872–1929), creator of the Ballets Russes, a ballet and opera company which introduced many aspects of Russian culture to the West through its celebrated performances in Paris on the eve of World War I.

Among those who contributed most to the revival of interest in liturgical music were Stefan Smolensky (1848–1909) and Aleksandr Kastalsky (1865–1926), both associated with the Moscow Synodal School, which became a center for study and performance. What they attempted to do was to retain as much as possible the original character of the music within the framework of Western-style diatonic harmony. Smolensky developed a theory of "native counterpoint" to explain how Russian liturgical music fundamentally differed from that of the West.

Among the School's graduates were Konstantin Shvedov (1886–1954) and Nikolai Golovanov (1891–1953). Interestingly, Shvedov chose to emigrate from Russia after the Bolshevik Revolution, but Golovanov stayed and turned his energies to conducting, becoming conductor of the orchestra of the leading opera and ballet theatre of the Soviet era, the Bolshoi Theatre. Golovanov wrote some important liturgical settings before 1917, notably the Op.1 "Six Liturgical Chants," but Soviet censorship prevented him from pursuing this aspect of his creativity.

Tragically, the work of the Moscow Synodal School was interrupted and halted by the Bolshevik Revolution. Its professors and students were forced either to emigrate, or to begin writing secular choruses in praise of the staunchly atheistic Soviet regime. Some, like the little-known composer G. Izvekov (1865–?), suffered an even worse fate. Persecuted and imprisoned by the Soviet government for his religious beliefs along with thousands of others during the 1920s and 1930s, Izvekov was sent to prison. He composed the choral concert piece "With mine tears I want to wash away the scrolls of my transgressions" with a piece of charcoal, writing on the wall of his prison cell. One week later, Izvekov died.

Happily, the fall of communism and the Soviet regime brought an end to ideological censorship and official atheism. Since the late 1980s, and particularly since the celebration of the millennium of Christianity in Russia in 1988, interest in all aspects of the Russian Orthodox tradition – including music – has been growing rapidly in Russia. Many previously closed churches have been restored and reopened, and numerous new performing groups specializing in the liturgical repertoire have been formed. This was the dawn of a promising new era in the study and performance of the music of Russian Orthodoxy.

There is much more to the history of modern Russian music, of course, than the evolution of Orthodox chant. Like other forms of modern Russian culture, Europeanized music developed primarily in two cities: Moscow and St. Petersburg. Separated by a mere 400 miles of flat northern fields and swamps, St. Petersburg and Moscow had, by 1900, evolved into distinct but hopelessly co-dependent capitals, the wheels of the axis upon which Russian literature, art, music and dance had turned ever since Peter I had created St. Petersburg from scratch in the early 1700s.

The age-old tension and competition between ancient holy Moscow (the seat of Russian Orthodoxy since the early 1300s) and rational "European" St. Petersburg also reveals the fundamental Russian cultural identity crisis – the struggle between East and West – that has in one way or another afflicted nearly every major Russian creative artist, including composers like Glinka, Mussorgsky, and Tchaikovsky. Where Moscow has always been chaotic, "organic," feminine, and Oriental, St. Petersburg has been ordered, "artificial," masculine, and Western.

For four centuries before St. Petersburg was founded, Moscow had been the center of Russian Orthodoxy, and therefore of Russian music. Foreigners who visited Moscow always marveled at the power and virtuosity of the singers in the capital's many church choirs. The basses were particularly impressive, and they became famous far and wide for their stamina, prodigious vodka consumption, and booming low notes. One such artist was Fedor Chaliapin (1873–1938), the quintessential Russian operatic bass, who did a great deal to popularize Russian music all over the world. His appearance as Tsar Boris in Mussorgsky's opera *Boris Godunov* (based on Pushkin's play of the same name and set during the "Time of Troubles" around 1600) at the Metropolitan Opera in New York in late 1921 was so sensational that it caused a near-riot.

Until Peter I came to the throne at the end of the 1600s, the tsars considered themselves servants of God and the spiritual leaders of the Orthodox Russian people. Tsar Ivan I ("The Terrible") was even an accomplished church musician who sang at services and composed a number of chants. Accordingly, the tsars were hostile to secular music, both of the imported Western and native folk variety. Those who dared to offer public performances of such music – like the *skomorokhi*, traveling minstrels – were persecuted as criminals.

But all of this changed when Peter took charge of Russia and immediately set about modernizing and Westernizing what he perceived to be a hopelessly backward and superstitious society. After moving the capital to St. Petersburg, he began ordering his reluctant aristocratic subjects to attend Western-style court balls, where they clumped through European dances like the minuet, polonaise, and anglaise. Peter also established German-style "staff orchestras" that accompanied his burgeoning army into the field and played at ceremonial court occasions. Finally, in 1721, Karl Friedrich, Duke of Schleswig-Holstein, hoping to persuade Peter to let him marry his daughter, arrived with a full-scale German chamber orchestra that became a regular fixture of aristocratic society, performing music by Corelli, Telemann, and other European composers of the day.

Peter's successors continued to import and lavishly subsidize musicians and composers. By the end of the eighteenth century, many wealthy Russian nobles had established their own domestic orchestras, choirs, and opera and ballet theatres on their estates. Many of the leading performers were serfs who had been trained by European teachers. Some of the peasant dancers even became favorites of the royal family; ballerina Mathilda Kschessinska (1872–1971) was a mistress of the future Tsar Nicholas II.

Because the young capital ("Russia's Window on the West") on the Neva River was clearly the center for this newly emerging secular culture, and because the tsar and the court were there, by the early nineteenth century most of the action in Russian music was happening in St. Petersburg. It was here that Mikhail Glinka (1801–57), known as the "Father of Russian Music," presided over the premieres of his groundbreaking operas *A Life for the Tsar* (1836) and *Ruslan and Ludmila* (1842).

Since there were no conservatories in Russia before the 1860s, Glinka received most of his musical education abroad, in a somewhat unsystematic fashion. In Italy, he studied with a number of distinguished teachers, and became acquainted with prominent operatic composers like Bellini and Donizetti. The influence of their melodic *bel canto* style is very strongly felt in both of Glinka's operas.

Glinka was an accomplished performer as both pianist and singer, undertook systematic study of folk music of various cultures, and knew many of the great European composers of his day. The Hungarian Franz Liszt, another "nationalistic" composer, called Glinka a "genius," and even devised an improvisation on themes from his two operas. The French composer and discerning critic Hector Berlioz also thought highly of his Russian contemporary and praised his ability as a "novel and vital" orchestrator in an 1845 article.[4]

Both personally and musically, Glinka exerted an enormous influence on the development of "serious" Russian music, and most of all, on opera, the genre in which Russian composers would first make their mark. Before the brilliantly successful premiere of *A Life for the Tsar* in St. Petersburg on 27 November 1836, Russia had no operatic tradition of its own to speak of. In the late eighteenth century, Catherine the Great had imported Italian composers to toss off imitative operas for her fashionable court, and a few Russian natives (notably Aleksei Verstovsky) had produced operettas employing folk tunes and subjects. No one, however, had come near Glinka's achievement. He succeeded in forging a uniquely Russian opera on a highly patriotic subject – the story of the simple old peasant Ivan Susanin who intentionally leads the invading Polish army astray, losing his life in the process. *A Life for the Tsar* was a work that drew upon all the composer had learned abroad of the Italian tradition and yet retained its own distinct national personality. With this opera, Glinka also initiated the splendid tradition of nationalistic Russian opera-epics that would eventually produce Mussorgsky's *Boris Godunov* and *Khovanshchina*; Borodin's *Prince Igor*; Rimsky-Korsakov's *The Tsar's Bride* and *Sadko*; Prokofiev's *War and Peace*, and others.

Similarly, *Ruslan and Ludmila*, performed for the first time in St. Petersburg in 1842 and based on a dramatic poem by Glinka's friend Pushkin, was to be the first in a long series of Russian fairy-tale operas. Many would follow in Glinka's footsteps: Rimsky-Korsakov in *The Golden Cockerel*; Stravinsky in *The Nightingale*; even Prokofiev, in a typically satirical vein, in *Love for Three Oranges*. Glinka's fondness for fairy-tale subjects also influenced Tchaikovsky, Stravinsky, and Prokofiev in their work as ballet composers. According to musicologist David Brown, Glinka was nothing less than "the father of the nineteenth-century Russian nationalist school."[5]

This nationalist school took definite shape during the 1860s, a dynamic and active period in the history of modern Russian music and culture. The decade's most important development for music was the opening of Russia's first two Conservatories: in St. Petersburg in 1862 and in Moscow in 1866. The Conservatories were founded by two brothers, Anton Rubinstein (St. Petersburg) and Nikolai Rubinstein (Moscow), who took a leading role in professionalizing the Russian musical scene.

Around the same time, a group of five St. Petersburg composers with similar (at least initially) aesthetic and political views united to form a group that would play a central role in Russian musical life until the turn of the century. In an 1867 article on one of the concerts sponsored by the group, the powerful and discerning critic Vladimir Stasov gave them the enduring name "*moguchaia kuchka*," meaning "The Mighty Fistful" or "The Mighty Handful." The *kuchka* is also known abroad as "The Five" (since there were five members), "The New Russian Musical School," and as "The Balakirev Circle," in tribute to its first leader, Mily Alekseevich Balakirev (1837–1910). Besides Balakirev, the group included Rimsky-Korsakov (1844–1908), Mussorgsky (1839–81), Borodin (1833–87), and Cesar Antonovich Cui (1835–1918).

What brought these composers together was a shared belief in certain basic principles. All were filled with democratic enthusiasm for Russia's future in the aftermath of the emancipation of the serfs in 1861 and the institution of social, political, and economic reforms under Tsar Alexander II. All believed that Russian composers should make much greater use of Russian folklore and folk music. They resented the domination of Russian music by imported European music and musicians, and advocated a more nationalistic approach in both musical style and subject matter. They favored the programmatic genres of opera, song, and symphonic poem, largely because of their ability to carry narrative messages. They declared themselves enemies of sterile academic routine and advocated a vague kind of musical "realism," an idea most fully realized in the works of Mussorgsky, surely the most naturally gifted of the five.

Significantly, all five composers had received little formal training, a fact which would to some extent limit their ability to fulfill their idealistic ambitions. Most were also only part-time composers: Borodin was a prominent chemist, Rimsky-Korsakov a navy man, and Mussorgsky a reluctant civil servant. Considering all these limitations, they managed to accomplish a great deal. Some of their compositions still rank among the greatest achievements of Russian music.

Although Balakirev was the group's early leader, he and his colleagues had fallen out by the mid-1870s, when the *kuchka* effectively ceased to exist. An isolated and deeply spiritual man, Balakirev claimed to be proud of his lack of formal musical education. His most productive period was in the 1860s, when he began his marvelously evocative symphonic poem *Tamara*, based on a romantic poem by Mikhail Lermontov about a mysterious erotic encounter in a remote Caucasus mountain pass. Begun in 1867 and completed in 1882, the languid, fresco-like *Tamara* became the touchstone for what would be a rich tradition of programmatic "Orientalism" in Russian music. Along with the celebrated *Islamey*, Balakirev's extremely difficult piano arrangement of two

"Eastern" folk tunes (one Caucasian and one popular among the Crimean Tartars), *Tamara* would directly influence such later popular "Oriental" works as Rimsky-Korsakov's *Scheherazade*, Borodin's *Prince Igor*, and even Prokofiev's *String Quartet No.2*.

In his later years, Balakirev, generally regarded as the greatest Russian composer-pianist of the nineteenth century, also devoted more time to composing for the piano, producing numerous pieces in more conventional forms – scherzos, nocturnes, waltzes, and mazurkas.

Balakirev's personal and ideological rigidity made it difficult for him to appreciate new developments in Russian music. Despite his early intimacy with Mussorgsky, he found his opera *Boris Godunov* unimpressive and claimed he could have helped Mussorgsky create more effective orchestration. Balakirev also rejected the significance of emerging pianist-composers like Rachmaninov (1873–1943) and the mystical-symbolist Aleksandr Nikolaevich Scriabin (1871–1915). What happened to Balakirev is that he was overtaken by the professionalization of Russian music that began in the mid-1860s with the founding of conservatories in St. Petersburg and Moscow. Like Glinka, whom he took as his model, Balakirev was largely an autodidact; he came of age in a romantic era when enthusiasm and ideological principles were considered more important than academic training. As the situation rapidly changed after 1870, he was unwilling or unable to reinvent himself, as Rimsky-Korsakov, seven years his junior, was able to do, and he did not die prematurely, as both Mussorgsky and Borodin did.

For many years, the popular image of Mussorgsky was of a disorganized, slovenly, but lovable alcoholic whose prodigious talent was finally flooded – oh, so romantically! – in a sea of vodka. His early, impoverished death and the frightening portrait painted by Ilya Repin in the last days of Mussorgsky's life contributed to this dime-novel image and for many years overshadowed serious consideration of his musical output and significance. But the fact is that during his short and sad life, Mussorgsky produced two of the greatest monuments of the "New Russian School": the historical operas *Boris Godunov* and *Khovanshchina*. He also wrote the very popular symphonic poem *Night on Bald Mountain* (*Ivanova noch' na Lisoi gore*); many pieces for piano, including the programmatic cycle *Pictures At An Exhibition*, later orchestrated by the French composer Maurice Ravel; and scores of songs, including the brilliant cycles "The Nursery," "Sunless," and "Songs and Dances of Death."

All of these works demonstrate the basic traits of Mussorgsky's aesthetic: "a disdain for formal beauty and technical polish and every other manifestation of 'art for art's sake'; the desire to relate his art as closely as possible to life, especially to that of the Russian masses; to nourish his art on events and in turn to employ it as a medium for communicating human experience; and a somewhat self-conscious and aggressive Russianness and an intense sympathy with the Russian peasant, newly freed from serfdom."[6] Another central ingredient of Mussorgsky's musical style was his fascination with human speech and language, whose intonations and colors he strove to convey in all his vocal (and even some of his non-vocal) compositions.

In both *Boris Godunov* and *Khovanshchina*, Mussorgsky created a new kind of historical-epic opera that rejects the "pretty" *bel canto* tradition favored by Glinka. Taking his inspiration from Russian folk culture, Mussorgsky sought to retain its characteristic verbal texture and rhythm, producing a vocal line that assumes the contours of the text. Another innovative aspect was the very prominent role given to "the people" (*narod*), whose many choruses are integral to the dramatic and emotional content. In *Boris*, Mussorgsky also showed a remarkable gift for psychological insight, portraying the tortured guilty conscience of the usurper-tsar with a graphic and gritty naturalism.

Both *Boris* and *Khovanshchina* encountered many obstacles on their way to the stage. Mussorgsky first presented *Boris* for production in St. Petersburg in 1869, but the opera was turned down because it lacked a prominent female role. After the composer added the role of the Polish Princess Marina Mniszek and the so-called "Polish act," *Boris* was staged at the Imperial Mariinsky Theatre, the most prestigious opera house in Russia, in 1874. After Mussorgsky's death, Rimsky-Korsakov, who found his colleague's musical style primitive and alien, undertook a revision of *Boris*, fundamentally altering the orchestration. It was in this Rimsky-Korsakov version that *Boris* first became known in the West, after Diaghilev staged it in Paris in 1908. More recently, however, the original Mussorgsky version has returned to favor.

The situation with *Khovanshchina* was even more complicated, since Mussorgsky left the opera unfinished and in considerable disarray at the time of his death. Rimsky-Korsakov, believing in Mussorgsky's genius but compelled to "correct" some of his more revolutionary musical ideas, produced a performing edition of *Khovanshchina* that was first staged in 1886. Dissatisfaction with Rimsky's editing job was widespread, however. In 1958, Soviet composer Dmitry Shostakovich completed an edition regarded by most critics as much closer to Mussorgsky's original intentions.

Uncompleted operas were, in fact, something of a specialty for the *kuchka* composers. When Aleksandr Borodin died at midnight on 28 February 1887, while attending a costume ball in Russian national dress, his only full-length opera, *Prince Igor*, was also far from finished. Once again, Rimsky-Korsakov, by this time a professor at the St. Petersburg Conservatory, came to the rescue, aided by another St. Petersburg composer, Aleksandr Glazunov (1865–1936). They pieced together the fragments Borodin had left behind, orchestrated many sections, and filled in the numerous gaps.

The rather confused and episodic story line of *Prince Igor* is based on an incident from twelfth-century Russian history immortalized in the epic poem "The Lay of the Host of Igor" (*"Slovo o polku Igoreve"*), regarded as perhaps the greatest work of medieval Russian literature. The hero is Igor Sviatoslavich (1151–1202), who ruled the small city of Novgorod-Seversk, found today near the Ukrainian-Russian border. The much greater cities of Kiev and Novgorod overshadowed Igor's realm, and he played an insignificant role in the complex politics of Kievan Russia. By the late twelfth century, constant feuding among the princes of the numerous small Russian city-states had disastrously weakened their collective military position. They were under constant threat from various nomadic tribes, who made frequent attacks on the Russian settlements, burning them to the ground, raping the women, and taking the inhabitants captive.

One of the most formidable of these tribes was the Polovtsy (also known as Kumans), of Turkic origin. In 1185, in a quixotic attempt to assert control over the area, Igor marched against the Polovtsy, without appealing for help to any other of Russia's princes. Igor's doomed campaign, which ended in his capture (and eventually escape), provided the basic material for "The Lay of the Host of Igor" and for Borodin's opera. Other sources confirm the basic facts of the story, including the kind and noble behavior of the Polovtsy toward Prince Igor while he was held captive, an aspect emphasized by Borodin in his operatic treatment. After all, it was in order to entertain Prince Igor that the victorious Khan Konchak ordered his lithe (if also enslaved) subjects to dance and sing.

The uninhibited and noble behavior of these half-wild nomads of the prairie clearly evoked a strong response in Borodin, who was himself the son of an elderly Caucasian prince. In his evocative "musical picture" *In the Steppes of Central Asia* (1880), perhaps his most popular composition, Borodin had already given evidence of his special affinity for "Eastern" material. All of Borodin's music (which includes three symphonies, two popular string quartets, and songs) is full of memorable and lyrical melodies.

It can be no coincidence that about half of the sections Borodin managed to orchestrate for *Igor* belonged to the Polovtsian acts (Acts 2 and 3), including what have become the opera's most celebrated pages: the scene of Polovtsian singing and dancing that concludes Act 2. For a supposedly Russian nationalistic opera, in fact, Borodin's pro-Polovtsian bias is somewhat surprising. In contrast with the decisive, romantically appealing Polovtsy, the Russians (with the exception of the stalwart Igor) come across as a debauched and querulous bunch of crybabies.

When *Prince Igor* received its premiere at the Mariinsky Theatre in 1890, the dances were lavishly choreographed by Lev Ivanov (1834–1901), who would become famous a few years later for his work on Tchaikovsky's ballets *The Nutcracker* and *Swan Lake*. But it was impresario Sergei Diaghilev, always on the lookout for new attractions, who came up with the idea of presenting the exotic Polovtsian dances as a separate ballet. (The scene can be performed without chorus, in which case the brass doubles the voice parts.) In 1909, Diaghilev commissioned Mikhail Fokine (1880–1942) to design new choreography; the piece was then used as part of the first of his famous Paris seasons. In this version, *The Polovtsian Dances* were presented with great success at the Théâtre du Chatelet in Paris on 19 May 1909, and played a central role in introducing the music of Borodin and his Russian nationalist colleagues to the Western audience.

Of all the members of the *kuchka*, Rimsky-Korsakov was unquestionably the most productive and disciplined. Although he initially set out to become a career navy man, Rimsky eventually abandoned the life of a sailor (after extensive cruises around the world, one of which brought him to New York) to pursue the less certain profession of composer. Exact and even excessively organized, Rimsky vowed to make up for his lack of formal musical training through accelerated study, and eventually became a professor at the newly founded St. Petersburg Conservatory, where, he later confessed, he stayed just one step ahead of his students at the beginning of his teaching career. In this capacity Rimsky was well situated to exercise a huge influence over the subsequent development of Russian music. His students eventually included such important future artists as Stravinsky and Prokofiev, while his writings on orchestration were the bible for generations of Russian composers and musicologists. His life spanned a long and seminal period in the history of Russian music, from the professional beginnings of the 1860s nearly until the Russian Revolution.

Artistically, Rimsky thought of himself first and foremost as a composer of operas. He wrote fifteen, in a wide variety of genres: historical (*The Maid of Pskov, The Tsar's Bride, Servilia, Pan Voyevoda*), fairy tale (*May Night, The Snow Maiden, Christmas Eve, The Tale of Tsar Saltan, The Golden Cockerel*), folk epic (*Sadko, The Tale of the Invisible City of Kitezh and the Maiden Fevronia, Mlada*), and even one psychological opera-drama (*Mozart and Salieri*) that treats the same subject of envy between composers as Peter Shaffer's hit Broadway play "Amadeus." Until recently, Rimsky's operas have been almost unknown abroad, but they have always occupied a central place in the repertoire of Russia's opera houses. As numerous critics have observed, most of the operas are in fact rather static "pictures" lacking in dramatic interest and strong characters. Where Rimsky excels (as in *Sadko, Christmas Eve*, and *Kitezh*) is in the portrayal of a particular milieu or atmosphere, often with the use of folk melodies and harmonies.

Outside of Russia, Rimsky is today best remembered for three colorful orchestral pieces: *Capriccio espagnol*, the "Russian Easter" Overture (*Svetlyi prazdnik*, making extensive use of Russian Orthodox chant), and the Symphonic Suite *Scheherazade*. All were written at about the same time, in 1887–88, fifteen years after Rimsky had completed the third of his three symphonies but before he had composed most of his operas. *Scheherazade* is one of the most successful works in the rich tradition of Russian musical "Orientalism," and reflected a growing interest among Russian artists in the Caucasus and Central Asia, areas that had been conquered and incorporated into the Russian Empire.

Based on episodes from the Arabian folk epic *Tales of 1001 Nights*, which was very popular in Russia, *Scheherazade* uses the solo violin to represent the narrator Scheherazade. Her "voice" links the various episodes, all of them ingeniously orchestrated. "I had in view the creation of an orchestral suite in four movements, closely knit by the community of its themes and motives, yet presenting, as it were, a kaleidoscope of fairy-tale images and designs of Oriental character," wrote Rimsky in his encyclopedic and informative autobiography *My Musical Life*.[7]

Also inspired by an "Oriental" subject was Rimsky's early *Symphony*

No.2 ("Antar"), based on the adventures of Antar, one of the most popular figures of Arabian legend. In fact, this was the first "Oriental" symphonic work produced by any member of the *kuchka*. Here, the composer made use of the ascending octatonic scale in order to give the work an Eastern character. Like so much of Rimsky's best music, "Antar" demonstrates a love of the fantastic; attraction to Arabian and Oriental characters and themes refracted through the lens of Russian romanticism; and colorful, light, and balanced orchestration.

By the 1870s, the *kuchka* was disintegrating and the situation in Russian music was becoming much more varied and professionalized. With the founding of the Moscow Conservatory in 1866, the musical balance between Russia's two capitals had also begun to shift. A major figure in this process was Tchaikovsky. Immediately upon graduation from the St. Petersburg Conservatory, Tchaikovsky was lured to Moscow to become a professor of composition there. His growing stature over the following years brought credit to the institution, and to the Moscow musical community in general. Significantly, the first four of his six symphonies, as well as the opera *Eugene Onegin* and the ballet *Swan Lake* received their premieres in Moscow. It seems Tchaikovsky also enjoyed being at a distance from the Petersburg-based *moguchaia kuchka*, with whose often dogmatic aesthetic of democratic "realism" and mild Slavophilism he had little sympathy.

For the rest of his career, Tchaikovsky divided his time and affections between Moscow and St. Petersburg. In this, he was somewhat unusual in the context of nineteenth century Russian cultural history. Cultural figures tended to be strongly identified either with one or the other: Dostoevsky, for example, found his inspiration solely in St. Petersburg (the setting of many of his stories and novels, including *Crime and Punishment*), while Tolstoy preferred Moscow, condemning Petersburg as artificial and un-Russian. Tchaikovsky's ability to create and work in both places is indicative of his role as a bridge between the two dominant strains in Russian music: Russian nationalism and European classicism.

As Russia's first truly "international" composer, Tchaikovsky represented a coming-of-age for his country's culture, and provided an example for his colleagues in the next century (Rachmaninov, Stravinsky, Prokofiev, Shostakovich) of how native Russian musical and literary traditions could be synthesized with broader European ones. Tchaikovsky always resisted regarding Russian music as somehow separate and isolated from other music. He once compared European music to a single large orchard having different trees: French, German, Italian, Russian, Polish, and so on.

Russian-American choreographer George Balanchine, founder of the New York City Ballet, who was born in St. Petersburg just eleven years after the composer died, aptly described Tchaikovsky, a composer whose works he often turned into ballets, as a "European from Russia."[8] Tchaikovsky's favorite composer was Mozart, the epitome of the European classical style, in whom he saw an idealized vision of a perfect and harmonious age infinitely superior to his own debased and vulgar era. Significant too is the fact that "progressive" Russians (like the members of the *kuchka*) found Tchaikovsky's music insufficiently Russian (Prokofiev would later be accused of the same failing), while German critics found him too crude.

Like Leo Tolstoy and Aleksandr Pushkin (whose novel in verse *Eugene Onegin* and story "Queen of Spades" he made into operas), Tchaikovsky had come of age in the post-Napoleonic era, when Russia had become an integral part of the European world. Also like Tolstoy and Pushkin, Tchaikovsky was a member of the privileged upper class, and received a European-style education along with a hefty dose of Russian reality. Tchaikovsky's mother was of French ancestry, and he was called Pierre as a boy. One of the composer's first literary compositions was a poem to his guardian angel, written in French.

As a result of this somewhat schizophrenic upbringing and education, Tchaikovsky, like so many members of the Russian upper class, felt emotionally torn between his backward native Russia and the greater sophistication and comfort of Europe. He spent long periods of time living abroad, but always returned to Russia, unable to bear prolonged separation. The idea of permanent emigration to Europe was profoundly distasteful to the composer, and he harshly judged his numerous countrymen who chose that path.

At the same time, Tchaikovsky found Russian chauvinistic anti-European nationalism equally uncongenial. He had no sympathy for the often dogmatic pro-Russian sentiment that arose in certain intellectual circles in St. Petersburg in the 1860s. This also helps to explain his often hostile relations with the members of the "Mighty Handful," who tended to reject and belittle European influence in their music. Most of all, this explains Tchaikovsky's deep antipathy to the music and aesthetic of Modest Mussorgsky. In a letter to his brother, Tchaikovsky wrote, "I send Mussorgsky's music to hell from the bottom of my heart; this is the most vulgar and base parody of music."[9] The ethnographic and

Russocentric approach of most of the *kuchka* composers was alien to Tchaikovsky. Their mutual lack of understanding can also be explained in part by their different social backgrounds. Tchaikovsky belonged to the upper classes, while the members of the *kuchka* were closer to the lower and emerging urban middle classes.

There was no question, then, that Tchaikovsky thought of himself and his music as part of the broader European tradition. This fact is obvious, too, in the subjects the composer chose for his operas and ballets. Unlike the members of the *kuchka*, who, as we have seen, wrote operas almost exclusively on old Russian, pre-Petrine subjects, Tchaikovsky preferred libretti focusing on stories occurring in more recent times and involving members of the Europeanized Russian aristocracy. *Eugene Onegin* (1878) and *The Queen of Spades* (1890) are the two best examples. In *The Queen of Spades*, Tchaikovsky shows a particular fondness for the last years of the eighteenth century, the Mozartian era. The small interpolated opera "The Faithful Shepherdess" with which the ball guests are entertained is nothing less than a loving musical tribute to Mozart. Both *Onegin* and *The Queen of Spades* also demonstrate Tchaikovsky's loyalty to the monarchy, and his allegiance to his aristocratic class. In fact, members of the *kuchka* were much less enthusiastic about the Romanov dynasty and used to accuse Tchaikovsky resentfully of having cornered the market on royal patronage.

In his love for ballet, too, Tchaikovsky was heavily influenced by European models. Significantly, none of the members of the *kuchka* showed strong interest in ballet, which they regarded as an applied art unworthy of a serious composer. Ballet had come to Russia in the eighteenth century from France and Italy, lavishly supported by the royal family and aristocracy, and the court choreographers and ballet composers were mostly imported from Europe. The romantic ballet *Giselle*, first produced in St. Petersburg in 1842 with a score by the French composer Adolphe Adam, was extremely popular on the Russian stage during Tchaikovsky's youth, and made a deep impression on him. So did the exotic "Indian" ballet *La Bayadère* (1877). Its bland and serviceable music was written by the Austrian composer Alois Louis Minkus, an Austrian who served as official composer for the Bolshoi Theatre in Moscow and the Mariinsky Theatre in St. Petersburg from the 1860s through the 1880s. Later, Tchaikovsky became friendly with Léo Delibes, the French composer of the ballet *Coppelia*, whose story of a doll come to life may well have influenced the concept of *The Nutcracker*.

It was with Tchaikovsky's brilliant scores for *Swan Lake* (1876), *Sleeping*

Beauty (1889), and *The Nutcracker* (1892) that the technically sophisticated Russian ballet at last found a Russian composer capable of producing music that was more than just superficial illustration. Credited as the "reformer" of ballet music, Tchaikovsky deepened its symbolic and conceptual aspects and almost single-handedly brought ballet to the same level of respectability as the opera and symphony. Largely owing to Tchaikovsky's groundbreaking work, many other Russian and Soviet composers subsequently produced major ballet scores, including Glazunov (*Raymonda*), Prokofiev (*Romeo and Juliet, Prodigal Son, Cinderella*), Stravinsky (*The Rite of Spring, Petrushka, The Firebird*), Shostakovich (*The Golden Age*), Reinhold Gliere (*The Red Poppy*), and Aram Khachaturian (*Gayane, Spartacus*). In fact, ballet music has become known as one of Russia's greatest contributions to the repertoire of classical music.

Tchaikovsky was the first Russian composer to become widely known and admired abroad; he conducted at the opening of Carnegie Hall in New York in 1891. When he came to America, Tchaikovsky was fifty-one years old, and at the very height of his career. He had already completed five of his six symphonies (all but the so-called "Pathétique"), seven of his eight operas, two of his three ballets, two of his three crowd-pleasing piano concerti, dozens of songs, the sensational *1812 Overture*, and many other overtures and works for orchestra, chamber ensemble and solo instruments. A respected pedagogue, he had been teaching at the Moscow Conservatory for twenty-five years.

But tragically, Tchaikovsky lived for only a little more than two more years after returning to Russia from the United States. Chronically depressed and unhappy in his closeted life as a homosexual, he died in St. Petersburg of what appears to have been cholera. Ever since his death, Tchaikovsky has been the subject of wild speculation in various biographical and fictionalized accounts, including several films. But much more important than Tchaikovsky's unorthodox personal life was the fact that his career signified a real turning point in the history of Russian music. His professionalism and international stature brought an end to the charges of "dilettantism" that had so long been leveled at Russia's composers.

Because of his prominence and influence, Tchaikovsky is also often called the head of the "Moscow School." This rather abstract and relative label is given to a loosely connected group of composers centered in Moscow around the turn of the century. Its members include composers extremely diverse in aesthetic and style: the conservative neo-romantic

Sergei Vasilievich Rachmaninov (1873–1943); Nikolai Karlovich Medtner (1880–1951), often called the "Russian Brahms" for his love of complex counterpoint; the neoclassical Sergei Ivanovich Taneyev (1856–1915); and the visionary mystic Aleksandr Nikolaevich Scriabin (1872–1915). What these artists shared was the city where they worked, a distaste for the obvious Russian nationalism associated with the *moguchaia kuchka*, an interest in writing for the piano, and a preference for classical rather than programmatic genres.

Rachmaninov and Medtner had perhaps the most in common. Both studied at the Moscow Conservatory with Taneyev; both rejected the stylistic innovations and aesthetic of the emerging modernist avant-garde; both were well known for a melancholy, introverted, and taciturn disposition. But perhaps their most crucial and bitter shared experience was living – and dying – in painful exile from the Russia they so adored.

For both artists, the Bolshevik Revolution of 1917 proved a personal and aesthetic watershed. When Tsar Nicholas II was overthrown, they were already mature, fully-formed artists, and they watched in bewilderment as Vladimir Lenin and his associates established the world's first socialist state. Belonging by birth, education, and temperament to the doomed world of gentry culture, both composers were political and cultural conservatives who knew they would be unable to remake themselves. Along with so many other of Russia's most brilliant creative minds (Stravinsky, Vladimir Nabokov, Vasily Kandinsky), they chose the terrible alternative of emigration.

There was no doubt in Rachmaninov's aristocratic mind that he did not belong in the new Soviet Union, with its frightening social instability and fierce promises of equality and anti-elitism. Only one month after the Revolution, he took advantage of concert dates in Sweden to take his family to the West. Eventually he settled in the United States, although the notoriously dour and phlegmatic Rachmaninov always found America something of a strain. Despite countless triumphant coast-to-coast tours as a pianist-conductor-composer that brought him renown, adulation, and sufficient money to purchase a home in Beverly Hills, Rachmaninov could never completely adapt to the materialistic style and competitive pace of the brash, booming country he once haughtily dismissed as "The Dollar Princess." For the relentlessly gloomy and nostalgic composer, America was too fast, too loud, and too mercenary. His heart would always belong to Russia – the Russia of his youth, a state of mind that no longer existed in real historical space.

That emigration – and the resulting financial need to make long and exhausting tours as a piano virtuoso – was hard on Rachmaninov is clear from the catastrophic decline in his rate of composition after he left Russia. Thirty-nine of Rachmaninov's forty-five opus numbers (including his three short operas, all of his songs, three of his four phenomenally popular piano concerti, and two of his three symphonies) were already composed by the time he left Russia at age forty-four.

Rachmaninov gained enormous fame during his lifetime on the strength of a handful of works: the *Piano Concerto No.2* (1901), the *Piano Concerto No.3* (1909), the *Rhapsody on a Theme of Paganini* (1934), the Second (1907) and Third (1936) Symphonies, and some virtuoso pieces for piano solo. Like Tchaikovsky, he had a remarkable gift for melody and for creating a strong sense of emotional atmosphere – so much so, in fact, that some critics dismissed him as too sentimental. The Second Piano Concerto shows Rachmaninov's style at its best. Written in three movements of approximately equal length, it is packed with unforgettable melodies, many of which have been shamelessly plundered over the years for such popular songs as "Full Moon and Empty Arms," "Ever and Forever," "If This Is Goodbye," and "This Is My Kind of Love."

The celebrated first movement opens with an unusual sequence of F-minor chords in the unaccompanied piano part which resemble the tolling of a bell. A surging, somber theme follows in the orchestra, a theme that sounds Russian to its very core, as Rachmaninov's long-time friend and fellow pianist Nikolai Medtner once pointed out:

> The theme of Rachmaninov's inspired Second Concerto is not only the theme of his life but always conveys the impression of being one of the most strikingly Russian themes, and only because the soul of this theme is Russian; there is no ethnographic trimming here, no dressing up, no decking out in national dress, no folksong intonation, and yet every time, from the first bell stroke, you feel the figure of Russia rising up to her full height.[10]

Medtner never enjoyed the popular or financial success achieved by Rachmaninov. Seven years younger than his friend and mentor, the equally apolitical Medtner left the USSR in 1921 after making a half-hearted attempt to participate in the proliferating official committees that were reorganizing Moscow's musical life. Following in Rachmaninov's footsteps to the United States, where many dispossessed Russian musicians had sought refuge, Medtner failed to make the kind of impression he had hoped for. Homesick for Russia, he returned to

Europe and settled in Paris, where there was a large and lively Russian *émigré* community including such prominent figures as Diaghilev, Stravinsky, and Prokofiev. Medtner focused almost exclusively on the piano. Virtually his entire output as a composer was dedicated to that instrument, with the exception of about 100 songs and seven works for chamber ensemble.

Although Aleksandr Scriabin was also a celebrated piano virtuoso who wrote many works for the instrument, spiritually and aesthetically this fascinating and revolutionary figure had little in common with the backward-looking Medtner and Rachmaninov. So avant-garde were the ideas and music of Scriabin, in fact, that Soviet radio chose to broadcast his vast orchestral work *Le poeme de l'extase* (*The Poem of Ecstasy*, 1908) as an accompaniment to the first manned spaceflight by Yury Gagarin. (Reportedly, it was simultaneously transmitted to Gagarin in the space-craft and to dazed earthlings by their radios below.) The choice was surely appropriate, since the music of this enormous, orgiastic symphony is not entirely of this planet. But what else should one expect from a composer who considered himself more mystic than musician, a wild Russian with a fondness for Satanism and altered states of consciousness, an ego-maniac who likened himself to the sun? For Scriabin, composing music was much more than putting notes together; it was a means to transform his audience, to transport them to realms far beyond the concert hall.

As he matured as a composer, Scriabin became increasingly drawn to various mystical schemes and utopian visions which he attempted to incorporate into his music. Correspondingly, the forms and genres in which he was composing tended to become less and less conventional. His Third Symphony (*Le divin poeme*), completed in 1904, uses poetic French phrases as titles for three of the four movements, and follows a spiritual-poetic (one might even call it New Age) text. Written in French and attached to the score, it describes the struggle between Man-God and Slave-Man, the two parts of the Ego, which eventually attain blissful unity and divine freedom. For the *Poem of Ecstasy*, Scriabin composed an accompanying 369-line poem dealing with pain, death, and sexual desire culminating in orgasmic release. Composed in free sonata form in a single movement, the work is structured around countless repetitions of a short opening theme that ascends by a fourth, a major third, and a minor third. Progressing through increasingly complex harmonic per-mutations, this striving theme becomes ever more insistent and ecstatic, finally reaching its triumphant "I am" conclusion (or, perhaps more accurately, orgasm) over the full orchestra, complemented by the pipe organ.

At one point while he was working on *The Poem of Ecstasy*, Scriabin, who had no interest in conventional politics, claimed that it was "music reeking of Revolution . . . the ideals for which the Russian people are struggling." Soviet critics and cultural bureaucrats would not agree with this assessment later on, however. Literal-minded and puritanical, they tended to see Scriabin's music and poetic visions as examples of the deplorable decadence of pre-revolutionary aristocratic society. Supremely egotistical and iconoclastic, Scriabin would have no real heirs in Russian music. His mystical approach found no imitators, and would even be banned for many years after the 1917 Revolution. According to musicologist Hugh Macdonald, "Scriabin can be seen as a truly visionary composer who initiated a new musical language, as Schoenberg and Debussy were doing at much the same time, no less radical and advanced than theirs, and like them breaking decisively with tonality."[11]

The collapse of the tsarist government and the establishment of the Soviet regime after the Bolshevik Revolution of 1917 turned Russian musical life upside down. As we have seen, many prominent composers and musicians chose to emigrate to the West rather than to live through the privations and uncertainty. Those who remained behind had to adjust to a new political and cultural order that became increasingly doctrinaire and totalitarian. Although most of the major musical institutions of tsarist Russia (conservatories, symphonies, opera and ballet companies) continued to exist, they had to cope first with drastically reduced resources and later with vastly increased official control. During the 1920s, a reasonable degree of variety still existed in Soviet musical life, but soon after Stalin's ascension to power in the late 1920s the situation became much more regimented and repressive. With the creation of the Union of Soviet Composers and its many satellite organizations, composers could be much more easily controlled, through a rather primitive system of punishment and reward. Soviet music became a state-subsidized and state-run monopoly.

The impact of the Russian Revolution can easily be seen in the lives and to a great extent the music of the three major composers of the twentieth century: Igor Stravinsky (1882–1971), Sergei Prokofiev (1891–1953), and Dmitry Shostakovich (1906–75). The not infrequently caustic impresario Sergei Diaghilev, never at a loss for *le mot juste*, once proclaimed of his star protégés, Stravinsky and Prokofiev: "The only thing they have in common is that both are Russian and both live in the same century."[12] Had Diaghilev known Shostakovich, who was younger than Prokofiev and Stravinsky, he would have recognized him as no less incomparable – personally, politically, musically. They were three musical planets following three different orbits. Granted, Stravinsky, Prokofiev, and Shostakovich did share a language and a nationality. All were born in tsarist Russia, and within only twenty-four years of each other. All three were trained in the same city: St. Petersburg (later called Petrograd, and then Leningrad). Each produced a large body of music in a wide variety of genres: opera, ballet, symphony, concerto, chamber music, incidental music for the theatre, film scores.

And yet these three Russian titans, each a major figure of twentieth-century world music, came from radically dissimilar backgrounds and developed in radically different directions. Stravinsky was an aristocrat at heart, a suave connoisseur who flourished among the wealthy patrons of St. Petersburg, Paris, and New York. Encouraged by the taste-maker Diaghilev, who dubbed him his "first son," Stravinsky pursued the life of a *déraciné* exile in the West, where he was eventually embraced and lionized, particularly in avant-garde and dance circles.

Diaghilev's "second son," Prokofiev, ever the *Wunderkind*, came from a provincial, earnest, middle-class family of uncertain social status. After passing through a long period of indecision in the 1920s and 1930s, traveling almost frantically between Europe, America, and Stalin's Soviet Union, he ultimately chose Moscow in 1936, on the eve of Stalin's purge of Soviet artists and intellectuals.

The younger, less pampered, and perhaps more cynical Shostakovich, on the other hand, grew up alongside, and in some sympathy with, the Russian revolutionary movement, nurtured by the urban intelligentsia of St. Petersburg. A child of the new Soviet Russia, where he lived for his entire career, Shostakovich made only brief, infrequent, and carefully controlled trips abroad.

All three composers shunned politics as much as possible – for the Soviet composers Prokofiev and Shostakovich this was far from easy – but the 1917 Russian Revolution proved a watershed event in their lives. At the risk of oversimplification, one could view Stravinsky as a representative of the last secure *fin de siècle* generation of tsarist Russian gentry culture; Prokofiev as a member of the "lost generation" caught between two worlds, too young to feel comfortable in the old traditions and too old to accept the new; and Shostakovich as an integrated (if not always happy) member of Soviet society. At the least, the Revolution forced Prokofiev and Stravinsky to make difficult early choices about their future careers and exerted a seminal influence on the aesthetic environment in which Shostakovich's would unfold.

In musical and dramatic style, as well as in the literary taste they showed in their choice of subjects for ballets and operas, these three Russians did, as Diaghilev noted, have little in common. Prokofiev was an eclectic, veering from the severe textual fidelity of his experimental opera *The Gambler* (1917, revised 1928) based on a Dostoevsky novella; to the satirical and highly self-conscious theatricality of his *commedia dell'arte* opera *Love for Three Oranges* (1919); to the sexual pathology of the expressionistic *The Fiery Angel* (1927) from a novel by the symbolist Valery Briusov; to the strained Soviet socialist realism of *Semeon Kotko* (1939); to the safe "Tchaikovskyism" of *War and Peace* (1941–53), a setting of Tolstoy's novel; and finally, to the embarrassing operetta-like simplicity of *Story of a Real Man* (1948), composed in the devastating aftermath of the 1948 Composers Congress at which Prokofiev and Shostakovich were criticized for writing inaccessible and "anti-Soviet" music.

Stravinsky long rejected the idea of full-length opera as *passé*. Under the spell of Diaghilev and his trend-setting Ballets Russes, Stravinsky from the beginning sought to break down the barriers between opera and other theatrical forms, using double casts of singers and dancers (as in *The Nightingale*, 1914), speaking narrators (as in *Oedipus Rex*, 1927), and staged folk rituals (as in *The Wedding*, 1923). Only at the end of his career did Stravinsky arrive at a more or less traditional opera, *The Rake's Progress* (1951), with an English-language libretto.

Shostakovich's development as an operatic composer began brilliantly with *The Nose* (1928), a daringly avant-garde setting of Nikolai Gogol's absurd short story of the same name. First performed in Leningrad in early 1930, *The Nose* was written for an unusual chamber-size orchestra including six percussionists, two harps, piano, balalaika, and domras (a Russian folk instrument). The music overflows with Chaplinesque gallops, offbeat polkas, and weird waltzes. But *The Nose* was strongly criticized by the official cultural establishment as a "childish attempt to flabbergast the audience," and vanished from the stage after a single season. Shostakovich's second attempt at opera was the tragic *Lady Macbeth of the Mtsensk District*, based on a short story of the same name by Nikolai Leskov. First performed in 1934, *Lady Macbeth* was a huge success with both audience and critics, and was quickly staged abroad.

But in a pattern that would become increasingly familiar in the USSR over the following years, *Lady Macbeth* was publicly censored and banned by Stalin in early 1936 on the grounds that its overt sexuality, raw language, and frequently dissonant musical style were inappropriate for a Soviet composer and audience. Terrified, Shostakovich believed he might be arrested or even executed, as many other "nonconformist" artists were at that time. Fortunately, he was spared, but the experience deeply scarred him as a man and an artist. Not surprisingly, he never again wrote another opera. Instead, he concentrated on genres that were somewhat more difficult to label as politically wayward, primarily symphonies and string quartets. He wrote fifteen of each. Like Prokofiev, who produced two of the greatest film scores ever written (*Aleksandr Nevsky* in 1938 and *Ivan the Terrible* in the early 1940s), Shostakovich also wrote many film scores, at least in part because the cinema was a "popular" art favored by the communist leadership.

Although Stravinsky was born and received his early training in Russia, he spent most of his life in Europe and America. Thus, his mature work really belongs as much – or even more – to the history of American/European music than to Russian music. He played a central role in the development of the New York City Ballet, which was founded by his long-time colleague and collaborator, George Balanchine. It is hard to overestimate Stravinsky's influence in twentieth-century "elite" culture – as a critic, writer, thinker, collaborator, and composer. His gift for self-promotion was almost as impressive as his ability to land in the most chic (and comfortable) environment at any given time: aristocratic St. Petersburg at the turn of the century, France between the wars, Los Angeles after 1939, and Venice after death.

Intellectually dexterous and meticulously schooled in the musical traditions of the past, Stravinsky knew also that traditions had to change or die. For him, conventions were meant not to be received or followed, but considered, dissected, dismantled – then put back together in an entirely new order and configuration, in combinations no one had imagined before.

Meanwhile, back in Stalin's USSR, the environment for composers and musicians became increasingly hostile and dangerous by the late 1930s. After the highly publicized attack on Shostakovich's *Lady Macbeth* in 1936, composers understood that every new work could become the occasion for an ideological dressing-down – or even worse. Shostakovich managed to resurrect his reputation with his heroic *Symphony No.5* (1937), deeply influenced by Beethoven and Tchaikovsky, while Prokofiev gained Stalin's praise for his music to the propagandistic historical epic film *Aleksandr Nevsky*, directed by Sergei Eisenstein. World War II also brought a certain degree of relaxation to the musical/cultural scene, as Stalin and his henchmen for a while turned their attention to external enemies.

But soon after the war ended, repression of composers returned and even intensified. In January 1948, Andrei Zhdanov, a member of the Party Central Committee and the official watchdog over cultural matters, summoned the leading Soviet composers to a closed meeting at which many of them were subjected to a crude verbal attack. Prokofiev and Shostakovich were harshly rebuked for writing "formalist" music, along with the Armenian Aram Ilych Khachaturian (1903–78) and the indefatigable symphonist Nikolai Iakovlevich Miaskovsky (1881–1950). More meetings followed in February, at which those criticized were pressured into reading official apologies. From this moment until the death of Stalin five years later, life for Prokofiev and Shostakovich was harrowing. Publication and performances of their music nearly ceased. Prokofiev's first wife was arrested on invented charges of spying and sentenced to twenty years in labor camp. For Prokofiev, who had suffered a stroke in early 1945, the pressure was simply too much. He died on 5 March 1953 – the same day as Stalin.

It is important to remember, however, that there was no shortage of Soviet composers willing to produce the kind of socialist realist music the Party censors and bureaucrats said they wanted. They turned out dutifully tendentious cantatas, songs, symphonic poems, ballets, and operas by the thousands. Musicologist Stanley Dale Krebs has provided a concise description of what socialist realism in music actually meant. Among the required ingredients were "nationalism, Party glorification and service, exclusive creative and critical recognition of the Russian nineteenth century, denial of Western influence and isolation from the West, methodical eclecticism, concentration on programme genres, high propaganda content, humourlessness, and simplicity of idiom geared to the widest audience of the moment."[13] Folklore and folk subjects were also highly desirable. Dissonance, atonality, and other styles and techniques used in European "avant-garde" music of the time were considered harmful and inappropriate to "the people."

With Stalin's death in 1953, the situation in Soviet music began to change. As in all areas of culture, "The Thaw" period of the late 1950s and early 1960s was an exciting and turbulent time. Shostakovich produced several of his greatest works, including the massive choral *Symphony No.13* ("Babi Yar," 1962), set to poems by the poet Evgeny Evtushenko dealing with the previously forbidden topic of anti-Semitism. Contact with the West became much easier. A new young generation of Soviet composers became familiar with and began to employ enthusiastically the music and techniques of European and American composers.

Among this group were several composers destined to become important artists in the *glasnost* period of the 1980s, when socialist realism was finally discredited and rejected as an outdated relic of the Stalinist and Brezhnev past. Alfred Schnittke (1934–98), Sophia Gubaidulina (born 1931), and Edison Denisov (born 1929) are regarded as the most significant composers of the post-Soviet period. Like Russian writers and painters, they have joined the international creative community, as Russian music emerges from seventy years of almost complete isolation into the new post-communist era.

NOTES

1. Alfred J. Swan, *Russian Music and Its Sources In Chant and Folk-Song* (London: John Baker, 1973), pp. 37–38.
2. Piotr Ilyich Tchaikovsky, *Piotr Ilyich Tchaikovsky: Letters to His Family, An Autobiography*, trans. Galina von Meck (New York: Stein and Day, 1981), pp. 263–64.
3. Swan, *Russian Music*, p. 139.
4. Alexandra Orlova, *Glinka's Life in Music: A Chronicle*, trans. Richard Hoops (Ann Arbor: UMI Research Press, 1988), p. 438.
5. David Brown, "Mikhail Glinka," *The New Grove Dictionary of Music and Musicians*, ed. Stanley Sadie, vol. VII (London: Macmillan, 1980), p. 434.
6. Gerald Abraham, "Musorgsky," *The New Grove Russian Masters I*, ed. Stanley Sadie (New York: Norton, 1986), pp. 131–32.
7. Nikolai Andreevich Rimsky-Korsakov, *My Musical Life*, ed. Carl Van Vechten, trans. Judah A. Joffe (London: Eulenburg Books, 1974), p. 294.
8. George Balanchine and Solomon Volkov, *Balanchine's Tchaikovsky: Interviews with George Balanchine* (New York: Simon and Schuster, 1985), p. 14.
9. Tchaikovsky, *Letters to His Family*, p. 89.
10. Z. A. Apetyan, ed., *Vospominaniia o Rakhmaninove*, vol. II (Moscow: Gos.muz.izd-vo., 1988), p. 350.
11. Hugh Macdonald, "Scriabin," *The New Grove Russian Masters II*, ed. Stanley Sadie (New York: Norton, 1986), p. 64.
12. *Observer* (London), 5 June 1921.
13. Stanley Dale Krebs, *Soviet Composers and the Development of Soviet Music* (London: George Allen and Unwin Ltd., 1970), p. 53.

11

Theatre

For decades, Soviet scholarship insisted that the national character of the Russian theatre was unmistakable and that its origins were to be found in pagan ceremonials and the agrarian cycles of peasant life. Actually, from the very beginnings, Russian performance, as opposed to ritual, was initiated and molded by foreign influences. The wandering jesters or *skomorokhi* had Byzantine antecedents; the occasional Orthodox liturgical "mysteries," as well as the first court dramas, were fashioned on Latin plays of the Jesuit academies in Poland and Ukraine. Even the earliest folk dramas can be shown to have been affected (contaminated, to use the term in its dramaturgical sense) by contact with non-Russian models drawn from the touring repertoires of the Englische Komedianten (professional companies of players from London) or European puppet shows.

What does make the Russian theatre stand out from other national theatres is its secular bias and the cross-fertilization of court and popular theatres. Theatre in the West can be shown to have evolved from two distinct strains, the professional (embodied by itinerant troupes of motley entertainers) and the amateur (represented by performances sponsored initially by church, then by school or court). In Russia, the two strains would coexist and commingle: although professional theatre was often hampered by its governmental ties, the amateur was frequently productive of reform and fresh impulses.

The Russian Orthodox Church was doctrinally hostile to any kind of enactment and countenanced plays within its precincts only for a brief period in the sixteenth century. Amateur performance was therefore to be found under the patronage of the court, and even when its subjects were biblical, the atmosphere was secular. The very terminology suggests that the "entertainment" component was paramount over any didactic or edificatory aims: the palace of Boris Godunov contained a *poteshnaia palata* or amusement hall; and in 1613 the court set aside *poteshnye khoromy* or amusement chambers where music and buffoons might be enjoyed. Long after Tsar Aleksei Mikhailovich had forbidden the performances of the *skomorokhi* as "devilish pastimes" (1648), he founded a court theatre, an act which marked his supremacy over mutinous commoners and the church's temporal influence. In the absence of native practitioners, in 1672 the tsar called upon a Lutheran pastor, Johann Gregory, to establish a troupe composed of the sons of European artisans domiciled in Moscow's "German" quarter.

A royal court, with its elaborate ceremonial and its clear-cut disposition of roles, is already a "performative" environment; to introduce into it a formal theatre is to provide a microcosmic mirror of its predilections and usages. Although Aleksei's son Peter the Great briefly returned theatre to the public with a short-lived German company situated in Red Square under the management of Johann Kunst, the autocrat's heart really lay in the elaborate open-air pageants and fireworks displays copied from European *trionfi* (baroque processionals), which celebrated his military victories. His female successors, Anna and Elizabeth, confined theatre to the palace, first with performances by courtiers and then with professional actors and musicians imported from Germany, Italy, and France. Foreigners implanted a neoclassical style in opera, ballet, stage architecture and design, and rhetorical declamation; as the preferred mode in court circles, it impeded a native school from developing. Nevertheless, training combining voice, body, and expression nurtured a "syncretic" performer who could bestride the genres and would later inspire the concept of the "synthetic actor" popular in the early revolutionary period.

On 30 August 1756 the Empress Elizabeth "established the Russian theatre"; but to date its foundation from this decree is highly arbitrary. Elizabeth's real innovation lay in braiding the two traditional strains by combining the professional troupe of Fedor Volkov with the aristocratic students of the Cadet School and opening up performance to a general public. Volkov, son of a Yaroslavl merchant, was a former amateur who had created his own professional theatre; once moved to Petersburg, his actors proved to be too "natural" for their imperial patron and had to be retrained in "embellishments of art." A distinctly Russian drama began to take shape, but, even when, as in the plays of Aleksandr Sumarokov, it drew on such historical matter as the Pretender Dmitry's assault on the throne, its form was dictated by neoclassical rules: unities, alexandrines, decorum. Satires, such as those of Vasily Kapnist and Denis Fonvizin, might attack fashionable francophiles but always did so within the bounds of French or Danish models. This was due partly to the inchoate state of the Russian literary language, but more to a national inferiority complex in the presence of highly developed European theatre.

Throughout the latter part of the eighteenth century, as the Russian theatre evolved, with ever more plays, players, and playhouses, the foreign influence reigned supreme. The actor Ivan Dmitrevsky went abroad to study Garrick and Le Kain; the leading managers in Moscow were an Italian, Giovanni Locatelli, and an Englishman, Michael Maddox; even the so-called "people's houses," under police supervision, played Molière for the most part. A few individual voices, like those of Petr Plavilshchikov and Vladimir Lukin, called for Russian life to be treated on stage, but only rarely did plays, usually comedies, draw on observed behavior.

When landowners, freed from government service, returned to their estates and set up serf theatres there, the repertoires were composed chiefly of Italian opera, French *opéra-comique*, lachrymose comedy, or imitations thereof. Soviet historians have posited a "serf intelligentsia" evolving out of this widespread pastime, but even those slaves who were well trained imitated the classic style and had no opportunity to innovate from their experience. Just as court ceremonials tended to theatricalize the lives of their participants, every squireen sought to erect a fantasy realm in his private domain. Despite governmental strictures on repertoire, the atmosphere was highly eroticized, for the stage display was less a pursuit of artistry than a demonstration of the serf-owner's power and potency. Still, the practice, carried out in at least 173 venues, began to develop a taste for playgoing in the provinces.

An abiding problem for the Russian theatre was the constricted size of its audience. Most spectators were drawn from the nobility or land-owning classes, with a penchant for luxury and aping European modes; the middle class was too rudimentary to interject its own tastes. Catherine the Great, fearful of freedom of thought, consolidated the Moscow and Petersburg theatres into a state bureaucracy, which eventually congealed into a monopoly in 1827. Actors and musicians were registered as members of the civil service, subject to an administration whose concerns were as much protocol as art. Theatrical censorship, managed by the Ministry of the Interior from 1819, grew stricter over the years, and even extended to periodicals which were rebuked when actors, i.e. government employees, were unfavorably criticized. Forcibly submissive to strict codes of conduct and aesthetics, the theatres in Moscow and Petersburg had difficulty in finding a national voice.

In the provinces, independent entrepreneurs were allowed to operate under police supervision, but the nature of their audiences and the talent available – strollers and local amateurs – prevented much in the way of innovation. However, remarkable actors, such as the former serf Mikhail Shchepkin and the itinerant Prov Sadovsky, polished their skills in these troupes and constituted a reservoir from which the imperial theatres could draw.

In St. Petersburg, in the shadow of the court, preference was given to ballet and opera, and to French and German companies at the Mikhailovsky (Grand Duke Michael) Theatre. The Russian company installed at the Aleksandrinsky (Empress Alexandra) had less prestige. Its style remained cool, classical, and restrained, as in the best work of Ekaterina Semenova, who introduced French neoclassic declamation, Pavel Karatygin, and Ivan Sosnitsky. Moscow, on the other hand, cherished the performances at the Maly (Little) Theatre, nicknamed "the second Moscow University." Shackled by the triviality of a repertoire composed chiefly of farces and melodramas adapted from European plays, actors such as the fiery Pavel Mochalov managed to bring spontaneity and vivacity to their impersonations.

Since playwrights were hampered by censorship and fashion, acting improved far more quickly than playwriting. Despite the occasional work of genius, such as Aleksandr Griboedov's *Woe from Wit* (1824) or Nikolai Gogol's *Inspector* (1836), which were distrusted at their premieres, the genius of the best Russian dramatists was deployed on vaudevilles and patriotic drama. The emergence of Aleksandr Ostrovsky, Aleksei Potekhin, Aleksei Pisemsky, and others in the 1850s and 1860s finally brought on to the stage Russian types, manners, and idioms hitherto seldom seen: peasants, rural gentry, Moscow merchants. In place of the generic emotional realism of Shchepkin and Mochalov, a new generation of actors transferred observed mannerisms and dialects to the stage. This was reflected in a new attention to local color in costume and set design, less in the dramatic theatre than in opera and ballet.

The general populace was debarred from these recreations for socioeconomic and political reasons. Popular entertainment had to be innocuous, but an indigenous type of performance developed in the fairground

11.1 Griboedov's "Woe from Wit" at the Moscow Maly Theatre in the 1850s: L. V.
Samarin as Chatsky, Mikhail Shchepkin as Famusov, and G. S. Olgin as Skalozub.

showbooth, primitive but lurid: limited to pantomime farces and harle-
quinades, mingling European themes with Russian folklore. A "grand-
dad" (*ded*) stood outside and improvised references to news of the day and
faces in the crowd; but even this nascent satire was put under state
control in 1855. About this time, the puppet Petrushka was introduced
into city streets, his knockabout antics and uncensored remarks much
appreciated by the crowd. The circus also thrived, again under the guidance of European impresarios like Ciniselli; it would prove a testing-
ground for such satiric clowns as the Durov brothers (Anatoly and
Vladimir).

After the abolition of serfdom in 1861, the populist movement promulgated the idea of a *narodny* or people's theatre that would serve less as
a leisure activity than as an educational tool. A theatre at popular prices
playing a classical repertory was first opened at the Polytechnic
Exhibition of 1872, under the aegis of the Ministry of the Interior, but it
could not be made permanent. The movement for an *obschedostupny* or
easily accessible theatre chimed in with a prevalent literary creed, propounded by Vissarion Belinsky and his followers, that art's chief claim to
significance was its ability to advance the progress of Russian society.
Belinsky preferred "realism" as the best conveyance of a critical view of

modern life; hence the promotion by the liberals of Ostrovsky's plays as true pictures of the "kingdom of darkness" that was unenlightened Russia. But the Slavophiles also embraced Ostrovsky, viewing him as a delineator of ethnic traditions and idioms.

To Ostrovsky's dismay, throughout the reign of Alexander II and well into that of his successor, the most popular shows throughout Russia were the comic operas of Offenbach, in Russified adaptations that conveyed an intoxicating whiff of Gallic spice. Nevertheless, the growth of private theatre clubs throughout the 1860s and 1870s testified to an enlarged and eager audience for serious drama. The development of the intelligentsia, a body of educated, literate persons often drawn from the *raznochintsy* or upwardly mobile lower ranks, was a prime contributory factor. By 1882, when the imperial monopoly was rescinded, there was a potentially sizable playgoing public, though not large enough to support enterprises with no source of funding but the box office. Impresarios such as Mikhail Lentovsky and Fedor Korsh survived by cannily offering the public a mixed diet of boulevard sensation and highminded drama; but it was only those theatres supported by self-made millionaires, such as Savva Mamontov, Aleksei Suvorin, and Savva Morozov, that had the freedom to experiment boldly.

The abolition of the imperial monopoly also gave renewed impetus to the people's theatre movement. Ostrovsky and others propagandized for the theatre as an essential nutriment of the social organism, and in this early phase of Russian industrialization, factory-owners sponsored theatres by and for the workers. Similar experiments mushroomed on estates, in army camps, and at universities. The repertoire ranged from Shakespeare, Molière, and Pushkin to such traditional folk plays as *Tsar Maksimilian*, but their popularity was genuine and undeniable.

A turning point came in 1897 with the First All-Russian Congress of Stage Workers, a convocation in Moscow of theatre people from all over the empire to deliberate on the theatre's educational goals, artistic aims, and professional standards. It affirmed the theatre's function of social betterment by calling for the creation of repertory theatres sworn to renounce the star system, to rehearse seriously the best classic and modern drama, and to uplift the public. The theatre was defined as a temple, and the actor as dedicated officiant to its lofty goals, an educated citizen to be treated with respect. Two such operations were founded in 1898: Aleksandr Lensky's New Theatre in St. Petersburg staggered on for a while, with a relatively inexperienced company; but it was the Moscow

11.2 Korsh's Theatre, Moscow, designed by the architect M. N. Chicagov.

Art Theatre (MAT), the brain-child of the amateur actor (and textile magnate) Konstantin Stanislavsky and the playwright Vladimir Nemirovich-Danchenko, that managed to survive. In part this was because the enterprise was supported by Morozov's millions, but also because the directors discovered in Anton Chekhov a playwright whose works inspired and perpetuated a house style. A realism of mood and environmental atmosphere prevailed, and ensemble feeling made up for deficiencies in the individual performances of the uneven company. Such innovations as the suppression of applause during acts and of music in the intervals were supposed to contribute to the illusion of reality into which the spectator was to be drawn. Its founders had originally hoped that the MAT would be a "people's" theatre at popular prices; but lack of state funding and local restrictions prevented that. Instead, it turned into an exemplary mouthpiece for the intelligentsia, which saw its own concerns and psychic states projected from its stage.

The Art Theatre also promoted the primacy of the stage director as the single mind whose vision was to infiltrate and unite the spectacle. Stanislavsky began as an imitator of the Meiningen school, with an emphasis on historical accuracy, deft deployment of crowds, and picturesque groupings. Gradually, he realized the need to stimulate the individual actor's creativity, and over the course of his lifetime tried to codify a system to achieve this result. The Art Theatre's high-minded

11.3 The last act of Chekhov's *The Three Sisters* at the Moscow Art Theatre, directed by Stanislavsky in the setting by Viktor Simov (1903).

program and its ideals were contagious and inspired many imitators before the Revolution.

The emergence of the director argued for visual as well as conceptual unity throughout a stage production. This was implemented by the *Mir iskusstva* or World of Art movement, which professed aestheticism, part eighteenth-century, part avant-garde. Its painters were invited to work at Mamontov's opera (where the brilliant bass Fedor Chaliapin exemplified the "syncretic" actor) and for the first time genuinely Russian motifs, drawn from folk art, *lubki* (tuppence-colored prints) and religious icons, began to appear in sets and costumes designed for works by Russian composers. The World of Art's greatest achievement was Sergei Diaghilev's introduction of Russian opera and the Ballets Russes to the West. The polychromatic designs of Leon Bakst, Aleksandr Golovin, Natalia Goncharova, and Alexandre Benois, along with the virtuosic dancing of Vatslav Nizhinsky, Mikhail Fokin, Tamara Karsavina, and Anna Pavlova, were often drawn from genuine Slavic sources, and had the effect of a highly spiced curry on jaded European palates. For the first time, Russian performance gained an ascendant influence over its Western counterparts.[1]

The notion of a unified vision also underlay the symbolist movement, which preached a religious communion (*sobornost'*) between stage and audience with the actor serving as officiating priest at the mystery, a return to an ostensible ancient theatre hypothesized by the poet and classicist

Viacheslav Ivanov. Attacked in 1902 by Valery Briusov for "superfluous truth," even the Art Theatre dabbled in symbolism in its productions of Maurice Maeterlinck, Knut Hamsun, and Leonid Andreev; but the fad was best incarnated by Vsevolod Meyerhold's static and sacerdotal productions at Vera Komissarzhevskaya's theatre in St. Petersburg (1906–07), which he characterized as "conventionalized" (*uslovnyi*). His *Hedda Gabler* subordinated the action to a spectrum of "impressionist" colors; his *Sister Beatrice* copied the flatness and arrangement of Quattrocento painting; the nuns in clinging blue-gray vestments acted in profile. The choreographed groups expressed themselves in incantatory cries of rhythmic ecstasy, long pauses, staccato gestures, and barely audible murmurs. The actors in *The Little Showbooth* (*Balaganchik*) by Aleksandr Blok played out a metaphysical Punch-and-Judy show, bleeding cranberry juice, their speeches uttered "like drops dripping in a deep well."

The millennial mood that fostered the more portentous symbolist pronouncements also generated a highly emotional style of acting, best exemplified by Pavel Orlenev, Vera Komissarzhevskaya, and Lidiia Yavorskaya; a new *emploi*, that of the neurasthenic young man who commits suicide by the play's end, came into being. This apocalyptic attitude somewhat dissipated after the failed Revolution of 1905; in an ensuing "Crisis in the Theatre" ideologues debated the questions, is the theatre relevant, does it have any meaning for contemporary society? One who loudly answered "yes" was Nikolai Evreinov, who argued that theatricality was a basic principle of life, and that an instinct for theatre lay at the origin of all rites and arts. Evreinov, like many of his colleagues, was steeped in the most parturient of modernist theories of theatre: they were eager to put the ideas of Adolphe Appia, Gordon Craig, Georg Fuchs, Emile Jaques-Dalcroze, and Isadora Duncan to the test. Pantomime was seriously analyzed, and the *commedia dell'arte*, researched by Konstantin Miklashevsky, plumbed for inspiration. Laboratory theatres proliferated, among them Evreinov's Antique Theatre (1907–11) dedicated to reconstructing premodern theatrical forms; Meyerhold's The Strand and Interlude House exploring *commedia* and Asian performance; along with the eclectic Free Theatre of Aleksandr Tairov and Konstantin Mardzhanov. Even Stanislavsky, despairing of the MAT's inertia, founded a Studio to try out his system with untried actors and invited Gordon Craig to stage an idiosyncratic *Hamlet* (1912). A rash of cubo-futurist experiments erupted, the most elaborate being Aleksei Kruchonykh's *Victory over the Sun* (1913), an "anti-aesthetic" *étude* in sound beyond meaning, with designs by the "suprematist" painter Kazimir Malevich.

The froth stirred up by this ferment of activity was channeled into "small forms" or "theatres of miniatures." Although the burgeoning music-halls and vaudeville theatres throughout Russia, featuring gypsy choruses and buxom *chanteuses*, were regarded as vulgar by many intellectuals, their vitality was infectious. Variety's exuberance was combined with theatrical sophistication to produce such cabarets as The Crooked Mirror in St. Petersburg, a forum for parodying current artistic trends and exploring Evreinov's concept of monodrama; The Stray Dog, a musky outlet for poets and avant-gardistes; and The Bat in Moscow, a more purely ornamental *divertissement* of song, dance, and skits. On the very eve of Revolution, the cabaret proved hospitable to Aleksandr Vertinsky, a minstrel in white-face and Pierrot costume, who crooned the praises of cocaine and blighted love in world-weary tones.

As if to ignore the deepening political crisis, many creative artists turned their backs on contemporary reality and indulged in a florid aestheticism. Hired by the State Aleksandra Theatre in 1909, Meyerhold spent its huge budgets on lavish recreations of a legendary past in Molière's *Don Juan* (1911), an evocation of Versailles, and Lermontov's *Masquerade* (1917), which rehearsed for four years. Inspired by Fuchs, Meyerhold placed the actor on the apron and used the depth of the stage to show off the brilliance of his designers. Both Fedor Komissarzhevsky and Aleksandr Tairov proposed a "synthetic actor," who could play everything from high tragedy to operetta. Komissarzhevsky's deliberately eclectic productions at his sister's theatre in Petersburg and Konstantin Nezlobin's in Moscow sought to incarnate each dramatist's idiosyncratic style. In 1914 Tairov founded the Moscow Kamerny (Chamber) Theatre, which offered a synthesis of the traditional with the modernist; the actor was to be exalted over the playwright or the designer through the exploitation of his three-dimensional body. Dance, gymnastics, gesture, mime and a symphonic melding of voices were the primary means, employed by Tairov on geometric constructions of levels and platforms allowing maximal physical expression. The actor's sheer virtuosity was supposed to stimulate the spectator without literary or mechanical aides. Tairov was fortunate that his players, headed by such virtuosi as his wife Alisa Koonen and Nikolai Tseretelli, and his designers, such painters as Natalia Goncharova, Mikhail Larionov and Aleksandra Exter, were capable of realizing these refinements, most successfully in Innokenty

Annensky's *Thamira the Cither Player* (1916), an antiphony of Dionysian and Apollonian rhythms.

On the threshold of revolution, the basic types of Russian dramatic performance could be categorized as: (1) the commercial theatre, presenting boulevard comedy or society melodrama; (2) the tendentious theatre, dominated by psychological realism, and expressing the intelligentsia's social concerns; and (3) the chamber theatre, stimulating experiments essentially aimed at *aficionados* of theatrical innovation. But in every case these theatres were patronized by a small percentage of the urban public; the huge mass of the Russian populace never set foot in them.

Masquerade, Meyerhold's sumptuous evocation of a decadent society, opened in St. Petersburg the same night that the February Revolution broke out, and its audience went home to the sound of gunfire. No sooner had the Bolsheviks seized power in October 1917 than they turned their attention to the theatre. As early as 9 November 1917, a decree of the Soviet of People's Commissars placed the theatres under the authority of the arts section of the newly formed State Commission (later Commissariat) for Education. A theatre section (TEO: *Teatralny Otdel*) was organized to consolidate and operate the theatres. At first, the TEO was run by experienced persons who had a real interest in the theatre's welfare: Meyerhold directed it from August 1920, and its repertoire section was under the control of the poet Aleksandr Blok, while Evgeny Vakhtangov, Stanislavsky's favorite pupil, ran the directing section.

The decree of 26 August 1919, "On the unification of theatrical activity," signed by Lenin and Commissar of Education Anatoly Lunacharsky, was in fact the constitutive charter for the Soviet theatre: "all theatrical holdings (buildings, accessories), given their cultural value" were declared national property and their finances centralized. Their repertoires were to be regularly inspected in the interest of social ideals. From the inception, the Party and the state regarded theatre as a means of raising the ideological and intellectual consciousness of the masses and indoctrinating them in socialism. This was to adopt to the ends of communism the long-standing views of the Belinsky school on the theatre's social mission; in so doing, it tacitly endorsed the value given to realism in that curriculum.

To promote popular education, free tickets were distributed to Party cadres, military units, factory workers, and other proletarian groups. Overnight, the Russian audience changed. Instead of well-read, highly educated spectators, actors were confronted with soldiers fresh from the front, illiterate mechanics, and old market-women. Unaccustomed to the etiquette and conventions of the theatre, these untutored playgoers ate, drank, responded vociferously, often to the shock of such as Stanislavsky. Amid the cold, privation, and uncertainties of the Civil War, theatres, dozens of them brand new, played to full houses.

In this first phase of the post-revolutionary Russian theatre, the growth of a mass audience avid for performance, the ferment of ideas and experiments of artists and *animateurs*, and the political needs of the unstable government produced a dynamic synergy. Inspired by such pre-revolutionary concepts as symbolist communion, the return to a "theatrical theatre," and Evreinov's "theatricality for oneself," artists argued that the political revolution should be seconded by a theatrical revolution, overthrowing all the old conventions. In fact, revolution in the theatre was most visible in an exciting pursuit of new forms, which quickly ran into the brick wall of Party imperatives and the aesthetic preferences of officialdom. The program adopted by the 8th Congress of the Bolshevik party in 1919 stipulated the necessity of "offering and making accessible to the workers all the treasures of art produced through the exploitation of their work and which have heretofore been kept for the exclusive disposition of the exploiters." So far as the government was concerned, theatre was not a question of finding new forms, but rather of allowing the disinherited to enter into possession of their sequestered legacy.

This process of restitution often involved the replacement and even the repudiation of the professional theatre in favor of amateurism, as was obvious in the activity of the Proletkult. The Proletkult (proletarian organizations of cultural education) movement was founded in September 1917 by Aleksandr Bogdanov. Independent of political parties, including the Bolsheviks, it covered the nation with a network of clubs, literary circles, and studio theatres, numbering almost a hundred in the provinces by late 1918; by 1920 more than 80,000 persons were taking part. The Proletkult claimed as its goal a total break with the bourgeois past, since, as Bogdanov put it, proletarian culture could be the work of no one but the proletariat. This meant the rejection of all existing professional theatre.

In actuality, the Proletkult's theatrical activity was directed by veterans of the professional stage: its first production, Romain Rolland's *The Storming of the Bastille* (Petrograd, 1 May 1918) was staged to celebrate the first anniversary of the October Revolution by Aleksandr Mgebrov, who had worked at the MAT and under Meyerhold in his symbolist phase. The Moscow Proletkult's first director was Valentin Smyshlaev, a product of Stanislavsky's Studio; in 1922 it was taken over by Meyerhold's pupil Sergei Eisenstein. His experiment to ground the theatre in a context of reality by staging Georg Kaiser's *Gas* in a Moscow gasworks was a total failure. Severely criticized by Lenin for its rejection of the heritage of the past, the Proletkult was condemned by the Central Committee of the Bolshevik Party on 1 December 1920 as "futurists, decadents, partisans of an idealist philosophy hostile to Marxism, mere losers," guilty of inculcating perverse tastes in the workers. The Bolshevik leadership did not share the iconoclasm of the theatrical leadership. To popularize past masterpieces, Maksim Gorky and Blok founded the Bolshoi Dramatic Theatre (BDT) in Petrograd (later, Leningrad) in 1919 as a haven of high culture. The scheme of its promoters was to house the heroic classical theatre of Shakespeare, Molière and Schiller, the only repertoire suitable, in their opinion, for an apocalyptic age.

The man most responsible for promulgating an artistic doctrine for the Party was the People's Commissar of Education, Lunacharsky. An old-style *intelligent* even to his pince-nez, Lunacharsky was tasked to preserve the monuments of Russian culture in the midst of a collapsing society. This meant an urgent concern to safeguard traditional theatres and maintain classic Russian and foreign works. The Art Theatre, for instance, floundering in the new era, restaging tired productions of Chekhov, and unable to mount a revolutionary play, was under heavy attack from the extreme left. Regarding the MAT, the Kamerny, and the former Imperial theatres as an endangered species, in 1921 Lunacharsky registered them as academic theatres under the direct administration of the Commissariat of Education, which kept them carefully sheltered from the frenetic innovation going on elsewhere.

One can hardly talk about a theatrical avant-garde after 1918, for those who had been in the vanguard in the pre-revolutionary period constituted the post-revolutionary mainstream. The suprematicists and futurists welcomed the Revolution enthusiastically. The young poet Vladimir Mayakovsky took on the task of consummating the social revolution by "an October 25th in the realm of art." For his part the designer Georgy Annenkov, quoting the manifesto uttered in 1913 by the Italian futurist Emilio Marinetti, proclaimed the music-hall the basis of the revolutionary theatre. Although it would be among the first movements to run afoul of the authorities, the cult of variety was widely promoted as "eccentrism" and "circusization." The Durovs' trained animals were recruited for allegorical attacks on the White Army, while the great clown Vitaly Lazarenko lent his talents to "agitation-propaganda" and Meyerhold's experiments. Eisenstein, during his stint with the Moscow Proletkult, enunciated the doctrine of "Montage of Attractions." A show was to be organized like a circus around a linked series of spectacular numbers, which required actors to have an acrobat's expertise. His staging in 1923 of Ostrovsky's comedy, *No Fool like a Wise Fool*, transformed it into a variety show with the addition of film strips and contemporary political figures standing in for the characters in the plays. Ironically, it was American movies and the overwhelming popularity of Charlie Chaplin and the athletic Douglas Fairbanks that spurred many of these novelties.

The cult of technology and machinery also had an enormous influence on Soviet theatre aesthetics. Rejecting capitalism as a system, Russian artists nevertheless eagerly embraced American industry's efficiency experts and assembly-line techniques; Taylorism, named after a manager at the Ford factory, became a term to conjure with. Meyerhold, in particular, wedded Taylorism to constructivism, a demystified, allegedly scientific approach to art, to create biomechanics, a mechanistic, highly kinetic style of acting.

There was also a fervent belief in the value of raw data. The "factographic" approach of Sergei Tretiakov as well as of many agitprop operations assumed that audiences needed information, sometimes conveyed in pure documentary form, but more often sugar-coated by entertainment. Under the leadership of professionals, amateur or *samodeiatelny* ("do-it-yourself") circles were created in the armed forces and factories; these clubs, organized under umbrella groups such as Proletkult or Teresvat (Theatre of Revolutionary Satire), played a large part in the agitprop movement. Tendentious skits on political topicalities might involve an "agitation tribunal" where the spectators were called on to try enemies of the people; a "theatrical lecture" which used slides, film clips, charts, and diagrams; literary montage employing choruses, declamation, and dialog; the "living newspaper," which was to be copied by the US Federal Theatre Project; and, in its hyperthyroid form, "mass spectacles."

These outdoor pageants strongly resembled the festivals of the French Revolution in their attempt to engender a new national mythology by simulating recent victories of the Bolsheviks. Combining such real-life elements as military troops and bands with *commedia dell'arte* elements (class enemies played by actors wearing grotesque masks), they deployed thousands of people. The first was *The Overthrow of the Autocracy*, staged by N. Vinogradov in Leningrad in February 1919; it was much imitated and similar spectacles were organized for anniversaries of such red-letter days in the history of revolutionary communism as the convocation of the Third International, Bloody Sunday, and the foundation of the Red Army. Directed by a consortium of stage managers who issued instructions via field-telephones or signal flags, mass spectacles took place in the open against the facade of a historic building with the crowd serving as an antiphonal chorus – Whites versus Reds, Europe versus the USSR – but as these shows grew vaster, the crowd's role became more peripheral. The culminating production was *The Taking of the Winter Palace* (19 July 1920) on the third anniversary of the October Revolution; Evreinov manipulated a cast of 8,000 within the actual presence of the Winter Palace.

Almost all the directors in this initial period were men who had made their reputations before the Revolution. Many of the youngsters trained by the inspiring Leopold Sulerzhitsky at Stanislavsky's First Studio (founded 1912) emerged as the most brilliant of the new generation. There Evgeny Vakhtangov staged Strindberg's *Erik XIV* (1921) with Michael Chekhov, the dramatist's nephew, in the title role; it was a stunning exploration of a schizoid mind torn between the courtier's world, depicted in a stylized fashion, and the commoner's world, depicted realistically. Chekhov, an actor of perfervid imagination, in 1922 took over the leadership of the Studio, which was later renamed the Second Moscow Art Theatre; there he excelled as a psychotic Hamlet.

Vakhtangov appreciated Stanislavsky's teachings on "inner technique," but, like Meyerhold, he preferred a "theatricalized" exterior, a synthesis of the human and the fantastic. Opposed to extremes of Stanislavskian psychology and Meyerholdian manipulation alike, he made the actor the star player in a game imbued with energized emotion. Racked by tuberculosis, Vakhtangov died too soon to fulfill all his promise, but he left a legacy of two seminal productions. Gozzi's *Princess Turandot* (1922, Third Studio) was the culmination of all those *fin de siècle* experiments in *commedia dell'arte*. High-spirited, improvisational, and playful, yet sophisticated in the sources of its fantasy, it brought a ray of sunshine into the lives of playgoers inured to hunger, darkness, cold, and imminent danger. Everything on stage was a pretext for stunts, pranks,

11.4 Michael Chekhov as Hamlet.

and tricks. Its unabashed theatricality offered a surrogate life to the denizens of a time of troubles.

Without knowing the language, Vakhtangov nevertheless agreed to direct the Hebrew theatre company Habima in S. An-ski's folkloric play of demonic possession *The Dybbuk* (1922). He molded the inexperienced actors into terrifying gargoyles, imbued with a genuine mysticism. The grotesque style was so dynamic that it influenced all of Habima's later work, and Vakhtangov's *Dybbuk* remained in its repertory long after it had become the State Theatre of Israel. After Vakhtangov's death, the troupe of his Third Studio carried on an autonomous existence and in 1926 took the name Vakhtangov Theatre. Drawing on the talents of such disciples as Boris Zakhava, Ruben Simonov, and Serafima Birman, for a while it preserved a tradition of gaudy, sharply etched comic performance, but eventually succumbed to the growing imposition of socialist realism.

Vakhtangov's influence was also evident in the work of the Jewish Chamber Theatre, founded by Aleksandr Granovsky. Performing in Yiddish, with the participation of fine actors like Solomon Mikhoels and

Veniamin Zuskin, it wallowed in sub-Dybbukian grotesquerie. Its house style was very derivative of the stage designs Mark Chagall had created for its first production, during his stint with Teresvat. This theatre progressed from ethnic material by Avrahm Goldfadn and Sholem Aleichem to a *King Lear* which Gordon Craig pronounced the best he had ever seen.

Part opportunist, part true believer, Meyerhold had been the first director to jump on the Bolshevik bandwagon. His production of Mayakovsky's *Mystery Bouffe* in collaboration with the author for the first anniversary of the Revolution (7–9 November 1918) was a landmark, the inaugural Soviet play performed in a poetic agitprop, poster style, initiating a productive collaboration between a futurist poet and a constructivist director. Mayakovsky himself defined *Mystery Bouffe* as the "heroic, epic and satiric enactment of our era."

Once he took over the TEO in 1920, Meyerhold became the most important person in Russian theatrical life. It was at this time that he launched the slogan "Theatrical October" (*Teatralnyi Oktiabr*); for him, as for the ideologues of the Proletkult, the Revolution had so far taken place only in the socioeconomic realm, and now had to be recapitulated in the realm of art, particularly in the theatre. He organized the Studio of Communist Drama (Mastkomdram), founded his own theatre, RSFSR1, which he was to run under various names from 1920 to 1938, and from 1922 to 1924 assumed the artistic direction of the newly founded Theatre of the Revolution. RSFSR1 opened with an adaptation of *Dawns* by Emile Verhaeren, its hortatory rhetoric set against a cubist design by Vladimir Dmitriev, motifs by Vladimir Tatlin, and hints of Greek tragedy played in agitprop style. For many years Meyerhold was to be the tutelary genius of the Soviet theatre, and his schools trained a vital generation of theatre practitioners.

In April 1922 with Fernand Crommelynck's *Magnificent Cuckold*, Meyerhold realized his first integrally "constructivist" and "biomechanical" staging, in which corporeal movement predominated over language; the stage "construction" was not a setting but a machine for acting, and costumes were replaced by blue overalls, true workclothes for actors. Biomechanics discarded the "psychological" acting founded on Stanislavskian "re-experiencing"; and replaced it with plastic physical expression, gymnastic training, *commedia* clowning, and Asian emblemata. Later, Meyerhold enunciated the concept of "pre-acting," an alienation device to detach the actor from his role and provide commentary on his rendition.

When Lunacharsky, anxious to put the brake on untrammeled experimentation, launched the slogan "Back to Ostrovsky" in 1923, Meyerhold challenged it with his unconventional staging of *The Forest* (1924), whose script he dismantled into a series of discrete episodes reconfigured as an exuberant harlequinade: its success was enormous. Meyerhold's self-aggrandizement as "author of the spectacle" culminated in a profound transformation of Gogol's *Inspector* in 1926: the text was disassembled, reassembled, and turned into a palimpsest interpolated with variant readings, commentary, quotations from the Gogolian canon, musical leitmotivs, and new characters created out of whole cloth. The idea was to illuminate the social and political meaning of a classic, but the practice tended to weigh down the original, as in Meyerhold's later productions of Griboedov and Sukhovo-Kobylin.

Constructivism was also ubiquitous at the Kamerny Theatre, where Anatoly Vesnin's setting for G. K. Chesterton's *The Man Who Was Thursday* (1923) was a complicated Tower of Babel, a stack of multiple levels, staircases, and elevators, an expressionist epitome of the modern metropolis. Although the Kamerny's director Tairov was another proponent of "theatrical theatre," he differed from Meyerhold in preferring the art of the word to that of gesture. Word was extended to mean declamation and song: it was not by chance that *Princess Brambilla* (1920), for instance, was named on the posters as a "capriccio by the Kamerny Theatre on themes by E. T. A. Hoffmann."

In his book *Notes of a Director* (1921), Tairov explained his idiosyncratic beliefs, exalting the "truth of art" over Stanislavsky's "truth of life." His choice of plays was, on principle, extremely eclectic and drew widely on the Western repertoire: although his cubist staging of Racine's *Phèdre* (1922) was much appreciated, he was more interested in promoting modern tragedy. His productions of Hasenclever's *Antigone* and Shaw's *St. Joan* (1924), always with Koonen as the heroine, wielded crowds and dialectic with great fluidity. Tairov's introduction of O'Neill to Russia, with *The Hairy Ape, Desire under the Elms* (both 1926), and *All God's Chillun* (1929), was his oblique way of responding to the call for social relevance. And although he was progressive enough to risk the first Russian staging of Brecht (*Threepenny Opera*), his most popular productions were Lecoq's frivolous operettas *Giroflé-Girofla* (1922) and *Night and Day*.

Stanislavsky and Nemirovich-Danchenko had at first been stranded by these creative upheavals. During the Civil War, the Art Theatre company had been split, half abroad, half at home; rejoined, it toured to

Europe and the United States under Stanislavsky's leadership (1922–24). Nemirovich took this opportunity to found his Musical Studio, dedicated to staging opera and operetta along psychologically and historically accurate lines. The MAT's first successful new production was Mikhail Bulgakov's *Days of the Turbins* (1926), based on his novel *The White Guard*; although attacked, by Mayakovsky and Lunacharsky among others, as too indulgent to the old regime, it became the MAT's biggest money-maker for a decade, and proved to be Stalin's favorite play. Stanislavsky emitted one belated burst of invention with colorful productions of Ostrovsky's *Ardent Heart* and Beaumarchais' *Marriage of Figaro* (1927); but as government interference grew more prevalent, he used the excuse of ill health to retire to his home, where he worked with an opera studio and exercised his system, especially his new theory of "physical actions." This reversed his earlier insistence on emotional recall by requiring actors to find a preliminary physical expression to evoke emotions.

Stanislavsky had always been hesitant about writing down his ideas in any definitive form, and only when others claimed to be his interpreter did he feel impelled to publish. In 1925, he issued the Russian version of his memoirs, *My Life in Art*, and this was followed by *An Actor Works on Himself*, a pedagogic tract introducing students to the "system."[2] Much vaguer and more porous than many of his disciples would grant, the system was neither a philosophy nor a textbook: mingling stage slang and the jargon of psychology, Stanislavsky coined his own vocabulary – "re-experiencing," "through action," "the task," "the super-objective," "the magic if" – to provide workers in the theatre with a common language and to probe the roots of creativity.

Enormous as is the residual effect of Stanislavsky's teachings, in the 1920s he was thoroughly eclipsed by Meyerhold. The external attributes of the latter's creations, with their geometric planes, bare utilitarian machinery, and hyperkinetic actors, were propagandized to the farthest reaches of the USSR, in a delirium of epigonism. The anti-theatre had a field day, tearing down prosceniums and traditional stages, exalting the importance of raw material. Psychology and the technique of interiority in creating a character were abandoned, and eccentric costume and makeup substituted for them. In Moscow, Meyerholdian clones were unavoidable: beside the "agitational" Theatre of Revolution, which staged German expressionist plays, and the Proletkult during Eisenstein's regime, there were, among others, Nikolai Foregger's

11.5   A Blue Blouse troupe demonstrating "Fordism in the factory."

Workshop (*Mastfor*); Vakhtang Mchedelov's Theatre of Masks (*Teatr Masok*), and the satirical miniature theatre Semperante. In Petrograd, Meyerhold's former collaborators Sergei Radlov and Vladimir N. Soloviev directed the Theatre of Popular Comedy (*Teatr Narodnoi komedii*, 1920–22), founded on principles of improvisation and circus routines, while his experiments, old and new, were recapitulated in Yury Annenkov's Hermitage Theatre and at the Factory of the Eccentric Actor (FEKS) of Grigory Kozintsev and Leonid Trauberg, inspired by Gogol and silent cinema. Even the Maly Theatre dabbled in constructivism, and the rage for innovation could be seen throughout the provinces and the other republics. Analogous novelties were devised by Les Kurbas in Kiev and Kote Mardzhanishvili in Tbilisi. Agitprop theatre persisted, but was now in the hands of such troupes as The Blue Blouses, who presented short sketches on topical subjects using biomechanical displays of gymnastic prowess.

The sum product was an exuberant, physical, caricatural theatre, exuding *joie de vivre* and an almost adolescent impetuosity. It is no accident that it was concurrent with the New Economic Policy (1921–28), propounded by Lenin as a short-term solution to Russia's ruined infrastructure; limited capitalism allowed a certain scope for individual initiative and private concerns. The abuses of NEP provoked a host of broad comedies, and even a space to play them in, the Theatre of Satire. But with Lenin's death, the accession of Stalin, and the cancellation of NEP, satire became a dangerous commodity. Bulgakov's comedy of con-men, opium dealers, and madams, *Zoya's Apartment* (1926), was closed after four performances at the Vakhtangov Theatre, condemned as "pornography"; his lampoon of censorship, *The Crimson Island* (1927), was not even allowed to open at the Kamerny. Meyerhold had staged *Credentials* (1924), Nikolai Erdman's farce about would-be Party members and hangers-on of the *ancien régime*, with great success; but he was prevented from presenting Erdman's more sardonic comedy, *The Suicide*, in 1928.

The change in climate was most evident in the reaction to Meyerhold's productions of Mayakovsky's last comedies. *The Bedbug* (1929), a "fairy tale" which starts in a Moscow full of predatory parasites and ends in a sterile future, was treated hostilely by an increasingly uniform press. *The Bathhouse* (1930), an attack on bureaucrats who are left behind when humanity is launched into space (much as the "Clean" had been left out of the ark in *Mystery Bouffe*), revealed how far Mayakovsky and Russia had traveled since his immediate post-revolutionary enthusiasm. The play was savaged, and Mayakovsky committed suicide shortly after the reviews appeared. Stalin had his sardonic revenge by elevating Mayakovsky to the posthumous status of poet laureate of the Soviet Union.

The new mood could be gauged in other respects. A ponderous solemnity began to pervade the theatre, even in Meyerhold's work. The makeshift, versatile "machines for acting" were replaced by complex revolves, elegant staircases, and mobile wagons, often decorated with sumptuous period properties and furniture, as in his *Inspector*. Hectic tempi were slowed down. The manic, spring-heeled acting of such vital performers as Igor Ilinsky, Maria Babanova, Boris Shchukin, and Iudif Glezer was discounted in favor of the nuanced psychological realism of a Nikolai Khmelev or Alla Tarasova.

Many of the most talented left the country. There had been a scattering of *émigrés* directly after the Revolution, chiefly to Berlin and Paris, when The Bat and The Blue Bird cabarets resettled in Europe. Tours of the Art Theatre and other companies to the US had left defectors behind. A last wave, just before emigration was banned, included Michael

Chekhov and Andrius Jilinsky. A handful of these exiles, such as Akim Tamiroff, Vladimir Sokoloff, and Eugenie Leontovich, made successful careers as actors, others such as Fedor (Theodore) Komissarzhevsky, Peter Sharoff, Tatiana Pavlowa, and Georges Pitoëff worked as directors, interpreting Russian culture to the English, Italians, and French. Cut off from their language and culture, many of these refugees, among them Richard Boleslavsky, Maria Ouspenskaya, Tamara Daykarhanova, Vera Soloviova, Leo and Barbara Bulgakov, even Chekhov, taught, disseminating the ideas of Stanislavsky in a garbled or partial form. These keepers of the flame had an immense influence on their host cultures, even if they occasionally suggested that Russian art had ended with their departure from the homeland.

Within the USSR, as Stalin consolidated his power, the gradual and ruthless purge of all, even imaginary opposition, the collectivization of agriculture, and the launching of the first Five Year Plan in 1928 all conduced to uniform effort or what was known in Marxist newspeak as the "socialist offensive on all fronts." In the arts, individual initiative came under suspicion and patterns were imposed upon both form and content.

For all the attempts at standardization, the Soviet stage of the 1930s occasionally provided opportunities for creative directors. Indeed, the level of playwriting was so pedestrian that it required ingenious staging to make the texts interesting. Vakhtangov's student Nikolai Akimov, in particular, ran in eccentric channels; originally a designer with cartoon proclivities, he became notorious for a *Hamlet* (1932) played as boisterous farce. Chased from the dramatic stage, social satire took refuge in the puppet theatre, with the ingenious artistry of Sergei Obraztsov; on the revue stage or *estrada* in the quick-change comedy of Arkady Raikin; and, briefly, in the children's theatre, in the resourceful productions of Natalia Sats.

Increased uniformity in drama was imposed in the name and with the abetment of Maksim Gorky. From the Revolution on, Gorky had proclaimed the need for a robust, melodramatic Soviet repertoire, drawing more on Dickens and Rostand than on Chekhov; but he did so from the safe remove of Capri. In 1928, his distrust of the regime overcome, Gorky returned to Russia and became head of the Union of Soviet Writers (founded in 1932). All pre-existing literary organizations, including the Proletkult and its successor RAPP (the Russian Association of Proletarian Writers), were suppressed.

11.6   Act II of *Armored Train 14–69* at the Moscow Art Theatre (1927).

It became dangerous to be too far left of center. The Theatre of Working Youth or TRAM (*Teatr rabochei molodezhi*) had been founded in 1925 as a cross between a "do-it-yourself theatre" and a biomechanical team; it rapidly grew from eleven organizations in 1928 to seventy in 1930. As the theatrical arm of RAPP, it waged war on the classics and professional theatre as vestiges of bourgeois culture. Holier than the Pope in its insistence that all workers in the theatre be of unimpeachably proletarian background, the Leningrad TRAM was on its way to becoming a powerful political voice when it was suppressed in 1932 by being absorbed into "theatres of the Lenin Komsomol" (Communist Youth League).

That same year Stalin for the first time described writers as "engineers of souls" and spoke of "socialist realism." "Socialist realism" differed from suspect "formalism" by advancing the primacy of content and message over style, and from "critical realism" by presenting a cleaned-up picture of how things ought to be in an ideal socialist world. Not only Party congresses and press hacks, but Gorky himself promulgated this doctrine. His programmatic article "On Plays" (1933) demanded a civic drama, rich in character conflicts and psychological realism. These moves were reinforced at the First Congress of Soviet Writers in August 1934, when Andrei Zhdanov's definition of socialist realism was included in the statutes of the Writers' Union. Socialist realism became henceforth the "fundamental method" – to use Zhdanov's term – of all the arts.

A bizarre doctrine of "conflictlessness" was introduced, which decreed the impossibility of conflicts in works about Soviet characters, on the pretext that Soviet society was exempt from contradictions. There followed a "varnishing" of reality, an idyllic representation of Soviet life. Plays of the lowest level about espionage or deviationism proliferated, as the satires of Mayakovsky, Nikolai Erdman, Yury Olesha, and Boris Romashov disappeared from the repertoire. The government now decreed that the classics were not to be tampered with except by Marxist exegesis; and the greatest safeguards of the classics were the "academic theatres," the MAT, the Maly, and the Leningrad BDT. The Art Theatre had been transmuted into a Soviet shrine in 1927, with its production of Vsevolod Ivanov's *Armored Train 14–69*, whose protagonists are Bolshevik partisans in Siberia. The images created by the actors Vasily Kachalov in the role of the partisan chief and Nikolai Khmelev in the role of the Bolshevik intellectual became sanctified icons. In 1932, the MAT was rebaptized in Gorky's name (his plays reentered its repertory for the first time since 1905) and its archaic brand of psychological realism prescribed as the best and only model for the Soviet theatre.

Just as traditional performance techniques were given priority over the experimental, so the author's script was privileged over the director's deconstruction of it. The exclusive themes of Soviet dramatists were to be building socialism through industrialization and collective farming, combat on the "ideological" front, and the apotheosis of Soviet leaders. The caroler of the first Five Year Plan was Nikolai Pogodin, whose characters, easily labeled black or white, often addressed the audience directly: in the last act of *The Epic of the Axe* (1930), the "director of the theatre" invites the spectators to visit a steelmill. The most memorable of the plays of the "ideological front" were Aleksandr Afinogenov's *Fear* (1931), about the reeducation of a scientist who fears the Soviet system, and *Aristocrats*, a "comedy" by Pogodin (1935) about the reclamation of political prisoners and common outlaws building a dam in the Far East. Whether this "Beggar's Opera" version of a labor camp run by the secret police, the Cheka, was the product of Pogodin's cynicism or idealism or sheer ignorance is hard to determine, but it is typical of the single-minded zeal promoted from above.

Propaganda for the Five Year Plans demanded heroic self-sacrifice on the part of the Soviet people, just as Gorky was calling for positive protagonists in literature. The modest champions of everyday life in the plays of Pogodin, Viktor Gusev, Konstantin Simonov, and Aleksei

Arbuzov were soon effaced by superheroes, and the theatre teemed with oversized figures of titanic will and plays of epic sweep, such as Vsevolod Vishnevsky's *Optimistic Tragedy* (1933). Its success at the Kamerny Theatre with Koonen as the resolute female commissar on a battleship finally won Tairov a modicum of governmental approval. A fictionalized Lenin first took stage in Pogodin's *Man with a Gun* (Vakhtangov Theatre, 1937), rapidly followed by a series of dramas showing him to be an omniscient combination of Socrates and Harun-al-Raschid, mingling with his subjects and soliciting their opinions. Certain actors, often for no reason but their bald heads, had to dedicate their careers to impersonating the lost leader. More uncertain were the careers of those actors selected to play Stalin when he too became a theatrical commonplace. Even when Stalin's character did not appear in person, great figures from the past were forged into precursors of the Man of Steel. Frequently evoked was Ivan the Terrible, most successfully in two plays by Aleksei Tolstoy: the tsar's repulsion of the Mongols, suppression of mutinous boyars, and diplomatic handling of the West were shown to be presages of Stalin's policies.

The proclamation of socialist realism entailed a war on all manifestations of "formalism." As waged by the press and the Committee for Artistic Affairs (*Komitet po delam isksusstva*) which administered the theatres, this meant the chivvying of any modicum of originality or novelty. A dreary sameness of playwriting and staging resulted, known in the USSR as "leveling" or "standardization." "Deviationists" and "internal *émigrés*" were expected to engage in self-flagellation and confessions of political betrayal. To avoid controversy, directors turned to adaptations of nineteenth-century novels, and the predominant directing style became a kind of timorous naturalism. Those who, like Meyerhold and Tairov, pursued a personal aesthetic were relentlessly criticized.

From 1933 on, Meyerhold staged no contemporary works: among his last finished productions were Dumas *fils*' tried-and-true melodrama, *The Lady of the Camellias* (1934) and a combination of three one-act farces by Chekhov entitled *33 Swoons* (1935); meanwhile he pursued plans for an up-to-date theatre building and productions of *Hamlet* and *Boris Godunov*. On 8 January 1938, the Meyerhold Theatre was closed by decision of the Committee for Artistic Affairs; the way had been paved for this decision by an article by the Committee's chairman, published in *Pravda* (17 December 1937) under the headline "An Alien Theatre." This article reproached Meyerhold for his inability to renounce his formalist past, for staging works of authors who were later condemned, for presenting petty bourgeois characters without providing a social rationale, for persisting in his errors despite the warnings he had received. Meyerhold, who had been generously protected and supported by Stanislavsky until the latter's death, was arrested in June 1939, tortured into a "confession," and then shot. Like many others, he became a "non-person"; he was expunged from print and public speech, and even a book-length study of his production of *Masquerade* managed never to mention his name.

Despite Tairov's success with *The Optimistic Tragedy*, he too continued to be assailed as the last holdout of bourgeois aestheticism; in 1938–39 the Committee for Artistic Affairs merged the Kamerny troupe with that of the small, inaptly named Realistic Theatre. The latter had been run by one of the few innovative directors to survive the 1930s with his career intact. Nikolai Okhlopkov, an eager destroyer of proscenium arches, sought to merge actor and spectator in a mix similar to the symbolist communion, but without any mystical overtones. Like his teacher Meyerhold, he borrowed freely from the Asian theatre and the *commedia dell'arte*, and spliced plays into discrete cinematic episodes. His troupe was made up primarily of young actors, supple to his will, and he preferred to adapt novels rather than cultivate the talents of playwrights. Okhlopkov's most successful experiments were with Gorky's *The Mother* (1933), staged in the round, Aleksandr Serafimovich's *The Iron Flood* (1934), in which the action took place on peninsulas of platform thrust into the audience, and Pogodin's *Aristocrats*, which incorporated the conspicuous props-man of the oriental stage. Okhlopkov's survival of the anti-formalist campaign seems due in part to the politically correct content of his plays, in part to the fact that (unlike the Armenian Vakhtangov, the Jewish Tairov, and the German Meyerhold), he looked and sounded like the strapping scion of Russian peasants.

A long, dark night fell on the Soviet theatre. Its intellectual and artistic poverty was concealed by a lavish, pompous realism which pretended to be the offspring of Stanislavsky. The cult of personality transformed theatres into rhetorical showwindows. The history of the Russian theatre was falsified. The instability of foreign policy affected the arts. When the non-aggression pact was signed between Hitler's Germany and the Soviet Union, Evgeny Shvarts' satirical fable of Nazi racial policies, *The Naked King*, was withdrawn. Eisenstein, whose talents had been limited to teaching from 1930, was recruited to stage *Die Walküre* at the Bolshoi; but once the treaty was abrogated and the Germans invaded the Soviet Union, his task became to film the ultra-patriotic epic *Aleksandr Nevsky*.

During the war itself, all efforts were bent to support the troops at the front or uplift morale at home. As the Germans struck deeper into Soviet territory, theatrical companies were evacuated to such remote towns as Tashkent, Irkutsk, and Omsk, which had the unlooked-for effect of bringing professionalism to the hinterlands. Performers were sent to the front, both to entertain the troops and to develop "do-it-yourself" brigades, in the interests of promoting the culture the nation was defending. The rough-and-ready conditions of performance on truck-beds or in forest clearings were most common to the concert brigade, the Soviet equivalent of the American USO, with the difference that instead of radio personalities the performers were often distinguished stage actors reciting classical poetry.

The wartime repertoire stuck to encouraging and unproblematic issues, depicting the feelings of defenders of hearth and home, whether infantryman, partisan, or civilian. Current events, such as the sieges of Sebastopol, Leningrad, and Stalingrad, were instantly mythologized in plays by Boris Lavrenev, Vsevolod Vishnevsky, and Yuly Chepurin, in the tradition of the Bolshevik mass spectacles. With news reportage severely limited and controlled, these works immediately transformed the topical into the epic. Ignoring Marxist condemnation of feudal princes and aristocrats, history itself was enlisted in the cause, and all successful military commanders of the Russian past, from Dmitry of the Don to Mikhail Kutuzov, converted into dramatic heroes.

The only significant experiment of the mid-1940s was Tairov's attempt at a stripped-down *Seagull* (1944), abbreviated to a Platonic dialog about the responsibilities of art, and staged against gray draperies and a grand piano. Few saw it, and the critics did not approve. A war-ravaged public preferred sheer entertainment, and they were catered to by the sentimental farces of Valentin Kataev and his ilk.

With the westward advance of Soviet troops into occupied territory and beyond, and the reopening of theatres in large cities, governmental control once more became stultifying. The brief interlude of mere amusement was ended by a decree of the Party Central Committee entitled "On the repertoire of dramatic theatres and how to improve it" (26 August 1945). In line with new principles laid down by Zhdanov, the theatre was reproached for avoiding topical themes, omitting ideological content, presenting honest Soviet citizens as buffoons, and blindly idealizing historical figures. The introduction of bourgeois foreign plays was also condemned. The new focus of attention was to be *homo sovieticus*, depicted with all the virtues he had displayed during the Great Patriotic War.

Zhdanov's imperatives coincided with a new reign of terror in Soviet society, in part prompted by the Cold War, in part by a campaign against "cosmopolitans," meaning Jews, intellectuals, and anyone who might have been tainted by contact with the West in wartime. The Kamerny Theatre, the last bastion of "formalism," was padlocked in 1950 and then reopened as the Pushkin Dramatic Theatre, a move which drove Tairov mad. The great Yiddish actor Solomon Mikhoels, who had spent the war touring the world raising money for the Soviet cause, was pushed in front of a truck; his colleague Veniamin Zuskin was also murdered.

In the face of such brutality against artistic incentives, and constrained by the dictum that all conflicts in Soviet society were solved, dramatists were hard put to deal with contemporary themes in any but the most stereotypical ways. The enemy now was shown to be Western capitalism and imperialism, especially the America of Truman and McCarthy. This Cold War trend was launched by Konstantin Simonov's *The Russian Question* (1947), which portrayed a New York journalist who pens libels of the USSR, until he discovers the truth and refuses to write any more lies for his Wall Street masters. These crude melodramas could hardly be made palatable even by the most sophisticated acting. Under the generic heading "realism," the theatre excelled in depicting a neverland, and any attempt to move into other realms was attacked with the all-purpose labels of formalism, bourgeois aesthetics, and cosmopolitanism. The result was general paralysis.

This became so patent that in 1952 the Party had to condemn the theory of "conflictlessness" and no less a politico than Malenkov called for "Soviet Gogols and Soviet Shchedrins," an oxymoron if ever there was one. Stalin's preferences continued to permeate the arts: they could be discerned in the stentorian tones of actors' voices, the monumental scenery, even the blocking directed at what had been his stage-box. Only with his death in 1953 could real change finally take place.

Gradually, experimentation stopped being equated with political deviation. In classes and productions, Stanislavsky's pupil Maria Knebel imparted a more accurate, living version of his legacy to such directors-to-be as Leonid Kheifets, Anatoly Efros, and Anatoly Vasiliev. Meyerhold's memory was rehabilitated and his writings published. Debates raged on the relative merits of Meyerhold and Stanislavsky; in practice, both schools converged and blended: acting remained psychologized, but directing began to recover its earlier theatricality.

Khrushchev's de-Stalinization speech at the twentieth Party congress (1956) ushered in the so-called "Thaw" in the arts, which precipitated a new lyricism and humanism in the theatre. The same year that Khrushchev denounced Stalin's crimes, the Sovremennik (Contemporary) Theatre-Studio was inaugurated by Viktor Rozov's *Alive Forever!* Headed by actor-director Oleg Efremov under the aegis of the arteriosclerotic Art Theatre, it was a youth-oriented collective with democratic principles, dedicated to portraying its own generation. Its motto – "if I am honest, I take responsibility" – embodied the first flush of post-Thaw optimism and self-criticism, some of it directed at the moribund "realism" of the MAT. A new identification with the man in the street and a colloquial intonation in stage speech replaced Stalinist grandiosity and declamation. The two house authors, Rozov and Aleksandr Volodin, were steeped in the sentimentalist tradition and their works usually pitted an idealistic younger generation against their compromised elders; in Rozov's dramatization of Goncharov's *The Same Old Story*, Oleg Tabakov as Aduev Jr. delineated a horrifying transformation from idealism to corruption.

These dramatists, along with the prolific, popular, and influential Aleksei Arbuzov, infused realism with theatricalist and cinematic elements recollected from the 1920s: they interpolated music, song and dance, pantomime and poetry, choruses, flashbacks, split focus, and montage. This breaking of the frame, even when halfhearted, emboldened a new generation of directors who often eschewed contemporary plays for adaptations of narrative fiction and revivification of the classics. Mayakovsky's comedies returned to the stage in Valentin Pluchek's revivals at the Theatre of Satire. At the Vakhtangov Theatre Nikolai Akimov mounted Shvarts' ironic fables *The Shadow* (1940, produced 1960) and *The Dragon* (1942, produced 1962) to great acclaim and staged the first production of Saltykov-Shchedrin's fantasia of officialdom *Shadows* (1953) at the Leningrad Comedy Theatre. Okhlopkov transferred his experiments in staging in the round to the Mayakovsky Theatre, most successfully with Arbuzov's *It Happened in Irkutsk* (1959).

In Leningrad, the dominant presence was that of Georgy Tovstonogov, who took over the BDT in 1956; a man of acute intelligence who knew how to work within the bureaucracy, he wielded a powerful authority not seen since Nemirovich-Danchenko. Starting with his revival of Vishnevsky's *Optimistic Tragedy*, he launched a series of productions noted for their sober and humanitarian depiction of a universal moral hebetude. He discovered and promoted the provincial actor Innokenty Smoktunovsky, a former prisoner-of-war, who brought a haunted lucidity to his Prince Myshkin in Dostoevsky's *Idiot* (1957), the one sane survivor in a mad world. Tovstonogov added existentialist overtones to Gorky's *Barbarians* and *The Petty Bourgeoisie* (1967) and Chekhov's *Three Sisters* (1965). His team of students and assistant directors, including Vladimir Vorobev, Efim Padve, Gennady Yudenich, Mark Rozovsky, and Mark Zakharov, would run the most vital theatres and studios of the next decades. Many of them found opportunities in the small studio and amateur groups devised to circumvent official restrictions on the repertoire and theatre organizations.

In Moscow, the controversial and peripatetic Anatoly Efros sought in his productions to capture the essence of contemporaneity by internalizing the *mise en scène* in the actor as a mass of anxieties and contradictions. He made a cult of rehearsals, relying on improvisation to lend spontaneity to his stagings; he disdained most Soviet playwriting, making an exception for Arbuzov, Rozov, and the suspect Edvard Radzinsky, whose plays often reexamined the role of the intellectual in repressive societies. During three seasons at the Lenkom, Efros outraged audiences with his productions of *The Seagull*, Bulgakov's *Cabal of Hypocrites* (1967), and Radzinsky's *Making a Movie* (1965).

Tempering the influences of the great Russian directors with that of Brecht, Yury Liubimov took over the Taganka Theatre in 1964,[3] and perfected a style which combined agitprop minstrelsy with revisionist cultural criticism. He rarely staged plays, preferring adaptations of novels (Dostoevsky, Bulgakov, Abramov, Trifonov) or, better yet, pastiches of literary and historical material (Mayakovsky, John Reed, Gogol). Aided and abetted by his designer David Borovsky, Liubimov did away with table rehearsals and shaped his actors like clay through vital work onstage. A kind of licensed rebel, tacitly tolerated by Brezhnev but hampered by the lower echelons of the *nomenklatura*, Liubimov was obsessed by the theme: how do artists survive in a bureaucratic regime?

The star of the Taganka troupe was Vladimir Vysotsky, whose Hamlet in a turtleneck or dressing-gown clad Svidrigailov in *Crime and Punishment* galvanized spectators. Vysotsky was perhaps the most subversive of a generation of *chansonniers*, a raw-voiced balladeer of bohemian protest. His songs, along with those of Bulat Okudzhava and

Aleksandr Galich, were not recognized by the official media, but were widely transmitted by *magnitizdat*, bootleg tape recordings.

This repression was typical of the late 1960s, when the theatre underwent a series of pogroms: major productions were banned or aborted in rehearsal. The process, usually spearheaded by the obstructive Mme. Furtseva, Minister of Culture, was explored in Galich's novel *Dress Rehearsal*, published in Germany only after he had been forced into emigration; a play of his, part of his long attempt to have Jewish war heroes officially recognized, was regularly thwarted, revised, and eventually proscribed. By 1967, Andrei Sinyavsky and Yuly Daniel were in the gulag, Aleksandr Solzhenitsyn was on his way into exile, and the progressive journal *Novy Mir* was in danger. Efros responded with a hysterical, sexually charged *Three Sisters* at the Malaya Bronnaya: an attack on the new torpor of the intelligentsia, it was severely criticized and canceled. The freeze congealed with the Prague invasion on 21 August 1968; reprisals in Russia came not in bloodshed but in stagnation.

In 1970, following a period of internecine strife, Efremov left the Sovremennik to head the bloated, moribund MAT; his reforms included dividing the swollen troupe into two, importing Smoktunovsky to play Chekhov's Ivanov (a character whose vacillations became emblematic for the times) and promoting two effective playwrights, Mikhail Roshchin and Aleksandr Gelman. But Efremov's most telling act might have been his own performance as the anti-hero Zilov in Aleksandr Vampilov's *Duck Hunting* (1967). Zilov was something new, a morally peccable protagonist who dwelt in a Dostoevskian realm of vulgar transgressions and humiliations. It was Erdman's *Suicide* transmogrified from farce to existential black comedy.

The Russian theatre of the 1970s experienced neither a counterculture nor an organic shift of generations. Reinterpretation of the classics became a major means of skirting censorship, and audiences became highly attuned to "Aesopic language," hints, and allegories. Brezhnev-era corruption and oppression were obliquely reflected in the Sovremennik's adaptation of satires by Saltykov-Shchedrin, *Balalaikin and Co.* (1973) and Tovstonogov's (and Rozovsky's) *Kholstomer*, (1975), the life-story of a horse, taken from Tolstoy. Nostalgia for the moral certainties of the Great Patriotic War blew through such plays as Roshchin's *Evacuation Train* (1975) at the MAT, while Gelman's moralities probed for flaws in the socialist infrastructure. The Sovremennik's production of *The Ascent of Mt. Fuji* by Chingiz Aitmatov and Kaltai Mukhamedzhanov

(1973), within a month of the twentieth anniversary of Stalin's death, symbolized the new standard for self-criticism, not only in its subject matter, collective guilt over compliance with Stalinist tyranny, but in its material, drawn from the biographies of the folk singer Okudzhava and the dissident Solzhenitsyn, and its plot, a reunion which devolves into the "truth game" from *The Idiot*.

Despite the congealed conservatism of the theatrical bureaucracy both before and after Brezhnev's death in 1982, fresh grass broke through the concrete, especially in the proliferating studio and laboratory theatres. A younger audience was attracted by the less extreme manifestations of Western rock and roll, and these tastes were catered to by the Soviet rock musical, which made up in exuberance what it lacked in technical slickness. The eclectic and inventive Mark Zakharov, artistic director of the Lenin Komsomol Theatre in Moscow from 1973, won great popular success with his musical spectacles *The Constellation and Death of Joaquin Murieta* (from Pablo Neruda, 1976) and *The Juno and the Avos* (from Andrei Voznesensky, 1981).

Vysotsky, the nation's clandestine teller of truths, died of alcoholism at the age of forty in July 1980. This was a watershed for the Taganka, which had become more assiduously persecuted and suffocated. In 1983, while in Italy, Liubimov was stripped of his Soviet citizenship, allegedly for comments made to the British press, and his theatre was turned over to Anatoly Efros. Efros had spent the previous years at the Malaya Bronnaya staging exquisitely acted, pictorially metaphoric productions of *Othello*, *Don Juan* (1973), Gogol's *Getting Married* (1974), and *A Month in the Country*, with designs by David Borovsky and Valery Levental. Transplanted to the Taganka, faced with a hostile and recalcitrant company, Efros was out of his element, and the level of his work there was abysmal; he died in office of a heart attack in 1989.

The political takeover by Mikhail Gorbachev in 1985, with its subsequent loosening of restraints in the arts, initially stirred great excitement. Plays which had been kept off the stage for years, whether classics or contemporaries, suddenly appeared in multiple productions. Previously proscribed comedies by Bulgakov and Erdman headed the season's lists. Russia's long suppressed surrealist tradition, the Oberiu of the 1920s, was rediscovered, with the effect that renditions of Daniil Kharms' *Elizaveta Bam* and Aleksandr Vvedensky's *Christmas at the Ivanovs'* burgeoned in the studios. A new strain of absurdism emerged in the plays of Andrei Amalrik and Nina Sadur. Liudmila Petrushevskaia's dour, hopeless portrayals of Soviet family life, enlivened by the "tape-recorder" effect of her Mamet-like dialog, were widely produced. The exciting directorial work carried on in the republics by the Georgians Robert Sturua and Timur Chkheidze and the Lithuanian Eimuntas Nekrošius, could be seen in the Russian capitals.

Subjects that had been taboo for decades suddenly were thrust to the fore. The myths of Bolshevik history were reexamined in Mikhail Shatrov's plays, beginning with *We Shall Overcome*, bringing on Trotsky and presenting a self-questioning (if still ultimately correct) Lenin. Traditional Jewish themes returned in Mark Zakharov's *Memorial Prayer*, knit together from Sholom Aleichem's tales of Tevye the dairyman. Prostitution, specifically the banishment of whores to the suburbs during the Moscow Olympics, was the subject of Aleksandr Galin's *Stars in the Morning Sky*, directed by Lev Dodin (the bulk of Galin's *oeuvre*, however, seems like Neil Simon flavored with a touch of Pirandello). An exotic treatment of homosexuality was showcased by the openly gay Roman Viktyuk in his productions of Genet's *The Maids* and Hwang's *M. Butterfly*, inspired by clown shows and discotheques.

Installed in the unfashionable Theatre of the Young Spectator, Kama Ginkas and his wife Genrietta Yanovskaya presented highly theatrical, sharply intelligent dramatizations of Bulgakov's *Heart of a Dog*, Dostoevsky's *Notes from Underground*, and Chekhov (*Ivanov and Others*). Anatoly Vasiliev, deprived of a theatre of his own, gave birth to stunning productions after long gestation periods; he discovered the talent of Viktor Slavkin, whose *A Young Man's Grown-up Daughter* turned the generational conflict of the 1950s on its head, presenting a middle-aged parent fixated on an idyllic America while his daughter is part of a cynical, disillusioned age. Slavkin's *Cerceau*, staged by Vasiliev in a tent, was a mock-Chekhovian exploration of the isolation and disintegration of his contemporaries.

The effects of *glasnost* had one unfortunate effect for the theatre: audiences no longer needed Aesopic discourse and hidden messages best conveyed from a living stage. Engaged in voluble debates over the latest revelations in print or on television, Soviet citizens found the theatre an irrelevance, and for a while it languished. Once they discovered the inability of politics to change the facts of their everyday life, the theatre enjoyed a resurgence. But this was in turn severely affected by the dissolution of the Soviet Union and the introduction of a market economy. In 1993 there were 600 state-supported professional theatres, some 400 of them devoted to drama, serving some 110 million spectators in forty languages, so that the collapse of the infrastructure was devastating and the box office became a potent factor. Actors were lured from their ensembles by commercial managements to enhance star-studded productions, and nude sex-shows with no pretensions to art cast their nets for the ticket-buyer. For every experimental studio production, confected by such talented young directors as Sergei Zhenovach, there would be a lavish, Hollywood-style revival aimed at the new capitalists who had more cash than taste. A second emigration of theatrical talent moved westward to take advantage of high fees and more controlled conditions.

In 1987, the Art Theatre had split in twain, ostensibly because its troupe was too large; in fact, the divorce resulted from a feud between Efremov and the actress Tatiana Doronina, and the two companies, the Chekhov and the Gorky (nicknamed "His and Hers") now reside in two separate buildings. Liubimov had celebrated his return to the Taganka with Erdman's *The Suicide*, but to a younger audience he seemed irrelevant, segregated from his historic moment; his very proprietorship of the theatre was threatened by a former bureaucrat who wanted to turn it into a nightclub. This is typical. Their subsidies cut to mere maintenance, theatre companies, voluntarily or under compulsion, rent out their buildings to the newly rich underworld for restaurants and casinos, and the venerable Kheifets was beaten nearly to death for resisting such an attempt at the Army Theatre. The lives of Russian theatre artists are threatened no longer by the political establishment, but by the "shadow government," the lawless entrepreneurs who actually run the country.

The new "revolution" failed to inspire the effusion of creativity that accompanied that of Red October. In an uncertain world, audiences required a "theatre of consolation," something to take their minds off the woeful state of their everyday lives. Politics was a bore, and the grand theatrical metaphors created by Efros and Liubimov were now out of fashion. There was a turn toward the personal and intimate. Numerous revivals of Ostrovsky reflected both the Russian need to find indigenous roots for capitalism and a renewed interest in family affairs. The so-called "pornographic" playwrights of the Silver Age were rediscovered, the neurasthenia of the past identified with the restless uncertainty of the present. Vasiliev stopped mounting finished productions and carried on master-classes instead, because he regarded his generation as a mere "bridge" to something new.

After a decade of stasis, Moscow theatregoers of 1995 were electrified by two openings: Oleg Antonov's *The Deadly Act or Salto Mortale*, directed by Vladimir Mashkov at the Tabakov Studio, and a student revival of Vladimir Kirshon's Stalinist-era play *The Miraculous Fusion* at the State Theatre Institute. The former, four clowns vying to take over the routine of a deceased colleague, is an exuberant, Felliniesque *tour de force* whose allegorical messages are submerged beneath the stunts. The Kirshon piece, concerning a team of young scientists trying to invent a new form of steel, is a coming-to-terms with the past, an acceptance of one's heritage, good, bad, and ugly. In its enthusiastic embrace of a bygone faith it proclaimed that the past seventy years had not been wasted. The Russian theatre may yet be reinvigorated by its life-enhancing tradition.

NOTES

1. The disciplined training of the imperial dance schools was maintained under the Soviets, so that the international influence of dancers and choreographers such as Leonid Massine and George Balanchine who had emigrated earlier was continued by the exquisite technique of Galina Ulyanova, Maia Plisetskaya, Natalia Danilova, Rudolf Nureyev, Mikhail Baryshnikov, and others.
2. Only the first part was completed and published after his death in 1938; the second part was revised by experts with a Stalinist bent. All current foreign translations are distortions of the original texts, which are at last being published in the new edition of Stanislavsky's works.
3. The Taganka and the Sovremennik were the only official new theatres to be opened after World War II.

12

Film

In any history of Russian film questions about boundaries arise, 299 directly or by implication. The subject cannot include all of the production of the Russian Empire, the old Soviet Union, and the Commonwealth of Independent States. Nonetheless, Aleksandr Dovzhenko, among the Fathers of Soviet film, is a fact of the Russian and Ukrainian cinemas; Mikhail Chiaureli, in the Stalinist generation, a fact of the Georgian and Russian cinemas; and later, Sergei Paradzhanov, from the generation that came to artistic maturity after Stalin's death, of the Armenian, Ukrainian, Georgian, and Russian cinemas. Iakov Protazanov is a pre-revolutionary filmmaker and a post-revolutionary one. The work of film artists in emigration or temporarily working in France, Germany, the United States, and elsewhere enters into various constructions of the subject. Ivan Mozzhukhin, Andrei Tarkovsky, and Andrei Konchalovsky are candidates for inclusion in histories in international contexts.

Questions about genres also arise. Avant-garde Soviet film challenged the dominant narrative models of bourgeois audiences, along with the conventions of film viewing. Agitprop in the twenties erased the boundaries between fiction and fact. Film became not a fiction or a document, but a tool in the reconstruction of reality; Sergei Eisenstein's films about revolution in the twenties and even Aleksandr Medvedkin's about collectivization in the thirties were part of this tradition. Children's films and animation and multiplication films – by Wladyslaw Starewicz (of Polish parentage), Yury Norshtein, and the *émigré*, Alexandre Alexéieff – should be remembered. The documentary tradition, too, now that it has emerged from the shadow of Party ideology, calls for reexamination in light of newly available archival resources (it includes the wartime documentary work of directors known for their feature films). A few television films have become "classics" alongside other feature films: for instance, Mikhail Kozakov's *Pokrovsky Gates* (1982). Since *glasnost* a vigorous independent film and video movement has developed with the "alternative" or "parallel" films of Gleb and Igor Aleinikov in Moscow, and the *necro* realist films of Evgeny Iufit and Andrei Mertvy in Leningrad. The boundaries of the field are porous and continually open to redefinition.

Pre-revolutionary cinema

Russian silent film before the Revolution has a rich history, with directors including Evgeny Bauer and Iakov Protazanov, stars, starlets, and notable actors. Within months of the first demonstrations of the Lumière brothers' invention to audiences in Paris in 1896, they were showing their films to audiences in St. Petersburg. Representatives of their company filmed some parts of the coronation of Tsar Nicholas II in 1898 (the footage often reappears in documentary compilations). The tsar, and following him the nobility, soon became film enthusiasts. But more importantly for the new film entrepreneurs, there was in Russia a huge market for cheap entertainment ready to be exploited. Several foreign companies, led by Pathé (starting in 1904) and Gaumont established themselves as distributors of foreign-made films. From distribution they turned to production to satisfy a demand abroad for exotic Russian films, as well as a demand in Russia for Russian films. In this they were spurred by the often opportunistic Aleksandr Drankov, who in 1907 advertised himself as the founder of the first Russian studio, and, starting in 1908, by Drankov's more artistically significant rival, Aleksandr Khanzhonkov. Further competition was offered by a Baltic German, Paul Thiemann (Timan), who established Thiemann and Reinhardt in 1909. Iakov Protazanov was one of the directors associated with this firm, while Wladyslaw Starewicz and Petr Chardynin were associated with Khanzhonkov. Evgeny Bauer began in the studios of Pathé and Drankov, and later worked for Khanzhonkov. Foremost among the stars and legends of Russian silent film were Vera Kholodnaia, loved for her pale face and large eyes, and Ivan Mozzhukhin, one of the recognized great actors. Both Kholodnaia and Mozzhukhin did much of their best work with Bauer.

More than 1,700 films were made between 1907 and 1917. The surviving legacy (nearly 300 films) has received considerable attention in recent years from scholars who have looked at the achievement of the early silent filmmakers in relation to that of their contemporaries elsewhere and also from scholars interested in contextualizing Soviet film within the whole of Russian film history and producing new, revisionist accounts. These studies suggest that Russian silent film was not simply an offshoot of European film, but rather a school in its own right. They also indicate that the pre-revolutionary producers and filmmakers provided an important link with Soviet film, particularly in the period 1917–21.

The Russian school of silent film

Russian silent film at the time of the Revolution was characterized by a deliberately slow pace which allowed for the playing out of emotions and, hence, was not primarily concerned with action or melodramatic posturing. It found its fullest expression in drawing-room dramas, but was not restricted to them. Evgeny Bauer (1865–1917) is the major director of this school to be rediscovered in recent years. Before his death (as a consequence of an injury sustained while filming), he made more than eighty films, of which at least twenty-six survive. Iakov Protazanov (1881–1945), another prolific director, began in this school of filmmaking. Protazanov's films in his first or "silent" period included *Nikolai Stavrogin* (from Dostoevsky's *The Devils*) in 1915, *Queen of Spades* (from Pushkin's tale) in 1916, and *Father Sergius* (from Tolstoy's tale) in 1918, with Ivan Mozzhukhin in the main roles in the first and last of these. His sentimental *Keys to Happiness* (1913), with Vladimir Gardin as co-director, was the greatest box-office success of pre-revolutionary film. After 1923, upon returning from emigration in Paris and Berlin, where he also made films, he proved that he could adapt to the shifting politicized conditions of the Soviet Union and directed a number of well-liked motion pictures (see below). He was a survivor and a notable bridging figure in Russian film history.

The early Russian directors were inventive *cinéastes*. Bauer's tracking shots and well-positioned lighting created a sense of spaciousness, depth, and even luxuriousness in interior scenes, without the need for elaborate sets. The investigation of acting especially for film was undertaken by the great director from the theatre, Vsevolod Meyerhold. A major loss among the many Russian silent films of this period is undoubtedly his *The Picture of Dorian Grey* (1915), particularly as in it Meyerhold made use of the biomechanical principles of acting, that he had developed in opposition to the psychological principles of Konstantin Stanislavsky and the Moscow Art Theatre. Explorations of the technical basis of film by Wladyslaw Starewicz (1882–1965) led to the development of animation film. Working with stop-motion photography in *Beautiful Liukanida* (1913), he animated carefully constructed models of beetles and got them to perform an array of remarkable tricks. In *Christmas Eve* (made the same year, from Gogol's tale, with Mozzhukhin playing the Devil), Starewicz used trick photography and manipulations of the images on the film strip to gain nearly as much control over his characters and objects as over his constructions of beetles, and to create a world corresponding to Gogol's fantastic imagination. Starewicz made fifty films in Russia before emigrating (after 1919 he pursued his career in France and Italy).

Russian film in the pre-revolutionary years and in the transition period ending in the second half of the twenties was a commercial enterprise, subject to censorship (proscriptive rather than prescriptive) and catering to a public that wanted entertainment and escape. Domestic production competed at the box office with foreign films and with foreign stars who were favorites of the Russian public (including Asta Nielsen and Valdemar Psilander from Denmark, and the French comedian, Max Linder). It was not isolated from but offered only an imperfect reflection of fashions, ideas, and trends in the other arts. The symbolism and decadence that prevailed in literature in the first decade of the century reached film during the years of the Great War, when it affected even the work of major directors, as in Starewicz's *Lily: An Allegory of Today* (1915), Bauer's *After Death* (1915), and Protazanov's *Satan Triumphant* (1917). A group of futurists, including Mikhail Larionov, Natalia Goncharova, and David Burliuk, joined forces to make *Drama in the Futurists' Cabaret No. 13* (1913). Another futurist, Vladimir Mayakovsky, waited until the Bolshevik Revolution to make a series of films (as writer and actor): *Creation Can't be Bought, The Lady and the Hooligan, Shackled by Film* (all in 1918, and all with small production companies). Many of the structures of the pre-revolutionary film industry, along with its administrators, directors, workers, and artists, continued to be needed after the Revolution. Soviet film with its organs of production and control did not, and could not, simply and suddenly emerge in 1917 (or in 1925).

Film: a revolutionary art

The importance of film was formally recognized immediately after the "October" Revolution. On 9 November came a decree establishing the

People's Commissariat of Enlightenment, with a sub-department for film. Over the coming days and months came various decrees aimed at establishing control over the film industry. In 1918 the government also established the State Film School in Moscow, that was to become famous for the experiments conducted in Lev Kuleshov's workshop. In August 1919 the government decreed the nationalization of film production and distribution under the aegis of the People's Commissariat of Enlightenment, headed by Anatoly Lunacharsky. The importance Lenin attached to film is reflected in often-cited words, which he reportedly said to Lunacharsky in 1922: "You must bear firmly in mind that, of all the arts, film is the most important for us." The difficulty the government faced in establishing control over the industry is reflected in his demand that same year for a "Leninist film-proportion" of propaganda to safe entertainment in movie theatre screenings. The first success of Soviet film, *Polikushka* (1919), an adaptation of a tale about a serf written by Tolstoy, was a production of the old *garde*; it came from Rus', a private studio which had been reconstituted as an artists' collective, and it introduced a major actor from the Moscow Art Theatre, Ivan Moskvin, to film. The proceeds from its sales abroad were used to buy much-needed stock. A film in 1923, Ivan Perestiani's *Red Imps* from the Film Section of the Georgian Commissariat of Enlightenment, dealing with the adventures of three children as Red Cavalry scouts, was a first token that directors were ready to make Soviet films. By 1925, the year commemorating the attempted revolution of 1905, a generation of Soviet filmmakers was ready to establish film as *the* art of the Revolution.

The removal of the seat of government to Moscow and the drive toward centralization had confirmed this city as the principal centre of film production. Leningrad, the former St. Petersburg, was the second centre (and yet over the years to come studios in Kiev, Tiflis [Tbilisi], Odessa and elsewhere challenged the new and old capitals). Moscow and Leningrad were filled with stage-actors, writers, musicians, set designers, critics, and theorists who eagerly turned to the new art form of the Revolution. In these two cities, in comparison with Hollywood, actors and even directors were freer to move between the stage and the screen. Among the directors, Eisenstein began in the avant-garde theatre, and then moved to film when he realized that no stage was adequate for the development of his ideas. Writers, as Mayakovsky had shown, who wanted to support the Revolution could reach a broader public through film. The Russian formalists, who had begun as literary theorists before the Revolution, turned to film theory and criticism; two of them, Yury Tynianov in Leningrad and Viktor Shklovsky, in Moscow, provided scripts for important films (including *The Overcoat* and *Bed and Sofa*). Futurist painting was available as a fashion (for Protazanov, in *Aelita*, 1924) and, more importantly, as a principle of construction (for Eisenstein and Dziga Vertov). The composer, Dmitry Shostakovich, produced a series of film scores, most particularly for Grigory Kozintsev and Leonid Trauberg, starting with a score for live orchestral accompaniment to *New Babylon* in 1929. Later Sergei Prokofiev, too, worked in film, notably with Eisenstein. Artists in many fields turned to film work when other doors were closed; film, often seen as a synthesis of the arts, had a vast pool of talent to draw on. But, in film as in the other arts, producers and consumers had to be found and, moreover, producers in the emerging structures of the Soviet film industry were exposed to political and bureaucratic attacks. On occasion, films depended on the reception they found abroad (the acclaim given to *Battleship Potemkin* in Berlin in 1926 facilitated its distribution at home). The freedom that Soviet filmmakers enjoyed was but a relative one even in their years of glory. The tensions and clashes over the function of art – and over who controlled it – that were to mark the history of Soviet film first appeared in these years.

The primacy of montage

Montage was established as a leading principle of Soviet film by the efforts of filmmakers who in the absence of film equipment and stock were driven to experiments and theoretical reflection. In its application in film, the term "montage" meant *editing*, but beyond that: it signified *rapid editing cuts* (deriving from American practice rather than the prevailing practice in early Russian films), and, secondly and more importantly, it took into account the way a bit of film changed in meaning depending on what preceded or followed it. Kuleshov was particularly impressed with the power available to him in montage. By splicing together different bits of film, he could freely construct both space ("creative geography") and time. He could even construct an utterly imaginary landscape out of elements of the real. He could also construct states of mind (the "Kuleshov effect"). An instance of creative geography in his work was the construction of a setting representing the Yukon from shots made on the Moscow river (in *By the Law*, 1926). As for the Kuleshov effect, a famous instance was described by Vsevolod Pudovkin (who trained as an actor in Kuleshov's Workshop before becoming a director): a single shot of the actor Ivan Mozzhukhin was projected once, followed by a shot of a woman in a coffin, then again, followed by a shot of a child skipping, and last, followed by a shot of a bowl of soup. To viewers it seemed that Mozzhukhin's fixed expression changed in each of the sequences: the sequences seemed another demonstration of his wonderful acting.

In his workshop Kuleshov developed principles of cinematic acting based on his principles of montage. Film did not require the reliving of experience that was at the heart of the Stanislavsky method in the Moscow Art Theatre. Meyerhold's principles of actors' movement provided a more useful model. Moreover, the movie camera could be used to frame different parts of the body, which had their own ways of indicating feeling and emotion. The stress in Kuleshov's work was on the many means of expression available to actors (who were *naturshchiks*, "types" subjected to highly disciplined physical training). The members of the workshop, known as the Kuleshov Collective, included the actors Aleksandra Khokhlova, Leonid Obolensky, Vladimir Fogel, and one other future director besides Pudovkin – Boris Barnet. During 1920–21, having no film stock, the Collective honed their craft in kino-plays performed before audiences, in which they demonstrated the principles of cinematic acting in scenes connected by rapid transitions corresponding to editing cuts.

Eisenstein differed from Kuleshov as to the meaning of montage but not as to its centrality. He, as Kuleshov, edited his own films (and to this day it is common practice for Russian directors, unlike Hollywood directors, to edit their own films). In defining montage, he compared the bits of film he edited together to cells waiting to explode, and charged Kuleshov with merely treating them as bricks to be linked in sequence. For Eisenstein conflict between cells was primary, and this depended on conflict within the shots: montage was also an internal principle of construction. And connected with his notion of montage as conflict – and finally explosion – was a principle of aggressive action on the viewer: his "montage of attractions," most nakedly displayed in *Strike* (1925), amounts to a variety of devices acting on the viewer's emotions. The term "attraction" in his usage came from the music-hall and the circus; it was equivalent to a turn or an act. The montage of attractions was tightly integrated into story in his later work, but expressiveness and action directed at the spectator remained central concerns. Film was an art of "pathos," or feeling. Eisenstein wanted his films to deliver a "kino-fist."

Kuleshov (1899–1970)

The director Lev Kuleshov began his film career before the Revolution as an actor and also as an artistic designer (with Evgeny Bauer). During the Civil War following the October Revolution he shot newsreels. His ideas on montage and on cinematic acting, noted above, are directly reflected in the two films for which he is best remembered, *The Extraordinary Adventures of Mr. West in the Land of the Bolsheviks* (1924) and *By the Law* (1926). The former is a free-spirited comedy (of which there are too few examples in Soviet film). Kuleshov followed Mr. West's comic adventures with a science-fiction adventure film, *Death Ray* (1925), which was above all an attempt to demonstrate the technical resources he had at his disposal in filmmaking. Critics and bureaucrats criticized it on the grounds of experimentalism and ideological inadequacy and, in result, Kuleshov's collective was in danger of being driven out of existence. They shot their next film, *By the Law* (1926), on a minimal budget, using a tight script adapted by Viktor Shklovsky from a story by Jack London ("The Unexpected"). This film, with its story of lawless behavior, met with more opposition and its distribution was restricted; it was better known abroad than at home.

The other films by Kuleshov include a first experiment with sound, *Horizon* (1933), set in an American city (constructed with the help of model skyscrapers), and *The Great Consoler* (1933), which drew on O. Henry's stories and led to persistent accusations that he was afflicted with "Americanitis." Then, when socialist realism was enshrined, Kuleshov's principal response was silence. He made a children's film, *Siberians* (1940), and two wartime films. He remained active as a teacher at the major Russian film school, the All-Union State Institute of Cinematography (VGIK), until his death. He left two classic works on the craft of film, *The Art of the Cinema* (1929) and *Fundamentals of Film Direction* (1941).

Eisenstein (1898–1948)

Sergei Eisenstein is, for many, the preeminent Russian filmmaker, both because of the films he made and because of the body of theoretical writing he produced (much of it during the intervals when he was not allowed to make films). He was ambitious for the scope of his chosen art, seeking to measure himself against major writers and artists (Zola, Dostoevsky, Joyce, Leonardo, El Greco, Piranesi, and the Russian constructivists, among others). He looked for what he could learn from other cultures (Chinese and Mexican) and times. After studying theatre with Meyerhold and designing costumes and directing plays for the Proletkult stage, he came to film because it offered him greater flexibility and many more ways to act on the spectator. With his cameraman Eduard Tisse, he explored the many resources of cinematography. For Eisenstein, however, the crucial creative experience was montage, which he first explored in 1923 and 1924 in work and experiments with Kuleshov and with Esfir Shub. The montage of his films gave him his fullest release as an artist. In his theoretical writings, "montage" served as a term of analysis whose reference extended beyond relationships between and within film shots; it appeared in some very fruitful discussions of literary texts and paintings. In film the concept soon carried a "vertical" reference to sound, words, and music. It was further amplified with the terms "polyphony" and "counterpoint" in order to describe the relationship between different elements or lines of significance in his own films.

The "pathos" that for Eisenstein was fundamental to film was connected with ideas and even with action. But the films were grounded in the inner world of feeling and emotion (even in the early films, in which he cast the masses as collective hero). Two influences on him in the exploration of the inner world were Freud and Joyce. Eisenstein was intrigued by Joyce's experiments in rendering "interior monologue," but felt that film provided a better medium than literature for these explorations. Joyce was sufficiently impressed by Eisenstein's ideas that, after the two met in Paris in 1929, he was ready to authorize the Russian director to make a film version of *Ulysses*. This project, along with an adaptation of Karl Marx's *Capital*, was one of many that Eisenstein entertained but did not finally realize.

Eisenstein's art was highly calculated (too much so for some critics), yet he found that its actual effect might be a dreamlike or synaesthetic state (this being the characteristic danger of art). He knew that his art was subversive. In his "Autobiographical Sketches," written in the last year of his life, he claimed that his aggressive artistic freedom had made him necessary to the Revolution, but that it had also led to his continually upsetting the authorities ("the forces which almost always have a name and address" with their "private, nighttime leg-dislocating business," he says in his *Memoirs*). Stalin and Stalinist bureaucrats usually distrusted his films. Directly or indirectly, Stalin aborted two film projects in which

Eisenstein had made major investments of creative energy: "Que Viva Mexico" in 1931 and "Bezhin Lug" in 1935 (and again in 1937). But Stalin also recognized Eisenstein's talent and sometimes needed his films.

Strike (1925) was nominally about a workers' strike in capitalist Russia and its bloody suppression. The film is noted for: (1) its continual development of metaphor and (2) its free experimentation with montage, in which action is continually fragmented, especially through the use of overlapping shots taken from different angles (Eisenstein's vision was poetic and constructivist). The film draws heavily on the circus and on Proletkult traditions of propaganda in the theatre. The story serves as a pretext for a montage of a variety of "attractions" provoking emotions and thought.

Battleship Potemkin (1925) has a well-established reputation as one of the important films in the history of cinema. It commemorated the Revolution of 1905, which in the new mythology was a precursor of the Bolshevik Revolution of October 1917. The film focused on a particular episode, a mutiny, that in the film leads to demonstrations of protest on land. Eisenstein's collective hero, comprised of sailors and of urban masses, looks strangely like a spontaneously acting brotherhood (bearing but a remote resemblance to a Marxist-Leninist proletariat led by the Communist Party). Untrained actors, selected as *typages*, represent the forces of confrontation and revolution. The long "Odessa Steps" sequence, with soldiers descending on and firing at a crowd of demonstrators, is one of the most complicated, thrilling, and studied montage sequences in the history of film.

October (1928) was one of the anniversary films designed to commemorate the tenth anniversary of the Revolution. It was based on historical events (but also on the reenactments of the Revolution involving thousands of people that were staged in 1920). In accordance with the principle of *typage*, Lenin was significant above all as a "type." This caused controversy, because the cult of Lenin had begun (and is also a source of difficulty for modern viewers who question Lenin's actual historical role). The film's completion was delayed by the necessity to eliminate the role of the "type" corresponding to Trotsky (to the extent possible) because, by the end of 1927, Stalin was consolidating his power and treating Trotsky as a saboteur of the Revolution.

More than any other film, *October* is constructivist in its images and structure. The collapse of tsarist power is depicted through the dismantling of the statue of Alexander III. Spinning bicycle wheels represent the Cyclists' Battalion. The raising of a drawbridge in order to cut off rebellious workers becomes an event in subjective time, with the characteristics of a nightmare. The film's most famous montage sequence, "God and Country," deconstructs and subverts the notion of God and is associated with the idea of a new "intellectual cinema," which Eisenstein thought he could develop in order to make a film of Marx's *Capital*.

Old and New (1929) focused on the peasants and on the problem of transforming agriculture through collectivization. The film was a comedy aiming for simplicity and intelligibility to mass spectators. Its central character was played by a farm laborer chosen after a long search, Marfa Lapkina (she gives vivid testimony to Eisenstein's ability to elicit a performance from an untrained actor). This heroine has to persuade poor, apathetic peasants to pool their resources in order to buy a cream-separator, a bull, and finally a tractor. She also has to overcome the indifference of office workers who must authorize the tractor sale. An erotic subtext is a source of energy underlying political conflicts (as often in Eisenstein's work). Relations with machinery are blatantly eroticized: Marfa's with the cream-separator (in the montage sequence that shows her waiting for the cream-separator to work), and the tractor driver's with the tractor. A montage sequence showing a procession of peasants praying for rain is another of Eisenstein's deconstructions of God and religion. Eisenstein experimented with deep focus in this film in order to show composition in depth.

Aleksandr Nevsky (1938) was the first film Eisenstein was allowed to complete after *Old and New*. It focused on a patriotic topic: a battle against the Teutonic knights led by a Russian hero of the thirteenth century. It is the most socialist realist of Eisenstein's films, although arguably its solemn socialist realism is undercut by a festive carnivalism. In editing the film, Eisenstein worked closely with Prokofiev, the composer of the film music (now famous in its own right as *The Aleksandr Nevsky Cantata*). The film was an experiment in audiovisual counterpoint, reaching its fullest development in the Battle-on-the-Ice sequence, in which the knights in heavy armor are lured to battle on a frozen lake and disappear into its waters when the ice cracks under their weight.

Eisenstein's major achievements are for many *Ivan the Terrible*, Part 1 (1944) and Part 2 (1946). A perpetual revolutionary, Eisenstein now called into question the premises of his first films; his hero in this film was not the masses, but rather the Great Man in History. Ivan fights external enemies in Part 1 and then strives to unify Russia against internal opposition in Part 2. But he is also a haunted, tragic character. In the carnivalistic Banquet Scene at the end of Part 2 (a sequence shot in color), we see Ivan as a deceiver, an actor, a lonely man condemned to have only substitutes for the satisfactions of love and friendship. In Eisenstein's intention the film was to have a third part, ending with Ivan breaking through to the Baltic Sea in a visionary anticipation of the battle won by Peter the Great. Stalin had hoped that Eisenstein's film about a Great Leader would prove, by analogy, a vindication of his own historical role. His hopes seemed to be realized by Part 1, but upon seeing Part 2 Stalin understood that his expectations had been misplaced; angry denunciations of the film followed. Eisenstein, who was ill following a heart attack, received permission to remake the film, but was unable to do so before his death in 1948. *Ivan*, Part 2, disappeared, but survived (with mutilations inflicted by Eisenstein in reediting the film) and was finally released in 1958. Almost all of the material shot for Part 3 of the film has been lost.

In the *Ivan* films Eisenstein sought to emphasize stylistic differences by having a second cinematographer, Andrei Moskvin (the FEKS cameraman, see below) shoot the indoor scenes, while Eisenstein's usual cinematographer, Eduard Tisse, shot the outdoor ones. Eisenstein himself wrote the script with its resounding dialog. Once again he collaborated closely with Prokofiev during the montage, continuing their explorations of audiovisual counterpoint. The Banquet Scene was an exercise in the use of color, seeking to detach it from objects in order to use it in the construction of images of the inner world.

Pudovkin (1893–1953)

Vsevolod Pudovkin first worked in film as an actor in 1920 and joined the Kuleshov group in 1922. He had acting parts in Kuleshov's *Extraordinary Adventures of Mr. West* and *Death Ray*, in Fedor Otsep's *Living Corpse* (1929) and, much later, in Eisenstein's *Ivan the Terrible*. He regularly played small roles in his own films. In his work as a director he applied Kuleshov's principles of montage, developing highly poetic and lyrical structures for his films.

Chess Fever (1925) is an amusing exercise, in which shots of a chess champion, José Capablanca, taken during a competition in Moscow, were used in piecing together a comedy involving an obsessive chess-player and the woman he loved. *Mother* (1926), based on Gorky's novel, is Pudovkin's best-loved and most lyrical work, with the performance of

Vera Baranovskaia in the role of the mother, and Nikolai Batalov in the role of the son. *The End of St. Petersburg* (1927), another film commemorating the Revolution, offers a richly symbolic picture of the old capital and the Revolution, with some good crowd scenes. *The Descendant of Genghis Khan* or *Storm Over Asia* (1928) carried the revolution to Buriat Mongolia. There is much exotic material here and amusing caricatures of the British interventionists. *The Deserter* (1933) is interesting for Pudovkin's experiments with the contrapuntal montage of image and sound. Among his later films, *Minin and Pozharsky* (1939), with a script by Shklovsky, co-directed by Mikhail Doller, celebrated a patriotic uprising against the occupying Poles and was intended as a rival to Eisenstein's *Aleksandr Nevsky*. Pudovkin's last film, *The Return of Vasily Bortnikov* (1953) raises questions about the meaning of public life: a man returning from the war finds that his wife is unfaithful and makes his work as chairman of the collective farm a substitute for his failed marriage. Pudovkin left a number of theoretical works. *Film Technique* and *Film Acting* (both 1949, English edition) served as basic handbooks for film students.

Dovzhenko (1894–1956)

Aleksandr Dovzhenko, born of Ukrainian peasant stock, began his working life as a teacher. During the Civil War he joined the Red Army and became a member of the Party. In reward for this service he was assigned to diplomatic missions in Poland and Germany in 1921–23, and in turn his postings led to an opportunity to study art in Munich. *Zvenigora* (1928), incorporating the revolutionary movement into Ukrainian legend and folk tale, brought instant recognition from major filmmakers because of its quest for a poetic film language. *Arsenal* (1928) was a further exploration of poetic language; in it the themes of war, suffering, and revolution were cut free from a dependence on story. *Earth* (1930) has proved the director's best-known and best-loved film. In this representation of a Ukrainian village on the eve of collectivization, Dovzhenko recreated a rural life that was still in touch with the rhythms of nature. While supporting collectivization on ideological grounds, the film is memorable for its long takes dwelling on the fertility and beauty of the land and for its scenes of an old man's death, a young man's dance of love on the road by moonlight, and a woman's primal, animal despair and grief when this man, who is her lover, is murdered. All these images, paradoxically, amount to a celebration of a village life on the eve of its destruction, yet this celebration transcends any parochial or nationalistic cause.

Dovzhenko further explored the transformation of the country in *Ivan* (1932) and *Aerograd* (1935), seeking Stalin's approval to film the latter of these. He made *Shchors* (1939), about an intellectual and Civil-War hero in response to a request from Stalin. Dovzhenko had Stalin's special license to pursue his distinctive poetic cinema; the price he paid was a growing conformity of themes. Indeed, Dovzhenko was the avant-garde director most identified with the Party and the Party line. His subsequent films included *Liberation* (1940) (about the unification of Western Ukraine with the Ukrainian SSR during the time the Molotov–Von Ribbentrop Pact was in effect). During the actual war years he supervised (rather than directed) a number of powerful documentaries. His biographical film in color, *Michurin* (1948), became embroiled in ideological controversies over Lysenko's biological dogmas about the genetic transmission of acquired characteristics and Dovzhenko finally lost directorial control over the film.

FEKS: Kozintsev (1905–73) and Trauberg (1902–90)

FEKS, the Factory of the Eccentric Actor, was established in 1921 by Grigory Kozintsev and Leonid Trauberg. Eisenstein, on a visit from Moscow, associated himself with the group. They were "eccentrics," with theatrical influences coming from the circus and music hall, and film influences from German expressionism. They sought to take the energy and rhythms of contemporary life onto the stage and onto the screen. The "Factory" produced several actors and also the director Sergei Gerasimov.

The Adventures of Oktiabrina (1924) was a joyful agit-film, in which a young woman fought and defeated leftover reprobates from pre-revolutionary Russia. *The Devil's Wheel* (1926) took a favorite NEP (New Economic Policy) theme of the twenties – the discovery and routing of a band of criminals. The cameraman for this film was Andrei Moskvin, henceforth generally associated with the work of the FEKS team. *The Overcoat* (1926) and *S.V.D.* (1927) had scripts by the formalist theorist, Yury Tynianov. *The Overcoat*, an adaptation of Gogol's short story, transformed the old imperial capital into a nightmare world through camera shots from strange angles and contrasts of scale and of light and darkness. Bureaucracy invaded the world of dreams; ordinary feelings of love found grotesque expressions. FEKS worked out a fantastic realism in film, which unfortunately was later buried by the emerging naturalistic and socialist realist tradition. *S.V.D.*, commemorating the Decembrist revolt of 1825, showed a grotesque Russia that was not prepared for revolution. *The New Babylon*

(1929), set in 1871, took a luxurious Parisian shop as a pretext for views of the Second Empire and the rise of the Paris Commune. The score for live orchestral accompaniment by Shostakovich developed the film's rhythms of decay and rebellion.

FEKS broke with their silent-film style when they made the *Maksim* trilogy. The first part, *The Youth of Maksim*, that came out the same month, January 1935, as socialist realism was proclaimed, immediately became part of the new canon and was followed by *The Return of Maksim* (1937) and *The Vyborg Side* (1939). It told the story of a mythical (composite) Old Bolshevik. Kozintsev and Trauberg's *Plain People*, however, made at the end of World War II, was caught up in the wave of repression in the arts. Trauberg, in particular, became a victim of the campaign against "cosmopolitism." Thenceforth the fates of the FEKS team were separated.

Documentary film: Vertov, Shub, Shklovsky

Dziga Vertov (1896–1954) began during the Civil War by making documentaries, including films for the agit-trains by means of which the message of the October Revolution was disseminated to civilians and soldiers. He was born Denis Kaufman in the Polish part of the old Russian Empire; his chosen name refers to the clicking of movie cameras. He founded the Kino-Eye group and in its name issued manifestos denouncing acted films (Vertov associated them with the surviving commercial cinema) and proclaiming that the material of revolutionary film was life, facts, and machines. The movie camera was a "perfectible eye" (in contrast with man's imperfect one). Montage, in Vertov's conception, was an all-encompassing process that began with the selection going into the preparation of a film and ended with the editing and final reorganizations of filmed material. Film recorded the socialist transformation of society and itself had to be part of the revolutionary process by helping people to see this transformation. This view of the montage and production of film readily suggests Vertov's affinity with the constructivists and the futurist Mayakovsky.

Vertov directed the production of the news compilation, *Kino-Pravda*, of which twenty-three installments appeared from June 1922 through 1925. Cameramen in different parts of the Soviet Union sent the material to Vertov for editing. They made considerable use of compact, hand-held cameras, in pursuit of the Kino-Eye goal of catching "life unawares." *Man With a Movie Camera* (1929), Vertov's most signally avant-garde work, sees both the camera and the process of filmmaking self-reflexively in the context of industrial production. Vertov's cameraman in this and other big films of the twenties was his brother, Mikhail Kaufman.

Vertov's self-reflexive structures did not open up a perspective allowing him to distinguish between revolutionary change and Stalin's or even Lenin's appropriations of communist ideals and revolution. *Enthusiasm* or *Symphony of the Don Basin* (1930) was a film about the "shockworkers" of the Don Basin, who aimed to fulfill their Five Year Plan in four. The film was also an experiment designed to bring to the recording of sound the same flexibility as the Kino-Eyes had achieved in silent film. *Three Songs of Lenin* (1934) was constructed out of "folk songs" about the deceased leader. *Lullaby* (1937) was supposedly about emancipated women, but ultimately about Stalin (and yet its reception by the Stalinist film establishment was lukewarm). Vertov's later career raises disturbing questions about the weaknesses of his political convictions.

Other documentary filmmakers of the first post-revolutionary generation made distinctive use of montage. From her beginnings as a title-writer and film editor, Esfir Shub (1894–1959) became a developer of the principles and craft of montage. She made feature-length films out of archival films and fragments, often poorly identified and preserved, and succeeded in giving new life and meaning to the material. *The Fall of the Romanov Dynasty* (1927) incorporated Nicholas II's home movies, which she had discovered. More pre-revolutionary material was edited into *The Russia of Nicholas II and Leo Tolstoy* (1928). In *The Great Road* (1927) Shub dealt with the period since the Revolution, making the film out of newsreels from this decade.

Turksib (1929), a collaboration between Viktor Shklovsky and Viktor Turin (1895–1945) celebrated the construction of the rail link between Turkestan and Siberia. Shklovsky's script and titles showed a formalist focus on *material* and a characteristic concern to "make it strange" (in this instance through a structure of contrasts). These same formalist concerns encouraged Shklovsky to salvage the footage Mikhail Kalatozov (1903–73) had brought back from Svanetia for an abandoned fictional film. Out of this film *material* Shklovsky edited *Salt for Svanetia* (1930), setting the isolation and harsh beauty of the region against its people's urgent need for links to the outside world.

Film: entertainment and education

The "avant-garde" directors who rose to prominence in the twenties were part of a larger group of filmmakers who shared common concerns to make films, to attract audiences, and to survive in times of unpredictable political and economic change. The separation of the "avant garde" from the larger group is in part an artificial one, stemming from the success of the former in obtaining a foreign following and in part, too, from their particular focus on refashioning spectators and politically educating them. The less famous directors were often happier to cater to the taste for entertainment of unregenerate spectators (and perhaps in the process educate them). In retrospect, moreover, the particular privileging of a narrower group may seem unwarranted. Media students and historians of popular culture who examine the productions of Soviet film in a spirit of relaxed tolerance readily find that distinctions break down. On political grounds, Fridrikh Ermler belongs with the leading revolutionary filmmakers, as does Boris Barnet through personal and professional ties. Some films designed for entertainment are now recognized to have artistic merits too. Moreover, critics note that in 1935, at the time of the imposition of socialist realism, model films were supplied by a variety of directors, from both the narrower and the broader categories. And within three years, Eisenstein and Dovzhenko, in one category, and Protazanov, in another, were all working within the new constraints; any commitment to testing and extending the limits of the permissible was an individual matter rather than a question of categorization.

Protazanov (from 1923 until his death in 1945)

Upon his return from emigration (see above), the resourceful and well-tested filmmaker Iakov Protazanov made a striking film, *Aelita* (1924), with constructivist sets by Aleksandra Exter and Isaak Rabinovich, about a revolution among Martians. Protazanov was necessarily viewed with suspicion as a representative of the old bourgeois cinema, but good political sense (and luck) allowed this filmmaker to survive. *His Call* (1925) attached a melodramatic story to an appeal for membership of the Communist Party. The heroine of *The Forty-First* (1927), a soldier in the Red Army, shoots her lover, a White Guard officer, at the end of a desert-island idyll (a poorer version in sound and color was made by Grigory Chukhrai in 1956 at the start of the Thaw). *The White Eagle* (1927), based on "The Governor" by Leonid Andreev, develops a story about a tsarist official who orders the shooting of some demonstrators and is later tormented by guilt (the film preserves a record of Meyerhold as an actor). *The Holiday of St. Iorgen* (1930) uses vaudeville in the cause of the campaign against religion. Protazanov's sound films included *Without Dowry* (1937), a good adaptation of Ostrovsky's play with the same name. *Nasreddin in Bukhara* (1943), made in Tashkent, is a humorous film based on Uzbek folk legends about a champion of the poor.

Ermler (1898–1967)

From 1919 Fridrikh Ermler was a committed Bolshevik and Party member, who during the Civil War even became a member of the secret police, the Chekha. In Leningrad in 1924 he founded KEM, the Workshop for Experimental Film, a student group which performed "films without film stock," or scenes performed as if for a camera. The films he completed had an ongoing concern with the Party, which was not seen as always infallible. In his early, silent productions – *Katka's Reinette Apple* (1926) and *Parisian Cobbler* (1928) – he formed a notable collaboration with Fedor Nikitin, whose background was in the Moscow Art Theatre and with whose help he developed characters that provide an unusual critical perspective on the emerging socialist society. *Fragment of an Empire* (1929), Ermler's last and greatest silent film, moved into different territory, notable for its cinematic handling of the problem of memory and, particularly, for its dual time scheme, worked out with the help of Eisenstein.

Ermler's name became associated with the transition to socialist realism. His film *Counterplan* (1932), which he co-directed with Sergei Iutkevich, was a recognized precursor of socialist realist aesthetics. Nonetheless, in his later work Ermler continued to go beyond the restrictions of the Party line.

Barnet (1902–65)

Boris Barnet was a member of Kuleshov's workshop (he acts the part of the cowboy in Kuleshov's *Extraordinary Adventures of Mr. West in the Land of the Bolsheviks*). He directed a series of films with good work by actors, dealing with such problems as the housing shortage, building the new society, and sabotage. They include *Girl With the Hat-Box* (1927) and *House on Trubnaia Square* (1928). His best film is his first in sound, *Outskirts* or *Patriots* (1933), about the upheavals brought by the Revolution in the life of a provincial town.

Room (1894–1976)

Abram Room had a steady career as a filmmaker. One of his early films was controversial, *Bed and Sofa* (1927), and was soon suppressed. Another, *The Stern Youth* (1936), was also suppressed and was scarcely known before *glas-*

nost. Room filmed *Bed and Sofa* (1927) to a script by Shklovsky (with whom he made another film, *Rocky Road*, 1929, which did not survive). *Bed and Sofa* was designed as an exercise for just three actors, portraying a man, his wife, and his best friend all sharing a one-room apartment. In this reworking of the drawing-room triangular love story, the wife walks out on the men, who regard her as mere property, at the same time as they refuse to take responsibility for the child she has conceived. Room's treatment of the script was unusual for its exploration of sensuality and particularly for the eroticization of relations between the two men. A homoerotic subtext in *The Stern Youth* is even more surprising given the very late date of the film as socialist realism came into force.

Others

Sergei Iutkevich (1904–85) is a figure who continually appears alongside members of the avant-garde. He studied under Meyerhold and joined FEKS together with Eisenstein. His many films include *Lace* (1928), about a member of the Komsomol's fight against theft in a lacemaking factory; *Counterplan* (1932), co-directed with Fridrikh Ermler (see below); and *Man With a Gun* (1938), about Lenin, with Maksim Straukh in the title-role.

Yury Tarich (1885–1967) was a representative of the traditional school of filmmaking. His film about Ivan the Terrible, *The Wings of a Serf* (1926), was a good melodramatic one, with violence, lust, and sadism predominant. A sub-theme dealing with the role of the tsar in industry and trade was introduced by the formalist Viktor Shklovsky, who was brought in for some rewriting of the script. A more sustained collaboration between Tarich and Shklovsky, an adaptation of Pushkin's *Captain's Daughter* (1928), included an interesting experiment in reversing the roles of the hero and the villain, but the film was ultimately buried by the *material* – Shklovsky's particular interest. Tarich remained highly productive during the war and postwar periods, redirecting his efforts to the area of Belorussian film.

Olga Preobrazhenskaia (1881–1971) was an actress in some of Protazanov's pre-revolutionary films and later a director. Her *Peasant Women of Riazan* (1927), co-directed with Ivan Pravov, was a traditional tale about a man's violent desire for his son's bride; it is memorable for montage rhythms in the scenes of peasants dancing. A later film with Pravov, *Stepan Razin* (1939), dealt with a dangerous topic, folk rebellion, and suffered in terms of criticism and distribution.

Nikolai Ekk (1902–76) is remembered for one good film, *Pass to Life*

(1931), about the taming and socialization of *bezprizorniki*, children who had lost their families during the years of upheaval and who had to fend for themselves. The film set a record for box-office receipts. It has a claim to be the first Soviet sound film, or the first film conceived as a sound film rather than as a silent film with sound added.

Socialist Realism (1935–85)

The struggle for Party control of the film industry unfolded in conjunction with the consolidation of Stalin's hold on power and the move toward the first Five Year Plan, providing for rapid industrialization and forced collectivization. The political struggle was also waged as an aesthetic one for films that would be accessible to the masses. Some advocates of realism, or "prosaic" cinema, wished to entrench their own kind of filmmaking. Defenders of poetic cinema were labeled as dangerous "formalists" (a term that was to receive sweeping application). The question of the direction of film was complicated by the introduction of sound. The "Statement on Sound Film," issued by Eisenstein, Pudovkin, and Grigory Aleksandrov in 1928, expressed the fear that the new medium would obliterate achievements in the development of contrapuntal montage and take film back toward static filmed theatre. The First Party Conference on Cinema in March 1928 was a turning point, with attacks on non-Party film workers who had succumbed to decadent filmmaking and complaints about foreign films. A naturalistic style based on undiscussed aesthetic preferences was generally advocated. Following the conference, more and more films were banned. Boris Shumiatsky, head of the film industry, boasted in 1933 that 50 percent of the production of the past few years remained on the shelf. The near collapse of production in that same year produced a crisis, in part because Stalin himself was an avid film watcher and demanded films for his private screenings.

The proclamation of socialist realism in January 1935 at the All-Union Conference on Cinematographic Affairs provided some direction for the development of the film industry. At the same time, the institutionalization of socialist realism provided instruments of direct bureaucratic and economic control over filmmakers. The guidelines reduced (but did not eliminate) arbitrariness in decisions to prevent or to shelve films. Censorship was not only proscriptive, but also prescriptive. Filmmakers now had to present "positive" heroes: fighters from the Revolution and the Civil War, Lenin and Stalin, precursory Great Men in Russian history, leaders in the struggles for industrialization and collectivization, Party heroes and workers, men and women committed to seeking out saboteurs and wreckers. Under the new aesthetic and the new bureaucratic regime some artists managed to develop and a few produced interesting work. Others did not submit to the new order or failed to adapt to it. Many films continued to be shelved after completion, since an aesthetic that was subservient to the Party was continually vulnerable to shifts in the Party line, which were capricious or the result of changing historical circumstance. One or two poetic filmmakers such as Aleksandr Medvedkin managed to make and release a film before it was denounced for subversiveness. A suppressed poetic talent, Eisenstein, was called upon when the shadow of war required that all talents be enlisted. Socialist realist film evolved a number of models, which formed the basis of genres. These genres offered some guarantee of stability.

Models and genres
Industrial struggle

In 1932, after a three-year interruption in his film career, Fridrikh Ermler returned to work with the help of Sergei Iutkevich. The film they co-directed, *Counterplan*, achieved unintended political importance when it became one of the acknowledged models of socialist realist film. It dealt with the building of a giant turbine, relations between the Party and the workers, and the struggle to get a sense of collective responsibility from older workers with pre-Revolutionary attitudes. The achievement was in part technical: one of the first sound films, *Counterplan,* perfected the recording of speech and achieved a quiet naturalism of manner. Shostakovich supplied the music.

Revolutionary heroes

Chapaev (1934) was one of the successes of socialist realist art, acclaimed by leading filmmakers and audiences alike. Its directors were Sergei Vasilyev (1900–59) and Georgy Vasilyev (1899–1946), who were known as "The Vasilyev Brothers" (although they were unrelated). The script came from a story by Dmitry Furmanov, an account of his relationship as political commissar with a fiery Red Army commander during the fight against the Czech armies under Kolchak. The film used sound and drew on the montage tradition of the twenties. In the work of the two Vasilyevs, *Chapaev* was an isolated success.

Positive heroes under socialism

Films with "positive heroes" for post-revolutionary society formed an important class. Two characteristic films were *The Baltic Deputy* (1937) and *Member of the Government* (1940), co-directed by Aleksandr Zarkhi (1908–   ) and Iasha Kheifits (1905–95). The former was about a member of the progressive intelligentsia faced with the need to accept the October Revolution, the second about a woman devoted to the ideals of collective farming. An obvious model of a positive character was provided by Gorky himself in the adaptations of his autobiographical trilogy made by Mark Donskoi (1901–81): *The Childhood of Gorky* (1938), *Among People* (1939), *My Universities* (1940). Donskoi followed these good, popular films with an adaptation of another socialist realist classic, Nikolai Ostrovsky's novel *How the Steel Was Tempered* (1942).

The Lenin and Stalin cults

A special subclass of positive-hero films was devoted to the Lenin and Stalin cults. Two examples of the former are *Lenin in October* (1937) and *Lenin in 1918* (1939), with Boris Shchukin as Lenin and Mikhail Romm (1901–71) as director. Romm was a respected filmmaker and teacher at the VGIK (All-Union Institute of Cinematography) film school (among his later students at VGIK were Andrei Tarkovsky and Vasily Shukshin).

The Stalin cult was consecrated by a director with achievements in Georgian and Russian cinema, Mikhail Chiaureli (1894–1974), in monumental films with Mikhail Gelovani in the main role: *The Great Dawn* (1938), *The Vow* (1946), and *The Fall of Berlin* (two parts, 1950).

Historical leaders

Russian history, too, was a source of other great leaders in the fight to make Russia strong against imagined and real internal and external threats. Such heroes appear in Vladimir Petrov's two-part film *Peter the Great* (1937, 1939), Pudovkin and Doller's *Minin and Pozharsky* and their *Suvorov* (1941), Eisenstein's *Aleksandr Nevsky*, and also (but ambiguously) his *Ivan the Terrible*.

Musical comedy

The musicals in film by Grigory Aleksandrov (1903–83) and Ivan Pyriev (1901–68) were tremendously popular; they satisfied the audience's need for entertainment and for escape into a fantasy world. Musical comedy was a mediating genre, through which the role of the positive heroine or hero in leading the collective toward socialism was normalized. The movies provided stars, most particularly Liubov Orlova in Aleksandrov's films and Marina Ladynina in Pyriev's. The resemblance of the movies to American musicals has been often commented on in recent years (along with the mechanisms of denial that they fulfilled). The composer Isaak Dunaevsky (1900–55) worked with Aleksandrov regularly, and with Pyriev sometimes.

Grigory Aleksandrov had been associated with Eisenstein as an actor in the Proletkult theatre and as his assistant in all his films up to "Que Viva Mexico" (which he completed in a crudely edited version in 1979). His musical comedies began with *Jolly Fellows*, or *Jazz Comedy* (1934), and continued with *Circus* (1936) and *Volga-Volga* (1938). Ivan Pyriev, for his part, enjoyed little success in his film career until he turned to musicals in 1938. Thereafter his position quickly rivaled Aleksandrov's. His musical comedies included *The Rich Bride* (1938), *The Tractor Drivers* (1939), *The Shepherd and the Swine Girl* (1941), all starring Marina Ladynina; the films continued after the war. Aleksandr Ivanovsky (1881–1968) and Herbert Rappaport (1908–83) had one isolated success in the genre in their co-directed *Musical Story* (1940), starring Zoia Fedorova.

Literary adaptations

A rich but not necessarily safe genre was the adaptation of Russian literary classics of the pre- and post-revolutionary periods. Here, too, socialist realist principles of selection and interpretation prevailed. Pudovkin's poetic (and silent) treatment of the major socialist realist classic, *Mother*, did not provide the desired model; *Petersburg Night* (1934), by Grigory Roshal (1898–1983) and Vera Stroeva (1903–   ), based on early works by Dostoevsky, came closer to a socialist realist aesthetic. Protazanov showed he could work in this genre in *Without Dowry* (1937). And as we have seen, Mark Donskoi devoted himself to classics of socialist realist literature.

In the later years of socialist realism, one well-established director who chose to work with literary texts was Ivan Pyriev. His last project, begun after Stalin's death, was a series of adaptations of novels by the ever controversial Dostoevsky: *Nastasia Filippovna* (1958, from *The Idiot*); *White Nights* (1959); and a three-part adaptation of *The Brothers Karamazov* (1968–69, with the last part completed after Pyriev's death by its two leading actors). It seems that, for all Pyriev's success in musical comedy, he was hoping to prove himself a significant artist. In his Dostoevsky films Pyriev escaped some of his own limitations (and the limitations of socialist realism) because he was drawn to the complexities of Dostoevsky's protagonists and because of some good casting choices (his principal successes, nonetheless, were with the more sensual characters and the buffoons). Another well-established director, Sergei Bondarchuk, sought to measure himself against *War and Peace*, in an expensive and cumbersome four-part adaptation (1966).

Cultural monuments

Particularly after Stalin's death (and perhaps out of a sense of exhaustion) socialist realist film was given latitude to record other classical achievements of Russian culture. Vera Stroeva directed well thought-out versions of Mussorgsky's *Boris Godunov* (1955) and *Khovanshchina* (1959), and Mikhail Shapiro directed a wide-screen, stereophonic version of Shostakovich's *Katerina Izmailova* (1967). Galina Ulanova's ballet art is preserved in *Romeo and Juliet* (1955), and Maia Plisetskaia's in *Anna Karenina* (1975).

War films

The making of films about The Great Patriotic War (or the Second World War, as it is known elsewhere) was complicated by the evacuation of film studios to Central Asia, by questions about the failure of Stalin and the Party to prepare for the German invasion, and by the consequent spontaneous resistance (or collaboration) of local populations. The major effort of filmmakers, including many fiction-film directors, initially concentrated on documentaries (here Dovzhenko distinguished himself once again). Later there came war films, such as *Zoia* (1944) by Leo Arnshtam (1905–79) and Ermler's *The Great Turning Point* (1946). Films dealing with much of the reality of the war were forbidden as long as socialist realism remained in force, as Aleksei German (1938–) discovered when he made *Trial on the Road* (1971).

Cold War films

With the return of repression in the arts at the war's end, film production declined. An all-time low was set in 1951, when only nine titles were released. The Cold War became the subject of a number of films. Kalatozov's *Conspiracy of the Doomed* (1950) reenacted, in an Eastern European setting, the ostensible reasons, including American conspiracy, that had justified the establishment of Stalinism at home.

Exceptions

Many films were stopped at some point, early or late, in the production process. Even under Stalin some exceptional films did get made – and were then shelved. *Ivan the Terrible*, Part 2, is the most famous of them. Another, completed just before the promulgation of socialist realism, is Aleksandr Fainzimmer's *Lieutenant Kizhe* (1934): a satire, with a score by Prokofiev, set in the reign of Tsar Paul and involving a character with a merely fictitious identity. A third is *Grabbers*, or *Happiness* (1935), by a true-believing communist and Bolshevik, Aleksandr Medvedkin (1900–89); it is a fable about a poor peasant (who it seems was doomed to be a victim not only before but also after collectivization), told with a wonderful stylization of character, performance, and setting. In other film work (on his "kino-train") Medvedkin sought to give to film the freedom that later became readily available with video and to engage in direct discussions with peasants and workers.

One film about the Terror was made and released: Ermler's *The Great Citizen*, Parts 1 and 2 (1938, 1939). The film began with the official version of the murder of Kirov, secretary of the Leningrad Communist Party; it laid the blame on disaffected Bolsheviks and Trotskyites and provided ample justification for the Purge Trials. But for an analogy with the situation during the Terror and to find models of the counter-revolutionary conspirators, Ermler turned to Dostoevsky's *The Devils* and, with its help, produced a picture of Stalinist myths of the One Leader and rituals of self-criticism. In the last two decades of socialist realism, many more exceptional films were made. Most of them were shelved.

The Thaw and the Stagnation

Khrushchev's speech denouncing Stalin at the Twentieth Party Congress in 1956 introduced what is called the "Thaw," that gradually came to an end between 1965 (the date Khrushchev was ousted from office) and 1969 (the date of the invasion of Czechoslovakia). The short-term effect of the Thaw was a certain relaxation of the ideological and aesthetic norms of socialist realism. In film, the individual and private life suddenly had more meaning. Kalatozov's *The Cranes Are Flying* (1957) measured the meaning of a soldier's death in terms of his fiancée's love for him. Kozintsev's film adaptation, *Don Quixote* (1957) allowed for the exploration of life outside of an ideological framework. Iuli Raizman (1903–) in *Communist* (1958) gave a picture of a communist as an ordinary man, who must provide leadership for the building of a power station. Grigory Chukhrai (1921–) in the popular *Ballad of a Soldier* (1959) showed a soldier on leave beginning to conceive the experiences of life he will probably never know. Mikhail Romm, who had directed films about Lenin, now made *Ordinary Fascism* (1966), using documentary materials from archives and Eisensteinian principles of montage in order to explore the functioning of fascist Germany and the popular support it enjoyed (parallels with the workings of totalitarianism at home readily suggested themselves). The Thaw allowed for a more honest picture of the West than earlier in Soviet culture, in *The Journalist* (1967) by Sergei Gerasimov (1906–85). The Thaw even allowed the exploration of tragedy, for which there was little room in a socialist realist aesthetic; Kozintsev made *Hamlet* (1964), with Innokenty Smoktunovsky in the title role, in which his reading of Shakespeare was inflected by his experience of totalitarianism. In 1971 he followed it with an even stronger *King Lear*, starring the Estonian Yury Iarvet. The political and bureaucratic structures governing the film industry, however, remained in place, and during the "Stagnation" under Brezhnev continued as a frequent and major source of interference.

In the longer term the Thaw released energies that were the basis of several careers in film despite the obstacles and restrictions in studios and at the level of the ministerial body, Goskino. Andrei Tarkovsky (1932–86), Vasily Shukshin (1929–74), and Gleb Panfilov (1934–   ) all got their beginning in these years. Other careers were cut off at their inception, or were suddenly interrupted. Aleksandr Askoldov's *Commissar* (1967), was not released until 1987 (the film breached taboos concerning women and Jews), and in the interim he was barred from the studios. The films of Kira Muratova (1934–   ) from the Odessa Film Studio were shelved, but despite obstacles she continued to work and was acclaimed after 1986 as a major filmmaker, whose work was of special interest to feminist criticism. Sergei Paradzhanov (1924–90), a Georgian of Armenian descent working in Kiev, had several projects blocked and spent several years in prison on a charge of homosexuality; nonetheless, he completed major films rooted in non-Russian traditions of legend and folklore. All in all, the film legacy of the Khrushchev and Brezhnev years when it was fully disclosed was large; it became available once *glasnost* was introduced to the film industry in 1986.

Subverting authority

Throughout the period of Stagnation the structures of control and the official aesthetics of film were under pressure from without and from within. The direction of the changes was often unclear. The new value placed on personal life could be used in the service of apologetics for the Brezhnev regime, as in the popular Vladimir Menshov's *Moscow Does Not*

Believe in Tears (1980). The attack on bureaucracy in Raizman's *Your Contemporary* (1967), pitting an engineer against bureaucracy in Moscow, still accorded with socialist realist norms, whereas the attack in *Garage* (1980) by Eldar Riazanov turned to savage satire. Moreover, during the years of Stagnation it seemed that the films and directors targeted for harassment were often arbitrarily chosen. Some directors enjoyed more freedom than others, while others proved astute fighters.

One director was notably successful in overcoming barriers and in challenging the socialist realist aesthetic. Andrei Tarkovsky became a major name at home and abroad after prizes for *Ivan's Childhood* (1962) in Venice and then for *Andrei Rublev* (1966) in Cannes in 1969 (when the film was obtained for the festival in spite of obstacles put up by Soviet officials). *Rublev* was eventually shown in Russia, but only with major cuts. A recurring theme in Tarkovsky's work is the necessity of the artist and the inevitable imperfection of art. Incomplete and ruined works of art indicate some greater perfection, but indicate, too, the uncertain place of art in human affairs (as with the revelation of fragments of Rublev's icons at the end of *Andrei Rublev*). Time is sometimes examined as synchronous or cyclical (rather than linear and progressive), as in *Solaris* (1972). The legacy of Stalinism haunts *The Mirror* (1975). The ambiguous Zone in *Stalker* (1979) is dangerous, and yet a potential source of good (it is perhaps a symbol of the gulag). The Russian artist is looked at in a European context in *Nostalgia* (1983) and *The Sacrifice* (1986), which were both made abroad. Cineastes were drawn to Tarkovsky not just by his ambiguous, puzzling stories, but also by his cinematic wizardry. Long, unedited shots create a totally cinematic space and time, connecting events and actions that cannot form any ordinary spatio-temporal continuity. A painterly use of color leads Tarkovsky to introduce sequences in color, often muted, into black-and-white films, while, more traditionally, he inserts black-and-white sequences into color films.

One myth under challenge during the Thaw and the Stagnation was that of the transformed countryside under communism. A filmmaker and writer of the "village prose school," Vasily Shukshin interrogated the vitality, brutality, and limitations of village life, into which he had been born and which endured as an alternative to the spiritually bankrupt urban world. His films were generally released after delays. They included: *Your Son and Brother* (1966), *Peculiar People* (1970), *Stoves and Benches* (1972), and *The Red Snowball Tree* (in color, 1974). But when Andrei Konchalovsky (1937–) brought a documentary style to collective-farm characters and life in *The Story of Anna Kliachina Who Loved But Did Not Marry* (1967), his film was shelved.

The challenges of other directors to socialist realist stereotypes were sometimes subtler. Larisa Shepitko (1933–79) inserted religious metaphor in a film about war, *The Ascent* (1977), in which the execution of partisans and Russians by Nazi forces became a Crucifixion. Panfilov focused on simple, unheroic characters in a series of films that explored the varied talents of Inna Churikova: *No Ford Through the Flames* (1968), *The Beginning* (1970), *I Want to Speak* (1973, released 1976), and a new *Mother* (1990).

On occasion, directors used positions of influence to extend the limits of the allowable. Lev Kulidzhanov (1924–   ) made a film at the very start of the Thaw about the war and its impact on the individual, *The House Where I Live* (co-director Iakov Segal, 1957). He was made First Secretary of the Filmmakers Union upon its foundation in 1965. In 1970 he made a good Dostoevsky adaptation, *Crime and Punishment*. Nikita Mikhalkov (1945–   ), who enjoyed official protection, shrewdly gauged the limits of the possible during the years of Stagnation. Two of his films which were out of the ordinary were *Unfinished Play for a Mechanical Piano* (1977) and *Oblomov* (1980), the former being a particularly successful rendition of Chekhov. Mikhalkov's political skills also served him in the making of *Burnt by the Sun* (1994), which had the necessary ingredients to find acclaim abroad, leading to an Oscar for best foreign film. It is a *Cherry Orchard* set in the thirties, with quotations from Fellini and Bergman, centering on the family of a Bolshevik revolutionary, who are all about to be sacrificed by the rising Stalinists. The film has topical allusions to the settling of scores in the post-communist period.

During the Brezhnev years Aleksandr Sokurov (1951–   ), among other directors, found opportunities in the film schools and in the studios to make films, and then regularly saw them shelved. He made a very powerful first film when he was a student at VGIK, *A Lonely Human Voice* (1978), that drew on the traditions of Eisenstein and FEKS, while treating impotence as a metaphor for development arrested by the Revolution. Sokurov was then forced to confine himself to documentary films – which in turn were also blocked – including *Alto Sonata: Dmitri Shostakovich* (1981) and *Elegy* (1985–86), the latter about Fedor Shaliapin, Russia's great basso who emigrated after the Revolution. With the advent of *glasnost* Sokurov returned to fiction film with the exception of his *Moscow Elegy* (1988), which commemorated Tarkovsky (who had seen Sokurov as his spiritual heir).

Several directors showed the destabilizing effect that voices from the margins could have. In Georgia, Iosif Ioseliani (1934–   ) made films highlighting the tenuousness of human relationships and gently questioning human verities, as in *Falling Leaves* (1966) and *Pastorale* (1976). Eventually he chose to pursue his career in France. Sergei Paradzhanov set his *Shadows of Forgotten Ancestors* (1965) in an idyllic Carpathian world out of time, which seemed to deny the existence of history and the fact of the Revolution, along with socialist realist principles of struggle and progress (moreover, the film was read as a Ukrainian nationalist text). In subsequent films, in a career interrupted by persecution and imprisonment, Paradzhanov turned to Georgian and Armenian tales and legends: *Color of Pomegranate* (1970), *The Legend of Suram Fortress* (1984), and *Ashik-Kerib* (or *Ashug Qaribi*, 1989), looking for a distinctive stylistic solution for each of the films. Another Georgian, Tengiz Abuladze (1924–   ), used his own explorations of the world of legend in *Prayer* (1969) and *The Wishing Tree* (1978) in order to develop a language of allegory through which to examine the figures of Stalin and Beria in *Repentance* (1984).

One Russian director who had a film that seemed ready-made for the age of *glasnost* was Aleksei German. *My Friend Ivan Lapshin* (completed 1983, released 1985) took for its hero a police officer sent to a provincial town on an assignment to wipe out a gang of bandits and focused on his romance with an actress in a local theatre. The film was set just before the Great Terror, and viewed in a tolerant, Chekhovian manner people who kept their faith in the cause of socialism and progress.

Glasnost and democracy

The Fifth Congress of the Filmmakers Union in May 1986 broke with the heritage of socialist realism and introduced the policies of *glasnost'* and *perestroika* into the film industry. One direct consequence of the congress was the establishment of a Conflict Commission to review and release shelved films (more than 170 were found). Another consequence was the founding of a film museum, whose mission has included the dissemination of the forgotten or suppressed heritage from the communist years. In stages, the powers of the ministerial body, Goskino, to control the production of films were lifted, its distribution monopoly was challenged, and censorship was eliminated. In stages, too, the organization of the industry was decentralized. Studios moved to a system of self-financing, while the breaking up of the Soviet Union spelled an end to the big all-union systems of organization. Among filmmakers, there was a wish to address openly the dark secrets of Stalinism and of more recent history: for instance, the war in Afghanistan, the patriarchal basis of Russian society and the position of women in it, social problems – sex, drink, drugs, the homeless, the youth culture at home and abroad. One difficulty for many filmmakers was to find a recognizable language and genres for addressing these problems; the socialist realist aesthetic had been addressed to very different problems. A related difficulty was to find audiences. It was clear that the mass-spectator wanted American movies, which were generally (and cheaply) available, and that distributors, whether controlled by Goskino or not, were interested in catering to that taste. Filmmakers needed to gain access to other, more specialized audiences at home and abroad, and also to compete with American releases. In both areas there have been some successes; there are even films that appeal both to cinematically sophisticated critics and to the moviegoing public.

In this period, Kira Muratova's strong feminist voice came to the fore in films such as *Asthenic Syndrome* (1989). The dark secrets of the labor camps were brought to light in Aleksandr Proshkin's *Cold Summer of '53* (1987), Vitaly Kanevsky's *Freeze/Die. Resurrect* (1991), and Marina Goldovskaia's documentary, *Solovki Power* (1988). A timely (or opportunistic), highly rhetorical documentary by Stanislav Govorukhin, *No Way to Live* (1990), presented archival pictures of the destruction wrought under Stalin. Westerns or "Easterns" were filmed, as in Alla Surikova's *Man From Boulevard des Capucines* (1987), that met a pent-up demand for American culture. (A better, earlier example of the use of the Western or "Eastern" genre was given in Vladimir Motyl's *White Sun of the Desert* [1970].) Rock music, sex, and youth culture were introduced with a vengeance in such films as Vasily Pichul's *Little Vera* (1988), Petr Todorovsky's *Intergirl* (1989), Rashid Nugmanov's *The Needle* (1989), which was a film in Russian by a young Kazakh director, starring a rock singer, Viktor Tsoi, Sergei Soloviev's *Assa*, and Sergei Livnev's *Hammer and Sickle* (1994). Nugmanov's film in particular showed that young filmmakers had absorbed the lessons of Godard. The war in Afghanistan was the subject of Sergei Lukianchikov's documentary *Pain* (1988) and Vladimir Khotinenko's fictional *Musulmanin* (1995). In *Caucasian Prisoner* (1996) Sergei Bodrov took a conflict much closer to the Russian heartland – the war in Chechnia – and challenged Russian stereotypes of the Chechens. Bodrov's script draws on a story by Tolstoy set in an earlier stage of Russia's imperial war against this mountain people.

Continuities: Russian and European

The question of Russian culture as discontinuous and therefore incomplete has exercised filmmakers since the sixties (along with the discontinuity and fragmentariness of Russian culture in exile). Oleg Kovalov's *Concert for a Rat* (1995) ambitiously seeks to establish lost continuities, both internal and external, turning to constructivism to show that its visual lessons were not exhausted by Eisenstein, and to Russian symbolism to suggest links with the surrealism of Buñuel and Cocteau. Kovalov hopes to develop a film language with which to explore the inaction and complicity of Russians under the Terror. Links are established, too, with the postmodernism of Stanley Kubrick's *Clockwork Orange* and with a feminism that questions the basis of Russian patriarchy and explores Russian sexual repression. Kovalov, and a number of other directors working at the end of the twentieth century, demonstrate that Russia in a postmodern and post-communist age has a distinctive claim to the heritage of European culture.

Suggested reading

330   **1 Russian cultural history: introduction**

Auty, Robert and Dmitry Obolensky, eds., *An Introduction to Russian Language and Literature*, Cambridge, 1977.

Bakhtin, Mikhail, *Art and Answerability: Early Philosophical Essays by M. M. Bakhtin*, eds. Michael Holquist, Vadim Liapunov, trans. Vadim Liapunov, Austin, TX, 1990. Other Bakhtin texts of this press edited by Holquist and Liapunov.

The Bakhtin Reader: Selected Writings of Bakhtin, Medvedev, and Voloshinov, ed. by Pam Morris. London; New York, 1994.

Rabelais and His World, trans. Helene Iswolsky, Bloomington, IN, 1984.

Berdiaev, Nikolai, *The Origins of Russian Communism*, Ann Arbor, MI, 1964.

The Russian Idea, Hudson, NY, 1992.

Berry, Ellen E. and Anesa Miller-Pogacar, eds., *Re-Entering the Sign. Articulating New Russian Culture*, Ann Arbor, MI, 1995.

Besançon, Alain, *The Rise of the Gulag: the Intellectual Origins of Leninism*, trans. Sarah Matthews, New York, 1980.

Billington, James H., *The Icon and the Axe: An Interpretive History of Russian Culture*, New York, 1966.

Clark, Katerina, *The Soviet Novel: History as Ritual*, Chicago, 1985.

Costlow, Jane T. and Stephanie Sandler, Judith Vowles, eds., *Sexuality and the Body in Russian Culture*, Stanford, CA, 1993.

Diment, Galya and Yury Slezkine, *Between Heaven and Hell: the Myth of Siberia in Russian Culture*, New York, 1993.

Emerson, Caryl, *The First Hundred Years of Mikhail Bakhtin*, Princeton, NJ, 1997.

Boris Godunov: Transpositions of a Russian Theme, Bloomington, IN, 1986.

Epstein, Mikhail, *After the Future: the Paradoxes of Postmodernism and Contemporary Russian Culture*, Amherst, MA, 1995.

Fedotov, G. P., *The Russian Religious Mind*, New York, 1960.

Florovsky, Georges, *Collected Works of Georges Florovsky*, Belmont, MA, 1972.

Groys, Boris, *The Total Art of Stalinism: Avant-Garde, Aesthetic Dictatorship, and Beyond*, trans. Charles Rougle, Princeton, NJ, 1992.

Hingley, Ronald, *Russian Writers and Society in the Nineteenth Century*, 2nd edn., London, 1977.

Holquist, Michael and Katerina Clark, *Mikhail Bakhtin*, Cambridge, MA, 1984.

Hosking, Geoffrey, *Russia: People and Empire, 1552–1917,* Cambridge, MA, 1997.

Hughes, Robert P. and Irina Paperno, eds., *Russian Culture in Modern Times. California Slavic studies 17,* 2 vols., Berkeley, CA; London, 1994.

Kalbouss, George, *A Study Guide to Russian Culture, Religious History and Theology,* Needham Heights, MA, 1991.

Karlinsky, Simon and Alfred Appel, Jr., eds., *Russian Literature and Culture in the West: 1922–1972,* 2 vols., *TriQuaterly* 27–28 (Spring–Fall 1973).

Kelly, Catriona et al., eds., *Constructing Russian Culture in the Age of Revolution, 1881–1940,* Oxford; New York, 1998.

Russian Cultural Studies: an Introduction. Oxford, NY: Oxford U. Press, 1988.

Lahusen, Thomas, ed., with Gene Kuperman, *Late Soviet Culture. From Perestroika to Novostroika,* Durham; London, 1993.

Leong, Albert, ed., *Oregon Studies in Chinese and Russian Culture,* New York, 1990.

Likhachev, Dmitrii Sergeevich, *Reflections on Russia,* ed. Nicolai N. Petro, trans. Christina Sever, with a foreword by S. Frederick Starr, Boulder, CO, 1991.

Lotman, Yury and Boris Uspenskii, Ann Shukman, *The Semiotics of Russian Culture,* Ann Arbor, MI, 1984.

Malia, Martin, *Alexander Herzen and the Birth of Russian Socialism.1812–1855,* Cambridge, MA, 1961.

Masaryk, Tomas, *The Spirit of Russia,* 3 vols., New York, 1961, 1967.

Miliukov, Pavel, *Outlines of Russian Culture,* 3 vols., New York, 1972.

Morson, Gary Saul and Caryl Emerson, *Mikhail Bakhtin: Creation of a Prosaics,* Stanford, CA, 1990.

Nakhimovsky, Alexander D. and Alice Stone, eds. ,*The Semiotics of Russian Cultural History: Essays by Iurii M. Lotman, Lidiia Ginsburg, Boris A. Uspenskii,* introduction by Boris Gasparov, Ithaca, NY, 1985.

Norman, John O., ed., *New Perspectives on Russian and Soviet Artistic Culture,* New York, 1994.

Paperno, Irina, *Chernyshevsky and the Age of Realism: a Study in the Semiotics of Behavior,* Stanford, CA, 1988.

Paperno, Irina and Joan Delaney Grossman, eds., *Creating Life: the Aesthetic Utopia of Russian Modernism,* Stanford, CA, 1994.

Cultural Mythologies of Russian Modernism: from the Golden Age to the Silver Age, Berkeley, CA, 1992.

Riasanovsky, Nicholas, *A History of Russia,* 4thedn., New York, 1984.

Rzhevsky, Nicholas, *Russian Literature and Ideology,* Urbana, IL, 1983.

Shalin, Dmitri N., *Russian Culture at the Crossroads: Paradoxes of Postcommunist Consciousness,* Boulder, CO; Oxford, 1996.

Shatz, Marshall and Judith E. Zimmerman, eds., *Landmarks (Vekhi): a Collection of Articles about the Russian Intelligentsia,* Armonk, NY, 1994.

Venturi, Franco, *Roots of Revolution,* New York, 1960.

Vernadsky, George, *A History of Russia,* 5 vols., New Haven, CT; London, 1987.

Vucinich, Alexander, *Science in Russian Culture, 1861–1917,* Stanford, CA, 1970.

Wachtel, Andrew, *An Obsession with History: Russian Writers Confront the Past,* Stanford, CA, 1994.

Weidle, Wladimir, *Russia: Absent and Present,* trans. A.Gordon Smith, New York, 1961.

West, James L. and Iurii A. Petrov, eds., *Merchant Moscow. Images of Russia's Vanished Bourgeoisie,* Princeton, NJ, 1998.

Zenkovsky, V., *A History of Russian Philosophy,* 2 vols., New York, 1953.

2 & 3 Language; religion

Benz, Ernst, *The Eastern Orthodox Church: Its Thought and Life*, New York, 1963.

Birnbaum, Henrik, *Common Slavic: Progress and Problems in its Reconstruction*, Cambridge, MA, 1979.

On Medieval and Renaissance Slavic Writing; Selected Essays, The Hague, 1974.

Birnbaum, H. and Peter Merill, *Recent Advances in the Reconstruction of Common Slavic. 1971–1982*, Columbus, OH, 1985.

Brumfield, W., *History of Russian Architecture*, Cambridge, 1993.

Chizhevsky, Dmitry. *History of Russian Literature from the Eleventh Century to the End of the Baroque*. Mouton: The Hague, 1960.

Comrie, Bernard, et al., *The Russian Language in the Twentieth Century*, 2nd edn., Oxford; New York, 1996.

Comrie, Bernard and G. Corbett, *The Slavonic Languages*, London; New York, 1993.

Comrie, Bernard, ed., *The World's Major Languages*, New York, 1987.

Conybeare, Frederick, *Russian Dissenters*, New York, 1962.

Crummey, Robert, *The Old Believers and the World of the Antichrist: The Vyg Community and the Russian State*, Madison, WI, 1970.

Danzas, Julia,*The Russian Church*, London, 1936.

DeBray, R. G. A., *Guide to the Slavonic Languages*, 3rd edn., Columbus, OH, 1980.

Elis, Jane, *The Russian Orthodox Church. Triumphalism and Defensiveness*, New York, 1996.

Fedotov, Georgii, *The Russian Religious Mind: Kievan Christianity, the Tenth to Thirteenth Centuries*, New York, 1946.

A Treasury of Russian Spirituality, London, 1952.

Fennell, John L. I. and Dimitri Obolensky, *A Historical Russian Reader: A Selection of Texts from the Eleventh to the Sixteenth Centuries*, Oxford, 1969.

Florovsky, Georges, *Ways of Russian Theology*, Belmont, MA, 1979.

French, Robert, *The Eastern Orthodox Church*, London, 1951.

Gorodetzky, Nadezhda, *The Humiliated Christ in Modern Russian Literature*, London, 1938.

Grunwald, Constantin de, *Saints of Russia*, London, 1960.

Hart, David K., *Topics in the Structure of Russian: An Introduction to Russian Linguistics*, Columbus, OH, 1996.

Jakobson, Roman, *Russian and Slavic Grammar Studies. 1931–1981*, eds. Linda Waugh and Morris Halle, Berlin; New York, 1984.

Lenhoff, Gail, *The Martyred Princes Boris and Gleb: A Sociocultural Study of the Cult and the Texts,* Columbus, OH, 1989.

Nichols, Robert Lewis, ed., *Russian Orthodoxy under the Old Regime*, Minneapolis, MN, 1978.

Obolenskii, Dimitri, *The Byzantine Commonwealth: Eastern Europe, 500–1411,* Crestwood, NY, 1982.

Payne, Robert, *The Holy Fire: The Story of the Eastern Church*, London, 1958.

Powell, David E., *Antireligious Propaganda in the Soviet Union: A Study of Mass Persuasion*, Cambridge, MA; London, 1975.

Schenker, Alexander M., *The Dawn of Slavic. An Introduction to Slavic Philology*, New Haven, CT; London, 1996.

Schenker, Alexander M. and E. Stankiewicz, eds., *The Slavic Literary Languages: Formation and Development*, New Haven, CT; Columbus, OH, 1980.

The Visage of Russian Orthodoxy, Moscow, 1993.

Vlasto, A. P., *A Linguistic History of Russia to the End of the Eighteenth Century*, Oxford; New York, 1986.

Ware, Timothy, *The Orthodox Church. Intellectual History and Philosophy*, New York, 1993.

Warhola, James W., *Russian Orthodoxy and Political Culture Transformation*, Pittsburgh, PA, 1993.

Worth, Dean ed. *Slavic Linguistics, Poetics, Cultural History: in Honor of Henrik Birnbaum on his Sixtieth Birthday*, Columbus, OH, 1986.

The Formation of the Slavonic Literary Languages: Proceedings of a Conference held in Memory of Robert Auty and Ann Pennington*, Columbus, OH, 1985.

On the Structure and History of Russian: Selected Essays. Munich: 1977.

The Origins of Russian Grammar: Notes on the State of Russian Philology before the Advent of Printed Grammars. Columbus, OH, 1983.

Zenkovsky, Sergei A., ed., *Medieval Russia's Epics, Chronicles, and Tales*, New York, 1974.

Zernov, Nicholas, *Eastern Christendom*, London, 1961.

The Russian Religious Renaissance of the Twentieth Century, New York, 1963.

4 & 5 Asia; the West

Avins, Carol, *Border Crossings: The West and Russian Identity in Soviet Literature, 1917–1934*, Berkeley, CA, 1983.

Bassin, Mark, "Russia between Europe and Asia: The Ideological Construction of Geographical Space," *Slavic Review* 50 (Spring 1991), pp. 1–17.

"Inventing Siberia: Visions of the Russian East in the Early 19th Century," *American Historical Review* 96 (June 1991), pp. 763–94.

Becker, Seymour, "Russia between East and West: the Intelligentsia, Russian National Identity, and the Asian Borderlands," *Central Asian Review* 10:4 (1991), pp. 47–64.

Billington, James H., *The Icon and the Axe: An Interpretive History of Russian Culture*, New York, 1966.

Brower, Daniel and Edward J. Lazzerini eds., *Russia's Orient. Imperial Borderlands and Peoples. 1700–1917*, Bloomington, IN, 1997.

Chizhevsky, Dmitry, *Outline of Comparative Slavic Literatures*, Boston, 1952, 1983.

Clark, Katerina, *Petersburg, Crucible of Cultural Revolution*, Cambridge, MA, 1995.

Dallin, David J., *The Rise of Russia in Asia*, New Haven, 1949.

Halperin, Charles J., *Russia and the Golden Horde: The Mongol Impact on Medieval Russian History*, Bloomington, IN, 1985.

Hauner, Milan, *What is Asia to Us? Russia's Asian Heartland Yesterday and Today*, London, 1990.

Hoffman, Stefani H., "Scythianism: A Cultural Vision in Revolutionary Russia," Ph.D. thesis, Columbia University, New York, 1975.

Kerr, David, "The New Eurasianism: The Rise of Geopolitics in Russia's Foreign Policy," *Europe-Asia Studies* 47:6 (1995), pp. 977–88.

Lantzeff, George V. and Richard A. Pierce, *Eastward to Empire. Exploration and Conquest on the Russian Open Frontier, to 1750*, Montreal, 1973.

Layton, Susan, *Russian Literature and Empire: Conquest of the Caucasus from Pushkin to Tolstoy*, Cambridge, 1994.

Lobanov-Rostovsky, A., *Russia and Asia*, Ann Arbor, MI, 1965.

Monas, Sidney and Grigorii Z. Kaganov., *Images of space: St. Petersburg in the Visual and verbal arts*, CA, 1997.
Riasanovsky, Nicholas V. "Russia and Asia: Two 19th-Century Views," *California Slavic Studies* 1 (1960), pp. 170–81.
"The Emergence of Eurasianism," *California Slavic Studies* 4 (1967), pp. 39–72.
Russia and the West in the Teaching of the Slavophiles, Cambridge, MA, 1952.
Rogger, Hans, *National Consciousness in Eighteenth-Century Russia*, Cambridge, MA, 1960.
Sarkisyznz, Emanuel, "Russian Attitudes toward Asia," *Russian Review* 13 (October, 1954), pp. 245–54.
Russland und der Messianismus des Orients, Tübingen: 1955.
Schiebel, Joseph, "Aziatchina: The Controversy concerning the Nature of Russian Society and the Organization of the Bolshevik Party," Ph.D. thesis, University of Washington, Seattle, 1972.
Slezkine, Yuri, *Arctic Mirrors: Russia and the Small Peoples of the North*, Ithaca, NJ, 1994.
Solzhenitsyn, Aleksandr Isaevich, *A World Split Apart: Commencement Address Delivered at Harvard University, June 8, 1978*, trans. Irina Ilovayskaya Alberti, New York, 1978.
Rebuilding Russia: Reflections and Tentative Proposals, trans. and annotated Alexis Klimoff, New York, 1991.
Stephan, John J., "Asia in the Soviet Conception," in Donald S. Zagoria, ed., *Soviet Policy in East Asia*, New Haven, CT, pp. 29–56.
Treadgold, Donald W. ,*The West in Russia and China : Religious and Secular Thought in Modern Times*, 2 vols., Cambridge; New York, 1973.
Trubetzkoy, Nikolai S., *The Legacy of Ghengis Khan and other Essays on Russia's Identity*, trans. Anatoly Liberman, Ann Arbor, MI, 1991.
Utechin, S. V., "The Russians in Relation to Europe and Asia," in Raghavah Iyer, ed., *The Glass Curtain between Asia and Europe*, London, 1965, pp. 87–101.
Vucinich, Wayne S., ed., *Russia and Asia: Essays on the Influence of Russia on the Asian Peoples*, Stanford, CA, 1972.
Wittfogel, Karl, "Russia and the East: A Comparison and Contrast," *Slavic Review* 22 (December 1963), pp. 627–56.
Wren, Melvin, *The Western Impact upon Tsarist Russia*, Chicago, 1971.

6 Ideological structures

Berlin, Isaiah, *Russian Thinkers,* ed. Henry Hardy and Aileen Kelly, London, 1978.
Boym, Svetlana, *Common Places: Mythologies of Everyday Life in Russia*, Cambridge, MA, 1994.
Cherniavsky, Michael, *Tsar and the People: Studies in Russian Myths*, New Haven, CT, 1961.
Chizhevsky, Dmitry, *Russian Intellectual History*, trans. John C. Osborn and Martin P. Rice, Ann Arbor, MI, 1978.
Clowes, Edith, Samuel D. Kassow and James L.West, *Between Tsar and People: Educated Society and the Quest for Public Identity in Late Imperial Russia*, Princeton, NJ, 1991.
Dunham, Vera, *In Stalin's Time: Middleclass Values in Soviet Fiction*, Cambridge, 1976.
Edie, James, James P. Scanlan, and Mary-Barbara Zeldin, *Russian Philosophy*, 3 vols., Chicago, 1965.
Engelstein, Laura, *The Keys to Happiness: Sex and the Search for Modernity in Fin-de-Siecle Russia*, Ithaca, NY, 1992.

Fitzpatrick, Sheila, *The Cultural Front: Power and Culture in Revolutionary Russia*, Ithaca, NY, 1992.

Florovsky, Georges, *Ways of Russian Theology*, Belmont, MA, 1979.

Frank, Joseph, *Dostoevsky*, 5 vols., Princeton, NJ, 1976–   .

Gleason, Abbott, *Young Russia*, New York, 1980.

Gleason, Abbott, Peter Kenez, and Richard Stites, eds., *Bolshevik Culture: Experiment and Order in the Russian Revolution*, Bloomington, IN, 1985.

Jones, W. Gareth, *Nikolay Novikov: Enlightener of Russia*, Cambridge, 1984.

Kuvakin, Valery A., *A History of Russia and Philosophy, From the Tenth Through the Twentieth Centuries*, 2 vols., Buffalo, NY, 1994.

Leatherbarrow, W. J., and D. C. Offord, eds. and trans., *A Documentary History of Russian Thought from the Enlightenment to Marxism*, Ann Arbor, MI, 1987.

Malia, Martin, *Alexander Herzen and the Birth of Russian Socialism*, Cambridge, MA, 1961.

The Soviet tragedy: a History of Socialism in Russia, 1917–1991, New York; Toronto, 1994.

Marker, Gary, *Publishing, Printing, and the Origins of Intellectual Life in Russia, 1700–1800*, Princeton, NJ, 1985.

Parthé, Kathleen, *Russian Village Prose: The Radiant Past*, Princeton, NJ, 1992.

Raeff, Marc, *Origins of the Russian Intelligentsia: The Eighteenth-Century Nobility*, New York, 1966.

Russian Intellectual History: an Anthology, New York, 1966.

Riasanovsky, Nicholas, *Nicholas I and Official Nationality in Russia, 1825–1855*, Berkeley and Los Angeles, CA, 1961.

Rogger, Hans, *National Consciousness in Eighteenth-Century Russia*, Cambridge, MA, 1960.

Rzhevsky, Nicholas, *Russian Literature and Ideology*, Urbana, IL, 1983.

Scanlan, James, *Russian Thought After Communism: the Recovery of a Philosophical Heritage*, Armonk, NY, 1994.

Stites, Richard, *The Women's Liberation Movement in Russia: Feminism, Nihilism and Bolshevism 1860–1930*, Princeton, NJ, 1978.

Revolutionary Dreams: Utopian Vision and Experimental Life in the Russian Revolution, New York, 1989.

Tumarkin, Nina, *The Living and the Dead: The Rise and Fall of the Cult of World War II in Russia*, New York, 1994.

Venturi, Franco, *Roots of Revolution*, New York, 1960.

Walicki, Andrej, *A History of Russian Thought from the Enlightenment to Marxism*, Stanford, CA, 1979.

The Slavophile Controversy, Oxford, 1975.

Zernov, Nicholas, *The Russian Religious Renaissance of the Twentieth Century*, New York, 1963.

7 Popular culture

Editions of primary material

Afanas'ev, A. N., *Erotic Tales of Old Russia*, trans. Yury Perkov, Oakland, CA, 1980.

Alexander, A. E., *Russian Folklore: An Anthology in English Translation*, Belmont, MA, 1975.

Bonnell, Victoria, ed., *The Russian Worker*, Berkeley, CA, 1983.

The Domostroi: Rules for Russian Households in the Time of Ivan the Terrible, trans. and ed. Carolyn Johnston Pouncy, Ithaca, NY, 1994.

Sadovnikov, D., *Riddles of the Russian People*, trans. Ann C. Bigelow, Ann Arbor, MI, 1986.
Silent Witnesses (10 videocassettes of early Russian films), London, British Film Institute, 1992.
Sytova, Alla, ed., *The Lubok: Russian Folk Pictures Seventeenth to Nineteenth Century*, Leningrad, 1984.
Taylor, Richard, and Ian Christie, eds., *The Film Factory: Russian and Soviet Cinema in Documents, 1896–1939*, London, 1988.
Warner, Elizabeth, *Heroes, Monsters and Other Worlds from Russian Mythology*, London, 1985.
Warner, Elizabeth, and Kustovskii, Viktor, *Russian Traditional Folksong*, Hull, 1990 (includes audio cassette).

Studies
General

Balzer, Marjorie Mandelstam, ed., *Russian Traditional Culture: Religion, Gender and Customary Law*, Armonk, NY, 1992.
Bonnell, Victoria E., ed., *Roots of Rebellion: Workers' Politics and Organizations in St. Petersburg and Moscow, 1900–1914*, Berkeley, CA, 1983.
Brower, Daniel, *The Russian City: Between Tradition and Modernity*, Berkeley, CA, 1990.
Bushnell, John, *Mutiny amid Repression: Russian Soldiers in the Revolution of 1905*, Bloomington, IN, 1985.
Engel, Barbara, *Between the Fields and the City: Women, Work and Family in Russia 1861–1914*, Cambridge, 1994.
Engelgardt, Aleksandr Nikolaevich, *Letters from the Country 1872–1887*, trans. and ed. Cathy A. Frierson, New York, 1994.
Engelstein, Laura, *Moscow 1905*, Stanford, CA, 1982.
Frank, Stephen P. and Steinberg, Mark D., eds., *Cultures in Flux: Lower-Class Values, Practices, and Resistance in Late Imperial Russia*, Princeton, NJ, 1994.
Glickman, Rose L., *Russian Factory Women: Workplace and Society, 1880–1914*, Berkeley, CA, 1984.
Johnson, Robert E., *Peasant and Proletarian: The Working Class of Moscow in the Late Nineteenth Century*, New Brunswick, NJ, 1979.
Kenez, Peter, *The Birth of the Propaganda State: Soviet Methods of Mass Mobilization 1917–1929*, Cambridge, 1985.
Koenker, Diane, *Moscow Workers and the 1917 Revolution*, Princeton, NJ, 1981.
Oinas, Felix J., *Essays in Russian Folklore and Mythology*, Columbus, OH, 1985.
Oinas, Felix J. and Soudakoff, Stephen, eds., *The Study of Russian Folklore*, The Hague, 1975.
Perrie, Maureen, *The Image of Ivan the Terrible in Russian Folklore*, Cambridge, 1987.
Propp, Vladimir, *Theory and History of Folklore*, trans. Aridne Y. Martin and Richard P. Martin, Manchester, 1984.
Smith, S. A., *Red Petrograd: Revolution in the Factories 1917–1918*, Cambridge, 1985.
Stites, Richard, *Russian Popular Culture: Entertainment and Society since 1900*, Cambridge, 1992.

Special topics

Brooks, Jeffrey, *When Russia Learned to Read: Literacy and Popular Literature, 1861–1917*, Princeton, NJ, 1985.

Bushnell, John, *Moscow Graffiti: Language and Subculture,* Boston, 1990.

Kelly, Catriona, *Petrushka, the Russian Carnival Puppet Theatre,* Cambridge, 1990.

McReynolds, Louise, *The News under Russia's Old Regime: The Development of a Mass-Circulation Press,* Princeton, NJ, 1991.

Mally, Lynn, *Culture of the Future: The Proletkult Movement in Revolutionary Russia,* Berkeley, CA, 1990.

Mehnert, Klaus, *The Russians and their Favorite Books,* Stanford, CA, 1983.

Neuberger, Joan, *Hooliganism: Crime, Culture, and Power in St. Petersburg, 1900–1914,* Berkeley, CA, 1993.

Propp, Vlamimir, *Morphology of the Folk Tale,* trans. Laurence Scott, ed. Louis A. Wagner, Austin, TX, 1968.

Smith, G. S., *Songs to Seven Strings: A History of Russian Guitar Poetry,* Bloomington, IN, 1985.

Smith, R. E. F. and David Christian, *Bread and Salt: A Social and Economic History of Food and Drink in Russia,* Cambridge, 1984.

Stites, Richard, *Revolutionary Dreams: Utopian Vision and Experimental Life in the Russian Revolution,* Oxford, 1989.

Thurston, Gary, "The Impact of Russian Popular Theater, 1886–1915," *Journal of Modern History* 55 (June 1983), pp. 237–67.

Warner, Elizabeth, *The Russian Folk Theatre,* The Hague, 1977.

Folk Theatre and Dramatic Entertainments in Russia, Cambridge, 1987.

White, Stephen, *The Soviet Political Poster,* New Haven, CT, 1988.

Youngblood, Denise, *Movies for the Masses: Soviet Popular Cinema in the Twenties,* Cambridge, 1993.

Soviet Cinema in the Silent Era, Ann Arbor, MI, 1985.

Zguta, Russell, *Russian Minstrels: A History of the Skomorokhi,* Oxford, 1978.

8 Literature

Anthologies

Brown, Clarence, ed., *The Portable Twentieth-Century Russian Reader,* London, 1993.

Gibian, George, ed., *The Portable Nineteenth-Century Russian Reader,* New York, 1993.

Rzhevsky, Nicholas, ed., *An Anthology of Russian Literature: Introduction to a Culture,* Armonk, NY, 1996.

Studies

Avins, Carol, *Border Crossings: The West and Russian Identity in Soviet Literature, 1917–1934,* Berkeley, CA, 1983.

Barnes, Christopher, *Boris Pasternak: A Literary Biography,* vol. I, Cambridge, 1989.

Bayley, John, *Pushkin: A Comparative Commentary,* Cambridge, 1971.

Beaujour, Elizabeth, *The Invisible Land: A Study of the Artistic Imagination of Iurii Olesha,* New York, 1970.

Bethea, David M., *Joseph Brodsky and the Creation of Exile,* Princeton, NJ, 1994.

The Shape of Apocalypse in Modern Russian Fiction, Princeton, NJ, 1989.

Boyd, Brian, *Nabokov,* 2 vols., Princeton, NJ, 1990–91.

Boym, Svetlana, *Death in Quotation Marks: Cultural Myths of the Modern Poet,* Cambridge, MA, 1991.

Bristol, Evelyn, *A History of Russian Poetry,* Oxford, 1991.

Brown, Clarence, *Mandelstam*, Cambridge, 1973.

Brown, Deming, *The Last Years of Soviet Russian Literature: Prose Fiction 1975–1991*, Cambridge, 1993.

Soviet Russian Literature Since Stalin, Cambridge, 1978.

Brown, E. J., *Mayakovsky: A Poet in the Revolution*, Princeton, NJ, 1973.

Russian Literature Since the Revolution, revised edn., Cambridge, MA, 1982.

Brown, William Edward, *A History of Russian Literature of the Romantic Period*, 4 vols., Ann Arbor, MI, 1986.

Carden, Patricia, *The Art of Isaac Babel*, Ithaca, NY, 1972.

Cavanagh, Clare, *Osip Mandelstam and the Modernist Creation of Tradition*, Princeton, NJ, 1995.

Chances, Ellen, *Andrei Bitov: The Ecology of Inspiration*, Cambridge, 1993.

Clark, Katerina, *The Soviet Novel: History as Ritual*, Chicago, 1981.

Cooke, Raymond, *Velimir Khlebnikov: A Critical Study*, Cambridge, 1987.

Costlow, Jane, *Worlds Within Worlds: The Novels of Ivan Turgenev*, Princeton, NJ, 1990.

Debreczeny, Paul, *Social Functions of Literature: Alexander Pushkin and Russian Culture*, Stanford, CA, 1997.

Driver, Sam, *Anna Akhmatova*, New York, 1972.

Ehre, Milton, *Oblomov and His Creator: The Life and Art of Ivan Goncharo*, Princeton, NJ, 1974.

Elsworth, John, *Andrey Bely: A Critical Study of the Novels*, Cambridge, 1983.

Erlich, Victor, *Modernism and Revolution: Russian Literature in Transition*, Cambridge, MA, 1994.

Ermolaev, Herman, *Mikhail Sholokhov and His Art*, Princeton, NJ, 1982.

Soviet Literary Theories 1917–1934: The Genesis of Socialist Realism Berkeley, CA, 1963.

Fanger, Donald, *Dostoevsky and Romantic Realism: A Study of Dostoevsky in Relation to Balzac, Dickens, and Gogol*, Cambridge, MA, 1965.

The Creation of Nikolai Gogol, Cambridge, MA, 1979.

Fitzpatrick, Sheila, ed., *Cultural Revolution in Russia, 1928–1931*, Bloomington, IN, 1984.

Fleishman, Lazar, *Boris Pasternak: The Poet and His Politics*, Cambridge, MA, 1990.

Frank, Joseph, *Dostoevsky*, 5 vols., Princeton, NJ, 1976– .

Freeborn, Richard, *The Rise of the Russian Novel: Studies in the Russian Novel from 'Eugene Onegin' to War and Peace*, Cambridge, 1973.

Turgenev: The Novelist's Novelist. A Study, London, 1960.

Fusso, Susanne, *Designing Dead Souls: An Anatomy of Disorder in Gogol*, Stanford, CA, 1993.

Garrard, John, ed., *The Russian Novel from Pushkin to Pasternak*, New Haven, CT, 1983.

Gillespie, David, *Iurii Trifonov: Unity through Time*, Cambridge, 1992.

Ginzburg, Lydia, *On Psychological Prose*, trans. Judson Rosengrant, Princeton, NJ, 1991.

Goscilo, Helena, ed., *Fruits of Her Plume: Essays on Contemporary Russian Women's Culture*, Armonk, NY, 1993.

Gregg, Richard, *Fedor Tiutchev: The Evolution of a Poet*, New York, 1965.

Grossman, Joan Delaney, *Valery Bryusov and the Riddle of Russian Decadence*, Berkeley, CA, 1985.

Gustafson, Richard, *The Imagination of Spring: The Poetry of Afanasy Fet*, New Haven, CT, 1966.

Heldt, Barbara, *Terrible Perfection: Women and Russian Literature*, Bloomington, IN, 1987.

Hoisington, Sona Stephan, ed., *A Plot of Her Own: The Female Protagonist in Russian Literature*, Evanston, IL, 1995.

Holmgren, Beth, *Women's Work in Stalin's Time: On Lidiia Chukovskaia and Nadezhda Mandelstam*, Bloomington, IN, 1993.

Hosking, Geoffrey, *Beyond Socialist Realism: Soviet Fiction Since Ivan Denisovich*, London, 1980.

Hubbs, Joanna, *Mother Russia: The Feminine Myth in Russian Culture*, Bloomington, IN, 1988.

Jackson, Robert Louis, *Dostoevsky's Quest for Form*, New Haven, CT, 1966.

Karlinsky, Simon, *Marina Tsvetaeva: The Woman, Her World and Her Poetry*, Cambridge, 1986.

Kelly, Catriona, *A History of Russian Women's Writing 1820–1992*, Oxford, 1994.

Kornblatt, Judith Deutsch, *The Cossack Hero in Russian Literature: A Study in Cultural Mythology*, Madison, WI, 1992.

Layton, Susan, *Russian Literature and Empire: Conquest of the Caucasus from Pushkin to Tolstoy*, Cambridge, 1994.

Ledkovsky, Marina, et al., eds., *Dictionary of Russian Women Writers*, Westport, CT, 1994.

Maguire, Robert, *Red Virgin Soil: Soviet Literature of the 1920s*, Princeton, NJ, 1968.

Exploring Gogol. Stanford, CA, 1994.

Markov, Vladimir, *Russian Futurism: A History*, Berkeley, CA, 1968.

Masing-Delic, Irene, *Abolishing Death: A Salvation Myth of Russian Twentieth-Century Literature*, Stanford, CA, 1992.

Matthewson, Rufus, Jr., *The Positive Hero in Russian Literature*, 2nd edn., Stanford, CA, 1975.

McLean, Hugh, *Nikolai Leskov: The Man and His Art*, Cambridge, MA, 1977.

Mersereau, John, Jr., *Mikhail Lermontov*, Carbondale, IL, 1962.

Milne, Lesley, *Mikhail Bulgakov: A Critical Biography*, Cambridge, 1990.

Mirsky, D. S., *A History of Russian Literature From its Beginnings to 1900*, New York, 1958.

Morris, Marcia A., *Saints and Revolutionaries: The Ascetic Hero in Russian Literature*, Albany, NY, 1993.

Morson, Gary, *The Boundaries of Genre: Dostoevsky's Diary of a Writer and the Traditions of Literary Utopia*, Austin, TX, 1981.

Hidden in Plain View: Narrative and Creative Potentials in War and Peace, Stanford, CA, 1987.

Moser, Charles, *Esthetics as Nightmare: Russian Literary Theory 1855–1870*, Princeton, NJ, 1989.

Moser, Charles, ed., *The Cambridge History of Russian Literature*, revised edn., Cambridge, 1992.

Murav, Harriet, *Holy Foolishness: Dostoevsky's Novels and the Poetics of Cultural Critique*, Stanford, CA, 1992.

Nepomnyashchy, Catharine Theimer, *Abram Tertz and the Poetics of Crime*, New Haven, CT, 1995.

O'Toole, Lawrence, *Structure, Style and Interpretation in the Russian Short Story*, New Haven, CT, 1982.

Pachmuss, Temira, *Zinaida Hippius: An Intellectual Profile*, Carbondale, IL, 1971.

Parthe, Kathleen F., *Russian Village Prose: The Radiant Past*, Princeton, NJ, 1992.

Poggioli, Renato, *The Poets of Russia, 1890–1930*, Cambridge, MA, 1960.

Pyman, Avril, *The Life of Alexander Blok*, 2 vols., Oxford, 1979–80.

Sandler, Stephanie, *Distant Pleasures: Alexander Pushkin and the Writing of Exile*, Stanford, CA, 1989.

Scammell, Michael, *Solzhenitsyn: A Biography*, New York, 1984.
Scherr, Barry, *Maxim Gorky*, Boston, 1988.
   Russian Poetry: Meter, Rhythm, and Rhyme, Berkeley, CA, 1986.
Seifrid, Thomas, *Andrei Platonov*, Cambridge, 1992.
Shane, Alex, *The Life and Works of Evgenij Zamjatin*, Berkeley, CA, 1968.
Shneidman, N., *Soviet Literature in the 1980s: Decade of Transition*, Toronto, 1989.
Slobin, Greta N., *Remizov's Fictions 1900–1921*, DeKalb, IL, 1991.
Terras, Victor, *Belinskij and Russian Literary Criticism: The Heritage of Organic Esthetics*,
   Madison, WI, 1974.
Terras, Victor, ed., *A Handbook of Russian Literature*, New Haven, CT, 1985.
Tertz, Abram, *On Socialist Realism*, New York, 1961.
Todd, William Mills, III, *Fiction and Society in the Age of Pushkin: Ideology, Institutions, and
   Narrative*, Cambridge, MA, 1986.
Wachtel, Andrew, *The Battle for Childhood: Creation of a Russian Myth*, Stanford, CA, 1990.
Wasiolek, Edward, *Dostoevsky: The Major Fiction*, Cambridge, MA, 1964.
   Tolstoy's Major Fiction, Chicago, 1978.
Woodward, James, *Ivan Bunin: A Study of His Fiction*, Chapel Hill, NC, 1980.
Ziolkowski, Margaret, *Hagiography and Modern Russian Literature*, Princeton, NJ, 1988.

9 Art

General reference works

Milner, J., *A Dictionary of Russian and Soviet Artists,* Woodbridge, 1993.

General histories with sections on the nineteenth century

Auty, R. and D. Obolensky, eds., *Companion to Russian Studies. 3. An Introduction to Russian
   Art and Architecture*, Cambridge, 1980.
Billington, J., ed., *The Horizon Book of the Arts of Russia*, New York, 1970.
Bird, A., *A History of Russian Painting*, Oxford, 1987.
Brumfield, W., *History of Russian Architecture* , Cambridge, 1993.
Moscow. Treasures and Traditions. Catalog of exhibition circulated by the Smithsonian
   Traveling Exhibition Service, Washington, DC, 1990.
Rice, T. Talbot, *A Concise History of Russian Art*, London; New York, 1963.
Sarabianov, D., *Russian Art. From Neo-Classicism to the Avant-Garde*, London, 1990.
Valkenier, E., *Russian Realist Art : the State and Society : the Peredvizhniki and their Tradition* ,
   New York, 1989.
   Ilya Repin and the World of Russian art, New York, 1990.

Modernism

Anikst, M. and E. Chernevich, *Russian Graphic Design 1880–1917,* New York, 1990.
Art and Revolution, Catalog of exhibition at the Seibu Museum of Art, Tokyo, 1982.
Art and Revolution II, Catalog of exhibition at the Seibu Museum of Art, Tokyo,1987.
The Avant-Garde in Russia 1910–1930. New Perspectives. Catalog of exhibition at the Los
   Angeles County Museum, Los Angeles; and the Hirshhorn Museum and
   Sculpture Garden, Washington, DC, 1980–81.
Borisova, E. and G. Sternin, *Russian Art Nouveau,* New York, 1988.
Bowlt, J., *The Russian Avant-Garde: Theory and Criticism 1902–34,* New York, 1976.

The Silver Age. Russian Art of the Early Twentieth Century and the "World of Art" Group, Newtonville, MA, 1979.

Bowlt, J. and N. Misler, *The Thyssen-Bornemisza Collection: Twentieth Century Russian and East European Painting*, London, 1993.

Brumfield, W., *The Origins of Modernism in Russian Architecture*, Berkeley, CA, 1991.

Compton, S., *The World Backwards. Russian Futurist Books 1912–16*, London, 1978.

Elliott, D., *New Worlds. Russian Art and Society 1900–1937*, London, 1986.

Gray, C., *The Russian Experiment in Art: 1863–1922*, revised edn., London, 1986.

The Great Utopia. The Russian and Soviet Avant-Garde 1915–1932. Catalog, New York, Solomon R. Guggenheim Museum, 1992–93.

Howard, J., *The Union of Youth*, Manchester, 1992.

Janecek, G., *The Look of Russian Literature. Avant-Garde Experiments 1900–1930*, Princeton, NJ, 1984.

Jewish Artists in Russia and the Soviet Union, 1890–1988. Catalog of exhibition at the Jewish Museum, New York, and other cities, 1995–96.

Lodder, C., *Russian Constructivism*, New Haven, CT, 1983.

Paris–Moscou 1900–1930. Catalog of exhibition at the Centre Pompidou, Paris, and the Pushkin Museum of Fine Arts, Moscow, 1979–81.

Roman, G. and V. Marquardt, eds., *The Avant-Garde Frontier. Russia Meets the West, 1910–1930*, Gainesville, Florida, FL, 1992.

Rudenstine, A., S. F. Starr, and G. Costakis, eds., *Russian Avant-Garde Art: The George Costakis Collection*, New York, 1981.

Twilight of the Tsars. Catalog of exhibition, Hayward Gallery, London, 1991.

Soviet Period

Anikst, M., ed., *Soviet Graphic Design of the Twenties*, New York, 1987.

Banks, M., ed., *The Aesthetic Arsenal: Socialist Realism under Stalin*, New York; and Moscow, 1993.

Bown, M. C. and B. Taylor, eds., *Art of the Soviets*, Manchester, 1993.

Golomshtok, I., *Totalitarian Art*, London, 1990.

Khan-Magomedov, S., *Pioneers of Soviet Architecture*, New York, 1987.

Taylor, B., *Art and Literature under the Bolsheviks*, London, 1991.

Tolstoy, V., I. Bibikova, and C. Cooke, *Street Art of the Revolution*, London, 1990.

10 Music

Abraham, Gerald, et al., *The New Grove Russian Masters 2: Rimsky-Korsakov, Skryabin, Rakhmaninov, Prokofiev, Shostakovich*, New York, 1986.

Bowers, Faubion, *Scriabin, a Biography*, 2nd edn., New York, 1996.

Brown, David, *Tchaikovsky Remembered*, Portland, OR, 1994.

Brown, David, et al., *The New Grove Russian Masters 1: Glinka, Borodin, Balakirev, Musorgsky, Tchaikovsky*, New York, 1986.

Campbell, Stuart, ed., *Russians on Russian Music, 1830–1880: An Anthology*, Cambridge, 1994.

Gordon, Stewart, *A History of Keyboard Literature: Music for the Piano and its Forerunners*, New York, 1996.

Haimo, Ethan, and Paul Johnson, eds., *Stravinsky Retrospectives*, Lincoln, NE, 1987.

Holden, Anthony, *Tchaikovsky: a Biography*, New York, 1996.

Martyn, Barrie, *Nicholas Medtner: His Life and Music*. Brookefield, VT, 1995.

Moldon, David, *A Bibliography of Russian Composers*, London, 1976.

Morosan, Vladimir, *Choral Performance in Pre-revolutionary Russia*, Madison, CT, 1994.

Newmarch, Rosa, *The Russian Opera*, Westport, CT, 1972.

Norris, Geoffrey, *Rachmaninoff*, New York, 1994.

Norris, Jeremy, *The Russian Piano Concerto*, Bloomington, IN, 1994.

Orlova, Alexandra, ed., *Musorgsky Remembered*, Bloomington, IN, 1991.

Poznansky, Alexander, *Tchaikovsky's Last Days: a Documentary Study*, Oxford, 1996.

Prokofiev, Sergei, *Selected Letters of Sergei Prokofiev*, Harlow Robinson, ed., Boston, 1998.

Ridenour, Robert, *Nationalism, Modernism and Personal Rivalry in Nineteenth Century Russian Music*. Ann Arbor, MI, 1981.

Roberts, Peter, *Modernism in Russian Piano Music: Scriabin, Prokofiev and their Russian Counterparts*, Bloomington, IN, 1993.

Robinson, Harlow, *Sergei Prokofiev: a Biography*, New York, 1987.

Schwartz, Boris, *Music and Musical Life in Soviet Russia: 1917–1981*, Bloomington, IN, 1983.

Seaman, Gerald, *History of Russian Music*, Oxford, 1967.

Sitsky, Larry, *Music of the Repressed Russian Avant-garde 1900–1929*, Westport, CT, 1994.

Taruskin, Richard, *Defining Russia Musically: Historical and Hermeneutical Essays*, Princeton, NJ, 1997.

  Stravinsky and the Russian Traditions: a Biography of the Works through Mavra, Oxford, 1996.

  Opera and Drama in Russia as Preached and Practiced in the 1860s, Ann Arbor, MI, 1981.

Wilson, Elizabeth, *Shostakovich: a Life Remembered*, Princeton, NJ, 1994.

Discography and scores

Bastable, Graham, ed., *Twelve Songs for Voice and Piano/A. P. Borodin*, New York:, 1994. 1 score.

Dmitri Pokrovsky Singers, *Les noces*, New York, 1994. 1 sound disc, digital.

Dolskaya, Olga, trans. and ed., *Vasily Titov and the Russian Baroque: Selected Choral Works*, Madison,CT, 1995.

Levasev, Evgenij, ed., *Complete Works/M. P. Mussorgsky*, The Institute of the Russian Federation for the Study of the Arts. Moscow, 1996. 1 score.

Lewin, Michael, *A Russian Piano Recital*, Baton Rouge, LA, 1992. 1 sound disc.

Morosan, Vladimir and Alexander Ruggieri, eds., *All-night Vigil: opus 37/Sergei Rachmaninoff*, Madison, CT, 1992.

Morosan, Vladimir, ed., *One Thousand Years of Russian Church Music, 988–1988*, Washington, DC , 1991.

  Ten Sacred Choruses/P. I. Tchaikovsky, Madison,CT, 1993.

  The Complete Sacred Choral Works/P. I. Tchaikovsky, Madison, CT, 1996. 1 score.

Morris, Richard, *Fugues, Fantasia and Variations*, New York, 1994. 1 sound disc, digital.

Nikitin, Sergei, *Vremena ne vybiraiut: pesni*, Moscow, 1994.

Rachmaninoff, Sergei, *The Complete Sacred Choral Works*, Madison, CT, 1994. 1 sound disc.

  Russische Rhapsodie: fur 2 klaviere vierhandig, Hamburg; New York, 1994.

Shostakovich, D. D., *Anti-Formalist Rayok for Reader, 4 Basses and Mixed Chorus with Piano Accompaniment*, London, 1991. 1 score.

Stravinsky, Igor, *Songs*, Moscow, 1993. 1 sound disc.

Yarbrough, Joan and Robert Cowan, eds., *Capriccio on Russian Themes: for 1 Piano, 4 Hands/M. Glinka*, New York, 1992.

11 Theatre

Alpers, Boris, *The Theatre of the Social Mask*, trans. M. Schmidt, New York 1934.

Baer, Nancy Van Norman, ed., *Theatre in Revolution: Russian Avant-garde Stage Design 1913–1935*, New York, 1991.

Bakshy, Alexander, *The Path of the Modern Russian Stage, and Other Essays*, London, 1916.

Benedetti, Jean Norman, *Stanislavski. A Biography*, London, 1988.

Benedetti, Jean Norman, ed. and trans., *The Moscow Art Theatre Letters*, New York 1991.

"Bibliography of Articles on Soviet Theatre 1955–1980," in Alma H. Law and C. Peter Goslette, eds., *Soviet Plays in Translation: an Annotated Bibliography*, New York,1981.

Bowers, Faubion, *Broadway U.S.S.R. Ballet, Theatre and Entertainment in Russia Today*, New York, 1959.

Braun, Edward, *Meyerhold, a Revolution in the Theatre*, London, 1995.

Braun, Edward, ed. and trans., *Meyerhold on Theatre*, London, 1969.

Brown, Ben W., *Theatre at the Left*, Providence, RI, 1938.

Carnicke, Sharon M., *The Theatrical Instinct: Nikolaj Evreinov and the Russian Theatre of the Early Twentieth Century*, New York, 1989.

Carter, Huntley, *The New Spirit in the Russian Theatre, 1917–28*, London, 1929.

Chaliapin, Fedor I., *Chaliapin. An Autobiography as Told to Maxim Gorky, with Supplementary Correspondence and Notes*, trans., comp. and ed. Nina Froud and James Hanley, New York, 1967.

Cherkasov, Nikolay, *Notes of a Soviet actor*, Moscow, 1953.

Clayton, J. Douglas, *Pierrot in Petrograd. Commedia dell arte/balagan in Twentieth-century Russian Theatre and Drama*, Montreal and Kingston, 1993.

Dana, H. W. L., *Drama in Wartime Russia*, New York, 1943.

Handbook of Soviet Drama, New York, 1938.

Davidow, Mike, *People's Theater: From the Box Office to the Stage*, Moscow, 1977.

The Drama Review 57 (March 1973), Russian issue; 68 (December 1975), eccentrism issue; 99 (Fall 1983), Michael Chekhov issue. Other articles in issues of: Spring 1967, Winter 1968, Fall 1971, March 1974, September 74, June 1975, December 1977, December 1979, September 1980, and Spring 1982.

Evreinov, N., *The Theatre in Life*, ed. and trans. A. Nazaroff, London, 1927.

Fülöp-Miller, René and Joseph Gregor, *The Russian Theatre, its Character and History with a Special Reference to the Revolutionary Period*, trans. P. England, New York, 1978.

Geldern, James von, *Bolshevik festivals, 1917–1920*, Berkeley, CA, 1993.

Gerould, Daniel and Julia Przyboś, "Melodrama in the Soviet theater 1917–1928: an Annotated Chronology," in Daniel Gerould, ed., *Melodrama*, New York, 1980, pp. 75–92.

Gershkovich, Alexander, *The theater of Yuri Lyubimov: Art and Politics at the Taganka Theater in Moscow*, trans. Michael Yurieff, New York, 1989.

Golub, Spencer, *The Recurrence of Fate. Theatre and Memory in Twentieth-century Russia*, Iowa City, 1994.

Gorchakov, Nikolai A., *Stanislavski Directs*, trans. Miriam Goldina, New York, 1962.

The Theater in Soviet Russia, trans. Edgar Lehrman, New York, 1957.

Hoover, Marjorie L., *Meyerhold and his Set Designers*, New York, 1988.

Meyerhold – the Art of Conscious Theater, Amherst, MA, 1974.

Houghton, Norris, *Moscow Rehearsals: an Account of Methods of Production in the Soviet Theatre*, New York, 1936.

Return Engagement, New York, 1962.

Jelagin, Jury, *Taming the Arts*, trans. Nicholas Wreden, New York, 1951.

Karlinsky, Simon, *Russian Drama from its Beginnings to the Age of Pushkin*, Berkeley and Los Angeles, CA, 1985.

Kleberg, Lars, *Theatre as Action. Soviet Russian Avant-garde Aesthetics*, trans. Charles Rougle, London, 1993.

Kleberg, Lars and Nils Åke Nilsson, eds., *Theatre and Literature in Russia 1900–1930*, Stockholm, 1984.

Komisarjevsky, Theodore, *Myself and the Theatre*, London, 1929.

Komissarzhevsky, Viktor, *Moscow Theatres*, trans. V. Schneierman and W. Perelman, Moscow, 1959.

Leach, Robert, *Meyerhold*, Cambridge, 1988.

Macleod, Joseph, *Actors Cross the Volga: a Study of the Nineteenth Century Russian Theatre and of Soviet Theatres in War*, London, 1946.

The New Soviet Theatre, London, 1943.

Marc Chagall and the Jewish Theatre. Catalog, New York: Guggenheim Museum, 1992.

Markov, Pavel A., *The Soviet Theatre*, New York, 1935.

Marshall, Herbert, *The Pictorial History of the Russian Theatre*, New York, 1977.

Meyerhold at Work, ed. Paul Schmidt, trans. Paul Schmidt, L. Levin, and V. McGee, Austin, TX, 1980.

Morozov, Mikhail M, *Shakespeare on the Soviet Stage*, trans. David Magarshack, London, 1947.

Nemirovich-Danchenko, Vladimir, *My Life in the Russian Theatre*, trans. J. Cournos, London, 1937.

Polyakova, Elena, *Stanislavsky*, Moscow, 1983.

Rudnitsky, Konstantin, *Meyerhold the Director*, trans. G. Petrov, ed. S. Schultze, Ann Arbor, MI, 1981.

Russian and Soviet Theatre. Tradition and the Avant-garde, trans. R. Fermer, ed. L. Milne, London, 1988.

Russell, Robert and Andrew Barratt, eds., *Russian Theatre in the Age of Modernism*, London, 1990.

Russian and East European Performance (periodical; formerly *Newsnotes on Soviet and East European Drama and Theatre*).

Segel, Harold B., *Twentieth-century Russian Drama from Gorky to the Present*, 2nd edn., New York, 1994.

Senelick, Laurence, *Anton Chekhov* (Macmillan Modern Dramatists), New York, 1985.

Gordon Craig's Moscow Hamlet: a Reconstruction, Westport, CT, 1982.

Senelick, Laurence, ed. *National Theatre in Northern and Eastern Europe, 1746–1900. Theatre in Europe: a Documentary History*, Cambridge, 1991.

Wandering Stars: Russian Emigré Theatre, 1905–1940, Iowa City, 1992.

Senelick, Laurence, ed. and trans., *Russian Dramatic Theory from Pushkin to the Symbolists: an Anthology*, Austin, TX, 1981.

Shevstova, Maria, *The Theatre Practice of Anatoly Efros*, Devon, 1978.

Simonov, Ruben, *Stanislavsky's Protegé: Eugene Vakhtangov*, trans. Miriam Goldina, New York, 1969.

Slonim, Mark, *Russian Theatre from the Empire to the Soviets*, New York, 1961.

Smeliansky, Anatoly, *Is Comrade Bulgakov Dead?*, New York, 1994.

Soviet Theaters 1917–1941, ed. Martha Bradshaw, New York, 1954.

Stanislavsky, K. S., *My Life in Art*, trans. J. Robbins, Boston, 1924.

Stanislavsky on the Art of the Stage, ed. and trans. David Magarshack, New York, 1961.

Tairov, A., *Notes of a Director*, trans. W. Kuhlke, Coral Gables, FL, 1969.

Theater. Russian and Soviet Classics issue (Spring 1991).

Theater Three 10/11. Russian Theatre and Drama at the End issue (1992).

Toporkov, Vasily, *Stanislavsky in Rehearsal: the Final Years*, trans. Christine Edwards, New York, 1979.

Tovstonogov, Georgy, *The Profession of the Stage-director*, trans. B. Bean, Moscow, 1972.

Tulane Drama Review 9, 1 and 2 (Fall and Winter 1964). Stanislavsky issues.

Vakhtangov, Evgeny, *Evgeny Vakhtangov*, comp. Lyubov Vandrovskaya and Galina Kapterova, trans. Doris Bradbury, Moscow, 1982.

van Gyseghem, André, *Theatre in Soviet Russia*, London, 1944.

Varneke, B. V., *History of the Russian Theatre Seventeenth through Nineteenth Century*, trans. Boris Brasol, New York, 1951.

Warner, Lisa, *The Russian Folk Theatre*, The Hague, 1977.

World Theatre 8, 1. The actor and Stanislavski issue (Spring 1959).

  12, 2. Stanislavski issue (1963).

Worrall, Nick, *Modernism to Realism on the Soviet Stage: Tairov–Vakhtangov–Okhlopkov*, New York, 1989.

Yershov, Peter, *Comedy in the Soviet Theater*, New York, 1956.

12 Film

Aumont, Jacques, *Montage Eisenstein*, trans. Lee Hildreth, Constance Penley and Andrew Ross, Bloomington, IN, 1987.

Babitsky, Paul and John Rimberg, *The Soviet Film Industry*, New York, 1955.

Barna, Yon, *Eisenstein: The Growth of a Cinematic Genius*, trans. Lise Hunter, Bloomington, IN, 1973.

Birkos, Alexander S., *Soviet Cinema: Directors and Critics*, Hamden, CT, 1976.

Bordwell, David, *The Cinema of Eisenstein*, Cambridge, MA, 1993.

Brashinsky, Michael, and Andrew Horton, eds., *Russian Critics on the Cinema of Glasnost*, Cambridge, 1994.

Christie, Ian, and Richard Taylor, eds., *Eisenstein Rediscovered*, London, 1993.

Cohen, Louis H., *The Cultural-Political Traditions and Developments of the Soviet Cinema, 1917–72*, New York, 1974.

Dickenson, Thorold and Catherine de la Roche, *Soviet Cinema*. London, 1948. Reprint, New York, 1972.

Eisenstein, Sergei, *Film Form*, ed. and trans. Jay Leyda, New York, 1949.

  Film Sense, ed. and trans. Jay Leyda, New York, 1947.

Eisenstein, Sergei, V. I. Pudovkin, and G. V. Aleksandrov, "A Statement on the Sound Film," in *Film Sense*, pp. 257–59.

Golovskoy, Val S. and John Rimberg, *Behind the Soviet Screen. The Motion Picture Industry in the USSR, 1972–82*, Ann Arbor, MI, 1986.

Heil, J. T., "No List of Political Assets: The Collaboration of Iurii Olesha and Abram Room on *Strogii Iunosha*," *Slavistische Beiträge* 248 (December 1989).

Horton, Andrew and Michael Brashinsky, *The Zero Hour: Glasnost and Soviet Cinema in Transition*, Princeton, NJ, 1992.

Johnson, Vida T. and Graham Petrie, *The Films of Andrei Tarkovsky: A Visual Fugue*, Bloomington, IN, 1994.

Kepley, Vance, Jr., *In the Service of the State: The Cinema of Alexander Dovzhenko*, Madison, WI, 1986.

Kuleshov, Lev, *Kuleshov on Film: Writings of Lev Kuleshov*, trans. and ed. Ronald Levaco, Berkeley and Los Angeles, CA, 1974.

Lary, N. M., *Dostoevsky and Soviet Film*, Ithaca, NY, 1987.

Lawton, Anna, *Kinoglasnost: Soviet Cinema in Our Time*, Cambridge, 1992.

Lawton, Anna, ed., *The Red Screen, Politics, Society, Art in Soviet Cinema*, London, 1992.

Le Fanu, Mark, *The Cinema of Andrei Tarkovsky.*, London, 1987.

Leyda, Jay, *Kino: A History of the Russian and Soviet Film*, rev. ed. Princeton, NJ, 1983.

Leyda, Jay and Zina Voynow, *Eisenstein at Work*, New York, 1982.

Liehm, Mira and Antonin Liehm.,*The Most Important Art: Soviet and East European Film After 1945*, Berkeley and Los Angeles, CA, 1977.

Mayne, Judith, *Kino and the Woman Question: Feminism and Soviet Silent Film*, Columbus, OH, 1989.

Michelson, Annette, ed., *Kino-Eye: The Writings of Dziga Vertov*, trans. by Kevin O'Brien, Berkeley and Los Angeles, CA, 1984.

Nizhny, Vladimir, *Lessons With Eisenstein*, ed. and trans. Ivor Montagu, New York, 1962.

Pudovkin, V. I., *Film Technique and Film Acting*, trans. by Ivor Montagu, New York, 1949.

Schnitzer, Luda and Jean, and Marcel Martin, eds., *Cinema in Revolution*, trans. by David Robinson, New York, 1973.

Shlapentokh, Dmitry and Vladimir, *Soviet Cinematography 1918–1991: Ideological Conflict and Social Reality*, New York, 1993.

Tarkovsky, Andrei, *Sculpting in Our Time: Reflections on the Cinema*, trans. by Kitty Hunter-Blair, London, 1989.

Taylor, Richard and Ian Christie, eds., *Inside the Film factory: New Approaches to Russian and Soviet Cinema*, New York, 1991.

Taylor, Richard, ed. and trans., and Ian Christie, ed., *The Film Factory: Russian and Soviet Cinema in Documents 1896–1939*, Cambridge, MA, 1988.

Tsivian, Yuri, *Early Cinema in Russia and its Cultural Reception*, trans. Alan Bodger, London and New York, 1994.

Silent Film Witnesses: Russian Films, 1908–1919, Bloomington, IN, 1990.

Turovskaya, Maya, *Tarkovsky: Cinema as Poetry*, London, 1989.

Youngblood, Denise J., *Movies for the Masses: Popular Cinema and Soviet Society in the 1920s*, Cambridge, 1992.

A select filmography

1908   *Stenka Razin*, Drankov: Vladimir Romashkov.

1909   *Death of Ivan the Terrible* (Smert' Ivana Groznogo), Thiemann and
Reinhardt: Vasili Goncharov.

1910   *Peter the Great* (Petr Velikii), Pathé Frères: Vasili Goncharov. *The Idiot*
(Idiot), Khanzhonkov: Petr Chardynin.

1911   *L'khaim*, Pathé Frères: Maurice Maître and Kai Hansen. *Kreutzer Sonata*
(Kreitserova sonata), Khanzhonkov: Petr Chardynin. *The Convict's Song*
(Pesnia katorzhnika), Thiemann and Reinhardt: Iakov Protazanov.

1912   *The Beautiful Liukanida* (Prekrasnaia Liukanida), Khanzhonkov:
Wladyslaw Starewicz. *The Escape of the Grand Old Man* (Ukhod velikogo
cheloveka), Thiemann and Reinhardt: Protazanov and Elizaveta
Thiemann (with Vladimir Shaternikov as Tolstoy).

1913   *Tercentenary of the Romanov Dynasty* (Trekhsotletie tsarstvovaniia doma
Romanovykh), Drankov and Taldykin: Aleksandr Ural'sky (with
Evgeni Bauer as art director, Mikhail Chekhov as Tsar Mikhail
Fedorovich). *Keys to Happiness* (Kliuchi schast'ia), Thiemann and
Reinhardt: Protazanov and Vladimir Gardin. *Terrible Revenge*
(Strashnaia mest'), Khanzhonkov: Starewicz. *Christmas Eve* (Noch'
pered rozhdestvom), Khanzhonkov: Starewicz.

1914   *Drama in the Futurists' Cabaret No. 13* (Drama v kabare futuristov No. 13),
Toporkov and Winkler: Vladimir Kas'ianov. *Child of the Big City* (Ditia
bol'shogo goroda), Khanzhonkov: Evgeni Bauer. *Woman of Tomorrow*
(Zhenshchina zavtrashnego dnia), Khanzhonkov: Chardynin (with
Vera Iureneva, Ivan Mozzhukhin). *Chrysanthemums: The Tragedy of a
Ballerina* (Krizantemy: Tragediia baleriny), Khanzhonkov: Chardynin
(with Vera Karalli, Ivan Mozzhukhin).

1915   *Nikolai Stavrogin* (from Dostoevsky's *Devils*), Ermoliev: Protazanov
(with Mozzhukhin). *Tsar Ivan Vasil'evich Grozny*, Sharez: A Ivanov-Gai
(with Fedor Shaliapin). *The Picture of Dorian Gray* (Portret Doriana

Greia), Russian Golden Series: Vsevolod Meyerhold. *Lily: An Allegory of Today,* Skobelev Committee: Starewicz. *After Death,* Khanzhonkov: Bauer.

1916   *Peasant Lady* (Baryshnia-krestianka, from Pushkin's tale), Vengerov and Gardin: dir. Ol'ga Preobrazhenskaia. *Queen of Spades* (Pikovaia dama, from Puskin's story), Ermol'ev: Protazanov (with Mozzhukhin, Vera Orlova). *A Life for a Life* (Zhizn' za zhizn'), Khanzhonkov: Bauer (with Vera Kholodnaia).

1917   *Revolutionary* (Revoliutsioner), Khanzhonkov: Bauer. *Satan Triumphant* (Satana likuiushchii), Ermol'ev: Protazanov (with Mozzhukhin, Orlova). *The King of Paris* (Korol' Parizha), Khanzhonkov: Bauer (with Karalli).

1918   *The Lady and the Hooligan* (Baryshnia i khuligan) Neptune: Vladimir Maiakovsky. *Shackled by Film* (Zakovannaia filmoi), Neptune: Maiakovsky. *Father Sergius* (Otets Sergei), Ermol'ev: Protazanov (with Mozzhukhin, Orlova). *Kaliostro,* Rus': Starewicz (with Ol'ga Chekhova). *Engineer Prait's Project* (Proekt inzhenera Praita), Khanzhonkov: Lev Kuleshov.

1919   *Polikushka,* Rus': Aleksandr Sanin (with Ivan Moskvin). *The Queen's Secret* (Taina korolevy), Ermol'ev: Protazanov (with Mozzhukhin).

1920   *Mother* (Mat', from Gorky's novel), Mos-kino-committee: Aleksandr Razumny. *On the Red Front* (Na krasnom fronte), Kino Section, Moscow Soviet and VFKO: Kuleshov (with Leonid Obolensky and Aleksandra Khokhlova).

1921   *History of the Civil War* (Istoriia grazhdanskoi voiny), All-Russian Kino Committee: Dziga Vertov. *Hunger–Hunger–Hunger* (Golod … golod … golod), Gos-Kino School and VFKO: Vladimir Gardin and Vsevolod Pudovkin (cameraman, Eduard Tisse).

1922   *Film-Truth* (Kino-Pravda), Vertov, numbers produced 1922–25.

1923   *Red Imps* (Krasnye diavoliata), Kinosektsiia Narkomprosa Gruzii: Ivan Perestiani. *Locksmith and Chancellor* (Slesar' i kantsler), VUFKU: Gardin (script co-written with Pudovkin, from play by Anatoly Lunacharsky).

1924   *Aelita,* Mezhrabpom-Rus: Protazanov (script co-written with Fedor Otsep, from novel by A.N. Tolstoy). *The Extraordinary Adventures of Mr. West in the Land of the Bolsheviks* (Neobychainye prikliucheniia mistera Vesta v strane bol'shevikov), Goskino: Kuleshov (with Khokhlova, Pudovkin, Obolensky, Boris Barnet). *Adventures of Oktiabrina* (Pokhozhdeniia Oktiabriny), Sezapkino and FEKS: Grigory Kozintsev and Leonid Trauberg.

1925   *Leninist Film-Truth* (Leninskaia Kinopravda) = *Kino-Pravda,* No. 25, Kul'tkino: Vertov. *Strike* (Stachka), Goskino and Proletkult: Sergei Eisenstein. *Chess Fever* (Shakhmatnaia goriachka), Mezhrabpon-Rus:

Pudovkin (with Jose Raoul Capablanca, Protazanov). *Battleship Potemkin* (Bronenosets Potemkin): Goskino: Eisenstein.

1926 *The Overcoat* (Shinel'), Leningradkino: Kozintsev and Trauberg. *Mother* (Mat'),Mezhrabpom-Rus: Pudovkin. *Wings of a Serf* (Krylia kholopa), Sovkino: Yuri Tarich (co-scripted by Viktor Shklovsky and Konstantin Shil'dkret).

1927 *The Forty-First* (Sorok pervyi), Mezhrabpom-Rus: Protazanov. *The Fall of the Romanov Dynasty* (Padenie dinastii Romanovykh), Sovkino: Esfir Shub. *Bed and Sofa* (Tretia Meshchanskaia), Sovkino: Abram Room (script by Shklovsky). *Mary Pickford's Kiss* (Potselui Meri Pikford), Mezhrabpom-Rus: Sergei Komarov. *The End of St. Petersburg* (Konets Sankt-Peterburga), Mezhrabpomfilm-Rus: Pudvkin, co.-dir. Mikhail Doller. *The White Eagle* (Belyi orel), Mezhrabpomfilm-Rus: Protazanov (with Vsevolod Meyerhold, also Anna Sten).

1928 *The Parisian Cobbler* (Parizhskii sapozhnik), Sovkino: Fridrikh Ermler (with Fedor Nikitin). *The House in the Snowdrifts* (Dom v sugrobakh, from Zamiatin's story "The Cave"), Sovkino: Ermler (with Nikitin). *Zvenigora*, VUFKU: Aleksandr Dovzhenko. *October* (Oktiabr'),Sovkino: Eisenstein and Grigorii Aleksandrov. *The Captain's Daughter* (Kapitanskaia dochka), Sovkino: Tarich. *The Descendant of Genghis Khan* (Potomok Chingis-khan; also: *Storm over Asia*), Mezhrabpomfilm: Pudovkin.

1929 *Man with Movie Camera* (Chelovek s kinoapparatom), VUFKU: Vertov. *New Babylon* (Novyi Vavilon), Sovkino: Kozintsev and Trauberg. *Arsenal*, VUFKU: Dovzhenko. *Old and New* (Staroe i novoe), Sovkino: Eisenstein and Aleksandrov.

1930 *Earth* (Zemlia), Vufko: Dovzhenko.

1931 *A Pass to Life* (Putevka v zhizn'), Mezhrabpomfilm: Nikolai Ekk. *The Quiet Don* (Tikhii Don, from Mikhail Sholokhov's novel), Soiuzkino, Moscow: Olga Preobrazhenskaia and Pravov.

1932 *Ivan*, Ukrainfilm: Dovzhenko. *The House of the Dead* (Mertvyi dom), Mezhrabpomfilm: V. Fedorov. *Counterplan* (Vstrechnyi), Rosfilm, Leningrad: Ermler and Sergei Iutkevich. *A Simple Case* (Prostoi sluchai), Mezhrabpomfilm: Pudovkin. *K.Sh.E.* or *The Komsolmol B Electification Leader*, Esfir Shub.

1933 *Outskirts* (Okraina, also: *Patriots*), Mezhrabpomfilm: Barnet. *The Great Consoler* (Velikii uteshitel', from O. Henry stories), Mezhrabpomfilm: Kuleshov.

1934 *Petersburg Night* (Peterburgskaia noch', from Dostoevsky's "White Nights" and *Netochka Nezvanova*), Soiuzfilm: Grigorii Roshal and Vera Stroeva. *Lieutenant Kizhe* (Poruchik Kizhe), Belgoskino: Aleksandr Feinzimmer (script by Iuri Tynianov, music by Sergei Prokofiev). *Three*

Songs of Lenin (Tri pesni o Lenine), Mezhrabpomfilm: Vertov. *Chapaev*, Lenfilm: Sergei and Georgi Vasilyev (the Vasilyev "Brothers"). *Jolly Fellows* (Veselye rebiata), Mosfilm: Aleksandrov (music by Isaak Dunaevsky).

1935   *The Youth of Maksim* (Yunost Maksima), Lenfilm: Kozintsev and Trauberg (Boris Chirkov, music by Dmitri Shostakovich). *Aerograd* Mosfilm and Ukrainfilm: Dovzhenko.

1936   *We from Kronstadt* (My iz Kronstadt), Mosfilm: Efim Dzigan. *Circus* (Tsirk), Mosfilm: Aleksandrov (music by Dunaevsky).

1937   *Without Dowry* (Bespridannitsa, from Ostrovsky's play), Mezhrabpomfilm: Protazanov. *Baltic Deputy* (Deputat Baltiki), Lenfilm: Aleksandr Zarkhi and Iosif Kheifits. *The Return of Maksim* (Vozvrashcheniye Maksima), Lenfilm: Kozintsev and Trauberg (with Boris Chirkov). *Peter the First* (Petr I), Part One, Lenfilm: Vladimir Petrov. *Lenin in October* (Lenin v oktiabre), Mosfilm: Mikhail Romm (with Boris Shchukin). *Lone White Sail* (Beleet parus odinokii, from Valentin Kataev's novel), Soiuzdetfilm: Vladimir Legoshin.

1938   *A Great Citizen* (Velikii grazhdanin), Part One, Lenfilm: Ermler. *The Rich Bride* (Bogataia nevesta), Ukrainfilm: Pyriev (with Marina Ladynina, music by Dunaevsky). *Volga-Volga*, Mosfilm: Aleksandrov (music by Dunaevsky). *Childhood of Gorky* (Detstvo Gor'kovo, from Gorky's *Trilogy*), Soiuzdetfilm: Mark Donskoi. *Alexander Nevsky* (Aleksandr Nevsky), Mosfilm: Eisenstein and Dmitri Vasiliev.

1939   *The Vyborg Side* (Vyborgskaia storona), Lenfilm: Kozintsev and Tauberg (with Boris Chirkov). *Peter the First* (Petr I), Part Two, Lenfilm: Petrov. *Lenin in 1918* (Lenin v 1918 godu), Mosfilm: Romm. *Shchors*, Kiev Studio: Dovshenko. *Minin and Pozharsky* (Minin i Pozharsky), Mosfilm: Pudovkin and Doller (script by Shklovsky). *The Tractor Drivers*, Mosfilm and Kiev Studio: Pyriev (with Ladynina).

1940   *My Universities* (Moi universitety), Soiuzdefilm: Donskoi. *Virgin Soil Upturned* (Podniataia tselina), Mosfilm: Yuli Raizman (script by Mikhail Sholokohov, from his novel). *Liberation* (Osvobozhdenie), Kiev Studio: Dovzhenko, co.-dir. Iulia Solntseva.

1941   *Masquerade* (Maskarad), Lenfilm: Sergei Gerasimov.

1942   *Murderers Are on Their Way* (Ubitsi vykhodiat na dorogu, from plays by Brecht) Combined Studio: Pudovkin.

1943   *Nasreddin in Bukhara* (Nasreddin v Bukhare), Tashkent Studio: Protazanov.

1944   *Zoia*, Soiuzdetfilm: Leo Arnshtam. *Ivan the Terrible* (Ivan Grozny), Part One, Combined Studio: Eisenstein (with Nikolai Cherkasov, Serafima Birman, Pavel Kadochnikov).

1945   *Berlin*, Central Newsreel Studio: Raizman.

1946   *The Great Turning-Point* (Velikii perelom), Lenfilm: Ermler. *Ivan the Terrible* (Ivan Grozny, shelved, released 1958), Part Two, Mosfilm: Eisenstein. *The Stone Flower* (Kamennyi tsvetok), Mosfilm: Aleksandr Ptushko. *Admiral Nakhimov*, Mosfilm: Pudovkin.

1947   *Village Schoolteacher* (Selskaia uchitel'nitsa), Soiuzdetfilm: Donskoi (with Vera Maretskaia).

1948   *Michurin*, Mosfilm: Dovzhenko, in color (the released version is not by Dovzhenko).

1949   *Meeting on the Elbe* (Vstrecha na El'be), Mosfilm: Aleksandrov (with Liubov' Orlova). *The Fall of Berlin* (Padenie Berlina, Parts One, Two, Mosfilm: Mikhail Chiaureli (with Mikhail Gelovani as Stalin).

1950   *Conspiracy of the Doomed* (Zagovor obrechennykh), Mosfilm: Mikhail Kalatozov.

1953   *The Return of Vasili Bortnikov* (Vozvrashchenie Vasiliia Bortnikova), Mosfilm: Pudovkin.

1955   *Romeo and Juliet* (Prokofiev's ballet), Mosfilm: Lev Arnstam and L. Lavrovsky (with Galina Ulianova). *Boris Godunov*, Mussorgsky's opera, Mosfilm: Vera Stroeva.

1956   *Othello* (Otello), Mosfilm: Sergei Iutkevich.

1957   *Carnival Night* (Karnaval'naia noch'), Mosfilm: Eldar Riazanov. *Don Quixote* (Don Kikhot), Lenfilm: Kozintsev. *The Cranes Are Flying* (Letiat zhuravli), Mosfilm: Kalatozov. *The House Where I Live* (Dom, v kotorom ia zhivu), Gorky Studios: Lev Kulidzhanov, co-dir. Iakov Segel.

1958   *The Communist* (Kommunist), Mosfilm: Raizman. *Nastasia Filippovna* (from Dostoevsky, *The Idiot*), Mosfilm: Pyriev.

1959   *Destiny of a Man* (Sud'ba cheloveka), Mosfilm: Sergei Bondarchuk. *Khovanshchina*, Mussorgsky's opera, Mosfilm: Stroeva. *Ballad of a Soldier* (Ballada o soldate), Mosfilm: Grigorii Chukhrai. *White Nights* (Belye nochi, from Dostoevsky's novel), Mosfilm: Pyriev.

1960   *Lady with the Little Dog* (Dama s sobachkoi), Lenfilm: Kheifits.

1961   *Peace to Those Who Enter* (Mir vkhodiashchemu), Mosfilm: Aleksandr Alov and Vladimir Naumov.

1962   *Ivan's Childhood* (Ivanovo detstvo). Mosfilm: Andrei Tarkovsky.

1964   *I Walk About Moscow* (Ia shagaiu po Moskve), Mosfilm: Georgi Daneliia. *Hamlet* (Gamlet), Lenfilm: Kozintsev (with Innokenti Smoktunovsky). *Shadows of Forgotten Ancestors* (Teni zabytykh predkov), Dovzhenko Studio: Sergei Paradzhanov.

1965   *Nasty Story* (Skvernyi anekdot, from Dostoevsky's story), released 1987, Mosfilm: Alov and Naumov.

1966   *War and Peace* (Voina i mir), in four parts, Mosfilm: Bondarchuk. *Wings*

(Krylia), Mosfilm: Larisa Shepitko. *Andrei Rublev*, released with cuts 1972, Mosfilm: Tarkovsky (with Anatoli Solonytsin).

1967   *Katerina Izmailova*, Shostakovich's opera, Lenfilm: Mikhail Shapiro (with Galina Vishnevskaia). *Your Contemporary* (Tvoi sovremennik), in two parts, Mosfilm: Raizman. *The Commissar* (Kommissar), released 1987, Gorky Studio: Aleksandr Askoldov. *The Story of Anna Kliachina Who Loved But Did Not Get Married* (Istoriia Asi Kliachinoi, kotoraia liubila da ne vyshla zamuzh), released 1987, Mosfilm: Andrei Konchalovsky. *Brief Encounters* (Korotkie vstrechi), released 1987, Odessa Film Studio: Kira Muratova (with Vladimir Vysotsky). *Beginning of an Unknown Era* (Nachalo nevedomogo veka), released 1987, Experimental Studio, Mosfilm: Larisa Shepitko and Andrei Smirnov (script based on stories by Platonov and Olesha).

1968   *Saiat Nova*, or *Color of Pomegranate* (Tsvet granata), national release 1971, Armenfilm: Paradzhanov. *The Brothers Karamazov* (Brat'ia Karmazovy), three parts, Mosfilm: Pyriev (Part 3 completed by Mikhail Ulianov and Kiril Lavrov, Mosfilm).

1969   *Prayer* (Mol'ba), Gruziiafilm: Tengiz Abuladze. *A Nest of Gentry* (Dvorianskoe gnezdo), Mosfilm: Konchalovsky. *Pirosmani*, Great Experimental Studio and Gruziiafilm: Georgi Shengelaia.

1970   *Crime and Punishment* (Prestuplenie i nakazanie, from Dostoevsky's novel), Mosfilm: Lev Kulidzhanov. *White Sun of the Desert* (Beloe solntse pustyni), Mosfilm: Vladimir Motyl.

1971   *Flight* (Beg, from Bulgakov), Mosfilm: Alov and Naumov. *King Lear* (Korol' Lir), Lenfilm: Kozintsev (with Iuri Iarvet). *Belorussian Station* (Belorusskii vokzal), Mosfilm: Andrei Smirnov.

1972   *Solaris* (from the novel by Stanislaw Lem), Mosfilm: Tarkovsky. *Stoves and Benches* (Pechki-lavochki), Gorky Studio: Vasili Shukshin.

1973   *I Want to Speak* (Proshu slova), released 1976, Lenfilm: Gleb Panfilov (with Inna Churikova, also Shukshin).

1974   *Mirror* (Zerkalo), Mosfilm: Tarkovsky. *The Red Snowball Tree* (Kalina krasnaia), Gorky Studio: Shukshin.

1976   *Slave of Love* (Raba liubvi), Mosfilm: Nikita Mikhalkov. *Pastorale*, released 1978, Gruziiafilm: Iosif Ioseliani.

1977   *The Ascent* (Voskhozhdeniye), Mosfilm: Shepitko. *Unfinished Play for a Mechanical Piano* (Neokonchennaia p'esa dlia mekhanicheskogo pianino), Mosfilm: Nikita Mikhalkov.

1978   *The Wishing Tree* (Drevo zhelania), Gruziiafilm: Abuladze. *A Lonely Human Voice* (Odinikii golos cheloveka), Aleksandr Sokurov.

1979   *Sibiriade*, in four parts, Mosfilm, Andrei Kanchalovsky. *Stalker*, Mosfilm: Tarkovsky.

1980   *Autumn Marathon* (Osennii marafon), Mosfilm: Georgi Daneliia. *Garage* (Garazh), Mosfilm: Riazanov. *Moscow Does Not Believe in Tears* (Moskva slezam ne verit), Mosfilm: Vladimir Menshov. *Some Days in the Life of I.I. Oblomov* (Neskol'ko deni iz zhizni I.I. Oblomova), Mosfilm: Mikhalkov.

1981   *Twenty-Six Days in the Life of Dostoevsky* (Dvadtsat' shest' dnei iz zhizni Dostoyevskovo), Mosfilm: Aleksandr Zarkhi. *Valentina*, Mosfilm: Panfilov (with Churikova).

1982   *My Friend Ivan Lapshin* (Moi drug Ivan Lapshin), released 1985, Lenfilm: Aleksei German. *Pokrovsky Gates* (Pokrovskie vorota), Mikhail Kozakov (TV film).

1983   *Nostalgia* (Nostalgiia), Opera Film (Rome): Tarkovsky.

1984   *The Legend of Suram Fortress* (Legenda o Suramskoi kreposti), Paradzhanov, co.-dir. David Abashidze. *Repentance* (Pokaianie), Gruziiafilm: Abuladze.

1986   *Elegy* (Elegiia), Association of Filmmakers of the USSR: Sokurov.

1987   *Assa*, Mosfilm: Sergei Soloviev. *Forgotten Tune for the Flute* (Zabytaia melodiia dlia fieity), Mosfilm: Riazanov. *A Twist of Fate* (Peremena uchasti), Odessa Film Studio: Kira Muratova. *Man From Boulevard des Capucines*, Alla Surikova. *Non-Professionals* (Neprofessionaly), Kazakhfilm: Sergei Bodrov.

1988   *The Needle* (Igla), Kazakhfilm: Rashid Nugmanov (with Viktor Tsoi). *Little Vera* (Malen'kaia Vera), Gorky Studio: Vasili Pichul. *Mother* (Mat', from Gorky's novel), Mosfilm/Cinecitta Raidue/Cinefin Ltd.: Panfilov (with Churikova).

1989   *Asthenic Syndrome* (Astenicheskii sindrom), Odessa Film Studio: Muratova. *Ashik-Kerib*, Paradzhanov. *Intergirl* (Interdevochka), Petr Todorovsky. *Soviet Elegy* (Sovetskaiia elegiia), Leningrad Documentary Film Studio: Sokurov.

1990   *Taxi Blues* (Taksi-bliuz), Lenfilm: Pavel Lungin, *This Is No Way to Live* (Tak zhit' nel'zia), Stanislav Govorukhin. *Card Sharpers* (Katala), Mosfilm: Bodrov. *Adam's Rib* (Rebro Adama), Mosfilm: Viacheslav Krichofovich (with Chrikova).

1991   *Stalin's Funeral* (Pokhorony Stalina), Mosfilm: Evgeny Evtushenko.

1992   *Daddy, Father Christmas Is Dead* (Papa, umer Ded Moroz), Lenfilm: Evgeni Iufit. *Luna-Park*, IMA Films/L, Productions (Moscow): Pavel Lungin. *The Tractor Drivers* (Traktoristy), Gleb and Igor Aleinikov. *Moscow Parade* (Prorva), East-West (France)/ Project Camps (Russia)/ Mosfilm: Ivan Dikhnovichny.

1993   *Island of the Dead* (Ostrov mertvykh), Soiuzitalofilm: Oleg Kovalov.

1994   *Hammer and Sickle* (Serp i molot), L-Film: Sergei Livnev. *Burnt by the Sun*

(Utomlennye solntsem), Studio "Tri-T" and Camera One (Franco-Russian co-production): Mikhalkov.

1995   *The Moslem* (Musulmanin), Vladimir Khotinenko. *Concert for a Rat* (Kontsert dlia krysy), Lenfilm: Kovalov.

1996   *Caucasian Prisoner* (Kavkazkii plennik), Sergei Bodrov.

Index

About True Christianity (Zadonsky) 51
Abramtsevo estate and workshops 207–08, 213, 231
absolutism 49, 51
Abuldaze, Tengiz 327
Academy of Agricultural Sciences *see* Lenin All-Union Academy
Academy of Arts 205–06, 208
acmeism 191, 193
Adam, Adolphe 253
Adrian, Patriarch 49
adventure narrative, popular 148
aesthetics 40, 87–88
Afanas'ev, A. N. 135
Afinogenov, Aleksandr 287
Afrika *see* Bugaev, Sergei
After Russia (Tsvetaeva) 194
age hierarchy 128
agitation-propaganda ("agitprop") 136, 277, 312
agriculture, large-scale colonization 65
Aitmatov, Chingiz 200, 294
Akhmadulina, Bella 200
Akhmatova, Anna 153, 173, 191, 193–94, 195
AKhRR (Association of Artists of Revolutionary Russia) 221–23
Akimov, Nikolai 228, 285, 292
Aksakov, Konstantin 109
Aksakov, Ivan 109
Aksyonov, Vasily 199, 200
Alaska 63, 64
Albert, Yury 233
Aleichem, Sholem 280, 296
Aleinikov, Gleb and Igor 300
Aleksandr Nevsky (Eisenstein) 262
Aleksandrinsky Theatre, St. Petersburg 267
Aleksandrov, Grigory 320–21
Aleksei, Tsar 87
Aleshkovsky, Yuz 200

Aleutian islands 64
Alexander I 52, 109
Alexander II 41, 189, 245
Alexandrine period 108–09
Alexéieff, Aleksandr 299
All Russian Artistic-Manufacturing Exhibition (1882) 97
All-Union Conference on Cinematograph Affairs (1935) 318
All-Union State Institute of Cinematography (VGIK) 306, 320
Alphabet of Russian Superstitions (Chulkov) 133
Altai mountain 65
Amalrik, Andrei 295
Ambrose, Father (ascetic hermit) 52
"American Painting and Sculpture" Exhibition, Moscow (1959) 229
Amur river valley 64, 65
Amvrosy, Bishop 47
anarchism 95
Ancient Russian Art Exhibition, Moscow (1913) 215
Andreev, Leonid 191, 272
Andrei Kkozhukhov (Stepnyak-Kravchinsky) 164
animals, cruelty to 128
Anna Karenina (Tolstoy) 186
Annenkov, Georgy 276
Annenkov, Yury 283
Annensky, Innokenty 191, 273–74
Annunciation church, Kremlin 40
anti-rationalism 142
anti-Semitism 115, 121, 263
Antique Theatre (1907–11) 272
Antonov, Oleg 298
Appia, Adolphe 272
Aral Sea 65
Arbuzov, Aleksei 287–88, 292
architecture 88–89

355

Archives of American Art 229
Arkhipov, Abram 223
Armenia 65
Army Theatre 297
Arndt, Johann 51, 106
Arnshtam, Leo 322
art; Abramtsevo and Talashkino 207–08,
    209; abstraction 213–14, 229; action
    painting 229; AKhRR 221; American
    influence 229; artifact, notion of 211–12;
    avant-garde 213–18, 223, 228; Blaue
    Reiter group 217; constructivism 208,
    219–20; and contemporary Western
    culture 228–29; cubism 216, 228;
    developments after Stalin 226–34;
    dilettantism 212; dissident art 226–33;
    divination theme 231; environmental
    art 229; exhibitions 206, 210, 214, 215,
    216, 221, 223, 224, 226–27; and film 304;
    futurism 191; gambling theme 231;
    geometrism 229; and Hegel 95–96;
    indigenous culture 215; Jack of
    Diamonds group 214; kinetic art 229,
    232–33; lyrical abstraction 229; magic
    realism 229; Manège exhibition (1962)
    226, 227; Movement group 232; and
    nationalism 91; neo-primitivist
    movement 213, 214; neo-Russian style
    205–8; October Revolution 218–21;
    photography 220; polygraphical
    design 220; post-impressionism 216,
    228; "primitive culture" 213;
    proletarian style 219; and religion
    215–16, 230; Soviet socialist realism
    221–26; stage design 220; studio art
    (1880s/1890s) 209–10; Svomas (Free
    Studios) 219; symbolist aesthetic
    208–13; *tematicheskaia kartina* 222; trade
    unions 222–23; Union of Youth 217;
    Unovis 217–18; "wanderers" movement
    206–07, 208; *see also names of artists and
    organizations*
art forms, elite and democratic 142
Art Theatre *see* Moscow Art Theatre (MAT)
Artsybashev, Mikhail 145
Arzhak, Nikolai *see* Daniel, Yuly
Ascension church, Kolomenskoe (nr.
    Moscow) 40
ascetics, monastic 44, 51
Asia; earliest contacts with 58–62; Russian
    relationship with 58, 66–68; as Russia's
    alternative to Europe 71–75
Askoldov, Aleksandr 324
assimilation of other groups, Russian 72
Assumption, Kremlin Cathedral of the 40
Assumption church, Novgorod 40

atheism 39, 54
Atlanticism 81
Aurelius, Marcus 89
Aurora, flagship of Revolution 145
Author Working Group (ARGO) 232
autocracy 93
Avvakum, Archpriest 46–47, 168, 172

Babel, Isaak 167, 197
Babi Yar (Evtushenko/Shostakovich) 263
Bakhtin, Mikhail 123, 155, 185, 188, 197
Bakst, Lev 209, 213, 271
Bakunin, Mikhail 95
Balakirev, Mily Alekseevich 245–46
Balanchine, George 252, 261
Balasoglo, Aleksandr 72
ballet 87, 251, 252, 253–54, 271, 322
Ballets Russes 208, 209, 241, 271
Balmont, Konstantin 191, 209, 212
Bandit Churkin 148
Baranov, Leonid 233
Baranovskaia, Vera 311
Baratynsky, Evgeny 178
Barliuk, David 192, 214
Barliuk, Vladimir 214
Barnet, Boris 305, 315, 316
baroque 90, 99
Bat cabaret, The, Moscow 273, 284
Batalov, Nikolai 311
Batiushkov, Konstantin 177
Bauer, Evgeny 149, 300, 301, 302
Bayadere, La (Tchaikovsky) 253
Beardsley, Aubrey 210
Beaumarchais, Pierre 282
beauty and religious faith 40–41
Bedny, Demian 142
belatedness in literature 169–70
belief systems, alternative 141
Belinsky, Vissarion 95–96, 111, 170, 171, 178,
    180–81, 268
Beliutin, Eli 226, 228, 231–22, 239
Bely, Andrei 99, 190, 191, 192, 210
Benois, Alexandre 99, 155, 209, 211, 212, 213,
    271
Benois, Leonty 99
Berberova, Nina 202
Berdiaev, Nikolai 41, 123, 165, 230
Beria, Lavrenty 223, 327
Bernshtam, T. A. 131
Bible 26, 164
Bilibin, Ivan 153, 211, 212
bilingualism 28
Birman, Serafima 279
birthplace, importance of 125–26
Bitov, Andrei 200
"Black Hundreds" 115, 126

Black Sea 64, 65, 73
Blaue Reiter group, Munich 217
Blok, Aleksandr 76–77, 82, 153, 167, 174, 190,
     191, 210, 274
Blue Bird cabaret 284
Blue Blouses troupe 283, *283*
Blue Rose mystical painters 210
Bodrov, Sergei 328
Boehme, Jacob 107
bogatyri (traditional folklore heroes) 136
Bogdanov, Aleksandr 275
Bogorodsky, Fedor 221, 226
Boileau, Nicolas 176
Boleslavsky, Richard 295
Bolsheviks 99, 100
Bolshoi Dramatic Theatre (BDT) 276
Bolshoi Theatre, Moscow 241, 253
Bonaparte, Napoleon (quotation) 57
books, copying of 42, 45
Boris and Gleb, Saints 29, 168
Boris Gudonov (Mussorgsky opera) 242,
     246
Boris Gudonov (Pushkin) 165
Borisov-Musatov, Viktor 210
Borodin, Aleksandr 236, 245, **248–49**
Borodin, Igor 153
Borovsky, David 293, 295
Borovsky, Pafnuty 42
Bortniansky, Dmitry 51, 239
Boym, Svetlana 195
Brainin, Vladimir 233
Brecht, Bertold 281, 293
Brezhnev, Leonid 150, 226, 293
Briullov, Karl 205
Briusov, Valery 141, 191, 209, 210, 272
Brodsky, Isaak 221, 222
Brodsky, Joseph 167, 190, 199, 200–01
"Bronze Horseman," "The" (Pushkin) 89
Brothers Karamazov, The (Dostoevsky) 164,
     176, 184
Brown, David 244
Bruskin, Grigory 227
Bugaev, Sergei ("Afrika") 233
Bulatov, Erik 229
Bulgakov, Leo and Barbara 285
Bulgakov, Mikhail 167, 188, 197, 198, 282,
     284, 293
Bulgakov, Sergei 230
Bulgarin, Faddei 178
"bulldozer" exhibition, Moscow (1974) 226,
     227
bullying 128
Bunin, Ivan 189, 191
Burliuk, David 302
bylina (folk epic) 136, 143
Byron, George Gordon, Lord 179

Byzantinization of religion 25
Byzantium 21, 85

Camus, Albert 114
Cancer Ward (Solzhenitsyn) 202
capitalism 80, 122; and Bolsheviks 117–18
card playing in art 231
Caspian Sea 65
Catherine II (the Great) 65, 89–90, 103–04,
     108, 133, 176, 266
Caucasus 65
Central Museum of the Armed Forces,
     Moscow 222
Chaadaev, Petr 69, 94–95, 169
Chachkin, Igor 233
Chagall, Marc 155, 214, 218, 280
Chaliapin, Fedor 242, 271, 326
Chardynin, Petr 300
Chashnik, Ilia 217
chastushka verse 136, 143–44
chauvinism 121, 126, 152, 252
Chekha secret police 316
Chekhov, Anton 153, 155, **187–88**, 270, 293;
     short stories 188
Chekhov, Michael *279*, 284–85
Chekrygin, Vasily 230
Chepurin, Yuly 290
Chernigov 25
Chernyshev, Mikhail 229
Chernyshevsky, Nikolai 112–13, 164, 167, 206
Cherry Orchard, The (Chekhov) 188
Chersonese 24
Chesterton, G. K. 281
Chevengur (Platonov) 197
Chiaureli, Mikhail 299, 320
Chkheidze, Timur 296
choral groups, Ukrainian 34
Christ the Savior, Cathedral of, St.
     Petersburg 41
Christianity 22–23, 50–51, 70, 241;
     Byzantine 39–43, 85; and pagan gods
     38; Roman 39; and Russian culture 21,
     24–25, 163
Chrysostomos, St. John 26
Chudakov, Aleksandr 187
Chuikov, Semeon 224
Chukrai, Grigory 323
Chulkov, Mikhail 133, 154
church, as building 40
churches *see denominations*: Greek Orthodox,
     Russian Orthodox, etc.; *individual
     names*
churches, reunion of Eastern and Western
     98
Churikova, Inna 326
cinema 142; popular 147–48

Ciniselli 268
Civil War, Russian 117, 127, 275, 281
Cixous, Hélène 195
Clark, Katerina 196–97
class 109, 125, 127, 131–33, 152
classicism in literary culture 105
clergy as social class 53
Cobbett, William 135
Cold War 82, 191
Coleridge, Samuel Taylor 134
collective farm literature 120
collectivization of villages 127
colonization 69–70
comedies 145
Committee for Artistic Affairs 288–89
Commonwealth of Independent States 233
communalism, social 110
Communism 80, 100, 101, 122; art and the
    Party 222, 223; fall in Eastern Europe
    189; and musical tradition 236–37; and
    theatre 276; and the village 117
Communist Youth League 286
compromise, political 116, 118
"conflictlessness" doctrine for artists and
    writers 287
conscience in literature, social 170–71
Constantinople 26, 40, 50
consumerism 120
Contemporary, The, journal 178, 182
copying of texts 42, 45
Cossacks 63–64
Costakis, George 228–29
Council of Florence 42
court society 104
Craft (Tsvetaeva) 194
crafts 207–08, 214–15
Craig, Gordon 106–07, 272, 280
Cranes are Flying, The (Kalatozov) 149
crime, violent 127
Crime and Punishment (Dostoevsky) 97, 184
Crimea 63, 64
Crimean War (1850s) 73, 114
Crommelynck, Fernand 280
Crooked Mirror cabaret, St. Petersburg 273
Crystal Palace, London 96
Cui, Cesar 245
culture; characteristics and genres of
    popular 141–55; early Russian native 22;
    early Russian spiritual 22–23;
    evolution of popular 131–40; peasant
    117, 136–37; principal difference
    between European and Russian 50–51;
    problems of terminology in popular
    125–31; Soviet political 121–22; Soviet
    variant of Russian 118–19
Cumans 59

customs, peasant 137–40
Cyril and Method, Saints 25, 27
Cyrillic writing 25

Dahl, Vladimir 135, 181
Daniel the Black (icon painter) 40
Daniel, Yuly 199, 294
Danilevsky, Nikolai 111, 112
Daykarhanova, Tamara 285
Dead Souls (Gogol) 169, 180
Decembrists 94, 109, 134, 178, 182–83, 189
deconstruction 184
dedovshchina (domination through bullying)
    128
Degas, Edgar 210
Deineka, Aleksandr 220, 225
dekulakization 127
Délibes, Léo 253
Delvig, Anton 178
Demon, The (Lermontov) 179
Denisov, Edison 263
deprivation 127
Derzhavin, Gavrila 41, 168, 169, 176–77
despotism 49, 62
Devils, The (Dostoevsky) 114, 184
Diaghilev, Sergei 209, 241, 249, 258–59, 271
dialectical materialism 198
dictionaries 35, 133
diglossia 27–29
discussion groups, political 109
Diveevsky Pustyn convent 53
divination as theme of art 231
Dix, Otto 220
Dmitrevsky, Ivan 266
Dmitriev, Vladimir 280
Dobrotoliubie (Love of God) 52
Dobuzhinsky, Mstislav 155, 211, 212
Dodin, Lev 296
doll, Russian (*matreshka*) 139
Doller, Mikhail 311, 320
Domostroi texts 44
"Donkey's Tail" Exhibition, Moscow (1912)
    215, 216
Donskoi, Mark 320, 321
Donskoy, Dmitry 119
Doronina, Tatiana 297
Dostoevsky, Fedor 40, 52, 74, 75, 96, 111–12,
    121, 167; and Age of Realism 182,
    184–85; novels filmed 301; sacred to
    secular writing 164
Dostoevsky and Romantic Realism (Fanger)
    178–79
Double, The (Dostoevsky) 181
Dovlatov, Sergei 200
Dovzhenko, Aleksandr 299, 311–12, 315
Doctor Zhivago (Pasternak) 169, 197

drama, in Moscow 34
Drankov, Aleksandr 300
dual-faith (*dvoeverie*) 23, 131
Dubroliubov, Nikolai 113, 170
Dugin, Aleksandr 82
dukhovnye pesni (devotional songs) 143
Dunaevsky, Isaak 321
Duncan, Isadora 272
Durov brothers (clowns) 268, 277
Dyshlenko, Yury 228

Eastern Christianity *see* Christianity,
    Byzantine
Eccentrics of Soviet cinema 154
Eckartshausen, Karl 52
Eckhart, Meister (Johann) 107
Economic Achievements, Exhibition of
    (1975) 227
education 47, 104–05, 121, 133; and literature
    34; universal elementary 142; and
    working-class people 130
Efremov, Oleg 292, 294, 297
Efros, Anatoly 291, 293, 294, 295
Eikhenbaum, Boris 188
Eisenstein, Sergei 154, 192, 236; films 262,
    299, 305, **306–10**, 315, 320; theatre 276,
    277, 289
Ekk, Nikolai 317–18
ekstrasensy (mesmerists and mediums) 141
Elagin, Ivan 202
Elinson, Genri 229
Elizabeth, Empress 89, 265
émigré movement (1920s) 81–82, 189, 202
empire, building of eastern 62–66, 69–70,
    72
Engels, Frederic 100
Enlightenment, the 90, 92, 104, 108–09, 111,
    176
entertainment 132, 133, 141, 147–51
Envy (Olesha) 165, 197
Ephraim the Syrian 53
epic (*bylina/stárina*) 23
Erdman, Nikolai 284
Ermler, Fridrikh 315, **316**, 317, 319, 322, 323
Erofeev, Venedikt 200, 203
eros-cum-national myth in literature
    172–74
Esenin, Sergei 167, 191
ethnography 120, 130, 136; *see also* folklore
etiquette 133
Eugene Onegin (Tchaikovsky) 251, 253
Eurasia, vision of (*Evraziistvo*) 75–79, 81
Europe; attitude to Russia 67; Russian
    attitude to 79, 85–87, 94
Europeanization of Russian society 67, 69,
    93

Evfimy, Patriarch 45
Evreinov, Nikolai 272, 273, 277
Evtushenko, Evgeny 200, 228, 263
Exter, Aleksandra 216, 273, 315

Factory of the Eccentric Actor (FEKS) 283,
    312–13
Fainzimmer, Aleksandr 323
fairgrounds 137
Falconet, Etienne-Maurice 89–90
Falk, Robert 228
Fanger, Donald 178
Father Gapon's Association of St.
    Petersburg Workers 127
Fatherland Notes, journal 182
Fathers and Children (Turgenev) 97, 114, 183
Fedorov, Nikolai 167
Fedorova, Zoia 321
Fedotov, Pavel 231
FEKS *see* Factory of the Eccentric Actor
feminism 118
Feodosy (Theodosius), Abbot of Kiev
    Monastery of the Caves 26, 42, 55
Fet, Afanasy 178, 187
fiction 93, 163–64; individuation (Bakhtin)
    185; popular 145–46, 147; popular
    Western 151; *see also names of authors*
film; acting 305; agitprop 299, 312;
    American movies 277; animation 302;
    boundaries and genres 299–300;
    Cannes film festival 325; censorship
    302; children's 299, 306; Cold War 322;
    on collectivization 309, 311;
    constructivism 308–09, 313;
    continuities (Russian and European)
    329; creative geography 304, 306;
    cultural monuments 322;
    documentaries 299–300, 313–14, 322;
    entertainment and education 314–15;
    exceptional films despite repression
    322–23; experiment with sound 306,
    318; fantastic realism 312–13; *glasnost'*
    and democracy 327–28; historical
    leaders 320; industrial struggle 319;
    kino-plays 305; Lenin and Stalin cults
    320; literary adaptations 321–22;
    Lumière brothers 300; mass-market,
    Indian 150; melodrama in popular
    culture 129; models and genres 319–23;
    montage 304–05, 307, 308, 313, 324;
    musical comedy 320–21; Oscar award
    326; poetic language 311–12; positive
    heroes under socialism 320; pre-
    revolutionary 300–01, 302; recent
    history events 328–29; revolutionary
    302–04, 313; as revolutionary art

film (cont.)
  302–04; revolutionary heroes 319;
  silent 300–02, 313; socialist realism 306,
  318–19, 321; stagnation period 324–27;
  subverting authority 324–27;
  symbolism and decadence 302;
  television 300; Thaw period 323–24;
  and village life 325–26; war films 322;
  see also names of people and organizations
Film-makers Union, Fifth Congress of
  (1986) 327
Filonov, Pavel 214, 220, 224
Fioravanti, Aristotle 40
First All-Russian Congress of Stage Workers
  (1897) 269
First Circle (Solzhenitsyn) 202
"First Fall Open Air Show of Paintings,"
  Moscow (1974) 227
First Party Conference on Cinema (1928) 318
First World War 76, 77, 302
Five Year Plans 118, 285, 287
Flavius 26, 29
Florence 86
Florensky, Pavel 41, 54, 164, 166, 171
Florovsky, Georges 107, 108
Fogel, Vladimir 305
Fokine, Mikhail 249, 271
folk songs 138, 236, 237
folklore 23, 129, 134–40, 143–44, 153, 214;
  and "fakelore" 137–40; imitations 153;
  and music 236, 237, 245; and theatre
  268, 271
Fonvizin, Denis 91–92, 266
fool, character of the wise 144
Foregger, Nikolai 282–83
formalists 192
Fourier, Charles 111
Free Theatre 272
Freeborn, Richard 186
Freemasonry 52, 91–92, 103, 105–09
Fuchs, Georg 272
fur trade 64
Furmanov, Dmitry 197, 319
Furtseva, Madame (Minister of Culture) 294

Gabo, Naum 218
Galaxy Kinetic Complex (1962) 232
Galich, Aleksandr 200, 294
Galin, Aleksandr 296
Galuppi, Baldassare 239
gambling as theme of art 231
game shows 148
Gan, Aleksei 219
Gardin, Vladimir 301
Garland, Judy 148
Garshin, Vsevolod 187

Gartman, Foma 211
Gaulle, Charles de 80
Gaumont film company 300
Gazeta-kopeika, newspaper 145
Gelman, Aleksandr 294
Gelovani, Mikhail 320
gender hierarchy 128–29
genetics 100–01
genre convention in popular culture 149
genres, literary 174–75
geographical position of Russia 57–58,
  68–69, 72–73, 80–81
Geok-Tepe (1881) 74
Georgia 65
Gerasimov, Aleksandr 221, 225
Gerasimov, Sergei 224, 225, 312, 324
German, Aleksei 322, 327
Ghengis Khan 59–60, 79
Gift, The (Nabokov) 197, 199
Ginkas, Kama 296
Ginzburg, Lydia 182, 188
Gippius, Zinaida 191, 209
Giselle (Tchaikovsky) 253
Gladkov, Fedor 144, 197
glasnost'/post-glasnost' eras 189, 199, 202, 263,
  296, 300, 324
Glazunov, Ilia 149, 228, 254
Glezer, Aleksandr 227, 229
Gliere, Reinhold 154
Glinka, Mikhail 236, 243–44
Gnezdovo 25
gods, pagan 22–23, 24, 38, 42, 172
Gogol, Nikolai 52, 154, 175, 178, **180–81**, 267,
  302
Golden Age of Russian literature 174, 187
Golden Horde 50, 60, 63, 64
Goldfadn, Avrahm 280
Goldovskaia, Marina 328
Golomshtok, Igor 229
Golovanov, Nikolai 241
Golovin, Aleksandr 208, 209, 271
Golubkov, Lenia 151
Goncharov, Ivan 153, 182
Goncharova, Natalia 155, 192, 271, 273, 302
Gorbachev, Mikhail 80, 189, 227, 295
Gorbanevskaia, Natalia 200
Goriunova, Nonna 233
Gorky, Maksim 121, 164, 191, 197, 223, **285–87**
Goskino 328
Govorukhin, Stanislav 328
grammars, early 34–35
Granovsky, Aleksandr 279
Great Patriotic War see Second World War
Great Schism 172
Grebenshchikov, Boris 146
Greek language 45, 87, 238–39

Greek Orthodox Church 24, 25
Gregory, Johann 265
Grek, Maksim 44, 45
Griboedov, Aleksandr 267, 281
Grigoriev, Vasily 70
Grigorovich, Dmitry 181
Gronsky, Ivan 196
Grossman, Vasily 200
Grosz, George 220
Group of Seven nations 81
Groys, Boris 197
Gubaidulina, Sophia 263
Gulag Archipelago, The (Solzhenitsyn) 169, 199, 202
Gumilev, Nikolai 173, 191
Gusev, Viktor 287

Hagia Sophia *see* St. Sophia Cathedral, Constantinople
hagiography 41, 164
Hamartolos Chronicle 26
Hamsun, Knut 272
Hanseatic League 85
Hasenclever 281
Hebrew Theatre company (State Theatre of Israel) 279
Hegel, Georg 95
Heldt, Barbara 195
Helvétius 108
Herald of Europe 182
hermit monasticism 43, 51
Hermitage Theatre 283
hero in literature, search for positive 171
Hero of Our Time, A (Lermontov) 179
heroines of literature and national myth 173
Herzen, Aleksandr 111, 169, 182
Hesychasm, South Slavic 32
heterodox literary forms 168–69
Hilarion, Metropolitan 31, 172
Hindu Kush 65
history, overview of Russian cultural 20–21
History of the Russian State (Karamzin) 169, 177
Hoffmann, E.T.A. 281
Holbach, Baron Paul 108
holy fool, concept of 165, 167
Holy Russia, myth of 115, 172
Holy Synod 50, 54
Holy Trinity Church, Nikitinki (Moscow) 40
Holy Trinity Monastery, nr. Moscow 42
humanism 86–88
Hypatian Chronicle (c. 1425) 29

"I. V. Stalin in the Visual Arts" Exhibition, Moscow (1949) 224
Iarvet, Yury 324

Iazykov, N. N. 135
icon, the 164–65
iconic space or liminality 164, 166
"Icons and *Lubki*" Exhibition, Moscow (1913) 216
identity; class *see* class identity; national *see* national identity
ideology, official Soviet 119
Idiot, The (Dostoevsky) 164, 184
Igor I 24–25, 27
Igor, Sviatoslavich, Prince 248
Igor Tale 29
Ilia the Prophet, Church of (Yaroslavl) 40–41
Imitation of Christ (à Kempis) 106
imperial Russia *see* empire, building of eastern
In the Steppes of Central Asia (Borodin) 249
individual experience, importance in literature 92–93
industrialization 109, 115, 116, 118, 207, 269; and popular culture 125–26; "smokestack culture" 121; and Soviet theatre 277
Infante, Francisco 229
InKhuK (Institute of Artistic Culture) 219
Inspector General, The (Gogol) 180
intellectuals in post-Soviet world 122
intelligentsia 53, 100, 103, 107, 142–43; Bolshevik variant 17; in post-Soviet world 122; and theatre 269
Interlude House theatre 272
International Exhibition 1851, London 96–97
Ioganson, Boris 225
Ioselani, Iosif 327
Iosif, Archbishop of Suzdal 34
irony 146–47
Isidor, Metropolitan 42
Iskander, Fazil 200
Islam 59
istoricheskie pesni (historical songs) 143
Iufit, Evgeny 300
Iutkevich, Sergei 317, 319
Ivan III 60
Ivan IV (Ivan the Terrible) 32, 45, 63, 86, 242, 288
Ivan Kupala (St. John's Night) 141
Ivanov, Aleksandr 205
Ivanov, Georgy 190
Ivanov, Lev 249
Ivanov, Viacheslav 75, 188, 190, 191, 212, 271
Ivanov, Vsevolod 287
Ivanovsky, Aleksandr 321
Izbornik (1073) 27
Izmaragd text 44
Izvekov, G. 241

"Jack of Diamonds" Exhibition, Moscow
    (1910) 214, 216, 217
Jacobins, Russian 114
Jakobson, Roman 188
James, Henry 168
Jaques-Dalcroze, Emile 272
Jawlensky, Aleksei von 210
Jesuits (Society of Jesus) 33, 52, 87, 265
Jewish Chamber Theatre 279–80
Jewish Wars (Flavius) 26, 29
Jews 121
Jilinsky, Andrius 285
jokes 144, 145, 152, 154
Jordan (Gothic chronicler) 21
journals 104
Journey to India 26
Joyce, James 307
Judaism 59
Jung-Stilling, Heinrich 52

Kachalov, Vasily 287
Kaiser, Georg 276
Kalatozov, Mikhail 148–49, 314, 322, 323
Kalinin, Viacheslav 226, 229
Kamchatka 64
Kamerny Theatre, Moscow 273, 281, 284,
    288, 289, 291
Kandinsky, Vasily 192, 210–11, 215
Kanevsky, Vitaly 328
Kapnist, Vasily 265
Karamzin, Nikolai 93, 154, 168, 169, 176–77
Karatygin, Pavel 267
Karelia 48
Karsavina, Tamara 271
kartinki (little pictures) 138
Kasatkin, Nikolai 223
Kastalsky, Aleksandr 241
Kataev, Valentin 290
Katsman, Evgeny 221
Kaufman, Denis *see* Vertov, Dziga
Kaufman, Mikhail 314
Kaufman, Rafail 224
Kazakov, Yury 200
Kazan 63
Kazan Cathedral, St. Petersburg 41
KEM *see* Workshop for Experimental Film
Kemenov, Vladimir 224
Keys of Happiness, The (Verbitskaia) 145
KGB interrogation of artists 227
Khachaturian, Aram 254, 262
Khanzhonkov, Aleksandr 300
Kharms, Daniil 154, 295
Khazars 59
Kheifets, Leonid 291, 297
Kheifits, Iasha 320
Khlebnikov, Velimir 191, 192–93, 217

Khmelev, Nikolai 287
Khodasevich, Vladislav 167, 189
Khokhlova, Aleksandra 305
Kholodnaia, Vera 129, 146, 300
Khomiakov, Aleksei 73, 109
Khotinenko, Vladimir 328
khozhdenie v narod (going among the people)
    135
Khrushchev, Nikita 150, 201, 225, 292, 323
Kiev 26; Monastery of the Caves 34, 42;
    scholars in 45–46
Kiev Museum of Art 224
Kiev-Moglia Academy 34
Kievan Caves Patericon 27
Kievan Rus' territory 21, 33, 59–62, 85–86
Kino-Eye group 313, 314
Kipling, Rudyard (quotation) 57
Kireevsky, Ivan 52, 109
Kireevsky, P. V. 135
Kirshon, Vladimir 298
Kliuchevsky, Vasily 61
Kliuev, Nikolai 153, 167, 191
Knebel, Maria 291
Knights Templar 106
Koleichuk, Infante and Viacheslav 232–33
Kolodzei, Tatiana 229
Kolomensky, Pavel 47
Kolychev, Metropolitan Filipp 42, 55
Kolyma Tales (Shalamov) 202
Komissarzhevskaya, Vera 272
Komissarzhevsky, Fedor 273, 285
Kon, Igor 122
Konchalovsky, Andrei 299, 325–26
Koonen, Alisa 273, 281, 288
Kooning, Willem de 229
Kopet Dag mountains 66
Korea 63
Korin, Pavel 225
Korolenko, Vladimir 187
Korovin, Konstantin 207, 209
Korsh, Fedor 269
Korzhavin, Naum 200
Kosoi, Vassian 44
Kovalov, Oleg 329
Kovanshchina (Mussorgsky) 237–38, 246,
    247–48
Kozakov, Mikhail 300
Kozintsev, Grigory 283, 304, **312–13**, 323–24
Kramskoi, Ivan 206
Krasnopevtsev, Dmitry 229
Krebs, Stanley Dale 262
Kremlin 40, 86
Krestovsky, V. V. 138
Kristeva, Julia 195
Kriukova, Marfa 136
Kropivnitsky, Lev 226, 230–31

Kruchonykh, Aleksei 191, 217, 272
Krylov, Porfiry 226
Kschessinska, Mathilda 243
Ksenia of Petersburg 42
Kubrick, Stanley 329
Kukryniksy trio of artists 225–26
Kulakov, Mikhail 228, 230–31
Kul'bin, Nikolai 211
Kuleshov, Lev 303, 304–05, **306**, 307, 310, 316
Kulidzhanov, Lev 326
Kulikovo, Battle of (1380) 60, 81
Kunst, Johann 265
Kupriianov, Mikhail 226
Kuprin, Ivan 191
Kurbas, Les 283
Kurbsky, Prince Andrei 32, 173
Kurella, Alfred 222
Kurganov, Nikolai 133
Kushner, Aleksandr 200
Kustodiev, Boris 155
Kutuzov, General 119
Kuzmin, Mikhail 191
Kuznetsov, Pavel 210, 228

labor and saintliness 42, 48
Lady Macbeth (Shostakovich) 260–61
Ladynina, Marina 321
Lake Balkhash 65
Landmarks symposium 116
language; administrative 31–32; alphabet
  for spoken 75; archaistic movement 31;
  bilingualism 28; chancery 31–32;
  dialectisms 32; dictionaries 133;
  diglossia 27–29; far-reaching changes
  30–31; grammars 34–35; influence of
  Polish 33, 34; in Mussorgsky's operas
  247; poetic language in film 311–12;
  revolution in 192–93; Russian and
  Slavic 19–20, 23–24; standardization of
  34–35; uses of Rusian 23–24;
  Westernization 33–35; written 25–26,
  27–29, 32–33, 35–36
Lapkina, Marfa 309
Larionov, Igor 155, 273
Larionov, Mikhail 192, 210, 214, 215, 216, 302
Last Thrust to the South, The (Zhirinovsky) 148
Latin 33, 87, 264
Laurentian chronicle (1377) 29
Lavrenev, Boris 290
Lazarenko, Vasily 277
Lazarevskaia, Yulianiia 42
Lecocq, Alexandre 281
legal codes 22, 23, 33, 133
Lenin All-Union Academy of Agricultural
  Sciences 100
Lenin Komsomol Theatre, Moscow 293, 295

Lenin, Vladimir 80, 112, 255, 303, 308
Leningrad *see* St. Petersburg
Leningrad Comedy Theatre 292
Lensky, Aleksandr 269
Lentovsky, Mikhail 269
Lentulov 216
Leon, Emperor 24
Leontiev, Konstantin 52, 53
Leontovich, Eugenie 285
Lermontov, Mikhail 41, 167, 178–79, 245
Leskov, Nikolai 182, 187
Letters of a Russian Traveler (Karamzin) 176–77
leveling-down tendency in peasant culture
  122
Levental, Valery 295
Levitan, Isaak 208
Lhériter, Jeanne-Marie 134
liberalism, "bourgeois" 116
Life of Feodosy 29
Life for a Life, A (Bauer) 149
Life of Prince Aleksandr Nevsky 27
Life of St. Cyril 25
Life of Stephen of Perm (Premudryj) 31
liminality or iconic space 164
Linder, Max 302
Lissitzky, El 217, 224
literacy 25–27, 85
literary societies 109
literature; acmeism 191, 193; Age of Realism
  182–85; ascetic 43; belatedness 169–70;
  categories of 174; and Catherine the
  Great 90; collective farm 120; and
  education 34; *émigré* 189–90, 202; epic
  96; eros-cum-national myth 172–74;
  exiled writers 200; formalists 192;
  formative influences 162–3; and
  Freemasonry 106–07; genres 174–75;
  Golden Age 174, 187; heterodox literary
  forms 168–69; historical consciousness
  197; historical fiction 93; the holy fool
  (*iurodivyi*) 165, 167; importance of
  individual experience 92–93; influx of
  Western 123; literary "martyrs" 167–68;
  maximalism 165–67; as mirror of
  society 161; modernism 189, 190;
  monastic 43–44; the novel 95; Old
  Russian 175–76; "pairing" of group
  leading figures 191–92; periods in 175,
  189; post-Stalinist 199–203; problem of
  personality (*lichnost'*) 171; recent
  "deconstruction" 203; religious
  sensibility 163–65; repression in 174;
  role of original work and mixed genres
  29–30; romantic realism 178–79;
  salient themes 162–74; as social
  conscience 170–71; and social

literature (*cont.*)
consciousness 96; socialist realism 189,
196–97; source of overall meaning
161–62, 166; space–time opposition
170–71; spirituality 163–65; twentieth-
century 188–90; *see also* fiction; *names of
authors*
Lithuania 33
Litovsky Statut legal codex 33
Liubimov, Yury 293, 295, 297
Livnev, Sergei 328
Locatelli, Giovanni 266
location (geographical position) of Russia
57–58
Lomonosov, Mikhail 35, 90, 176
Lopukhin, Ivan 107
Lotman, Yury 109, 166, 188
lower class 131–32, 135
lubok (popular print) 138, 149, 214, 215
Lukianchikov, Sergei 328
Lukin, Vladimir 266
Lumière brothers 300
Lunacharsky, Anatoly 218, 274, 276, 281
Lysenko, T. D. 101, 312

Macdonald, Hugh 258
Mchedelov, Vakhtang 283
Mackintosh, Charles Rennie 210
Maddox, Michael 266
Maeterlinck, Maurice 272
Magdeburg, bronze foundry in 86
magic tales, traditional 153
Maistre, Joseph De 52
Makary (Optyna elder) 52
Makovsky, Konstantin 207
Maksimov, Vladimir 200
Malaya Bronnya theatre 294, 295
Malevich, Kazimir 192, 214, 215, 216, 217–18,
220–21, 231, 273
Maliutin, Sergei 208
Maly Theatre, Moscow 267, 283
Mamontov family 48, 207
Mamontov, Savva 207, 269
Manchuria 63
Mandelstam, Nadezhda 169, 188
Mandelstam, Osip 167, 170, 173, 191, **193–94**,
195, 202
Marcus Aurelius 89
Mardzhanishvili, Kote 283
Mardzhanov, Konstantin 272
Mareev, Aleksandr 233
Mariinsky Theatre, St. Petersburg 247, 249,
253
martyrology, literary 167–68
Marx, Karl 113
Marxism 80, 116, 184, 190, 198

Marxist-Leninism 100
Mashkov, Vladimir 298
Masonry *see* Freemasonry
Master and Margarita (Bulgakov) 188, 197
Masterkova, Lidiia 229, 230–31
MAT *see* Moscow Art Theatre
Matisse, Henri 216
Matiushin, Mikhail 192, 217
matreshka (Russian doll) 139
Matveev, Artemon 87
maximalism in literature 165–67
Mayakovsky, Vladimir 167, 191, 192–93, 195,
280, 284, 302
media, modern, and popular culture 138,
143
medicine, alternative 141
Medtner, Nikolai 255, 256–57
Medvedkin, Aleksandr 153, 299, 319, 323
Meire, A. 54
Memoir on Ancient and Modern Russia
(Karamzin) 93
Mendeleeva, Liubov 192
Menshov, Vladimir 324–25
Merezhkovsky, Dmitry 185, 191, 209
Mertvy, Andrei 300
Meyerhold, Vsevolod 192, 220, 238, 273,
274, 280–82, 284, 288–89; films 301,
305, 315
Mgebrov, Aleksandr 275–76
Miaskovsky, Nikolai 262
middle classes 118
Mikhailov, Georgy 229
Mikhailovich, Tsar Aleksei 46, 50
Mikhailovsky Theatre, St. Petersburg 267
Mikhalkov, Nikita 326
Mikhnov-Voitenko, Evgeny 229
Mikhoels, Solomon 279, 291
Miklashevsky, Konstantin 272
Ministry of Culture of the USSR 226
Minkus, Alois 253
Mir iskusstva, magazine 207, 209
Mochalov, Pavel 267
modernism, Russian 190
modernist movement 136
modernization, economic 115
Molière (Jean Baptiste Poquelin) 34
monasteries 42–43
monasticism 43, 47; non-possessors
movement 44
Monet, Claude 210
Mongol invasion 59–62, 78, 98, 169, 237
Mongolia 63
Morganists 101
Morits, Yunna 200
Morozov, Ivan 216
Morozov, Savva 48, 269

Morshen, Nikolai 202
Moscow; and development of language 31–32; and film production 303; music and 242–43, 251
Moscow Art Theatre (MAT) 48, 270, 276, 281–82, 284, 287–88, 294; split into two companies 297
Moscow Institute of Painting, Sculpture, and Architecture 208
Moscow Polygraphical Institute 231
"Moscow School" (of composers) 254–55
Moscow Synodal School 239, 241
Moscow-Tartu School of Semiotics 188
Moskovsky komsomolets, newspaper 145
Moskvin, Andrei 310
Moskvin, Ivan 303
Mother Damp Earth (*Mat' syra zemlia*) 131, 172
Mother of God 131
Mother (Gorky) 164, 223
Mother Russia (*Rodina-mat'*) idea 131
Motyl, Vladimir 328
Mozzhukhin, Ivan 299, 300, 301, 305
Mstislav, Vladimirovich, Prince 30
Mt. Athos, Greece 33, 34, 52
Mukarovsky, Jan 188
Mukhamedzhanov, Kaltai 294
multifaith (*mnogoverie*) 131–32
Mumford, Louis 88
Muratova, Kira 324, 328
Muscovy, principality of 62, 63, 67, 79, 86
music; ballet 253–54; classical 237; Conservatories founded 244, 246; film 304; and folk sources 236, 237; in Moscow 242; Moscow and St. Petersburg rivalry 242–43; nationalist school 244; notation 239; opera 243–44, 246–48, 250, 253, 260, 266, 269; professionalization of 246, 251; and religion 236, 237–41; rock music 295; singing 237–40; *skomorokhi* 243; socialist realist 262–63; "The Five" composers (*kuchka*) 244–45, 251, 252–53; and Westernization 237–38; *znamenny raspev* (chant) 238; *see also* names of composers and musicians
Mussorgsky, Modest 153, 236, 237, 245, 246–47, 252
mystical idealism 98, 109
myths 137, 145, 165–66, 172–74

Nabokov, Vladimir 188, 190, 197
Nadson, Semeon 187
Naked Year, The (Pilnyak) 197
Napoleon Bonaparte 93, 94

narrative perspective 147
national identity; and Asia 66–71; and Europe 71–73, 80; growing sense of 87, 105, 111; and literature 161
National Radical Party 152
nationalism 119, 121, 126
Nazarenko, Tatiana 233
Nechaev, Sergei 114
Negoda, Natalia 146
Neizvestny, Ernst 226, 227, 228, 231
Nekrasov, Nikolai 181
Nekrasov, Viktor 200
Nekrosius, Eimuntas 296
Nemirovich-Danchenko, Vladimir 270, 281–82
Nemukhin, Vladimir 226, 228, 231
neo-Kantian revival 115
neo-Russian art 205–08
neoclassicism 90–91, 92, 176
Neoplatonism, Renaissance 106, 107
neoslavonisms 30–31
Nesterov, Mikhail 153
New Economic Policy (1921–28) 283–84
New Theatre, St. Petersburg 269
New York City Ballet 252, 261
Nezlobin, Konstantin 273
Nicholas I 94, 110, 135
Nicholas II 116, 255, 314
Nielsen, Asta 302
Nietzsche, Friedrich 184, 190
nihilism 87, 113
Nikitin, Fedor 316
Nikon, Patriarch 46
Nissky, Georgy 224
Niva, magazine 137
Nizhinsky, Vatslav 271
No. 4 art group 216
nomads 59, 61, 75, 78
non-possessors movement (Trans-Volga Elders) 44
Norshtein, Yury 299
Northern Flowers, journal 178
Norton Dodge Collection, Zimmerli Art Museum (USA) 230, 231
Notes from Underground (Dostoevsky) 184
novelization 185
Novgorod 59–60, 85
Novgorod Chronicles 30
Novikov, Nikolai 91, 92, 104, 109
Novoselov, M. A. 54
Novy mir 201, 294
Novyi put' (New Way) 54
Nugmanov, Rashid 328
Nusberg, Lev 229, 232
Nutcracker, The (Tchaikovsky) 253, 254
Nutovich, Evgeny 229

Oblomov (Goncharov) 153, 183
Obolnsky, Leonid 305
Obraztsov, Sergei 285
occultism, Western mystical 107
Odessa Film Studio 324
Odoevsky, Vladimir 174
Offenbach, Jacques 269
O'Keefe, Georgia 229
Okhlopkov, Nikolai 289
Okudzhava, Bulat 200, 293, 295
Old Believers 44–49, 138, *140*, 238
Old Church Slavonic (OCS) 27
Oldest Russian Poems, The (Kirsha Danilov)
    133–34
Olesha, Yury 165, 197
Olga, widow of Igor I 24–25, 27
On the Corruption of Morals in Russia
    (Shcherbatov) 104
On the Red Steed (Tsvetaeva) 195
On True Christianity (Arndt) 106
One Day in the Life of Ivan Denisovich
    (Solzhenitsyn) 201, 202
O'Neill, Eugene 281
opera 208, 243–44, 246–48, 250, 253, 260,
    266, 269
Optyna Pustyn monastic community 52
Orenburg 65
Orlenov, Pavel 272
Orlova, Liubov 146, 321
OST *see* Society of Studio Artists
Ostroukhov, I. 48
Ostrovsky, Aleksandr 153, 182, 197, 267, 269,
    282, 297, 316
Otsep, Fedor 310
Ottoman Empire 65
Ouspenskaya, Maria 285
Ovchinnikov, Vladimir 229
"Overcoat," "The" (Gogol) 180

Padve, Efim 293
paganism 22–23, 38–39, 131–32, 172
"pairing" of group-leading figures 191–92
Pamir mountains 65
Panfilov, Gleb 324
Panina, Vera 129, 142
Panslavism 121
Paracelsus 107
Paradzhanov, Sergei 299, 324, 327
parody 146–47
Parthé, Kathleen 120
Pasternak, Boris 169, 191, 193, 197, 199
Pathé film company 300
"Pauk" (Wolfspider) 152
Paustovsky, Konstantin 200
Pavlova, Anna 271
Pavlowa, Tatiana 285

Peace, Richard 181
peasant culture 117, 125–27
Pechenegs 59
people of the soil (*pochvenniki*) 112
People's Commissariat of Enlightenment
    218–19, 303
Perestiani, Ivan 303
Perov, Vasily 206
Perovsky, General 65
persecution; of artists and writers 167, 169,
    227, 241, 285–86, 289, 291, 295;
    religious 55–56, 241
Persia 63
personality in literature, problem of 171
Peter I (the Great) 35, 39, 71, 79, 86; and
    music 242–43; persecution of Old
    Believers 48; and religion 49, 50–51,
    166, 172; and St. Petersburg 88–89, 93;
    and Slavophilism 110; social reforms of
    67, 103–04, 109, 133; statue of 89–90, 99;
    and theatre 265
Peterburgskii listok, newspaper 145
Petersburg (Bely) 99, 190
Petrashevsky Circle 111, 201
Petrashevsky, Mikhail 71, 72, 74–75, 182
Petrine legacy/project *see* Peter I (the Great)
Petrograd *see* St. Petersburg
Petrov, Vladimir 320
Petrov-Vodkin, Kuzma 224
Petrushevskaia, Liudmila 202, 295–96
Petrushka 137, 148, 268
philanthropic activities 107, 130
philosophes 90, 108
Philosophical Letters (Chaadaev) 94
philosophy 95, 98; "of feeling" 92
Photius 24
Piaf, Edith 148
Pichul, Vasily 328
Pietism 52, 106–07, 109
Pikul, Valentin 146
Pilnyak, Boris 197
Pimenov, Yury 220, 255
Pisarev, Dmitry 98, 113
Pisemsky, Aleksei 182, 267
Pitoeff, Georges 285
Plan of Monumental Propaganda, Lenin's
    219
plant-breeding 100
Plastov, Arkady 224, 225
Platonov (Andrei) 197, 198
Plavilshchikov, Petr 266
Plavinsky, Dmitry 226, 229
Plekhanov, Georgy 115
Plisetskaia, Maia 322
Pluchek, Valentin 292
Pobedonostsev, K. 54

Poem without a Hero (Akhmatova) 194
poetry 34, 35, 133–34, 170, 174, 192–96;
    modernist/postmodernist 188;
    symbolist 210
Pogodin, Mikhail 73–74
Pogodin, Nikolai 287, 288, 289
Poland 33, 87
politics; discussion groups 109; passivity of
    Russian church 110; political extremes
    115–16; *see also names of groups*
Pollock, Jackson 229
Polonsky, Vitold 149
Polotsky, Simeon 34
Polovtsy 59
Polytechnic Exhibition (1872) 268
Poor Folk (Dostoevsky) 181
pop groups, Western 150
Poplavsky, Boris 202
Popova, Liubov 214, 218, 220
popular culture as concept and reality
    131–40
populism 112, 113–14, 115, 120, 127; as
    political ideology 135–36
poststructuralism 184
Potekhin, Aleksei 267
poverty 127
Prague School structuralists 188
Pravov, Ivan 317
Premudryj, Epifany 31
Preobrazhenskaia, Olga 317
"Priestless"/"Priestly" sect
    (*Bespopovtsy/popovtsy*) 47
Prigov, Dmitry 203
Primary Chronicle 22, 24, 25, 27, 29–30
Prince Igor (Borodin) 248–49
printing 34–35, 45, 138
Printing House, Moscow 45
prints and paintings, popular 138, 149–50,
    150
Prokhanov, Aleksandr 82
Prokofiev, Sergei 236, 254, 258–59, 260, 262,
    304, 309, 310
Prokopovic, Feofan 35, 50, 51
Proletkult 275–76, 277, 285, 307, 321
propaganda 152, 277–78, 280, 285–88
"Prophet," "The" (Pushkin) 167
Proshkin, Aleksandr 328
Protazanov, Iakov 299, 300, 301, 302, 315–16,
    321
protiazhnaia pesn' (melodies of woe) 143
proverbs or sayings 144–45
Psilander, Valdemar 302
Pudovkin, Vsevolod 304–05, **310–11**, 320, 321
Pugachev, Emelyan 166
Pugacheva, Alla 146, 150
Purchas, Samuel 67

puritanism of Soviet culture 118
Pushkin, Aleksandr 34, 41, 53–54, 89, 153,
    167–68, 175, **177–78**; tales filmed 301
Pushkin Dramatic Theatre (formerly
    Kamerny) 291
Pustozersk 47
Put' publishing firm 54
Puvis de Chavannes, Pierre 210
Pyriev, Ivan 320–21, 321–22

Queen of Spades (Tchaikovsky) 253

Rabin, Oskar 227, 228, 229
Rabinovich, Isaak 315
Rachmaninov, Sergei 236, 246, 255, **255–56**
radicalism 112, 113–14
Radio Erevan 144
Radishchev, Aleksandr 93, 108, 109, 167
Radlov, Sergei 283
Radonezhsky, Sergei 43
Radzinsky, Edvard 293
Raikin, Arkady 145, 285
Raizman, Iuli 323, 325
RAKhN (Russian Academy of Artistic
    Sciences) 219
RAPP (Russian Association of Proletarian
    Writers) 285–86
Rappaport, Herbert 321
raree shows 143
Rasputin, Grigory 54
Rasputin, Valentin 200
Rastrelli, Francesco Bartolomeo 41, 89
rationalism 109
Razin, Stenka 166
Reaction in Germany (Bakunin) 95
realism *see* socialist realism
Realism, Age of (literature) 182
Realistic Theatre 289
Red Cavalry (Babel) 197
Red Wheel, The (Solzhenitsyn) 202
Reformation 169
religion; alternative belief systems 141; and
    art 215–16, 230; atheism 39, 54;
    Byzantinization of 25; Great Schism
    172; Judaism 59; and literature 163–65;
    maximalism in spirituality 165–66;
    monasteries 42–43; monastic ascetics
    44, 51; monasticism 43, 44, 47;
    multifaith (*mnogoverie*) 131–32; and
    music 236, 237–41; pagan gods 22–23,
    24, 38, 42, 172; paganism 22–23, 38–39,
    131–32, 172; secularization policy 142;
    sensibility in literature 165; and theatre
    264–65; theology 41; *see also*
    Christianity
religious revival 52, 103, 115, 202

Remizov, Aleksei 189
Renaissance, Italian 21, 94, 169
Renovationists 55
Repin, Ilia 206–07, 208, 246
repression in literature 174
Requiem (Akhmatova) 193–94
Rerikh, (Roerich) Nikolai 153, 208
Resurrection, Church of the, St. Petersburg
    41
Revolution; French 93, 134; Russian (1905)
    115, 116; Russian (1917) 77, 100, 127, 189:
    and art 218–21; and film 302–04; and
    music 236–37, 255, 258; and theatre 274
"Revolution, Life, and Labor Exhibition"
    (1924) 221
revolutions, European (1848) 95, 189
Reyn, Evgeny 200
Riabushinsky, Nikolai 48, 209
Riangina, Serafima 224
Riasanovsky, Nicholas 59
Riazanov, E. 144
Riazhsky, Georgy 221
Riches (Pikul) 146
Rilke, Rainer M. 195
Rimsky-Korsakov, Nikolai 236, 244, 245,
    249–51
rites of passage in popular culture 128–29
rituals, religious 46, 51
Rodchenko, Aleksandr 218, 219–20, 224
Roginsky, Mikhail 229
Roman Catholic Church 42
Romanov family 86–87, 113
romanticism, nostalgic 115
Romm, Mikhail 320, 323
Room, Abram 316–17
Roshal, Grigory 321
Roshchin, Mikhail 294
Rosicrucian Order 92, 106
Rostovsky, Dmitry 51
Rozanov, Vasily 174, 190, 210
Rozanova, Olga 231
Rozov, Viktor 292
Rozovsky, Mark 293
Rubinstein, Anton 244
Rubinstein, Nikolai 244
Rubinstein, Yakov 228
Rublev, Andrei 21, 40
Rukhin, Evgeny 226, 228
Russia and Europe (Danilevsky) 112
Russian Academy 133
Russian Folk Tales (*Narodnye russkie skazki*) 135
Russian Folklore, journal 143
Russian Herald 182
Russian Idea, The (Berdiaev) 165
Russian Museum, St. Petersburg 225–26,
    231

Russian Orthodox Church 40
Russian Social Democracy 115
Russian Village Prose (Parthé) 120
Russian Word, journal 182
Russo-Japanese War (1904–05) 98

Sadovsky, Prov 267
Sadur, Nina 154, 295
Safe Conduct (Pasternak) 193
St. Basil's Cathedral, Moscow 40
St. Isaac's Cathedral, St. Petersburg 41
St. Petersburg 88–89, 93, 99–100; centre of
    Westernization 104; and film
    production 303; music in 242; peasant
    culture in 126
St. Petersburg Academy of Arts 214
St. Sophia Cathedral; Constantinople 40,
    86; Kiev (1037) 25, 40; Novgorod (1045)
    40, 86
Saints Peter and Paul Cathedral, St.
    Petersburg 41
Saltykov-Shchedrin, Mikhail 182, 292, 294
Samarkand 65
samizdat (self-printed material) 199
Sanin (Artsybashev) 145
Sarai 60
Sarovsky, Seraphim 53, 55
satire 90, 284, 287
Sats, Natalia 285
Scandinavian conquest 21–22
Scheherazade (Rimsky-Korsakov) 250–51
Schism (*Raskol*) 46, 47
Schnittke, Alfred 263
Scott, Walter 93, 134
Scriabin, Aleksandr 246, 255, **257–58**
Scythian Dances, A (Ivanov) 76
Scythianism and the vision of Eurasia 75–79
Seagull, The (Chekhov) 188
Second World War 79, 119, 129, 189; and film
    313, 322; and musical tradition 236; and
    Soviet art 225–26; and theatre 290
secularization policy 142
Seifrid, Thomas 198
*Selected Passages from Correspondence with
    Friends* (Gogol) 180
Semenov, Iulian 148
Semenov, Petr 72
Semenova, Ekaterina 267
Semperante satirical miniature theatre 283
sensation and novelty, demand in popular
    culture 149–50
Sentimentalism, English 92
Serafimovich, Aleksandr 197, 289
serfs, liberation of 189, 245, 268
Sergius of Radonezh 42
Sermon on Law and Grace (Hilarion) 31

Serov, Valentin 208, 225
Seventeen Moments of Spring (Semenov) 148
Severyanin, Igor 191
sexual sinner as popular character in fiction
    148–49
Shalamov, Varlam 167, 200, 202
Shapiro, Mikhail 322
Sharoff, Peter 285
Shatov, Mikhail 296
Shaw, George Bernard 281
Shchepkin, Mikhail 267
Shcherbatov, Mikhail 104
Shchukin, Boris 320
Shchukin, Sergei 48, 216
Shemiakin, Mikhail 229
Shepitko, Larisa 326
Shevchenko, Aleksandr 214
Shklovsky, Viktor 188, 304, 306, 314, 317
Sholokhov, Mikhail 197
Shostakovich, Dmitry 155, 236, 254, **258–61**,
    263; film music 304, 312, 322
Shteinberg, Eduard 229
Shterenberg, David 218
Shub, Esfir 307, 314
Shukshin, Vasily 320, 324, 325
Shvarts, Evgeny 289, 292
Shvedov, Konstantin 241
Siberia 63–64, 69
Silver Age; of Russian culture 53, 54, 123; of
    Russian literature 174
Simonov, Konstantin 287, 291
Simonov, Ruben 279
Sinyavsky, Andrei 167, 168, 190, 196, 199, 200,
    200–01, 294
Sketches from a Hunter's Album (Turgenev) 120
Skify (Blok) 76–77, 82
skomorokhi (wandering players) 143, 264,
    265
slang (*zhargon*) 128
Slavic languages 19–20, 27, 29, 239
Slavonic, normalization of 34–35
Slavonicisms, problem of 27
Slavophilism 109–13, 115, 120, 182
and belatedness debate 169
and nationalism 121
Sleeping Beauty (Tchaikovsky) 253
Sluchevsky, Konstantin 187
Slutsky, Boris 200
Smoktunovsky, Innokenty 293, 324
Smolensky, Stefan 241
Smolny Cathedral, St. Petersburg 41
Smotritsky, Melety 33, 35
Smyshlaev, Valentin 276
soap operas 148, 151
social clubs 109
socialism, Russian 113, 115

socialist realism 118, 286; and art 221–26; in
    literature 196–97
Socialist Revolutionaries 127
Society of Jesus *see* Jesuits
Society of Studio Artists (OST) 220
Society of Wandering Exhibitions 206, 221
Sokoloff, Vladimir 285
Sokolov, Nikolai 225
Sokolov, Sasha 200
Sokurov, Aleksandr 326
solidarity in popular culture 126, 128
Sologub, Fedor 191
Solovetsky Monastery 47
Soloviev, Sergei 328
Soloviev, Vladimir 39, 40, 41, 52, 98, 167, 187,
    190–1, 230, 283
Soloviova, Vera 285
Solzhenitsyn, Aleksandr 101, 167, 168, 169,
    190, 199, **200–02**, 294
Somov, Konstantin 209, 211, 212, 213
song-books, printed 137–38
songs, folk 23
Sooster, Ullo 228
Sorokin, Vladimir 203
Sorsky, Nil 32, 44, 52
Sosnitsky, Ivan 267
Sotheby's auction, Moscow (1988) 227
Soviet Novel: History as Ritual (Clark) 196
Sovremennik (Contemporary) Theatre-
    Studio 292, 294
space–time opposition in literature 170–71
Spengler, Oswald 112
Spiritual Order for Russian Orthodox Church
    50
spirituality (*dukhovnost'*) 163–65
Stage Workers, First All-Russian Congress
    of (1897) 269
Stalin, Josef 80, 118, 119, 224–25, 226; and
    Soviet film 307–08, 310, 312, 314, 327;
    and Soviet theatre 285, 286, 291
Stanislavsky, Konstantin 270, 272, 278,
    281–82
Stankevich, Nikolai 182
star cults, popular 146
Starewicz, Wladyslaw 299, 300, 302
Stasov, Vladimir 206
State Aleksandra Theatre 273
State Commission for Education 274
State Film School, Moscow 303
State Museum of Russian Art, Kiev 231
State Theatre Institute 298
State Theatre of Israel (formerly Hebrew
    Theatre company) 279
Steiner, George 185
Stepnyak-Kravchinsky, Sergei 164
stereotypes in fiction and drama 147–48

Sterligov, Vladimir 228
Sterne, Laurence 92, 93
Stevens exhibition, Moscow (1970) 226
Stoglav Council (1550) 45
Stolypin, Petr 116, 117
Stone (Osip Mandelstam) 194
Storm, The (Ostrovsky) 182
Strand Theatre, The 272
stratification, social 133
Stravinsky, Igor 153, 155, 236, 244, 254,
    258–59, 260–61
Stray Dog cabaret 273
Strike (Eisenstein film) 154
Stroeva, Vera 321, 322
Studio of Communist Drama
    (Mastkomdram) 280
Studite statutes 26
Sturua, Robert 296
subcultural groups 128
Sue, Eugène 96
Suetin, Nikolai 217
Sukhanov, Arseny 45
Sukhovo-Kobylin (Aleksandr) 281
Sulerzhitsky, Leopold 278
Sumarokov, Aleksandr 91, 176, 265
superstitions 38, 133, 141
Surikova, Alla 328
Suvorin, Aleksei 269
Suvorov, General 119
Sviatoslav 59
Svomas (Free Studios) 219
Swan, Alfred J. 238
Swan Lake (Tchaikovsky) 253
symbolism 98–99, 115, 208–13
symbolism/decadence movement 191,
    271–72, 302
symbols, Stalinist governing 130–31
Synkel Chronicle 26
Syr Darya 65

Tabakov, Oleg 292
Tabakov Studio theatre 298
Taganka Theatre 293, 295, 297
Tairov, Aleksandr 272, 273, 281, 289, 290
Talashkino estate and workshops 208, 213
Tale of the Destruction of Rjazan (1237) 29,
    60–61
Tale of the Loss of the Russian Land 27
Tale of the Priest and his Servant Balda
    (Pushkin) 134
Talochkin, Leonid 229
Tamiroff, Akim 285
tamizdat (printed abroad) 200
Taneyev, Sergei 255
tape recordings, bootleg 294
Tarabukin, Nikolai 219

Target art group 216
Tarich, Yury 317
Tarkovsky, Andrei 299, 320, 324, 345
Tarkovsky, Arseny 200
Tashkent 65
Tatars 42–43, 75
Tatischev, Vasily N. 68, 79
Tatlin, Vladimir 192, 218, 220–21, 280
Tatlin's Monument to the III International
    219
Taylorism and acting 277
Tchaikovsky, Petr Ilych 153, 236, 240, **251–54**
technology 96
television 151, 300
Tenisheva, Princess Mariia 207, 208
TEO (*Teatralny Otdel*) 274, 280
Teresvat (Theatre of Revolutionary Satire)
    277, 280
terminology of popular culture 125–31
Terts, Abram *see* Sinyavsky, Andrei
"thaws" of Soviet era 189, 323–24
theatre; 1970s period 294–95; 1995
    landmarks 298; "academic" 276, 287;
    acting 267, 272, 277, 280, 284, 293;
    agitprop 277–78, 280, 293; amateurism
    favored 275; audience 266–67, 267–68,
    269, 274–75; cabaret 273; categories at
    time of Revolution 274; censorship
    266–67, 284–91, 294; children's 285;
    Cold War period 291; "conflictlessness"
    doctrine 287, 291; constructivism
    280–83; "Crisis in the Theatre" debate
    272; dissolution of Soviet Union
    296–97; Englische Komedianten 264;
    fairground showbooths 267–68;
    foreign influence 266; Gorbachev
    period 295–96; industrial technology
    influence 277; laboratory 272; "long
    dark night" 289–91; Meiningen school
    270; music hall 273, 276–77; national
    character 264–66; Oberiu (1920s) 295;
    pageants 277–78; Petrushka 268;
    playwriting 285, 287; popular 147–48,
    268–70; post-revolutionary 275;
    present-day entrepreneurs 297; private
    clubs 269; provincial 267; puppet 285;
    and religion 264–65; repertory 269–70;
    royal court setting 265; in St.
    Petersburg 267; satire 284, 287; serf
    theatre 266; staging 280–81, 282, 284,
    285, 289; street comedies 143, 145;
    symbolist movement 271–73; "Thaw"
    period 292; "Theatrical October" 280;
    unification decree (1919) 274; workers'
    146, 274–75, 277–78; *see also names of
    organizations, people and theatres*

Théâtre du Chatelet, Paris 249
Theatre of Popular Comedy 283
Theatre of the Revolution 280
Theatre of Satire 284, 292
Theatre of Working Youth (TRAM) 286
Theatre of the Young Spectator 296
themes in literature 162–74
theology 41
Theophanes the Greek 40
Thiemann (Timan), Paul 300
"Thirty Years of the Moscow Union of
  Artists" Exhibition (1962) 226
Three Sisters (Chekhov) 153, 188
Thyssen-Bornemisza Collection, Madrid
  215, 217
Tian-Shan mountains 65
Tikhon, Patriarch 53, 55
Time of Troubles (seventeenth century) 45,
  242
Tisse, Eduard 307, 310
Tiulpanov, Igor 229
Tiutchev, Fedor 41, 179
Todorovsky, Petr 328
Todorsky, Simeon 51
Tolstaya, Tatiana 202
Tolstoy, Aleksei 288
Tolstoy, Leo 53, 146, 164, 182, 183, **185–86**;
  works filmed 301
Tolstoy movement 127, 164
Toporov, Vladimir 188
Tovstonogov, Georgy 292–93, 294
Toynbee, Arnold 112
Trans-Volga Elders 32
Transfiguration of the Savior, Church of the
  (Kizhi) 41
translation 27, 29, 52, 175, 188
Trauberg, Leonid 283, 304, **312–13**
Trediakovsky, Vasily 34, 35, 36, 167, 176
Tretiakov Gallery, Moscow 206, 211, 217
Tretiakov, Pavel 206
Tretiakov, Sergei 48, 277
Trezzini, Domenico 41
Trifonov, Yury 200
Trinity-Sergius Monastery (formerly
  Troitsky cloister) 43
Trismegistus, Hermes 107
Tristia (Osip Mandelstam) 194
Trivolis, Mikhail *see* Grek, Maksim
Troitsky, Artemy 44
Tselkov, Oleg 227, 228
Tseretelli, Nikolai 273
Tsoi, Viktor 328
Tsvetaeva, Marina 153, 167, 173, 188, 189,
  194–96
Turgenev, Ivan 97, 114, 120, 182
Turin, Viktor 314

Turkestan 65
Turkey 63
Tvardovsky, Aleksandr 201
"Twenty Years of the Red Army and Navy"
  Exhibition, Moscow (1938) 224
Tynianov, Yury 188, 304
Tyshler, Aleksandr 155, 228

Ukraine 34, 51
Ulanova, Galina 322
Uncle Vanya (Chekhov) 188
Union; of Soviet Artists 223, 226; of
  Soviet Composers 258; of Soviet
  Socialist Republics *see* USSR; of Soviet
  Writers 222–23, 285, 286; of Youth
  group 217
Unovis (Affirmers of the New Art) 217–18
Ural mountains 65, 69
urban myths 145
urbanized popular culture 129, 140, 151–55
US Federal Theatre Project 277
Uspensky (Assumption) Cathedral,
  Vladimir (1158–60) 40
Uspensky, Boris 109, 172, 188
Uspensky, Petr 211
USSR 80–83
USSR in Construction, propaganda magazine
  224
Ussuri valley 64
utopianism 111

Vakhtangov, Evgeny 274, 278–79
Vakhtangov Theatre 284, 292
Vampilov, Aleksandr 294
Van'ka the Steward ballad 138
Vasiliev, Anatoly 291, 296
Vasilyev, Georgi 319
Vasilyev, Sergei 319
Vasnetsov, Viktor 153, 207, 209, 210
Vavilov, Nikolai 100
Vekhi (Landmarks) 54
Velichkovsky, Paissius 52
Venetsianov, Aleksei 231
Venice 87
Verbitskaia, Anastasiia 145
Verhaeren, Emile 280
Vernadsky, George 106
Vertinsky, Aleksandr 142, 273
Vertov, Dziga 304, 313–14
Vesnin, Anatoly 281
Viktyuk, Roman 296
village and politics 117
village prose movement 119–21
Vinkovetsky, Yakov 227, 228, 231
Vinogradov, N. 278
violence and crime 127–28

Virgin of the Intercession Cathedral (St.
Basil's, Moscow) 40
Virgin of the Intercession church
(Novgorod) 40
Virgin Mary 131
Vishnevsky, Vsevolod 288, 290, 293
Vitebsk Practical Art Institute, St.
Petersburg 217
Vladimir I, Prince of Kiev 22, 24–25, 38,
39–40, 163
Vladimov, Georgy 200
Volkov, Fedor 265
Volocky, Joseph 32
Volodin, Aleksandr 292
Vorobev, Vladimir 293
Voznesensky, Andrei 200, 228
Vrubel, Mikhail 153, 208, 209, 210
Vsemirnaia illiustratsiia, magazine 137
Vvednsky, Aleksandr 295
Vyazemsky, Petr 178
Vysotsky, Vladimir 142, 146, 148, 200, 293,
295

"wanderers" movement in art 206–07, 208,
221, 240
War and Peace (Tolstoy) 153, 169, 186
We (Zamyatin) 197
Weber, Max 110
West, Russian attitude to the 85–87
Western Christianity *see* Christianity,
Roman
Westernization 49, 103–04, 113; of language
33–35; of popular culture 150–51
What Is Art? (Tolstoy) 146
What Is Oblomovism? (Dobroliubov) 171
What Is to Be Done? (Chernyshevsky) 113, 164,
169, 171, 176
When Will the Real Day Come? (Dobroliubov)
171
Who Is to Blame? (Herzen) 170
Winter Notes on Summer Impressions
(Dostoevsky) 96, 97
Witte, Sergei 116
Witte system of industrialization 115
Wittfogel, Karl 62
women; heroines in literature 173; role of
129, 130; strong woman in literature 171
Wordsworth, William 134
work and popular culture 141
working class 117, 122, 130, 142;
manipulation of 130–31
"Works by Georgian Artists" Exhibition,
Moscow (1937) 223
Workshop for Experimental Film (KEM) 316

World of Art, The, periodical 98–99
World of Art movement 208–13, 271
World Wars I and II *see* First/Second World
War
writing 35–36; creative 120; early 25–26,
27–29; exiled writers in post-Stalinist
period 200; and film 303–04; First All-
Union Congress of Soviet Writers (1934)
222–23, 286; and Freemasonry 106;
"martyred" writers 167; medieval
forms of secular 164; new genres of
written language 32–33; persecution of
writers 169; Russian relationship to
written word 161; sacred status of 163;
writer as secular saint 167–68
Writing Manual (Pis'movnik) 133

xenophobia, Russian 100, 126, 130, 152
Xoiroboskos 26

Yakulov, Georgi 216
Yankilevsky, Vladimir 226
Yanovskaya, Genrietta 296
Yaroslav the Wise, Prince 26, 59
Yavorskaya, Lidiya 272
Yavorsky, Stephan 50, 51
Yeats, W. B. 190
Yeltsin, Boris 121, 148
Yermak (Cossack) 63
Young, Edward 92
Yudenich, Gennady 293

Zadonsky, Tikhon 51–52
Zakharina-Unkovskaia, Alexandra 211
Zakharov, Mark 293, 295, 296
Zakharov, Vadim 233
Zakhava, Boris 279
Zamyatin, Evgeny 167, 197
Zarkhi, Aleksandr 320
Zavtra (formerly *Den'*) 82
Zen Buddhism in art 230
Zhdanov, Andrei 223, 262, 286, 290–91
Zhenovach, Sergei 297
Zhilinsky, Dmitry 233
Zhirinovsky, Vladimir 148, 152
Zhukovsky, Vasily 177
Zinoviev, Aleksandr 200
Zizany, Lavrenty 35
Znanie (knowledge) group 191
Zolotoe runo, magazine 209
Zoshchenko, Mikhail 127
Zuskin, Benjamin/Veniamin 280, 291
Zvezdochetov, Konstantin 233